T0234791

Lecture Notes in Computer Science　　9694

Commenced Publication in 1973
Founding and Former Series Editors:
Gerhard Goos, Juris Hartmanis, and Jan van Leeuwen

More information about this series at http://www.springer.com/series/7409

Selmin Nurcan · Pnina Soffer
Marko Bajec · Johann Eder (Eds.)

Advanced Information Systems Engineering

28th International Conference, CAiSE 2016
Ljubljana, Slovenia, June 13–17, 2016
Proceedings

 Springer

Editors
Selmin Nurcan
Université Paris 1 Panthéon-Sorbonne
Paris
France

Pnina Soffer
Department of Information Systems
University of Haifa
Haifa
Israel

Marko Bajec
University of Ljubljana
Ljubljana
Slovenia

Johann Eder
Alpen-Adria Universität Klagenfurt
Klagenfurt
Austria

ISSN 0302-9743   ISSN 1611-3349   (electronic)
Lecture Notes in Computer Science
ISBN 978-3-319-39695-8   ISBN 978-3-319-39696-5   (eBook)
DOI 10.1007/978-3-319-39696-5

Library of Congress Control Number: 2016939988

LNCS Sublibrary: SL3 – Information Systems and Applications, incl. Internet/Web, and HCI

Printed on acid-free paper

This Springer imprint is published by Springer Nature
The registered company is Springer International Publishing AG Switzerland

Preface

This volume of the LNCS series contains the papers accepted for presentation at the 28th International Conference on Advanced Information Systems Engineering (CAiSE 2016), held in Ljubljana, Slovenia, during June 13–17, 2016. CAiSE has established itself as a leading venue on information systems engineering. It serves as a forum for the exchange of ideas for researchers, practitioners, and students, where the most recent results in the domain are presented and discussed. In addition, it is a place to learn, meet the community, start new projects, and identify future trends.

Information systems are developed by people and for people. The CAiSE 2016 theme was "Information Systems for Connecting People," emphasizing the wish to satisfy the needs and requirements of people, both as individuals and as parts of organizations, which are socio-technical systems. In particular, this theme emphasized the role of information systems in communication among individuals, organizational units, and organizations themselves. It could also imply knowledge building and knowledge sharing, all kinds of decision making, negotiating and reaching agreements, bridging differences and distances among various points of view, perspectives, positions, and/or cultures.

Following this theme, the scientific program of CAiSE 2016, whose papers appear in this volume, included "traditional" topics associated with information systems engineering, as well as more contemporary topics and ones specifically related to the theme. The program included the following paper sessions:

- Collaboration
- Innovation, gamification
- Cloud and services
- Open source software
- Requirements engineering
- Business process modelling
- Business process management
- Variability and configuration
- Process mining
- Mining and business process performance
- Mining and decision support
- Conceptual modelling

CAiSE 2016 received 211 full-paper submissions from all over the world: papers were submitted from 48 countries in all five continents. After a rigorous reviewing process, involving the CAiSE Program Committee and Program Board, 35 high-quality papers were selected for presentation at the conference (acceptance rate of 16.5 %). Notably, the papers accepted for publication in the conference include representatives of all five continents, demonstrating how international CAiSE is.

The scientific program also included three keynotes and four tutorials, whose abstracts appear in this volume. The keynotes are: "Three Projects and a Projection" by Jonathan Grudin, "Making Your Users and You Tick" by Igor Benko, and "Processes and Quality of Data" by Barbara Pernici. The tutorials are: "Sustainability in Information Systems Engineering and Research" by Sergio España, Patricia Lago, and Sjaak Brinkkemper; "Quality of Business Process Models" by John Krogstie; "ICT-Based Creativity and Innovation" by Michele Missikoff; "Capability-Driven Development for Building Sustainable Information Systems" by Janis Stirna, Jelena Zdravkovic, and Hrvoje Simic.

In addition, the conference featured a variety of workshops, three attached working conferences, an industry track, a doctoral consortium, and a forum devoted to fresh research ideas. Separate proceedings have been published for all these events.

As editors of this volume, we would like to thank all the members of the Program Board and of the Program Committee, as well as external reviewers for their dedication in providing thorough and fair evaluations. Our deepest thanks to Richard van de Stadt, who helped us with the CyberChairPRO conference management system in an extremely effective way. We also warmly thank the local organization team and the CAiSE webmaster, publicity chairs, workshop organization chairs, forum chairs, tutorial and panel chairs, doctoral consortium chairs, publication chair, and industry chairs. Last but not least, we thank the general chairs, Marko Bajec and Johann Eder, who helped us with patience and dedication, combining experience with enthusiasm, to deliver a program that we are sure the community found interesting and inspiring.

April 2016   Selmin Nurcan
                                                                    Pnina Soffer

Organization

Steering Committee

Barbara Pernici	Politecnico di Milano, Italy
Óscar Pastor	Universitat Politècnica de València, Spain
John Krogstie	Norwegian University of Science and Technology, Norway

Advisory Committee

Janis Bubenko Jr.	Royal Institute of Technology, Sweden
Arne Sølvberg	Norwegian University of Science and Technology, Norway
Colette Rolland	Université Paris 1 Panthéon Sorbonne, France

General Chairs

Marko Bajec	University of Ljubljana, Slovenia
Johann Eder	University of Klagenfurt, Austria

Program Chairs

Selmin Nurcan	University of Paris 1 Panthéon-Sorbonne, France
Pnina Soffer	University of Haifa, Israel

Organization Chairs

Vida Groznik	University of Ljubljana, Slovenia
Slavko Žitnik	University of Ljubljana, Slovenia
Marko Janković	University of Ljubljana, Slovenia

Workshop Chairs

Haris Mouratidis	University of Brighton, UK
Jianwen Su	University of California at Santa Barbara, USA
John Krogstie	Norwegian University of Science and Technology, Norway

Forum Chairs

Sergio España	Universidad Politécnica de Valencia, Spain
Mirjana Ivanović	University of Novi Sad, Serbia

Doctoral Consortium Chairs

Roel Wieringa   University of Twente, The Netherlands
Stefanie Rinderle-Ma   University of Vienna, Austria
Óscar Pastor   Universidad Politécnica de Valencia, Spain

Tutorial and Panel Chairs

Xavier Franch   Universitat Politècnica de Catalunya, Spain
Jolita Ralyté   University of Geneva, Switzerland

Publicity Chairs

Rébecca Deneckère   Université Paris 1 Panthéon-Sorbonne, France
Marta Indulska   The University of Queensland, Australia
Renata Guizzardi   Federal University of Espírito Santo, Brazil

Publication Chair

Saïd Assar   Mines-Telecom Institute, France

Industry Chairs

Dimitris Karagiannis   University of Vienna, Austria
Niko Schlamberger   Slovenia Society Informatica, Slovenia

Webmaster

Marko Janković   University of Ljubljana, Slovenia

Program Committee Board

Sjaak Brinkkemper, The Netherlands   Óscar Pastor, Spain
Eric Dubois, Luxembourg   Barbara Pernici, Italy
Marlon Dumas, Estonia   Klaus Pohl, Germany
Xavier Franch, Spain   Manfred Reichert, Germany
Giancarlo Guizzardi, Brazil   Hajo Reijers, Netherlands
John Krogstie, Norway   Colette Rolland, France
Pericles Loucopoulos, UK   Janis Stirna, Sweden
Raimundas Matulevičius, Estonia   Mathias Weske, Germany
Haralambos Mouratidis, UK   Roel J. Wieringa, The Netherlands
Andreas L. Opdahl, Norway

Program Committee

Wil van der Aalst, The Netherlands
João Paulo Almeida, Brazil
Daniel Amyot, Canada
Yuan An, USA
Eric Andonoff, France
Saïd Assar, France
Paris Avgeriou, The Netherlands
Luciano Baresi, Italy
Carlo Batini, Italy
Zohra Bellahsene, France
Boualem Benatallah, Australia
Balázs Benyó, Hungary
Giuseppe Berio, France
Ilia Bider, Sweden
Nacer Boudjlida, France
Jordi Cabot, Spain
Albertas Caplinskas, Lithuania
Silvana Castano, Italy
Corine Cauvet, France
Lawrence Chung, USA
Isabelle Comyn-Wattiau, France
Panos Constantopoulos, Greece
Alfredo Cuzzocrea, Italy
Fabiano Dalpiaz, The Netherlands
Maya Daneva, The Netherlands
Valeria De Antonellis, Italy
Rébecca Deneckère, France
Michael Derntl, Germany
Neil Ernst, USA
Sergio España, Spain
João Falcão e Cunha, Portugal
Kathrin Figl, Austria
Ulrich Frank, Germany
Avigdor Gal, Israel
Paolo Giorgini, Italy
Claude Godart, France
Cesar Gonzalez-Perez, Spain
Michael Grossniklaus, Germany
Francesco Guerra, Italy
Renata Guizzardi, Brazil
Irit Hadar, Israel
Anne Hakansson, Sweden
Chihab Hanachi, France
Brian Henderson-Sellers, Australia

Jennifer Horkoff, UK
Marta Indulska, Australia
Matthias Jarke, Germany
Manfred Jeusfeld, Sweden
Paul Johannesson, Sweden
Ivan Jureta, Belgium
Haruhiko Kaiya, Japan
Dimitris Karagiannis, Austria
Evangelia Kavakli, Greece
David Kensche, Germany
Larry Kerschberg, USA
Marite Kirikova, Latvia
Christian Kop, Austria
Agnes Koschmider, Germany
Lea Kutvonen, Finland
Marcello La Rosa, Australia
Regine Laleau, France
Alexei Lapouchnian, Canada
Dejan Lavbič, Slovenia
Julio Cesar Leite, Brazil
Sotirios Liaskos, Canada
Kalle Lyytinen, USA
Michel Léonard, Switzerland
Alexander Mädche, Germany
Heinrich Mayr, Austria
Jan Mendling, Austria
Miguel Mira da Silva, Portugal
Isabelle Mirbel, France
John Mylopoulos, Italy
Moira Norrie, Switzerland
Michael Pantazoglou, Greece
Jeffrey Parsons, Canada
Anna Perini, Italy
Gilles Perrouin, Belgium
Anne Persson, Sweden
Geert Poels, Belgium
Jaroslav Pokorny, Czech Republic
Artem Polyvyanyy, Australia
Erik Proper, Luxembourg
Christoph Quix, Germany
Jolita Ralyté, Switzerland
Gil Regev, Switzerland
Iris Reinhartz-Berger, Israel
Dominique Rieu, France

Stefanie Rinderle-Ma, Austria
Thomas Rose, Germany
Michael Rosemann, Australia
Gustavo Rossi, Argentina
Antonio Ruiz Cortés, Spain
Irina Rychkova, France
Shazia Sadiq, Australia
Motoshi Saeki, Japan
Camille Salinesi, France
Rainer Schmidt, Germany
Michael Schrefl, Austria
Samira Si-Said Cherfi, France
Vítor E. Silva Souza, Brazil
Guttorm Sindre, Norway
Monique Snoeck, Belgium
Arnon Sturm, Israel
Angelo Susi, Italy

David Taniar, Australia
Ernest Teniente, Spain
Denis Trček, Slovenia
Juan-Carlos Trujillo Mondejar, Spain
Aphrodite Tsalgatidou, Greece
Francisco Valverde Girome, Spain
Irene Vanderfeesten, The Netherlands
Olegas Vasilecas, Lithuania
Panos Vassiliadis, Greece
Gianluigi Viscusi, Switzerland
Barbara Weber, Austria
Alain Wegmann, Switzerland
Matthias Weidlich, Germany
Hans Weigand, The Netherlands
Yijun Yu, UK
Eric Yu, Canada
Jelena Zdravkovic, Sweden

Additional Reviewers

Manel Achichi
Basmah Almoaber
Areti Ampatzoglou
George Athanasopoulos
Fatma Başak Aydemir
Zia Babar
Christian Bartelt
Malak Baslyman
Maria Bergholtz
Devis Bianchini
Alexander Bock
Dominik Bork
Andrej Bugajev
Andrea Burattin
Federico Cabitza
Javier Canovas
Victorio A. Carvalho
Sofia Charalampidou
Marco Comerio
Mario Cortes Cornax
Xavier Devroey
Mohamed Ben Ellefi
Walid Fdhila
Pablo Fernandez
Alfio Ferrara

José María García
Frédéric Gervais
Mohamad Gharib
Mahdi Ghasemi
Christophe Gnaho
Vangelis Gongolidis
Bénédicte Le Grand
Jens Gulden
Antonio-Manuel Gutierrez-Fernandez
Mehdi Haddad
Fayçal Hamdi
Median Hilal
Tobias Hildebrandt
Monika Kaczmarek
Georg Kaes
Sybren de Kinderen
Eleni Koutrouli
Martin Kretzer
Alexei Lapouchnian
Dirk van der Linden
Angela Locoro
Ioanna Lykourentzou
Abderrahmane Maaradji
José Antonio Parejo Maestre
Fabrizio Maria Maggi

Petros Manousis
Christian Manteuffel
Salvador Martinez
Andrea Maurino
Michele Melchiori
Stefano Montanelli
Carlos Müller
Mario Nolte
Kestutis Normantas
Elda Paja
Óscar Pastor
Jesús Peral
Marcela Ruiz
Mattia Salnitri

Titas Savickas
Silvia Schacht
Christoph G. Schuetz
Arik Senderovich
Zhou Shao
Dieter Steiner
Florian Stertz
Jonathan Svirsky
Nikolaos Tantouris
Chouki Tibermacine
Christina Tsagkani
Maria Jose Villanueva
Michael Walch
Andreas Weiler

Keynotes

Three Projects and a Projection

Jonathan Grudin

Microsoft Research, USA
jgrudin@microsoft.com

Abstract. Thirty years ago, working as a software engineer, I was asked to help develop information systems for connecting people—a range of communication and collaboration support applications and features. It proved difficult to develop systems that people wanted to use. To understand why I gravitated to research, continuing to work with developers and HCI practitioners when opportunities arise. In this talk I will discuss three favorite projects in recent years that had directly applied goals. The goals were fully realized in one case, partly realized in a second, and the third is a favorite because of what we learned. The project areas were an enterprise email system extension, an enterprise 'serious game' platform, and K-12 (primary and secondary) education. I will then step back to describe changes over thirty years that seem salient, and some of the challenges and opportunities confronting us today.

Making Your Users and You Tick

Igor Benko

Google, USA
ibenko@google.com

Abstract. A successful system delights its users, makers, and operators. Making such a system requires melding of different disciplines, practices, a good timing, perseverance, social responsibility, risk management, and some luck. The challenge amplifies when the system targets users across continents and vastly different cultures. In this talk we will illustrate some of the challenges with lessons from Google Search and Google Maps. In particular, we will look into features that help connecting people and that help connect people to the issues they care about. As examples we will use My Maps that connect people over social issues. We will also look at experimental features in Google Search where we enabled interactions between people and cultural moments, and where we enabled American presidential candidates post content directly to Google Search.

Processes and Quality of Data

Barbara Pernici

Politecnico di Milano - DEIB
Piazza Leonardo da Vinci 32, 20133 Milano, Italy
barbara.pernici@polimi.it

Abstract. While a great emphasis has been given in the literature on modeling and analyzing the structure of processes, data being processed and managed within processes are often considered with less attention. In the talk, the importance of data in processes will be analyzed mainly from the point of view of its quality. The data being considered include both the ones directly managed by the process and also the ones that are available in the process execution environment, providing information about its context of execution. In particular the presentation will discuss the issues and possible techniques that can be adopted for evaluating the impact of poor data quality on processes, for assessing the importance of different data quality dimensions, such as, for instance, accuracy, consistency, and completeness, for improving processes adding data quality controls, for repairing processes when failures due to poor data quality occur during execution. Finally, future directions for research considering the opportunities and issues arising from the larger and larger amounts of data available in process environments from different sources will analyzed and discussed.

Tutorials

CAiSE 2016 Tutorials

This section contains the abstracts of the tutorials accepted for presentation at the 28th International Conference on Advanced Information Systems Engineering (CAiSE 2016), held in Ljubljana, Slovenia, from the 13th to the 17th of June, 2016.

The objective of the tutorials is offering new insights, knowledge and skills to managers, teachers, researchers, and students seeking to gain a better understanding of the state-of-the-art in Information Systems engineering. They are a good way to get a broad overview of a topic beyond a current paper presentation.

This year, 9 tutorial proposals were submitted for consideration at CAiSE 2016. The tutorials were evaluated according to several criteria: relevance to CAiSE, structure and contents of the proposal, attractiveness, novelty of the topic, perceived importance in the field, methodology for the presentation, background of the speaker(s) and past experience.

As a result, 4 tutorials were selected for presentation at the conference: "Sustainability in Information Systems Engineering and Research", by Sergio España, Patricia Lago and Sjaak Brinkkemper; "Quality of Business Process Models", by John Krogstie; "ICT-based Creativity and Innovation", by Michele Missikoff; "Capability Driven Development for Building Sustainable Information Systems", by Janis Stirna, Jelena Zdravkovic and Hrvoje Simic. All the tutorials were assigned 90 minutes for presentation and were included in the main conference program.

We would like to thank all the people involved in the organization of the event: the CAiSE 2016 Program Chairs, Selmin Nurcan and Pnina Soffer; the CAiSE 2016 General Chairs, Marko Bajec and Johann Eder; and all the colleagues who submitted their tutorial proposal for consideration to the conference.

Barcelona/Geneva, March 2016

Xavier Franch, Universitat Politècnica de Catalunya, Spain
Jolita Ralyté, University of Geneva, Switzerland

Sustainability in Information Systems Engineering and Research

Sergio España[1], Patricia Lago[2], Sjaak Brinkkemper[1]

[1] Department of Information and Computing Sciences, Utrecht University,
The Netherlands
s.espana@uu.nl, s.brinkkemper@uu.nl
[2] Department of Computer Science, VU University Amsterdam, The Netherlands
p.lago@vu.nl

Abstract. Academic and industrial interest in sustainability-related topics is increasing. There is a growing awareness that, when it comes to improving the impact in our surroundings, every little helps. This tutorial provides an overview of sustainability in the realm of information systems, both from a research perspective and from the point of view of industry practitioners. Starting from the basics of sustainability and its relation with information technology, we then review methods and technologies applicable to this domain. Moreover, we will discuss the current challenges in sustainable information systems research and development. Interlarded with examples and interactions with the participants, our ultimate goal is to motivate you to take part in this interesting area with a strong societal impact.

Keywords: Sustainability · Green IT · Information systems · Responsible software · Responsible enterprise · Socio-environmental impact · Tutorial

1 ICT Sustainability Is Not Only a Hot Topic, but also Necessary

The behaviour of enterprises and citizens has an impact on the sustainability of the economic, social and environmental systems [1]. Responsible enterprises and well-informed citizens are agents of change towards a better world. Given the great challenges to be faced, their efforts need to be supported by the appropriate information and communication technology (ICT).

The impressive advances in ICT over the last few decades have brought big threats and opportunities. Among the threats, data centres serving the ever-growing demand for information are now responsible for around 2 % of greenhouse gas emissions, a similar share to aviation [2]. Advances in energy-efficient hardware and software are expected to alleviate this problem [3]. Among the opportunities, the emerging second wave of sustainable ICT is becoming more externally focused and service-oriented, applying technology not only to exploit enterprise and customer opportunities but also to address broader societal problems [4]. In this promising landscape there are many opportunities for successful innovations to be applied in sectors such as agriculture, construction, power, consumer services, manufacturing or transportation.

2 Overview of the Tutorial: From Basics to Challenges

The tutorial aims to raise awareness on the role that advanced information systems research and engineering can have in creating a more sustainable world. It is a call for participation in a growing movement to save the planet and its people, while keeping profit in mind. The main intended learning outcomes of the tutorial are the following:

- Know the basics of sustainability from the economic, social and environment points of view (a.k.a. triple bottom line).
- Understand the role played by information systems research and engineering in technical sustainability.
- Be aware of the relevant toolset of methods and technologies applicable to this research domain.
- Be able to outline past and current trends on sustainable software, as well as the open challenges of the area.

The tutorial provides a bird's eye view on sustainable information systems engineering and research. It intends to produce insights in the audience on how they can contribute to a more sustainable world as researchers and as individuals, presenting the necessary methods and tools to do so.

Eventually, we intend to motivate you to participate in improving our world: practitioners will learn what they can do to improve the responsibility of their enterprises (well-established practices and tools); researchers will learn how they can expand the frontiers of knowledge on sustainable software (relevant theories, research methods and challenges).

References

1. Gibson, R.B.: Beyond the pillars: sustainability assessment as a framework for effective integration of social, economic and ecological considerations in significant decision-making. J. Environ. Assess. Policy Manage. **8**(3), 259–280 (2006)
2. Global e-Sustainability Initiative -GeSI- and Boston Consulting Group: SMARTer 2020: the role of ICT in driving a sustainable future (2012). http://gesi.org/portfolio/report/72
3. Procaccianti, G., Lago, P., Lewis, G.A.: Green architectural tactics for the cloud. In: 11th Working IEEE/IFIP Conference on Software Architecture. WICSA 2014, pp. 41–44. IEEE (2014)
4. Harmon, R.R., Demirkan, H.: The next wave of sustainable IT. IT Prof. **13**(1), 19–25 (2011)

Quality of Business Process Models

NTNU, Trondheim, Norway
John.krogstie@idi.ntnu.no

Abstract. The goal of the tutorial was to discuss issues of quality of business process models, and how the SEQUAL framework on quality of models and modeling languages can be used in practice to assess and evaluate a business process model. Based on the tutorial and accompanying material, the participants should be able to use the framework in their own work. The expected audience of the tutorial was people with intermediate or advanced background in (process) modeling, although anyone with some familiarity with modeling, and in particular business process modelling should be able to benefit from the tutorial.

Keywords: Business process modelling · Quality of models · Modeling languages

Tutorial Details

Business processes is at the core of organizational activities. A (business) process is a collection of related, structured tasks that produce a specific service or product to address a certain (organizational) goal for a particular actor or set of actors. The management of business processes receives increasing interest [2]. An important area in this regard is the modelling of processes - Business Process Modelling. Although a lot of work is done in this area, we still have not developed a common agreement relative to central notions such as:

- Quality of business process models so they can be used to achieve their purpose.
- Appropriate modelling formalisms and extensions of modelling formalisms and approaches to support achieving and maintaining model quality.
- Needs for tools and methods to support process modelling.

Within process modeling we have found the move towards standardization, e.g. to the use of BPMN, but it can be argued that BPMN do not address all the goals of modeling [1]. To understand the issues of quality of conceptual models we have for many years worked with SEQUAL, a framework for understanding the quality of models and modeling languages, which we have seen can subsume all main aspects relative to quality of models. SEQUAL builds on early work on quality of model [7], but has been extended based on theoretical results [8, 9, 10] and practical experiences [3, 4, 6, 11] with the original framework.

SEQUAL has three unique properties compared to other frameworks for quality of models:

- It distinguishes between quality characteristics (goals) and means to potentially achieve these goals.
- It is closely linked to linguistic and semiotic concepts. In particular, the core of the framework including the discussion on syntax, semantics, and pragmatics is parallel to the use of these terms in the semiotic theory of Morris.
- It is based on a constructivistic world-view, recognizing that models are usually created as part of a dialogue between those involved in modeling, whose knowledge of the modeling domain changes as modeling takes place.

Work to specialize SEQUAL for investigating the quality of business process models is the topic of an upcoming book [5] and is the basis for this tutorial which contains the following parts:

1. Characteristics of business process models
2. Quality of models relative to different goals of business process modeling
3. Overall presentation of the SEQUAL framework
4. Exemplifying the different aspects of the framework
5. Extensive examples of how the framework has been used in industrial settings
6. Summary with a quiz and take home lessons

References

1. Aagesen, G., Krogstie, J.: Analysis and design of business processes using BPMN. In: vom Brocke, J., Rosemann, M. (eds.) Handbook on Business Process Management. Springer, Berlin (2010)
2. Von Brocke, J., Rosemann, M. (eds.): Handbook on Business Process Management, 2nd edn. Springer, Berlin (2015)
3. Heggset, M., Krogstie, J., Wesenberg, H.: Understanding model quality concerns when using process models in an industrial company. In: Gaaloul, K., Schmidt, R., Nurcan, S., Guerreiro, S., Ma, Q. (eds.) EMMSAD 2015. LNBIP, vol. 214, pp. 395–409. Springer, Berlin (2015)
4. Krogstie, J.: Model-driven development and evolution of information systems. In: Konstantas, D., Léonard, M., Pigneur, Y., Patel, S. (eds.) Object-Oriented Information Systems. LNCS, vol. 2817, p. 2. Springer, Berlin (2012)
5. Krogstie, J.: Quality in Business Process Modeling. Springer (2016)
6. Krogstie, J., Dalberg, V., Jensen, S.M.: Process modeling value framework. In: Manolopoulos, Y., Filipe, J., Constantopoulos, P., Cordeiro, J. (eds.) ICEIS 2006. LNBIP, vol. 3, pp. 309–321. Springer, Berlin (2008)
7. Lindland, O.I., Sindre, G., Sølvberg, A.: Understanding quality in conceptual modelling. IEEE Softw. 11(2), 42–49 (1994)
8. Moody, D.L.: Theorethical and practical issues in evaluating the quality of conceptual models: current state and future directions. Data Knowl. Eng. 55, 243–276 (2005)
9. Nelson, H.J., Poels, G., Genero, M., Piattini, M.: A conceptual modeling quality framework. Softw. Qual. J. 20, 201–228 (2012)

10. Price, R., Shanks, G.: A semiotic information quality framework: development and comparative analysis. J. Inf. Technol. **20**(2), 88–102 (2005)
11. Moody, D.L., Sindre, G., Brasethvik, T., Sølvberg, A.: Evaluating the quality of process models: empirical testing of a quality framework. In: Spaccapietra, S., March, S.T., Kambayashi, Y. (eds.) ER 2002. LNCS, vol. 2503, pp. 214–231. Springer, Berlin (2002)

ICT-Based Creativity and Innovation

Michele Missikoff

Institute of Sciences and Technologies of Cognition, CNR, Rome, Italy
michele.missikoff@cnr.it

1 Framing Innovation

Innovation is a key factor to relaunch the EU industrial system. In particular SMEs, that represent the 99 % of the enterprises active in Europe, need to systematically adopt innovation as part of their everyday business (see: *continuous innovation* [1]). To this end, SMEs need to rethink their culture, organization and, overall, their strategies in adopting advanced ICT infrastructures. Hence, ICT plays a central role in carrying out successful innovation; in particular, there is a new generation of ICT-based socio-technical platforms that are proving to be very effective in supporting the challenging activities of an innovation project.

This tutorial illustrates some of the key competences necessary to carry out a successful innovation project. Some of them are directly derived from the experience in Information Systems Engineering, but need to be revisited in the light of the advent of a new breed of socio-technical systems, aimed at supporting innovation in networked organizations (i.e., SMEs, but also large highly decentralised corporations, public institutions, etc.).

Carrying out an innovation project is not an easily job for a single enterprise, then it is really a challenge for a network of enterprise, having the problem of achieving the necessary coordination and synergy in a distributed, multi-player operational and decisional context. Managing an innovation project requires approaches, methods and tools inherently different from those used in 'traditional' Project Management. It is necessary a deep rethinking of existing tools and methods and, at the same time, new tools and methods need to be developed. The BIVEE (Business Innovation in Virtual Enterprise Environment) platform, developed by an European project (that received the European Excellence Award), represents a valid example [2].

2 Objectives of the Tutorial

The objectives of this tutorial is to illustrate the opportunities that advanced ICT solutions can offer to improve the innovation capacity of complex organizations, in particular SMEs organized in virtual (networked) enterprises. To this end, the tutorial starts with a reflection on the nature of Innovation, since this term represents a rich and articulated domain, often addressed without the awareness of its complexity. Then, the tutorial proceeds addressing the following topics.

- Nature and essence of Innovation.
- Different types of innovation and the main approaches that can be used to address them.
- Focusing on selected topics, e.g., how to improve creativity, by using game-based technique, how to promote divergent thinking and serendipity in innovation.
- ICT methods and tools able to support the various activities found in the different phases of the lifecycle of Innovation: from its inception (e.g., Creativity phase) to its conclusion (e.g., Engineering and transfer to production).
- Practical issues to be considered when developing an ICT-based platform for innovation support and management, starting from a specific case: the European project BIVEE.
- Sharing conclusions on how to starting and carrying out an Innovation project.

The core of the presentation will be based on the 5-dimensional Open Innovation Space. The 5 dimensions are: *(i) key supporting disciplines* (from Economics to Design Science, from Art and Creativity to Engineering), *(ii) enterprise facets* (Process, Product, Service, Organization, Market, Technology), *(iii) digital enablers* (from Collaboration platform to Knowledge Management, from Big Data Analytics to Decision Support Systems), *(iv) application domains* (see below), *(v) enterprise innovation lifecycle* (where the core is represented by the BIVEE Innovation Waves: *Creativity, Feasibility, Prototyping, Engineering*).

It is important to remark once more that the approach and the addressed topics are positioned at a meta-level, therefore the presentation is not concerned with innovation in a specific application domain, such as automotive, health, agro-food, or aerospace. We concentrate on innovation as a discipline per se, addressing it in a sufficiently general fashion to seize the commonalities, principles, guidelines, but also methods and tools, that are valid for a large variety of enterprises operating in different application domains. But, naturally, the tutorial does not pretend to be exhaustive over all the problems and solutions connected to innovation (that include, e.g., from change management to HR, from organizational issues to business models); similarly, despite the generality of the adopted approach and the proposed solutions, when such solutions are actually applied to a concrete situation, a number of refinements, integrations and customization need to be carried out.

References

1. Boer, H., Gertsen, F.: From continuous improvement to continuous innovation: a (retro)(per)spective. Int. J. Technol. Manage. **26**, 8 (2003)
2. Missikoff, M., Canducci, M., Maiden, N. (eds.): Enterprise Innovation: from Creativity to Engineering. Wiley (2015)

Capability Driven Development for Building Sustainable Information Systems

Janis Stirna[1], Jelena Zdravkovic[1], Hrvoje Simic[2]

[1] Department of Computer and Systems Sciences, Stockholm University,
Forum 100, SE-16440, Kista, Sweden
{js, jelenaz}@dsv.su.se
[2] Croz d.o.o., Lastovska 23, 10000 Zagreb, Croatia
hsimic@croz.net

Abstract. The notion of capability has emerged in information system (IS) engineering as the means to support development of context dependent organizational solutions and supporting IS applications. To this end a Capability Driven Development (CDD) has been proposed. The CDD methodology supports IS development and designing as well as running applications that need to be adjusted according to changes in the context. This tutorial presents the methodology, demonstrates the tool support for CDD, as well as summarizes our experiences of using CDD in four companies.

Keywords: Enterprise modeling · Capability design · Capability development

Introduction

A significant objective of today's enterprise Information Systems (IS) is to be sustainable, which entails producing value to their stakeholders over time. A major concern is how IS can successfully support constant variations in business conditions originating, for instance, from changes in customers' demand, environmental aspects, regulations, etc. A key challenge is the need to adjust according to change at runtime.

Capability as a concept originates from competence-based management and military frameworks. It offers a complement to traditional Enterprise Modeling (EM) approaches by representing organizational knowledge from a result-based perspective. Lately, the notion has emerged in IS engineering as an instrument to context-dependent business and application design. To ensure the needs of business stakeholders for the variety of business contexts that an enterprise faces and thus facilitate sustainable application delivery, we see the capability notion as the central concept to enable a holistic approach to model-oriented IS development that integrates both the business and technological development perspectives. Capability is seen as *the ability and capacity that enable an enterprise to achieve a business goal in a certain context* [1]. It is operationalized in a capability-oriented approach that integrates organizational development with IS development taking into account changes in the application context of the solution. This is referred to as Capability Driven Development (CDD). It requires a number of organizational concepts to be modeled, such as business goals, processes, resources, Key Performance Indicators (KPIs), as well as the parameters for describing business environmental contexts for organizations capabilities. CDD consists of the following method components:

- *Capability Design* for design, evaluation and development of capabilities by using process models, goal models and other types of models.
- *Enterprise Modeling* is included in CDD for the creation of enterprise models that are used as input for capability design.
- *Context Modeling* for analyzing the capability context, and the variations needed to deal with variations.
- *Reuse of Capability Design* for elicitation and documentation of patterns for capability design.
- *Run-time Delivery Adjustment* for defining capability adjustments at runtime.

The CDD methodology is supported by the CDD environment consisting of the following key components:

- *Capability Design Tool (CDT):* a graphical modelling tool for supporting the creation of models according to the capability meta-model. The CDT will provide the developers with a suitable notation for EM and capability design.
- *Capability Navigation Application (CNA):* an application that uses the models created in the CDT to monitor relevant context and handle run-time capability adjustments.
- *Capability Context Platform (CCP):* the context platform supports capturing and distributing context information to the CNA.
- *Capability Delivery Application (CDA):* the business application that are used to support the capability delivery. This can be a custom-made IS, or a configured IS such as an ERP. The CNA communicates, or configures the CDA to adjust for changing contexts during capability design and delivery.

CDD been applied in the following cases: SIV AG (Germany) for standard business processes execution capability; FreshTL Ltd (UK) for maritime compliance capability; CLMS Ltd (UK) for collaborative IS development using the MDD technology; Everis (Spain) for service promotion capability, marriage registration capability, and SOA platform capability.

References

1. Bērziša, S., Bravos, G., Gonzalez, T., Czubayko, U., España, S., Grabis, J., Henkel, M., Jokste, L., Kampars, J., Koç, H., Kuhr, J., Llorca, C., Loucopoulos, P., Juanes, R., Pastor, O., Sandkuhl, K., Simic, H., Stirna, J., Valverde, F., Zdravkovic, J.: Capability driven development: an approach to designing digital enterprises. Int. J. Bus. Inf. Syst. Eng. (BISE) **57/1**, 15–25 (2015)

Contents

Conceptual Modeling

Mining and Decision Support

Cloud and Services

Variability and Configuration

Open Source Software

Business Process Management

Collaboration

View-Based Near Real-Time Collaborative Modeling for Information Systems Engineering

Petru Nicolaescu[1(✉)], Mario Rosenstengel[1], Michael Derntl[2], Ralf Klamma[1], and Matthias Jarke[1,3]

[1] RWTH Aachen University, Lehrstuhl Informatik 5, Ahornstr. 55,
52074 Aachen, Germany
{nicolaescu,rosenst,klamma,jarke}@dbis.rwth-aachen.de
[2] Eberhard Karls Universität Tübingen,
eScience-Center, Wilhelmstr. 32, 72074 Tübingen, Germany
michael.derntl@uni-tuebingen.de
[3] Fraunhofer FIT, Birlinghoven Castle, Sankt Augustin, Germany

Abstract. Conceptual modeling is a creative, social process that is driven by the views of involved stakeholders. However, few systems offer view-based conceptual modeling on the Web using lock-free synchronous collaborative editing mechanisms. Based on a (meta-)modeling framework that supports near real-time collaborative modeling and meta-modeling in the Web browser, this paper proposes an exploratory approach for collaboratively defining views and viewpoints on conceptual models. Viewpoints are defined on the metamodeling layer and instantiated as views within a model editor instance. The approach was successfully used for various conceptual modeling languages and it is based on user requirements for model-based creation and generation of next-generation community applications. An end-user evaluation showed the usefulness, usability and limitations of view-based collaborative modeling. We expect that Web-based collaborative modeling powered by view extensions will pave the way for a new generation of collaboratively and socially engineered information systems.

Keywords: Views · Viewpoints · Collaborative conceptual modeling

1 Introduction

Conceptual modeling is a key tool for representing domain-specific information during the requirements elicitation and design phases of information systems [16]. With the increased collaboration between stakeholders from different geographical locations and the emergence of Web technologies that enable near real-time (NRT) communication and offer a proper medium for collaboration and information exchange, new research opportunities emerge in the field of collaborative conceptual modeling. Usually, (meta-)models are used to create abstract representations of a system and to address different groups of stakeholders,

S. Nurcan et al. (Eds.): CAiSE 2016, LNCS 9694, pp. 3–17, 2016.
DOI: 10.1007/978-3-319-39696-5_1

e.g. developers, project managers, customers, partners, or investors. The complexity of models and metamodels representing these systems is increasing rapidly. Thus, it is often necessary to look at a complex system or application from different points of view. Moreover, certain stakeholders may prefer or require a different view to express their concerns [11,17]. Views (also referred to as viewpoints) are used to deal with this complexity in (meta-)modeling frameworks. View-based modeling aims at creating partial metamodels and models, each one of them reflecting a set of concerns of the modeled system [17]. Previous research during the late '90 s covers viewpoints and the generation of views from metamodels, especially from a requirements engineering perspective [15,16]. The works also explore the generation of views from metamodels, in various industry or academia-driven information systems. However, as aforementioned, the Web 2.0 uprise has reshaped the social work behavior, making systems available for heterogeneous communities free or at a low cost, on the Web, which is also valid in the conceptual modeling case.

The motivation underlying this work is taken from a Model Driven Web Engineering scenario where developers and end users collaboratively built a Web application [4]. In this setting, a study was carried out using thirteen user evaluation sessions in groups of two or three, with a total of 36 participants. We observed how collaborative modeling can be leveraged by different stakeholders during the design phase of an information system. We provided both non-technical users and software developers with an NRT collaborative editor for modeling and generating Web applications. Based on a common application metamodel, they were given separate parts of a model for modeling the frontend and backend of the application. In a first stage, participants were allowed to model the backend of a given information system in NRT (services, database, service interface, etc.). Then, they were asked to model in the same way the interface for the already designed backend. The results show that many end users perceived parts of the model as too complicated or were finding the representation not relevant or intuitive for them. As such, they expressed the desire to reduce complexity of a model by only being presented with relevant aspects, which in the specific case were mostly considered to be HTML5 frontend elements. Furthermore, many end users expressed the desire to have familiar representations of such objects. Following these outcomes, this paper explores the NRT collaborative definition of views through a metamodel-based approach and their usage in NRT collaborative modeling scenarios.

We formulate three research questions:

- How can various stakeholders collaboratively define views as part of a metamodel in NRT? (*RQ1*);
- How to generate customized views based on the metamodel definition where stakeholders can further collaboratively edit parts of a generated model? (*RQ2*);
- Do views impact NRT collaborative modeling with respect to user experience improvement and the modeling process speed (*RQ3*)?

In order to explore the collaborative work with custom-defined views, the paper presents a view extension framework for NRT collaborative modeling in the Web browser. The framework facilitates a collaborative, graphical definition of views on the metamodel layer. This allows metamodelers to redefine entities (e.g. objects and relationships of a metamodel) in custom viewpoints and then apply these viewpoints to the models. In previous work [5], we presented SyncMeta, a Web-based NRT collaborative (meta-)modeling tool. SyncMeta allows the collaborative creation of metamodels in NRT based on a visual language specification (VLS) and the generation of model editors based on the defined metamodels. The view extension was implemented on top of this framework.

This paper is structured as follows. In the next section we introduce the SyncMeta framework that offers the foundation for our collaborative view-based modeling extension. Section 3 introduces viewpoints and views and provides a formalization on view-based metamodeling. Section 4 then describes the architecture and implementation of the framework and discusses the limitations of our approach. Section 5 presents an end-user evaluation of the implementation. Section 6 shows how the view-based extension goes beyond the state of the art. Finally, Sect. 7 concludes the paper and outlines the future work.

2 SyncMeta: Near Real-Time Collaborative (Meta-)Modeling and the Views Extension

SyncMeta is a Web-based metamodeling framework that allows users to create modeling languages collaboratively with NRT synchronization of edits. An illustration of the concepts and roles in the SyncMeta framework is given in Fig. 1. On the metamodeling layer metamodelers use the Meta-Model Editor for collaborative authoring of a metamodel, represented by a VLS. This builds the basis

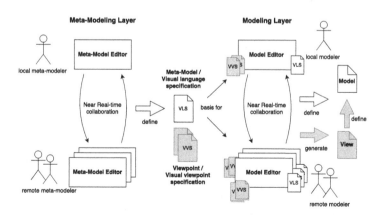

Fig. 1. Concepts and roles in the SyncMeta (meta-) modeling process [5], enhanced with views extension

for a model editor for the specified modeling language. A VLS is defined visually using a graph-based visual modeling language (VML). An arbitrary number of model editors can be generated based on the defined VLS. The NRT collaboration takes place at both metamodeling and modeling layers. The implementation details, architecture and interface offered by SyncMeta are detailed in the previous work [5]. The gray elements in Fig. 1 depict the view extension integrated into the SyncMeta framework. These also reflect the contributions of this work. On the metamodeling layer metamodelers may collaboratively define viewpoints in SyncMeta's metamodel editor. For the definition of a viewpoint the underlying VML was extended with additional view types. The view types define references to classes of the metamodel and offer to define conditions on the attributes of the referenced class (*RQ1*). Additionally the appearance and rules for each view type can be redefined in a view. To facilitate the metamodeling process a Closed-View Generation (CVG) algorithm based on [20] was implemented to automatically add classes and relationships to the viewpoint when a reference to an object or relationship is defined in the metamodel (*RQ1*).

Similar to the VLS generated for a metamodel, for each viewpoint a visual view specification (VVS) is generated which consists of a construction plan for the view in the modeling layer (*RQ2*). Here, an existing model can be used in combination with a certain VVS to generate a view on the model. Modelers may collaboratively edit any view or the model itself in NRT, with all actions being propagated to collaborators and reflected in all views and in the model (*RQ2*).

A simple example is given by the model-based community application design. Domain-specific experts from a certain community, software architects and software developers can define a metamodel for the information systems which should be developed in the respective community. For that, they create the metamodel collaboratively on the Web in NRT. Then, more VVS are defined in the metamodel, e.g. a view for frontend elements as modeling objects for community end users, a backend view for developers and a communication view between frontend and backend. Based on the defined VVS, a model editor is generated together with corresponding views. Community end users can collaboratively create the frontends they require on the frontend view, together with developers. Developers can give immediate feedback on the functionality required by end users. Developers can also edit in NRT the application backend and the communication between the backend and frontend, while architects can see in NRT the entire model and check the integrity of the modeled system. The view extension framework – following the same implementation policies of SyncMeta – is Web-based and fully open source (available in GitHub[1]).

3   Views and Viewpoints

The terms *view* and *viewpoint* are used interchangeably in many different reports and are often just introduced as examples. We therefore offer formal definitions for these terms and explain the relations between the different concepts used in

---

[1] https://github.com/rwth-acis/syncmeta

the visual modeling approach (*RQ1, RQ2*). The definitions are used in Sect. 4 for explaining the implementation of the viewpoint modeling and the view generation.

As in [7] a *viewpoint* is defined as a language which represents a metamodel. A viewpoint can restrict the original metamodel and it addresses a set of concerns of one or more stakeholders.

A *view* is the presentation of a model by applying a specific viewpoint. Thus, a view is a concrete instance of a viewpoint. A viewpoint is defined by a collection of view types.

A *view type* is a meta-class whose instances a view can display [8]. Thus, a view type is an object or a relationship class which comprises a set of rules. These rules can be "selectional" or "projectional" predicates that determine the representation of a object within the view.

In the following we introduce the formal definitions for the terms introduced above. First we define the sets of classes, properties and types and then define the formal concept of a metamodel.

Let P be an infinite set of properties. Each $p \in P$ can be an arbitrary complex function or a simple value from an enumeration type. We only require that each p has a label, a type and a unique identifier.

Let T be the set of all types defined in the VML on the metamodeling layer of SyncMeta, e.g., $T = \{Object, Relationship, NodeShape, Generali$ $zation, Association, \dots \}$. An overview of all types in the VML is depicted in Fig. 3.

Let C be an infinite set of classes. Any class $c \subseteq C$ has a unique name, a type description, and a set of properties.

We define $\textbf{label}(c) = l$ for $c \in C$. Analogously, we define $\textbf{label}(C) = \{label(c) \mid c \in C\}$ as the set of all unique identifiers of all classes in C. Thus, we define the signature of a class c as a triplet with $c = (l, t, A)$, where l is the unique name of the class, $t \in T$ is the name of a type associated with the class, and $A \subset P$ a finite set of properties. We define $\textbf{type}(c) = t$ as the type of class c. Analogously, we define $\textbf{type}(C) = \{type(c) \mid c \in C\}$. Similar definitions can be found in [20].

Definition 1. *A* **metamodel** *is a directed graph* $G = (V, E)$ *with* $V \subset C$ *a finite set of nodes and* $\forall c \in V : \textbf{type}(c) \in T$. *E is a finite set of edges with* $E = \{(l, t, c_i, c_j, A) \mid c_i, c_j \in V, c_i \neq c_j, t \in T, l$ *an identifier,* $A \subset P\}$.

We assume that a metamodel may consist of an arbitrary number of classes and each class may consist of an arbitrary number of properties. We only require that the type of each class belongs to the VML. Analogously we can define a viewpoint. A viewpoint is a metamodel on its own. We just require that a viewpoint consists of at least one view type. Thus, we formally define a view type before we give a formal definition of a viewpoint. We define a function φ that transforms an object class or a relationship class into a ViewObject or ViewRelationship class, respectively. On other classes the function φ is the identity function.

Definition 2. *Let* $VT_C = \{\varphi(c) \mid c \in C\}$ *and* $\varphi(l, t, A) = (l', t', A', l)$ *with* l' *the new unique label,* t' *is ViewObject or ViewRelationship if* t *is Object or Relationship, else* $t = t'$. *Obviously,* $A' \subseteq A \subset P$.

A view type class of a viewpoint consists of a reference to a class in the metamodel. The reference is the unique name l. Thus, a viewpoint is not independent of the metamodel.

Definition 3. *A* **viewpoint** *with respect to* VT_C *is a metamodel with* $G' = (V', E')$, *and* $\exists c \in V' : c \in VT_C \wedge$ **type**$(c) = ViewObject$.

Based on these formal definitions of the concepts at the metamodeling layer we can define the concept of viewpoint applied to a model of the modeling layer of SyncMeta (*RQ1*). For the generation of the model editor instance a VLS of the metamodel is generated. For simplicity we think of the VLS as the metamodel described in Definition 1. First we formally define the relation between the metamodel defined in the metamodeling layer and the model.

Definition 4. *Based on graph* $G = (V, E)$ *of a metamodel, a* **model** *is a directed graph* $M = (V', E')$ *with* $\forall v \in V' : type(v) \in label(V)$ *and* $\forall e \in E' : type(e) \in label(E)$.

We require each node and each edge of the *model* to be an instance of a node type or edge type defined in the metamodel. To generate views we first need to define a function which applies a view type to an entity within the model:

Definition 5. *Let* $VP = (V, E)$ *be a VVS of a viewpoint. Let* $\phi_v(n) \colon (l, t, A) \mapsto (l, type(v), A')$, $v \in VT_V$ *is a view type class of* VP. $A' \subset P$ *is the new set of properties defined by view type* v. *Analogously, the function for edges is defined as* $\phi_v(e) \colon (l, t, c_1, c_2, A) \mapsto (l, type(v), c_1, c_2, A'))$, *where* A' *is generated from the attributes defined for* v.

With this helper function we can define a view as follows:

Definition 6. *Let* $VP = (V_{VP}, E_{VP})$ *be a VVS of a viewpoint and* $M = (V_M, E_M)$ *a model. A* **view** $V = (V_V, E_V)$ *is a subgraph of* M *with* $V_V = \{\varphi_v(c) \mid v \in V_{VP} \wedge c \in V_M\} \subseteq V_M$ *and* $E_V = \{\varphi_v(e) \mid v \in V_{VP} \wedge e \in E_M\} \subseteq E_M$.

The resulting view is a subgraph of the model it is applied on. Each node/edge whose type is referenced to a view type in the VVS is part of the view (RQ2). For the view generation we need a VVS and a existing model as input.

4   Architecture and Implementation

Widgets. Figure 2 depicts an overview of the widgets offered by SyncMeta with the view extension. The canvas widget visualizes the current state of the model and provides mechanisms to manipulate the model–e.g. adding nodes and edges, drag & drop, and similar. Each edit that alters the model is propagated locally

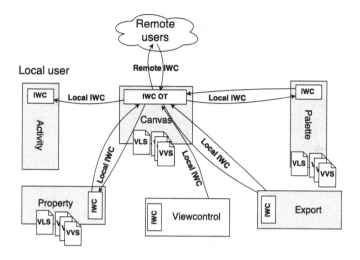

Fig. 2. Widget components of Syncmeta with the view extension

to other widgets and remotely to other collaborators. The property editor widget allows editing properties of node and edges selected in the canvas widget. Each property modification (e.g., changing the title of a node) is propagated back to the canvas widget. On the metamodeling layer the canvas widget saves and retrieves all nodes and edges of the metamodel and the viewpoints. The palette widget provides the nodes and edge types defined in the metamodel. Additionally the palette dynamically adjusts to the types defined in a particular VVS whenever a viewpoint is applied to a model. The activity widget tracks and displays the edits made by all collaborators. This is mainly for awareness purposes. SyncMeta consists of several additional widgets which serve special purposes, for example the export widget allows to export a model in JSON or PNG format. The view control widget allows to generate, export, and import a viewpoint metamodel or a VVS.

Conflict Resolution. SyncMeta enables non-locking collaboration— that is, each user can manipulate any part of the model at any time. The mechanisms to resolve editing conflicts are achieved using the OpenCoWeb JavaScript Operational Transformation (OT) Engine API [18], which is based on a decentralized peer-to-peer architecture. The details for the conflict resolution in the NRT modeling are given in [5] and are not repeated here due to space restrictions. The view extension uses also these mechanisms for modeling tasks and the view definitions. All operations are propagated to all other collaborators. At each receiving client the OT algorithms detect and resolve any occurring conflicts. The OT engine ensures a congruent model state after processing all operations at all client sides, following an optimistic approach (i.e. as opposed to approaches which use locking for all or parts of the model [3], changes are propagated in NRT andtherefore almost instantly visible at all sites).

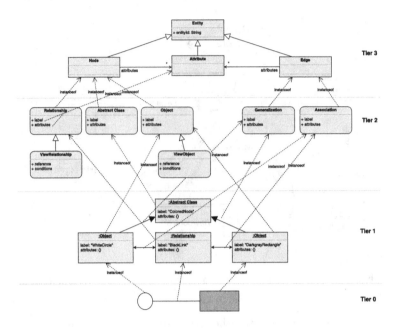

Fig. 3. Simplified extended metamodel hierarchy with view types

Metamodeling and Viewpoint Modeling(*RQ1*). In the previous section we have presented the formal definitions of viewpoints, views and view types and shown that we can apply the NRT collaborative modeling approach of SyncMeta also to the view extension. SyncMeta implements a four-tier metamodel hierarchy, which is depicted in Fig. 3. *Tier 3* defines the basic elements of a graph-based modeling language. *Tier 2* defines the node and edge types of the VML as well as the view types of the viewpoint models. As stated in Sect. 3, Definition 2, a viewpoint does not contain any *Object* or *Relationship* types. We replace them by using the *ViewObject* and *ViewRelationship* types, which are a specialization of *Object* and *Relationship*, respectively. These contain a reference to a node type or an edge type in the metamodel. It is also possible to define conditions on the attributes of the referenced class, i.e. in contrast to a simple object class a view-object offers functionalities to customize the attributes of a view. Meta-modelers are able to hide and rename attributes. The *Conjunction* attribute determines the logical connector of the conditions. This can be either the logical AND or OR. Thus, we can build a formula with the predicates $\varphi_1, .., \varphi_n$, either with a conjunction over all predicates $\varphi_1 \wedge ... \wedge \varphi_n$ or with a disjunction over all predicates $\varphi_1 \vee ... \vee \varphi_n$. Conditions on attributes allow metamodelers to make simple queries on the attributes of an object class and filter the entities of this class in the view canvas of the model editor.

With auxiliary classes it is possible to define custom node and edge shapes for each view type. *Tier 1* defines the actual metamodel or viewpoint. Metamodelers are allowed to develop an arbitrary number of viewpoints in the same NRT

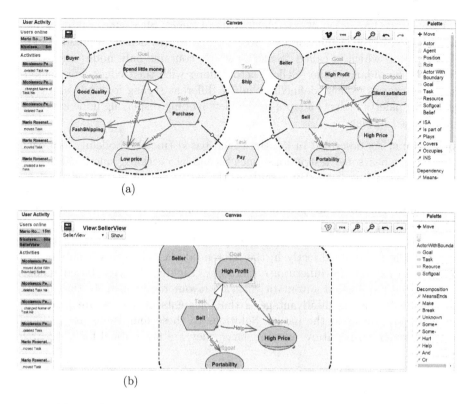

Fig. 4. (a) An i^* model of buyer-seller relationships. (b) Applied *SellerView* to the model above

collaborative fashion they are used to define metamodels. The metamodel is the input for the model editor instantiation and each viewpoint is generated to a VVS. *Tier 0* is the actual model of the modeling layer. On Tier 0 a viewpoint is applied to the model. The resulting view supports NRT collaborative modeling as well. While concepts on Tiers 2 and 3 are implemented in the framework, models on Tier 0 and 1 are defined by modelers and metamodelers, respectively.

View Generation(*RQ2*). On the modeling layer modelers may apply the viewpoints defined on the metamodeling layer. This is done for any existing model by selecting the desired view from a drop-down menu (see Fig. 4(b)). As described in Sect. 3, Definitions 5 and 6 all nodes and edges of the model that are associated with a view type in the viewpoint are then a part of the view, while all other nodes and edges are hidden. In addition to filtering on the type level, the framework also allows filtering nodes and edges on instance level based on the values of their properties. The selected view applies custom styles like adjusting the color, shape, labels or connectors. The following steps are used:

- Filter nodes/edges regarding the ViewObjects/ViewRelationships of the VVS
- Filter nodes/edges by conditions defined on their attributes
- Apply custom styles for each node/edge

Figure 4(a) shows a small i^* model [21] about buyer-seller relationships, which was also used in the evaluation (see Sect. 5). Figure 4(b) depicts a possible view on the model, which is called "SellerView". It contains only nodes and edges within the boundary of the "Seller" actor, along with their edges. For demonstration purposes we also defined a slightly different styling for node and edge types. The palette widgets adapts to the view by only displaying node and edge types defined in view.

Limitations. As described in [5], the visual-based (meta-) modeling approach of SyncMeta has some restrictions, such as model checking functionalities on the (meta-)modeling layer. By extension, the views do not allow the specification of cardinalities or multiplicities with regard to the relationships and view-relationships. Also, it is not possible to define conditions on inherited attributes of super classes. Currently, only the definition of conditions for the attributes of the referenced class is allowed. A simple solution for this problem is that we define the attribute directly in the referenced class, but this is suboptimal and fails to exploit the inheritance hierarchy. Finally, the view-based modeling approach requires an automatic diagram layout mechanism. In the current implementation, a big disadvantage is that elements of a view are placed at the same position as in the model. Solutions to these limitations are planned to be implemented in future versions, since they are not critical for a research prototype.

5 Evaluation

We performed an end user evaluation of the model editor. The main goal was to evaluate the usability and usefulness of the view-based modeling approach and monitor the NRT collaboration features (*RQ3*).

Participants. The end user evaluation comprised four sessions with four participants each with a total of 16 participants, who were recruited from researchers and students of our department. Their expertise in conceptual modeling, i^* and SyncMeta was measured using seven-point Likert scale (from 1=novice to 7=expert). The results show that users had varying existing knowledge of modeling. As such, expertise with graphical editors is quite high, but has a high standard deviation ($M = 4.38; SD = 2.42$). The same holds for user's general expertise in conceptual modeling ($M = 4.5; SD = 2.46$). However, the level of expertise with i^* is rather low ($M = 2.44; SD = 2.5$).

Methodology. In each session, the four participants were split into two groups (*Group Alpha* and *Group Beta*) with two people each. Both groups had to complete two tasks of comparable scope. Each task comprised a list of detailed instructions to extend a given i^* model with additional nodes and edges. This could be performed without any i^* expertise. The collaborators could decide for themselves how to complete the instructions by communicating with each other via chat or just start modeling and let SyncMeta resolve potential conflicts. The first task was solved by Group Alpha and consisted of a predefined view applied,

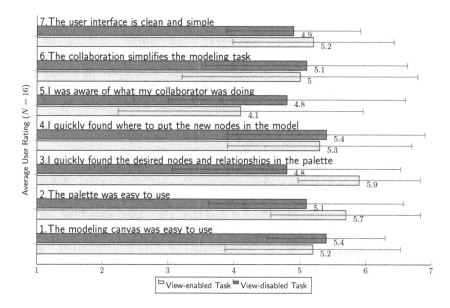

Fig. 5. Survey results of i^* group sessions (quantitative items).

which customized the model editor regarding the requirements of the task (see Fig. 4(b)). Group Beta solved the same task without any view on the original model (see Fig. 4(a)). For the second task, they switched roles: Group Beta used a predefined view, while Group Alpha solved the task without a view.

After each task the session participants were asked to rate statements regarding their experience with and without views. The ratings were made using a seven-point Likert scale ranging from "strongly disagree" (1) to "strongly agree" (7). During the evaluation the working times for each task and group was recorded to determine whether the views had an impact on the time it took modelers to complete the tasks.

Results. The mean ratings for tasks solved with and without views are plotted as series "view-enabled task" and "view-disabled task", respectively, in Fig. 5. For most statements there is little difference between the ratings for view-enabled vs. view-disabled task. We ran paired-sample t-tests for view-enabled vs. view-disabled ratings to identify significant differences. Two statements exposed significant differences at $p < .05$, namely statement 3, revealing that views helped to find nodes and relationships quicker in the palette ($p = .01$), and statement 5, revealing that the views actually hampered the awareness of the collaborator's edits ($p = .04$)

Additionally the working times for each group and task were recorded. The average working time of Alpha groups for Task 1 without views ($M = 253\,\text{s}; SD = 39$) was on average 82 s or 52 % longer than the average working time for Task 2 with view enabled ($M = 171\,\text{s}, SD = 19$). The average working time of the Beta groups for Task 2 without views ($M = 191\,\text{s}; SD = 22$)

was on average about 24 s or 15 % longer in comparison to Task 1 with views enabled ($M = 167$ s; $SD = 31$) . The lower improvement factor for the Beta groups compared to the Alpha groups can be explained by a learning curve. The Alpha groups used the views during the second task, where they were more familiar with how to work with the tool. Conversely, the Beta groups used the views during the first task when it was the first use with the tool for most of them. This actually shows that modeling with views speeds up the modeling process even for users who are unfamiliar with the tool (*RQ3*).

The findings are that views can improve user experience and speed up the modeling process; they can also be used to customize the model editor in order to ease adoption and to improve stakeholder involvement during the collaborative modeling process. Participants also provided some textual comments about the view-based modeling approach. They stated that they liked switching between views and that the reduced palette gives a better orientation, which may explain the faster modeling times with views enabled. The NRT collaboration features were already evaluated in SyncMeta [5], but challenges were also encountered. In the evaluation, NRT collaboration and edits awareness were only available between views and the entire model editor. However, the evaluation results have shown that users require also collaboration directly between individual views and this feature was implemented as consequence (*RQ3*).

6   Related Work

Table 1 demonstrates that views and related concepts have been successfully used in many research fields, including object-oriented databases (OODB) [2, 20], enterprise architecture (EA) [10,22] and corresponding frameworks and in conceptual modeling (CM) [1,6,9,12,13].

OODBs fully support general concepts of object-oriented programming languages. One of the most popular view extensions is called MultiView [2], a simple and powerful tool for supporting multiple views in the Gemstone OODB [19]. Multiview introduced the CVG-algorithm to facilitate the definitions of viewpoints. A similar approach is provided by our view extension (cf. Sect. 2).

EA frameworks are used to look at complex information systems from different point of view—e.g. data, function, networks, organizational, structures, schedules and strategy. The ARIS Framework [10] provides various model editors to build complex enterprise architectures, e.g. location allocation diagram, network diagram, technical resource model. All entities of these model editors are integrated into one comprehensive metamodel. The *Zachman Framework* [22] is a two dimensional classification schema for descriptive representations of an organization. It is an abstract guideline which proposes perspectives on a particular system of an enterprise in different development stages.

Finally, a plethora of CM tools also provide view extensions. *MetaEdit+* [9] is a tool set to define modeling languages and generate model editors. Unlike SyncMeta only a locking collaboration approach is used. $AToM^3$ [12] and *ADOxx* [6] are domain-independent metamodeling frameworks with focus on

Table 1. Comparison of related tools and frameworks.

Tool/Framework	Type	Domain-independent	Graphical view editing	Conditional filters	Conditional styles	Collab. viewpoint definition	Collab. view manipulation	NRT editing
Abiteboul &Bonner [2]	OODB	•		•				
Multiview [20]	OODB	•	•					
ARIS Framework [10]	EA		•					
Zachman Framework [22]	EA	•	•	-	-			
MetaEdit+ [9]	CM	•	•			•	•	
AToM³ [12]	CM	•		•	•			
ADOxxx [6]	CM	•		•				
Sirius [1]	CM	•	•	•	•			
CO2DE [13]	CM		•			•	•	
SyncMeta Views	CM	•	•	•	•	•	•	•

simulation of models. $AToM^3$ allows to transform a model expressed in a certain formalism to an equivalent model in another formalism. ADOxxx [6] provides a query language called AQL for the generation of views on these models. In contrast to SyncMeta Views these frameworks do not provide any NRT collaboration features. *Sirius* [1] uses the Eclipse Modeling Framework (EMF) as basic infrastructure. It offers fully customizable viewpoints on complex models. Modelers can define conditional styles and filters for entities based on their attributes. It is possible to generate a subset of the available palette and define optional layers to show additional content. Sirius lacks NRT collaboration features, but it offers many customization options which makes the framework very powerful. *CO2DE* is a desktop collaborative modeling application. Similar to SyncMeta it provides awareness features to help users recognize edits of model elements and a chat room. CO2DE doesn't support metamodeling. However, it does not automatically solve editing conflicts. It uses a locking approach for enabling collaboration, which is therefore not in NRT. The philosophy is that users have to discuss about conflicts and deal with them on their own.

As this comparison shows, the views framework we implemented exhibits the key features for view definition, editing and use found in literature. As a highly distinguishing feature, SyncMeta Views enables non-locking NRT collaboration during view definition and use, which is not supported in any of the existing tools.

7 Conclusion and Future Work

In this work, we explored how metamodel-based view generation can be effectively combined with NRT collaboration in modeling for teams with different competences and roles. For this purpose, we presented a view extension for the SyncMeta metamodeling framework which allows the generation of views for focusing on particular aspects of a complete model. The views are editable and all edits are reflected in all views and in the model. Thus, we offer a unique approach of NRT collaboration for free conceptual model editing on the Web using optimistic concurrency control mechanisms, combined with known techniques for views definition and generation from information systems domain. The view-based extension was evaluated in group sessions using an instance of the i^* language generated and initialized with a simple model and views. The evaluation results show that NRT collaboration for view-based authoring is possible, that by using views the modeling speed is slightly improved and that the views are useful for reducing complexity, especially when dealing with big models.

The view-based modeling proposed also opens many relevant new research directions. We plan to enhance the expressiveness of the conditions on a view type to allow more complex queries and model perspectives. Moreover, to improve the NRT collaboration features of the framework we have replaced the OpenCoWeb implementation and are currently evaluating SyncMeta Views with Yjs [14], a real-time P2P shared editing framework for arbitrary data types, as it overcomes scalability drawbacks and is much easier to use by developers. Furthermore, in order to improve the feedback during collaborative modeling and to support end-users working with the views extension, we are currently developing an intelligent assistant system for collaborative modeling scenarios to guide collaborators during the modeling process using different strategies like remote support or conflict avoidance. Together with an automatic distributed approach to deal with co-evolution of metamodels and models, these improvements will gear the framework towards use in real-world information systems engineering projects.

Acknowledgments. This research was co-funded by the European Commission through the FP7 Integrated Project "Learning Layers" (grant no. 318209).

References

1. Sirius - The easiest way to get your own modeling tool: Graphical Editors for your DSL (2014). https://www.eclipse.org/sirius/features.html
2. Abiteboul, S., Bonner, A.: Objects and Views. In: York, A.N. (ed.) ACM International Conference On Management Of Data (SIGMOD), pp. 238–247. ACM, New York (1991)
3. Chechik, M., Dalpiaz, F., Debreceni, C., Horkoff, J., Rath, I., Salay, R., Varro, D.: Property-based methods for collaborative model development. In: Joint Proceedings of the 3rd International Workshop on the Globalization Of Modeling Languages and the 9th International Workshop on Multi-Paradigm Modeling, pp. 1–7 (2015)

4. De Lange, P., Nicolaescu, P., Derntl, M., Jarke, M., Klamma, R.: Community application editor: collaborative near real-time modeling and composition of microservice-based web applications. In: Modellierung (2016)
5. Derntl, M., Nicolaescu, P., Erdtmann, S., Klamma, R., Jarke, M.: Near real-time collaborative conceptual modeling on the web. In: Johannesson, P., et al. (eds.) ER 2015. LNCS, vol. 9381, pp. 344–357. Springer, Heidelberg (2015). doi:10.1007/978-3-319-25264-3_25
6. Fill, H.G., Karagiannis, D.: On the conceptualisation of modelling methods using the ADOxx meta modelling platform. Enterp. Model. Inf. Syst. Architect. **8**(1), 4–25 (2013)
7. Fischer, K., Panlenko, D., Krumeich, J., Born, M., Desfray, P.: Viewpoint-Based Modeling - Towards Dening the Viewpoint Concept and Implications for Supporting Modeling Tools (2012)
8. Goldschmidt, T., Becker, S., Burger, E.: Towards a tool-oriented taxonomy of view-based modelling. In: Sinz, E.J., Schürr, A. (eds.) Modellierung (2012)
9. Kelly, S., Lyytinen, K., Rossi, M., Tolvanen, J.P.: MetaEdit+ at the age of 20. In: Bubenko, J., Krogstie, J., Pastor, O., Pernici, B., Rolland, C., Sølvberg, A. (eds.) Seminal Contributions to Information Systems Engineering, pp. 131–137. Springer, Heidelberg (2013)
10. Kozina, M.: Evaluation of ARIS and zachman frameworks as enterprise architectures. J. Inf. Organ. Sci. **30**(1), 115–136 (2006)
11. Kurpjuweit, S., Winter, R.: Viewpoint-based meta model engineering. In: Reichert, M. (ed.) Proceedings of the 2nd International Workshop on Enterprise Modelling and Information Systems Architectures, GI-Edition/Proceedings, vol. 119, pp. 145–158. Ges. für Informatik (2007)
12. de Lara, J., Vangheluwe, H.: $AToM^3$: a tool for multi-formalism and meta-modelling. In: Kutsche, R.-D., Weber, H. (eds.) FASE 2002. LNCS, vol. 2306, p. 174. Springer, Heidelberg (2002)
13. Meire, A.P., Borges, M., de Araújo, R.M.: Supporting multipleviewpoints in collaborative graphical editing. Multimedia Tools and Appl. **32**(2), 185–208 (2007)
14. Nicolaescu, P., Jahns, K., Derntl, M., Klamma, R.: Yjs: a framework for near real-time P2P shared editing on arbitrary data types. In: Cimiano, P., Frasincar, F., Houben, G.-J., Schwabe, D. (eds.) ICWE 2015. LNCS, vol. 9114, pp. 675–678. Springer, Heidelberg (2015)
15. Nissen, H.W., Jarke, M.: Repository support for multi-perspective requirements engineering. Inf. Syst. **24**(2), 131–158 (1999)
16. Nissen, H.W., Jeusfeld, M.A., Jarke, M., Zemanek, G., Huber, H.: Managing multiple requirements perspectives with meta models. IEEE Softw. **13**(2), 37–48 (1996)
17. Nuseibeh, B., Kramer, J., Finkelstein, A.: ViewPoints: meaningful relationships are difficult!. In: Proceedings of the 25th International Conference on Software Engineering, 2003, pp. 676–681 (2003)
18. OpenCoWeb: Open Cooperative Web Framework 1.0 Documentation
19. Rundensteiner, E.A., Kuno, H.A., Ra, Y.G., Crestana-Taube, V., Jones, M.C., Marron, P.J.: The MultiView project. ACM SIGMOD Rec. **25**(2), 555 (1996)
20. Rundensteiner, E.A.: MultiView: a methodology for supporting multiple views in object-oriented databases. In: Kaufmann, M. (ed.) Proceedings of the 18th VLDB Conference, pp. 187–198. Morgan Kaufmann (1992)
21. Yu, E.: From organization models to system requirements: a 'cooperating agents' approach. In: Cooperative Information Systems (1995)
22. Zachman, J.A.: The Zachman Framework: A Primer for Enterprise Engineering and Manufacturing. Zachman Framework Associates, Toronto (2003)

A Framework for Model-Driven Execution
of Collaboration Structures

Christoph Mayr-Dorn[(✉)] and Schahram Dustdar

Distributed Systems Group, TU Wien, 1040 Vienna, Austria
{mayr-dorn,dustdar}@dsg.tuwien.ac.at

Abstract. Human interaction-intensive process environments need collaboration support beyond traditional BPM approaches. Process primitives are ill suited to model and execute collaborations for shared artifact editing, chatting, or voting. To this end, this paper introduces a framework for specifying and executing such collaboration structures. The framework explicitly supports the required human autonomy in shaping the collaboration structure. We demonstrate the application of our framework to an exemplary collaboration-intensive hiring process.

Keywords: human Architecture Description Language · Collaboration patterns · Collaboration configuration · Scripting collaborations

1 Introduction

Medical diagnosis, paper authoring, and peer reviewing are examples of collabora-tion-intensive tasks. Such tasks increasingly require multiple participants who benefit more from dedicated collaboration support than from rigid control and data flow specification. Collaboration support ranges across distinct forms and patterns [11] such as *Shared Artifact, Social Network, Secretary/Principal, Master/Worker,* or *Publish/Subscribe.* Contemporary process technology is ill equipped to provide such collaboration support in a general manner.

Business Process Management (BPM) approaches traditionally assume a single executing entity per task or activity. In the rare cases where multiple human process participants work on a joint task [12,20,21], process specifications per se contain no details with respect to the applicable communication, coordination, or collaboration structures. The core question we address in this paper is thus: how can we set-up and control flexible collaboration instances at runtime in support of joint task execution?

Our solution is a framework for model-driven execution of collaboration mechanisms. A collaboration model specifies an arbitrary combination of collaboration mechanisms such as shared artifacts, messages, streams, requests, and the corresponding user roles expressed in the human Architecture Description Language (hADL) [9]. At runtime, a client (i.e., a process) requests instantiation of a hADL model with actual users and maintains control over the collaboration instance via our framework.

© Springer International Publishing Switzerland 2016
S. Nurcan et al. (Eds.): CAiSE 2016, LNCS 9694, pp. 18–32, 2016.
DOI: 10.1007/978-3-319-39696-5_2

Our approach is complementary to existing process modeling and execution techniques. We don't need to awkwardly model collaboration aspects in terms of fine-grained task, control flow, or data flow primitives. Instead, we specify how a process obtains control over who, when, and how to involve particular users in a particular collaboration.

The evaluation use case demonstrates how our proof-of-concept framework may facilitate the collaboration in multi-participant tasks. Our approach thus provides processes along the specificity frontier [2]—from rigorously defined workflows to ad-hoc activities—a novel capability for configuring collaborations depending on process context: from automatically wiring up process participants and collaboration objects to providing collaboration guidance.

The remainder of this paper is structured as follows. Section 2 motivates our work based on a running scenario. We provide necessary background information in Sect. 3. Section 4 outlines the architecture, models, and internal workings of our framework. Section 5 demonstrates the application of our framework to a use case from the motivating scenario. We discuss related work in Sect. 6 before concluding this paper with a summary and outlook on future work in Sect. 7.

2   Motivating Scenario

Assume a collaborative employment process for a vacant post-doc position at a university department. The department is interested in obtaining consensus on the set of candidates invited for interviews and aims at executing the decision process in a transparent manner. The hiring committee establishes a set of criteria against which to evaluate the candidates. Each application is assigned to a team of two department members for preparing a detailed assessment report. All department members may give comments on any applicant such as whether they know them from conferences, co-authoring, etc.

All assessment reports are discussed by the hiring committee. Committee members are expected to prepare by reading through the reports prior to the meeting. The university's minority awareness officer inspects every assessment for ensuring that evaluations are free from bias and that a sufficiently diverse candidate set is considered for interviewing. When supported by a traditional process-centric system without integrated collaboration support, such a process very probably causes awkward handling of feedback into assessments, participants lacking process awareness and thus missing out on discussions or working on out-dated information, as well as delays due to limited potential for parallel work.

There is no single mechanism for collaboration that would fit the overall process. We exemplify the benefit of introducing shared artifacts (here documents that allow synchronous editing and commenting) as well as communication streams (here chat rooms) for discussions (Fig. 1). Shared artifacts primarily enable parallel work while limiting the potential for write conflicts and access to out-dated information. Chat rooms provide a well-known, well-scoped mechanism for discussing, enabling late participants to quickly catch up with

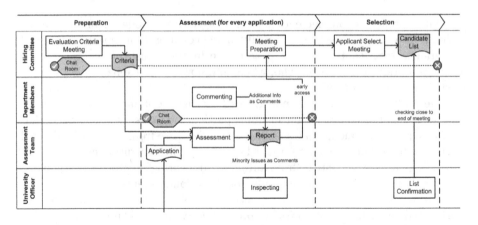

Fig. 1. Excerpt of a collaboration-intensive hiring process applying shared documents (shaded) and chat rooms (with dashed, horizontal life-lines). Process language specific details are omitted on purpose in order to abstract from integrations details and focus on the collaboration aspects and their potential impact instead.

the current state of the collaboration. The minority awareness officer may start early inspecting the reports without waiting for their finalization thus avoiding an overload on the assessment due date. Additionally, and more importantly, rather than escalating biased assessments after the deadline, any such concerns can be swiftly dealt with through timely feedback on a continuous basis. Similarly, the hiring committee can access the assessment reports early and just need to read-up on any last changes after the deadline (ultimately reducing the time needed to prepare for the application selection meeting). Realizing such a scenario requires a dedicated framework for managing the collaboration structure.

3   The human Architecture Description Language

We provide a brief introduction to hADL [9] as our approach makes heavy use of it. hADL provides a collaboration-centric equivalent of a software architecture "component & connector" view. A hADL model describes a collaboration structure in terms of interacting user roles and their available collaboration mechanisms. Figure 2 provides the hADL meta model (*elements in italics*). Figure 3 depicts the hADL model for the collaboration-intensive aspects of our motivating scenario (`elements in teletype`). Note that hADL's canonical representation is provided as an XML schema, available for download among the supporting online material (SOM) at http://wp.me/P1xPeS-6L.

hADL distinguishes between *HumanComponent*s (e.g., `DocUser` and `ChatUser`) and *CollaborationConnector*s to emphasize the difference between the primary collaborating users and non-essential, replaceable users that facilitate the collaboration. Collaboration connectors are responsible for the efficient and effective interaction among human components, respectively ensuring desirable collaboration outcome.

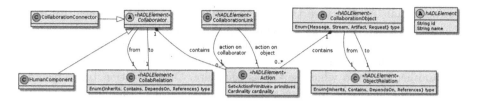

Fig. 2. Simplified and condensed hADL meta model displaying the elements relevant for the execution framework.

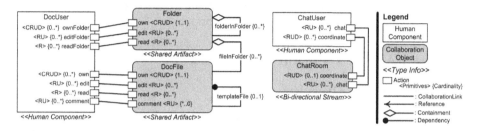

Fig. 3. hADL model excerpt that describes the main collaborators, collaboration objects and capabilities involved in the motivating scenario. DocUsers have either the capabilities to own, to edit, or to read Folders and Docfiles, or additionally to comment on the latter. ChatUsers have the ability to coordinate or to chat in a ChatRoom.

Humans employ diverse collaboration mechanisms that range from emails, shared wiki pages, social network activity streams, to Q&A forums and vote collection. These means implement vastly different interaction semantics: a message is sent and received, a shared artifact is edited, a vote can be cast. hADL makes these differences explicit by means of *CollaborationObjects*. CollaborationObjects are first class modeling constructs which abstract from concrete interaction tools and capture the semantic differences in various subtypes such as *Message*, *Stream* (e.g., ChatRoom), or *SharedArtifact* (e.g., DocFile).

hADL Actions specify what capabilities a HumanComponent or CollaborationConnector requires for fulfilling their associated role, e.g., document authoring or providing comments. Complementary, actions on CollaborationObjects determine the offered capabilities. For example, editing a shared document (i.e., DocFile) requires the ability of performing a DocUser's **edit** action, while a ChatRoom offers the **coordinate** and **chat** actions. Additionally, hADL distinguishes among create (C), read (R), update (U), and delete (D) *primitives* to indicate the intended effect of an action. Further, action *cardinalities* specify the upper and lower boundaries on the number of collaborators which may simultaneously have obtained the action's capabilities. For example, exactly one user might own a document {1..1}, but many users might edit it {0..*}. *CollaborationLinks* subsequently connect actions that belong to HumanComponents or CollaborationConnectors to actions that belong to CollaborationObjects.

The human Architecture Description Language provides `CollabRelations` for modeling relations among HumanComponents and CollaborationConnectors as well as `ObjectRelations` among CollaborationObjects. For example, the specific `templateOf` relation may be applied for modeling that one `DocFile` *dependsOn* another `DocFile` which serves as template. Other relation types include *references* for specifying uni-directional relations between CollaborationObjects and *contains* for modeling hierarchical substructures.

Together, all these elements establish the blueprint of a collaboration structure. Note that hADL specifies the a-priori defined collaboration object types to be used at runtime (e.g., a `DocFile`), rather than their specific purpose within the (process) context (e.g., an assessment report).

4   The hADL Execution Framework

4.1   Architectural Overview

The primary purpose of model-driven collaboration execution is separating the specification of a collaboration structure (the what) from its realization on specific collaboration platforms (the how). This enables the hADL client—such as a process—to focus on the desired structure, the involved collaborators, and how the overall collaboration should evolve. Low-level details such as interacting with the various collaboration platforms through their APIs, maintaining collaboration state throughout the process' lifetime, or adaptation due to platform API changes remain hidden. Figure 4 depicts this separation of concerns. The main architectural elements and their duties are:

- the hADL client: requests instances of hADL elements to be created, re/wired, and released.
- the hADL Collaboration Linkage Connector (CLC): manages the collaboration structure, ensures valid client requests, and forwards those to surrogates for enactment.
- the Surrogates: translate hADL-centric client requests into invocations of the collaboration platforms.
- the hADL Runtime View: stores the current collaboration structure.

A hADL model describes the available element types (e.g., ChatUser, DocUser, ChatRoom, etc.) and their possible wiring but not an actual runtime topology involving actual humans. It's up to the **hADL client** to specify what instances of hADL elements from a particular hADL model it requires and how and when to wire them. To this end, the hADL client issues "acquisition" requests to the CLC which concrete users to involve in what collaboration-specific role (i.e., HumanComponent or CollaborationConnector) and what collaboration mechanism (i.e., CollaborationObjects) to utilize. A hADL client, for example, requests to involve user `Bob` as *Chat User*, and acquire a *Chat Room* with name `PreMeeting`. Here `Bob` and `PreMeeting` represent so-called *ResourceDescriptors* that describe identity and properties of users and collaboration mechanisms (see Fig. 5 middle). Once acquired, the hADL client determines

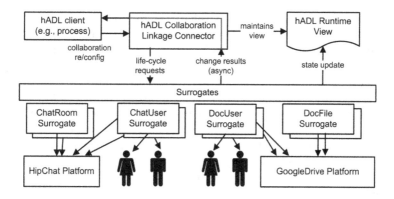

Fig. 4. Conceptual architecture of the hADL execution framework.

the wiring among instances of human component, collaboration connectors, and collaboration objects according to hADL actions, links, or relations. Wiring, gor example, ChatUser Bob to ChatRoom PreMeeting via action *coordinate*.

The **hADL Collaboration Linkage Connector** (CLC) takes the client's acquisition and rewiring requests and ensures they are valid according to the underlying hADL model. Its main purpose is maintaining the "prescribed" view of the current collaboration structure, i.e., creating, updating, and removing *hADL element instances* of the **hADL Runtime View** as pending to existing (i.e., *prescribed*) or pending to be released (i.e., *prescribed removed*) (see Fig. 5 right). Elements remain in the prescribed state until the corresponding change at the collaboration platform has occurred and then enter the *described* state. To this end, the CLC doesn't invoke the collaboration platforms directly but delegates any valid client request to surrogates (see below) which ultimately update the instances' status from *prescribed* to *described*.

Note that the CLC remains external to the actual ongoing collaboration. It's limited to setting up and evolving the collaboration structure. The collaboration itself, such as joint content production, chat discussions, or message authoring and dispatching, is subject to the involved users via the respective collaboration platforms. The CLC's name is inspired by software architecture terminology as it assumes the role of a *linkage connector* but at the level of collaboration entities rather than software components:

> Linkage connectors are used to tie the system components together and hold them in such a state during their operation. [...] a linkage connector may disappear from the system or remain in place to assist in the system's evolution [26, p. 168].

We introduce **Surrogates** as the key mechanism for mapping a high-level collaboration model in hADL to the implementation-level collaboration platforms. Typically, a hADL model will specify a separate surrogate for each HumanComponent, CollaborationConnector, and CollaborationObject (see Fig. 5 left). A surrogate is responsible for acquiring access to a collaborator (i.e., a ChatUser), respectively creating an instance of a CollaborationObject (e.g., a ChatRoom), wiring up these elements, and eventually releasing them again. To this end, surrogates exhibit sophisticated capabilities around a collaboration platform's (web) API. A *DocFile* surrogate, for example, knows which GoogleDrive collaboration platform API methods to invoke in order to establish/remove a *own*, *edit*, *read*, and *comment* link with a *DocUser* as well as *templateFile* and *fileInFolder* relations. In contrast, the *DocUser* surrogate encapsulates all logic required to contact a user and invite him/her to join the collaboration structure such as becoming editor of a document, and so on. It is up to the surrogate's implementation what communication protocol to use for interacting with a collaboration platform (typically JSON/XML over HTTP) and users (typically SMTP, XMPP, or SMS). Eventually, at runtime, there exists a surrogate instance for each instance of HumanComponent, CollaborationConnector, and CollaborationObject.

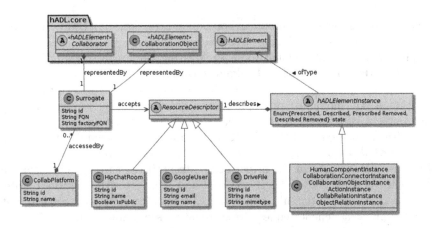

Fig. 5. Simplified UML model depicting the extensions to the core hADL model and example realizations of abstract classes. Surrogates describe what ResourceDescriptors they accept. At runtime, the CLC creates hADLElementInstances with reference to their type and their ResourceDescriptor. Subclasses of hADLElementInstance are identical to their counterpart in the hADL core model and thus are depicted as a single class for sake of brevity.

Our framework is designed to remain independent from specific process languages and engines. Hence how the process conducts the assignment of actual tasks to users is out of scope of this paper and requires process-specific mechanisms, e.g., WS-HumanTask [18] or BPMN2 user tasks [1]. In the remainder of this section, we describe how the framework's main software components interact and how to get from model to execution.

4.2   hADL Framework Component Interactions

We outline the interaction among our framework's software components based on a typical interaction sequence depicted in Fig. 6 (also found in our motivating scenario and use case implementation).

A interaction session starts with the hADL client acquiring (1) HumanComponents, CollaborationConnectors, and CollaborationObjects. Specifically, the client passes one or more tuples specifying which ResourceDescriptor describes a particular hADL element type. Here the client asks for `Bob` becoming a *ChatUser* and a *ChatRoom* with name `PreMeeting`. The hADL CLC checks the request whether hADL element types and ResourceDescriptors match (2), etc., and subsequently add instances to the hADL Runtime View (3). These instances exist in the "descriptive" state, i.e., pending to exist. The CLC then initiates the matching surrogates that will handle the individual hADL element instances (4). But first, it returns an "observable" back to the client (5).

An observable is a subscription endpoint for the client to receive events from the CLC and surrogates. We use this event-driven mechanism for asynchronous notification of successful and failed request processing. Request processing at a surrogate usually involves invoking the collaboration platform API and hence potentially requires a significant amount of time. Request completion takes even longer when the surrogate contacts a user for confirming the participation in a collaboration. A client thus doesn't block on a request but may process results (e.g., successful setup of a chat room) or react to failures (e.g., user declined to join a chat room) as these events arrive.

Next, the CLC passes all acquisition request together with the respective hADL element instance, ResourceDescriptor, and observable to the individual surrogates who process these in parallel (6,7). Surrogate A for ChatUser Bob invokes the HipChat API to check whether the user (as described in the ResourceDescriptor) already exists or has to be invited (8). In the former case the surrogate can immediately mark the hADL instance element as "descriptive", i.e., confirmed to exist (9). Subsequently, the surrogate dispatches an event back to the client (via the observable mechanism) that the acquiring was successful and includes a reference to the HumanComponentInstance representing ChatUser Bob (10). Note that the observable mechanism strongly decouples client and surrogates. The client remains unaware of surrogates—it only cares about the request outcome—and surrogates remain unaware of event consumers.

Note that from here on, we no longer depict request checks, collaboration platform invocations, or observables due to space limits.

In our example, the client continues to wireup chat room and chat user. It does so by passing the source and destination hADL instances, and link type to be established (14). Remaining at the hADL level, the CLC has no insights into how a surrogate brings about changes. Hence, for establishing links (or relations), it always triggers the surrogates of both involved endpoint instances (16,17). The surrogates' logic determines whether any action is required. For example, Surrogate B checks whether the ChatUser Bob may obtain "coordinate" capabilities and signals success (18) while Surrogate A "knows" that in this case no action is required (the surrogate implementation assumes here that the user always agrees to become coordinator of a chat room). Note that no interaction between any two surrogates occurs for establishing links (or relations). The surrogates remain completely decoupled and any implicit information exchange occurs only via the well defined ResourceDescriptors. That is, for example, Surrogate B receives a *wire* request which contains the reference to the opposite endpoint (a HumanComponentInstance of type ChatUser, here Bob). It extracts the ResourceDescriptor—Bob's details—and thus obtains all the necessary information to determine locally (and via the collaboration platform API) whether the link may be established or not.

Note that so far no actual wiring has occurred. The client has the opportunity for further rewiring before calling *start*. Upon start (19), the CLC triggers all surrogates with pending changes to execute the rewiring (20+). Any subsequent changes require first calling *stop*. Stopping (23) signals the CLC and surrogates that the client is about to request changes to, or final releasing of, the hADL instances. A surrogate may then decide that its local view of the collaboration is outdated and pulls in the latest updates from the collaboration platform.

In our example, the client intends to release ChatUser Bob (26). The CLC marks this human component instance and all its links as "removed prescriptive" (27) and first requests all links to be removed (28,29). Unwiring works exactly like wiring. Only then does the CLC ask the surrogate to release ChatUser Bob (32). For the various CollaborationObject types, releasing typically means closing a stream, deleting or archiving a shared artifact, aborting a request, or removing a message channel. For HumanComponents and CollaborationConnectors, on the other hand, releasing implies notifying them on the ending collaboration and removing their access rights to the various collaboration object instances. Finally, upon completing the release procedure, the surrogate instance terminates (34).

4.3   From Model to Execution

From a developer's perspective, model-driven execution of collaboration structures consists of three phases: modeling the collaboration types, scripting the hADL client, and executing the collaboration structure at runtime.

The **modeling phase** comprises all activities necessary to (i) create the hADL model, (ii) specify the collaboration platform-specific ResourceDescriptors (i.e., GoogleUser, DriveFile, HipChatRoom), (iii) implement the corresponding surrogates (i.e., surrogates for DocUser, ChatUser, DocFile, Folder, and ChatRoom), and (iv) extend the hADL model with surrogate and ResourceDescriptor details (see Fig. 5). We assume in this bottom-up approach, that the utilized collaboration platforms (i.e., HipChat and GoogleDrive) already exist and expose an API suitable for invocation by the surrogates. The methodology for specifying the hADL model and aligning the surrogates is out of scope of this paper.

In the **scripting phase**, the developer implements the hADL client's logic as a set of steps that setup and modify the collaboration structure. Typically each step defines the required input (e.g., the ResourceDescriptors of the users to invite to a chat room and the chatroom's name) and the expected output,

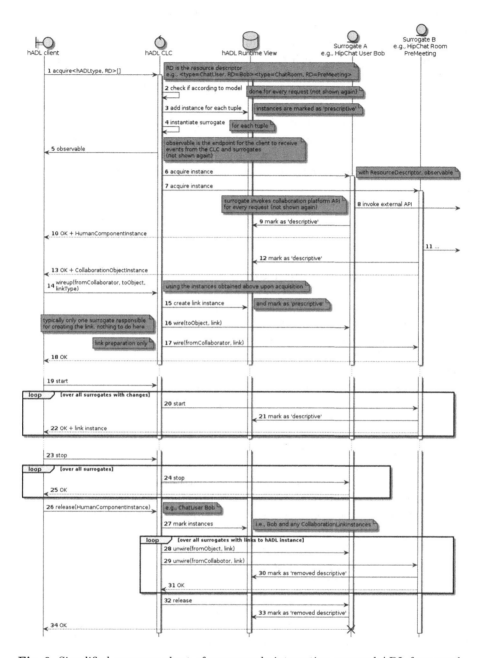

Fig. 6. Simplified sequence chart of an example interaction among hADL framework components. The hADL client requests a user and chat room, wires the user to the chat room, and ultimately removes the user again. The sequence chart is available in high resolution among the supporting material at http://wp.me/P1xPeS-6L.

i.e., the hADL element instances for use in subsequent steps (e.g., the chat user instance and chat room instance). The developer inspects the extended hADL model to learn what elements are available, how these can be linked (i.e., actions, links, and relations), and which resource descriptors match. S/he subsequently extracts the element identifiers for invoking the hADL CLC. For example, the developer learns that a GoogleUser ResourceDescriptor may be used to acquire a ChatUser and a DocUser. No insights into surrogate implementation or collaboration platform API are required. Listing 1 demonstrates how to invoke the CLC purely using model information. Note that in this listing all steps are condensed into a single script for sake of brevity. The resulting hADL client script (currently plain java) becomes integrated into the application's logic or a business process specification.

Finally, in the **execution phase** the hADL client script is executed as regular source code, requiring only that the surrogate implementations are accessible to the CLC for instantiation.

5   Use Case Implementation

We demonstrate the basic capabilities of our framework and the feasibility of our approach through the proof-of-concept implementation of a use case and hADL execution platform. Specifically, we showcase the setup, rewiring, and releasing of two distinctly different collaboration mechanisms—Google Drive documents and HipChat chat rooms—as described in the example process[1] in Fig. 1. We provide all hADL models, extensions, source code, and configurations for replicating the use case as supporting online material (SOM) available at http://wp.me/P1xPeS-6L.

We implemented surrogates for Google Drive files and HipChat chat rooms. The file surrogate makes use of the official java client for Google Drive[2], while we extended a third-party java library[3] for implementing the chat room surrogate. Both platforms automatically send notification emails to users when they obtain access to files, respectively chat rooms. Hence our HumanComponent surrogates are minimal implementations. The use case introduces ResourceDescriptors for the Google Drive file (id, name, and mime type), the HipChat chat room (id, name, and topic), and user identification (by email address, applied for Google Drive and HipChat users); see also Fig. 5 middle. Setup includes registration of the same five users for Google Drive and HipChat: two committee members, two assessment team members (for one exemplary job application), and the minority officer.

Listing 1 summarizes the hADL framework client pseudo code for supporting the process in the motivating scenario. The pseudo code lacks use of our framework's asynchronous communication mechanism (i.e., observables and events)

---

[1] No process engine was used for our use case implementation as this paper addresses the collaboration structure execution aspect only.

[2] https://developers.google.com/api-client-library/java/apis/drive/v2.

[3] https://github.com/evanwong/hipchat-java/tree/java7.

for sake of clarity and brevity. Note how collaboration changes are typically enforced at the begin and end of process steps: lines 1–4 describe preparations for the *Evaluation Criteria Meeting*, lines 5–11 list the post-meeting changes to document and chatroom. Lines 12–22 show the setup of the assessment team and department members with access to report and chatroom. Lines 23–28 reduce access upon the assessment deadline, and lines 29–33 setup the *Applicant Selection Meeting*, then the listing skips a few steps before lines 34–35 completely close down the collaboration instance. The full script is available in the SOM.

Listing 1. Pseudo code for managing collaboration structures in support of a hiring process: variables with 'I'-postfix are hADL model runtime instances; resource descriptors are reduced to simple strings, e.g., 'Bob'.

```
 1: file1I = acquire(Model.DOCFILE,' EvalCriteriaReport') {prepare meeting}
 2: users1I[] = acquire(Model.DOCUSER, ['Alice',' Bob']) {hiring committee}
 3: link(users1I, file1I, Model.EDITING)
 4: start() {ready for meeting}
 5: stop() {upon meeting end}
 6: unlink(users1I, file1I, Model.EDITING)
 7: link(users1I, file1I, Model.COMMENTING)
 8: room1I = acquire(Model.CHATROOM,' CriteriaDiscussionRoom')
 9: users2I[] = acquire(Model.CHATUSER, ['Alice',' Bob'])
10: link(users2I, room1I, Model.CHATTING)
11: start() {chatroom setup completed}
12: stop() {assessment phase begins}
13: file2I = acquire(Model.DOCFILE,' Assessment1') {for job application 1}
14: users3I[] = acquire(Model.DOCUSER, ['Carol',' Dave']) {assessment team}
15: user5I = acquire(Model.DOCUSER,' Eve') {minority officer}
16: link(users3I, file1I, Model.READING) {access to eval criteria}
17: link(users3I, file2I, Model.EDITING) {access to assessment report}
18: link(users1I + user5I, file2I, Model.COMMENTING) {commenting access for department members and
    minority officer}
19: room2I = acquire(Model.CHATROOM,' Application1DiscussionRoom') {application specific discussion
    room}
20: users4I[] = acquire(Model.CHATUSER, ['Carol',' Dave']) {acquire remaining department members}
21: link(users2I + users4I, room2I, Model.CHATTING) {all department member may discuss}
22: start() {assessment scope setup completed}
23: stop() {assessment deadline reached}
24: unlink(users3I, file2I, Model.EDITING)
25: unlink(users1I, file2I, Model.COMMENTING)
26: link(user1I + users3I, file2I, Model.READING) {read access for department members, commenting remains
    for officer}
27: release(room2I) {close chatroom for application 1}
28: start() {execute changes}
29: stop() {before selection meeting}
30: file2I = acquire(Model.DOCFILE,' CandidateList')
31: link(users1I, file3I, Model.EDITING)
32: link(user5I, file3I, Model.COMMENTING) {minority officer can comment before meeting completion}
33: start() {execute changes}
34: stop() {skipping steps here ...}
35: releaseAll() {... ultimately, shutting down collaboration: files and chatroom}
```

---

6   Related Work

Managing human work dependencies is not limited to processes. Brambilla and Mauri integrate social network-centric actions into web applications via social primitives [5]. Their focus is on making commenting, posting, voting, and searching capabilities of public social platforms available as WebML operations. Our approach, in contrast, focuses on specifying and executing the collaboration structures, leaving the actual collaboration per se to the users via the actual, underlying platforms. Activity-centric approaches such as [2,12] put control into the hands of users for flexibly defining and deviating from (ad-hoc) processes.

Human and Artifact-centric BPM. Even traditional workflow description languages dedicated to modeling human involvement such as Little-JIL [6], BPEL4People [15], or WS-HumanTask [18] foresee no explicit communication among process participants outside of tasks. Although BPEL4people supports four eyes, nomination, escalation, and chained execution scenarios—and WS-HumanTask allows attaching comments to tasks—all interaction is purely task-centric. Similarly, La Rosa et al. [20] demonstrate how EPC-based models may involve multiple users in a task including artifacts but neither how multiple participants collaborate, nor their capabilities on the artifacts. In contrast, Liptchinsky et al. model the impact of social relations on software artifacts and the respective engineering process [21]. The collaboration mechanisms that give rise to social relations and process execution support remain out of scope. Subject-oriented BPM [14] models all data flow exclusively with messages between process participants. Hence other collaboration mechanisms such as shared artifacts, chat rooms, etc. are extremely awkward to represent.

Artifact-centric BPM approaches [17] (aka document-centric, data-centric, or object-centric) focus on specifying artifact structure, states, and access rights. Examples such as the Business Entity Definition Language [23], Philharmonicflows [19], FlexConnect [24] or ad-hoc processes driven by documents [8] remain restricted to artifacts and leave aside other collaboration mechanisms such as chatting, voting, or direct messaging. These approaches, however, model artifacts in much more detail compared to hADL.

Social BPM and Crowd Sourcing. Recent research efforts started explicitly targeting the integration of social media into business process management (BPM) technology. Brambilla et al. present design patterns for integrating social network features in BPMN [4]. A social network user may engage in task-centric actions such as voting, commenting, reading a message, or joining a task. Böhringer utilizes tagging, activity streams, and micro-blogging for merging ad-hoc activities into case management [3]. Dengler et al. utilize Wikis and social networks for coordinating process activities [7]. oBPM [16] relies on task and artifact abstractions for coordinating business process modelling.

These approaches differ in several crucial aspects from our work: (i) they integrate collaboration mechanisms only in single tasks, (ii) these mechanisms are typically hard-wired social media connectors with no abstraction, (iii) and/or collaboration aspects support the process design phase [13] only.

To the best of our knowledge, no contemporary research approaches address the issue of modeling and executing collaboration structures. We focused in our own, previous work on establishing a passive runtime view of the ongoing collaboration from monitoring a system's software architecture [10] and addressed the aspect of configuration and deployment of collaboration systems, i.e., provisioning the technical infrastructure [25]. Our approach in this paper is completely independent of either works. The discussed work above presents primarily orthogonal approaches worthwhile investigating for future integration.

7   Conclusions and Outlook

In this paper[4], we presented a first framework for model-driven execution of collaboration structures. We demonstrated how to specify collaboration structures on an abstract level subsequently grounded in concrete collaboration platforms via surrogates. The preliminary evaluation use case demonstrated the application of our framework for supporting a hiring process via Google Drive documents and HipChat chat rooms. The current implementation puts a significant burden on the framework client for error handling and correct model usage. Future work will explores the use of a Domain-Specific Language for expressing and generating the source code for type safe collaboration modification. Additionally, we will focus on adding sophisticated error handling strategies and investigating the integration with a process engine.

References

1. BPMN 2.0. http://www.omg.org/spec/BPMN/2.0/PDF/
2. Bernstein, A.: How can cooperative work tools support dynamic group process? bridging the specificity frontier. In: Proceedings of ACM Conference on Computer Supported Cooperative Work, CSCW 2000, pp. 279–288. ACM, New York (2000)
3. Böhringer, M.: Emergent case management for ad-hoc processes: a solution based on microblogging and activity streams. In: zur Muehlen and Su [22], pp. 384–395
4. Brambilla, M., Fraternali, P., Vaca, C.: BPMN and design patterns for engineering social BPM solutions. In: Daniel, F., Barkaoui, K., Dustdar, S. (eds.) BPM Workshops 2011, Part I. LNBIP, vol. 99, pp. 219–230. Springer, Heidelberg (2012)
5. Brambilla, M., Mauri, A.: Model-driven development of social network enabled applications with WebML and social primitives. In: Grossniklaus, M., Wimmer, M. (eds.) ICWE Workshops 2012. LNCS, vol. 7703, pp. 41–55. Springer, Heidelberg (2012)
6. Cass, A.G., Lerner, B.S., Sutton Jr., S.M., McCall, E.K., Wise, A.E., Osterweil, L.J.: LittleJIL/Juliette: a process definition language and interpreter. In: Ghezzi, C., Jazayeri, M., Wolf, A.L. (eds.) ICSE, pp. 754–757. ACM (2000)
7. Dengler, F., Koschmider, A., Oberweis, A., Zhang, H.: Social software for coordination of collaborative process activities. In: zur Muehlen and Su [22], pp. 396–407
8. Dorn, C., Dustdar, S.: Supporting dynamic, people-driven processes through self-learning of message flows. In: Mouratidis, H., Rolland, C. (eds.) CAiSE 2011. LNCS, vol. 6741, pp. 657–671. Springer, Heidelberg (2011)
9. Dorn, C., Taylor, R.N.: Architecture-driven modeling of adaptive collaboration structures in large-scale social web applications. In: Wang, X.S., Cruz, I., Delis, A., Huang, G. (eds.) WISE 2012. LNCS, vol. 7651, pp. 143–156. Springer, Heidelberg (2012)
10. Dorn, C., Taylor, R.N.: Coupling software architecture and human architecture for collaboration-aware system adaptation. In: Notkin, D., Cheng, B.H.C., Pohl, K. (eds.) ICSE, pp. 53–62. IEEE/ACM (2013)
11. Dorn, C., Taylor, R.N.: Analyzing runtime adaptability of collaboration patterns. Concurrency Comput. Pract. Experience **27**(11), 2725–2750 (2015)

---

[4] This research was partially supported by the EU FP7 SmartSociety project (600854).

12. Dustdar, S.: Caramba process-aware collaboration system supporting ad hoc and collaborative processes in virtual teams. Distrib. Parallel Databases 15(1), 45–66 (2004)
13. Erol, S., Granitzer, M., Happ, S., Jantunen, S., Jennings, B., Johannesson, P., Koschmider, A., Nurcan, S., Rossi, D., Schmidt, R.: Combining BPM and social software: contradiction or chance? J. Softw. Maint. Evol. Res. Pract. 22(6–7), 449–476 (2010)
14. Fleischmann, A., Schmidt, W., Stary, C., Obermeier, S., Börger, E.: Subject-Oriented Business Process Management. Springer, Heidelberg (2012)
15. Ford, M., Endpoints, A., Keller, C.: WS-BPEL extension for people (BPEL4People), version 1.0 (2007)
16. Grünert, D., Brucker-Kley, E., Keller, T.: oBPM an opportunistic approach to business process modeling and execution. In: Workshop on Business Process Management and Social Software (BPMS2 2014) (2014)
17. Hull, R.: Artifact-centric business process models: brief survey of research results and challenges. In: Meersman, R., Tari, Z. (eds.) OTM 2008, Part II. LNCS, vol. 5332, pp. 1152–1163. Springer, Heidelberg (2008)
18. Ings, D., Clement, L., König, D., Mehta, V., Mueller, R., Rangaswamy, R., Rowley, M., Trickovic, I.: Web services human task (WS-HumanTask) specification version 1.1. Technical report, OASIS, July 2012. http://docs.oasis-open.org/bpel4people/ws-humantask-1.1.html
19. Künzle, V., Reichert, M.: Philharmonicflows: towards a framework for object-aware process management. J. Softw. Maint. Evol. Res. Pract. 23(4), 205–244 (2011)
20. La Rosa, M., Dumas, M., ter Hofstede, A.H.M., Mendling, J., Gottschalk, F.: Beyond control-flow: extending business process configuration to roles and objects. In: Li, Q., Spaccapietra, S., Yu, E., Olivé, A. (eds.) ER 2008. LNCS, vol. 5231, pp. 199–215. Springer, Heidelberg (2008)
21. Liptchinsky, V., Khazankin, R., Truong, H.-L., Dustdar, S.: A novel approach to modeling context-aware and social collaboration processes. In: Ralyté, J., Franch, X., Brinkkemper, S., Wrycza, S. (eds.) CAiSE 2012. LNCS, vol. 7328, pp. 565–580. Springer, Heidelberg (2012)
22. zur Muehlen, M., Su, J. (eds.): BPM Workshops. LNBIP, vol. 66. Springer, Heidelberg (2011)
23. Nandi, P., Koenig, D., Moser, S., Hull, R., Klicnik, V., Claussen, S., Kloppman, M., Vergo, J.: Data4BPM, part 1: introducing business entities and the business entity definition language (BEDL), April 2010. http://ibm.co/1QTR0IH
24. Redding, G., Dumas, M., ter Hofstede, A.H.M., Iordachescu, A.: A flexible, object-centric approach for business process modelling. SOCA 4(3), 191–201 (2010)
25. Sungur, C.T., Dorn, C., Dustdar, S., Leymann, F.: Transforming collaboration structures into deployable informal processes. In: Cimiano, P., Frasincar, F., Houben, G.-J., Schwabe, D. (eds.) ICWE 2015. LNCS, vol. 9114, pp. 231–250. Springer, Heidelberg (2015)
26. Taylor, R.N., Medvidovic, N., Dashofy, E.M.: Software Architecture: Foundations, Theory, and Practice. Wiley Publishing, New York (2009)

Social Business Intelligence in Action

Matteo Francia, Enrico Gallinucci, Matteo Golfarelli, and Stefano Rizzi$^{(\boxtimes)}$

DISI, University of Bologna, V.le Risorgimento 2, 40136 Bologna, Italy
{matteo.francia3,enrico.gallinucci2,matteo.golfarelli,
stefano.rizzi}@unibo.it

Abstract. Social Business Intelligence (SBI) relies on user-generated content to let decision-makers analyze their business in the light of the environmental trends. SBI projects come in a variety of shapes, with different demands. Hence, finding the right cost-benefit compromise depending on the project goals and time horizon and on the available resources may be hard for the designer. In this paper we discuss the main factors that impact this compromise aimed at providing a guideline to the design team. First we list the main architectural options and their methodological impact. Then we discuss a case study focused on an SBI project in the area of politics, aimed at assessing the effectiveness and efficiency of these options and their methodological sustainability.

Keywords: Social Business Intelligence · User-generated content · OLAP

1 Introduction

An enormous amount of *user-generated content* (UGC) related to people's tastes, opinions, and actions has been made available thanks to the omnipresent diffusion of social networks and portable devices. This huge wealth of information is raising an increasing interest from decision makers because it can give them a timely perception of the market mood and help them explain the phenomena of business and society. *Social Business Intelligence* (SBI) is the discipline that aims at combining corporate data with UGC to let decision-makers (simply called *users* from now on) analyze and improve their business based on the trends and moods perceived from the environment [4].

In the context of SBI, the most widely used category of UGC is the one coming in the form of textual *clips*. Clips can either be messages posted on social media or articles taken from on-line newspapers and magazines, or even customer comments collected on the corporate CRM. Digging information useful for users out of textual UGC requires first crawling the web to extract the clips related to a *subject area*, then enriching them in order to let as much information as possible emerge from the raw text. The subject area defines the project scope

Partially supported by the "WebPolEU: Comparing Social Media and Political Participation across EU" FIRB Project funded by MIUR.

and extent, and can be for instance related to a brand or a specific market, or to a wider domain such as EU politics. Enrichment activities may simply identify the structured parts of a clip, such as its author, or even use NLP techniques to interpret each sentence, find the *topics* it mentions, and if possible assign a *sentiment* (also called *polarity*, i.e., positive, negative, or neutral) to it [10]. For instance, the tweet "UKIP's Essex county councillors stage protest against flying of EU flag at County Hall. Well done to them", in the subject area of EU politics, mentions topics "UKIP" and "protest" and has positive sentiment.

We call *SBI process* the one whose phases range from web crawling to users' analyses of the results. In the industrial world, the SBI process is often implemented in the so-called *social media monitoring tools* [16], i.e., commercial tools and platforms available for the analysis of UGC, such as Brandwatch, Tracx, and Clarabridge. Their main feature is the availability of a fixed set of dashboards that analyze the data from some fixed points of view (such as topic usage, topic correlation, and brand reputation) and rely on some ad-hoc KPIs (e.g., topic counting and sentiment), so they lack in providing flexible user-driven analyses.

In the academic world, the SBI "big picture" has not been deeply investigated so far. In [2] we proposed a reference architecture and an iterative methodology for designing SBI applications, and showed how its adoption can make the activities for developing and maintaining SBI processes more efficient and the SBI process itself more effective. However, we also concluded that SBI projects come in a variety of shapes, characterized by different relevance and sophistication degrees for each design task and architectural component, which results in quite different demands in terms of skills, computing infrastructure, and money. Hence, finding the right cost-benefit compromise depending on the project goals, on its time horizon, and on the available resources may be quite hard for the designer.

During the last few years we have been involved in different SBI projects. In particular, in the context of the WebPolEU project we developed an SBI platform aimed at investigating the connection between politics and social media. The project used UGC written in three languages and was focused on the 2014 European Election. This experience has motivated us in writing this paper, whose goal is to discuss the main factors that impact the above-mentioned compromise aimed at providing design guidelines to the SBI design team. To this end, first we list the main technical options for each architectural component together with their methodological implications. Then we discuss a case study focused on the WebPolEU project, aimed at assessing the effectiveness and efficiency of these options as well as the overall sustainability of the methodological approach, based on a qualitative and quantitative analysis of the critical issues related to each architectural component and design activity.

2   Architectural and Methodological Framework

The reference architecture we proposed in [2] to support the SBI process is depicted in Fig. 1. Its main highlight is the native capability of providing historical information, thus overcoming the limitations of social media monitoring tools

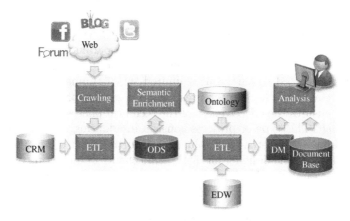

Fig. 1. A reference architecture for the SBI process

in handling the data reprocessing typically required by cleaning and semantic enrichment needs. In the following we briefly comment each component.

– The *Operational Data Store* (ODS) stores all the relevant data about clips, their authors, and their source channels; the ODS also represents all the topics within the subject area and their relationships.
– The *Data Mart* (DM) stores integrated data in the form of a set of multidimensional cubes which support the decision making process.
– The *Document-Base* stores the clips in textual form and the related meta-data to be used for text search.
– *Crawling* carries out a set of keyword-based queries aimed at retrieving the clips (and the available meta-data) that are in the scope of the subject area. The target of the crawler search could be either the whole web or a set of user-defined web sources (e.g., blogs, forums, web sites, social networks).
– *Semantic Enrichment* works on the ODS to extract the semantic information hidden in the clip texts. Such information can include its topic(s), the syntactic and semantic relationships between words, or the sentiment related to a whole sentence or to each single topic it contains.
– The *ETL* process turns the semi-structured output taken from either the crawler or the CRM into a structured form and loads it onto the ODS. Then it integrates data about clips and topics with the business data extracted from the EDW (Enterprise Data Warehouse), and loads them onto the DM.
– *Analysis* enables users to explore the UGC from different perspectives and control the overall social mood.

From the methodological point of view, we observe that the roles in charge of designing, tuning, and maintaining each component of the SBI process may vary from project to project, and so may vary the complexity of each design activity and the control the designer and the user have over it. Specifically, as claimed in [2], SBI projects can be classified into:

– *Best-of-Breed.* A best-of-breed policy is followed to acquire tools specialized in one of the parts of the SBI process. In this case, the designer has full control of the SBI process by finely tuning all its critical parameters.
– *End-to-End.* Here, an end-to-end software/service is acquired and tuned. Designers only need to carry out a limited set of tuning activities that are typically related to the subject area, while a service provider or a system integrator ensures the effectiveness of the technical phases of the SBI process.
– *Off-the-Shelf.* This type of projects consists in adopting, typically in a *as-a-service* manner, an off-the-shelf solution supporting a set of standard reports and dashboards. The designer has little or no chance of impacting on activities that are not directly related to the analysis of the final results.

Moving from level best-of-breed to off-the-shelf, projects require less technical capabilities from designers and users and ensure a shorter set-up time, but they also allow less control of the overall effectiveness and less flexibility.

3 A Case Study on EU Politics

The WebPolEU Project (http://webpoleu.altervista.org) aims at studying the connection between politics and social media. By analyzing digital literacy and online political participation, the research evaluates the inclusiveness, representativeness, and quality of online political discussion.

SBI is used in the project as an enabling technology for analyzing the UGC generated in Germany, Italy, and UK during a timespan ranging from March, 2014 to May, 2014 (the 2014 European Parliament Election was held on May 22–25, 2014). In the architecture we adopted, topics and related taxonomies are defined through Protégé; we use Brandwatch as a service for keyword-based crawling, Talend for ETL, SyN Semantic Center by SyNTHEMA for semantic enrichment (specifically, for labeling each clip with its sentiment), Oracle to store the ODS and the DM, MongoDB to store the document database for full-text search, and Mondrian as the multidimensional engine. Given the nature of the subject area, no EDW and no CRM are present in the architecture. We used the Indyco CASE tool to design the DM, and we developed an ad-hoc OLAP & dashboard interface using JavaScript, D3, and Saiku.

To enable topic-based aggregations of clips in the OLAP front-end, the classes in the domain ontology describing the subject area (that was designed together with the domain experts by classifying the topics emerged during macro-analysis) have been arranged into a *topic hierarchy* (see Fig. 2(a)). To effectively model the topic hierarchy, taking into account its specificities (it is heterogeneous, dynamic, non-onto, non-covering, and non-strict), the meta-star approach has been used [4].

4 Architectural Options

The techniques to be used to support the processes appearing in Fig. 1 may change depending on the context of each specific project, resulting in heavier or

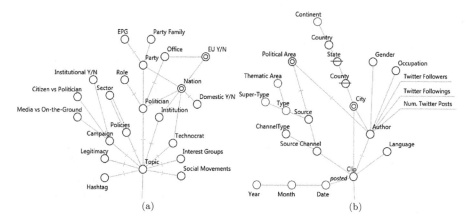

Fig. 2. A DFM representation of the topic (a) and clip (b) hierarchies for WebPolEU

lighter architectures. In the light of our experience with SBI projects of different types, in the following subsections we discuss the main options available to the design team, as well as their methodological impact.

4.1 Analysis

A component for analyzing the UGC is always present in SBI architectures, and it can take a variety of shapes characterized by quite different capabilities:

- **Dashboards** effectively summarize the trends and behaviors within the subject area, but only support a small number of predefined views and navigations (e.g., by topic or by geography).
- **Text search** enables very detailed analyses of the UGC up to the single-clip level, by supporting searches on both the clip text and its related meta data.
- **OLAP** provides very flexible analyses based on the multidimensional metaphor, which enables users to understand in depth the market mood by slicing and drilling according to different dimensions such as time, topic, geography, UGC source, and the related hierarchies.
- **Text mining** enables advanced analyses on textual data such as clip clustering and new topic discovery [5].

Standard commercial SBI systems normally provide only dashboards and text search, and only a few of them support text mining (e.g., SAS Text Miner and Temis). Providing OLAP capabilities requires an additional layer of multidimensional data to be added to the architecture, as well as additional ETL processes that obviously increase the overall complexity. In the WebPolEU implementation, a set of cubes (see Fig. 3) are provided; noticeably, their schemata are largely project-independent, except for the topic hierarchy whose content and structure strictly depends on the domain ontology. Besides, to enable text search functionalities, the relational ODS is coupled with a document-oriented database.

4.2 ODS

In principle, the ODS component could even be dropped (in which case, the two ETL processes in Fig. 1 could be unified) since the users do not access it directly. However, the presence of the ODS—in compliance with three-tier data warehouse architectures—is warmly recommended in SBI for several reasons:

- **Buffering and early analysis.** Crawling and semantic enrichment activities have a very different timing due to the complexity of enrichment. The ODS can be seen as the *buffer* that makes the two phases independent of each other, so as to give users the possibility of timely accessing a subset of information that (i) enables some relevant early analyses; (ii) has a key methodological role for tuning the crawling and enrichment processes at the next iteration. Such information ranges from the clip meta-data returned by the crawler (e.g., source, author, and clip count) to some *quick-and-dirty* semantic enrichment.
- **Clip reprocessing.** Semantic enrichment is inherently an iterative process, due to changes in topics and in the domain ontology which may occur even months after the clips were retrieved. Storing clips in an ODS, where they can be easily queried at any time, makes reprocessing feasible.
- **Data cleaning.** It is well known that data cleaning techniques are more effective when applied to materialized data rather than when they are applied on-the-fly to a data flow. In the specific case of SBI, cleaning is necessary, for instance, to correct wrong character sequences, to repair enrichment/crawling errors which may produce wrong or incomplete results, and to filter off-topic clips based on relevance measures computed on both text and meta-data.

In our prototypical implementation, a relational ODS is used to store clips and their meta-data together with topics and their relationships. However, other alternatives could be explored. Choosing a NoSQL repository is mainly a matter of scalability, strictly related to the quantity of data to be stored and processed. In WebPolEU, about 10 millions of raw clips were retrieved and about 1.3 billions of entity occurrences were produced by semantic enrichment. Although this size is still manageable with traditional RDBMS, larger projects may make NoSQL solutions more attractive. In our experience, the main advantages of using an RDBMS are:

- The ODS plays the role of a hub for ETL data flows, and its tuples are subject to several updates to trace the process steps. This determines a transactional workload which is better handled if the ACID properties are preserved.
- The presence of a well-defined, structured, and normalized schema is very useful to process the clip meta-data.

4.3 Crawling

The crawling component is the main entry point to the SBI system for all the data that will be analyzed. From a technical point of view, the problem with crawling is to ensure that a satisfactory compromise is achieved between retrieving too much content (which adds harmful noise and leads to useless efforts during semantic enrichment and analysis, as well as during all test activities) and retrieving too little content (which may dramatically reduce the reliability of analysis results). The two drivers that can be used to tune this compromise are *clipping* and *querying*.

Clipping is the process through which an indexed web page is parsed and every building section of the page itself is identified in order to exclude from the information extraction process all those contents that are not relevant and do not contain any useful information [19,20]. Bad clipping implies that the crawler will introduce into the system UGC filled with useless text such as hyperlinks, which will make the information almost incomprehensible for the semantic enrichment engine and often also for a human being—and also negatively affect the performance and quality of semantic enrichment activities.

Besides an accurate page clipping, the other ingredient for an effective crawling is a proper set of crawling queries. The standard way to identify relevant UGC from the web is by using Boolean keyword-based queries, where keywords considered as relevant or descriptive for the project scope are combined using different operators to instruct the crawler on the topics we are interested in and the ones that are out of scope. The operators typically provided by crawlers can be roughly classified into *Boolean* (e.g., AND, OR, NOT), *proximity* (e.g., NEAR/n), *meta* (e.g., country, site, author); wildcards are supported.

In the light of the above, it is apparent that managing and tuning the specific features of crawling to ensure its effectiveness is a burdensome and very time-consuming task. Noticeably, the roles in charge of these activity drastically depend on the project type as defined in Sect. 2: (1) in best-of-breed projects, all technical activities are in charge of the designer; (ii) in end-to-end projects, crawling templates are created and maintained by a service provider who is responsible of the clipping quality, but crawling queries are managed by the designer; (iii) in off-the-shelf projects, designers and users jointly carry out macro-analysis, but all other activities are largely in the hands of the service provider—which means that the designer can control the crawling effectiveness only to a limited extent [2]. So, from a project management point of view, the main trade-off involved in crawling is between (i) *do it yourself—but it will take a lot of time and effort* and (ii) *let the provider do it for you—but then you will have little control on the overall quality.*

4.4 Semantic Enrichment

The semantic enrichment process is maybe the one showing the widest spectrum of possible technological alternatives, with a very relevant impact on the expressiveness of the supported OLAP queries and on the accuracy of the results. Basic semantic enrichment techniques may be sufficient if users are only interested in analyzing raw data (e.g., counting the number of occurrences of each topic in the UGC); in some cases (for instance, for languages—like German—whose inherent complexity discourages automated analysis and interpretation of sentences), semantic enrichment is done by manually tagging each sentence with its sentiment. In our WebPolEU project, semantic enrichment is achieved as the combination of different (and possibly alternative) techniques:

- **Crawler meta-data:** Each clip is equipped with several meta-data, which are mainly related to the web source (e.g., http address and web site nation), to the author (e.g., name, sex, and nationality), and to the clip itself (e.g., its language). As shown in Fig. 2(b), in WebPolEU these meta-data are used to build the clip hierarchy.

- **Information retrieval:** The content of the clips can be analyzed by searching the raw text for user-defined topics (or their aliases). Although this type of analysis is not based on an in-depth comprehension of clip semantics, it returns a quick and valuable first level of analysis of the texts. In particular it allows to count the number of occurrences of a given topic and the number of co-occurrences of a pair of topics in a clip. Figure 3(a, b) shows the IR Clip and IR Topic Occurrence cubes of the DM; each event of IR Clip represents a clip and its topics, while each event of IR Topic Occurrence represents the occurrence of a single topic within a clip.

- **Crawler sentiment:** The crawler often provides its own sentiment score. In WebPolEU we use Brandwatch, whose sentiment analysis module is based on mining rules developed for each supported language and assigns a single sentiment to each clip. In both the IR Clip and IR Topic Occurrence cubes, the crawler sentiment for each clip is modeled as a measure.

- **NLP analysis:** It is the deepest analysis raw texts undergo. As shown in Sect. 2, the commercial system SyN Semantic Center is in charge of extracting the single entities, their part-of-speech, and their semantic relationships from the raw data. Two cubes are derived through NLP analysis. The first one, NLP Entity Occurrence (Fig. 3(c)), differs from IR Topic Occurrence since it also stores all the entities (i.e., lemmas, annotated with their part-of-speech) discovered in the text. The second one, NLP Semantic CoOccurrence (Fig. 3(d)), stores semantic relationships and explicitly models couples of topics/entities in the same sentence together with an optional qualifier (e.g., Angela Merkel had lunch with Matteo Renzi).

- **Domain expert:** differently from social media monitoring solutions, SBI projects allow additional meta-data to be provided by domain experts by means of the domain ontology coded in the topic hierarchy (see Fig. 2(a)) and by additional meta-data to be added to the other hierarchies.

5 Case Study Analysis

Carrying out an SBI project requires to find the right trade-off between its effectiveness, efficiency, and sustainability, respectively expressed in terms of correctness of the results obtained, appropriateness of the response time, and time/money required to run the project. In this section we provide a quantitative evaluation of these aspects with reference to our case study.

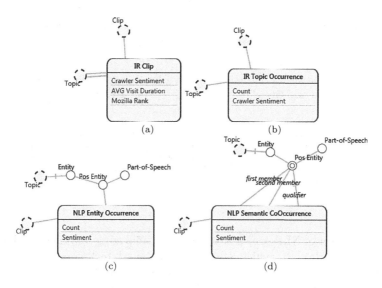

Fig. 3. A DFM representation of IR and NLP cubes. Topic and clip hierarchies have been hidden to simplify the picture

Overall, the number of collected clips in WebPolEU was around ten millions, which decreased to six millions after dropping non-relevant sources and duplicate clips. Noticeably, the quantity of information generated by the semantic enrichment process is much larger (|NLP Entity Occurrence| ≈ 500 M for each language) and places the project on the edge of big data. The topics were provided by the team of socio-political researchers involved in WebPolEU; the number of topics is about the same (around 500) for Germany, Italy, and UK, since the same issues were discussed in the three nations. Although the number of clips collected for Germany (933 K) is quite lower than that for Italy and UK (about 3 M each), the number of occurrences generated is not so different; this is because the lower number of clips for Germany is counterbalanced by their greater average length.

5.1   Effectiveness

Our first goal is to evaluate different semantic enrichment techniques in terms of the trade-off they offer between added value on the one side, and resource demand/effort on the other. In particular, we will compare the approach based on crawler meta-data, crawler sentiment, and information retrieval (called IR in the following) against the approach based on NLP analysis (called NLP). We will focus on the Italian and English clips since they were both enriched using the same tools (Brandwatch for IR and SyN Semantic Center for NLP). As shown in Table 1(a), the two techniques find the same topic occurrences in a clip in most cases. This shows that the KPIs based on topic counting, which are widely adopted for UGC analysis, does not necessarily require the adoption of sophisticated ontology-based techniques and a full comprehension of sentence syntax and semantic. Conversely, these techniques are required when analyzing semantic co-occurrences is one of the users' goals.

Table 1. Number of topic occurrences detected by IR and NLP (a) and number of positive, neutral, and negative clips detected by NLP, by IR, and agreed upon by NLP and IR (b)

	ITA	ENG
# Topic Occ. NLP	14 215 K	23 399 K
# Topic Occ. IR	15 401 K	25 006 K
# Shared Occ.	12 922 K	21 497 K

(a)

Sentiment	ITA			ENG		
	NLP	IR	Agreed	NLP	IR	Agreed
Positive	566 K	36 K	19 K	1090 K	142 K	107 K
Neutral	893 K	2340 K	888 K	1368 K	2973 K	1337 K
Negative	934 K	17 K	14 K	817 K	159 K	112 K

(b)

The real power of NLP comes into play when analyzing sentiment. Table 1(b) shows that Brandwatch, which adopts a rule-based technique for sentiment analysis, hardly assigns a non-neutral sentiment to a clip: most of the clips that Brandwatch labels as positive/negative are positive/negative for SyN too, while the two systems often disagree on neutral clips.

There is not much point in discussing the differences in IR and NLP sentiment without knowing which is the correct one. For this reason we evaluated the accuracy of the returned sentiment by asking five domain experts to manually tag a sample of the clips. The sample includes about 600 clips from the English corpus, equally divided by media type and NLP sentiment (as computed by Syn). Besides defining the clip sentiment as either negative, neutral, or positive, the domain experts were also asked to rate, for each clip, its *clipping quality* (i.e., the amount of non-relevant text present in the clip), which could impact on the difficulty of assigning the right sentiment, and its intrinsic *text complexity* (i.e., the effort of a human expert in assigning the sentiment due to irony, incorrect syntax, abbreviations, etc.). Table 2 shows the IR and NLP sentiment accuracy (i.e., percentage agreement with the consensus sentiment) for each sub-sample; a correct interpretation of the results requires some further explanation due to the different cardinalities of the sub-samples. It is apparent that the experts rated most of the clips as neutral—thus, a dummy classifier always stating *neutral* would most probably be very successful! Before commenting the tables, we recall that the lower bound on accuracy is 33 %, which is the percentage of success of a random classifier.

- The high accuracy achieved by IR on neutral clips is not actually due to its real capability of discerning between negative, neutral and positive clips, but rather to its inability/caution in assigning a non-neutral sentiment. Indeed, its accuracy on negative and positive clips is below that of a dummy classifier.
- When using NLP, detecting positive sentiments turns out to be much easier than identifying negative ones. This happens because positive opinions are normally characterized by enthusiastic words, while negative ones are often blurred by irony, which can hardly be detected. This is confirmed by the experts, that mostly label positive clips as having standard complexity.

- For clips whose texts complexity has been classified as hard, both IR and NLP often fail in assigning the right sentiment.
- The clipping quality impacts more on NLP than on IR accuracy. It would be interesting to investigate if this is related to the deeper level of text understanding NLP tries to achieve.

Table 2. IR and NLP sentiment accuracy for each sub-sample

Clipping Quality	Text Complexity	Negative		Neutral		Positive	
		IR	NLP	IR	NLP	IR	NLP
High	Standard	16.7%	62.7%	85.1%	39.9%	21.7%	68.3%
	Hard	15.2%	36.4%	100.0%	44.4%	0.0%	100.0%
	Overall	15.9%	49.5%	92.5%	42.2%	10.8%	84.2%
Low	Standard	20.0%	55.0%	87.8%	54.9%	28.6%	57.1%
	Hard	0.0%	0.0%	100.0%	0.0%	–	–
	Overall	10.0%	27.5%	93.9%	27.4%	28.6%	57.1%

Text Complexity	Negative		Neutral		Positive		IR	NLP
	IR	NLP	IR	NLP	IR	NLP		
Standard	18.3%	58.8%	86.4%	47.4%	25.1%	62.7%	43.3%	56.3%
Hard	7.6%	18.2%	100.0%	22.2%	0.0%	100.0%	43.0%	36.2%
Overall	13.0%	38.5%	93.2%	34.8%	16.7%	75.2%	43.2%	47.2%

As to analysis, the last phase of the SBI process, we can only give some qualitative assessment. Moving from standard dashboards to user-driven OLAP analysis has been recognized as truly valuable by the WebPolEU users since it enables them to flexibly and autonomously navigate data to get a deeper insight on the ongoing trends, leaning on hierarchies to better analyze data.

5.2 Efficiency

We start this section by mentioning how the architecture in Fig. 1 has been implemented in the WebPolEU project. ETL and analysis run on an 8-cores server with 64 GB of RAM; the text search engine runs on a 7-nodes cluster (each node equipped with a 4-cores processor and 32 GB of RAM); the semantic enrichment component runs on a 6-nodes virtual cluster (each node equipped with a 12-cores processor and 10 GB of RAM). As to the data volume, the raw crawler files take 79 GB, the ODS 481 GB, the DM 116 GB, and the documents for text search 65 GB. Noticeably, since the OLAP cubes in the DM mainly store numerical data, their required storage is lower than that of the ODS.

Table 3 shows the time required for running the main ETL flows with reference to all clips (a 20 × parallelization was adopted to maximize the throughput) and the time for the bi-directional ETL flow between the ODS and NLP semantic enrichment as a function of the clip length (here times were measured on a single-process basis). These results confirm that NLP semantic enrichment deeply impacts on the time and space required to feed the DM, so its adoption

Table 3. Average processing time in seconds for 10 000 clips; to the right, average time for NLP semantic enrichment of one clip

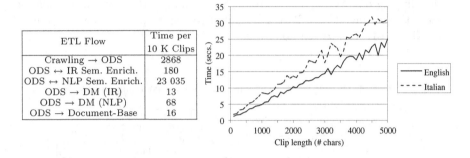

ETL Flow	Time per 10 K Clips
Crawling → ODS	2868
ODS ↔ IR Sem. Enrich.	180
ODS ↔ NLP Sem. Enrich.	23 035
ODS → DM (IR)	13
ODS → DM (NLP)	68
ODS → Document-Base	16

Table 4. Execution time for chart, OLAP and free-text queries

Query type	Exec. time (s)			Query example
	Min	Avg	Max	
IR charts	1.2	7.4	25.5	Daily trend of UK topic occurrences for each channel type and party
NLP charts	0.8	62.2	288.7	Top 5 entities related to the "Cameron" topic
IR OLAP	0.3	7.7	50.1	Average crawler sentiment for each party and country
NLP OLAP	0.4	14.7	79.4	Average sentiment for each topic sector and clip type
Free-text	0.2	1.1	2.9	"Europe" AND "Politics" (filter on Clip.Source = "telegraph.co.uk")

should be carefully evaluated. Interestingly, both processing time and data size are higher for Italian clips due to the greater complexity of the Italian language.

We close our efficiency analysis by showing, in Table 4, the execution time for an analysis workload including 33 queries, which can be classified into three groups corresponding to the main functions of a typical SBI platform: charts, OLAP analysis, and free-text search. The first group includes the queries whose output is used to draw the charts available in the WebPolEU interface (e.g., tag cloud, trends, etc.), while the other two groups were created by auditing and sampling the queries actually issued by WebPolEU users. Although the average query time is higher for NLP queries (because the corresponding cubes have higher cardinalities), all the groups are compatible with interactive analyses.

5.3   Sustainability

The first design iteration for WebPolEU took 84 person-days overall; of these, 18 were for designing the domain ontology (including topic definition), 21 for designing and testing semantic enrichment (in particular for tuning the dictionary), and 26 for designing and testing crawling queries. The second iteration was mostly used for tuning the ETL (20 person-days out of 30). The main critical issues related to each activity are listed below:

– Ontology design: the correctness of the results is deeply affected by the number of topics and aliases defined. For example, with reference to Fig. 2, the number of occurrences for each topic sector depends on the topics and aliases summarizing that sector, hence, including an unbalanced number of topics for the different sectors may lead to an unfair analysis. Keeping a proper level of detail for different sectors requires a deep knowledge of the domain and related vocabulary.

- Crawling design: commercial solutions (like Brandwatch) normally limit the length of the crawling queries; this makes it harder to properly define the subject area, which is necessary to filter off-topic clips. Finding the proper formulation of queries with constraints on their length and number may become a real nightmare.
- ETL & OLAP design: although parsing a JSON file is a trivial task, handling all the possible unexpected character sequences is more tricky and requires continuous tuning along the whole project. On the other hand, unexpected character sequences often determine a failure of semantic enrichment.

6   Related Literature and Conclusion

As stated in the Introduction, only a few papers have focused on the full picture of SBI so far. Complete architectures for SBI have been proposed in [6,13]; in both cases, the basic blocks of the architecture have been identified, but still with a limited expressiveness. In particular, in [13] a comprehensive solution for the extraction of Twitter streams and the enhancement and analysis of their metadata is presented; the approach of [6] extracts sentiment data about products and their features from selected opinion websites and builds *opinion facts*. An important step towards increasing the expressiveness of SBI queries has been taken in [1], where a first advanced solution for modeling topic hierarchies has been proposed. Another step in this direction has been made in [4], where topic hierarchies are modeled by handling their dynamics and irregularity so as to enable full OLAP analyses of social data. In terms of OLAP analysis over UGC, a cube for analyzing term occurrences in documents belonging to a corpus is proposed in [9], although term categorization is very simple and does not support analyses at different levels of abstraction. In [12] the authors propose to use textual measures to summarize textual information within a cube.

As to the enabling technologies for the SBI process, a number of academic works have focused on specific issues that find application on strictly correlated fields. First of all, web crawling is a central issue in information retrieval, in whose context powerful languages to automatically and precisely capture the relevant data to be extracted were studied (e.g., [3]). In terms of semantic enrichment of raw clips and text understanding, different techniques have been studied in several areas of computer science. Whereas most of these techniques are typically tuned to perform well on a limited set of selected (web) sources, their accuracy tends to decrease when applied to a heterogeneous collection of documents extracted from multiple kinds of sources. In general, NLP approaches try to obtain a full text understanding [18], while text mining approaches rely on different techniques (e.g., n-grams) either to find interesting patterns in texts

Table 5. Summary of main architectural options

Component	Option	Pros	Cons
Analysis	Dashboard	Effective summary of trends	Low flexibility
	Text search	Detailed content analyses	Increased storage
	OLAP	High flexibility	Increased storage; extra ETL
ODS	Text mining	Enables advanced analyses	Complexity; expert analyst required
	Relational	Clip buffering, reprocessing, and cleaning; structured	Increased storage; performances
Crawling	NoSQL	Clip buffering, reprocessing, and cleaning; scalability	Low control of data transformation and quality
	Designer-managed	Good control of quality	Large effort
Sem. Enr.	Provider-managed	Small effort	Low control of quality
	Crawler meta-data	Enables clip classification and aggregation	Some complexity in collecting
	Crawler sentiment	Enables analysis of sentiment; no tuning	Unreliable for non-neutral clips
	Inf. retrieval	Enables topic occurrence analysis	Low text understanding
	NLP analysis	Enables analysis of sentiment; also reliable for non-neutral clips	Complex tuning; affected by clipping quality
	Domain expert	Enables analysis of sentiment; fully reliable	Costly; subjective

(e.g., named entities [14], relationships between topics [15], or clip sentiment [11]) or to classify/cluster them [17]. Also hybrid approaches between classical NLP and statistical techniques have been tried, either user-guided, as in [8], or automated and unsupervised, as in [6].

In this paper we have analyzed the main factors that impact on the costs and benefits of the main architectural options for SBI. A summary of the pros and cons of the different options, as emerging from our case study, is shown in Table 5. Remarkably, it turned out that crawling and semantic enrichment are the components that impact the most on the overall cost-benefit compromise. Here we summarize a few rules of thumb for making a good choice:

– The accuracy of both NLP and IR sentiment can be high on very specific sources and closed domains (such as the CRM of a bank or the movie reviews [7]), but it easily drops as soon as the domain becomes wider. Since a relevant effort is required to properly handle sentiment, the design team should carefully evaluate the use of sentiment analysis techniques by trading-off the accuracy achievable with the related costs.
– Although Twitter provides a partial analysis of the social environment, the shortness of tweets and the high percentage of non-neutral clips make it a good candidate to be the main source for an effective sentiment analysis. Indeed, experimental data show that Twitter clips yield the highest accuracy for NLP sentiment (56.6 %, vs. 51.5 % of forums and 42.4 % of news).
– Dashboards are the standard way for visualizing and analyzing data in SBI projects since they yield an immediate, easy-to-understand, and well-focused representation of results. However, as the role of SBI systems becomes more

important in companies, full-OLAP capabilities will increasingly be provided because they clearly enable more flexible and accurate analyses of the UGC.

– Off-the-shelf projects provide *quick-and-dirty* answers but preclude the possibility of carrying out in-depth analysis, tuning, reprocessing, and integration with enterprise data. They should be pursued either at an early stage of adoption of SBI solutions to assess the real value of social data for the company, or if the available resources are very limited.

References

1. Dayal, U., Gupta, C., Castellanos, M., Wang, S., Garcia-Solaco, M.: Of cubes, DAGs and hierarchical correlations: a novel conceptual model for analyzing social media data. In: Atzeni, P., Cheung, D., Ram, S. (eds.) ER 2012 Main Conference 2012. LNCS, vol. 7532, pp. 30–49. Springer, Heidelberg (2012)
2. Francia, M., Golfarelli, M., Rizzi, S.: A methodology for social BI. In: Proceedings of IDEAS, Porto, Portugal, pp. 207–216 (2014)
3. Furche, T., Gottlob, G., Grasso, G., Schallhart, C., Sellers, A.J.: OXPath: a language for scalable data extraction, automation, and crawling on the deep web. VLDB J. **22**(1), 47–72 (2013)
4. Gallinucci, E., Golfarelli, M., Rizzi, S.: Advanced topic modeling for social business intelligence. Inf. Syst. **53**, 87–106 (2015)
5. Gao, W., Li, P., Darwish, K.: Joint topic modeling for event summarization across news and social media streams. In: Proceedings of CIKM, Maui, HI, pp. 1173–1182 (2012)
6. García-Moya, L., Kudama, S., Aramburu, M.J., Llavori, R.B.: Storing and analysing voice of the market data in the corporate data warehouse. Inf. Syst. Front. **15**(3), 331–349 (2013)
7. Hu, M., Liu, B.: Mining and summarizing customer reviews. In: Proceedings of SIGKDD, Seattle, WA, pp. 168–177 (2004)
8. Kahan, J., Koivunen, M.R.: Annotea: an open RDF infrastructure for shared web annotations. In: Proceedings of WWW, Hong Kong, China, pp. 623–632 (2001)
9. Lee, J., Grossman, D.A., Frieder, O., McCabe, M.C.: Integrating structured data and text: a multi-dimensional approach. In: Proceedings of ITCC, Las Vegas, USA, pp. 264–271 (2000)
10. Liu, B., Zhang, L.: A survey of opinion mining and sentiment analysis. In: Aggarwal, C., Zhai, C. (eds.) Mining Text Data, pp. 415–463. Springer, New York (2012)
11. Pang, B., Lee, L., Vaithyanathan, S.: Thumbs up? sentiment classification using machine learning techniques. CoRR cs.CL/0205070 (2002)
12. Ravat, F., Teste, O., Tournier, R., Zurfluh, G.: Top_Keyword: an aggregation function for textual document OLAP. In: Song, I.-Y., Eder, J., Nguyen, T.M. (eds.) DaWaK 2008. LNCS, vol. 5182, pp. 55–64. Springer, Heidelberg (2008)
13. Rehman, N.U., Mansmann, S., Weiler, A., Scholl, M.H.: Building a data warehouse for Twitter stream exploration. In: Proceedings of ASONAM, Istanbul, Turkey, pp. 1341–1348 (2012)
14. Ritter, A., Clark, S., Mausam, E., O.: Named entity recognition in tweets: an experimental study. In: Proceedings of EMNLP, Edinburgh, UK, pp. 1524–1534 (2011)
15. Rosenfeld, B., Feldman, R.: Clustering for unsupervised relation identification. In: Proceedings of CIKM, Lisbon, Portugal, pp. 411–418 (2007)

16. Stavrakantonakis, I., Gagiu, A.E., Kasper, H., Toma, I., Thalhammer, A.: An approach for evaluation of social media monitoring tools. Common Value Manag. **52**, 52–64 (2012)
17. Wang, X., McCallum, A., Wei, X.: Topical n-grams: phrase and topic discovery, with an application to information retrieval. In: Proceedings of ICDM, Washington, DC, USA, pp. 697–702 (2007)
18. Yi, J., Nasukawa, T., Bunescu, R.C., Niblack, W.: Sentiment analyzer: extracting sentiments about a given topic using natural language processing techniques. In: Proceedings of ICDM, Melbourne, Florida, pp. 427–434 (2003)
19. Yi, L., Liu, B.: Web page cleaning for web mining through feature weighting. In: Proceedings of IJCAI, Acapulco, Mexico, vol. 3, pp. 43–50 (2003)
20. Yi, L., Liu, B., Li, X.: Eliminating noisy information in web pages for data mining. In: Proceedings of KDD, Washington DC, USA, pp. 296–305 (2003)

Business Process Modeling

To Integrate or Not to Integrate – The Business Rules Question

Wei Wang[1], Marta Indulska[2], and Shazia Sadiq[1(✉)]

[1] School of Information Technology and Electrical Engineering,
The University of Queensland, Brisbane, Australia
`w.wang9@uq.edu.au`, `shazia@itee.uq.edu.au`
[2] University of Queensland Business School,
The University of Queensland, Brisbane, Australia
`m.indulska@business.uq.edu.au`

Abstract. Due to complex and fragmented enterprise systems and modelling landscapes, organizations struggle to cope with change propagation, compliance management and interoperability. Two aspects related to the above are business process models and business rules, both of which have a role to play in the enterprise setting. Redundancy and inconsistency between business rules and business process models is prevalent, highlighting the need for consideration of integrated modelling of the two. An important prerequisite of achieving integrated modelling is the ability to decide whether a rule should be integrated into a business process model or modelled independently. However, in the current literature, little guidance can be found that can help modellers to make such a decision. Accordingly, our aim is to empirically test factors that affect such decisions. In this paper, we describe 12 such factors and present the results of an empirical evaluation of their importance. Through our study, we identify seven factors that can provide guidance for integrated modelling.

Keywords: Business process management · Business rule management · Integrated modelling

1 Introduction

The modelling of business processes and business rules has been an important topic of Information Systems and Computer Science research over the last two decades [1–3]. Traditionally, business rules are modelled in a standalone fashion using rule modelling notations. In more recent years, as new modelling languages and methods have been developed [3], researchers have argued that business rules can be modelled independently or integrated into business processes [4, 5]. Several researchers have motivated integrated modelling of business processes and business rules [6, 7]. Such integration is posited to result in improved model understanding, increased interoperability capacity, better change propagation of new requirements and increased capacity for compliance management [8–10]. Previous research has made several contributions towards this end through analyzing the representational capacity, deficiency and overlap of process and rule modelling languages [11], with a view towards their integrated use. Several initial

© Springer International Publishing Switzerland 2016
S. Nurcan et al. (Eds.): CAiSE 2016, LNCS 9694, pp. 51–66, 2016.
DOI: 10.1007/978-3-319-39696-5_4

approaches for the integration of business process models and business rules have also been proposed [12].

Empirical findings [13] indicate that process designers often have the need to represent in a process model business rules that go beyond control flow rules. Although all process models contain some business rules in the way of control flow, other rules may be, and often are, documented separately. Representing process models graphically without all relevant rules or operational constraints can result in flawed decision making and non-compliant process execution. It is also a roadblock to achieving a holistic understanding of the process, and thus affects shared understanding of requirements between stakeholders. In turn, incomplete requirements lead to incomplete system implementation, in which business processes might be executed without necessary constraints and monitoring mechanisms and, thus, might lead to high costs due to operational and compliance risks.

We argue, along the lines of [3], that there are situations under which a business rule is better modelled independently from a business process model, and situations under which it is more appropriate to integrate the rule with a business process model. It follows then that an important aspect of integrated modelling is the understanding of such situations and how they influence business rule representation. While the decision in regards to how a rule should be modelled is not a straightforward one, little guidance exists that can help modelers make such a decision. This shortcoming results in fragmented and inconsistent business process and rule models. In our earlier work [14] we identified the factors that are likely to affect such decisions. In this paper, our aim is two-fold: (1) to empirically evaluate the factors; (2) to identify guidelines for better business rule modelling decisions.

This paper unfolds as follows. The next section provides an overview of business process and business rule modelling, as well as prior efforts to identify factors that influence integration in the context of modelling. Section 3 overview the methodology used earlier for factor identification, and presents the methodology for empirical evaluation of the factors. Section 4 summarizes the factors and Sect. 5 discusses the empirical evaluation. Section 6 provides an empirically-grounded discussion on how these factors should affect rule modelling. Finally, we summarize the results of our study in terms of the evaluation results and provide some guidelines for modeling of business rules. We conclude the paper with a discussion of the findings and future outlook.

2 Background Concepts and Related Work

A business process model is a structured collection of activities that accomplishes a specific goal that will create value for an organization. Such structures also involve business rule models, which describe the constraints and requirements guiding and controlling the behavior of business activities, and can be integrated into related business process models or modelled independently. Business process modelling and business rule modelling both focus on creating a representation of the organization's current and future practices. They are complementary approaches as they address distinct aspects of organizational practices. However, the two approaches evolved separately over the last few decades and failed to integrate into a more powerful approach.

Three types of methods for integrated business process and rule modelling have been developed in literature *viz. annotation, encapsulation* and *extension* [12]. *Annotation* is the use of additional textual elements to represent other aspects that are beyond the representational capacity of the selected modelling language. The textual elements are typically attached to graphical symbols within the process model to represent extra information. *Encapsulation* is the embedding of related business rules into a specific element in business process models. The embedded rules can be folded and unfolded, thus allowing users to easily switch focus between the overall structure and detailed parts of a process model. *Extension* either creates new elements or combines existing meta-elements from other languages to increase the representation capability of the underlying language to represent both business activities and business rules. Figure 1 is a simplistic illustration of a business process model with rule integration, using *annotation, encapsulation,* and *extension* methods.

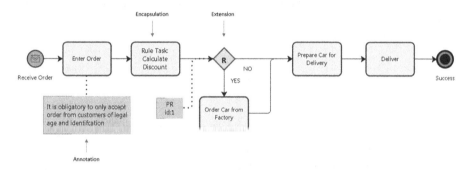

Fig. 1. Illustration of a business process model with rule integration

Although the benefits and methods of integrated business rule modelling have been well studied as stated Sect. 1, there is a paucity of research that examines or consolidates factors that are relevant for business process model and business rule integration. zur Muehlen *et al.* [3] were the first to argue the need for guidelines to inform such integration. They identified five potential factors expected to influence the representation of a business. However, without proper evaluation, the validity of each factor cannot be fully established. Investigation and validation of each factor's decision-influence on the representation of a business rule is also needed, which is the aim of our work as presented in the following sections.

3   Methodology

Our study involves two phases, *viz.* factor identification and factor validation. The first phase is based on a review and analysis of existing literature and is documented in [14], while the second is an empirical study of business rule experts in the form of academics and practitioners. In the following sub-sections, we outline our methodology.

3.1   Factor Identification

In our earlier work we embarked on a systematic identification of factors [14]. To identify these factors, we conducted a systematic literature review based on a comprehensive set of well-regarded Information Systems and Computer Science journals and conferences (see www.aisnet.org and www.core.edu.au) published between 1990–2013, a period of time after the initial proposal of integration of the two approaches [2]. Our data set consisted of 43,021 full-text articles (see Table 1). Each article was prepared (with OCR) for a full-text search. Subsequently, a full-text search was conducted using the term 'business rule'. We regarded a paper as relevant if the keyword 'business rule' occurred 3 times or more within the body of the text and only selected those papers for the next round of analysis that met this criterion. Based on this elimination process, 255 relevant papers were identified. For each of the 255 papers, we read the abstract, the introduction of the paper, and each paragraph where the term "rule" occurred to determine if the paper was relevant to our purpose. A paper was identified as relevant if a characteristic of a business rule like change frequency, reusability or impact is discussed or mentioned in the paper. This step resulted in the identification of 78 papers.

Table 1. Dataset of 1990–2013 publications

Type	Acronym	# of papers	# of relevant papers
Conferences	ACIS, AMCIS, CAiSE, ECIS, ER, HICSS, ICIQ, ICIS, IFIP, IRMA, IS Foundations, PACIS, BPM, WIDM, WISE, CIKM, SIGIR, VLDB	27,326	29
Journals	BPMJ, CAIS, EJIS, I&M, ISF, ISJ (Blackwell), ISJ (Sarasota), JAIS, ISR, MISQ, MISQ Executive, TKDE, DKE, CACM, DSS, TOIS	15,695	49

The set of 78 relevant papers was then read in full and manually coded with a dedicated coding protocol implemented via an Excel spreadsheet. The coding protocol was designed and agreed by the three researchers after an initial coding of several articles to refine the protocol and contained a field for a factor, the title of the paper, context, and other comments. One researcher carried out the initial coding exercise through iterative coding of the papers to identify all relevant factors and then refined the result with the two researchers. The refinement included (1) selecting business rule characteristics that had the potential to be factors and excluding unrelated characteristics, (2) identifying and clustering synonymous factors and (3) selecting a representative label for each factor and clarifying its definition. The result was refined over three iterations until all three researchers were satisfied with the selection and definition of each factor. Twelve factors were identified in total through this process, as summarized in Sect. 4 and detailed in full in [14].

3.2 Empirical Evaluation

To validate the identified factors for relevance and investigate their relative importance, we designed an empirical evaluation instrument. The authors of the 78 papers relevant for the factor identification were the target participants of the empirical evaluation. These academics and professionals were invited to participate in an online survey through invitation emails. In the invitation email, participants were informed about the background and nature of the study, for which no incentives were offered. We used Qualtrics[1] as the platform to deliver the survey and collect data.

The survey was designed, pilot-tested and revised through two iterations. In the first round of pilot testing, 3 PhD students with knowledge of conceptual modeling were asked to complete the survey and provide feedback on clarity of factor definitions and questions. In the second round, the revised survey was pilot-tested with 2 PhD students and a Master student by research, with knowledge of conceptual modelling and an international expert in requirements modelling. The revisions as a result of the pilot studies included changes to the definitions of factors and to questions so as to improve clarity as well as research rigor (e.g. randomization of questions was introduced through the pilot study). With our finalized survey instrument, we collected (1) the importance of factors, (2) an importance ranking of the factors from each participant and (3) expert opinions on how rules should be modelled given each factor.

We sent invitations to 112 authors of the 78 papers, and received 35 responses in total, of which 13 were incomplete and had to be removed. Thus, we received 22 usable responses, which represents a response rate of 23.08 % when calculated as responses per paper. While low, it is hard to achieve high response rates in empirical research and many consider any response rate of approximately 20 % to be usable [15–17].

4 Business Rule Modelling Factors

In total, twelve factors were identified. For further discussion of the factors, and the sources/papers in which they were identified, please refer to [14]. In the following we provide as a summary the definition of each factor, with arguments collected from the literature review. Only the definitions (in italics) are used in the survey and the argument statements or examples are excluded to avoid possible introduction of bias in the responses.

Accessibility. *Accessibility refers to the user's need to view and manipulate a business rule. If a stakeholder can easily view or manipulate a rule in a format that is suitable to his or her need, then the rule has high accessibility, otherwise, the rule has low accessibility.* Making business rule repositories accessible to stakeholders whenever required, as well as in a format that is suitable to their needs, is a basic requirement of information systems [18]. Separating the rules can make rules easily accessible to business users, and potentially reduce the complexity and waiting times in making changes required in response to specific external or internal changes in requirements [19].

---

[1] Qualtrics is a web-based survey platform. See: www.qualtrics.com.

Agility. *Agility refers to how quickly a business rule can be adapted to a change. Rate of change deals with how frequently the rule needs to be changed, and agility deals with how long will it take for each change to be modelled in a rule.* Some business rules are required to take effect immediately to ensure the agility of the system [19]. Similarly, there can be others that may not have strict constraints on time of initiation [20–22].

Aspect of Change. *Aspect of Change refers to the component of the rule that can be changed. The components of a rule that could change are the trigger condition, the reaction, or the values of parameters, as well as rule phrases and design elements* [23]. *Depending on the component, the change might be simple or complex.* While a graphical process model may expose some simple configuration to business users, more complex business rule changes may only be possible at a deeper level that may need a business rule language representation.

Awareness of Impact. *Awareness of Impact refers to how comprehensively the implications of a business rule, or its revisions, are understood. Some business rules have a direct and clear impact, while other rules may have an indirect or unclear impact. Thus, the impact may or may not be clear to the stakeholders.* Business users may have to bring to bear their additional external knowledge to understand the implications of a business rule [24]. If the impacts of a business rule are not comprehensively understood, e.g. a change in one department's business practices is necessitated by a change in another department and the effects cannot be safely predicted, then the deployment and implementation of the rule may need justification or re-engineering in the future [3]. The advantage of rule models is "easier and faster implementation in case adjustments needs to be made" [3].

Complexity. *Complexity refers to the level of difficulty in defining or understanding a business rule. Some rules are simple and some rules can be complex in nature.* Thus, the clarity and simplicity of business rules may differ based on the chosen representation [25]. Certain kinds of business rules cannot be clearly expressed in a business process modelling language due to language representation limitations, while others may be easily modelled as a standalone rule due to the more precise representation capability [26].

Criticality. *Criticality refers to the importance of the rule. Violation of critical rules can lead to severe consequences for the organization, while violation of non-critical rules may be less severe.* Integrating a business rule into a business process model can ensure that the business rule is implemented enterprise-wide. A standalone business rule, on the other hand, has a risk of being overlooked when users perform manual tasks relying on process models as guidelines for operations.

Governance Responsibility. *Governance Responsibility refers to who ensures that business activities are in accordance with business rules. Rules can be governed automatically by programs/systems, or manually by humans* [27, 28]. If the business rule is to be checked automatically in the system, machine readability and execution will be a basic requirement, while context availability and user-friendly representation will be more important if the rule is to be checked by a human.

Implementation Responsibility. *Implementation Responsibility refers to who is charged with implementing or updating the business rule. Both business users and technical users could be responsible for the implementation of a business rule.* Business users generally have the configuration responsibility over business rules in business rule repositories [3] and may not have process modelling expertise, whereas technical staff or the IT department may be responsible for the implementation of business processes [29].

Rate of Change. *Rate of Change refers to the frequency at which a business rule requires modification. Business rules can change in response to changes in regulations and policies.* Frequent business rule change requires mechanisms that support easy modification and propagation. It is possible that frequently changed business rules could be modelled in a stand-alone fashion, rather than being integrated into graphical process models where they could be labor-intensive and cumbersome to update [30], while stable business rules could be integrated into a business process model.

Reusability. *Reusability refers to the potential for a rule to be used in new contexts. An existing business rule may be adapted or modified to fit new contexts and scenarios to reduce the resources required in developing new rules.* Scattered [26, 31] and duplicated [23] rules make it difficult to evaluate and maintain the integrity and consistency [32, 33]. If a reusable business rule is integrated into a business process model, the development, testing, and maintenance efforts may be increased when that rule changes and requires update [23, 34]. On the contrary, modelling such a rule in a business rule notation and storing it in a business rule engine could ease maintenance efforts.

Rule Source. *Rule Source refers to the origin of the business rule. Rule sources could be external or internal – e.g. laws and regulations or internal policies and standards.* Requirements defined by external regulatory bodies can be "critical to the organization, while being outside the scope of their control. Particularly when the changes pertain to compliance with regulations" [3]. According to [3] modelling external business rules as part of a business process ensures that an audit trail is created, and thus facilitates compliance management and audit.

Scope of Impact. *Scope of Impact refers to the breadth of the impact of the rule. The impact of a business rule can be focused on an activity, an entire process, a department or the entire organization* [3]. If an organization-wide business rule is integrated into a large number of business process models any update to the rule will lead to a change in a large number of models, thus triggering re-work and risk of inconsistency [3, 35]. If the same business rule resides in a business rule repository, the update effort will be limited to an individual business rule instance, while being linked to potentially several process models.

5   Empirical Evaluation

In this section we present the empirical validation of the twelve factors. The main aim of the empirical study was to derive a ranking of factors based on their perceived importance by experts and capture expert indications as to how these factors affect modelling business rules in practice. To this end, in the following we first present a discussion of the relative ranking of the twelve factors, considering also the level of expert agreement in their ranking lists, and then explore the indications as to how these factors affect modelling of business rules.

5.1 Demographics

Our survey was aimed at academics and practitioners who authored the 78 papers relevant to this study. Table 2 shows that the overall business process modelling experience of our participants is higher than in other similar studies, e.g. [13]. However, the experience of standalone rule modelling is slightly lower than that of processes modelling, indicating that less participants are familiar with standalone rule modelling.

Table 2. Participant demographics

Aspect	Values	Percentage	Aspect	Values	Percentage
Responses	22	23 %	Years of experience in business process modelling overall	<2 years	14 %
Number of business process modelling notations used	1	9 %		2–5 years	18 %
	2	32 %		5–10 years	18 %
	3	14 %		>10 years	50 %
	4	14 %	Years of experience in business rule modelling notations overall	None	14 %
	5	18 %		<2 years	9 %
	>5	14 %		2–5 years	27 %
Number of business rule modelling notations used	0	23 %		5–10 years	27 %
	1	14 %		>10 years	23 %
	2	27 %	Number of business process models created	<10	18 %
	3	23 %		10–25	41 %
	4	9 %		25–50	9 %
	5	5 %		>50	32 %

5.2 Factor Importance

To distinguish the relative importance of each factor, we asked the participants to select at least 5 most important factors and rank them according to their relative importance. As current top-k ranking comparison algorithms require a constant k across all rankings [36], only the top-5 factors are calculated in the ranking and agreement analysis. We note that one participant selected 6 factors and two participants selected 7 factors in this question, but these factors are already in top 50% of factors based on importance (see Table 5).

To calculate consensus between the participants, the rankings provided by all participants are aggregated into a single score. Consensus ranking [37] is used as it can help minimize the overall distances between rankings. Since this is an NP-Hard problem, some relaxed methods are used to find the approximate closest distance [37].

We adopted the classical positional Borda's method [38] to calculate the aggregated ranking, which is well adopted in literature [37, 39].

Following this method, for a factor which ranked $i <= 5$ in an individual ranking, we assign $5-i$ points to the factor. For a factor which is not ranked within the top 5, we assign 0 points. The total points of each factor are a sum of the factor's points in each individual ranking.

As shown in Table 3, *agility* is ranked as the most important factor, with 42 points, and *criticality* is a close second. The factors *rate of change* and *reusability* are jointly ranked third, with 37 points. *Accessibility, awareness* of *impact, complexity, governance responsibility* and *scope of impact* follow in that order. The lowest ranked three factors are found to be those of *aspect of change, implementation responsibility* and *rule source*.

Table 3. Aggregated ranking using Borda's method

Factor	Total points	Rank	SD	Factor	Total Points	Rank	SD
Agility	42	1	2.05	Complexity	25	7	1.16
Criticality	41	2	2.19	Governance responsibility	21	8	1.61
Rate of change	37	3	2.00	Scope of impact	17	9	1.79
Reusability	37	4	1.87	Aspect of change	9	10	1.05
Accessibility	32	5	1.79	Implementation responsibility	9	11	1.39
Awareness of impact	27	6	1.73	Rule source	2	12	0.31

While Borda's method allows us to identify the relative ranking, it is important to determine whether there is an adequate level of agreement between experts' individual rankings. The concordance of the rankings is an indicator of such agreement. We use *compactness*, defined in [40], to calculate the degree of agreement as suggested in [41].

$$compactness = \sqrt{\frac{\sum_{i=1}^{m} \sum_{j=1}^{m} \left(r_i - r_j \right)^2}{m(m-1)}} \tag{1}$$

Normalized compactness ranges from 0 to 1, where 0 means the ranking lists are identical with each other (i.e. participants agree with each other) while 1 means they share nothing in common. Since for normalized concordance, 1 represents total agreement and 0 represents total disagreement semantically, concordance has an inverse relationship with compactness. Thus we use $1 -$ compactness to measure concordance.

In formula (1), m is the number of factors, compactness is the average coupled distance between all factors, and $r_i - r_j$ is the distance between two rankings r_i and r_j.

Weber *et al.* [36] provide a detailed classification of ranking distance measures in different dimensions according to the nature of the rankings. The dimensions are (1) conjoint and unconjoint ranking, (2) tied and untied ranking and (3) partial and full ranking. In our case, each ranking is selecting top-5 factors from all 12 factors, thus the ranking is a partial and conjoint ranking without ties. So we adopt the widely used Kendall's tao method introduced in [42] to calculate $r_i - r_j$. Kendall's tao distance is calculated using formula (2). x, y are elements in the set P which consists of elements in ranking r_i and r_j. p is assigned ½ as the neutral approach. The detailed algorithm to calculate $\bar{K}$ is described in [42].

$$r_i - r_j = \sum_{\{x,y\} \in P(r_i, r_j)} \bar{K}_{i,j}^{(p)}(r_i, r_j) \tag{2}$$

Combining formulas (1) and (2), the compactness of all the rankings is 0.36, resulting degree of agreement among the participants' rankings is 0.64, which is deemed acceptable [41]. In addition to the compactness of all rankings, we can reason about the compactness, or agreement, of the importance of each individual factor by considering the standard deviation of its ranking position. Accordingly, Table 3 also shows the standard deviation for each factor to provide an indication of the level of agreement on that factor.

6   Factors Informing Business Rule Modelling

In the first part of our empirical analysis we were able to identify a relative ranking of the factors. While this ranking provides an indication as to which factors should be considered when modelling business rules, it does not provide any guidance as to how a rule should be modelled given a particular factor. To carry out such an analysis we must first determine the set of factors that had consistency of responses in terms of their effect on business rule modelling. Thus, we first distinguish between 'affecting' factors and 'non-affecting' factors. A factor is considered to be non-affecting if there is no significant difference in expert opinion as to how that factor affects modelling. For example, experts are asked to indicate for the *aspect of change* factor, which has two circumstances: simple and complex, if the rule (to be changed or added) should be modelled in an integrated manner or modelled separately (see Table 4).

Table 4. Vote distributions for non-affecting factors (When a participant indicated that a factor is not important (importance rated as 1 or 2), this question was not applicable (N/A).)

Aspect of change	Integrated	Independent	I don't know	N/A
Simple	4	11	3	4
Complex	4	11	3	4

The decision distributions are identical regardless of the complexity of change, thus the factor *aspect of change* is considered to be a non-affecting factor because regardless of the circumstance (i.e. simple or complex), experts favor independent modelling. We

Table 5. Factor importance and effect matrix

	Affecting	Non-affecting
Top 50 % of factors based on importance	Agility Rate of change Reusability Accessibility	Criticality Awareness of impact
Bottom 50 % of factors based on importance	Rule source	Complexity Governance responsibility Scope of impact Aspect of change Implementation responsibility

use the difference of votes across the two opposite values of a factor as the metric of factor effect. If the differences of votes are within or equal to 3 (the roundup integer of 10% of the number of participants) both for integrated and independent modelling, then the factor is considered non-affecting.

We combine the importance and effect of factors in Table 5 (factors in each cell are ordered by their rankings in Table 3). The table shows that 4 factors in the 6 top 50% are affecting, and 5 factors in the 6 bottom 50% are not affecting. *Criticality* and *awareness of impact* are not affecting although ranked high on importance, and *rule source* is affecting although ranked lowest of importance.

In the following we will analyze the affecting factors to determine modelling guidance given the factors' circumstances.

In Table 6, 'vote difference' is the difference between the number of votes for independent modelling and for integrated modelling, which is used as an indication of modelling decision. A modelling decision for either type of modelling can be derived if the difference in votes is at least 3 (the roundup integer of 10% of the number of participants), otherwise the data can be interpreted as not providing any dominant view of the type of modelling that is appropriate (noted in Table 6 as "Either"). For example in Table 6, for the agility factor, where the need of agility is high, there are 13 more

Table 6. Dominant modeling preferences

Factor	Factor value	Vote difference	Dominant view
Agility	High	13	Independent
	Low	1	Either
Rate of change	Frequent	17	Independent
	Infrequent	−5	Integrated
Reusability	High	20	Independent
	Low	−3	Integrated
Accessibility	High	8	Independent
	Low	1	Either
Rule source	Internal	1	Either
	External	10	Independent

votes for independent modelling than for integrated modelling, so independent modelling is the dominant view for modeling.

Based on this analysis, the modelling decision is analysed for each circumstance of a given factor. While there are three situations in which the experts could not agree on a modelling decision, modelling guidance can be derived for the following seven situations:

1. When a rule has relatively high agility, it should be modelled independently.
2. When a rule changes frequently, it should be modelled independently.
3. When a rule changes infrequently it should be integrated in a business process model.
4. When a rule is highly reusable, it should be modelled independently.
5. When a rule's reusability is low, it should be integrated in a business process model.
6. When a rule requires relatively high accessibility, it should be modelled independently.
7. When a rule comes from an external source, it should be modelled independently.

To provide further insights into the rationale of the responses, in the following we briefly highlight relevant insights for non-affecting factors, which were collected through open-ended comment sections for each factor in our survey. We use the symbol *P* and a number to represent the participant number.

Criticality. The opinions on factor criticality are conflicting. Participants argue that "*it's obviously more important that critical business rules are modelled in safe and reliable ways than for less critical roles*" (*P20*) and "*criticality is important for the enforcement or monitoring of rule violations*" (*P11*), but "*that doesn't tell us anything about whether the rule can be embedded in the business process or not*" (*P20*), and "*whether this is done through a BRMS or a BPMS or manually does not matter, as long as it is effective.*" (*P11*).

Awareness of impact. Awareness of impact "*could not always be estimated and could not be easily represented*" (*P10*), and "*a rule may impact a process or something else*" (*P11*), thus it is considered as a less important factor.

Complexity. Since "*BPMN is not suitable for BR modelling*" (*P17*), simple and complex rules can be easier to handle in a dedicated rule representation than integrated into a business process.

Governance Responsibility. The importance of governance responsibility is challenged as "*a business rule can be modelled separately and be embedded in a business process at the same time*" (*P20*), and "*it depends on if the process model executed by a BPMS or will a rulebook be used*". (*P16*).

Scope of Impact. Participants admit that "*it might be easier to see which swim lanes are affected by the rule change and how a separately modelled and maintained BR scopes is hard to understand from a single BR out of context*" (*P17*). However, they believe this factor "*has more to do with governance and documentation than with modelling*" (*P17*).

Aspect of change. "*If the rule logic changes, it's easier to handle in the dedicated rule representation. If a single parameter changes, it's still easier to handle in a dedicated rule representation*" (*P11*). So the preference is independent modelling regardless of whether the change is complex or simple.

Implementation Responsibility. Participants argue that "*business and technical users have different responsibilities for the same set of rules*" (*P12*), with the underlying assumption that modelling process and implementation process are separated.

7   Conclusions and Future Work

This paper recapped twelve factors that are thought to potentially influence decisions on whether a business rule is modelled independently or modelled in a business process model [14]. We explored empirically the relative importance of the identified set of factors with academic experts and identified *agility* as the most important factor, followed by *criticality, rate of change* and *reusability. Accessibility, awareness of impact, complexity, governance responsibility* and *scope of impact*, with *aspect of change, implementation responsibility* and *rule source* being the least important factors. We also explored expert indications of how a business rule should be modelled given each factor, which lead us to derive seven guidelines for business rule modelling.

Our work is not without limitations. First, this study focuses on the factors which have a relatively high level of influence. Different modelling languages, tools and integrated modelling methods will affect these factors differently and will be a promising topic for future research. Second, we limit our scope of rules to those that can be both modelled independently as well as modelled with a business process. The rules that do not have the capability to be modelled into processes are beyond our discussion since there is no option for an alternative modelling decision. Although semantics and types of rule can be used to distinguish these rules in some cases, modelers still need to judge each rule individually according to its characteristics. Last, our study participants are predominantly academic experts in the field. The views of common practice are also critical to understand and are the next step in our study. Following that step, we plan to develop a decision framework and prototype to guide business rule modelling decisions. We expect that further empirical study will help to extend the decision framework through deeper insights into the decision processes.

References

1. Zoet, M., Versendaal, J., Ravesteyn, P., Welke, R.J.: Alignment of business process management and business rules. In: Proceedings of the 19th European Conference on Information Systems, Helsinki, Finland, p. 34 (2011)
2. Krogstie, J., McBrien, P., Owens, R., Seltveit, A.H.: Information systems development using a combination of process and rule based approaches. In: Andersen, R., Bubenko Jr., J.A., Sølvberg, A. (eds.) Advanced Information Systems Engineering. LNCS, vol. 498, pp. 319–335. Springer, Heidelberg (1991)

3. Zur Muehlen, M., Indulska, M., Kittel, K.: Towards integrated modeling of business processes and business rules. In: Proceedings of the 19th Australasian Conference on Information Systems (ACIS)-Creating the Future: Transforming Research into Practice, Christchurch, New Zealand, pp. 690–697. Citeseer (2008)

4. Green, P., Rosemann, M.: An ontological analysis of integrated process modelling. In: Jarke, M., Oberweis, A. (eds.) CAiSE 1999. LNCS, vol. 1626, pp. 225–240. Springer, Heidelberg (1999)

5. Milanovic, M., Gasevic, D., Wagner, G.: Combining rules and activities for modeling service-based business processes. In: 2008 12th Enterprise Distributed Object Computing Conference Workshops, pp. 11–22 (2008)

6. Mickevičiūtė, E., Butleris, R.: Towards the combination of BPMN process models with SBVR business vocabularies and rules. In: Skersys, T., Butleris, R., Butkiene, R. (eds.) ICIST 2013. CCIS, vol. 403, pp. 114–121. Springer, Heidelberg (2013)

7. Bona, D.D., Re, G.L., Aiello, G., Tamburo, A., Alessi, M.: A methodology for graphical modeling of business rules. In: 2011 Fifth UKSim European Symposium on Computer Modeling and Simulation (EMS), pp. 102–106. IEEE (2011)

8. Di Bona, D., Lo Re, G., Aiello, G., Tamburo, A., Alessi, M.: A methodology for graphical modeling of business rules. In: Proceedings of the 5th European Symposium on Computer Modeling and Simulation, Madrid, Spain, pp. 102–106 (2011)

9. De Nicola, A., Missikoff, M., Smith, F.: Towards a method for business process and informal business rules compliance. J. Softw. Evol. Process **24**, 341–360 (2012)

10. Xiao, X., Su, S.Y.W.: Meta-rule enhanced interoperation of operations, rules and processes for achieving dynamic inter-organizational collaboration. In: 2012 IEEE 13th International Conference on Information Reuse and Integration (IRI), pp. 533–540 (2012)

11. Zur Muehlen, M., Indulska, M.: Modeling languages for business processes and business rules: a representational analysis. Inform. Syst. **35**, 379–390 (2010)

12. Wang, W., Indulska, M., Sadiq, S.: Integrated modelling of business process models and business rules: a research agenda. In: Proceedings of the 25th Australasian Conference on Information Systems (ACIS). University of Auckland Business School, Auckland, New Zealand (2014)

13. Recker, J., Rosemann, M., Green, P.F., Indulska, M.: Do ontological deficiencies in modeling grammars matter? MIS Q. **35**, 57–79 (2011)

14. Wang, W., Indulska, M., Sadiq, S.: Factors affecting business process and business rule integration. In: Proceedings of the 25th Australasian Conference on Information Systems (ACIS). University of Auckland Business School, Auckland, New Zealand (2014)

15. Wallace, R.O., Mellor, C.J.: Nonresponse bias in mail accounting surveys: a pedagogical note. Brit. Acc. Rev. **20**, 131–139 (1988)

16. Malhotra, N.K.: Marketing Research: An Applied Orientation, 5th edn. Pearson Education India, New Delhi (2008)

17. Davies, I., Green, P., Rosemann, M., Indulska, M., Gallo, S.: How do practitioners use conceptual modeling in practice? Data Knowl. Eng. **58**, 358–380 (2006)

18. Kim, J.W., Jain, R.: Web services composition with traceability centered on dependency. In: Proceedings of the 38th Annual Hawaii International Conference on System Sciences, HICSS 2005, pp. 89–89. IEEE (2005)

19. van Roosmalen, M.W., Hoppenbrouwers, S.: Supporting corporate governance with enterprise architecture and business rule management: a synthesis of stability and agility. In: Proceedings of the International Workshop on Regulations Modelling and Deployment (ReMoD 2008) Held in Conjunction with the CAiSE 2008 Conference, Montpellier (2008). http://sunsite.informatik.rwth-aachen.de/Publications/CEUR-WS

20. Cappelli, C., Santoro, F.M., Cesar Sampaio do Prado Leite, J., Batista, T., Medeiros, A.L., Romeiro, C.S.C.: Reflections on the modularity of business process models: the case for introducing the aspect-oriented paradigm. Bus. Process Manag. J. **16**, 662–687 (2010)
21. Weigand, H., van den Heuvel, W.-J., Hiel, M.: Rule-based service composition and service-oriented business rule management. In: Proceedings of the International Workshop on Regulations Modelling and Deployment (ReMoD 2008), pp. 1–12. Citeseer (2008)
22. Witman, P.D.: Software product lines and configurable product bases in business applications-a case from financial services. In: 42nd Hawaii International Conference on System Sciences, HICSS 2009, pp. 1–10. IEEE (2009)
23. Loucopoulos, P., Kadir, W.M.N.W.: BROOD: business rules-driven object oriented design. J. Database Manag. (JDM) **19**, 41–73 (2008)
24. Taveter, K., Wagner, G.: Agent-oriented enterprise modeling based on business rules. In: Kunii, H.S., Jajodia, S., Sølvberg, A. (eds.) ER 2001. LNCS, vol. 2224, pp. 527–540. Springer, Heidelberg (2001)
25. Lu, R., Sadiq, W.: A survey of comparative business process modeling approaches. In: Abramowicz, W. (ed.) BIS 2007. LNCS, vol. 4439, pp. 82–94. Springer, Heidelberg (2007)
26. Kontopoulos, E., Bassiliades, N., Antoniou, G.: Deploying defeasible logic rule bases for the semantic web. Data Knowl. Eng. **66**, 116–146 (2008)
27. Ho, D.T.-Y., zur Muehlen, M.: From the stone age to the cloud: a case study of risk-focused process improvement. In: Proceedings of Australasian Conference on Computer and Information Science, Shanghai, China, pp. 144–160 (2009)
28. Iwaihara, M., Shiga, T., Kozawa, M.: Extracting business rules from web product descriptions. In: Zhou, X., Su, S., Papazoglou, M.P., Orlowska, M.E., Jeffery, K. (eds.) WISE 2004. LNCS, vol. 3306, pp. 135–146. Springer, Heidelberg (2004)
29. Leymann, F., Roller, D.: Production Workflow: Concepts and Techniques. Prentice Hall PTR, Upper Saddle River (2000)
30. Moreira, A., Fiadeiro, J.L., Andrade, L.: Evolving requirements through coordination contracts. In: Eder, J., Missikoff, M. (eds.) Advanced Information Systems Engineering. LNCS, vol. 2681, pp. 633–646. Springer, Heidelberg (2003)
31. Ofner, M.H., Otto, B., Österle, H.: Integrating a data quality perspective into business process management. Bus. Process Manag. J. **18**, 1036–1067 (2012)
32. Nelson, M.L., Peterson, J., Rariden, R.L., Sen, R.: Transitioning to a business rule management service model: case studies from the property and casualty insurance industry. Inf. Manag. **47**, 30–41 (2010)
33. Norta, A., Eshuis, R.: Specification and verification of harmonized business-process collaborations. Inf. Syst. Front. **12**, 457–479 (2010)
34. Mammar, A., Ramel, S., Grégoire, B., Schmitt, M., Guelfi, N.: Efficient: a toolset for building trusted B2B transactions. In: Pastor, Ó., Falcão e Cunha, J. (eds.) CAiSE 2005. LNCS, vol. 3520, pp. 430–445. Springer, Heidelberg (2005)
35. Kovacic, A., Groznik, A.: The business rule-transformation approach. In: 26th International Conference on Information Technology Interfaces, 2004, vol. 1, pp. 113–117 (2004)
36. Webber, W., Moffat, A., Zobel, J.: A similarity measure for indefinite rankings. ACM Trans. Inf. Syst. **28**, 1–38 (2010)
37. Dwork, C., Kumar, R., Naor, M., Sivakumar, D.: Rank aggregation methods for the web. In: Proceedings of the 10th International Conference on World Wide Web, pp. 613–622. ACM (2001)
38. Dummett, M.: The Borda count and agenda manipulation. Soc. Choice Welfare **15**, 289–296 (1998)
39. Young, H.P.: An axiomatization of Borda's rule. J. Econ. Theor. **9**, 43–52 (1974)

40. Xiaoyun, C., Yi, C., Xiaoli, Q., Min, Y., Yanshan, H.: PGMCLU: a novel parallel grid-based clustering algorithm for multi-density datasets. In: 1st IEEE Symposium on Web Society. SWS 2009, pp. 166–171 (2009)
41. Chen, L., Li, X., Han, J.: Medrank: discovering influential medical treatments from literature by information network analysis. In: Proceedings of the Twenty-Fourth Australasian Database Conference, vol. 137, pp. 3–12. Australian Computer Society, Inc. (2013)
42. Fagin, R., Kumar, R., Sivakumar, D.: Comparing top k lists. SIAM J. Discrete Math. **17**, 134–160 (2003)

Micro-Benchmarking BPMN 2.0 Workflow Management Systems with Workflow Patterns

Marigianna Skouradaki[1]([✉]), Vincenzo Ferme[2]([✉]), Cesare Pautasso[2], Frank Leymann[1], and André van Hoorn[3]

[1] Institute of Architecture of Application Systems (IAAS), University of Stuttgart, Stuttgart, Germany
marigianna.skouradaki@iaas.uni-stuttgart.de
[2] Faculty of Informatics, University of Lugano (USI), Lugano, Switzerland
vincenzo.ferme@usi.ch
[3] Institute of Software Technology (ISTE), University of Stuttgart, Stuttgart, Germany

Abstract. Although Workflow Management Systems (WfMSs) are a key component in workflow technology, research work for assessing and comparing their performance is limited. This work proposes the first micro-benchmark for WfMSs that can execute BPMN 2.0 workflows. To this end, we focus on studying the performance impact of well-known workflow patterns expressed in BPMN 2.0 with respect to three open source WfMSs. We executed all the experiments under a reliable environment and produced a set of meaningful metrics. This paper contributes to the area of workflow technology by defining building blocks for more complex BPMN 2.0 WfMS benchmarks. The results have shown bottlenecks on architectural design decisions, resource utilization, and limits on the load a WfMS can sustain, especially for the cases of complex and parallel structures. Experiments on a mix of workflow patterns indicated that there are no unexpected performance side effects when executing different workflow patterns concurrently, although the duration of the individual workflows that comprised the mix was increased.

Keywords: Benchmarking · Micro-benchmark · BPMN 2.0 · Workflow Patterns · Workflow Management Systems

1 Introduction

Despite the current trend of utilizing BPMN 2.0 as a common modeling and execution language for business processes [17], there are no means to measure and compare the performance of Workflow Management Systems (WfMSs). However, the need for a benchmark is regularly affirmed by the literature [21]. Before proceeding with the development of a standard complex benchmark one needs to understand the individual characteristics of the workload components. As a first approximation, the workload of a WfMS benchmark mainly consists of the workflow models to be executed and the frequency of their execution. However, we are

© Springer International Publishing Switzerland 2016
S. Nurcan et al. (Eds.): CAiSE 2016, LNCS 9694, pp. 67–82, 2016.
DOI: 10.1007/978-3-319-39696-5_5

currently lacking any information regarding the impact of individual BPMN 2.0 constructs on the performance of a WfMS. Micro-benchmarks aim to stress fundamental concepts of a system such as single operations or target narrow aspects of more complex systems. Therefore, we consider a micro-benchmark the appropriate tool for our goal as it targets the specific performance evaluation of atomic operations [20]. Workflow patterns can be seen as generic, recurring concepts and constructs that should be implemented by any workflow language [19]. In our context and given the complexity of the BPMN 2.0 language, we focus on the basic control-flow workflow patterns that apply on the core of the BPMN 2.0 language. Targeting to the simple workflow patterns we follow the assumption that these are the simplest and more frequent atomic operations that a WfMS would use. The main contribution of this paper is thus the first micro-benchmark for BPMN 2.0 WfMSs based on the following workflow patterns: sequence flow, exclusive choice and simple merge, explicit termination, parallel split and synchronization, as well as arbitrary cycle. Similar efforts for different systems [1,12] or languages (e.g., WS-BPEL [2]) have revealed fundamental bottlenecks in the corresponding engines, and have therefore been proven beneficiary to improve the tested systems. The main goal of this work is to enable further research in the performance engineering of the BPMN 2.0 WfMSs, by examining three state-of-the-art open-source WfMSs and providing the first insight on which BPMN 2.0 language factors impact the WfMSs performance.

This work focuses on studying the performance of the Process Navigator, a core WfMS component responsible for driving the execution of the tasks of each workflow instance with respect to the semantics of BPMN 2.0. More particularly, the research questions that our work aims to answer are: *(i)* what is the impact of individual or a mix of workflow patterns on the performance of each one of the benchmarked BPMN 2.0 WfMSs? *(ii)* are there performance bottlenecks in the selected WfMSs? We consider it important to understand the performance behaviour of the WfMS fundamental components before proceeding to more complex performance measurements that will also include external interactions. To do so, BPMN 2.0 workflows that implement the selected workflow patterns are given as input to two sets of experiments. The first set of experiments aims to execute a large load of workflow instances for each workflow pattern and investigate the behavior of the WfMSs. The second set of experiments studies the behavior of the WfMSs when they execute a uniformly distributed mix of all workflow patterns. For all the experiments we have calculated the throughput, the process execution time, and resource utilization from raw measurements, obtained using a reliable benchmarking environment presented in previous work [6]. The results revealed bottlenecks on architectural design decisions, wasteful resource utilization, and load limits for specific workflow patterns.

To summarize, the original, scientific contributions of this work are: *(i)* providing the first micro-benchmark for BPMN 2.0 WfMS; *(ii)* analyzing the effect of selected core BPMN 2.0 language constructs on the WfMS performance; *(iii)* defining meaningful candidate constructs for BPMN 2.0 complex benchmarks; *(iv)* running experiments on a reliable environment; *(v)* conducting a thorough analysis on the results of the performance evaluation of the selected WfMSs to reveal performance bottlenecks. The remainder of this paper is structured as follows: Sect. 2 presents the workload mix of the experiments and Sect. 3 explains the setup of the benchmark environment and of the experiments. The analysis of the results as well as possible threats to validity are discussed in Sect. 4. Section 5 overviews the related work and Sect. 6 concludes and presents our plans for future work. Moreover, supplementary material of the raw data and aggregated metrics can be found at: http://benchflow.inf.usi.ch/results/2015/caise-microbenchmark.tgz

2   Experiments Workload Mix

The workflows making up the workload of the micro-benchmark are designed to comply with these constraints: *(i)* Maximize the simplicity of the model expressing the workflow pattern; *(ii)* Omit the interactions with external systems. All tasks are implemented as script tasks, while human tasks and Web service invocations are excluded. This way we stress mainly the Process Navigator, since script tasks are fully automated and only use embedded application logic that is co-located with the engine. *(iii)* Most script tasks are empty. Only the ones required to implement the workflow pattern semantics contain the minimal amount of code and produce the minimum amount of data to do so. *(iv)* Define equal probability of passing the control flow to any outgoing branch of the gateways. *(v)* As it is recommended by the BPMN 2.0 Standard [9, p. 90], the exclusive choice is combined with the simple merge [EXC] workflow pattern and the parallel split is combined with the synchronization [PAR] workflow pattern.

In the scope of this work, we focus on the basic control flow and structural workflow patterns that can be expressed by BPMN 2.0 [22]. We have excluded the deferred choice, multiple instances without synchronization, and synchronization merge because the BPMN 2.0 elements that are used to implement them are not widely used in practice [15]. The workflows designed for our experiments are shown in Fig. 1. In the rest of this section we present the workflow models that comprise the workload mix of the micro-benchmark and define our hypotheses concerning their expected performance.

Sequence Flow [SEQ] - This workflow consists of two sequential empty script tasks. Since this is the simplest structure a workflow model may have, we expect that the execution times should be similar and stable on all three WfMSs [HYP1]. **Exclusive Choice and Simple Merge [EXC]** - The first script task randomly generates with uniform probability the numbers 1 or 2, according to which the upper or the lower branch is chosen. In both cases an empty script task is executed. The evaluation of the condition of the exclusive choice is expected to have an impact on the performance [HYP2]. **Parallel Split and Synchronization [PAR]** - This workflow executes in parallel two empty script tasks. As parallelism generally demands more CPU power we expect this to reflect on the performance measurements [HYP3]. **Explicit Termination Pattern**

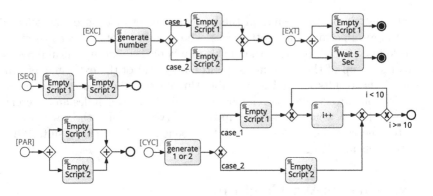

Fig. 1. Defined patterns for the workload mix

[**EXT**] - This workflow executes two branches concurrently and according to the BPMN 2.0 language semantics when one of these branches ends it will also terminate the rest of the executing branches and the overall workflow instance will be completed successfully. The "Empty Script 1" is an empty script task, while the "Wait 5 Sec" task waits for five seconds. The value of five seconds was chosen to guarantee that the lower branch will be slower than the upper one. As the "Empty Script 1" is the fastest, we expect that the workflow will be completed with the completion of the path containing the "Empty Script 1", and then the terminate event will interrupt the "Wait 5 Sec" task. The workflows in [PAR] and [EXT] have very similar structure, although they represent different workflow patterns. We expect that the concurrent execution of tasks should demonstrate similar performance behavior [HYP4]. **Arbitrary Cycle [CYC]** - Cycles are not expressed through any specific BPMN 2.0 construct but through a combination of exclusive gateways that form a cyclic structure that has at least two entries or two exits. The [CYC] is implemented with two entry points at the second and third exclusive gateways and starts by a script task that randomly generates the integer number $x = 1$ or $x = 2$ and initializes a variable $i = 0$. With respect to the value of the x variable the upper or the lower branches are followed (cf. [EXC]). The lower branch executes the "Empty Script 2". The upper branch executes an "Empty Script 1" and then increases the variable i. This path will be followed until the variable $i == 10$. To have a different but deterministic behavior of the branches we have implemented the "Empty Script 2" to assign $i = 5$. In this case the cycle will be repeated fewer times, until the variable $i == 10$. In terms of size [CYC] represents a slightly more complex structure than the other structures defined under the scope of this work. This might contribute towards revealing performance bottlenecks due to the usage of nested exclusive gateways, or sequential decision points [HYP5].

3   Experiments Setup

3.1   WfMS Configuration

The complex architecture of the WfMS introduces a set of challenges to be addressed by the design of the benchmark: *(i)* controlling the initial condition of the experiments is difficult due to the distributed nature of the WfMS; *(ii)* variable combinations of configuration parameters may have a significant impact on the performance; *(iii)* a standard API to interact with the WfMSs and to access the execution data is not available; and *(iv)* the asynchronous execution of processes introduces additional challenges for handling the performance data collection. In previous work we have therefore introduced the BenchFlow framework [6], that addresses the above challenges and provides a complete solution for benchmarking WfMS. Moreover, BenchFlow is compliant with the main requirements of a benchmark: portability, scalability, simplicity, vendor neutrality, repeatability, and efficiency [10].

To automate the configuration and deployment of the WfMS before the execution of benchmark, BenchFlow [7] uses the lightweight containerization technology Docker [13]. The execution of the benchmark is driven by Faban [4], a framework for performance workload creation and execution, used in industry benchmarks such as SPECjEnterprise2010 and SPECjms [18]. The load drivers provide the infrastructure needed to issue the load to the WfMS. To the rest of this paper the load drivers are also referred to as instance producers, as they are sending the requests for the workflow instance initiation. In order to ensure the reproducibility of the benchmark results one needs to explicitly describe the benchmark environment and configurations. Thus, in the following we provide this information.

The BenchFlow framework is used in this work for benchmarking three open-source WfMSs: WfMS A, WfMS B and Camunda 7.3.0 [3][1]. These WfMSs are widely used in industry and have a large user community according to the vendors' websites. The selected engines are also already tested against conformance to the BPMN 2.0 standard [8]. This makes them a suitable starting point for our defined workload and ensures the possibility to execute more diverse, complex workload in future versions of the benchmark. Moreover, WfMS B and Camunda are provided in Docker containers with vendor-suggested configurations, a fact that improves the reproducibility of our benchmark.

We benchmark these WfMSs on top of Ubuntu 14.04.01, using Oracle Java Server 7u79. WfMS A and Camunda were deployed on top of Apache Tomcat 7.0.62, while WfMS B was deployed on top of Wildfly 8.1.0.Final. All these WfMS utilise a MySQL Community Server 5.6.26 as Database Management System (DBMS), installed in a Docker container[2]. For WfMS B and Camunda[3] we have used the official Docker images, and we have followed the vendor-suggested

---

[1] At the time of publication some of the vendors we contacted did not explicitly agree to be named when presenting the results of the benchmark.

[2] https://hub.docker.com/_/mysql/.

[3] https://hub.docker.com/r/camunda/camunda-bpm-platform/.

configurations. We configured WfMS A as suggested from the vendor's website, and we deployed it using the most popular Docker image. We have updated the dependencies on the operating system and Java to be identical to the other two WfMS, to reduce possible discrepancies introduced by using different versions.

Every WfMS was given a maximum Java heap size of 32 GB, and the connection to the DBMS uses the MySQL Connector/J 5.1.33 with 10 as value for initial thread pool size, 100 as maximum number of connections, and 10 minimum idle connections. For WfMS A, we enabled the "Async executor" as suggested on the vendor's website. The other configurations are as provided in the mentioned Docker images. In particular, all the WfMSs log a complete history of the workflows execution to the database (i.e., details on the execution of the workflow instances as well as all the initial business process models). The containers are run by using the *host* network option of Docker. This option enables the containers to directly rely on the network interfaces of the physical machine hosting the Docker Engine, and has been proven not to add performance overhead in the network communications [5].

The benchmark environment is distributed on three servers: one for Faban that executes the instance producers, one for the WfMS, and one for the database of the WfMS that maintains the execution information of the workflows. All the servers use Ubuntu 14.04.3 LTS (GNU/Linux 3.13.0-33-generic x86_64) as operating system and the Docker Engine version 1.8.2. The WfMS is deployed on a 12 CPU Cores at 800 Mhz, 64 GB of RAM. In this way we ensure that the machine where we deploy the instance producer (64 CPU Cores at 1400 MHz, 128 GB of RAM) can issue sufficient load to the WfMS and the database (64 CPU Cores at 2300 MHz, 128 GB of RAM) and handle the requests from the WfMS. For the interaction of the WfMS with the DBMS and of the Instance Producers (IP), with the WfMS we use two different dedicated networks of 10 Gbit/s. Since the BenchFlow environment guaranties a repeatable benchmark, any test that follows the suggested configuration should reproduce the same results.

3.2 Experiments Methodology

We define two scenarios for the micro-benchmark. *Scenario 1* issues a large load to the WfMSs and investigates their behavior for individual patterns ([SEQ], [EXC], [EXT], [PAR], [CYC]). In some cases a WfMS does not sustain the predefined load. Then we re-execute the experiments with a lower load and observe the WfMS behavior for this execution. *Scenario 2* studies the performance behavior when different workflow patterns run concurrently [MIX]. More particularly, we test if the performance of a workflow pattern is affected when it runs concurrently with other types of workflow patterns. For this purpose, we benchmark a mix of all the workflow patterns distributed uniformly (i.e., 20 % of instances for each workflow pattern). The load of this experiment corresponds to the large load defined in Scenario 1. Both scenarios are executed three times for each WfMS to verify that the behavior is similar among the runs. The maximum standard deviation allowed among the repetitions was set to 5 %, but it was approximately 3.5 % on average.

For each benchmark run we collect the raw execution data for each workflow instance execution, and with these we calculate meaningful statistical data on the workflow instance duration ($WIDuration$), which is defined as the time difference between the start and the completion of a workflow instance; the resource utilization, in terms of CPU $utilization$ and $Memory$ $utilization$; the absolute number of the executed workflow instances by the WfMS per benchmark run ($\#WorkflowInstances(wi)$); and the number of executed workflow instances per time unit ($Throughput = \frac{\#WorkflowInstances(wi)}{Time(s)}$) [11].

The load function (T_l) we use consists of an experiment duration time of 10 min (cf., Experiment Duration of Table 1) with 30 s of ramp-up period (T_r). During the experiment the instance producers (u) perform up to 1 request per second (req/s) when the response time of the WfMS is low, and comprises the variable for which we execute the performance test. Whereas a load time of 10 min might not be representative of a real execution time, we consider it adequate for the micro-benchmark, as bottlenecks are already revealed within this time period (cf. Sect. 4). Given the used load function and the workload mix with only one workflow, the expected number of started workflows (S) is computed as $S = \sum_{j=1}^{u-1} \frac{T_r}{u} rj + (T_l - T_r)ru$ where T_r is the ramp-up period, T_l is the load time, and r is the user requests/s. The actual number can be less or equal than the expected one, since it depends on the resource availability of the servers where the instance producers are deployed, and the response time of the WfMS. We have also set a connection time-out period T_o of 20 s. According to our experiments it is an adequate time to indicate that the WfMS cannot handle the issued load. At the end of the run we are collecting the data, and analyze them to compute the relevant performance metrics. For all the data that are collected for the statistical analysis we have removed the first one minute ($2 * T_r$). This way we make sure that the analyzed results correspond to a stable state of the WfMS.

4 Evaluation

4.1 Results

For each workflow pattern and each WfMS, we show the duration (milliseconds, Fig. 2(a)), the CPU utilization (%, Fig. 2(b)), and the mean amount of RAM that was allocated by the engine (MB, Fig. 3(a)). Table 1 shows the statistics [14] of the duration computed for each workflow pattern and for every WfMS. The data provided in Table 1 correspond to the means of measurements obtained under the maximum load each WfMS could sustain, shown in terms of the number of concurrent instance producers. In some cases the WfMS could not handle the maximum load (1,500 concurrent instance producers), and we had to reduce the number of concurrent instance producers. These cases and the resulting data are discussed in detail in the following subsections. For every experiment, the total number of completed workflow instance requests from all WfMSs is listed in Table 1 in column $\#Workflow(wi)$. We also include the total duration of

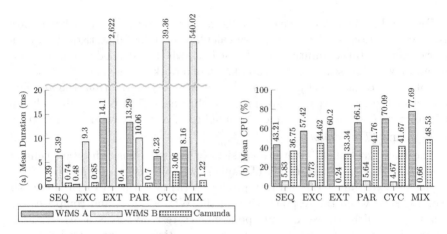

Fig. 2. (a) Mean duration (ms) per workflow pattern and (b) Mean CPU (%) Usage per workflow pattern

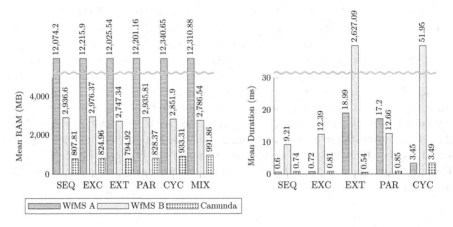

Fig. 3. (a) Mean RAM (MB) Usage per workflow pattern and (b) Mean duration (ms) per workflow pattern in [MIX]

each experiment (in seconds) and the average throughput in terms of workflow instances per second.

Similar statistics have been respectively calculated for CPU and RAM usage but they are omitted for space reasons, and they are provided with the supplementary material. The behaviour of all the WfMSs is discussed thoroughly in Sect. 4.3.

4.2   Results Analysis

Sequence Flow Pattern [SEQ]. The [SEQ] workflow pattern lasted on average 0.39 ms for WfMS A, 6.39 ms for WfMS B and 0.74 ms for Camunda. The short

Table 1. Workflow instance duration and experiment execution statistics

		Workflow Instance Execution Duration Statistics (ms)								Experiment Execution Statistics			
		Mean & CI T ($\alpha = 0.95$)	Mode	Min	Max	Sd	Q1	Q2	Q3	Max Load (IPs)	#Workflow (wi)	Experiment Duration (s)	Throughput (wi/s)
SEQ	A.	0.39 ± 0.01	0	0	561	1.70	0	0	1	1,500	781,736	540	1,447.66
	B.	6.39 ± 0.43	6	4	82	1.21	6	6	7	1,500	35,516	561	63.31
	C.	0.74 ± 0.01	1	0	682	2.29	0	1	1	1,500	786,664	540	1,456.79
EXC	A.	0.48 ± 0.01	0	0	485	2.07	0	0	1	1,500	775,455	540	1,436.03
	B.	9.30 ± 0.05	9	6	131	2.11	9	9	10	1,500	27,805	567	49.04
	C.	0.85 ± 0.01	1	0	627	2.51	0	1	1	1,500	765,274	540	1,417.17
EXT	A.	14.10 ± 0.06	10	5	858	13.45	10	11	14	1,500	770,229	540	1,426.35
	B.	2,622.00 ± 237.68	11	8	5,047	2,500.44	13	5,012	5,016	1,500	1,703	4,498	0.38
	C.	0.40 ± 0.01	0	0	74	1.03	0	0	1	1,500	784,614	539	1,455.68
PAR	A.	13.29 ± 0.06	8	4	456	11.99	9	10	13	1,500	772,013	540	1,429.65
	B.	10.06 ± 0.06	10	7	145	2.22	9	10	10	1,500	27,718	567	48.89
	C.	0.70 ± 0.01	1	0	691	2.10	0	1	1	1,500	773,883	540	1,433.12
CYC	A.	6.23 ± 0.13	2	0	478	18.68	1	2	3	800	347,770	540	644.02
	B.	39.36 ± 0.40	50	25	146	9.52	30	43	47	1,500	8,695	646	13.46
	C.	3.06 ± 0.04	2	0	353	4.43	2	2	3	600	177,770	542	327.99
MIX	A.	8.16 ± 0.07	0	0	663	14.65	1	2	12	1,500	758,659	541	1,402.33
	B.	540.02 ± 122.3	11	6	5,195	1,525.27	10	12	38	1,500	2,392	1,343	1.78
	C.	1.22 ± 0.02	0	0	434	4.21	0	1	1	1,500	575,210	542	1,061.27

WfMS A: *A.*, **WfMS B:** *B.*, **Camunda:** *C.*

duration of this workflow pattern justifies the low mean CPU usage which is 43.21 % for WfMS A, 5.83 % for WfMS B and 36.75 % for Camunda. WfMS B also has a very low average throughput of 63.31 wi/s while for the other two WfMS the average throughput is similar. Concerning the memory utilization under the maximum load WfMS A needed in average 12,074, WfMS B 2,936 and Camunda 807.81 MB of RAM respectively. As observed from the Table 1 [SEQ] is the workflow pattern with the highest throughput for all the WfMS under test.

Exclusive Choice & Simple Merge Patterns [EXC]. Before proceeding to the results analysis of the [EXC], we should consider that the first script task of the workflow pattern generates a random integer, which is given as an input to the very simple evaluation condition of the exclusive choice gateway. This was expected to have some impact on the performance. However, Fig. 2(a) shows that the duration times are not notably affected as the values are close to those of [SEQ]. More particularly, we have a mean of 0.48 ms for WfMS A, 9.30 ms for WfMS B and 0.85 ms for Camunda. Concerning the CPU and RAM utilization, we see a slight increase with respect to the [SEQ]. WfMS A uses an average of 57.42 % CPU and 12,215 MB RAM for executing 775,455 workflow instances in 540 s, WfMS B takes approximately the same amount of time (562 s) to execute 27,805 workflow instances. For this, it utilizes a mean of 5.73 % CPU and $2,976.37$ MB of RAM, and Camunda 43.21% of CPU and 824.96 MB of RAM for executing $765,274$ workflow instances in 540 s.

Explicit Termination Pattern [EXT]. As discussed in Sect. 2 the [EXT] executes concurrently an empty script and a script that implements a five seconds wait. According to the BPMN 2.0 execution semantics, the branch of the [EXT] that finishes first terminates the rest of the workflow's running branches. We have therefore designed the model considering that the fastest branch (empty script) will complete first, and stop the slow script on the other branch when the terminate end event following the empty script is activated. This was the case for WfMS A and Camunda, which executed the workflow patterns in an average of 14.11 ms and 0.4 ms respectively. The resource utilization of these two WfMSs also increases in this workflow pattern, i.e., we have 60.20% mean CPU usage and $12,025$ MB mean RAM usage for WfMS A and 33.34% mean CPU usage and 794.92 MB mean RAM usage for Camunda. We can already see an interesting difference on the performance of the two WfMS as [EXT] constitutes the slowest workflow pattern for WfMS A and the fastest for Camunda.

As seen in Fig. 2(a), WfMS B has very high duration results for this workflow pattern. We have investigated this matter in more detail and we have observed that over the executions WfMS B chooses the sequential execution of each path with an average percentage of 52.23% for following the waiting script first and 47.77% for following first the empty script. Since the waiting script takes five seconds to complete, every time it is chosen for execution it adds a five seconds overhead, and thus the average duration time is so high. This alternate execution of the two branches also explains the rest of the statistics. For example, we observe a very high standard deviation of 2500.44 that indicates that there is a very large spread of the values around the mean duration. Concerning the resource utilization we can observe a very low average usage of CPU at 0.24% and a mean RAM usage similar to the rest of the workflow patterns at $2,747.34$ MB. In Sect. 4.3 we attempt to give an explanation of this behavior for WfMS B.

Parallel Split and Synchronization Patterns [PAR]. The [PAR] executes two empty scripts concurrently. For WfMS A and WfMS B we observe an increase in the duration times to 13.30 ms for WfMS A and 10.07 ms for WfMS B. Camunda handles parallelism very fast, with a mean duration of 0.71 ms. Although WfMS B seems faster by looking the duration results, we should take into consideration that it has a total execution of $27,718$ workflow instances in 567 s while WfMS A executed $772,013$ workflow instances in 540 s. Moreover, it is noteworthy that WfMS A has a standard deviation of 11.99 which indicates that there were executions for which the parallelism introduced more overhead in duration than the average value. WfMS B has a 5.64% mean CPU and $2,935.81$ MB mean RAM usage and Camunda has a 41.67% mean CPU and 828.37 MB mean RAM usage. For both WfMSs these values are in the same range as the values resulted for the execution of the other workflow patterns. WfMS A utilizes in average 66.10% of CPU and $12,201.16$ MB of RAM. For WfMS A the values of utilized resources are relatively higher than these obtained from the other workflow patterns.

Arbitrary Cycle Pattern [CYC]. The performance of the [CYC] workflow pattern cannot be directly compared to the other workflow patterns, because it contains a higher number of language elements and demonstrates a more complex structure. The [CYC] is also expected to have some extra overhead because of the number generation and the script that increases the value of the variable. Finally, the duration of this workflow pattern is dependent on the generated number, as in the one case it executes 10 cycles while in the other it will execute 5 cycles. During the execution of [CYC], Camunda showed connection timeout errors for a load greater than 600 instance producers. For this reason, we had to reduce the load to 600 instance producers for testing the other two WfMS. The load for the results shown in Figs. 2(a), (b) and 3(a) for this workflow pattern is thus 600 instance producers. Table 1 shows the results for the maximum load each WfMS could sustain: 800 instance producers for WfMS A, 1500 instance producers for WfMS B and 600 for Camunda,. As expected, the mean [CYC] execution duration is higher than the other workflow patterns. WfMS A has a mean duration of 6.23 ms and Camunda a marginally bigger mean duration of 3.06 ms for this number of instance producers. WfMS B has a mean duration of 39.36 ms for approximately 600 instance producers.

Concerning the resource utilization, WfMS B and Camunda remain stable to the same range of mean CPU usage (4.67 % for WfMS B and 41.67 % for Camunda) as with the other workflow patterns. WfMS B remains on the same range of mean RAM usage (2, 851.9 MB), while we observe an increase for Camunda to an average of 933.31 MB. Concerning WfMS A's resource utilization, we observe a tendency to increase in comparison with the rest of the workflow patterns. For approximately 600 instance producers, WfMS A uses in average 70.09 % of CPU and 12, 201.16 MB RAM. We consider it also interesting to report how the results evolved for WfMS A and WfMS B when we increased the load to the maximum (1500 and 800 instance producers respectively). Then, we observe WfMS A doubling the mean duration time from 2.92 ms to 6.23 ms. The CPU is also more stressed reaching 83.93 % while the mean memory usage is only slightly increased to 12, 429.67 MB. WfMS B remains in the same range of the previous values with scarcely any increase to its performance. It uses in average 4.59 % of CPU and 2, 897.72 MB of RAM. This is because its response time increases while adding instance producers.

Mix [MIX]. By a quick overview of the [MIX] statistics, one could conclude that they express the mean duration times of the individual workflow patterns shown in Fig. 3(b). The throughput of the mix, is also a bit smaller for all the WfMSs, although WfMS A keeps it on the same range as the previous values at 1, 402.33 wi/s. In Fig. 3(b) we can observe the separate duration times of the workflow patterns for the case that they are executed in the uniformly distributed mix. As seen in Fig. 3(b), all workflow patterns have a slight increase in their duration times with respect to the execution as a single workflow pattern.

4.3   Discussion

As reported in Sect. 4.2, the BPMN version of WfMS B presents some pecu-
liarity in its behaviour. This was also noticed by Bianculli et al. [2] on their
performance measurements on the WS-BPEL version of the WfMS B. According to the WfMS B documentation the REST API calls to the execution server
will block until the process instance has completed its execution. We observed
the effects of this synchronous API in our experiments. All instance producers
send requests to the WfMS using the REST API with a think time of 1 s. The
instance producers need to wait for the completion of their previous request
before sending a new one, but in the case of WfMS B the clients that are waiting for the entire execution of the workflow instance to finish introduce a high
overhead. This overhead causes a delay that burdens the WfMS's performance.
In order to investigate this further we have executed a scalability test to analyze the WfMS behavior under different load intensity levels. The goal of this
experiment was to examine, whether by increasing significantly the number of
instance producers we could achieve a number of executed workflow instances
that can be more comparable to those of WfMS A and Camunda. We executed
the experiment for 500, 1000, 1500, and 2000 instance producers and observed
a mean response time of 7.15, 15.19, 22.58 and 30.89 s respectively, while the
throughput remained stable to an average of 62.23 workflow instances per second. These data basically show that *(i)* it is pointless to increase the number of
instance producers and target to the execution of more workflow instances; and
that *(ii)* the fact that WfMS B is the only WfMS of the three under test using a
synchronous REST API does not impact the comparability of the measurement.

Another issue discussed concerning WfMS B was the inconsistent execution
behaviour of the [EXT]. Although the expected execution of [EXT] is that when
the path with the empty script ends the execution of the path with the 5 s script
will also be terminated, we have observed many executions with the opposite
behavior. The path with the wait script was executing "first" and then, after
5 s, followed the execution of the empty script. In this case, the end event that
corresponded to the empty task was never executed. This behavior of WfMS B
was also explained in their documentation. WfMS B basically chooses to dedicate
a single thread to the parallel execution of scripts, leading to a non-deterministic
serialization of the parallel paths. Indeed data showed that in about 50 % of the
cases, the fast path is chosen to be executed first (cf., Sect. 2). When the branch
with the 5 s waiting script is chosen then as expected the execution of the WfMS
needs to wait 5 s until this branch is completed. This explains the very high
duration of the [EXT], as half of the executions have the 5 s duration.

At this point we can draw some conclusions. Regarding the behavior of
WfMS B on the duration of the workflow execution we observe much higher values for all the workflow patterns. The CPU and memory utilization of WfMS B is
always on much lower limits when compared to the other two WfMSs because of
the lower throughput. However, this is reasonable since every workflow instance
is executed sequentially and the actual executed load is lower compared to the
other two WfMSs, because of the higher response time. WfMS A and Camunda

share many architectural similarities because Camunda was originally a fork of WfMS A. Still their behaviour is not identical and leads to some interesting points. Camunda kept the duration values low for all the workflow patterns, but for [SEQ] and [EXC] WfMS A executed slightly better. However, we note large differences in the duration values for [EXT], [PAR], and [MIX], that indicate an impact of parallelism on the performance of the WfMS A, and increased resource utilization. The parallelism does not seem to have much impact on Camunda, as it remained relatively stable in all tests. Concerning the resource utilization in general we observe WfMS B and Camunda having a more stable behaviour, while WfMS A shows a direct increase when it is more stressed. In general, we may conclude that Camunda performed better and more stable for all metrics when compared with WfMS A and WfMS B.

Finally, concerning our hypotheses (cf., Sect. 2), [SEQ] resulted in the workflow pattern with the lowest and most stable performance for all WfMSs [HYP1]. Also it was the workflow pattern with highest throughput for all tested WfMSs. Concerning the [EXC], our hypothesis was affirmed (cf., [HYP2]) as there is a slight impact on the performance, which we connect with the evaluation of the condition. The [HYP3] and [HYP4] that the [PAR] and [EXT] will have similar impacts on performance holds basically for WfMS A and Camunda. Our [HYP4] and [HYP5] for parallelism and complex structures having an impact on the performance seems to hold for WfMS A, while for Camunda no conclusions can be drawn with respect to this point. These results indicate that sequential workflows (i.e., [SEQ]) may help towards discovering the maximum throughput of the WfMSs. Parallelism (i.e., [PAR]|[EXT]) may affect the WfMSs in terms of throughput and resource utilization, while more complex structures (i.e., [CYC]) are better candidates for stressing the WfMSs in terms of resource utilization. These conclusions should be considered when designing the workload for more complex, realistic cases and macro-benchmarks.

4.4 Threats to Validity

A threat to external validity is that we evaluate three WfMSs, which is the minimum number of WfMS for drawing initial conclusions. For generalizing our conclusions more WfMS are needed, and for this we are designing the BenchFlow environment to allow the easy addition of more WfMSs. Moreover, our simple workload models threaten the construct validity. Although the micro-benchmark does not correspond to real-life situations, we consider it fundamental for the purposes of our work. Using this knowledge as a basis, we plan to test more complex, realistic structures such as nested parallelism and conditions, as well as combinations of them in diverse probabilistic workload mixes [17].

5   Related Work

Röck et al. [16] conduct a systematic review on approaches that test the performance of WS-BPEL WfMSs, and stress the need for improvement on WfMSs baseline tests. Micro-benchmarks target to test the performance of atomic operations and assists performance engineers towards a deep comprehension of the evaluated system, in order to assure correct and reliable results. Especially in the case of modern, complex middleware systems, micro-benchmarks are usually preferred for satisfying this goal [20]. For example Mendes et al. [12] apply several micro-benchmarks on event processing systems to answer fundamental questions on their performance concerning scalability and bottlenecks. Another micro-benchmark is introduced by Angles et al. [1] based on social networks, and define the best candidates for macro-benchmarks. Another case of micro-benchmarking is proposed by Waller and Hasselbring [20] for measuring the overhead of application-level monitoring. The proposed micro-benchmark identifies three causes of monitoring overhead, and sets the basis for a reliable macro-benchmark. Regarding WfMSs Bianculli et al. [2] ran a micro-benchmark for WS-BPEL. In this work, the goal is to rank the WfMS with respect to their performance. To the extent of our knowledge we propose the first micro-benchmark for BPMN 2.0 WfMS, with respect to the language characteristics and we are confident that it is a strong contribution for more reliable, complex macro-benchmarks in the field of WfMSs.

6   Conclusion and Future Work

In this work we have presented a micro-benchmark for BPMN 2.0 WfMSs. To the extent of our knowledge this is the first attempt to investigate the impact of BPMN 2.0 language constructs on the WfMSs performance. We ran a set of experiments on a reliable benchmarking environment and among many important observations our results showed important bottlenecks due to architectural design decisions for WfMS B and that resource utilization can be a potential issue for WfMS C. We also discovered load bottlenecks for Camunda during the execution of the arbitrary cycle pattern. Consequently, despite the simplicity of the micro-benchmark we argue that it is a potentially suitable choice for benchmarking fundamental behavior or complex real-world WfMS.

Regarding individual workflow patterns we observed that the sequential workflow pattern revealed the maximum throughput for all of the WfMSs. Parallelism (i. e., explicit termination and parallel pattern) affected two of the three WfMSs in terms of throughput and resource utilization. More complex structures, such as the arbitrary cycle, also seem impact the resource utilization, thus they can be better candidates to stress the WfMS. Finally, the mix execution helped us conclude that there are no adverse performance effects when executing different workflow patterns concurrently. While there are no side-effects when executing different types of workflows concurrently, we did observe a slight increase on individual performance metrics when compared to the homogeneous experiments with individual patterns. The above results provide the first insights on which constructs constitute meaningful candidates for building more complex benchmarks. For example, a test aiming to measure the throughput or resource utilization of the WfMS should preferably choose complex, parallel structures.

We are currently working towards a public release of the BenchFlow environment in the near future. In future work we plan to exploit the conclusions of this work to execute macro-benchmarks on BPMN 2.0 WfMSs with more complex and realistic workflows that will also contain events and web service invocations.

Acknowledgements. This work is funded by the "BenchFlow" project (DACH Grant Nr. 200021E-145062/1) project and is supported by the SPEC research group.

References

1. Angles, R., Prat-Pérez, A., et al.: Benchmarking database systems for social network applications. In: Proceedings of GRADES 2013, pp. 15:1–15:7. ACM (2013)
2. Bianculli, D., Binder, W., Drago, M.L.: Automated performance assessment for service-oriented middleware: a case study on BPEL engines. In: Proceedings of WWW 2010, pp. 141–150 (2010)
3. Camunda Services GmBH: Camunda BPM, October 2015. https://camunda.org/
4. Faban: Performance framework, December 2014. http://faban.org
5. Felter, W., Ferreira, A., et al.: An updated performance comparison of virtual machines and Linux containers. Technical report, IBM, July 2014
6. Ferme, V., Ivanchikj, A., Pautasso, C.: A framework for benchmarking BPMN 2.0 workflow management systems. In: Motahari-Nezhad, H.Z., Recker, J., Weidlich, M., et al. (eds.) BPM 2015. LNCS, vol. 9253, pp. 251–259. Springer, Heidelberg (2015)
7. Ferme, V., Pautasso, C.: Integrating faban with docker for performance benchmarking. In: Proceedings of the 7th ACM/SPEC International Conference on PerformanceEngineering, Delft, The Netherlands, March 2016
8. Geiger, M., Harrer, S., Lenhard, J., Casar, M., Vorndran, A., Wirtz, G.: BPMN conformance in open source engines. In: Proceedings of the 9th IEEE International Symposium on Service-Oriented System Engineering (SOSE 2015), SOSE 2015, March 30–April 3 2015. IEEE, San Francisco Bay (2015)
9. Jordan, D., Evdemon, J.: Business Process Model And Notation (BPMN) Version 2.0. Object Management Group, Inc. (2011). http://www.omg.org/spec/BPMN/2.0/
10. von Kistowski, J., Arnold, J.A., et al.: How to build a benchmark. In: Proceedings of ICPE 2015, pp. 333–336 (2015)
11. Lazowska, E.D., Zahorjan, J., et al.: Quantitative System Performance: Computer System Analysis Using Queueing Network Models. Prentice-Hall, Englewood Cliffs (1984)
12. Mendes, M.R.N., Bizarro, P., Marques, P.: A performance study of event processing systems. In: Nambiar, R., Poess, M. (eds.) TPCTC 2009. LNCS, vol. 5895, pp. 221–236. Springer, Heidelberg (2009)
13. Merkel, D.: Docker: Lightweight Linux containers for consistent development and deployment. Linux J. **2014**(239), 2 (2014)
14. Montgomery, D.C., Runger, G.C.: Applied Statistics and Probability for Engineers. Wiley, New York (2003)
15. Muehlen, M.Z.: Workflow-Based Process Controlling. Logos, Berlin (2004)
16. Röock, C., Harrer, S., Wirtz, G.: Performance benchmarking of BPEL engines: a comparison framework, status quo evaluation and challenges. In: Proceedings of SEKE 2014, pp. 31–34 (2014)

17. Skouradaki, M., Roller, D.H., et al.: On the road to benchmarking BPMN 2.0 workflow engines. In: Proceedings of ICPE 2015, pp. 301–304 (2015)
18. Standard Performance Evaluation Corporation: SPEC's Benchmarks (SPEC). https://www.spec.org/benchmarks.html
19. Van Der Aalst, W.M.P., Hofstede, T., et al.: Workflow patterns. Distrib. Parallel Databases **14**(1), 5–51 (2003)
20. Waller, J., Hasselbring, W.: A benchmark engineering methodology to measure the overhead of application-level monitoring. In: KPDAYS. CEUR Workshop Proceedings, vol. 1083, pp. 59–68. CEUR-WS.org (2013)
21. Wetzstein, B., Leitner, P., et al.: Monitoring and analyzing influential factors of business process performance. In: Proceedings of EDOC 2009, pp. 141–150 (2009)
22. Wohed, P., van der Aalst, W.M.P., Dumas, M., ter Hofstede, A.H.M., Russell, N.: On the suitability of BPMN for business process modelling. In: Dustdar, S., Fiadeiro, J.L., Sheth, A.P. (eds.) BPM 2006. LNCS, vol. 4102, pp. 161–176. Springer, Heidelberg (2006)

Improving Understandability of Declarative Process Models by Revealing Hidden Dependencies

Johannes De Smedt[(✉)], Jochen De Weerdt, Estefanía Serral,
and Jan Vanthienen

Department of Decision Sciences and Information Management, Faculty of Economics
and Business, KU Leuven, Naamsestraat 69, 3000 Leuven, Belgium
{johannes.desmedt,jochen.deweerdt,estefania.serral,
jan.vanthienen}@kuleuven.be

Abstract. Declarative process models have become a mature alternative to procedural ones. Instead of focusing on what has to happen, they rather follow an outside-in approach based on a rule base containing different types of constraints. The models are well-capable of representing flexible behavior, as everything that is not forbidden by the constraints in the model is possible during execution. These models, however, are more difficult to comprehend and require a higher mental effort of both the modeler and the reader. Since constraints can be added freely to the model, it is often overseen what impact the combination of them has. This is often referred to as hidden dependencies. This paper proposes a methodology to make these dependencies explicit for the declarative process modeling language Declare by considering a Declare model as a graph and relying on the constraints' characteristics. Moreover, this paper also contributes by empirically confirming that a tool that can visualize hidden dependency information on top of a Declare model has a significant positive impact on the understandability of Declare models.

Keywords: Declarative process modeling · Declare · Hidden dependencies · Empirical evaluation

1 Introduction

Declarative process models have been proposed to counter the flexibility limitations of procedural modeling languages. Instead of modeling predetermined paths of activities, declarative process models use constraints to express what can, cannot, and must happen. Every execution sequence that is not strictly forbidden by the constraints can be enacted by the model. This makes declarative models much more flexible indeed, but also more difficult to comprehend. To put it simplistically, it is not possible to 'find an execution path by following your finger along the arcs'. There are many possible outcomes due to the interaction of the constraints over the activities.

© Springer International Publishing Switzerland 2016
S. Nurcan et al. (Eds.): CAiSE 2016, LNCS 9694, pp. 83–98, 2016.
DOI: 10.1007/978-3-319-39696-5_6

In different works approaches to deal with the understandability problems of declarative models have been proposed. For instance in [1], the impact of hierarchy is investigated and in [2] the typical pitfalls of understanding declarative models are pointed out.

This paper proposes an approach capable of improving the understandability of models expressed in Declare [3], one of the most widely used declarative process modeling language. The approach deals with hidden dependencies [2,4,5], one of the main reasons that make Declare models difficult to understand. Hidden dependencies pose a significant challenge for humans: it is not sufficient to rely on the information explicitly indicated by the constraints, but one has to carefully analyze all the defined constraints for understanding all the dependencies that are not explicitly visible (i.e., that are hidden). The contribution of this paper consists of a methodology to build so-called constraint dependency structures in order to reveal all hidden dependencies and make them explicit in a Declare model. Furthermore, this methodology is developed into the Declare Execution Environment[1], a tool that supplements an existing Declare model with visual and textual annotations to clarify which behavior is allowed or disallowed by the model. In an experimental evaluation with 95 novice Declare modelers, we show that the methodology to make hidden dependencies explicit and visually annotating a Declare model with this information, has a significant positive impact on the understandability of Declare models.

The structure of the paper is as follows. First, the concept of Declare constraints is briefly summarized and relevant characteristics are explained. Next, Sect. 3 explains how to capture and formalize dependency structures, followed by Sect. 4, which shows the implementation and tool. This tool is used for experimental validation in Sect. 5. Finally, Sect. 6 summarizes the related work and Sect. 7 discusses future work and the conclusion.

2   Declare Constraints and Their Characteristics

Declare models are constructed using a fixed set of constraints, which are summarized in Table A1 in [6]. They range from unary constraints, indicating the position and cardinality of an activity, to n-ary constraints, which capture typical sequential behavior such as precedence and succession relationships. A Declare model $DM = (A, \Pi)$ can be represented as follows:

- A is a set of activities from the alphabet Σ,
- Π is the set of Declare constraints defined over the activities.

In this paper we assume $n \leq 2$. A Declare graph can be represented as a directed graph $DG = (A, \Pi)$. Hence the activities and constraints map one-to-one onto the graph in case of $n = 2$, given that unary constraints are considered as self-loops. We denote all incoming arcs of $a \in A$ as $\bullet a \subseteq \Pi$ and outgoing arcs as $a \bullet \subseteq \Pi$. The antecedent and consequent of $\pi \in \Pi$ are denoted as π_a and π_b.[2]

---

[1] http://www.processmining.be/declareexecutionenvironment.

[2] Our interpretation of these concepts differ from, e.g., [7], as we consider a the antecedent in $Precedence(a, b)$ relationships, rather than b for notational simplicity.

The execution of a Declare model can be realized by constructing an automaton (either a Büchi [8] or finite state automaton [9,10]) by conjoining the different constraints' automata to obtain the behavior that is allowed for by all of them. This conjunction actually abolishes the notion of the separate constraints and thus throws away the information of how the separate constraints interact. One technique to mitigate this is to color the constraints [11] by keeping both the global and separate automata, but still the interactions remain untraceable.

Declare constraints exhibit a hierarchy, which is well-explained in [8,9]. For unary constraints, *Existence(A,n)* and *Absence(A,n)* together form *Exactly (A,n)*. Binary constraints are divided in different classes, for which every class depends on the previous one: *Unordered (Responded/co-existence)*, *Simple ordered (Precedence (p), Response (r), Succession (s))*, *Alternating ordered (Alternate p,r,s)*, and *Chain Ordered (Chain p,r,s)*. Next to these constraints, there exist negative versions for three of them *(Not co-existence, Not succession, Not chain succession)*. Finally, the *Choice* constraint exists, which is comparable with a branched unary constraint *Existence({A,B},n)*.

For binary constraints, *(Alternate/Chain) Response(A,B)* and *(Alternate/ Chain) Precedence(A,B)* form *(Alternate/Chain) Succession*. When a property is discussed for, e.g., *Chain succession*, this also includes *(Chain/Alternate) precedence/response* and vice versa.

Furthermore, each constraint has specific characteristics that are discussed in [12]. Some constraints have an impact on the temporary violation aspect of the model (the constraint is not in an accepting state and requires an activity to resolve it, e.g. *Response* or *Choice*), some constraints can disable activities for the remainder of the execution (such as *Exactly* and *Not succession*), and some constraints can temporarily block all other activities (*Chain* constraints). These different characteristics all impose certain dependencies among constraints that are not directly visible through a single constraint (arc). E.g., a model consisting of $A = \{a, b, c\}$ and $\Pi = \{Response(a, b), Response(b, c), Exactly(c, 2)\}$ contains a hidden dependency between a and c. When c is fired once (and hence can only fire one time anymore), and a has fired without b firing already, c should not fire before b resolves the temporary violation of $Response(a, b)$, since after firing c, c cannot resolve $Response(b, c)$ anymore (as it can only fire two times) and b should not fire to avoid another temporary violation of $Response(b, c)$.

The hidden dependencies caused by all these characteristics can be made explicit. In the following section, it is explained how they relate to the activities in a declarative model.

3 Declare Dependency Structures

This section discusses how dependency structures retrieved from Declare models can be constructed (Sect. 3.1), how they can aid interpretation of the model and the way in which constraints interact (Sect. 3.3). Before constructing the structures, however, the unary constraints in the model need to be propagated to achieve the correct interpretation, as explained in Sect. 3.2.

3.1   Construction

A hidden dependency can be defined as an interaction between constraints and their activities that is not made explicit as such in the model itself. They are the outcome of conjoining the separate constraints to avoid permanent violation, as explained earlier. Hence, it is paramount to find the ways to avoid permanent violation to occur. There are three types of resolution strategies to resolve temporary violations:

1. **An activity must still happen:** after firing the antecedent in *Responded existence, Co-Existence, (Alternate/Chain) Response*, the consequent must fire afterwards.
2. **An activity must still happen a certain amount of times:** *Existence, Exactly, Choice*.
3. **An activity must still happen at a fixed moment in time:** *Chain response*.

Note that combining different constraints could lead to coalesced resolution strategies: *Chain response(a,b)* coupled with *Existence(a,2)* requires firing b at least twice on certain fixed moments (directly after a) as well.

Now we construct the set of dependency structures DP for DM with $DS = (\pi^{DS}, \Pi_{dep}^{DS}, DS_{dep}^{DS}), DS \in DP$ with

- π^{DS} the constraint triggering the structure,
- Π_{dep}^{DS} the set of dependent constraints, and
- DS_{dep}^{DS} the set of nested dependency structures dependent of π^{DS}.

To fill Π_{dep}^{DS} and DS_{dep}^{DS}, Algorithm 1 creates a dependency structure for every activity that is involved in at least one of the five constraints that can permanently disable it. Hence, a structure is created for a in *Absence/Exactly(a,n)*, a and b in *Exclusive choice/Not co-existence(a,b)*, and for b in *Not succession(a,b)* as can be seen on lines 7–25.

First, all backward-propagating constraints are considered ($\Pi_{BW} \subseteq \Pi$, inferred from resolution strategy 1) and used for recursive search, as well as stored in Π_{dep} (Algorithm 2, lines 1–22). During this procedure, all incoming *Existence* and *Choice* constraints (as in 2) are stored as well (Algorithm 2, lines 16–18). They also need to be fulfilled, but do not propagate due to their unary nature. When *Responded existence* is encountered, a new dependency structure $DL \in DS_{dep}^{DS}$ is constructed because when the constraint becomes satisfied (by firing its consequent), it is satisfied indefinitely (unlike, e.g., *Response* which can become temporarily violated again) and its propagation is also abolished (Algorithm 2, lines 6–10).

For every activity that is encountered by the algorithm, a forward-dependency search is performed for all forward-propagating constraints $\Pi_{FW} \subseteq \Pi$, which include all *(Alternate/Chain) precedence* constraints and *Co-existence*. These constraints need to be activated (the antecedent has to be fired, in the case of alternating variant possibly multiple times) to resolve dependencies

Algorithm 1. Retrieving Dependency Structures

Input: $DM = (A, \Pi)$
Input: $\Pi_{BW} \leftarrow \Pi_{Resp/CoEx} \cup \Pi_{(C/A)Response}$ ▷ Backward-propagating constraints
Input: $\Pi_{FW} \leftarrow \Pi_{CoEx} \cup \Pi_{(C/A)Precedence}$ ▷ Forward-propagating constraints
Output: DP ▷ The set of dependency structures for DM
 1: **procedure** RETURNDEPTRANS(DM)
 2:     $DP \leftarrow \emptyset$ ▷ The set of all dependency structures of the model
 3:     **for** $\pi \in \Pi$ **do**
 4:        $DS \leftarrow \emptyset$ ▷ The dependent structure for π
 5:        $V^l \leftarrow \emptyset$ ▷ Set of visited activities for left search
 6:        $V^r \leftarrow \emptyset$ ▷ Set of visited activities for right search
 7:        **if** $\pi \in \Pi_{Abs} \vee \pi \in \Pi_{Exa}$ **then**
 8:           $\pi^{DS} \leftarrow \pi$
 9:           $DS \leftarrow SearchLeft(\pi_a, V^l, DS) \cup SearchRight(\pi_a, V^r, DS)$
10:           $DP \leftarrow DS$
11:        **end if**
12:        **if** $\pi \in \Pi_{NotSuc}$ **then**
13:           $\pi^{DS} \leftarrow \pi$
14:           $DS \leftarrow SearchLeft(\pi_b, V^l, DS) \cup SearchRight(\pi_b, V^r, DS)$
15:           $DP \leftarrow DS$
16:        **end if**
17:        **if** $\pi \in \Pi_{ExclChoi} \vee \pi \in \Pi_{NotCoEx}$ **then**
18:           $\pi^{DS} \leftarrow \pi$
19:           $DS \leftarrow SearchLeft(\pi_a, V^l, DS) \cup SearchRight(\pi_a, V^r, DS)$
20:           $DP \leftarrow DS$
21:           $DS_2 \leftarrow \emptyset$
22:           $\pi^{DS_2} \leftarrow \pi$
23:           $DS_2 \leftarrow SearchLeft(\pi_b, V^l, DS) \cup SearchRight(\pi_b, V^r, DS_2)$
24:           $DP \leftarrow DS_2$
25:        **end if**
26:     **end for**
27:     **return** DP
28: **end procedure**

---

from backward-propagating constraints. The constraints dependent of them are linked to them through a separate, nested dependency structure $DL \in DS_{dep}^{DS}$ (Algorithm 2, lines 22–36).

Example. Consider the model in Fig. 1a. *Not succession(c,b)*, meaning any occurrence of c cannot be followed eventually by b, causes the algorithm to construct a dependency structure for b. Backward-searching will reveal *Response(a,b)* and *Exactly(a,1)* as dependent constraints. c cannot fire before a has resolved *Exactly(a,1)*, which will render *Response(a,b)* temporarily violated and requires b to resolve it. Hence sequences such as $\sigma = e \to b$ or $\sigma = a \to e$ are not possible. In a forward search, *Precedence(b,d)* requires a new dependency structure, nested in $DS_{Not\_succession(C,B)}$. Firing e requires d to resolve *Response(e,d)*. Hence, firing c before firing e would render e disabled, as b can never fire anymore due to *Not succession(c,b)*, so the *Precedence(b,d)* can never be activated. Firing b before c would resolve this, as d can then fire an unlimited amount of times. The full dependency structure present in the model is $DS = \{\pi = Not\_succession(c,b), \Pi_{dep} = \{Response(a,b), Exactly(a,1)\}, DS_{dep} = \{\pi = Precedence(b,d), \Pi_{dep} = Response(e,d), \emptyset\}\}$.

Algorithm 2. Search for Dependency Constraints

```
1:  procedure SEARCHLEFT(a, V, DS)
2:      if ¬(a ∈ V) then                        ▷ Do if a is not visited yet, avoids infinite loops
3:          V ← a
4:          for π ∈ •a do                       ▷ Scan all incoming Declare constraints of activity a
5:              if π ∈ Π_BW then
6:                  if π ∈ Π_RespEx then
7:                      DL ← ∅                   ▷ Create new nested dependency structure
8:                      π^DL ← π
9:                      DL ← SearchLeft(π_a, V, DL) ∪ SearchRight(π_a, V, DL)
10:                     DS^DS_dep ← DL           ▷ Add nested structure to main structure DS
11:                 else
12:                     Π^DS_dep ← π
13:                     DS ← SearchLeft(π_a, V, DS) ∪ SearchRight(π_a, V, DS)
14:                 end if
15:             end if
16:             if π ∈ Π_Exis ∨ π ∈ Π_Exa ∨ π ∈ Π_Choi then
17:                 Π^DS_dep ← π
18:             end if
19:         end for
20:     end if
21:     return DS
22: end procedure

23: procedure SEARCHRIGHT(a, V, DS)
24:     if ¬(a ∈ V) then
25:         V ← a
26:         for π ∈ a• do                        ▷ Scan all outgoing Declare constraints of activity a
27:             if π ∈ Π_FW then
28:                 DL ← ∅
29:                 π^DL ← π
30:                 DL ← SearchLeft(π_b, V, DL) ∪ SearchRight(π_b, V, DL)
31:                 DS^DS_dep ← DL
32:             end if
33:         end for
34:     end if
35:     return DS
36: end procedure
```

3.2   Unary Propagation

The construction and use of dependency structures depends on the correct propagation of all unary relations inside of the model. E.g., consider the model in Fig. 1b. Changing *Precedence(b,d)* and *Response(e,d)* to their alternating variant and adding *Existence(e,2)* would require d and hence b to fire at least twice as well. In general, unary constraints that are not present in the original model are added in the following fashion for $a, b \in A$:

- *Responded existence(a,b)*, if a occurs at least or exactly n times, then b has to occur at least once.
- *Co-existence(a,b)*, if a or b occurs at least or exactly n times, then b respectively a has to occur at least once.
- *Response(a,b)*, if a occurs at least or exactly n times, then b has to occur at least once.
- *Precedence(a,b)*, if b occurs at least or exactly n times, then a has to occur at least once.

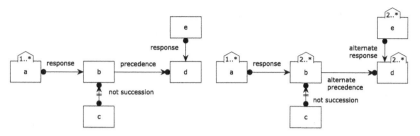

(a) Simple example with *Not succession* inflicting hidden dependencies.

(b) The same example with unary and alternating constraints.

Fig. 1. An example of a small Declare model with hidden dependencies in two variants.

- *Succession(a,b)*, if a or b occur at least or exactly n times, then the other activity has to occur at least once.
- *Alternate response(a,b)*, if b occurs at most or exactly n times, then a can occur at most n times. If a occurs at least or exactly m times, then b has to occur at least m times.
- *Alternate precedence(a,b)*, if b occurs at least or exactly n times, then a has to occur at least n times.
- *Alternate succession(a,b)*, both a and b have to have the same unary restrictions.
- *Chain response(a,b)*, if a occurs at least or exactly n times, then b has to occur at least n times. If b occurs at most or exactly m times, then a can only occur at most m times.
- *Chain precedence(a,b)*, if a occurs at most or exactly n times, then b can occur at most n times.
- *Chain succession(a,b)*, both a and b have to have the same unary restrictions.

Every unary constraint has a lower bound *Existence(n)* and upper bound *Absence(m)*, and they are combined and replaced by an *Exactly* constraint when $n = m - 1$. These rules are applied to the model until no unary constraint changes anymore. If there would be an activity for $n > m - 1$, this would mean the model would end up in a permanently violated state.

This propagation is done before the model is used in the algorithms in order to have consistent dependency structures. Next, the same procedure is repeated to calculate for each activity how many times it still has to execute in the following execution steps. This helps the dependency structures to recognize whether a certain nested structure can be cast off because it can fire a sufficient amount of times.

Example. Returning to the example, *Existence(e,2)* is propagated to d, yielding an *Existence(d,2)* and next to b yielding *Existence(b,2)*. The minimum amount of occurrences is also calculated and updated throughout the execution per activity. This way, the dependency structures will incorporate the unary constraints into the model and indicate that c cannot fire before b has fired its appropriate amount of times to enable d and e to fire at least twice. Initially, b, d, and e must execute a minimum of 2 times. b can be disabled after d and e have fired at least once, and b has fired at least two times (once before d fired and once after d fired to grant d another execution because of *Alternate precedence(b,d)*), for example sequence $\sigma_1 = b \rightarrow e \rightarrow d \rightarrow b \rightarrow c$ or $\sigma_2 = e \rightarrow b \rightarrow d \rightarrow b \rightarrow c$. After this execution, d cannot fire until e is fired because they can both fire only once anymore (d because of *Alternate precedence(b,d)* and hence e through *Alternate response(e,d)*) and d has to be able to resolve *Alternate response(e,d)*, e.g. $\sigma_1 \rightarrow e \rightarrow d$ and not $\sigma_1 \rightarrow d \rightarrow e$.

3.3 Interpretation

Constructing dependency structures can already give extra information by displaying them in a graph showing which constraints interact with the main constraint (π^{DS}) in the structure. However, they can be expressed in extra descriptions to annotate the model in order to help understand why constraints are related and what combined impact they have.

First of all, for *Exclusive choice(a,b)* and *Not co-existence(a,b)*, the structures reflect that whenever an activity from either structure is fired (either the one for a or b), the activities in the other structure become disabled permanently. Indeed, firing any activity in the dependency structure of a or b requires them to fire, hence activating *Exclusive choice* or *Not co-existence*. If the structures of a and b share activities, this means the net is not deadlock-free.

Secondly, for *Not succession(a,b)*, a becomes disabled whenever a constraint $\pi \in \Pi^{DS}_{dep}$ is temporarily violated and needs b to resolve it. Also, dependent structures in $d \in DS^{DS}_{dep}$ cannot contain any violations in their Π^d_{dep} unless the antecedent of the main constraint $\pi^d \in DS^d_{dep}$ is activated and can execute a minimum number of times required (as explained in Sect. 3.2). For unary constraints, *Absence(A,n)* and *Exactly(A,n)*, this applies as well, with the exception that a becomes disabled when a constraint relies upon it to become satisfied again.

Finally, every execution of activities in *Chain* constraints should be checked for executions one step ahead. For each of them, it is calculated whether the consequent is available to fire for *Chain response*, or is the only one available for *Not chain succession* in order to avoid deadlock.

4   Tool Support

The construction of the dependency structures has been implemented in a Declare execution environment, of which the implementation can be found by following the link in the introduction. The tool can read a Declare model saved from Declare Designer [13], which, during execution, is supported by descriptions for the hidden dependencies. A screenshot and an example can be found in Fig. 2.

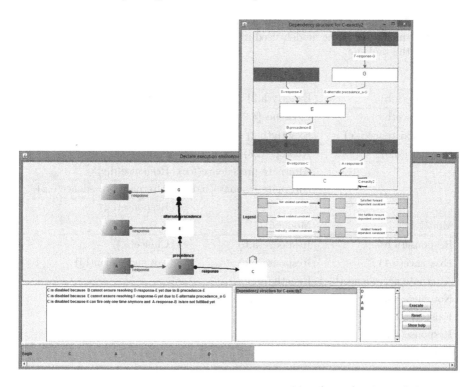

Fig. 2. An example of a small Declare model with hidden dependencies and the corresponding dependency graph for *Exactly(c,2)*.

Furthermore, the dependency structures can be visualized next to the model as a directed graph as well. Finally, the trace created over the model by the user is displayed below the model, aiding the user in understanding the history of the current situation displayed over the model.

The execution semantics are provided by dk.brics.automaton [14] and consists of the conjunction of the separate Declare automata expressed in regular expressions, as can be found in [9,10].

5 Empirical Evaluation

Making hidden dependencies explicit by annotating Declare models can significantly improve their understandability. In this section, it is empirically demonstrated that novice process modelers are indeed better capable of understanding Declare models when they are provided with an environment that makes hidden dependencies explicit through text and figures.

5.1 Experimental Setup

In the experiment, 95 students (see Table 2) enrolled in KU Leuven's *Business Analysis* course, in which both procedural and declarative process modeling are

Table 1. The different Declare models used during the experiments. High-resolution versions of the figures of the models used in the experiment can be found by following the link to the tool site.

Model 1	Model 2	Model 3
Response(a,b)	Exactly(a,2)	Response(a,b)
Precedence(b,c)	Existence(c,2)	Response(b,c)
Not co-existence(b,e)	Exactly(b,2)	Exactly(c,2)
Response(d,e)	Absence(d,3)	Precedence(b,e)
	Alternate precedence(a,c)	Response(d,e)
	Alternate response(b,d)	Alternate precedence(e,g)
		Response(f,g)
Model 4	**Model 5**	
Response(a,b)	Response(a,b)	Choice(a,j)
Existence(b,1)	Response(b,c)	Not succession(i,j)
Alternate precedence(b,c)	Exactly(c,2)	
Not succession(b,e)	Precedence(b,e)	
Existence(c,1)	Response(d,e)	
Response(d,c)	Alternate precedence(e,g)	
Existence(d,2)	Response(f,g)	

taught, were asked to solve five questions for each of five different Declare models in a timespan of two hours. The students have the same modeling experience and background and can be considered novice business process modelers. The models, as represented in Table 1, are of increasing complexity and are tailored towards assessing different kinds of dependencies:

- **Model 1:** focuses on the impact of the *Not co-existence* constraint.
- **Model 2:** focuses on the impact of unary constraint propagation.
- **Model 3:** focuses on the impact of simple forward and backward dependencies induced by *Exactly(c,2)*.
- **Model 4:** focuses on the impact of more advanced forward and backward dependencies induced by *Not succession(b,e)*.
- **Model 5:** focuses on the same impact as models 3 and 4, with an added *Choice* constraint.

At the start of the test, students were provided instructions making use of the example used in Sect. 2, a model which was used as a foundation for models 3–5, but without the additional constraints and activities added. As such, the idea behind hidden dependencies was explained, as well as how to make use of the tool they were provided with.

In order to measure the impact of handing natural language descriptions and the visualization of dependency graphs, the students were divided into three groups which received a different version of the Declare Execution Environment. Group A could only see the Declare model and the constraint descriptions, but no color annotation nor dependency structure visualizations. Group B received a tool in which the enabled activities were colored green, and temporarily violated constraints were colored red, in a fashion described in [11] and similar to Declare Designer [13]. Also, the constraint descriptions were given. Finally, group C was given an environment with the same functionality as group B, but with extra descriptions concerning hidden dependencies, as well as the possibility to open a dynamic visualization of the dependency structures.

Table 2. The students were selected from 3 different programs, however, it was made sure their distribution could not skew the results. More info can be found by following the provided link in Sect. 1.

Group	Participants	Gender		Program		
		Male	Female	IS	Business	CS
A	36	25	11	5	31	0
B	32	23	9	6	26	0
C	27	15	12	5	21	1

The questions were aimed at uncovering to which extent the participants grasped the full impact of the blend of different constraints. They were asked to indicate which activities were enabled after firing a certain sequence, and why or how to reach a certain firing sequence. Since two out of three groups knew which ones were enabled, they could focus more on the second part of the question. An example question used for model 1 was 'After firing d, which activities are still enabled? Explain'.

Each question was scored on a 0 to 1 scale, where incomplete answers (usually because of overlooked hidden dependencies or incorrect use of constraints) were still awarded a score higher than 0. E.g., a student from group B who provides the correct set of enabled activities but fails to state that activity c in model 3 is not enabled because of hidden dependencies was still awarded 0.6. The explanation was taken into account so as to make a fair comparison with students in group A, who got no extra information, and therefore many times missed even these basic answers. Group C students that just copied extra descriptions provided by the tool also did no receive a grade of 1, as they did not prove to understand the model.

5.2 Results

Quantitative Results. Given this setup, an experimental analysis can be conducted to investigate the impact of the environment students were given (i.e. group) on the score, where a higher score reflects a better level of understanding. Figure 3 shows boxplots of the average scores over 5 questions, per model and per group. From the figure, it can be seen that for each model, an increase

94   J. De Smedt et al.

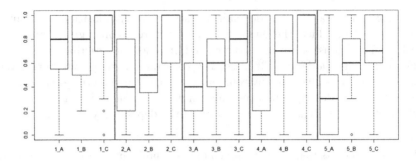

Fig. 3. Boxplot of the scores of 5 questions per model (1–5) and per group (A–C).

Table 3. Linear regression model based on the data gathered from the experiment with significance scores '***' 0, '**' 0.001, and '*' 0.01.

Coefficients	Estimate	Std. errror	t value		Pr(>|t|)	
(Intercept)	0.64092	0.01583	40.498	<	2.00E-16	***
Model2	-0.17082	0.01939	-8.81	<	2.00E-16	***
Model3	-0.17082	0.01939	-8.81	<	2.00E-16	***
Model4	-0.10498	0.01943	-5.403	<	7.22E-08	***
Model5	-0.21555	0.01964	-10.977	<	2.00E-16	***
GroupB	0.15811	0.01463	10.81	<	2.00E-16	***
GroupC	0.26522	0.01524	17.4	<	2.00E-16	***

Residual standard error: 0.2986 on 2340 degrees of freedom

Multiple R-squared: 0.1658

Adjusted R-squared: 0.1636

F-statistic: 77.49 on 6 and 2340 DF, p-value: < 2.2e-16

is observed in terms of the score when students are provided with additional hidden dependency-based annotations. Note that the data is available on the tool's web site.

So as to evaluate the statistical significance of this pattern, a linear regression ($Score = \alpha \times model + \beta \times group + \epsilon$) was fitted on the data. From the results in Table 3, it is clear that both the impact of the model as well as the group (and hence tool) is highly significant. Observe that the data was also fitted for a model with interaction between *model* and *group* and also for a model with *gender* and *program* included. These models did not raise the R-squared values much (<0.18), hence hinting at little extra explanatory power. Running a Durbin-Watson-test also rejected the hypothesis for correlation among the residuals. Finally, it was tested whether the error terms were normally distributed, as can be seen in Fig. 4a.

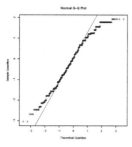

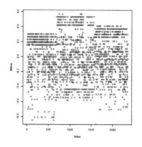

(a) Q-Q plot of the error terms showing they are close to a normal distribution.

(b) Plot of the residuals, showing no noticeable patterns.

Fig. 4. Descriptive statistics of the results of the linear regression model.

Qualitative Results. Since the participants did not just give an answer in the form of 'A is now enabled' but had to motivate their answers, some extra observations could be made concerning the results. Although it was the case that the two groups with the more elaborate tool were better capable of seeing which activities are enabled and which constraints are violated, they still seemed to ignore these annotations. Especially group B sometimes ignored the coloring of the model as they did not understand some implications of the constraints. Participants often also bended the descriptions of the Declare constraints towards their understanding, hence starting to discuss irrelevant parts of the model. For the third group, this behavior was still present, although to a much lesser extent. Group A participants often found the hidden dependencies in the easier examples. Because they had no support they analyzed the models thoroughly, but failed to find any hidden relations in the elaborate examples.

Remarks. As for all empirical studies, there are threats to validity that need to be addressed, the main ones in our case are:

– **Internal validity:** Our experiment had the maturation threat because subjects may react differently as time passes (because of boredom or fatigue). We solved this threat by dividing the experiment into different questions per model. Next this threat, we made sure there could be no interaction between the students of different sessions.
– **Construct validity:** Our experiment was threatened by the hypothesis guessing threat because students might figure out what the purpose of the study is, which could affect their guesses. We minimized this threat by hiding the goal of the experiment. Since the R-squared values were not very high, it might also be interesting to include the time spent on the questions and the grades of the final exam of the students to explain the score through the capabilities to learn and think logically in general.
– **External validity:** Our experiment might suffer from interaction of selection and treatment: the subject population is limited to students. Although the

number of subjects is quite high and their profiles balanced, we can only generalize the results to students. The subjects might not be representative to generalize the results to professional modelers as well. It is, e.g., not possible to claim that the tool can help or improve Declare modeling efforts of more experienced users.

6   Related Work

Declare, introduced as DecSerFlow and ConDec in [15,16], has become one of the most widely-used declarative process languages in research. Some competing approaches exist such as DCR Graphs [17], which are comparable to a slimmed-down version of Declare for improving understandability and setup, and the more data-oriented language Guard-Stage-Milestone [18].

Declare and its understandability has been researched for a test case-driven approach [4], the impact of hierarchies [1], and its common understandability challenges [2]. While these works clearly state the presence of hidden dependencies, with [2] explicitly mentioning this as a common pitfall for understandability, they have not provided a way to capture them. This work continues on the preliminary approach for retrieving hidden dependencies of [19].

Many other works on Declare mining exist as well, which have led to a better understanding of the properties of the language. Most notably the hierarchy [9] and semantics [10,20,21] and the transitivity properties [22] have brought clarification as to how constraints behave in a model.

7   Conclusion and Future Work

This paper shows how to retrieve and use dependency structures and unary propagation in Declare models to increase understandability. It offers a theoretic aspect in explaining how to construct and interpret the relations of constraints and their hidden dependencies in ways that have not been proposed yet, and was validated on novice users in an experiment. This showed that explaining and visualizing hidden dependencies and constraint structures rendered users significantly better capable of understanding the models.

Future work includes analyzing the results further by using extra user statistics such as average grades, as well as including new observations from expert users. Next, it is also straightforward to extend these findings to n-ary constraints, which changes only the propagation and interpretation slightly. Furthermore, constructing the hidden dependencies has numerous other applications. By understanding in which way constraints are related, it becomes easier to grasp the complexity of conjoining the separate Declare constraints' automata and hence it is possible to score the impact of different constraints on, e.g., the performance of calculating the global automaton of the whole model. Furthermore, these insights can be used to score a Declare model for simplicity., i.e., models which contain more hidden dependencies can be scored lower for this metric.

References

1. Zugal, S., Pinggera, J., Weber, B., Mendling, J., Reijers, H.A.: Assessing the impact of hierarchy on model understandability – a cognitive perspective. In: Kienzle, J. (ed.) MODELS 2011 Workshops. LNCS, vol. 7167, pp. 123–133. Springer, Heidelberg (2012)
2. Haisjackl, C., Zugal, S., Soffer, P., Hadar, I., Reichert, M., Pinggera, J., Weber, B.: Making sense of declarative process models: common strategies and typical pitfalls. In: Nurcan, S., Proper, H.A., Soffer, P., Krogstie, J., Schmidt, R., Halpin, T., Bider, I. (eds.) BPMDS 2013 and EMMSAD 2013. LNBIP, vol. 147, pp. 2–17. Springer, Heidelberg (2013)
3. Pesic, M., Schonenberg, H., van der Aalst, W.M.: Declare: full support for loosely-structured processes. In: 11th IEEE International Enterprise Distributed Object Computing Conference, EDOC 2007, pp. 287–300. IEEE (2007)
4. Zugal, S., Pinggera, J., Weber, B.: The impact of testcases on the maintainability of declarative process models. In: Halpin, T., Nurcan, S., Krogstie, J., Soffer, P., Proper, E., Schmidt, R., Bider, I. (eds.) BPMDS 2011 and EMMSAD 2011. LNBIP, vol. 81, pp. 163–177. Springer, Heidelberg (2011)
5. Montali, M., Pesic, M.M., Aalst, W., Chesani, F., Mello, P., Storari, S.: Declarative specification and verification of service choreographies. ACM Trans. Web 4(1), 1–62 (2010)
6. De Smedt, J., De Weerdt, J., Vanthienen, J.: Fusion miner: process discovery for mixed-paradigm models. Decis. Support Syst. 77, 123–136 (2015)
7. Burattin, A., Maggi, F.M., van der Aalst, W.M., Sperduti, A.: Techniques for a posteriori analysis of declarative processes. In: 2012 IEEE 16th International Enterprise Distributed Object Computing Conference, pp. 41–50. IEEE (2012)
8. Pesic, M.: Constraint-based workflow management systems: shifting control to users. Ph.D. thesis, Technische Universiteit Eindhoven (2008)
9. Di Ciccio, C., Mecella, M.: A two-step fast algorithm for the automated discovery of declarative workflows. In: 2013 IEEE Symposium on Computational Intelligence and Data Mining (CIDM), pp. 135–142. IEEE (2013)
10. Westergaard, M., Stahl, C., Reijers, H.A.: Unconstrainedminer: efficient discovery of generalized declarative process models. Technical report BPM-13-28, BPMcenter (2013)
11. Maggi, F.M., Montali, M., Westergaard, M., van der Aalst, W.M.P.: Monitoring business constraints with linear temporal logic: an approach based on colored automata. In: Rinderle-Ma, S., Toumani, F., Wolf, K. (eds.) BPM 2011. LNCS, vol. 6896, pp. 132–147. Springer, Heidelberg (2011)
12. De Smedt, J., De Weerdt, J., Vanthienen, J., Poels, G.: Mixed-paradigm process modeling with intertwined state spaces. Bus. Inf. Syst. Eng. 58(1), 19–29 (2016)
13. Westergaard, M., Maggi, F.M.: Declare: a tool suite for declarative workflow modeling and enactment. BPM (Demos) 820, 1–5 (2011)
14. Møller, A.: dk. brics. automaton-finite-state automata and regular expressions for Java (2010). Accessed 30 Aug 2014
15. van der Aalst, W.M.P., Pesic, M.: DecSerFlow: towards a truly declarative service flow language. In: Bravetti, M., Núñez, M., Zavattaro, G. (eds.) WS-FM 2006. LNCS, vol. 4184, pp. 1–23. Springer, Heidelberg (2006)
16. Pesic, M., van der Aalst, W.M.P.: A declarative approach for flexible business processes management. In: Eder, J., Dustdar, S. (eds.) BPM Workshops 2006. LNCS, vol. 4103, pp. 169–180. Springer, Heidelberg (2006)

17. Hildebrandt, T.T., Mukkamala, R.R.: Declarative event-based workflow as distributed dynamic condition response graphs. In: PLACES, pp. 59–73 (2011)
18. Hull, R., et al.: Introducing the guard-stage-milestone approach for specifying business entity lifecycles (invited talk). In: Bravetti, M. (ed.) WS-FM 2010. LNCS, vol. 6551, pp. 1–24. Springer, Heidelberg (2011)
19. De Smedt, J., De Weerdt, J., Serral Asensio, E., Vanthienen, J.: Gamification of declarative process models for learning and model verification. In: Business Process Management Workshops. Springer (2015). Accepted
20. De Giacomo, G., Masellis, R.D., Montali, M.: Reasoning on LTL on finite traces: insensitivity to infiniteness. In: Proceedings of the Twenty-Eighth AAAI Conference on Artificial Intelligence, pp. 1027–1033, 27–31 July 2014, Québec City, Québec, Canada (2014)
21. Di Ciccio, C., Mecella, M., Mendling, J.: The effect of noise on mined declarative constraints. In: Ceravolo, P., Accorsi, R., Cudre-Mauroux, P. (eds.) Data-Driven Process Discovery and Analysis, pp. 1–24. Springer, Heidelberg (2015)
22. Maggi, F.M., Bose, R.P.J.C., van der Aalst, W.M.P.: A knowledge-based integrated approach for discovering and repairing declare maps. In: Salinesi, C., Norrie, M.C., Pastor, Ó. (eds.) CAISE 2013. LNCS, vol. 7908, pp. 433–448. Springer, Heidelberg (2013)

Innovation, Gamification

The Authentication Game - Secure User Authentication by Gamification?

Frank Ebbers and Philipp Brune[(✉)]

University of Applied Sciences Neu-Ulm,
Wileystraße 1, 89231 Neu-Ulm, Germany
f.ebbers@yahoo.de,
Philipp.Brune@hs-neu-ulm.de

Abstract. Knowledge-based authentication with username and password still is the predominant authentication method in practice. As the number of online accounts increases, users need to remember more and more passwords, leading to the choice of better memorable but insecure passwords. Therefore, it is important to take into account the users' behavior to improve IT security. While gamification has been proposed as a concept to influence users' behavior in various domains, it has not been applied to user authentication methods so far. Therefore, in this paper an approach for a gamified authentication method is presented. Using a prototype implementation, a qualitative evaluation in an empirical study is performed. Results illustrate the general feasibility of the proposed approach.

Keywords: Information security · User authentication · Graphical passwords · Biometrics · Gamification

1 Introduction

For many years, knowledge-based authentication using username and password is the predominant authentication method in practice [2]. In recent years, also biometric and token-based approaches have become increasingly important, but textual passwords remained frequently used despite their well-known disadvantages [33]. As the number of mobile devices, web services and other online accounts increases, users need to remember more and more passwords. An average US user has 25 password-protected accounts and has to enter a password eight times a day [15]. Therefore, many people choose memorable but insecure passwords, built a mnemonic aid [28], write passwords down or use one password for many different services [17]. This leads to increasing security risks for private and business computing and illustrates the importance of "human factor in security" [39].

Security cannot be achieved by technological solutions alone [34]. It is important to take into account the users' behavior and security awareness regarding password usage. However, existing attempts like security awareness trainings often failed to successfully change users habits [21].

© Springer International Publishing Switzerland 2016
S. Nurcan et al. (Eds.): CAiSE 2016, LNCS 9694, pp. 101–115, 2016.
DOI: 10.1007/978-3-319-39696-5_7

In recent years, gamification has been proposed as a concept to influence peoples behavior in different contexts [49]. It denotes the process of adding game elements to a non-gaming environment [11] to influence users through intrinsic motivation. Although gamification already has been used in various contexts, in particular for educational purposes [42], few attempts have been made to apply it in the domain of IT security so far.

Therefore, in this paper an approach for a gamified authentication method is presented and evaluated. It requires a user to successfully complete a computer game to authenticate to a system. Using a prototype implementation of this authentication game, the approach is qualitatively evaluated in an empirical study. The results indicate the general feasibility of the proposed approach and show its perception by different potential users.

The rest of this paper is organized as follows: In Sect. 2 the related work is discussed in detail and Sect. 3 explains the design and implementation of the proposed authentication game. The design and data collection of the empirical study is described in Sect. 4, while Sect. 5 discusses the obtained results. We conclude with a summary of our findings.

2   Related Work

Traditionally, user authentication to an application or service is performed using a combination of a username and a secret password chosen by the user (the so-called user credentials), mainly since it is cheap and easy to use [19]. However, the weaknesses and risks of this approach have been discussed for many years [37,48]. Passwords may be easily forgotten, stolen or guessed by an attacker, i.e. using dictionary attacks [31,37]. The security of a password increases with its length, which in turn makes it harder to remember. In addition, the number of passwords an average user has to remember strongly increased in the last years [31]. Maintaining their various passwords therefore is an increasing challenge for most users [9,10]. The usability [32] of information security measures, in particular the traditional password-based authentication is being discussed for some years [3,46]. In particular, various alternatives to the standard username/password credentials have been proposed, namely biometrics and graphical passwords.

Graphical passwords are methods of image-based authentication first proposed in 1996 [4], which are based on the fact that humans can remember pictures much better than letters [8]. There exist different variants for graphical passwords, in particular recognition-based authentication [5], recall-based authentication [47] like the Draw-a-Secret (DAS) method [13,25], and pass-point methods [23,26]. Graphical passwords, in particular DAS are commonly used today in practice to protect mobile devices [12,30]. However, despite their better usability compared to using a conventional password, also the graphical password approaches like DAS have some security [44] as well as usability problems (i.e. the difficulty to draw precisely) [36].

"Biometrics is the science of establishing the identity of an individual based on the physical, chemical or behavioral attributes of the person" [24]. Physical and chemical characteristics could be fingerprints, voice, veins, iris prints or even ones DNA [45]. Another method for biometrical authentication is keystroke analysis. It has been demonstrated that human key stroke behavior is unique for a person [6,29]. However, the accuracy of keystroke-based approaches is inferior to other biometric characteristics. On the other hand the keystroke behavior could not be copied or stolen. The human way of pressing and releasing keys on a keyboard is unique and can be captured and replayed only be means of a key logger installed on the system. In the future, a logical continuation of keystroke patterns may be the use of gestures for user authentication [40].

However, in general still better technologies which improve the memorability of a user's credentials while improving the security of the authentication process are required [38]. Gamification may provide a promising approach for that purpose [1].

In recent years, Gamification has been studied by various authors. One major field of research is its application for educational purposes, denoted by terms like Serious Gaming, Edutainment or Learning Games [42]. While first applications of Gamification in the information security domain have been proposed [49], they mainly are related to information security trainings for improving security awareness [1,7,14]. Despite the fact that Gamification may provide a mean to improve IT security enormously [43] and that all existing alternatives to textual passwords like biometrics and graphical passwords have serious security or usability flaws, it has rarely been applied to user authentication so far [16,18].

Therefore, in the present paper the question is addressed how a gamified authentication method with additional keystroke pattern recognition could be designed for improving the security and usability of user authentication simultaneously.

3   Design and Implementation of the Authentication Game

This paper proposes a game-like solution for users to authenticate themselves with any web service or personal computer called the Ariadne PathLogin. Referring to the password management life cycle [9] it uses a holistic approach taking into account all human factors influencing the password generation and maintenance phase by means of Gamification. In addition, since it has been demonstrated that human muscle movements improve the ability to remember the password [9], the approach utilizes also users keystroke patterns as an additional biometric authentication factor.

Therefore, the proposed approach uses a chessboard game-like scenario as illustrated in Fig. 1. After selecting a specific avatar character, the user has to move it on an individual, secret path across the game board. During this movement, the user might also have to perform special actions (i.e. jumping) on certain fields. The specific avatar character and the path including the special actions have been individually selected by the user during the registration phase, therefore serving as part of the secret information identifying the user. The

Fig. 1. Design of the avatar character selection and playing field screens in the proposed Ariadne PathLogin game for user authentication. After selecting a specific avatar character as a "playing figure", the user has to move it on an individual, secret path across the game board for authentication using the keyboard's arrow keys.

additional special tasks further support the creation of highly individual and better memorable secrets by the users [9,20].

Ariadne PathLogin uses a board dimensioned to a 10×10 fields square (see right part of Fig. 1). Although the board itself thus offers only $10 \times 10 = 100$ fields, the number of selectable paths is theoretically infinite, since at every field the character might move to 4 possible neighboring fields (including fields already visited before) and the number of steps forming a path is also variable and unlimited. The goal of Ariadne PathLogin is to access to the Ariadne Castle at the end of the login process, which is accompanied by a fanfare sound, giving users a feeling of success. In a real-world application this corresponds to being granted access to the system.

Users control the character on the board by the arrow- or space keys on the keyboard. The user's characteristic keystroke pattern while doing so is also captured during the enrollment phase for subsequent comparison in every authentication process as an additional biometric signature.

3.1   Registration Phase

Like any other authentication method each user has to register first. For the Ariadne PathLogin, three different steps are required:

1. Specifying a unique textual username,
2. Selecting a specific "playing figure" or avatar character (called Ariadne),
3. Defining a specific path across the playing board.

The user can only perform one steps at once. In the game, each step is represented by a part of a treasure map (see Fig. 1), which may foster curiosity, learnability and memorability [32]. Furthermore, by displaying only one step at a time the user will not be distracted by too much information and the process is more secure since less information is unveiled.

The user has to select a personal avatar character out of four predefined characters. Choosing a unique character seen as a playing figure is important for creating a personal touch for the user [27]. Ariadne is the character of this game. She is a female character representing different and funny attitudes, designed by the authors. The user can choose between four different variants of the character as illustrated in the left part of Fig. 1. All variants are rather similar in shape and color in order to make character guessing or shoulder-surfing attacks by a third party more unlikely.

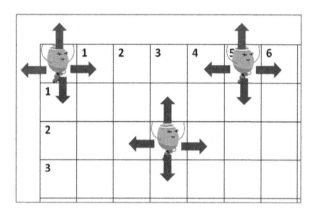

Fig. 2. Possible moves of the Ariadne avatar character during its path across the board. Red arrows indicate visible moves while the blue ones correspond to "hidden" moves to confuse a possible shoulder surfing attacker. (Color figure online)

Third, the user has to move the avatar character across the chess-like board to define an individual secret path, optionally including special actions like jumping on certain fields. The character's initial position is in the left upper corner of the board. The character can be moved only via the arrow keys. For each keystroke, the actual key and the corresponding time stamp are captured by the system. The user can choose the path freely with the character moving visibly only within the board area. However, if the user types a key sequence corresponding to the character moving outside the playing field, these keystrokes are still captured without moving the character visibly to enable using "hidden" paths for additional security. These different types of move operations are illustrated in Fig. 2. Here, red arrows symbolize visible movements while blue ones refer to invisible movements forming the hidden path.

To capture a characteristic individual keystroke pattern and to ensure that a user memorizes the selected path well, the user has to repeat this path five times. This can be compared to the traditional registration phase using text-based passwords, where any user also has to enter a new password at least twice in order to exclude mistakes. This first path is considered as the basis for the upcoming paths. If the user changes the path or the character in a subsequent iteration, the system will prompt the user by a popup message and cancel the path capture. After the fifth successful iteration, the characteristic keystroke pattern will be calculated and the captured data will be stored in the user database. For obtaining this characteristic keystroke pattern for a user's path, the arithmetic mean values of the time differences (in milliseconds) between subsequent distinctive keystrokes are calculated.

3.2 Authentication Phase

In the authentication phase, a user is authenticated by repeating the same three steps as in the registration phase, now entering the correct username, avatar character and path as previously captured. For comparison with the stored characteristic keystroke pattern, again the time differences between subsequent keystrokes are calculated and compared with the values stored in the database. However, since the measured time differences never will be exactly the same for a human (i.e. due to external factors and personal condition) [9], some tolerance interval needs to be used in the comparison. Previous results suggest a time tolerance interval of about 160ms for biometric keystroke patterns [41], which was adopted for the current implementation of Ariadne PathLogin. If all data are correct, the user is prompted about the successful login.

If the login process fails, the user has to start right from the beginning again. The reason is that in this case either the user name or the character or the path or multiples of these may be wrong. Since an attacker should not be revealed any information which of these are wrong, no clue is given and all data entries have to be repeated.

3.3 Prototype Implementation

For the experimental evaluation of the proposed approach, a prototype of the Ariadne PathLogin game was implemented as a browser-based web application. The purpose of this implementation is not to provide a production-ready solution, but to serve as the basis for evaluation of the concept.

The user interface of the prototype is implemented using HTML5, CSS and JavaScript. This frontend interacts with a server-side backend implemented in the widely used PHP language[1]. All data used within the authentication process are stored in a MySQL database accessed by the PHP code, using the InnoDB storage engine[2].

The users' characteristic keystroke patterns are stored in this database as strings consisting of a sequence of the numerical key codes pressed and the corresponding time passed since the previous keystroke in milliseconds. Since the pupose of the prototype implementation was to evaluate the feasibility of the approach from a user's perspective and not to provide a production-ready solution, implementation-related security issues like of this underlying storage mechanism are not discussed in this paper.

---

[1] See http://www.php.net.

[2] See http://www.mysql.com.

4   Evaluation

To evaluate the proposed approach, a qualitative, explorative empirical study was performed using the described prototype implementation. The purpose of the evaluation was twofold: First, the proposed approach was evaluated with respect to its effectiveness from a user's perspective regarding its usability and Gamification. This was done using a questionnaire the participants had to fill out. Second, its effectiveness as an authentication scheme needed to be analyzed regarding the reliability of clearly identifying a specific user. Therefore, the participants had to practically use the prototype implementation to register and authenticate themselves at the system.

A convenience sample of 51 participants with different occupation, social background and gender took part in the study. All participants were between 15 and 67 years old, with the majority being between 20 and 30. 41 of these participants (approx. 80 %) were male.

To have comparable results and exclude environmental influences, all participants had to use the Ariadne PathLogin in an identical work environment. A desktop workplace with always the same computer equipment was set up for them in a neutral surrounding. Only one participant was inside the room at a time to avoid mutual influences between participants.

Fig. 3. Setup of the participants' desktop for the empirical evaluation. Two different keyboards have been used to study the influence of the keyboard type on the users' keystroke patterns.

The computer used for the evaluation was a Notebook (Acer Aspire V3-571G with Intel i5-3210M CPU and Seagate Momentus XT 750 GB SSHD solid-state hybrid drive) running with Microsoft Window 8.1 64 Bits, a Firefox web browser 35.0.1 without any add-ons and the Ariadne PathLogin application running within the XAMPP 5.6.3 environment. In order to analyze the possible influence of keyboard types, two (new) USB keyboards were used with strongly

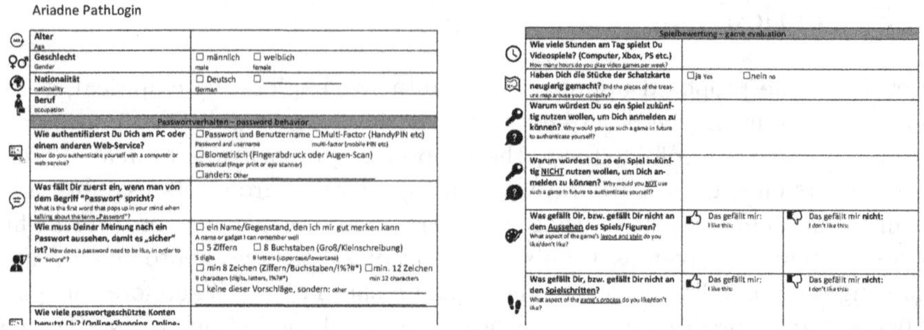

Ariadne PathLogin

Alter Age	
Geschlecht Gender	☐ männlich male ☐ weiblich female
Nationalität nationality	☐ Deutsch German ☐ ____
Beruf occupation	
Passwortverhalten – password behavior	
Wie authentifizierst Du Dich am PC oder einem anderen Web-Service? How do you authenticate yourself with a computer or web service?	☐Passwort und Benutzername Password and username ☐Multi-Factor (HandyPIN etc) multi-factor (mobile PIN etc) ☐Biometrisch (Fingerabdruck oder Augen-Scan) Biometrical (finger print or eye scanner) ☐anders: Other ____
Was fällt Dir zuerst ein, wenn man von dem Begriff "Passwort" spricht? What is the first word that pops up in your mind when talking about the term „Password"?	
Wie muss Deiner Meinung nach ein Passwort aussehen, damit es „sicher" ist? How does a password need to be like, in order to be "secure"?	☐ ein Name/Gegenstand, den ich mir gut merken kann A name or gadget I can remember well ☐ 5 Ziffern 5 digits ☐ 8 Buchstaben (Groß/Kleinschreibung) 8 letters (uppercase/lowercase) ☐ min 8 Zeichen (Ziffern/Buchstaben/!%?#*) 8 characters (digits, letters, !%?#*) ☐min. 12 Zeichen min 12 characters ☐ keine dieser Vorschläge, sondern: other ____
Wie viele passwortgeschützte Konten benutzt Du? (Online-Shopping, Online-	

Spielbewertung – game evaluation		
Wie viele Stunden am Tag spielst Du Videospiele? (Computer, Xbox, PS etc.) How many hours do you play video games per week?		
Haben Dich die Stücke der Schatzkarte neugierig gemacht? Did the pieces of the treasure map arouse your curiosity?	☐ja Yes ☐nein no	
Warum würdest Du so ein Spiel zukünftig nutzen wollen, um Dich anmelden zu können? Why would you use such a game in future to authenticate yourself?		
Warum würdest Du so ein Spiel zukünftig NICHT nutzen wollen, um Dich anmelden zu können? Why would you NOT use such a game in future to authenticate yourself?		
Was gefällt Dir, bzw. gefällt Dir nicht an dem Aussehen des Spiels/Figuren? What aspect of the game's layout and style do you like/don't like?	Das gefällt mir: I like this:	Das gefällt mir **nicht:** I don't like this:
Was gefällt Dir, bzw. gefällt Dir nicht an den Spielschritten? What aspect of the game's process do you like/don't like?	Das gefällt mir: I like this:	Das gefällt mir **nicht:** I don't like this:

Fig. 4. Excerpts of the first (left) and second page (right) of the questionnaire handed out to the participants before and after the practical usage of the prototype, respectively. The first page contains questions related to personal data and previous experiences regarding user authentication. The second page is devoted to the actual evaluation of the game. Questions are stated in German and English language.

differing types of keys (rather flat vs. high), namely Hama Basic Keyboard K 210, USB and an Apple Keyboard A1242. The complete described setup for the evaluation environment is displayed in Fig. 3.

In addition to using the tool, the participants had to fill out the two-page questionnaire shown in Fig. 4.

Each participant first was introduced into the topics of authentication, passwords and the purpose of the Ariadne PathLogin. Afterwards he or she had to fill out the first page of the questionnaire. When starting to use the prototype, the web browser was already opened in full-screen mode, displaying the main page of Ariadne PathLogin containing an overview of all functions to ensure an identical starting point for all participants.

Now the participants were asked to do a tutorial first to get familiar with the approach. No data was logged during this step.

After that, the participants should perform the described registration and login steps. In order to collect comparable data, all participants were asked to use the same predefined path, presented to them on a piece of paper. During these steps, the entered data was logged by the system for evaluation.

After the registration phase, users were asked to do the login. They were given the choice to select one of the two different keyboards. It was not necessary to login using both of them. If the user passed the login after a maximum of three tries, the login was considered as successful.

Finally, the users were asked to fill out the second page of the questionnaire.

5 Results

5.1 User Perception

Regarding previous experiences with different authentication methods, username and password are used by all participants, as one would expect. Due to the popularity of smartphones and mobile devices, 20 % also use finger print sensors. Multi-factor authentication has been used by about 22 % of the participants. These numbers are in agreement with previous findings indicating that 27 % of users use multi-factor authentication on their smartphones [35] and 22 % use of biometrical authentication [22].

Almost half of the participants immediately associated the term security with passwords. Despite this fact, nearly one fifth of the participants is annoyed by using text-based passwords, which supports the request for better authentication methods.

Table 1. Participants' opinions of Ariadne PathLogin as a computer game.

Positive	Negative
"Easy and clear to understand"	"Entering a new password (registration step) takes too long"
"Freedom of decision which character and path to choose"	"You can walk a wrong path"
"You can choose the security by yourself by defining a path or secret path"	"The icon's jump is confusing"
"Speed and sounds fit to the game"	"Too little action"
"Easy to reproduce"	

However, only about 50 % of the participants stated that they would be interested or willing to use Ariadne PathLogin in the future. Figure 5 shows a more detailed analysis of the reasons given by the participants for acceptance of the game.

The reasons for refusal of the approach are strongly varying between the different age groups (see Fig. 5). A majority of the 15–50 year-old participants considers it is too time consuming. As one participant formulated it: "I would use it for accounts I do not use very often, but which are very safety-critical like my online banking". The older the participants were, the fewer security doubts they had.

On the other hand, the older participants found the approach increasingly difficult to use.

Regarding their perception of the Ariadne PathLogin as a computer game, the structure and rules seemed clear for the majority of the participants. They liked also the possibility to choose the password strength by adjusting the path. On the negative side, users stated that the process takes too long and there are too few but still confusing actions, e.g. a jump is executed on the same field. The pros and cons of the approach as perceived by the participants are summarized in Table 1.

65 % of the participants claimed that they could remember the graphical path in Ariadne PathLogin better than a complex textual password. Two participants

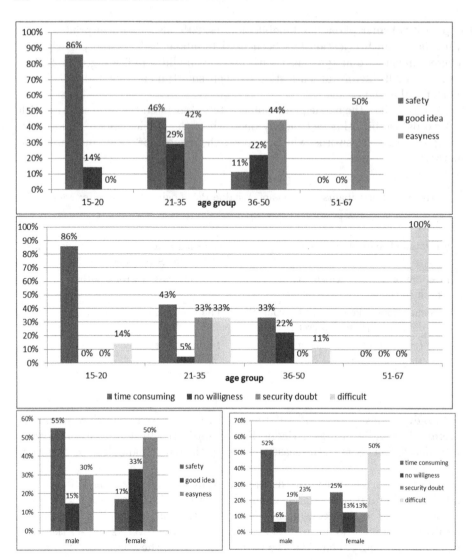

Fig. 5. Participants' reasons for their willingness to use or not use Ariadne PathLogin in the future depending on age (above) and gender (below).

even stated "Hey, that is cool. I can connect the path with a rhythm or beat" and "I would connect this path with my favorite song, that will surely help me".

5.2   Effectiveness of the Authentication Mechanism

Figure 6 shows the number of successful logins of the participants while using the Ariadne PathLogin prototype implementation depending on age and gender.

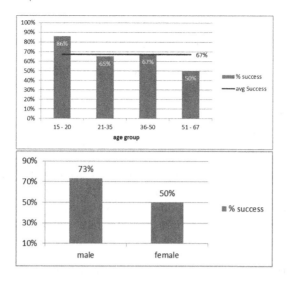

Fig. 6. Number of successful logins by the participants using Ariadne PathLogin depending on age (above) and gender (below).

The authors consider the login success rate as the main indicator for the effectiveness of the proposed approach.

The average success rate was 67%, with a variance of 2% and a standard deviation of 15%. Within the age group of 15 to 20 the rate was sufficiently high (86%). But even for elderly persons the login was successful in one out of two tries. Generally speaking, no critical difference can be found between age groups, whereas male users succeed almost 25% more often than female ones.

However, these results for the success rates should be considered critically. First, the number of participants was not equal for age groups and genders, and second users were presented a predefined path for this evaluation. It is likely that the memorability of the path and thus the success rate improves when users have to choose a path by their own.

It was also observed that the login success rate is strongly dependent on the numerical tolerance value used while comparing the keystroke pattern captured during login to the one previously stored in the database. The initial tolerance value used was 160 ms (see above). When increasing it to 250 ms, around 50% of those who failed before also succeeded. And even 70% were successful after changing the tolerance to 450 ms. However, increasing the tolerance on the other hand reduces the security of the approach, as it increases the probability of false positive matches.

Regarding the keyboard used, no significant influence was observed. Users typed on average 6% (25.81 ms) faster on the keyboard with the flat keys than on those with the higher keys. However, this small difference can be neglected.

To evaluate the risk due to false positive matches during the keystroke pattern comparison, the authors also tried to login to the users accounts. Although the authors knew all the credentials information of the users (username, chosen character, the path and the approximate typing speed at least from subjective cognition), they succeeded only in two out of 51 cases. This emphasizes the additional security gained by the biometric keystroke pattern comparison.

6   Conclusion

In conclusion, in the present paper an approach for a gamified authentication method has been presented and evaluated, which requires the user to successfully complete a computer game to authenticate to a system. The authentication mechanism used by the game is a combination of a biometric and a knowledge-based factor. To successfully log in, the user has to possess the secret knowledge of the correct username, avatar character and path across the playing board as well as to control the character with the corresponding personal keystroke pattern.

The feasibility of the proposed approach was evaluated by an empirical study, in which the participants had to use a prototype implementation of the game to log in, as well as to answer a questionnaire to assess the perceived quality of the game. The evaluation results suggest that despite some differences between participants of different ages the approach is feasible in general. However, it was considered rather time-consuming by many participants, so probably its application will remain restricted to scenarios where a higher level of security is required (i.e. online banking or access to mission-critical applications).

However, the validity of these findings is still limited due to the limited number of the participants in the empirical study and its qualitative nature. The evaluation still needs to be extended by further research efforts to verify the obtained results.

References

1. Amorin, J.A., Hendix, M., Andler, S.F., Gustavsson, P.M.: Gamified training for cyber defence: Methods and automated tools for situation and threat assessment (2013)
2. Andress, J.: The Basics of Information Security: Understanding the Fundamentals of InfoSec in Theory and Practice, 2nd edn. Elsevier Science, USA (2014)
3. Balfanz, D., Durfee, G., Smetters, D., Grinter, R.: In search of usable security: five lessons from the field. IEEE Secur. Priv. 2(5), 19–24 (2004)
4. Blonder, G.E.: Graphical password (1996). http://www.google.com/patents/US5559961
5. Brostoff, S., Sasse, M.A.: Are passfaces more usable than passwords? a field trial investigation. In: McDonald, S., Waern, Y., Cockton, G. (eds.) People and Computers XIV – Usability or Else!, pp. 405–424. Springer, London (2000)
6. Brown, M., Rogers, S.J.: User identification via keystroke characteristics of typed names using neural networks. Int. J. Man Mach. Stud. 39(6), 999–1014 (1993)
7. Burke, M., Hiltbrand, T.: How gamification will change business intelligence. Bus. Intell. J. 16(2), 8–16 (2011)

8. Chaki, N.: Computer Networks & Communications (NetCom): Proceedings of the Fourth International Conference on Networks et Communications. Lecture Notes in Electrical Engineering, vol. 131. Springer, New York (2013)
9. Choong, Y.-Y.: A cognitive-behavioral framework of user password management lifecycle. In: Tryfonas, T., Askoxylakis, I. (eds.) HAS 2014. LNCS, vol. 8533, pp. 127–137. Springer, Heidelberg (2014)
10. Das, A., Bonneau, J., Caesar, M., Borisov, N., Wang, X.: The tangled web of password reuse. In: Symposium on Network and Distributed System Security 2014, Washington, D.C. (2014)
11. Deterding, S., Sicart, M., Nacke, L., O'Hara, K., Dixon, D.: Gamification: using game-design elements in non-gaming contexts. In: Tan, D., Amershi, S., Begole, B., Kellogg, W.A., Tungare, M. (eds.) The 2011 Annual Conference Extended Abstracts, pp. 2425–2428 (2011)
12. Dunphy, P., Heiner, A.P., Asokan, N.: A closer look at recognition-based graphical passwords on mobile devices. In: Cranor, L.F. (ed.) SOUPS 2010. ACM International Conference Proceedings Series, p. 1. ACM, New York (2010). http://dl.acm.org/citation.cfm?id=1837114
13. Dunphy, P., Yan, J.: Do background images improve draw a secret graphical passwords?. In: Ning, P., Capitani, D., di Vimercati, S., Syverson, P., Capitani, D., di Vimercati, S., Syverson, P.F., Evans, D. (eds.) Proceedings of the 14th ACM conference on Computer and Communications Security, pp. 36–47. ACM Digital Library, New York (2007). http://dl.acm.org/citation.cfm?id=1315252
14. Fernandes, J., Duarte, D., Ribeiro, C., Farinha, C., Pereira, J.M., da Silva, M.M.: ithink: A game-based approach towards improving collaboration and participation in requirement elicitation. Procedia Comput. Sci. **15**, 66–77 (2012)
15. Florencio, D., Herley, C.. A large-scale study of web password habits. In: Williamson, C., Zurko, M.E. (eds.) Proceedings of the 16th International Conference on World Wide Web 2007, pp. 657–666. ACM, New York (2007)
16. Forget, A., Chiasson, S., Biddle, R.: Persuasion as education for computer security. In: World Conference on E-Learning in Corporate, Government, Healthcare, and Higher Education, vol. 2007(1), pp. 822–829 (2007)
17. Fortinet: Multiple password tendencies of gen x online users in the united states, as of February 2014· Statista (2014). http://www.statista.com/statistics/305462/generation-x-multiple-internet-account-passwords/
18. Gallego, A., Saxena, N., Voris, J.: Playful security: a computer game for secure wireless device pairing. In: 2011 16th International Conference on Computer Games (CGAMES), pp. 177–184, July 2011
19. Hari, K.K.K., Anbuoli, P., Manikandan, A., Saikishore, E. (eds.): Computer Applications I: Proceedings of the International Conference on Computer Applications, 24–27 December 2010, Pondicherry, India. Research Pub. Services, Singapore (2011)
20. Helkala, K., Svendsen, N.K.: The security and memorability of passwords generated by using an association element and a personal factor. In: Laud, P. (ed.) NordSec 2011. LNCS, vol. 7161, pp. 114–130. Springer, Heidelberg (2012)
21. Herold, R.: Managing an Information Security and Privacy Awareness and Training Program, 2nd edn. CRC Press, Boca Raton (2011)
22. InformationWeeks Analytics: Analytics report: Identity management - saas, mobility add urgency (2011). http://www.exactidentity.com/wp-content/uploads/2012/07/InformationWeek-Identity-Management.pdf
23. Iranna, A., Pankaja, P.: Graphical password authentication using persuasive cued click point. Int. J. Eng. Res. Appl. **2**, 2963–2974 (2013)

24. Jain, A.K., Flynn, P.J., Ross, A.A.: Handbook of Biometrics. Springer, New York (2007)
25. Jermyn, I., Mayer, A.J., Monrose, F., Reiter, M.K., Rubin, A.D., et al.: The design and analysis of graphical passwords. In: Association, U. (ed.) Proceedings of the 8th USENIX Security Symposium, Washington, D.C., USA, vol. 8. (1999)
26. Khot, R.A., Srinathan, K., Kumaraguru, P.: Marasim: a novel jigsaw based authentication scheme using tagging. In: Tan, D.S., Fitzpatrick, G., Gutwin, C., Begole, B., Kellogg, W.A. (eds.) CHI 2011, pp. 2605–2614 (2011). http://dl.acm.org/citation.cfm?d=1978942.1979322
27. Kroeze, C., Olivier, M.S.: Gamifying authentication. In: Venter, H.S., Loock, M., Coetzee, M. (eds.) 2012 Information Security for South Africa, pp. 1–8. IEEE, Piscataway (2012)
28. Kuo, C., Romanosky, S., Cranor, L.F.: Human selection of mnemonic phrase-based passwords. In: Cranor, L.F. (ed.) SOUPS 2006: Proceedings of the Second Symposium on Usable Privacy and Security, pp. 67–78. ACM, New York (2006)
29. Loy, C.C., Lai, W.K., Lim, C.P.: Keystroke patterns classification using the artmap-fd neural network. In: Liao, B.Y. (ed.) IIHMSP 2007, pp. 61–64. IEEE Computer Society, Los Alamitos (2007)
30. Luca, A.D., Hang, A., Brudy, F., Lindner, C., Hussmann, H.: Touch me once and i know it's you! implicit authentication based on touch screen patterns. In: Konstan, J.A., Chi, E.H., Höök, K. (eds.) Proceedings of the SIGCHI Conference on Human Factors in Computing Systems, pp. 987–996. ACM, New York (2012). http://dl.acm.org/citation.cfm?id=2208544
31. Newman, R.: Security and Access Control Using Biometric Technologies. Cengage Learning, New Delhi (2009)
32. Nielsen, J.: Usability Engineering. Morgan Kaufmann Publishers, San Francisco (1994). Updated edn
33. O'Gorman, L.: Comparing passwords, tokens, and biometrics for user authentication. Proc. IEEE **91**(12), 2021–2040 (2003)
34. Parsons, K., McCormac, A., Butavicius, M., Ferguson, L.: Human factors and information security: Individual, culture and security environment (2010)
35. SafeNet Inc.: Multi-factor authentication: Current usage and trends (2013). http://www2.safenet-inc.com/email/pdf/Multi_Factor_Authentication_WP_EN_A4_v3_3Apr2013_web.pdf
36. Sarohi, H.K., Khan, F.U.: Graphical password authentication schemes: current status and key issues. Int. J. Comput. Sci. Issues (IJCSI) **10**(2), 437 (2013)
37. Schneier, B.: Secrets and Lies: Digital Security in a Networked World. Wiley, New York (2011)
38. Schneier, B.: Secrets and Lies: Digital Security in a Networked World. Wiley, New York (2000)
39. Schultz, E.: The human factor in security. Comput. Secur. **24**(6), 425–426 (2005)
40. Shahzad, M., Liu, A.X., Samuel, A.: Secure unlocking of mobile touch screen devices by simple gestures: you can see it but you can not do it. In: Proceedings of the 19th Annual International Conference on Mobile Computing & Networking, MobiCom 2013, pp. 39–50. ACM, New York (2013). http://doi.acm.org/10.1145/2500423.2500434
41. Sharif, M., Faiz, T., Raza, M.: Time signatures - an implementation of keystroke and click patterns for practical and secure authentication. In: Third International Conference on Digital Information Management (ICDIM 2008), pp. 559–562. IEEE, Piscataway (2008)

42. Thiebes, S., Lins, S., Basten, D. (eds.): Gamifying information systems - a synthesis of gamification mechanics and dynamics. In: ECIS, Tel Aviv, Israel (2014)
43. Thornton, D., Francia, G.I.: Gamification of information systems and security training: Issues and case studies. Inf. Secur. Edu. J. **1**(1), 19–29 (2014)
44. Uellenbeck, S., Dürmuth, M., Wolf, C., Holz, T.: Quantifying the security of graphical passwords: the case of android unlock patterns. In: Proceedings of the 2013 ACM SIGSAC Conference on Computer & Communications Security, CCS 2013, pp. 161–172. ACM, New York (2013). http://doi.acm.org/10.1145/2508859.2516700
45. Wang, P.: Pattern Recognition, Machine Intelligence and Biometrics. Springer, Heidelberg (2012)
46. Yee, K.P.: Aligning security and usability. IEEE Comput. Soc. **2**(5), 48–55 (2004)
47. Zakaria, N.H., Griffiths, D., Brostoff, S., Yan, J.: Shoulder surfing defence for recall-based graphical passwords. In: Cranor, L.F. (ed.) Proceedings of the Seventh Symposium on Usable Privacy and Security, vol. 2011, pp. 1–12. ACM, New York (2011)
48. von Zezschwitz, E., De Luca, A., Hussmann, H.: Survival of the shortest: a retrospective analysis of influencing factors on password composition. In: Kotzé, P., Marsden, G., Lindgaard, G., Wesson, J., Winckler, M. (eds.) INTERACT 2013, Part III. LNCS, vol. 8119, pp. 460–467. Springer, Heidelberg (2013)
49. Zichermann, G., Cunningham, C.: Gamification by Design: Implementing Game Mechanics in Web and Mobile Apps, 1st edn. O'Reilly Media, Sebastopol (2011)

Improving the Length of Customer Relationships on the Mobile Computer Game Business

Erno Vanhala and Jussi Kasurinen[✉]

LUT School of Business and Management, Lappeenranta University of Technology,
P.O. Box 20, 53851 Lappeenranta, Finland
{erno.vanhala, jussi.kasurinen}@lut.fi

Abstract. Long lasting customer relationships have proven to be beneficial to the success of a company. The computer game business has traditionally been about developing and then selling products to the customers, but today the games apply different marketing strategies such as free-to-play model, which changes the role of a customer. The Existence, Relatedness and Growth (ERG) theory provides a model to assess how the customer could be understood, and why the game companies should implement features that support growth of the customers' presence and make them a critical component to the developer. In this article we compare five game companies to find out how they understand their customers, how they build their relationships and let customers to grow their online identity. The results show that the growth is still minor concern, but companies have plans to improve this aspect.

Keywords: Computer games · Customer relationship · Customer-driven innovation · ERG

1 Introduction

Creating computer games is not only a decision of selecting the right technologies and drawing fancy user interfaces with characters, it also requires other areas of expertise such as design and marketing. The software development side of games has been studied, for example, from the viewpoints of information systems, psychology, management, computer science and sociology [1]. In general, the computer games are a mixture of storytelling, community management and software application, with the same life cycles and success models than any other information system [1]. When developing such an application, the suitable technologies are only one part of the entire system. If the game application aims for long-lasting customer relationships, the developers need to think also business models [2] and social interactions.

Not many games are played ten years after their release. However, there are success stories which defy the expected life cycles; for example the World of Warcraft (WoW, released 2005) has managed to maintain a constant customer base, especially if compared to the Final Fantasy XI (released 2002), or to the Lord of the Rings Online (released 2007) which are comparable products. Constantly updating the content and

S. Nurcan et al. (Eds.): CAiSE 2016, LNCS 9694, pp. 116–132, 2016.
DOI: 10.1007/978-3-319-39696-5_8

the players' ability to build identity in WoW is different from the others, and they either have been financially appalling, or have declined in the user numbers.

In this research we studied five computer game companies and what their CEOs and game designers think about the role of their customer in their business and in their mobile games. We also wanted to study how customers' game experience is compared to the real-life experiences. To achieve this we used Existence, Relatedness and Growth (ERG) theory [3] to map the game environment to the real-life environment.

The research questions are *"How is the role of customers understood in a mobile game business?"* and *"How do customers build their identities in the mobile games?"*. This work is also a continuance study on our previous work [2], which studied the business and revenue models of the game companies. The computer and console gaming industry has 30–40 years of history and customer experiences, but the mobile game business is less than 15 year old, especially if considering only the ability to sell third party products for the mobile devices, while discounting the purpose-built handheld consoles. During this time, the high growth rate has made the game industry both economically relevant, and interesting for the scientific research.

In the field of information systems and software engineering it is considerably easy to benefit from the customers in the product development, especially when compared to shipbuilding or construction business. This can be achieved, for example, by having continuous discussion with the customer (e.g. feedback in app stores) or by building analytical tools inside the product that can report, for example, how the customers use the product and what are the design problems with the product.

2   Related Research

Computer games and customer relationships are not a very thoroughly studied topic, since only a handful of articles discussing the related areas were discovered, and they all were written after the year 2000. Although the topic is new, Henfridsson and Holmström [4] reported already in 2002 a study where one computer game company included customers in their development process before the release of a product. They built community for the players and received ideas, bug reports and votes for different new features. In addition, Desouza et al. [5] argue that software industries are moving from the customer-focused innovation to the customer-driven innovation. They use a case of a computer game company as an example on how innovations are gathered from their customers. In a literature review conducted by Bogers et al. [6] the users utilized as innovators was studied. Besides being the sources of innovation and design, they can also act as innovators. Von Hippel [7] continued this concept by describing how innovative users are often the ones who are early adopters of new things. He also argues how these early adopters may value the process of innovation, just because of the enjoyment it brings to them.

Jung et al. [8] present a study on how the intention to play is dependent on the user-centric design, technological capability and product capability. Fang and Zhao [9] had a similar study, where they argue that the player, game technology, social influence and the perceived ease of use affect the intention to play. Finally, Lewis et al. [10] analyzed how Zynga's 'Ville-game family (e.g. FarmVille) engage and retain customers. They study these games from the viewpoints of behavioral economics and behavioral psychology, and found out how these games use many motivational techniques such as progress bars, several in-game resources, bonuses and "altruistic" social actions to engage the customers and gain concrete income from them.

Although the computer games are built with technological solutions, the technology itself does not provide entertaining experience for the players nor does it provide income for the developers [11, 12]. In general, the game development work is somewhat different from the conventional software development as it includes parts such as graphical aspects, story design and sound work which are closer to the domain of movie business rather than software. Also, the computer game industry business models have changed significantly over the years: the business has moved from pay-to-play to free-to-play, where the revenues are not directly related to the units sold, but instead are based on the advertising and in-app-purchases from the product [13].

Extensive research has been carried out on how people interact and develop their presence in the online communities [14–16], and Hsiao and Chiou [17] argue that communities generated by computer games also fulfil the definition of an online community. Different sized communities work with different methods and goals, and it is important to design the communal and social aspects from the beginning.

In some cases, when the purpose is strong enough, the computer game does not necessarily have to have a special techniques for building identity. This can happen, for example, in a game that focuses on very narrow field like very realistic war simulations. Some players and their input is respected more than others, and they might become the rule policy makers in their community. Niche games can also grow to become widely played, when the community around the game is dynamic and has the necessary tools. This happened with Minecraft, where the developer allowed the users to do modifications and build communities, videos, tools and other things [18].

Part of the process is also getting recognition. Studies [19, 20] have indications on how members find the recognition as an important part of being in an online community. These communities build their online presence and even do self-marketing. Recognition in this environment can even increase member's own self-esteem, as getting recognition builds one's role and helps in the process of building online identity.

In our previous study [2] we discovered how the role of customer is defined in the computer game organizations. All the elements of the business models are not directly related to customers, but the elements like customer relationship and customer segment are parts that include customers. These elements were not considered the most important ones but in the end, the customers fund the games and validate the results of the innovation process. Usually the aim is not to serve everyone as it is not economically feasible, but to concentrate on strengths such as own niche, understanding the markets [21] and trying to engage more potential users. Still, a game surpassing the intended target audience or gathering customers from every demographic is not unheard of; some famous digital games such as the Angry Birds or FarmVille are basically played by everyone. The concept of business model combines all these elements and provides the company a view on how the business is run, what value is provided by whom, and what is got in return [22].

3   Research Process

This study follows the multiple case study method based on frameworks presented by Gable [23] and Eisenhardt [24]. We followed seven steps: defining the strategy, reviewing the literature, developing the case study protocol, conducting a pilot case study, conducting a multiple case study, developing a conceptual model and interpreting the findings. Our research questions, presented in the Sect. 1, determined the overall strategy. Section 2 shed light on the related literature. This case study was based on two interview rounds, where the first discussed general topics of the computer game business and the second focused deeply on the role of a customer. Data was collected through series of interview rounds where one or two researchers interviewed company representatives such as lead designers, owners, and developers. The companies for these interviews were selected from our pool of existing research partners, and supplemented with contacts from business conferences and trade fairs. The amount of interviewees fluctuated between one to three people based on who the company decided to send, based on the given outline of topics that would be covered in the interview. Typically one interview lasted one hour, and included approximately 20–25 semi-structured questions which allowed also open discussions. The questionnaires are available at http://www2.it.lut.fi/GRIP

The transcriptions were then coded and analyzed following the principles of Straussian Grounded Theory analysis [25] with open, axial and selective coding. Based on this work, the conceptual models presented in the Sects. 4 and 5 were defined. Principles derived from [23, 26, 27] were utilized to guarantee the validity. Our choices included selection of interviews as the data collection method, coding as the data analysis method and utilizing several researcher in the interview, analysis and writing process to avoid bias.

To analyze human needs, motivations and satisfaction, science has developed a variety of methods. There are Maslow's hierarchy of needs [28], Herzberg's two-way theory [29], Alderfer's ERG (existence, relatedness and growth) theory [3] and technology acceptance model (TAM) from Davis [30] – to name a few. Although all these are used in research, we decided to concentrate on ERG theory, as it is simpler than Maslow's hierarchy of needs and considered reliable [3].

In the ERG theory three categories of human needs are used [3]: Existence is the lowest level and it includes the basic physiological and material desires. Relatedness, the second level, includes relationships and sharing of thoughts. The second level cannot be achieved without mutuality. Growth is the highest level and includes desires to be creative and productive. The model is built in a simple format so that it can be straightforwardly adapted to other environments, for example to be used by companies improving their customer relationship. We selected ERG so that it would be the most beneficial also to computer game industry.

3.1   ERG in Digital Environment

Kim [31] described the hierarchy of needs in both offline and online environments, into which our work defined the computer game context. It is worth noting that in the online or in the game environment the needs are not the same as offline, but work on the same principle. For example, offline we do not need system access, but online and in games it is the first requirement. Similarly, in online context the food as a physical concept is not needed, but in offline the nutrition is important. After the essential components are working, it is possible to start developing of relatedness and growth features to the computer games. As ERG theory has only three different parts, its application does not require large changes, just the fulfillment of the hierarchy levels: the lower level needs have to be fulfilled before advancing to the higher levels. For example, when the criteria for the existence level have been met, the developers can start to think how they can give players a way to express relatedness inside the game. The model is summarized in the Table 1.

Table 1. Needs of different ERG levels and different systems. Based on [3, 31].

Need	Offline (Alderfer 1973)	Online (Kim 2000)	Computer game
Existence	Food, sex, health and protection from weather and crimes	System access. Protection from hacking and personal attacks	Access to the game – knowledge about the game and device to run it. Protection of personal information inside the game and inside the marketplace
Relatedness	The ability to love, feel belongingness to a community. Ability to receive respect and contribute to society	The ability to build one's online identity. Belongingness to a community and its sub groups. Ability to contribute and be recognized for those contributions	Ability to build one's identity inside game, i.e. to be able to build character throughout the game. Ability to contribute and interact with different gamers and be recognized for those contributions
Growth	The ability to be creative and fulfill one's potential	The ability to take role in the community and take advantage of opportunities by improving skills and learning new things	The ability to take role in the game community and take advantage of opportunities to be able to contribute to game development and learn new skills

3.2 Case Organizations

Our study had five participating game organizations. Some of these organizations have a catalogue of games, some are developing their first product. The priority platform indicates the focus platforms, for which the companies design and develop their products. The products may be later migrated to other platforms if the product is successful or commercially interesting in another platform. Based on this definition, Case A is a PC and game console company, cases B, D and E mobile game developers and Case C browser-game developer, although every organization has launched at least one product on a mobile platform. Table 2 illustrates some key figures.

Table 2. Summary of case organizations

	Case A	Case B	Case C	Case D	Case E
Years in business	More than 5	3	3	3	Less than 2
Team size*	Large	Medium	Medium	Small	Small
Priority platform	PC, game consoles	Mobile devices, PC	Browser, mobile devices	Health-care environment, mobile devices	Mobile devices
Number of released products	More than 10	2 released, 2 under development	2 released, 1 under development	Various health-care projects done	Developing its first release
Ways to collect gamer feedback	App stores, reviews, social media, early prototype testing by players	Facebook, app stores	Facebook, Twitter, Blog, app stores, own feedback channel	Customers can write memos, give oral feedback or take photos	Facebook, Twitter
Ways to collect analytical data	Nothing right now, statistical analysis in the future	Use of 3rd party tool to see how players play the game	Statistics are collected inside the game to see how gamers play the game	No direct access to data but only through health-care professionals	Statistics are collected inside the game to see how gamers play the game

* Small is less than 10 persons working for the game product, medium is 10 to 50 persons and large is more than 50 persons, including outsourced workers and developers of the bought assets.

4   Customers Role and Possibilities in Computer Games

The identity building inside game is not a new concept. Even old games like Quake (1996) let players to customize their game character in the multiplayer sessions and thus build their identity. Newer games, such as StarCraft II (2010), engage their users more via online multiplayer options and give active players badges, which are used to open new modification options. The growth level has been achieved in many games through modability. With the modern games the modding tools provide ways to develop whole new content, providing the players a method to grow their presence in the game community. The mobile games are still a new and rapidly growing industry, and these relatedness and growth issues have not been implemented in most of the games – although exceptions like Clash of Clans (2012) or Candy Crush Soda Saga (2013), which utilize players combined effort, exists.

4.1   Who is the Customer?

As the revenue models, especially in mobile gaming, have changed from the direct sales to the free-to-play concept [13], where the revenue is gained from in-app-purchasing and advertising while the game itself is provided for free. This introduces the dilemma if the customer of the game company is the player of the game, or the advertiser who generates the company's income?

The general view in this study was that the players are the real customers although not all of them are generating revenue. For example, the Case C identifies game players as their customers and describe how they focus their game development on ideas from this audience. For Case C it is the key point of their business to have a working relationship with the customers, which in practice means that the organization listens and actively collects input from their customers. For Case C there exists two kinds of players: those who use the in-app-purchases, and those who just play with the free features.

> *"We live from the masses. We are doing multiplayer games. Players need to have other players as enemies; whether they are paying players or not. Thus it is very important for us that we have a lot of players. The paying customer is important, but non-paying are also crucial."* -CEO, Case C.

Case B sees the players as their customers and they have created an online presence where players can communicate their thought concerning the game. They have found it difficult to respond to the feedback when it is written in a system that gives no possibility for an answer. It creates frustration among the developers as they would like to reply, but are unable.

> *"The <platform's> appstore system is a bit nasty in sense that we cannot give feedback through it. If someone asks a question there we have no way to answer."* -CEO, Case B.

Most of the case organizations consider the players as their customers – with the exception of Case D, which lists the health-care providers as their customers. All the players were seen as important whether they are paying or not. Mainly the reason is that the games require sufficient player base, and it can only be reached when the non-paying gamers are also treated as importantly as the paying ones. In other business models, such as the pay-to-play-model for the console games, this consideration is not as relevant; everybody pays to use the software, so all players are also customers.

4.2 Customers Role in Game Development

Our earlier study illustrated the role of the customer relationship as it was described as one of the elements the computer game business model is built on [2]. All of the cases have thought the data collecting process, and have built ways to collect data from the players. Reviews in the app stores and gaming websites are important sources of feedback. Also direct feedback in the social media is considered useful, and Case C has even build its own channel to get direct feedback. As Case D is doing serious games their data collection process is different. They get memos and photos from the customers and can have meetings with them. This is not widely available with the other cases, who make games for global markets.

> "We have a feedback system where a patient can give daily feedback on how the exercise has been and they can give oral or written feedback or take a pic and ask help. But no real content creation exists." -CEO, Case D

> "We have our own feedback channel where gamers can put their reports to. Our game has link to that. Then of course the reviews in app stores where we cannot answer but we get feedback from the comments. We have <social media> pages and game pages from where we get some comments." -Lead designer, Case C.

Besides the direct feedback from players, cases have ways to collect analytical data from the games. They get data to show for example how much the different levels are played, what brings the game to an end and how long the game sessions last. Case A did not have any analytical modules installed, but they were planning to do so in the future. Case D could only get data through their health-care organizations.

The collected data was mainly used to improve the game and the gaming experience to be more entertaining. This can be done for example by removing too difficult places from the game levels or adjusting parameters like health bars or points.

Virtually all the cases used statistical analysis on the collected metrics to understand how the players behave, where they get stuck and what features they mostly used. The Case B had dialogue with players and they also spent resources to analyze their own games to identify how players feel towards the newly introduced features, whether or not they used them, or if some parts were too difficult or easy.

> "We have used <analytics tool>. We follow where players die in different levels and thus we can analyze whether some sector is too hard if too much players have difficulties" -CEO, Case B.

> "Statistics tell us how the game is played. Whether players get stuck, do they like the game, how long they play... The collected data leads the game design – especially in free-to-play world." -CEO, Case E.

Our cases report to value the players and their feedback. Still, the actual player contribution to the game development is narrow. None of the case companies supported user-generated content (e.g. levels, characters, items). The only reported cases were Case A, which allowed players to make their own maps in their previous games, and Case C, which used graphics drawn by one of the fans of their game. It seems that the players cannot take active role in the development process, but their current role is to give feedback and ideas. We can argue that customers are taken into account in the innovation process, but the criteria for the customer-driven innovation is not met. From all the cases only A and C could be categorized in customer-centric innovation, and the rest are still working in the customer-focused innovation.

Additionally, there is a difference between the single player and multiplayer games. In a single player game it is easier to let players create content, but in the multiplayer games the game content, for example levels, need to be well balanced and cannot include cheats that would benefit one gamer over others.

> *"In single player game it is ok to do mods and share them to other players but in our case it is not possible as the players could create a cheat mode and gain benefit over other players."* - Lead designer, Case C.

4.2.1   Existence

The existence level is easy to achieve, as the game industry is moving towards the digital distribution models. This makes games available for everyone who has a device that can run the game. When talking about the mobile games, many of them are made with the technical solutions that allow cross-platform development options, which promotes the concept of developing the same game for different operating systems. The revenue model can be different between platforms, even if the game itself remains the same, like in Case B:

> *"Both of our first two games started as pay-to-play and they had also in-app-purchases options from the beginning. Now the both are also pay-to-play – the first game was free in the middle - but we put it back to paid one when we released the second game. In few weeks we will offer the games with free-to-play model. … 60–70 percent of revenue comes from in-app-purchases."* - CEO, Case B.

For both the Cases B and C the problem is not the access to the game, but the knowledge of the game. In our previous study, marketing was ranked as the second most important element in the business model amongst the start-up computer game companies [2]. When a game is released in the mobile application store, it is just one app within thousands of rivals, and making the potential players aware of the new game is hard. To raise awareness of a game among the players is not easy, and it seems that the computer game start-ups are aware of this problem [2].

> *"<Platform's> promotion is very important. If you get your game to 'New and noteworthy" it raises revenues and after that it will take it high for a while. Or if you get Editor's Choice it is even better."* -CEO, Case B.

> *"We have been going with the idea that we are unknown – invisible – and we don't have marketing know-how. The first games are exported to different countries via a publisher, who then gives us the coverage"* -CEO, Case C.

To have the protection of the personal information is difficult, but as the mobile games are targeted towards casual gamers, personal information is not always required. The privacy issues are getting more and more important and that was why the case organizations had also thought about it, although it was not a major problem. None of the case organizations was acutely worried that their systems might leak data. Third party services are used to handle money transactions, and no meaningful personal information is collected by the developer themselves.

"We do not store credit card information but use well-known third party service providers, such as PayPal." -Lead designer, Case C.

"Of course we need to have some kind of disclaimer to tell what data is collected but we are not interested on individual players. We have no way to identify a specific player. ... Individuals are not important but the mass data. ... Advertisers would not even benefit from our data. No one but us is interested in how 14 % of gamers get stuck on level 18." -CEO, Case E.

We also considered localization to be on the existence level as players are unable to play the game if they do not understand the language. All our case organizations localized their games to various languages, usually at least English, German, French, Russian, (Brazilian) Portuguese and Korean. Interviewees commented that although English is widely spoken, the situation is not the same in every country.

"It can be noted when we haven't made localization to some appstore description and when the localization is done later there is a spike [in downloads]." -CEO, Case B.

4.2.2   Relatedness

After the foundation of existence has been reached and the players have access to the game and they feel secure, the developers can start to work on providing features that give the feeling of relatedness. Our case organizations use achievements and grades, which give the player one to three stars from each level they pass based on the certain criteria. If these achievements and grades can be shared, then the feature supports relatedness amongst the players. For Case D, the achievements were themed around exercising so that health-care professionals could see how patients are doing.

"In a way we have achievements as the game will tell how many training exercises you have done in a row and applauds the person." -CEO, Case D.

Cases A and B use integration to social media instances so that the players can build profiles for example in the Facebook and communicate it with their friends. Case A also lets players to chat with each other inside the game. This is different from for example Case C, which sees that the in-game chat could be misused, so they only plan to build emotion based chat, that would not need any form of moderating.

"At the moment we do not have chat in our games. We have thought about it but not implemented as it will bring the problem of moderation. Players could shout obscenities that could bring problems. We are probably not implementing any clear chat." -Lead designer, Case C.

Building an identity inside the game could be started by letting the players customize their game character. Only Case C has implemented this feature, and even it was completed in a small scale. Case E had the idea to utilize this feature in the future, and Case B argued that it did not fit to their games, which were story based around the existing characters. They also mentioned that a game under development will include characters that will allow customization.

"Player can do some customization. They can for example select what kind of armor the game character has. It has both the action aspect and the visual aspect." -CEO, Case B.

In computer games, one form of interaction is the players competing against each other. Cases A and C have been building multiplayer games where the players are against other real individuals. When the game requires gamers to be online at the same time, it means that there needs to be large number of players to play the game. This has been challenging to Case C.

"Our philosophy has been that player will get an opponent in quick response. If no human player is available an AI will play against the player. Now we are actually implementing system where AI will play actual player account when real player has not logged in lately." -Lead designer, Case C.

Case E is concentrating on the single player games, and Case B has also been building single player game, but is now developing in parallel a game including interaction and competition between gamers.

"[This new game] has been developed based on social interaction. It is more social than Clash of Clans. The aim has been that player stay in the game if they feel like being part of a community. We aim that everyone does one's bit." -CEO, Case B.

4.2.3   Growth

After achieving the feeling of relatedness, the players aim for growth. On one hand, the short mobile games do not necessary have features for supporting this kind of behavior, but on the other hand larger games, such as StarCraft II, have features enabling players to engage themselves with other players; to build teams and arrange tournaments. Some mobile games, like Clash of Clans, have introduced these team building concepts also to the games where playing session is shorter.

Cases D and E had no real plans to provide features that would enable players to grow their presence in the games. Especially CEO of Case D did not see it happening in the near future, as the main aim for their product was to heal patients. Case E had some ideas which could be provided at some point, but as they were just releasing their first product, they did not have resources to implement anything non-critical.

"[User generated levels and map editor] have been thought but we would need someone to program it, develop the UI and we would need to have server backend to provide all the content. Right now we don't have the resources. We need to concentrate on what we have." -CEO, Case E.

CEO of Case B described how their forthcoming mobile game will rely heavily on the social aspect and require players to co-operate to achieve success in the game. Instead of playing as an individuals, players build a role in the community, and can lead the group if chosen so.

"On regular intervals there will be decision on whether the group will continue with the old leader or is there going to be new one on the lead" -CEO, Case B.

Similar ideas were presented by Case C, as they wanted to extend their mobile game to include clans and four-level leader-hierarchy in them.

"We are designing a system to fit multiplayer concept where individuals in clan could exchange objects. The clan could also work together and play against another clan." -Lead designer, Case C.

4.3 Summary of Findings

The observations lead us to consider that the mobile games are gaining features from the bigger games to support growth of players' identities. The first mobile games 15–20 years ago were just simple games designed to fit the small screen, but today mobile games are as important market segment as the dedicated game consoles. This has also created a need for improved methods to immerse the players in the game. However, as identified in the previous study analyzing business models and factors in the business activities [2], the role of a customer – player – is still not one of the main concerns driving the business decisions. The customer concerns are not considered important in the game development process, but inside the game product, players have some ways to build identity and get recognized. Example of this is that several games from our case organizations include various features that can be categorized with the ERG theory. Table 3 describes these features.

In the interviews, the game company representatives described how they value players and want to be in touch with them. Yet, it seems that they are not letting their customers to contribute to the actual game development process. This behavior differs from the "open source spirit" which can be characterized as the "customer-driven development", meaning that our case organizations are mostly customer-focused, not customer-driven. Players' feedback is valued and it can change the game design over some time, and statistics from games are used to improve games, but it in general the players have quite passive role with the product.

5 Discussion

All our case organizations have found a way to meet the existence level with the access, localization and security, but the knowledge has been more problematic. As a solution for this, all the organizations mention marketing and advertising, which increases the awareness of potential players. It seems that especially the designers of young organizations do not see it important to build features to support growth, or even relatedness. This is partly explained by the haste of getting the products to the market, since when the business starts to get in shape, the designers can also put more effort to design the features for the growth. Yet we still argue that mobile games are just getting the features of social interaction that the console, PC and Internet games have had for years. One of the biggest difference is the time spend with the game session, as the mobile games can be played when waiting for coffee, but the console games require more time spend with the product. This makes it easier for the console game developers to build features for support relatedness and growth. The new first person shooters have in-game voice-chats, which can be used when playing. The designers of short mobile games have to develop a method of communication that can be used in seconds with just few thump swipes.

Table 3. Features in games in different levels

	Case A	Case B	Case C	Case D	Case E
Existence	Games available on various formats on various platforms; games are localized to different languages (5+)	Games available on most popular platforms and publisher doing marketing; games are localized to different languages (10+)	Promotion by platform owner; security by using money transfers services; games are localized (10+)	Devices and games available through health-care institutions; games are localized to different languages	Games are available through app stores; no personal information is collected or stored; games are localized
Relatedness	Achievements; integrated to Facebook and other social media to identify oneself and invite friends and interact with them; gamers can communicate through in-game chats; competing against other gamers	Achievements; communication through 3rd party service with friends; competing against other gamers*; tasks that can be completed only with help of other gamers*; game character can be customized*	(Achievements); game character can be customized; competing against other gamers; emotion based chat*	Achievements: how much exercising has been done	Achievements; game character can be customized*
Growth	Maps in the previous games	Gamer groups have a leader who will be re-elected on constant intervals*	Four different levels of leaders in a clan*	None identified	None identified

* denotes feature-in-development

Still, in the end we believe that mobile games are gaining these features and play sessions are also getting longer.

Currently, the mobile games are basically played by everyone. This is a big difference from the 80's, when games were limited mostly to the special interest hobby groups. Current game designers have to take into account both casual gamers who are not very invested in the product, and the hard-core players, who spend hours per day in the game and learn all the details of the game mechanics.

5.1   ERG and Customers

The customers are seen as a part of the business model [2], but to be able to generate revenue from the players, there needs to exist some form of working game and the business logic, which transform users to profit. This is especially important when the free-to-play model is utilized, since there are business reports (e.g. [32]) which indicate that only less than three percent of the player population actually pays for the product, and less than half a percent of the players actually generate serious income. At the same time, almost half of the users open it less than five times.

Even if majority of the players are just free-riders, maintaining the player population is the strategy which is critical to the free-2-play games. In this article we have presented how ERG theory can be utilized to help the design to support long customer relationship within the game, and thus improve the possibility to generate more revenue from retaining the players and providing them with more meaningful tasks.

As we utilized three level ERG theory, it is also noteworthy how it has similarities to the customer-focused, customer-centric and customer-driven development of computer games. We argue that moving from the existence to the relatedness and growth requires also moving from the customer-focused design to the customer-centric, and even to the customer-driven design. To engage players in games it is important to let them fulfil their objectives, and allow them to build their identities and generate content. By providing techniques for the players to grow their online identity, developers also provide a way to build lasting customer relationships as the user has personal interest to stay with the game. This should be addressed when the business decisions are made in design, and the business model is being build. When games include online identity for the players, it binds them deeper into the game, possibly increasing the retention rate of players. Besides business model, these issues need to be designed into game and business logic.

5.2   Limitations of the Study

Qualitative studies are not without their threats and limitations. For example, Robson [33] in his classification and explanation identified three main types of threats: researcher bias, observational bias and reactivity. The researcher bias is considered to be the most dangerous as it represents a situation where researchers aim to enforce their own ideas and opinions. In this study, the researcher bias was taken into account by conducting the data collection in cooperation with another research group and the initial data analysis included three researchers, so that no one could push their own agenda. The data collection setups and instruments were also designed by at least two researchers. The interviewed organizations represent different sizes, release platforms and maturities of organizations, and interview sessions included several different stakeholders in the companies thus decreasing the interviewee bias. Although all the case organizations are located in Finland, they work in the global markets and represent a wide scale of industry practitioners. However, there might be some underlying peculiarities imposed by the business culture, education system or local authorities. Additionally, the results presented here present the viewpoint of the game developers on the customer roles and participation. Because of privacy issues, the actual customers were not used in this study. Qualitative studies also have their own limitations in the applicability of the results. Whittemore et al. [34] argue how the objective of qualitative studies is to describe chain-of-evidence what the studied phenomenon represents. In any case, the observations perceived are only applicable in the context of the observed phenomenon. If these results are interpreted outside the original scope they should only be applied as recommendations or suggestions.

6   Conclusion

This study presented how different sized and aged game developers focus on their customers in the development of new product combining information systems and software engineering. The results indicate that the mobile game development is not providing as much possibilities to the players to build their virtual identity as games that are played with dedicated consoles or PCs. The ERG (existence, relatedness and growth) theory provides a way to analyze how the customers can build their virtual identity. As the lower level needs has to be fulfilled first, it provides the game developers a framework or roadmap to consider when moving from the customer-focused development to the customer-driven development should be considered. This aims to build longer customer relationships, which provides more revenue. This would also benefit the mobile developers directly, since the current business model of free-2-play heavily depends on the acquisition of player population, and better retention means achieving meaningful volume with smaller population of players, also requiring smaller advertisement budget for visibility.

This study raises questions and recommendations on how to design mobile games in the future, when the markets are saturated and the players expect more options. However, more research is required to compare the growth of mobile games to the conventional PC and console games before making any strong suggestions.

References

1. Iriberri, A., Leroy, G.: A life-cycle perspective on online community success. ACM Comput. Surv. **41**(2), 1–29 (2009)
2. Vanhala, E., Kasurinen, J.: The role of business model and its elements in computer game start-ups. In: Lassenius, C., Smolander, K. (eds.) ICSOB 2014. LNBIP, vol. 182, pp. 72–87. Springer, Heidelberg (2014)

3. Schneider, B., Alderfer, C.P.: Three studies of measures of need satisfaction in organizations. Adm. Sci. Q. **18**(4), 489–505 (1973)
4. Henfridsson, O., Holmström, H.: Developing e-commerce in internetworked organizations: a case of customer involvement throughout the computer gaming value chain. ACM SIGMIS Database **33**(4), 38–50 (2002)
5. Desouza, K.C., Awazu, Y., Jha, S., Dombrowski, C., Papagari, S., Baloh, P., Kim, J.Y.: Customer-driven innovation. Res. Technol. Manag. **51**(3), 35–44 (2008)
6. Bogers, M., Afuah, A., Bastian, B.: Users as innovators: a review, critique, and future research directions. J. Manag. **36**(4), 857–875 (2010)
7. von Hippel, E.: Democratizing Innovation. MIT Press, Cambridge (2005)
8. Jung, H.S., Kim, K.H., Lee, C.H.: Influences of perceived product innovation upon usage behavior for MMORPG: product capability, technology capability, and user centered design. J. Bus. Res. **67**(10), 2171–2178 (2014). doi:10.1016/j.jbusres.2014.04.027
9. Fang, X., Zhao, F.: Personality and enjoyment of computer game play. Comput. Ind. **61**(4), 342–349 (2010)
10. Lewis, C., Wardrip-Fruin, N., Whitehead, J.: Motivational game design patterns of 'ville games. In: Proceedings of the International Conference on the Foundations of Digital Games, Raleigh, North Carolina, p. 172 (2012). http://dx.doi.org/10.1145/2282338.2282373
11. Chesbrough, H.: Business model innovation: it's not just about technology anymore. Strategy Leadersh. **35**(6), 12–17 (2007)
12. Yuan, Y., Zhang, J.J.: Towards an appropriate business model for m-commerce. Int. J. Mob. Commun. **1**(1), 35–56 (2003)
13. Ren, J.Q., Hardwick, P.: Revenue model innovations in the Chinese online game market. In: Proceedings of the 12th International Conference on Entertainment and Media in the Ubiquitous Era, Tampere, Finland, p. 44 (2008) http://dx.doi.org/10.1145/1457199.1457209
14. Dippelreiter, B., Grün, C., Pöttler, M., Seidel, I., Berger, H., Dittenbach, M., Pesenhofer, A.: Online tourism communities on the path to web 2.0: an evaluation. Inf. Technol. Tour. **10**(4), 329–353 (2008)
15. O'Donnell, D., Porter, G., McGuire, D., Garavan, T.N., Heffernan, M., Cleary, P.: Creating intellectual capital: a Habermasian community of practice (CoP) introduction. J. Eur. Ind. Training **27**(2/3/4), 80–87 (2003)
16. Preece, J.: Online Communities: Designing Usability, Supporting Sociability. John Wiley, New York (2000)
17. Hsiao, C.-C., Chiou, J.-S.: The impact of online community position on online game continuance intention: do game knowledge and community size matter? Inf. Manag. **49**(6), 292–300 (2012)
18. Lastowka, G.: Minecraft as web 2.0: amateur creativity & digital games. SSRN Electron. J. (2011). http://dx.doi.org/10.2139/ssrn.1939241
19. Butler, B., Sproull, L., Kiesler, S., Kraut, R.: Community Effort in Online Groups: Who Does the Work and Why? Human-Computer Interaction Institute (2007)
20. Hars, A., Ou, S.: Working for free? Motivations for participating in open-source projects. Int. J. Electron Commer. **6**(3), 25–39 (2002). http://www.jstor.org/stable/27751021
21. Kotler, P.: A generic concept of marketing. J. Mark. **36**(2), 46–54 (1972)
22. Vanhala, E., Määttänen, M., Smolander, K.: In-service promotion as a business model for social web applications. In: Advances in Business-Related Scientific Research Conference 2013, Venice, Italy (2013)
23. Gable, G.G.: Integrating case study and survey research methods: an example in information systems. Eur. J. Inf. Syst. **3**, 112–126 (1994)

24. Eisenhardt, K.M.: Building theories from case study research. Acad. Manag. Rev. **14**(4), 532 (1989)
25. Strauss, A.L., Corbin, J.M.: Basics of Qualitative Research: Grounded Theory Procedures and Techniques. Sage Publications, Newbury Park (1990)
26. Klein, H.K., Myers, M.D.: A set of principles for conducting and evaluating interpretive field studies in information systems. MIS Q. **23**(1), 67 (1999)
27. Meyer, C.B.: A case in case study methodology. Field Methods **13**(4), 329–352 (2001)
28. Maslow, A.: A theory of human motivation. Psychol. Rev. **50**, 370–396 (1943)
29. Herzberg, F.: One more time: how do you motivate employees? Harvard Bus. Rev. **46**(1), 53–62 (1968)
30. Davis, F.D.: Perceived usefulness, perceived ease of use, and user acceptance of information technology. MIS Q. **13**(3), 319–340 (1989)
31. Kim, A.: Community Building on the Web. Peachpit Press, Berkeley (2000)
32. Swrve: The Swrve New Players Report. http://landingpage.swrve.com/rs/swrve/images/new-players-report-0414.pdf. Accessed 04 Nov 2015
33. Robson, C.: Real World Research, 2nd edn. Blackwell Publishing, Hoboken (2002)
34. Whittemore, R., Chase, S.K., Mandle, C.L.: Validity in qualitative research. Qual. Health Res. **11**(4), 522–537 (2001)

ADInnov: An Intentional Method to Instil Innovation in Socio-Technical Ecosystems

Mario Cortes-Cornax[1(✉)], Agnès Front[1], Dominique Rieu[1],
Christine Verdier[1], and Fabrice Forest[2]

[1] LIG, Univ. Grenoble Alpes, 38000 Grenoble, France
{mario.cortes-cornax,agnes.front,dominique.rieu,
christine.verdier}@univ-grenoble-alpes.fr
[2] SFR INNOVACS, MSH-Alpes, 38040 Grenoble, France
fabrice.forest@univ-grenoble-alpes.fr

Abstract. This paper presents an intentional-based modelling method aimed to support the analysis, the diagnosis and innovations for socio-technical ecosystems. Understanding and improving socio-technical ecosystems is still indeed a major challenge in the information systems domain. Current information systems' methods do not consider the particularities of socio-technical ecosystems where breakthrough innovation is not always possible. The proposed method called ADInnov aims at guiding a continuous innovation cycle in socio-technical ecosystems by focusing on the resolution of their blocking points. It combines different user-centred techniques such as interviews, serious games or storyboarding. The method, represented with the MAP formalism, results from the lessons learned in a healthcare domain project (InnoServ). Through an empirical study, project managers evaluated the method appropriateness.

Keywords: Analysis · Diagnosis · Continuous innovation cycle · Socio-technical ecosystem · Organizational innovation · Service innovation · MAP

1 Introduction

Understanding, modelling and improving Socio-Technical (ST) ecosystems is still a major challenge in different information systems' areas such as virtual organizations (VO) [1], collaborative business processes (choreographies) [2] or multi-agent systems [3]. ST ecosystems refers to *an intricate ecosystem with a large number of actors playing various and variable functions, diversity of scenarios and special cases, abundance of flows, various interaction kinds, etc.* [4]. In particular, when trying to improve ST ecosystems such as healthcare, automating is not always possible and process-oriented approaches are extremely difficult to apply because of the afore-mentioned complexity [5]. When dealing with human-centred ecosystems, resistance to change is an important risk [6] and the integration and the mobilization of a wide group of stakeholders to support the potential improvements is critical [7]. In this context, breakthrough innovations are not always suitable. The innovations must be thought, accepted and ranked collectively. They must ensure the resolution of blocking points

© Springer International Publishing Switzerland 2016
S. Nurcan et al. (Eds.): CAiSE 2016, LNCS 9694, pp. 133–148, 2016.
DOI: 10.1007/978-3-319-39696-5_9

that are consensually recognized. In this context, our position is not to offer a method dedicated to innovation projects limited by time and costs and managed by a project team, but rather to instil in the ecosystems' heart an innovation culture. This is especially true in the current social innovation dynamics that impact many business ecosystems where traditional stakeholders and newcomers try to reinvent their businesses in order to optimise the "highest possible use value for the longest possible time while consuming as few material resources and energy as possible" [8].

Figure 1 presents a general view of the ADInnov method using the MAP formalism [9]. MAP models are directed graphs with nodes representing intentions and labelled edges capturing strategies. The main strategies presented in the paper are represented with thicker lines. The traditional approach *As-Is/To-Be* [10] is transformed into iterative cycles *As-Is/As-If*. The aim is to imagine innovation scenarios based on the question "And if?" that could be deployed in more or less long terms (even very long terms if the innovation requires legal or economic evolutions). Innovations should therefore be organized in a road map specifying when and how to be deployed. This could introduce new blocking points that require newer iterations implying new analysis and diagnosis and eventually the application of new innovation strategies. The iterative method will stop by choice of the consortium.

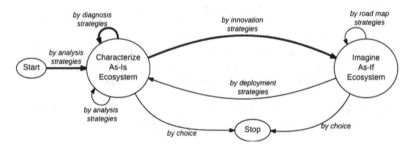

Fig. 1. General view of the *ADInnov* method

More specifically, the ADInnov method is dedicated to support the analysis and the diagnosis of ST ecosystems as well as to propose consensual innovations. *Analysis* explores the domain, identifies actors and their functions and divides the ecosystem in different views (responsibility networks and concerns) in order to manage its complexity. *Diagnosis* focuses on finding blocking points and inferring goals dedicated to resolve them. *Innovation* proposes organizational innovations (new functions, new groups of actors, etc.) and innovation services. ADInnov arises from the empirical user-centred method used during the InnoServ project[1] (*Innovation in Services for Frail People*). This project aimed to find organizational and low-tech-based solutions to maintain as long as possible frail people at home in total autonomy [11]. Soon became clear in this project that the traditional work-packages division was not adapted to the

---

[1] http://bit.ly/InnoServ_project.

project because a common understanding was essential. Instead, we adopted multi-disciplinary workshops with representation of the different partners of the project: the research laboratories, an innovation research federation, an association, a local authority and two private companies. Actors in the field such as physicians, nurses, council administrators or caregivers were integrated in the project progression and put forward essential information to understand and improve the ecosystem.

In a previous work [12], the main activities performed in the InnoServ project were extracted and represented as a BPMN business process diagram. In this paper, we aim to abstract and consolidate this previous work so that the method can be applied to other ecosystems. We use here the MAP formalism that allows achieving the desired level of abstraction, to easily support variability and to better represent the intentional considerations of innovative ecosystems, which tend to continuously innovate in an inductive way (based on inductive hypothesis or trials/errors). Moreover, compared to [12], this paper presents the ecosystem meta-model and a qualitative evaluation that we lead with innovation project managers in order to evaluate the appropriateness of the ADInnov method.

In the rest of the paper, Sect. 2 formalizes the main concepts of the method. Section 3 describes the ADInnov method, explaining the three main strategies (Analysis, Diagnosis and Innovation) and illustrating them through the InnoServ ecosystem. In order to prove the quality of the method, Sect. 4 details a qualitative study that we lead with several innovation project-managers (Sect. 4). The results of the InnoServ project were also evaluated and prove the efficiency of the method. Related works are presented in Sect. 5, where we give an overview of different methods, mostly focused on one of the three aforementioned strategies that we propose. Finally, we draw out conclusions and future work in Sect. 6.

2 Key Concepts Used in the ADInnov Method

This section presents the key concepts used in the ADInnov method. First, Sect. 2.1 gives the definition of the ecosystem according to the key concepts and presents our consideration of innovation in the context of ST ecosystems. Section 2.2 presents the detailed meta-model of an ecosystem and gives an instantiation example using the InnoServ ecosystem.

2.1 Innovation in an Ecosystem

Our focus is about intricate *ecosystems (Ec)* with a large number of actors playing various and variable functions, diversity of scenarios and special cases, abundance of flows, various interaction kinds, etc. [4]. Relying on this definition, an *actor (A)* is a type of physical or legal person who operates under its own business. Note that we call « actor » a type of actor. For instance, "nurse", or "physician" are (types of) actors. A *function (F)* corresponds to a skill or responsibility in the *Ec* involved in the realization of a service. This notion is equivalent to the well-known notion of "role" in the business process management domain [13]. In order to manage the *Ec* complexity, a decomposition approach is needed [14]. We propose the concept of *responsibility networks (RN)* to tackle this problem. A *RN* is a view on the *Ec* determined by the proximity (national, regional, individual, etc.) to the target (e.g., the frail person) and the actors involved on it. A *concern (C)* relates to a cross-cutting issue in the *Ec* that determines a point of interest of a provided service (e.g., financial, medical). A *blocking point (BP)* corresponds to a concrete problematic in the context of a *RN*. Several *BP* can be identified in a *RN*. *Goals (G)* are prescriptive statements about the system, capturing desired states or conditions [10]. Goals are hierarchically organized, starting from high level goals which can be iteratively refined into sub-goals. Goals do not define here the intentional process level, but the aim to resolve *BP*. A *service (S)* relates to a delivery consisting in the provision of technical and/or intellectual capacity or the provision of useful work for a beneficiary. It helps resolving a goal. A service contains a set of *concern services (CS)* that deals with the different concerns of the service. This leads us to the definition of the As-Is ecosystem that results from the application of the analysis and diagnosis strategies illustrated in Fig. 1 and detailed latter. The As-Is *ecosystem* is a set of *actors, functions, responsibility network, concerns, blocking points* and *services*. We consider a *blocking point* as a set of *goals* that resolve it, and a *service* as a set of *concern services:*

$$As\_Is(Ec) : \{\{A\}, \{F\}, \{RN\}, \{C\}, \{BP\}, \{S\}\}$$
$$BP : \{G\} \qquad S : \{CS\}$$

The innovation strategies (Fig. 1) transform an ecosystem *Ec* in an As-If ecosystem by the identification of a new set of *actors ({A'}), functions ({F'}), responsibility networks ({RN'}), concerns ({C'}), blocking points ({BP'})* and *services ({S'})*. The resulting set of blocking points ($\{BP'\}$) should be a subset of the previous one ($\{BP\}$) or the resulting goals linked to the blocking points *({G'})* have to be contained in the previous set *({G})*:

$$As\_If(Ec) = \{\{A'\}, \{F'\}, \{RN'\}, \{C'\}, \{BP'\}, \{S'\}\}$$
$$\{BP'\} \subset \{BP\} \vee \exists\, BP \in \{BP\} \wedge BP' \in \{BP'\}/\{G'\}_{BP'} \subset \{G\}_{BP}$$

The latter statement means that innovation leads to the identification of new actors, functions, responsibility networks, concerns or services but can also imply removals. For example a possible innovation could be to remove a (type of) actor in the ecosystem. The main objective of innovation, and therefore of our method, is to reach an ecosystem with less blocking points than before, or at least to have less goals to be achieved. Note that the deployment strategies of the imagined innovations can produce new blocking points that will have to be treated in a new iteration of the method. The adoption of risk management methods in the road map strategies could anticipate and therefore limit the introduction of these new blocking points.

This definition of an *Ec (As_Is or As_If)* is limited to the objectives of the method. More complex models would be more suited in case of different objectives. For instance, the requirements elicitation of the information system supporting the ecosystem may require the use of more complex modelling languages such as KAOS [10], URN [15] or i* [21].

2.2   Ecosystem Meta-Model

This section presents a generic ecosystem meta-model. Figures 2 and 3 capture the meta-model and provide two instantiation examples based on the InnoServ ecosystem. As a reminder, the InnoServ project seeks to understand and support innovation strategies and services around a frail person at home. Figure 2 instantiates *actors*, *functions*, *responsibility networks* and *concerns*. The latter ones are inspired from an organizational meta-model proposed by Russell et al. [13]. An actor can be qualified for several functions and a function can be played by several actors. Figure 2 shows that a nurse and a physician are both health professionals (the explanation of the defined functions is out of the scope of this paper, a more detailed information about the InnoServ functions is found in [1]). Responsibility networks (RN) are represented as ellipsis more or less close to the frail person. RNs can be composed of other RNs. In the InnoServ ecosystem, the following responsibility networks are identified: *Regulation*, which deals with new laws and rules concerning home care for frail people; *Coordination*, which deals with home care organization for frail people; and *Execution*, which focuses on the direct interaction with the frail person. Seven concerns were identified: *Social, Medical, Human Resources, Technological, Financial, Legal* and *Strategic*. Several functions can be necessary in a RN and zero or more functions can be part of it. An actor can be involved in several RNs and a RN can have several actors.

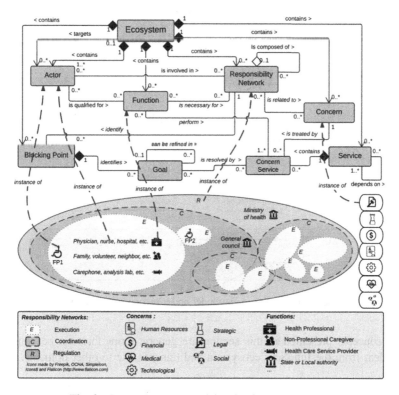

Fig. 2.   Ecosystem meta-model and a first instantiation

Figure 3 presents the notions of *blocking point* and *goal*, both related to *responsibility network*. An example of blocking point for the *Execution* RN is: *"There are skill's identification problems for the care activity"*, which is translated in a positive form (*"Identify function"*). Figure 3 shows an excerpt of the execution goal model. Note that the root and the first level goals respectively correspond to the responsibility network and the blocking points. Figure 3 also gives an example of *services* and *concern services*. The refinement of the blocking points results in a set of goals that overtake the blocking points. The meta-model also shows that a concern service is performed by zero or more functions and treats one concern in the context of one service. Figure 3 illustrates the service: *"Improve the recognition and salary of healthcare acts"*. This recognition points out a human resource concern (*recognition of the caregiver status*) and a financial concern (*increase salary or tax reduction for caregivers*).

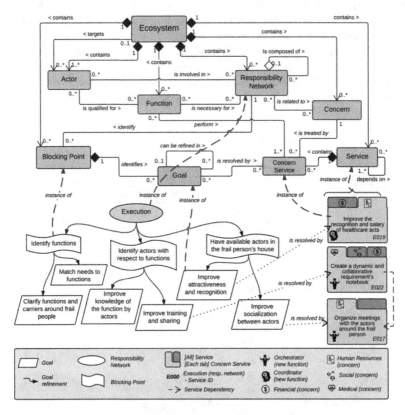

Fig. 3. Ecosystem meta-model and a second instantiation

The concepts presented in this section are generic terms that can be considered independent from the InnoServ ecosystem and transposable to other domains.

3   The *ADInnov* Method

We detail the three main sections presented in Fig. 1 that give the name to the *ADInnov* method: *Analysis*, *Diagnosis* and *Innovation*. The other sections presented in Fig. 1 (concerning road map and deployment) have not yet been studied in detail because they need long term implementation. For each section, application examples in the context of the *InnoServ* project are presented.

3.1   Analysis of the Ecosystem

Figure 4 refers to the section <*Start, Characterize the As-Is Ecosystem, **by analysis strategies**>* of Fig. 1. This section analyses the As-Is ecosystem. The results expected for this phase are: the characterization of the elements in the ecosystem (*glossary of terms*), a *list of actors and their functions*, a views separation in order to manage complexity (*responsibility networks and concerns*), and the *services* provided by the ecosystem. The resulting model corresponds to the one presented in Fig. 2. Table 1 summarizes the main sections highlighted in Fig. 4 with thicker arrows.

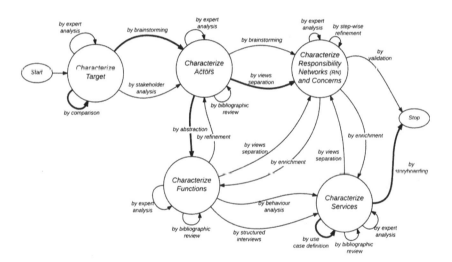

Fig. 4. Analysis of the ecosystem

3.2   Diagnosis of the Ecosystem

Figure 5 refines the section <*Characterize the As-Is Ecosystem, Characterize the As-Is Ecosystem, **by diagnosis strategies**>* of Fig. 1. This section corresponds to the diagnosis of the As-Is ecosystem. The results of the diagnosis should provide insights about the *major blocking points* and *the elicitation of goals in order to achieve them*. Table 2 summarizes the main sections highlighted in Fig. 5 with thicker arrows.

Table 1. Description of the selected analysis sections

Section	Description
<Characterize Target, Characterize Target, **by comparison**>	Identifies and describes the target comparing with similar ecosystems in other countries. *The target in the InnoServ project was the frail person*
<Characterize Target, Characterize Actors, **by brainstorming**>	Identifies and defines the actors in the ecosystem by spontaneous ideas in a grouped session. *Some actors of the InnoServ ecosystem (e.g., hospital, nurse, etc.) are illustrated in Fig. 2*
<Characterize Actors, Characterize Functions, **by abstraction**>	Identifies and describes functions gathering several actors and proposing a generic concept. *Some functions of the InnoServ ecosystem (e.g., health professional) are illustrated in Fig. 2*
<Characterize Functions, Characterize RN and concerns, **by views separation**>	Decomposes the ecosystem in different views in order to manage complexity. *The RNs (Execution, Coordination and Regulation) and Concerns (financial, social, medical, etc.) of the InnoServ ecosystem are illustrated in Fig. 2*
<Characterize Services, Characterize Services, **by use case definition** >	Identifies and defines several use cases to find concrete services of the ecosystem. *The InnoServ project used 4 use cases (homecoming, toilet, Alzheimer, and diabetes) described in [11] to provide a list of services*
<Characterize Services, Stop, **by story boarding**>	Creates a story board to illustrate the use cases. *The InnoServ project developed in detail 2 of the 4 use cases*

3.3   Design Innovations

Figure 6 refines the section *<Characterize the As-Is Ecosystem, Imagine the As-If Ecosystem, **by innovation strategies**>* of Fig. 1. This section corresponds to the design of the innovations in the As-Is ecosystem in order to reach the As-If ecosystem. The results expected for this phase are *a set of services* that help achieving the goals defined in the previous phase (each service responds to a specific goal and proposes a set of alterations on the ecosystem) and *a set of organizational innovations* in terms of alterations of the actors, functions, responsibility networks or concerns. In the InnoServ ecosystem, several organizational changes were proposed, such as the introduction of new functions. For example, we proposed the new function of *Orchestrator* that uses the resources near the frail person and performs the prescription services for a frail person. New functions imply extending the prerogatives of some actors. Nurses, for instance, could become orchestrators. Table 3 summarizes the main sections highlighted in Fig. 6 with thicker arrows.

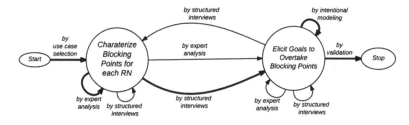

Fig. 5. Diagnosis of the ecosystem

Table 2. Description of the selected diagnosis sections

Section	Description
<Characterize BPs for each RN, Characterize BPs for each RN, by expert analysis>	Identifies and describes a set of blocking points guided by the responsibility networks and the concerns. *Some BPs of the InnoServ ecosystem are illustrated in* Fig. 3
<Characterize BPs for each RN, Elicit Goals to overtake BP, by structured interviews>	Inquires actors in the field considering their responsibility network in order to cover all of them. *In the InnoServ project, we performed 22 interviews of a representative panel of actors in the homecare service domain. We relied on actors to validate and identify blocking points and to imagine possible solutions*
<Elicit Goals to overtake BP, Elicit Goals to overtake BP, by intentional modelling>	Proposes goals that overtake the blocking points. Simple goal models can be built relying on responsibility networks. Figure 3 *provides an excerpt of the goal model used in the InnoServ ecosystem. Sub-goals are developed by analyzing the interviews, so they will correspond to a potential solution of the BP*
<Elicit Goals to overtake BP, Stop, by validation>	Validates the goal models by comparing the identified goals with the solutions proposed by actors' interviews. *The InnoServ project worked on the correspondence between the solutions proposed by actors in the field and leaf goals by double transcription*

4   Evaluation of the ADInnov Method

We evaluated the ADInnov method thanks to a qualitative methodology recommended by sociology and also by computer designers: the semi-structured interviews [17]. We conducted 8 interviews with senior researches that lead innovation projects such as the

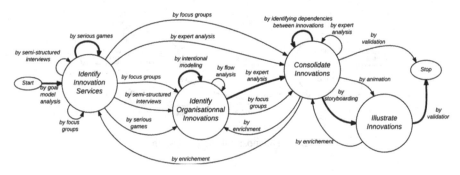

Fig. 6. Design innovations

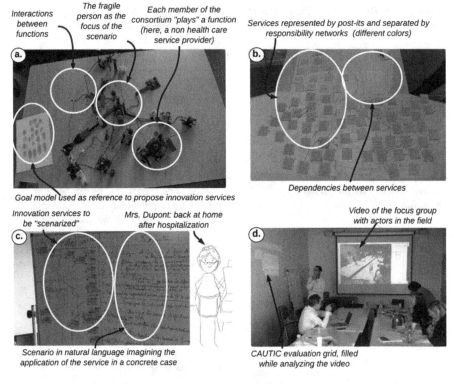

Fig. 7. Different innovation strategies used in the InnoServ ecosystem: (a) Lego serious play (b) Identification of dependencies (c) Storyboarding (d) CAUTIC method for validation

Nexus project[2], focused on the identification of innovations in eco-districts or the ACIC project[3] focused on the improvement of knowledge absorptive capacity for

---

[2] http://www.nexus-energy.fr/.

[3] http://bit.ly/acic_project.

Table 3. Description of the selected innovation sections

Section	Description
*<Start, Identify Innovation Services, **by goal model analysis**>*	Chooses the more fine grained goals to infer concrete solutions. *In the Innosev ecosystem, we relied on leaf goals to infer concrete services (cf.* Figure 3*). For each leaf goal, we tried to propose a concrete solution in terms of new service or organisational innovation*
*<Identify Innovation Services, Identify Innovation Services, **by serious games**>*	Uses Lego Serious Play[a], a serious game where the different participants put on a function hat in order to propose innovation services to resolve the blocking points in the context of a use case. *In the InnoServ ecosystem, subjects relied on use cases and goals extracted in the previous phase to infer services.* Figure 7(a) *shows a resulting model from a serious game session*
*<Identify Organizational Innovations, Identify Organizational Innovations, **by intentional modelling**>*	Identifies functions that contribute to reach the identified goals. *In the InnoServ ecosystem, attaching functions to the leaf-goals highlighted potential lacks that implied the proposition of new functions such as the Orchestrator*
*<Identify Organizational Innovations, Consolidate Innovations, **by expert analysis**>*	Consolidates propositions by checking with experts the coherence and the good alignment between goals and innovation services. *In the InnoServ ecosystem, a workshop implying healthcare experts from the consortium's socio-economic partners was organized to check the overall coherence*
*<Consolidate Innovations, Consolidate Innovations, **by identifying dependencies between innovations**>*	Identifies dependencies ("proceeds", "composes") between innovations. *In the InnoServ ecosystem, we used post-its to analyze dependencies between services.* Figure 7(b) *depicts the result of this workshop*
*<Consolidate Innovations, Illustrate Innovations, **by storyboarding**>*	Defines storyboards relying on dependency relations between services. *In the InnoServ ecosystem, scenarios in natural language completed with illustrations were proposed in order to imagine the implementation of the proposed services as well as organizational innovations.* Figure 7(c) *shows the storyboards and one of the two illustrated characters (Mrs. Dupont)*

(Continued)

Table 3. (*Continued*)

Section	Description
<*Illustrate Innovations, Stop, **by validation**>*	Validates the evolution scenarios by actors in the field before building the animated scenario that serves as demonstrator of the project's innovations. *In the InnoServ ecosystem, we used the CAUTIC method* [16] *to evaluate innovations in a focus group taking into account the following aspects: Assimilation (to the subject's technical know-how), Integration (with the subject's daily practices), Appropriateness (with regard to the subject's role and identity), Adaptation (to the subject's environment)* Figure 7(d) *shows one of the analysis sessions where 2h30 of focus groups implied 25 h of analysis*

a http://www.lego.com/fr-fr/seriousplay/.

innovation projects in collaborative SMEs networks. Table 4 shows the evaluation protocol, where we asked subjects to face the evaluation with an innovation project in mind. Data was gathered following an interview grid, where we asked subjects about the appropriateness of the proposed formalism and the proposed intentions, strategies and results. Due to the lack of space, we summarize the important points of the results.

The evaluation permitted to validate important aspects of the method but also highlighted some limits. A good point is the support of iterations, as new blocking points could be induced by the proposition of innovations. The simplicity of the MAP formalism was also appreciated. However, three researchers highlighted the difficulty to follow the models sequencing. The clear link between intentions and the expected results simplified the method understanding. Subjects highlighted the necessity to define different categories of blocking points (ex. financial, cultural, dysfunctions, etc.). In the same line, several researchers pointed out the necessity to analyze the risks as well as the potential opposite goals of the different actors as for example between private, public and associative actors.

This evaluation confirmed the appropriateness of our method, and helped us to understand its value and possible application. Moreover, the subjects described organisational mechanisms in which the method could work as a machine to permanently innovate in the ecosystem. The method was seen as a heuristic toolbox that the ecosystem can use in order to continuously think about its future and to find innovative ways to make it happen. By enabling this continuous and reflexive innovation loop process in the ecosystem, ADInnov supports the dissemination of the innovation culture in the organisation. Describing these mechanisms, the subjects characterized some improvement perspectives for the method. In particular, the method should supports characterizing the "stop" outputs in order to build a roadmap or a strategy that support decision-making when implementing innovations in the ecosystem. These "stop" could

Table 4. Evaluation protocol of the ADInnov method

Hypothesis
The ADInnov method is useful and can be applied in multi-disciplinary innovation projects
Protocol
Method Presentation ~ 20min
Evaluation ~ 1h30min — Questionnaire about the innovation project (goals, components, research methods) — Question about the appropriateness of the use of the MAP formalism. — Analysis of the *intentions* proposed in ADInnov. — Analysis of the *strategies* proposed in ADInnov. — Analysis of the *results* proposed in ADInnov. — Global appropriateness of the method and its applicability in other domains.

be characterized with regard to the responsibility networks (RN) so we can infer the feasibility framework. For instance the innovations concerning the *Execution* RN are supposed to be achievable in a short-term perspective involving a reduced number of actors, while outputs concerning the *Regulation* RN should involve a representative number of actors over a long time period. In addition, it should be possible to characterize the innovations depending of their class in terms of "products", "services", "infrastructure" or "financial and legal rules": this classification can help the actors to prioritize the implementation of innovations into the ecosystem.

5   Related Works

Several domains offer methodological tools that can be used in our method. Some are relevant because of the used language or by the steps they propose. Others propose participative techniques that make sense in our context.

Domain analysis methods in the Information System's community such as Merise [18] or SSADM [19] provide systems' analysis techniques relying on sub-problem decomposition. This decomposition is governed by the flow of information between the system and its environment or between different actors in the ecosystem. Kang et al. [20] proposed FODA (*Feature Oriented Domain Analysis*), in order to analyze the scope of the system and the functionality requirements. **Goal-modelling approaches** such as KAOS [10], URN [15], i* [21] or MAP [9] are also well known methods to study a system by focusing on its goals or intentions. The aforementioned methods facilitate the understanding of the studied ecosystem, the delimitation and the modelling of the domain. They may be useful to improve the system (as they help to understand it). Nevertheless they are limited when it comes to guide innovation. Note that our method is strongly inspired (in terms of concept usage) by the GORE method [10]. For instance, the term "blocking point" is similar to the KAOS obstacle [22]. However, these domain analysis methods focus on information systems requirements engineering, while we focus on innovation in ST ecosystems.

Multi-agents methods such as DIAMOND [23] are also considered as analysis methods. The latter proposes a spiral method with the following phases: *definition of the needs, analysis, generic design, and implementation.* An interesting point here is the decomposition approach into agents in order to build a system with a bottom-up approach. In our case, we are not in a building-from-scratch approach: the studied ecosystem is already established, like most of the current systems [24].

In the innovation domain, empirical methods such as CAUTIC [16] have been proposed. Serious games or focus groups are also commonly used to infer innovations and their effectiveness was already proved in the context of business process management (BPM) [25]. Creativity methods [26] are also well known to help inducing innovations. However, these methods focus in a very specific area and a one-shot view of innovation. In addition, they do not contemplate a rigorous analysis (and modelling) of the actual system or product. **User-centred methodologies** used for example to build domain specific languages [7, 26] propose similar phases as the previous ones: *Analysis, Design, Implementation* and *Testing.* These approaches show the benefits to integrate the end-user in the understanding and co-construction of a complex task. However, these approaches are not generic enough to be adapted to the evolution of ST ecosystems.

Generic methods in business process management domain promote continuous improvement. The PDCA method (Plan Do Check Act) [27] or the one described by van der Aalst (*Process Design, System Configuration, Process Enactment and Diagnosis*) [24] are well known examples. In the healthcare domain, Winge et al. [5] rely on PDCA to propose a generic process that supports care process conglomerations, referring to the tangle of processes around a patient. We think that process oriented approaches are limited for ST ecosystems, where automation is not always possible, in particular for the configuration and the enactment phases.

To resume, to our knowledge, there is no method accompanying iterative innovation for ST ecosystems. The ADInnov method mobilizes different methodological tools from different spectrums such as domain analysis, multi-agent, business process management and innovation domains.

6   Conclusion and Future Work

Understanding and improving ST ecosystems, where many entities interact in different ways and where a lot of special cases exist, is still a great challenge. To overtake this complexity, this paper presents *ADInnov*, an iterative method that supports the analysis, diagnosis and the design of innovations in such ecosystems. Our goal is to assist the study and guide the improvement of ST ecosystems by instilling an innovation culture that allows the stakeholders to permanently improve the ecosystem. The notion of As-If ecosystem appears to represent an improved vision of the As-Is ecosystem where innovations are introduced in order to resolve blocking points. The As-if ecosystem becomes an As-Is ecosystem when innovations have been deployed. New blocking points may appear implying an iterative process of innovation. This work is the consolidation and abstraction of an empirical method with the aim of applying it to other innovation projects. The method is represented using the MAP formalism and relies on a generic ecosystem meta-model where blocking points are considered as an inner part.

At present, the analysis/diagnosis/innovation strategies are limited by the best practices used in the InnoServ project. A larger deployment of the method is needed in order to improve it and study its applicability in other ecosystems such as smart-cities and eco-cities. The qualitative evaluation of the method with innovation project managers helped us to position the method with respect to other ecosystems and gave us some valuable clues to improve the method. The current strategies must be completed, in particular by creativity methods [26]. Road-map and deployment strategies have to be defined by integrating risk management methods. In addition, metrics regarding the resolution of blocking points have to be introduced in order to measure the grade of innovation.

References

1. Priego-Roche, L.-M., Verdier, C., Front, A., Rieu, D.: A virtual organization modeling approach for home care services. In: Demey, Y.T., Panetto, H. (eds.) OTM 2013 Workshops 2013. LNCS, vol. 8186, pp. 373–377. Springer, Heidelberg (2013)
2. Decker, G., Kopp, O., Barros, A.: An introduction to service choreographies. Inf. Technol. **50**(2), 122–127 (2008)
3. Kolp, M., Giorgini, P., Mylopoulos, J.: Multi-agent architectures as organizational structures. Auton. Agent. Multi. Agent. Syst. **13**(1), 3–25 (2006)
4. Newman, M.E.J.: Complex systems: a survey. Phys. Rep. **79**(I), 10 (2009)
5. Wingo, M., Porjono, E., Wangler, B.: Understanding core work and the coordination of care process conglomerations. In: Jeusfeld, M.A., et al. (eds.) ER 2015 Workshops. LNCS, vol. 9382, pp. 26–37. Springer, Heidelberg (2015). doi:10.1007/978-3-319-25747-1_3
6. Bateh, J., Castaneda, M.E., Farah, J.E.: Employee resistance to organizational change. Int. J. Manag. Inf. Syst. **17**(2), 113–116 (2013)
7. Villanueva, M.J., Valverde, F., Pastor, O.: Involving end-users in the design of a domain-specific language for the genetic domain. In: Escalona, M.J., Aragón, G., Linger, H., Lang, M., Barry, C., Schneider, C. (eds.) Information System Development, pp. 99–110. Springer, Switzerland (2014)
8. Giarini, O., Stahel, W.R.: "Hidden Innovation," in Science and Public Policy, Special Issue on the "Hidden Wealth, vol. 13, no. 4 (1986)
9. Rolland, C.: Capturing system intentionality with maps. In: Krogstie, J., Opdahl, A.L., Brinkkemper, S. (eds.) Conceptual Modelling Information Systems Engineering, pp. 141–158. Springer, Heidelberg (2007)
10. van Lamsweerde, A.: Goal-oriented requirements engineering: a guided tour. In: International Symposium on Requirements Engineering, Toronto, Canada. IEEE 2001, pp. 249–262 (2001)
11. INNOSERV, C.: InnoServ Livrable 1: livrable 1, rapport bibliographique Innovation de Service pour les personnes fragiles. Coordonné par Christine Verdier (2013)
12. Cortes-Cornax, M., Rieu, D., Verdier, C., Front, A., Forest, F., Mercier, A., Benoit, A.M., Faravelon, A.: A method to analyze, diagnose and propose innovations for complex ecosystems: the InnoServ project. In: Jeusfeld, M.A., et al. (eds.) ER 2015 Workshops. LNCS, vol. 9382, pp. 38–48. Springer, Heidelberg (2015). doi:10.1007/978-3-319-25747-1_4
13. Russell, N., van der Aalst, W.M., ter Hofstede, A.H., Edmond, D.: Workflow resource patterns: identification, representation and tool support. In: Pastor, Ó., Falcão e Cunha, J. (eds.) CAiSE 2005. LNCS, vol. 3520, pp. 216–232. Springer, Heidelberg (2005)

14. Moody, D.: The 'physics' of notations: toward a scientific basis for constructing visual notations in software engineering. IEEE Trans. Softw. Eng. 35(6), 756–779 (2009)
15. Amyot, D., Mussbacher, G.: User requirements notation : the first ten years, the next ten years. J. Softw. 6(5), 747–768 (2011)
16. Forest, F., Mallein, P., Arhippainen, L.: Paradoxical user acceptance of ambient intelligent systems: sociology of user experience approach. In: Proceedings of International Conference on Making Sense of Converging Media, pp. 211–218 (2013)
17. Hindus, D., Mainwaring, S.D., Leduc, N., Hagström, A.E., Bayley, O.: Designing social communication devices for the home. In: SIGCHI Conference on Human Factors in Computing Systems, pp. 325–332 (2001)
18. Nanci, D., Espinasse, B., Cohen, B., Asselborn, J.-C.: HeckenrothHenri: Ingénerie de Systèmes d'Information: Merise Deuxième génération, 4th edn. Paris (2001)
19. Ashworth, C.M.: Structured systems analysis and design method (SSADM). Inf. Softw. Technol. 30(3), 153–163 (1988)
20. Kang, K.C., Cohen, S.G., Hess, J.A., Novak, W.E., Peterson, A.S.: Feature-oriented domain analysis (FODA) feasibility study. Distribution 17, 161 (1990)
21. Castro, J., Kolp, M., Mylopoulos, J.: Towards requirements-driven information systems engineering: the Tropos project. Inf. Syst. 27(6), 365–389 (2002)
22. van Lamsweerde, A., Letier, E.: Handling obstacles in goal-oriented requirements engineering. IEEE Trans. Softw. Eng. 26(10), 978–1005 (2000)
23. Jean-Paul, J., Michel, O.: A multiagent method to design open embedded complex systems. In: Tools in Artificial Intelligence, pp. 205–222. InTech (2008)
24. van der Aalst, W.M.: Business process management demystified: a tutorial on models, systems and standards for workflow management. In: Desel, J., Reisig, W., Rozenberg, G. (eds.) Lectures on Concurrency and Petri Nets. LNCS, vol. 3098, pp. 1–65. Springer, Heidelberg (2004)
25. Front, A., Rieu, D., Santorum, M., Movahedian, F.: A participative end-user method for multi-perspective business process elicitation and improvement. Softw. Syst. Model. 1–24 (2015)
26. Maiden, N., Jones, S., Karlsen, K., Neill, R., Zachos, K., Milne, A.: Requirements engineering as creative problem solving: a research agenda for idea finding. In: Proceedings of the 2010 18th IEEE International Requirements Engineering Conference, RE 2010, pp. 57–66 (2010)
27. Deming, W.E.: Out of the Crisis, vol. 4. MIT Press, Cambridge (2000)

Mining and Business Process Performance

A Visual Approach to Spot Statistically-Significant Differences in Event Logs Based on Process Metrics

Alfredo Bolt[(⊠)], Massimiliano de Leoni, and Wil M.P. van der Aalst

Eindhoven University of Technology, Eindhoven, The Netherlands
{a.bolt,m.d.leoni,w.m.p.v.d.aalst}@tue.nl

Abstract. This paper addresses the problem of comparing different variants of the same process. We aim to detect relevant differences between processes based on what was recorded in event logs. We use transition systems to model behavior and to highlight differences. Transition systems are annotated with measurements, used to compare the behavior in the variants. The results are visualized as transitions systems, which are colored to pinpoint the significant differences. The approach has been implemented in ProM, and the implementation is publicly available. We validated our approach by performing experiments using real-life event data. The results show how our technique is able to detect relevant differences undetected by previous approaches while it avoids detecting insignificant differences.

Keywords: Process variants comparison · Annotated transition system · Statistical significance · Process mining

1 Introduction

Process mining is a relatively young research discipline that aims at discovering, monitoring and improving real processes by extracting knowledge from the behavior as recorded in the event logs readily available in today's systems [1]. The field of process mining puts forward techniques for discovering process models from event logs, for checking the conformance of normative models against the behavior observed in the event logs and analyzing bottlenecks and other *Key Performance Indicators* (KPIs).

Traditional process-mining techniques typically rely on the assumption that, within any organization, all executions of a certain process are characterized by an homogenous behavior, which can be easily compared. This assumption is often not met in reality: several variants of the same process may exist even within the same organization. As an example, consider an organization, such as a bank, that is composed by dozens of geographically spread branches. The same process, e.g., the loan's management, can be executed differently in these branches. Even within a branch, the observed behavior can vary according to

© Springer International Publishing Switzerland 2016
S. Nurcan et al. (Eds.): CAiSE 2016, LNCS 9694, pp. 151–166, 2016.
DOI: 10.1007/978-3-319-39696-5_10

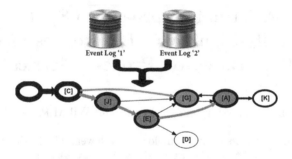

Fig. 1. Overview of the approach: two event logs are compared, producing a single annotated transition system, where the colors of nodes and edges represent the relevance of the differences found. (Color figure online)

different criteria; for example, the behavior may change over time or depend on the amount involved.

The comparative analysis of different process variants is obviously relevant and through the availability of event data also possible. This paper presents a generic technique to compare process variants by identifying statistically significant differences. Figure 1 sketches the idea: two event logs are compared for differences that are projected onto a transition system where states and transitions are colored to highlight differences. The thickness of the node's borders and arcs indicates the frequencies with which states and transitions are respectively visited or occur. The portions of behavior that are rarely observed are filtered out. Also, differences are not highlighted if they are not statistically significant. The visual properties of these transition systems, and their meaning, are discussed in Sec. 3.

The two event logs that are used for comparison can have actually been extracted from different information systems, e.g. of two branches of the same company or of different companies. Alternatively, they can be extracted from a process cube [2,3] using the typical operations of, e.g., dicing, slicing and filtering. In the case that more than two event logs need to be compared, they can be grouped and merged into two event logs.

As detailed in Sect. 6, existing work mainly focuses on reporting differences for what concerns the control flow, meaning the frequency with which activities occur and the causal relations between activities (i.e., which activities are typically observed to follow given activities). However, differences can be regarded from other viewpoints based on other process metrics, such as the time between activities and the overall process performance. Our approach allows end users to use several process metrics for detecting such differences. Figure 1 shows an overview of the approach: two event logs are taken as input and an annotated transition system showing the differences is produced as output.

In order to assess the practical relevance of the differences highlighted by our technique, we used real-life event data extracted from the information system of an Italian local police, which records the executions of the process of handling road-traffic fines. In particular, we show how the management of high fines varies from that of low fines, including differences in the behaviors of offenders in paying the fines.

The remainder of this paper is structured as follows. Section 2 introduces the basic concepts that are used throughout the papers, whereas Sect. 3 details our technique for comparing the behaviors observed in two event logs. Section 4 describes the software tool that implements this approach, whereas Sect. 5 presents the evaluation discussed above. Section 6 discusses related work; in particular, using the same dataset of an Italian local police, we illustrate how existing approaches highlight insignificant differences instead of highlighting many of the relevant differences, which conversely, our approach can. Finally, Sect. 7 summarizes our contributions and discusses future work.

2   Transition Systems as a Process Representation

The behavior observed in an event log can be summarized as a *transition system* [4]. Section 2.1 introduces the formalisms used to represent event logs. Section 2.2 describes how transition systems are created. Sections 2.3 and 2.4 illustrate how measurements can be annotated into the states and transitions of a transition system.

2.1   Event Log

Let $\mathcal{E}$ be the universe of events. Events may have *attributes* (e.g., the person who executed it, associated cost, timestamp). Attribute values are related to events through the function $att_a \in \mathcal{E} \to \mathcal{V}$, where a is an attribute name and $\mathcal{V}$ is the set of possible attribute values. In this paper we do not impose a specific set of attributes. However, given the focus of this paper, we assume that each event has at least the following attributes: *activity name* and *timestamp* (denoted as $att_n(e)$ and $att_t(e)$ respectively).

Let $\sigma \in \mathcal{E}^*$ be a trace. A trace records the execution of an *instance* of a process and is a finite sequence of events. The kth event of a trace is denoted as $\sigma(k)$. The length of a trace is denoted as $|\sigma|$. We

Table 1. A fragment of an event log represented as a table: each row corresponds to an event and each column corresponds to an event attribute. Events with the same *trace id* correspond to the same trace (i.e., process instance).

Trace id	Activity	Timestamp	...
1	A	28-12-2015:06.30	...
1	B	28-12-2015:06.45	...
1	C	28-12-2015:07.20	...
1	D	28-12-2015:08.05	...
2	A	29-12-2015:10.10	...
2	C	29-12-2015:10.30	...
2	B	29-12-2015:11.15	...
2	D	29-12-2015:12.10	...
3	A	30-12-2015:09.30	...
3	D	30-12-2015:09.40	...

assume that events in traces are ordered by timestamp i.e., $\forall \sigma \in \mathcal{E}^*, 1 \leq i < j \leq |\sigma| : att_t(\sigma(i)) \leq att_t(\sigma(j))$. The prefix of a trace containing its first k events is defined by the function $pref^k \subseteq \mathcal{E}^* \to \mathcal{E}^*$, with the special case $pref^0(\sigma) = \langle \rangle$. The set of all the prefixes of a trace σ is defined as $pref^\diamond(\sigma) = \bigcup_{k=0}^{|\sigma|} \{pref^k(\sigma)\}$.

The postfix of a trace containing its last k events is defined by the function $postf^k \subseteq \mathcal{E}^* \rightarrow \mathcal{E}^*$.

Let $L \in \mathbb{B}(\mathcal{E}^*)$ be an event log. An event log is a multiset of traces. The set of all the prefixes of traces of an event log L is defined as $P_L = \bigcup_{\sigma \in L} pref^\diamond(\sigma)$. The set of all the events in an event log L is defined as $E_L = \bigcup_{\sigma \in L} \{e \in \sigma\}$. Table 1 shows an example of an event log represented as a table. This event log will be used as a running example through the remainder of this section.

2.2   Transition Systems

Transition systems are composed of *states* and of *transitions* between them. A transition is defined by an activity being executed, triggering the current state to move from a *source* to a *target* state. Figure 2 shows two possible transition system representations of the event log presented in Table 1. The nodes indicate the *states* and the arcs indicate the *transitions* between them. Prefixes of traces can be mapped to states and transitions using representation functions that define how these prefixes are interpreted.

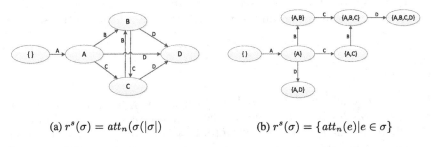

(a) $r^s(\sigma) = att_n(\sigma(|\sigma|))$ (b) $r^s(\sigma) = \{att_n(e)|e \in \sigma\}$

Fig. 2. Examples of transition systems obtained from the event log L presented in Table 1 using different *state representation* functions $r^s(\sigma), \sigma \in P_L$. In both cases, the *activity representation* function used is $r^a(e) = att_n(e), e \in E_L$.

The *state representation* function is defined as $r^s \in \mathcal{E}^* \rightarrow \mathcal{R}^s$ where $\mathcal{E}^*$ is the universe of possible traces and $\mathcal{R}^s$ is the set of possible representations of states. This function relates (prefixes of) traces to states in a transition system.

The *activity representation* function is defined as $r^a \in \mathcal{E} \rightarrow \mathcal{R}^a$ where $\mathcal{E}$ is the set of possible events and $\mathcal{R}^a$ is the set of possible representations of activities (e.g., *activity name* or *event id*).

When using a state representation function r^s and an activity representation function r^a together, (prefixes of) traces can be related to transitions in a transition system, as the activity and the source and target states of the transition can be identified using r^s and r^a. The set of all possible representations of traces is defined as $\mathcal{R}^t \subseteq \mathcal{R}^s \times \mathcal{R}^a \times \mathcal{R}^s$. A transition $t \in \mathcal{R}^t$ is a triplet (s_1, a, s_2) where $s_1, s_2 \in \mathcal{R}^s$ are the source and target states and $a \in \mathcal{R}^a$ is the activity executed.

Figure 2a shows the transition system that represents the event log L shown in Table 1 using the state representation function $r^s(\sigma) = att_n(\sigma(|\sigma|)), \forall \sigma \in P_L$

and the activity representation function $r^a(e) = att_n(e), \forall e \in E_L$. In this transition system, (prefixes of) traces are mapped into states and transitions as the activity name of their last event.

Figure 2b, shows a different representation of the same event log L. For this transition system the state representation function used is $r^s(\sigma) = \{att_n(e)|e \in \sigma\}, \sigma \in P_L$ and the activity representation function used is $r^a(e) = att_n(e), e \in E_L$. In this transition system, (prefixes of) traces are mapped into states as the set of activity names of all their events, and into transitions as the activity name of their last event.

Definition 1 (Transition System). *Let r^s be a state representation function, r^a an activity representation function and L an event log. A transition system $TS^{(r^s, r^a, L)}$ is defined as a triplet (S, A, T) where $S = \{s \in R^s | \exists_{\sigma \in P_L} s = r^s(\sigma)\}$ is the set of states, $A = \{a \in R^a | \exists_{e \in E_L} a = r^a(e)\}$ is the set of activities and $T = \{(s_1, a, s_2) \in S \times A \times S | \exists_{\sigma \in P_L, \sigma \neq \langle \rangle} s_1 = r^s(pref^{|\sigma|-1}(\sigma)) \wedge a = r^a(\sigma(|\sigma|)) \wedge s_2 = r^s(\sigma)\}$ is the set of valid transitions between states.*

Note that the structure of a transition system is affected by the state and activity representation functions used to create it. A thorough discussion on state and event representations in transition systems is presented in [4].

2.3   Measurements

In order to compare event logs, we need to introduce the measurements used for comparison. Measurement functions are computed as functions of event attributes contained in the events of a trace.

Given a state representation function r^s a *state measurement* function $sm_{r^s} \in \mathcal{E}^* \times \mathcal{R}^s \to \mathbb{B}(\mathbb{R})$, is a function that relates traces $\sigma \in \mathcal{E}^*$ and states $s \in \mathcal{R}^s$ to multisets of numerical measurements. For example, it is possible to measure whether or not a certain state s in a state representation r^s is reached during the process' execution recorded in a trace σ:

$$sm_{r^s}^{occur}(\sigma, s) = \begin{cases} [1] & \text{if } \exists \sigma' \in pref^\diamond(\sigma) : r^s(\sigma') = s \\ [0] & \text{otherwise} \end{cases} \tag{1}$$

It is also possible to measure the *elapsed time* between the beginning of a trace σ and the visit of a state s using a state representation r^s:

$$sm_{r^s}^{elapsed}(\sigma, s) = \biguplus_{\substack{\sigma' \in pref^\diamond(\sigma), \sigma' \neq \langle \rangle \\ r^s(\sigma') = s}} [att_t(\sigma'(|\sigma'|)) - att_t(\sigma'(1))] \tag{2}$$

Given a state representation function r^s and an activity representation r^a, a *transition measurement* function $tm_{(r^s, r^a)} \in \mathcal{E}^* \times \mathcal{R}^t \to \mathbb{B}(\mathbb{R})$, is a function that relates traces $\sigma \in \mathcal{E}^*$ and transitions $t \in \mathcal{R}^t$ to multisets of numerical measurements. For example, it is possible to measure whether a certain transition t is executed in a given trace σ:

$$tm^{occur}_{(r^s,r^a)}(\sigma,t) = \begin{cases} [1] \text{ if } \exists_{\sigma' \in pref^\diamond(\sigma), \sigma' \neq \langle\rangle} \left(r^s(pref^{|\sigma'|-1}(\sigma')), r^a(\sigma'(|\sigma'|)), r^s(\sigma') \right) = t \\ [0] \text{ otherwise} \end{cases}$$

(3)

It is also possible to measure the *elapsed time* of a trace until a transition is triggered within the trace:

$$tm^{elapsed}_{(r^s,r^a)}(\sigma,t) = \biguplus_{\substack{\sigma' \in pref^\diamond(\sigma), \sigma' \neq \langle\rangle \\ \left(r^s(pref^{|\sigma'|-1}(\sigma')), r^a(\sigma'(|\sigma'|)), r^s(\sigma') \right) = t}} [att_t(\sigma'(|\sigma'|)) - att_t(\sigma'(1)]$$

(4)

2.4   Annotations

As mentioned before, states and transitions can be *annotated* with the measurements obtained from an event log. Given a state measurement function sm, a transition measurement function tm and an event log L, an *annotation* function $an^{(sm,tm,L)} \in (\mathcal{R}^s \cup \mathcal{R}^t) \to \mathbb{B}(\mathbb{R})$, is a function that, given a state $s \in \mathcal{R}^s$ or transition $t \in \mathcal{R}^t$, produces a multiset of numerical measurements. The annotation function is defined as:

$$an^{(sm,tm,L)}(x) = \begin{cases} \biguplus_{\sigma \in L} sm(\sigma,x) \text{ if } x \in \mathcal{R}^s \\ \biguplus_{\sigma \in L} tm(\sigma,x) \text{ if } x \in \mathcal{R}^t \end{cases}$$

3   Comparison and Visualization of the Differences in Process Variants

Given two event logs L_1 and L_2, our approach produces comparison results (as shown in Fig. 1) in three steps:

1. Create an *annotated transition system* (i.e., a transition system with multiple annotation functions) from L_1 and L_2 using the state and activity representation functions r^s and r^a and the state and transition measurement functions sm_{r^s} and $tm_{(r^s,r^a)}$.
2. *Compare* the annotations of each state or transition of the annotated transition system.
3. *Visualize* the differences in the annotated transition system.

In order to compare process variants, we need to compare the annotations that are produced for the states and transitions of a transition system. Hence, we introduce *annotated transition systems* which allows to annotate a transition system with multiple annotation functions.

Definition 2 (Annotated Transition System). *Given two event logs L_1 and L_2, state and activity representation functions r^s and r^a, state and transition measurement functions sm and tm, we define an* annotated transition sys*tem* $ATS^{(r^s, r^a, L_1, L_2, sm, tm)}$ *as the triplet* $(TS^{(r^s, r^a, L_1 \uplus L_2)}, an^{(sm_{r^s}, tm_{(r^s, r^a)}, L_1)}, an^{(sm_{r^s}, tm_{(r^s, r^a)}, L_2)})$, *where* $TS^{(r^s, r^a, L_1 \uplus L_2)} = (S, A, T)$ *is a transition system and* $an^{(sm_{r^s}, tm_{(r^s, r^a)}, L_1)}$, $an^{(sm_{r^s}, tm_{(r^s, r^a)}, L_2)}$ *are annotation functions denoted as* an_1 *and* an_2 *respectively.*

Note that the transition system uses all the traces contained in the union of the event logs L_1 and L_2. Also, note that an_1 and an_2 use only the traces contained in one event log (L_1 and L_2 respectively).

Figure 3 shows an example of annotated transition system created using the event log L_1 and L_2 are created from the event log presented in Table 1 (the first two traces belong to L_1 and the third trace belongs to L_2), the state representation function $r^s(\sigma) = \{att_n(e) | e \in \sigma\}, \forall \sigma \in P_L$, the activity representation function $r^a(e) = att_n(e), \forall e \in E_L$, the state measurement function sm_{r^s} defined in Eq. 1 and the transition representation function $tm_{(r^s, r^a)}$ defined in Eq. 3. Only annotations of the function an_1 are represented (i.e., as text below the node and arc labels).

State and Transition Comparison Using Annotations. The comparison of annotations can be abstracted as a *comparison oracle* that is defined as the function $\textit{diff} \subset \mathbb{D}(\mathbb{R}) \times \mathbb{D}(\mathbb{R}) \to \textit{Bool}$, which given two multi-set of numerical measurements (i.e., annotations) decides whether there are differences between them (i.e., *true*) or not (i.e., *false*).

Given an $ATS = ((S, A, T), an_1, an_2)$, for each element $x \in S \cup T$ we want to detect differences by evaluating $\textit{diff}(an_1(x), an_2(x))$.

In order to avoid detecting irrelevant differences between the means of the annotations, *statistical significance tests* are used as the comparison oracle. We have opted for the two-tailed "Welch's T-test", also known as the "two-tailed

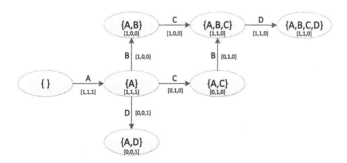

Fig. 3. Transition system annotated with the *occurrence* state and transition measurement functions defined in Eqs. 1 and 3. Annotations are represented as text under the node and edge labels.

T-test with different variances" [5] because it is suited when the two sets of measurements come from independent populations, such as when they are extracted from two event logs from different branches of a company.

Visualizing Differences in Annotated Transition Systems. Annotations and comparison results of states and transitions can be represented using visual properties (i.e., *thickness* and *color*) of nodes and arcs.

Given an $ATS = ((S, A, T), an_1, an_2)$, for each element $x \in S \cup T$, the *thickness* of the corresponding node (if $x \in S$) or arc (if $x \in T$) is proportional to the mean value of $an_1(x) \uplus an_2(x)$ i.e., the average value of the annotations associated with x and computed on the merged log. The thickness property provides insights about the overall behavior of both variants.

Figure 4 illustrates an example of this visualization using the ATS presented in Fig. 3. In this case, the annotations obtained from an_1 and an_2 are represented as thickness instead of text.

Given an $ATS = ((S, A, T), an_1, an_2)$, for each element $x \in S \cup T$, the corresponding node (if $x \in S$) or arc (if $x \in T$) will be colored black or white (depending whether it is an arc or a node) if $diff(an_1(x), an_2(x)) = false$, or it will be colored using other colors if $diff(an_1(x), an_2(x)) = true$. In the latter case, the color used will depend on the measurement function used and on the *effect size* of the difference.

The effect size oracle is defined as the function $eff \in \mathbb{B}(\mathbb{R}) \times \mathbb{B}(\mathbb{R}) \to \mathbb{R}$, which given two multisets of measurements, returns the size of the effect (i.e., how small or large is the difference) and the sign of the difference (+/-) in a certain scale. In this paper, we used Cohen's d [6] to measure effect size, which measures the difference of sample means in terms of pooled standard deviation units. Cohen relates ranges of d values to effect size categories: $d = \pm 0.2$ is considered as a *small effect*, $d = \pm 0.5$ is considered as a *medium effect* and $d = \pm 0.8$ is considered as a *large effect*. However, other effect size measurements could be used instead.

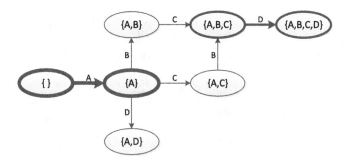

Fig. 4. An example of how the annotations are translated to the thickness of the transition's arcs and state's node borders using the annotated transition system shown in Fig. 3.

Currently, we support two measurement functions and, hence, two color intervals are used, as shown in Fig. 5[1]. In Fig. 5a, *occurrence* measurement functions (Eqs. 1 and 3) were used. Blue-based colors mean that the occurrence of a state or transition in a first event log is higher than in a second event log and red-based colors mean the opposite. In Fig. 5b, *elapsed time* (performance) annotation functions (Eqs. 2 and 4) were used. Green-based colors mean that the elapsed time of reaching a state or executing a transition in a first event log is higher than in a second event log and purple-based colors mean the opposite. Note that within the color intervals, different colors are used according to Cohen's d ranges of effect size values. Colors with higher intensity (i.e., darker) represent larger effect sizes (i.e., more relevant differences), whereas colors with low intensity (i.e., lighter) represent smaller effect sizes (i.e., less relevant differences).

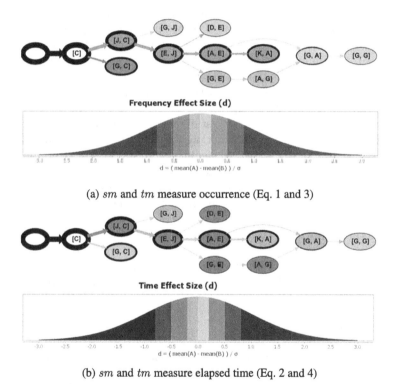

(a) *sm* and *tm* measure occurrence (Eq. 1 and 3)

(b) *sm* and *tm* measure elapsed time (Eq. 2 and 4)

Fig. 5. Example of an annotated transition system colored with the results of statistical significance tests and effect size oracle using different state and transition measurement functions. (Color figure online)

---

[1] Note that the example transition system used in this figure is different than previous examples, and it is used for illustration purposes only.

4   Implementation

Our approach has been implemented as the *Process Comparator* plugin in the ProM [7] framework. ProM allows researchers to implement process mining techniques in a standardized environment, providing several functionalities that can be used by the implementations, and also providing a distribution platform for other researchers to use these developments. The ProM framework is considered as the *de-facto* standard for process mining, and it can be freely downloaded form http://promtools.org.

The tool takes two event logs as input. However, more than two event logs can be compared. This is handled by requesting the user to group these event logs into two groups. Each of these groups is then merged into a single event log and then compared against each other. The tool also provides a "hint" functionality for the users that do not have context knowledge or do not know which processes to compare. This functionality suggests to compare a single process against all the others by calculating *similarity scores* between each process and the union of the $n - 1$ remaining processes. Similarity score is calculated based on the percentage of elements that present statistically significant differences. Finally, the process that has most differences with the rest is suggested to the user as a starting point for comparative analysis.

Our tool allows the user to change state and event representation functions, state and transition measurement functions and several useful parameters (e.g., the significance level of the statistical significance tests) in order to provide flexible representations for the event logs, as shown in Fig. 6. Our tool also provides frequency filtering capabilities where all the nodes and arcs with lower frequency than a defined threshold will be hidden from the visualization. This allows to filter out rare behavior and to produce clearer visualizations. Also, the elements of the annotated transition system presented as result are *interactive*. The user can click on any state or transition, and a data table will pop-up showing the values of the annotations of such state or transition for both event logs (e.g., frequency of occurrence, elapsed time, remaining time, number of traces).

5   Evaluation

In order to show the usefulness of our approach in practice, we performed experiments using multiple real-life event logs. Here we report on a log extracted from an Italian Municipality's information system that handled the "road fines management" process [8]. For showing the comparison capabilities of our approach, we split the event logs into two sub logs (i.e., *variants*): the first one contains all the cases where the fine amount was lower than 50 euros (i.e., *low fines*) and the second contains all the cases where the amount of the fine was equal or higher than 50 euros (i.e., *high fines*). The two event logs were then compared against each other using our tool, and the differences were projected into an annotated transition system. We performed two sets of experiments:

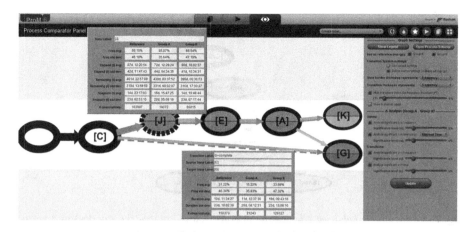

Fig. 6. Screenshot of the *Process Comparator* plugin in the ProM framework. Detailed data tables pop-up when the user clicks on states or transitions.

- The first was based on an abstraction where the last event of the trace is considered. We used the following state and transition abstraction: given an event log L, a trace $\sigma \in P_L$ and an event $e \in E_L$, $r^s(\sigma) = att_n(\sigma(|\sigma|))$ and $r^a(e) = att_n(e)$. As measurement for comparison, elapsed time was used as defined in Eqs. 2 and 4, thus comparing the time differences when activities were executed.
- The second was based on an abstraction where the last two events were considered: $r^s(\sigma) = \langle att_n(\sigma(|\sigma|)), att_n(\sigma(|\sigma| - 1)) \rangle$ and $r^a(e) = att_n(e)$. The occurrence measurements for comparison were used as defined in Eqs. 1 and 3.

In both of experiments, we used a confidence level $\alpha = 0.05$ for the Welch's T tests.

Figure 7 shows the results of the first experiment, where many relevant performance differences were detected. As previously shown in Fig. 5b, green colors are assigned to states and transitions that are reached or executed statistically significantly earlier in low fines, whereas purple colors are assigned when the opposite occurs. The green color assigned to state *Payment* indicates that payments were received significantly earlier for low fines (99 days versus 151 days)[2]. Conversely, the purple-colored transition *(Create Fine, Send Fine)* indicates that high fines are sent to offenders significantly earlier (72 days versus 90 days)[2]. The thickness of this arc also indicates that, overall, sending the fine after creating is a more frequent behavior. The fact that the *Create Fine* state is white indicates that there is no statistically significant difference in how early *Create Fine* is executed.

---

[2] This is not observable in the picture but, in the implementation, by clicking on a state/transition, one can read this information in a popup equivalent to the two shown in Fig. 6.

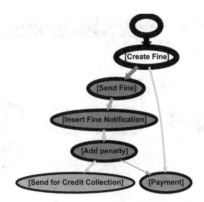

Fig. 7. Performance (*elapsed time*) comparison. Colored states (i.e., nodes) and transitions (i.e., edges) contain statistically significant differences between the two event logs. Purple shades represent earlier executions of activities or reaching of states in *high* fines. Green shades represent the other way around. White indicates that no significant differences can be observed. The shades become darker and darker with increasingly statistically significant differences. (Color figure online)

Fig. 8 illustrates the output of the second experiment. Orange shade ovals and arcs represent states reached or transitions executed significantly more often in low fines compared with high fines. Blue shades refer to the opposite. The first observation is that low fines are usually immediately paid without requiring the local police to send a copy of fine to the offender. This can be seen through the orange-colored state *[Payment, Create Fine]* and the transition from *[Create Fine]* to this state. Conversely, high fines are more often sent to the offender than low fines, as one can observe through the blue-colored state *[Send Fine, Create Fine]*. Similar observations can be derived by looking at the other states and transitions. Figure 8 highlights part of the transition system (red rectangle). It indicates that, for low fines, it happens significantly more often that offenders perform incomplete payments, which cause a penalty to be added[3], which are subsequently followed by a second payment to probably complete the fine payment. Conversely, for high fines, it is significantly more frequent that payments only occurs after adding the penalty. This can be seen from the blue color associated with the transition between states *[Add Penalty, Insert Fine Notification]* and *[Payment, Add Penalty]*. Please observe that the latter finding could not be observed if we used an abstraction solely based on the last occurred event.

6   Related Work

Earlier work has been done on comparing process variants. The corresponding papers can be grouped in two category: model-based and log-based comparison.

---

[3] According to the Italian laws, if a fine is not paid in full within 90 days, a penalty is added so that the due amount doubles.

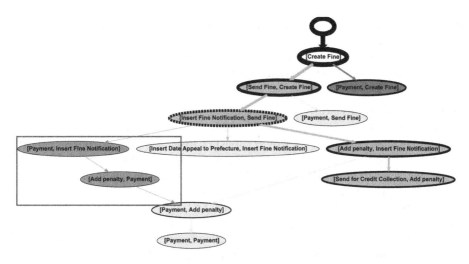

Fig. 8. *Occurrence* frequency comparison. Colored states (i.e., nodes) and transitions (i.e., edges) contain statistically significant differences between the two event logs. Blue colors represent a higher occurrence in *high* fines. Orange colors represent a higher occurrence in *low* fines. (Color figure online)

The main difference between these two categories is that model-based approaches require process models as inputs and log based approaches require event logs as inputs. Indirectly, model-based approaches can also be used starting from event logs. Models can be discovered from logs and then used as inputs for the approach. However, the obtained insights should be validated since the structure of the models (hence, the detected differences) can be drastically affected by the choice of the discovery technique or its parameters.

Model-Based Comparison. Model-based comparison techniques have been developed in recent years [9–12]. La Rosa et al. [11] provide a complete overview of the different ways to compare and merge models. Most of them are based on control-flow comparison, where the structural properties of the models (represented as graphs) are compared (e.g., nodes and edges present in one of the models, but not in the other one).

A drawback of model-based approaches is that they are unable to detect differences in terms of frequency or any other process metrics (e.g., elapsed time). For example, in Sect. 5, we detected a frequency difference on the payment of a fine directly after being created (34 % of the *low* fines versus 15 % of the *high* fines). This difference is not detected by model-based approaches, since in both variants the activity "Create Fine" is followed by "Payment" in at least 15 % of the cases, so this behavior would be present in the models of both variants. A severe drawback of employing model-based comparison is related to the fact that the variants are compared in terms of their model structure whereas we aim to compare the behavior. This motivates why, in this paper, we have opted for a low-level behavioral representation, i.e., transition systems, instead of high-level process modelling languages, such as BPMN or Petri nets. For instance, they are unable to detect that low-fine offenders perform incomplete payments that need to be integrated after receiving a penalization.

Log-Based Comparison. The most recent approach for log-based behavior comparison is by van Beest et al. [13]. This technique is able to identify differences between two event logs by computing *frequency-enhanced prime event structures* (FPES) from the corresponding event logs, comparing the obtained FPES and report the results using two sets of textual statements: *control-flow* differences and *branching frequency* differences.

This approach has some advantages, such as the handling of concurrency in process behavior. However, it presents three main limitations described as follows. First, the technique looks at the relative frequency, only. As such, when looking at branching frequency, it possibly returns a difference (if any), even though the branching point is actually reached very rarely. Also, no statistical significant tests are employed. Second, to determine branching points, they only look at the last activity independently of what activities were previously executed. As such - as we have verified by testing the reference implementation - it is unable to detect differences that refer to the activities preceding the last, such as, in the road-traffic case study, a number of low-fine offenders perform incomplete payments that need to be integrated after receiving a penalization. Third, the approach considers event logs as sequences of event labels, thus ignoring all other event attributes (e.g., timestamp, event payload). This limits the approach to detect only frequency differences. Differences in performance or other process metrics cannot be obtained.

Other approaches based on *sequence mining* such as [14–17] obtain rules that are overcomplicated and not valuable from a business perspective (as indicated in [13,14]).

7   Conclusion

The problem of comparing process variants is highly relevant. Many companies are observing that the executions of their processes are not always optimal and subject to variations. Processes may change because of the influence of several factors, such as the year period, the geographical location of the process' execution or the resource unit in charge. Some recent approaches aim to compare the execution of the different process variants. Most existing approaches tend to focus on the control-flow perspective or to detect differences that are statistically insignificant.

To our knowledge, no current approach is able to detect the relevant behavioral differences between process variants in terms of any process metric (e.g., performance) based on their recorded event logs. To address this issue, we developed a new technique based on annotated transition systems that detects statistically significant differences between process variants in terms of any process metric, using event logs as input. We used annotated transition systems to avoid being mining algorithm specific.

Our implementation is provided with two concrete metrics, which are related to the control-flow frequency (in the paper, named *occurrence*) and to the time perspective (the *elapsed time* metric). However, the framework allows one to easily add new measurement functions.

The evaluation and the related-work analysis has clearly shown that the approach is relevant and allows one to pinpoint differences that previous approaches fail to provide. Also, our approach excludes all differences that are in fact statistically insignificant, which are conversely returned by other approaches.

As future work, we aim to evaluate to what extent this visual approach scales when processes get larger and more complex. In this way, we can obtain direct feedback about whether business stakeholders can understand and benefit from our visual approach. Also, we aim to integrate it with *process cubes*, thus providing a complete suite to slice, dice, drill down, roll up and compare process variants.

References

1. van der Aalst, W.M.P.: Process Mining: Discovery, Conformance and Enhancement of Business Processes, 1st edn. Springer, Heidelberg (2011)
2. Bolt, A., van der Aalst, W.M.P.: Multidimensional process mining using process cubes. In: Gaaloul, K., Schmidt, R., Nurcan, S., Guerreiro, S., Ma, Q. (eds.) BPMDS 2015 and EMMSAD 2015. LNBIP, vol. 214, pp. 102–116. Springer, Heidelberg (2015)
3. van der Aalst, W.M.P.: Process cubes: slicing, dicing, rolling up and drilling down event data for process mining. In: Song, M., Wynn, M.T., Liu, J. (eds.) AP-BPM 2013. LNBIP, vol. 159, pp. 1–22. Springer, Heidelberg (2013)
4. van der Aalst, W.M.P., Schonenberg, M.H., Song, M.: Time prediction based on process mining. Inf. Syst. **36**(2), 450–475 (2011). Special Issue: Semantic Integration of Data, Multimedia, and Services
5. Welch, B.L.: The generalization of 'student's' problem when several different population variances are involved. Biometrika **34**(1–2), 28–35 (1947)
6. Cohen, J.: Statistical Power Analysis for the Behavioral Sciences. Lawrence Erlbaum Associates, Hillsdale (1988)
7. van Dongen, B.F., de Medeiros, A.K.A., Verbeek, H.M.W.E., Weijters, A.J.M.M.T., van der Aalst, W.M.P.: The ProM framework: a new era in process mining tool support. In: Ciardo, G., Darondeau, P. (eds.) ICATPN 2005. LNCS, vol. 3536, pp. 444–454. Springer, Heidelberg (2005)
8. de Leoni, M., Mannhardt, F.: Road traffic fine management process (2015). doi:10.4121/uuid:270fd440-1057-4fb9-89a9-b699b47990f5
9. Kriglstein, S., Wallner, G., Rinderle-Ma, S.: A visualization approach for difference analysis of process models and instance traffic. In: Daniel, F., Wang, J., Weber, B. (eds.) BPM 2013. LNCS, vol. 8094, pp. 219–226. Springer, Heidelberg (2013)
10. Cordes, C., Vogelgesang, T., Appelrath, H.-J.: A generic approach for calculating and visualizing differences between process models in multidimensional process mining. In: Fournier, F., Mendling, J. (eds.) BPM 2014 Workshops. LNBIP, vol. 202, pp. 383–394. Springer, Heidelberg (2015)

11. La Rosa, M., Dumas, M., Uba, R., Dijkman, R.: Business process model merging: an approach to business process consolidation. ACM Trans. Softw. Eng. Methodol. **22**(2), 11:1–11:42 (2013)
12. Ivanov, S., Kalenkova, A., van der Aalst, W.M.P.: BPMNDiffViz: a tool for BPMN models comparison. In: Proceedings of the BPM Demo Session 2015 Co-located with the 13th International Conference on Business Process Management (BPM 2015), Innsbruck, Austria, 2 September 2015, pp. 35–39 (2015)
13. van Beest, N., Dumas, M., García-Bañuelos, L., La Rosa, M.: Log delta analysis: interpretable differencing of business process event logs. In: Proceedings of the 13th International Conference on Business Process Management (BPM 2015), pp. 386–405 (2015)
14. Nguyen, H., Dumas, M., La Rosa, M., Maggi, F.M., Suriadi, S.: Mining business process deviance: a quest for accuracy. In: Meersman, R., Panetto, H., Dillon, T., Missikoff, M., Liu, L., Pastor, O., Cuzzocrea, A., Sellis, T. (eds.) OTM 2014. LNCS, vol. 8841, pp. 436–445. Springer, Heidelberg (2014)
15. Lakshmanan, G.T., Rozsnyai, S., Wang, F.: Investigating clinical care pathways correlated with outcomes. In: Daniel, F., Wang, J., Weber, B. (eds.) BPM 2013. LNCS, vol. 8094, pp. 323–338. Springer, Heidelberg (2013)
16. Jagadeesh Chandra Bose, R.P., van der Aalst, W.M.P.: Abstractions in process mining: a taxonomy of patterns. In: Dayal, U., Eder, J., Koehler, J., Reijers, H.A. (eds.) BPM 2009. LNCS, vol. 5701, pp. 159–175. Springer, Heidelberg (2009)
17. Swinnen, J., Depaire, B., Jans, M.J., Vanhoof, K.: A process deviation analysis – a case study. In: Daniel, F., Barkaoui, K., Dustdar, S. (eds.) BPM Workshops 2011, Part I. LNBIP, vol. 99, pp. 87–98. Springer, Heidelberg (2012)

Business Process Performance Mining
with Staged Process Flows

Hoang Nguyen[1](✉), Marlon Dumas[2], Arthur H.M. ter Hofstede[1],
Marcello La Rosa[1], and Fabrizio Maria Maggi[2]

[1] Queensland University of Technology, Brisbane, Australia
huanghuy.nguyen@hdr.qut.edu.au,
{a.terhofstede,m.larosa}@qut.edu.au
[2] University of Tartu, Tartu, Estonia
{marlon.dumas,f.m.maggi}@ut.ee

Abstract. Existing business process performance mining tools offer various summary views of the performance of a process over a given period of time, allowing analysts to identify bottlenecks and their performance effects. However, these tools are not designed to help analysts understand how bottlenecks form and dissolve over time nor how the formation and dissolution of bottlenecks – and associated fluctuations in demand and capacity – affect the overall process performance. This paper presents an approach to analyze the evolution of process performance via a notion of Staged Process Flow (SPF). An SPF abstracts a business process as a series of queues corresponding to stages. The paper defines a number of stage characteristics and visualizations that collectively allow process performance evolution to be analyzed from multiple perspectives. It demonstrates the advantages of the SPF approach over state-of-the-art process performance mining tools using a real-life event log of a Dutch bank.

Keywords: Process mining · Performance analysis · Multistage processes · Cumulative flow · Queuing theory

1 Introduction

Process mining is a family of techniques designed to extract insights from business process event logs [1]. *Process Performance Mining* (PPM) is a subset of process mining techniques concerned with the analysis of processes with respect to performance dimensions, chiefly *time* (how fast a process is executed); *cost* (how much a process execution costs); *quality* (how well the process meets customer requirements and expectations); and *flexibility* (how rapidly can a process adjust to changes in the environment) [2].

Along the time and flexibility dimensions, one recurrent analysis task is to understand how the temporal performance of a process evolves over a given period of time – also known as *flow performance* analysis in lean management [3]. For example, a bank manager may wish to know how the waiting times in a loan

© Springer International Publishing Switzerland 2016
S. Nurcan et al. (Eds.): CAiSE 2016, LNCS 9694, pp. 167–185, 2016.
DOI: 10.1007/978-3-319-39696-5_11

application process have evolved over the past month in order to adjust the resource allocation policies so as to minimize the effects of bottlenecks.

Existing PPM techniques are not designed to address such flow performance questions. Instead, these techniques focus on analyzing process performance in a "snapshot" manner, by taking as input an event log recorded during a period of time and extracting aggregate measures such as mean waiting time, processing time or cycle time of the process and its activities. For example, both the Performance Analysis plugins of ProM [4] and Disco [5] calculate aggregate performance measures (e.g. mean waiting time) over the entire period covered by an event log and display these measures by color-coding the elements of a process model. These tools can also produce animations of the flow of cases along a process model over time. However, extracting flow performance insights from these animations requires close and continuous attention from the analyst in order to detect visual cues of performance trends, bottleneck formation and dissolution, and phase transitions in the process performance. In other words, animation techniques allow analysts to get a broad picture of performance issues, but not to precisely quantify the evolution of process performance over time.

In this setting, this paper presents a PPM approach designed to provide a precise and quantifiable picture of flow performance. The approach relies on an abstraction of business processes called *Staged Process Flow* (SPF). An SPF breaks down a process into a series of queues corresponding to user-defined stages. Each stage is associated with a number of performance characteristics that are computed at each time point in an observation window. The evolution of these characteristics is then plotted via several visualization techniques that collectively allow flow performance to be analyzed from multiple perspectives in order to address the following questions:

Q1. How does the overall process performance evolve over time?
Q2. How does the formation and dissolution of bottlenecks affect the overall process performance?
Q3. How do changes in demand and capacity affect the overall process performance?

The rest of this paper is organized as follows. Section 2 reviews existing PPM techniques with respect to the problem of flow performance analysis. Section 3 describes the SPF concept and associated characteristics and visualizations. Section 4 discusses an evaluation of the approach based on a real-life log. Finally, Sect. 5 summarizes the contributions and outlines future work directions.

2   Related Work

Existing PPM tools support the analysis of entire processes or activities thereof with respect to performance measures such as cycle time, processing time and waiting time. Some PPM tools display the distribution of performance measures in the form of dashboards (e.g. bar charts) alongside aggregate statistics (e.g. mean and median) [5]. Others overlay the performance measures on top of a process model, for example by replaying the log on the process model [4,6] and calculating aggregate performance measures for each element in the process model during replay. Techniques for enhancing the quality of log replaying based on clustering techniques have been proposed [7]. All these techniques are designed to summarize the performance of the process over the entire time period covered by the event log. They can pinpoint bottlenecks, resource underutilization and other performance issues observed across said time period. However, they do not allow one to analyze how those bottlenecks form and dissolve, and more generally, how the performance of the process varies over time.

There is a range of techniques to extract and analyze process performance characteristics (incl. performance measures) from event logs. For example, de Leoni et al. [8] propose a framework to extract process performance characteristics from event logs and to correlate them in order to discriminate for example between the performance of cases that lead to "positive" outcomes versus "negative" outcomes. Meanwhile, Pika et al. [9] propose a framework to extract performance characteristics along the resource perspective. These proposals however are not designed to provide insights into the evolution of process performance over time.

A related technique supported by contemporary PPM tools is log animation. Log animation displays in a movie-like fashion how cases circulate through the process model over time [7,10,11]. However, extracting flow performance insights from these animations requires the analyst to: (i) manually look for visual cues in the animation that indicate trends, phase transitions or bottlenecks in the process' performance; and (ii) run additional queries to locate and quantify the observed performance phenomena.

Process performance has also been approached from the perspective of queuing theory. Senderovich et al. [12] propose a method to discover characteristics of "work queues" from event logs at the level of an entire process or of individual activities. Meanwhile, de Smet [13] proposes a method to discover collections of queues from event logs. This latter method discovers queues by grouping resources and activities into clusters based on cohesion metrics. The queuing models produced by the above methods are used for prediction (e.g. of waiting times) rather than performance analysis. As such these methods are only marginally related to the problem of flow performance analysis.

The concept of SPF presented in this paper is inspired by flow performance analysis techniques from the fields of lean management and agile software engineering. The idea of decomposing the process into stages and analyzing flow metrics at each stage can be found in various embodiments in contemporary lean and agile management tools, e.g. Kanban Flow[1] and ActionableAgile[2]. The concept of SPF formalized in this paper in the context of business process event logs, provides a generic framework that brings together flow performance analysis techniques found across these tools.

---

[1] http://kanbanflow.com.

[2] http://www.actionableagile.com.

3   Approach

In this section, we introduce the concept of SPF and its formalization before describing our SPF-based approach to process performance mining.

3.1   SPF Overview

An SPF is a partitioning of the set of log events into consecutive *stages* with a defined order (e.g. $\langle s_1, s_2, s_3, s_4 \rangle$). For each trace, all events in one stage must precede all events in the subsequent stage (in our example all events in s_1 must have a causal relation with all events in s_2). A trace does not need to have all stages, so long as its stages follow the defined order (in our example a trace with $\langle s_1, s_2 \rangle$ is possible but not a trace with $\langle s_1, s_2, s_4 \rangle$). We model a stage as a *queuing system*, where the queuing items are cases and the service facility is the set of resources available to handle cases in the stage in question. Each stage has an *arrival flow* via which new cases arrive to the stage in question and a *departure flow* via which cases depart. In addition, a stage may have *exit flows*, capturing the fact that a case may leave the process abnormally after being serviced at a stage. This will be the cases for traces that do not finish all stages.

For illustration, we use the loan origination process of a Dutch bank, which was the subject of the BPI Challenge 2012 log.[3] As depicted in the SPF in Fig. 1, a case in this process is a loan application that goes through four stages: Pre-Assess (s_1), Assess (s_2), Negotiate (s_3) and Validate (s_4), in this order. In the "Pre-Assess" stage, the bank checks the completeness of the loan application and requests the customer to provide sufficient documents before their application can proceed to the next stage. Next, in the "Assess" stage, the bank checks the eligibility of the loan application. In the "Negotiate" stage, the bank and the customer discuss the terms and conditions of the loan until it is ready for validation. Finally, in the "Validate" stage, a bank controller reviews and decides to approve or reject the loan application. At the end of any stage, a loan application can either be declined by the bank or canceled by the customer, which leads to interrupting the process at that point.

In this example, each stage has an exit flow consisting of loan applications that are declined or canceled. Thus, a trace recording a loan application that is canceled after the assessment, will only have the first two stages.

Flow performance in an SPF is determined by a set of *characteristics* capturing the interplay between the arrival flow on the one hand and the departure and exit flows on the other. One such characteristic is the *Cases In Progress* (in reference to "Work-in-Progress"), that is, the set of cases found in a stage at a given point in time. Another characteristic is the *Time in Stage*: the time between the arrival and the departure/exit of a case for a given stage. Each case spends a certain amount of time waiting in a stage, and another amount of time being processed in that stage. *Flow Efficiency* is the ratio between the processing time of a case in a stage and the Time in Stage. Below we formally define how an SPF and its characteristics are extracted from an event log.

---

[3] http://dx.doi.org/10.4121/uuid:3926db30-f712-4394-aebc-75976070e91f.

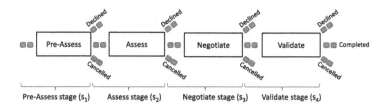

Fig. 1. SPF model of a loan origination process.

3.2 SPF Formalization

An event log is the starting point of any process mining task. Figure 2 shows an event log of a loan origination process. An event log consists of a set of *cases*, where a case is a uniquely identified instance of a process. For example, the loan application identified by code c_4 is a case. Each case consists of a sequence of *events*. An event is the most granular element of a log and is characterized by a set of attributes such as *activity*, *resource* (the entity that performed the activity associated with the event, which can be human or non-human), and *timestamp* (the moment when the event occurred). *Event type* represents the association between an event and its activity's lifecycle, such as "schedule", "start", and "complete". In this paper, we assume that "start" and "complete" are the only event types associated with activities.

Case ID	Case Status	Reason	Stage	Event ID	Event Type	Timestamp	Activity Name	AID	Res.
c_1	Incomplete	Declined	Pre-Assess (S_1)	e_1	start	05.10 09:00:00	Update application	a_1	Rob
				e_2	complete	05.10 10:00:00	Update application	a_1	Rob
c_2	Incomplete	Declined	Pre-Assess (S_1)	e_3	start	06.10 09:00:00	Update application	a_2	Rob
				e_4	complete	06.10 10:00:00	Update application	a_2	Rob
			Assess (S_2)	e_5	start	08.10 09:00:00	Check application	a_3	Sara
				e_6	complete	08.10 10:00:00	Check application	a_3	Sara
				e_7	start	09.10 08:30:00	Check application	a_4	Sara
				e_8	complete	09.10 09:00:00	Check application	a_4	Sara
c_3	Incomplete	Canceled	Pre-Assess (S_1)	e_9	start	08.10 09:00:00	Update application	a_5	Rob
				e_{10}	complete	08.10 10:00:00	Update application	a_5	Rob
			Assess (S_2)	e_{11}	start	09.10 09:00:00	Check application	a_6	Sara
				e_{12}	complete	09.10 09:15:00	Check application	a_6	Sara
			Negotiate (S_3)	e_{13}	start	11.10 09:00:00	Follow up offer	a_7	Sara
				e_{14}	complete	11.10 10:00:00	Follow up offer	a_7	Sara
c_4	Complete		Pre-Assess (S_1)	e_{15}	start	09.10 08:00:00	Update application	a_8	Rob
				e_{16}	complete	09.10 09:00:00	Update application	a_8	Rob
			Assess (S_2)	e_{17}	start	09.10 09:00:00	Check application	a_9	Tim
				e_{18}	complete	09.10 10:00:00	Check application	a_9	Tim
			Negotiate (S_3)	e_{19}	start	10.10 09:00:00	Follow up offer	a_{10}	Tim
				e_{20}	complete	10.10 10:00:00	Follow up offer	a_{10}	Tim
			Validate (S_4)	e_{21}	start	12.10 09:00:00	Validate application	a_{11}	Mike
				e_{22}	complete	12.10 10:00:00	Validate application	a_{11}	Mike

Fig. 2. Example event log for a loan origination process.

Formally, an event log EL is a tuple $(E, ET, A, R, C, time, act, type, res, case)$, where E is a set of events, $ET = \{start, complete\}$ is the set of event types, A is a set of globally (i.e. across cases) unique activity identifiers (AID), R is a set of resources, C is a set of cases, $time : E \to \mathbb{R}_0^+$ is a function that assigns a timestamp to an event, $act : E \to A$ is a function that assigns an AID to an event, $type : E \to ET$ is a function that assigns an event type to an event, $res : E \to R$ is a function that assigns a resource to an event, and $case : E \to C$ relates an event to a case. We write $e \lesssim_E e'$ iff $time(e) \leq time(e')$.

In our model, events are associated with *stages*. For example, a particular "Check application" event occurs at the "Assess" stage of a loan application. A completed case is one that passed all stages and has a "complete" status, otherwise, the case is considered to have exited the process prematurely and will have the status "incomplete".

Stage-Based Enhancement. In our approach, an event log must firstly be enhanced with stage information. A *stage-based enhancement* SE of an event log $EL = (E, ET, A, R, C, time, act, type, res, case)$ is defined as a tuple $(S, CS, <_S, stage, status)$, where S is a set of stages, $CS = \{complete, incomplete\}$ a set of case statuses, $<_S \subseteq S \times S$ a strict total order over S (with $\leq_S$ the corresponding total order), $stage : E \to S$ assigns stages to events, and $status : C \to CS$ assigns statuses to cases. For convenience, we write $E^{c,s} = \{e \in E \mid case(e) = c \wedge stage(e) = s\}$ to denote the set of all events of case c that occurred in stage s, and $E^{start} = \{e \in E \mid type(e) = start\}$ is the set of all "start" events.

While there can be a number of ways to arrive at a stage-based enhancement of an event log, there are a number of rules that need to be satisfied. First of all, if a case covers a stage s, i.e. there is at least one event belonging to that stage, there must be events associated with all stages preceding s in that case:

$$\forall c \in C \ \forall s \in S[E^{c,s} \neq \varnothing \Rightarrow \forall s' \in S[s' <_S s \Rightarrow E^{c,s'} \neq \varnothing]].$$

The stages covered by a case must observe the defined order $<_S$ over S:

$$\forall e, e' \in E[(case(e) = case(e') \wedge e \lesssim_E e') \Rightarrow stage(e) \leq_S stage(e')].$$

Events related to the same activity must belong to the same stage:

$$\forall e, e' \in E[act(e) = act(e') \Rightarrow stage(e) = stage(e')].$$

If a case has a complete status, it should have gone through all the stages:

$$\forall c \in C[status(c) = complete \Rightarrow \forall s \in S \ \exists e \in E[case(e) = c \wedge stage(e) = s]].$$

SPF Characteristics. The start of stage s in case c, $T_{AR}(c, s)$, is defined as $\min_{e \in E^{c,s}} time(e)$ if $E^{c,s} \neq \varnothing$ and is undefined ($\perp$) otherwise. Similarly, the end of a stage s in case c, $T_{DP}(c, s)$, is $\max_{e \in E^{c,s}} time(e)$ if $E^{c,s} \neq \varnothing$ and is undefined otherwise.

For all timestamps t neither $t < \perp$ nor $t > \perp$ holds. The last stage of case c is s, $laststage(c, s)$, iff $\neg(\exists s' \in S \; \exists e \in E[s <_S s' \wedge case(e) = c \wedge stage(e) = s'])$.

The set $C_{AR}(s, t)$ consists of all cases that have reached stage s on or before t, i.e. $C_{AR}(s, t) \triangleq \{c \in C \mid \exists e \in E^{c,s}[time(e) \leq t]\}$. Similarly, the set $C_{DP}(s, t)$ consists of all cases that have gone beyond stage s on or before time t, i.e. $C_{DP}(s, t) \triangleq \{c \in C \mid \forall e \in E^{c,s}[time(e) \leq t]\}$. The set $C_{EX}(s, t)$ consists of those cases that have completed stage s on or before time t, have not gone beyond stage s, and are considered to be incomplete: $C_{EX}(s, t) \triangleq \{c \in C \mid \forall e \in E^{c,s}[time(e) \leq t] \wedge laststage(c, s) \wedge status(c) = incomplete\}$.

The *Arrival/Departure/Exit Rate* X (X stands for AR, DP, and EX) is the average number of cases arriving at/departing from/exiting after a stage s per unit of time Δ at a given point in time t:

$$X(s, t, \Delta) \triangleq \frac{|C_X(s, t)| - |C_X(s, t - \Delta)|}{\Delta}.$$

It is required that $\Delta > 0$ here and elsewhere, and $t - \Delta$ is not before all case start times in the log, i.e. $\exists e \in E[time(e) \leq (t - \Delta)]$.

Cases in Progress is the number of cases present at a stage s at a point in time t:

$$CIP(s, t) \triangleq |C_{AR}(s, t)| - |C_{DP}(s, t)|.$$

The *Time in Stage* for a point in time t and a stage s is the minimal duration that one needs to wait to see the number of departing cases from s equal or greater than the number of cases that arrived in stage s on or before time t. Formally, let t' be the minimal timestamp such that $t' = t + i\Delta(i = 1 \ldots n)$ and $|C_{DP}(s, t')| \geq |C_{AR}(s, t)|$, then $TIS(s, t, \Delta) = t' - t$. $TIS(s, t, \Delta)$ is undefined if no such t' exists.

Finally, the *Flow Efficiency FE* of a stage s during an interval $[t - \Delta, t]$ is the sum of all durations of activities that occurred in that stage and that interval divided by the sum of all case durations for that stage in the said interval. To be able to determine the durations of activities, we have to impose further requirements on an event log: (1) for every activity in the log there is at most one corresponding "start" event and one corresponding "complete" event, i.e. $\forall e \in E \; \nexists e' \in E[e \neq e' \wedge act(e') = act(e) \wedge type(e') = type(e)]$, (2) for every "start" event of an activity there is a corresponding "complete" event and vice versa, i.e. $\forall e \in E \; \exists e' \in E[act(e) = act(e') \wedge type(e) \neq type(e')]$, and (3) for every activity its corresponding "start" event should occur before its corresponding "complete" event, i.e. $\forall e \in E \; \forall e' \in E[(type(e) = start \wedge type(e') = complete \wedge act(e) = act(e')) \Rightarrow time(e) < time(e')]$. Then, any activity $a \in ran(act)$ has exactly one corresponding "start" event e_s and exactly one corresponding "complete" event e_c. The duration of a during a closed time interval $[t_1, t_2]$, denoted $dur(a, t_1, t_2)$, is defined as $[t_1, t_2] \cap [time(e_s), time(e_c)]$. In addition, the duration of case c at stage s within interval $[t_1, t_2]$, written $dur(c, s, t_1, t_2)$, is defined as $[t_1, t_2] \cap [T_{AR}(c, s), T_{DP}(c, s)]$ if $E^{c,s} \neq \varnothing$ and is zero (0) otherwise.

Case ID	$T_{AR}(c,s_1)$	$T_{DP}(c,s_1)$	$T_{AR}(c,s_2)$	$T_{DP}(c,s_2)$	$T_{AR}(c,s_3)$	$T_{DP}(c,s_3)$	$T_{AR}(c,s_4)$	$T_{DP}(c,s_4)$
c_1	05.10 09:00:00	05.10 10:00:00	$\perp$	$\perp$	$\perp$	$\perp$	$\perp$	$\perp$
c_2	06.10 09:00:00	06.10 10:00:00	08.10 09:00:00	09.10 09:00:00	$\perp$	$\perp$	$\perp$	$\perp$
c_3	08.10 09:00:00	08.10 10:00:00	09.10 09:00:00	09.10 09:15:00	11.10 09:00:00	11.10 10:00:00	$\perp$	$\perp$
c_4	09.10 08:00:00	09.10 09:00:00	09.10 09:00:00	09.10 10:00:00	10.10 09:00:00	10.10 10:00:00	12.10 09:00:00	12.10 10:00:00

Fig. 3. Stage-based timetable.

$$FE(s,t,\Delta) \triangleq \frac{\sum\limits_{e \in E^{start}, stage(e)=s} dur(act(e), t - \Delta, t)}{\sum\limits_{c \in C} dur(c, s, t - \Delta, t)}.$$

Note that at least one case should have events in the interval $[t - \Delta, t]$ in stage s to avoid the denominator evaluating to zero.

The formulae above can be illustrated with the example log given in Fig. 2. First, the log is summarized by stages and cases as shown in Fig. 3 for ease of computation. With $t_1 = 09.10\ 08{:}15{:}00, t_2 = 09.10\ 09{:}15{:}00, \Delta = 1h$, the values of the SPF characteristics are computed as follows:

- $C_{AR}(s_2, t_1) = \{c_2\}, C_{AR}(s_2, t_2) = \{c_2, c_3, c_4\}$
- $C_{DP}(s_2, t_1) = \{\}, C_{DP}(s_2, t_2) = \{c_2, c_3\}$
- $C_{EX}(s_2, t_1) = \{\}, C_{EX}(s_2, t_2) = \{c_2\}$
- $AR(s_2, t_2, \Delta) = 2$ cases/h, $DP(s_2, t_2, \Delta) = 2$ cases/h, $EX(s_2, t_2, \Delta) = 1$ case/h
- $CIP(s_2, t_2) = 1$ case, $TIS(s_2, t_2, \Delta) = 1h$ (at $t' = 09.10\ 10{:}15{:}00$, $C_{DP}(s_2, t') = C_{AR}(s_2, t_2)$)
- $FE(s_2, t_2, \Delta) = \frac{dur(a_3, t_1, t_2) + dur(a_4, t_1, t_2) + dur(a_6, t_1, t_2) + dur(a_9, t_1, t_2)}{dur(c_1, s_2, t_1, t_2) + dur(c_2, s_2, t_1, t_2) + dur(c_3, s_2, t_1, t_2) + dur(c_4, s_2, t_1, t_2)} = \frac{0 + 30\,min + 15\,min + 15\,min}{0 + 45\,min + 15\,min + 15\,min} = 0.8.$

3.3 SPF-Based Performance Mining Approach

Our approach to process performance mining follows three steps: (i) construct flow cells; (ii) measure SPF characteristics; (iii) visualize SPF characteristics for user consumption.

Construct Flow Cells. First, the log is enhanced with stage information. This is currently done via preprocessing, which consists in adding two stage-based attributes: a "stage" attribute for each event, indicating which stage it belongs to, and a "status" attribute to the case, indicating if the case is complete.

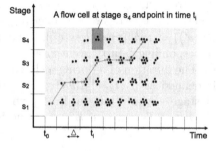

Fig. 4. Flow cells.

Next, the timeline of the log is divided into equal time intervals Δ. The stages and time intervals create a two-dimensional space (see Fig. 4), in which a cell at the intersection of a stage and an interval located at $t_i = t_o + i\Delta$ ($i = 0 \ldots n$, and t_o is the starting time of the log) is called a *flow cell*. From the stage-based timetable (e.g. Fig. 3), it is possible to check exactly which flow cells a case falls in during its lifecycle.

Measure SPF Characteristics. SPF characteristics are computed first at every flow cell, then rolled up to the stage and process level (also called system level). At a particular flow cell located at a stage s and a point in time $t_i = t_o + i\Delta$ ($i = 0 \ldots n$), the formulae presented in Sect. 3.2 can be applied as exemplified above. At a stage s, the SPF characteristics of s for a time interval are computed as a statistic (e.g. max, min, and mean) of the corresponding SPF characteristics of all flow cells located at stage s and fully contained within the time interval. Similarly, at the system level, the SPF characteristics of the system are computed as a statistic of the corresponding characteristics of all stages, except that the Arrival Rate and Departure Rate at the system level are the Arrival Rate at the first stage and Departure Rate at the last stage, respectively.

Visualize SPF Characteristics. Based on the above formalization, we provide three visualizations to support the analysis of SPF characteristics at different levels of abstraction and periods of time.

Cumulative Flow Diagram (CFD): A CFD is an area graph used in queueing theory [14] to visualize the evolution of flow performance over time. Figure 5 depicts how some SPF characteristics are related to the geometry of the CFD. In our case, each area, encoded with a different color, represents the number of cases queuing for a given process stage (*queue flow*), being worked in that stage (*service flow*) or exit-

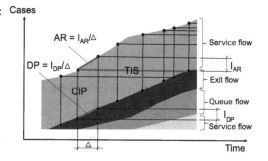

Fig. 5. CFD structure.

ing from that stage (*exit flow*). The service flow and the queue flow are actually two sub-stages of a process stage with similar SPF characteristics. The CFD is particularly suitable for examining the flow performance. For example, one can observe the process evolution over time through the development trend of different flows, identify the formation and dissolution of a bottleneck through widening and shrinking areas on a queue and service flow, and detect patterns of changes in the arrival rate and departure rate as well as their correlation with the process performance.

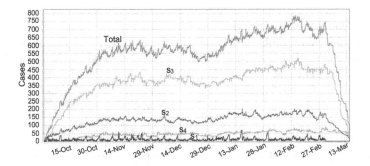

From Sat, 1 Oct 2011 00:38:44 +0200 To Wed, 22 Feb 2012 18:24:21 +0100 (144 days) (Mean/Median)					
	AR(cases/day)	DR(cases/day)	ER(cases/day)	CIP(cases)	TIS(hours)	FE(%)
System	84.73 / 72.00	18.62 / 0.00	65.72 / 24.00	702.26 / 723.00	550.33 / 546.00	2.92
s1-queue	84.73 / 72.00	84.73 / 72.00		3.53 / 3.00	0.69 / 0.00	
s1-service	84.73 / 72.00	84.69 / 48.00	37.10 / 24.00	12.19 / 10.00	4.13 / 2.00	9.25 / 1.35
s2-queue	47.59 / 24.00	47.55 / 24.00		4.44 / 3.00	2.69 / 1.00	
s2-service	47.55 / 24.00	46.38 / 0.00	14.05 / 0.00	132.53 / 136.00	67.58 / 68.00	0.86 / 0.63
s3-queue	32.33 / 0.00	31.49 / 0.00		96.98 / 97.00	72.64 / 71.00	
s3-service	31.49 / 0.00	28.39 / 0.00	9.22 / 0.00	362.85 / 379.00	285.25 / 296.00	0.23 / 0.19
s4-queue	19.17 / 0.00	19.03 / 0.00		48.88 / 52.00	61.40 / 58.00	
s4-service	19.03 / 0.00	18.62 / 0.00	5.35 / 0.00	41.66 / 43.00	55.95 / 50.00	1.32 / 0.94

Fig. 6. Performance Summary Table (AR = Arrival Rate, DR = Departure Rate, ER = Exit Rate, CIP = Cases in Progress, TIS = Time in Stage, FE = Flow Efficiency). For example, AR = 84.73/72.00 indicates that the mean arrival rate is 84.73 cases per day and the median rate is 72 cases per day.

Performance Summary Table (PST): The PST (Fig. 6) provides a quick and exact measurement of the flow performance in figures, at the stage and system levels. It also allows one to measure the flow for any time interval of the log.

Time Series Charts (TSCs): As most SPF characteristics are time-dependent, TSCs (Fig. 7) can be used to investigate the evolution of SPF stage characteristics over time, such as viewing the development of arrival rate, the difference between departure and arrival rate at different intervals, or the formation of bottlenecks over time. Figure 7 gives a multiple-series TSC showing the evolution of various SPF characteristics over time.

Fig. 7. Time series chart of various SPF characteristics.

4   Evaluation

We implemented our approach as a ProM plugin, namely the "Performance Mining With Staged Process Flows" plugin, as well as a standalone Java application.[4] In the following, we use this implementation to answer the questions raised in Sect. 1 using the BPI Challenge 2012 log, and compare the results with those

---

[4] Available from http://promtools.org (ProM) and http://apromore.org/platform/ tools (standalone Java application).

obtained from two state-of-the-art PPM tools. For space reasons, the results of a second evaluation, using the BPI Challenge 2013 log,[5] are provided in a technical report [15], though they are in line with those reported in this paper.

The BPI Challenge 2012 log records cases of a loan origination process at a Dutch bank (see Sect. 3 for a description). It contains 13,087 loan applications with a total of 193,208 events occurring from 1 Oct 2011 to 15 Mar 2012. Every case must pass four stages. The completion of each stage is marked by a special event such as A_PREACCEPTED, A_ACCEPTED, and A_ACTIVATED. We preprocessed this log to enhance it with stage information, including adding a "stage" attribute for events and a "status" attribute for cases.

The PPM tools evaluated are the "Performance Analysis with Petri Net" plugin of ProM 5.2 [4] (PEP for short), and Fluxicon's Disco [5]. PEP requires a Petri net discovered from an event log as input. The net can be obtained by using any of the available discovery algorithms of ProM that either directly discovers a Petri net or whose result can be converted into a Petri net, such as the Heuristics Miner. PEP can be run to internally replay the log on the Petri net, in order to align the log with the model, compute time-related performance information and overlay it to the model. Specifically, processing time is assigned to Petri net transitions (capturing process activities) while waiting time is assigned to places (capturing states). Arrival rates for these elements are also provided. Moreover, places are color-coded based on the length of the waiting time (blue for short waits, yellow for medium and red for long). The thresholds for the colors can be set automatically or manually by the user. The tool also provides overall performance measures such as arrival rate and statistics on cycle time.[6]

Similar to PEP, Disco's performance measurements are mainly based on a process model. The tool takes an event log as input and discovers a Fuzzy net, which provides an abstract representation of the process behavior, by showing the process activities and paths connecting these activities. This model is enhanced with frequency information and statistics on performance measures at the level of individual process activities (processing time) and paths (waiting time). The complexity of the discovered model can be adjusted based on case frequency, in order to obtain a simpler process model that abstracts away infrequent cases. Different types of filters besides frequency can be used to create model projections which can be used to compare process variants on the basis of their performance, e.g. focusing on all cases that have a duration or a number of events within a given range. In addition, Disco can replay the log on the discovered model.

For each question, we evaluated each tool along the quality dimensions of *ease of use* and *usefulness*, widely used in technology acceptance models [16]. In our context, ease of use refers to the effort required from the user to retrieve and to interpret data in order to answer a given question. Usefulness on the other

---

[5] http://dx.doi.org/10.4121/uuid:a7ce5c55-03a7-4583-b855-98b86e1a2b07.

[6] The "Replay a Log on Petri Net for Performance/Conformance Analysis" plugin of ProM 6 works in a similar way to PEP, though it provides less performance information.

hand refers to the extent the tool provides data that allows the user to answer the question in a precise (i.e. quantitatively) and informative manner. Below we evaluate the three tools for each question.

Q1: How does the overall process performance evolve over time?

SPF. The evolution of the process is depicted on a CFD (Fig. 8). The shape of the CFD reflects the development of the process at each stage. The characteristics, such as arrival rate (AR) and cases in progress (CIP), can be seen at any point in time as a tooltip. The CFD can be zoomed in to investigate patterns of evolution at different intervals (e.g. weekly, daily and hourly). The evolution can also be viewed on the plot of flow efficiency over time. The PST (Fig. 6) provides a summary of the flow performance at any time interval. From these visualizations, we can draw the following observations:

- The process has a stable trend indicated through the even height of service flows shown in Fig. 8 (bands named as s_i-Service). Further evidence is provided by the average arrival and departure rates, which are comparable at each stage in Fig. 6, and by the fact that there is little variation between the average mean and median value of CIP and TIS.
- There are strong exit flows throughout the period from s_1 (strongest) to s_4 (bands named as s_i-Exit on the CFD). Apparently, these exit flows contribute to keeping the arrival of cases at each stage on a par with their departure.
- The CFD and PST show that the waiting queue is negligible at stage s_1 but starts to emerge at stage s_2 and becomes considerable at stages s_3 and s_4, meaning that the process has slower response in the later stages.
- The process has very low flow efficiency (3 %), i.e. 97 % of time a case stays idle. The problem seems to be with frequent waits for customer response.

As shown above, the SPF proposes an easy way to understand how the overall process performance evolves over time. The output is easy to interpret, as it is based on visual cues and performance measures; precise, as it is supported by numeric measurements; and most importantly, it leads to various insightful observations.

PEP. An excerpt of the Petri net enhanced with performance information provided by PEP is shown in Fig. 9. This model was obtained by first discovering a Heuristics net from the log and then converting it to a Petri net. However, in order to obtain a model that is easy to interpret, we had to incrementally filter the log, as the first model discovered was a spaghetti-like model too dense to understand. Eventually, we ended up retaining only those events that mark the end of each stage in the log (i.e. the "gate" events), in a similar vein to our approach. A drawback of this operation is that the fitness of the model decreases as some traces of the log can no longer be replayed on the model. As a result, the performance measures provided by the tool are only approximate, as they only refer to those traces that perfectly fit the model.

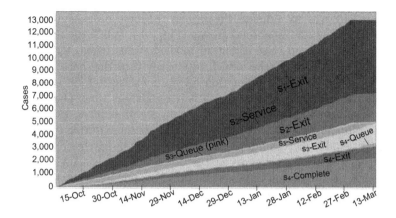

Fig. 8. CFD for the BPI Challenge 2012 log. Each stage s_i has a queue, service and exit flow. Some flows such as s_1-Queue, s_1-Service, s_2-Queue, and s_4-Service are fast and not observable on the normal scale.

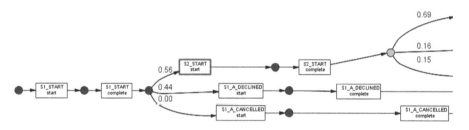

Fig. 9. Discovered process model in PEP, using gate events only.

Coming back to Q1, from the enhanced Petri net and associated performance measures, we were unable to answer Q1 as PEP does not offer any support to profile the process evolution over time. We concluded that PEP is unable to answer Q1.

Disco. Similar to PEP, the model discovered by Disco from the unfiltered log was rather complex, with 50 activities and over 150 paths. Hence, we also decided to retain the gate events only, leading to a rather simple model with 11 activities and 19 paths (Fig. 10a). Based on this model, we found two ways to answer Q1. One way was using the filter by timeframe provided by Disco to select different process variants by time intervals, e.g. by months from Oct 2011 to Mar 2012. After each interval, we recorded the performance measures manually for each process variant. At the end of this procedure, we obtained a set of monthly performance measures which we could use for trend analysis. While this approach could provide a precise measurement of process evolution, the results are not easy to retrieve and interpret from the figures manually calculated. We were unable to discover any insights because of the limitation of this manual review.

Another way was to animate the log on top of the discovered model, to identify any normal and abnormal trends (Fig. 10b). While the animation was running, we had to keep close attention to the various tokens flowing towards different directions through the model, to identify recurring patterns as well as deviations. To complete the animation for six months, it took approximately four minutes at maximum speed which is a reasonable time. One insight was that the cases seem to flow to the end of the process in batches. However, it was not easy to pinpoint the recurrent timing of these batches during the animation. We were also unable to compute the volume of cases in batches due to the lack of supporting performance figures in the animation. In conclusion, we found that although the animation in Disco can provide some insightful clues w.r.t. to process evolution, it is not possible to precisely characterize this evolution.

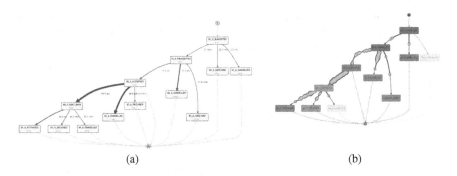

(a)   (b)

Fig. 10. (a) Filtered process model in Disco with highlighted bottlenecks and (b) its animation.

Q2: How formation and dissolution of bottlenecks affects overall performance?

SPF. We can observe signs of bottlenecks on the CFD when the queue band and/or service band become wider, meaning that the process has slower response to the arrival of new cases. The formation of bottlenecks can be identified from the time series charts of CIP and TIS of the queue and service stages, particularly at the peak points. The exact measurement of these effects is provided via the on-screen tooltips and by the PST with the time interval scale. The formation of bottlenecks generally leads to an increase of CIP and TIS in the queue and service period of a stage and possibly to a decrease of FE. Conversely, these effects gradually diminish when the bottleneck dissolves.

Although the log exhibits a stable process evolution, there are signs of bottlenecks. For example, Fig. 11a shows that at stage s_4, the queue (s_4-Queue) widens from 24 Oct and peaks on 27 Oct (CIP $= 120$ cases, see Fig. 12b) and then slowly decreases onwards. The time series chart of the flow efficiency for this stage (see Fig. 12a) also shows a fall on 26 and 27 Oct (around 0.55 % fall as measured by

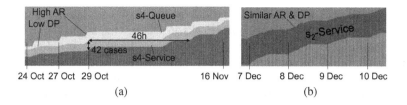

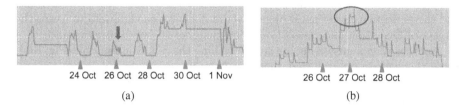

Fig. 11. (a) Example of widening queue at s_4 and (b) very minor queue at s_2.

Fig. 12. (a) Flow efficiency at s_4-Service and (b) CIP at s_4-Queue.

the PST). Our measurement also shows that the CIP and TIS of s_4-Service do not increase immediately from 26–27 Oct (ca. CIP $= 27$ cases, TIS$=20$ hours) but only afterwards (ca. CIP $= 42$ cases, TIS$=46$ hours from 29 Oct to 6 Nov 2011) as the aftermath of the previous congestion (Fig. 11a). The bottleneck then slowly dissolves towards 16 Nov (Fig. 11a) as the process increases its departure rate at s_4-Service after the bottleneck (from ca. 20 cases/day during 23–27 Oct to ca. 24 cases per day during 28 Oct-16 Nov). We observe that the FE has recovered and CIP and TIS have diminished during the period 28 Oct-16 Nov (Fig. 12a and b). Similar bottleneck phenomena are visible in stage s_4 at different times.

In conclusion, with our approach it is easy to retrieve data with interpretable and precise information to answer Q2, deriving information on how bottleneck formation and dissolution affect process performance.

PEP. Continuing from the enhanced model in Q1, PEP can highlight the bottlenecks on the model by coloring the places of the Petri net based on their associated waiting time (see Fig. 9). This information is enriched by detailed performance measurements at the level of individual elements (see e.g. Fig. 13).

However, we found no ways to reason about the impact of the formation and dissolution of bottlenecks on the process performance as the measures shown on the model are only aggregate values over the whole

Performance information of the selected place:

Frequency: 4763 visits
Arrival rate: 1.29 visits per hour

	Waiting time (hours)	Synchronization time (ho...	Sojourn time (hours)
avg	353.14	0.0	353.14
min	7.07E-3	0.0	7.07E-3
max	2149.17	0.0	2149.17

Fig. 13. Performance measures in PEP.

log timespan. It is not possible to drill down to lower levels of granularity, e.g. checking the daily arrival rate at a given place, and profile this over time. Thus, we conclude that PEP is unable to answer Q2.

Disco. Continuing from Q1 with the discovered high-level process model, we identified two ways of detecting bottlenecks in Disco. One is displaying performance measures on the model (Fig. 10a). Disco can highlight in red the exceptionally high values of activity and path durations as signs of bottleneck. We found that the paths for canceled cases at stages s_2, s_3 and s_4 take too long, e.g. 21 days at stage s_3. In addition, the path for cases going from s_3 to s_4 is also longer than average (11.9 days). While the use of filters allow one to measure the impact of a bottleneck on overall performance (e.g. by measuring how much the average cycle time improves by removing slow cases), based on the process model and the performance measures alone, we did not have enough data to assess the impact of formation and dissolution of bottlenecks on overall performance.

Another way of answering Q2 is by watching the replay animation (Fig. 10b). From this we can observe that there are busy flows of canceled cases at stages s_2, s_3 and s_4, and from s_3 to s_4. The tokens following these paths seem to be moving slower than those on other paths. However, we were unable to quantify these signs of bottleneck such as number of cases and waiting time, as well as the impact of these bottlenecks.

Q3: How do changes in demand and capacity affect overall process performance?

SPF. The demand and capacity are represented by the arrival (AR) and departure rate (DR), respectively. The arrival rate at the first stage is the customer demand while the departure rates at different stages are their corresponding capacities. They can be observed on the CFD, as well as in the time series charts of these characteristics. Any change in these characteristics will affect the overall process performance, including the CIP, TIS and FE of the queue and service periods, and lead to the formation and dissolution of bottlenecks.

Overall, the PST in Fig. 6 shows that the process under exam has a much higher AR at s_1-Queue as customer demand rate (84.73 cases/day), than DR at s_4-Service as final output rate (18.62 cases/day). However, the process maintains a stable evolution without congestion because there are strong exit flows as shown in Fig. 8. This mechanism effectively reduces the strain of high customer demand on the process.

As such, the impact of demand and capacity is visible locally at a stage only. For example, in relation to the bottleneck reviewed in Q2, the differential chart in Fig. 14 shows that the bottleneck appears due to the stronger dominance of the arrival rate over the departure rate prior to the bottleneck period (14–24 Oct). The difference between arrival and departure

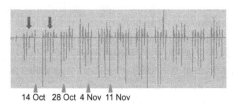

14 Oct 28 Oct 4 Nov 11 Nov

Fig. 14. Differential chart (DR-AR) at s_4-Queue.

patterns also has impact on the process performance. For example, Fig. 11a shows that the arrival rate AR at s_4-Queue is high within a short time (ca. 14 cases/day) while the departure rate DR is low (ca. 5 cases/day) and spreads over a longer time. This difference explains why there is a permanent long queue before s_4-Service, which we identified when answering Q2. In contrast, the AR and DR at s_2-Queue are approximately equal with the same distribution (see Fig. 11b). That is why there is a very minor queue at stage s_2.

PEP. We found no ways in PEP to investigate the impact of changes in demand and capacity on the process performance since this tool only captures one average value at every place/transition for the whole period. Hence, we are unable to answer Q3.

Disco. We replayed the animation in Disco while focusing on the speed of the token flows at the start activity of each stage and tried to learn how this relates to the flow of tokens departing from the last activity of each stage (Fig. 10b). However, we found it is very challenging to spot any patterns on the animation, since it is hard to capture the timing of tokens flowing at two different locations at the same time. We concluded that Disco is unable to answer Q3.

5   Conclusion

We presented an approach to analyze flow performance from event logs based on the concept of SPF, which transpose ideas found in lean management and agile software development to the field of PPM. The evaluation on real-life event logs puts into evidence qualitative advantages of this approach with respect to existing PPM techniques.

A key limitation of the SPF approach is the assumption that the log is divided into user-defined stages. In some cases, such stages may be already known (e.g. because they are captured in a process model), but in other scenarios the stages need to be discovered. A direction for future work is to design techniques for automated identification of *candidate stages* from a log. One possible approach is to cluster activities based on which resources most often perform them, as in [13]. An alternative is to cluster activities according to data dependencies, as in [17] where event types are grouped into clusters (corresponding to candidate sub-processes) based on shared data attributes.

Another limitation is that the approach still requires the user to manually identify patterns from the stage characteristics and visualizations, particularly patterns associated with formation and dissolution of bottlenecks. There is an opportunity to extend the SPF approach with techniques from statistical process control and change point analysis, such as CUSUM charts [18], to support the identification of such patterns. Another future work avenue is to conduct a usability evaluation of the SPF approach via controlled experiments in order to validate major design choices, such as the choice of stage characteristics and visualizations.

Acknowledgments. This research is funded by the Australian Research Council Discovery Project DP150103356 and the Estonian Research Council (grant IUT20-55).

References

1. van der Aalst, W.: Process Mining: Discovery, Conformance and Enhancement of Business Processes. Springer, Heidelberg (2011)
2. Dumas, M., La Rosa, M., Mendling, J., Reijers, H.: Fundamentals of Business Process Management. Springer, Heidelberg (2013)
3. Modig, N., Ahlström, P.: This is lean: resolving the efficiency paradox. Rheologica (2012)
4. Hornix, P.T.: Performance analysis of business processes through process mining. Master's thesis, Eindhoven University of Technology (2007)
5. Gunther, C.W., Rozinat, A.: Disco: Discover your processes. In: Proceedings of BPM Demos. CEUR Workshop Proceedings, vol. 940, pp. 40–44 (2012)
6. van der Aalst, W., Adriansyah, A., van Dongen, B.: Replaying history on process models for conformance checking and performance analysis. Wiley Interdisc. Rev. Data Mining Knowl. Disc. **2**(2), 182–192 (2012)
7. van Dongen, B.F., Adriansyah, A.: Process mining: fuzzy clustering and performance visualization. In: Rinderle-Ma, S., Sadiq, S., Leymann, F. (eds.) BPM 2009. LNBIP, vol. 43, pp. 158–169. Springer, Heidelberg (2010)
8. de Leoni, M., van der Aalst, W.M.P., Dees, M.: A general framework for correlating business process characteristics. In: Sadiq, S., Soffer, P., Völzer, H. (eds.) BPM 2014. LNCS, vol. 8659, pp. 250–266. Springer, Heidelberg (2014)
9. Pika, A., Wynn, M.T., Fidge, C.J., ter Hofstede, A.H.M., Leyer, M., van der Aalst, W.M.P.: An extensible framework for analysing resource behaviour using event logs. In: Jarke, M., Mylopoulos, J., Quix, C., Rolland, C., Manolopoulos, Y., Mouratidis, H., Horkoff, J. (eds.) CAiSE 2014. LNCS, vol. 8484, pp. 564–579. Springer, Heidelberg (2014)
10. Günther, C.W., van der Aalst, W.M.P.: Fuzzy mining – adaptive process simplification based on multi-perspective metrics. In: Alonso, G., Dadam, P., Rosemann, M. (eds.) BPM 2007. LNCS, vol. 4714, pp. 328–343. Springer, Heidelberg (2007)
11. Conforti, R., Dumas, M., La Rosa, M., Maaradji, A., Nguyen, H., Ostovar, A., Raboczi, S.: Analysis of business process variants in apromore. In: Proceedings of the BPM Demos. CEUR, vol. 1418 (2015)
12. Senderovich, A., Weidlich, M., Gal, A., Mandelbaum, A.: Queue mining – predicting delays in service processes. In: Jarke, M., Mylopoulos, J., Quix, C., Rolland, C., Manolopoulos, Y., Mouratidis, H., Horkoff, J. (eds.) CAiSE 2014. LNCS, vol. 8484, pp. 42–57. Springer, Heidelberg (2014)
13. de Smet, L.: Queue mining: combining process mining and queueing analysis to understand bottlenecks, to predict delays, and to suggest process improvements. Master's thesis, Eindhoven University of Technology (2014)
14. Reinertsen, D.: Managing the Design Factory: A Product Developers Tool Kit. Simon & Schuster Ltd, New York (1998)
15. Nguyen, H., Dumas, M., ter Hofstede, A., La Rosa, M., Maggi, F.: Business process performance mining with staged process flows. QUT ePrints Technical report 91110, Queensland University of Technology (2015). http://eprints.qut.edu.au/91110
16. Venkatesh, V., Bala, H.: Technology acceptance model 3 and a research agenda on interventions. Decis. Sci. **39**(2), 273–315 (2008)

17. Conforti, R., Dumas, M., García-Bañuelos, L., La Rosa, M.: BPMN miner: automated discovery of BPMN process models with hierarchical structure. Inf. Syst. **56**, 284–303 (2016)
18. Reynolds, M., Amin, R., Arnold, J.: CUSUM charts with variable sampling intervals. Technometrics **32**(4), 371–384 (1990)

Minimizing Overprocessing Waste in Business Processes via Predictive Activity Ordering

Ilya Verenich[1,2(✉)], Marlon Dumas[1,2], Marcello La Rosa[1],
Fabrizio Maria Maggi[2], and Chiara Di Francescomarino[3]

[1] Queensland University of Technology, Brisbane, Australia
{ilya.verenich,m.larosa}@qut.edu.au
[2] University of Tartu, Tartu, Estonia
{marlon.dumas,f.m.maggi}@ut.ee
[3] FBK-IRST, Trento, Italy
dfmchiara@fbk.eu

Abstract. Overprocessing waste occurs in a business process when effort is spent in a way that does not add value to the customer nor to the business. Previous studies have identified a recurrent overprocessing pattern in business processes with so-called "knockout checks", meaning activities that classify a case into "accepted" or "rejected", such that if the case is accepted it proceeds forward, while if rejected, it is cancelled and all work performed in the case is considered unnecessary. Thus, when a knockout check rejects a case, the effort spent in other (previous) checks becomes overprocessing waste. Traditional process redesign methods propose to order knockout checks according to their mean effort and rejection rate. This paper presents a more fine-grained approach where knockout checks are ordered at runtime based on predictive machine learning models. Experiments on two real-life processes show that this predictive approach outperforms traditional methods while incurring minimal runtime overhead.

Keywords: Process mining · Process optimization · Overprocessing waste

1 Introduction

Overprocessing is one of seven types of waste in lean manufacturing [1]. In a business process, overprocessing occurs when effort is spent in the performance of activities to an extent that does not add value to the customer nor to the business. Overprocessing waste results for example from unnecessary detail or accuracy in the performance of activities, inappropriate use of tools or methods in a way that leads to excess effort, or unnecessary or excessive verifications [2].

Previous studies in the field of business process optimization have identified a recurrent overprocessing pattern in business processes with so-called "knockout checks" [3,4]. A knockout check is an activity that classifies a case into "accepted" or "rejected", such that if the case is accepted it proceeds forward,

© Springer International Publishing Switzerland 2016
S. Nurcan et al. (Eds.): CAiSE 2016, LNCS 9694, pp. 186–202, 2016.
DOI: 10.1007/978-3-319-39696-5_12

while if rejected, all other checks are considered unnecessary and the case is either terminated or moved to a later stage in the process. When a knockout check rejects a case, the effort spent in previous checks becomes overprocessing waste. This waste pattern is common in application-to-approval processes, where an application goes through a number of checks aimed at classifying it into admissible or not, such as eligibility checks in a University admission process, liability checks in an insurance claims handling process, or credit worthiness checks in a loan origination process. Any of these checks may lead to an application or claim being declared ineligible, effectively making other checks irrelevant for the case in question.

A general strategy to minimize overprocessing due to the execution of unnecessary knockout checks is to first execute the check that is most likely to lead to a negative ("reject") outcome. If the outcome is indeed negative, there is no overprocessing. If on the other hand we execute first the checks that lead to positive outcomes and leave the one that leads to a negative outcome to the end, the overprocessing is maximal – all the checks with positive outcome were unnecessary. On the other hand, it also makes sense to execute the checks that require less effort first, and leave those requiring higher effort last, so that the latter are only executed when they are strictly necessary. These observations lead to a strategy where knockout checks are ordered according to two parameters: their likelihood of leading to a negative outcome and the required effort.

Existing process optimization heuristics [3,5] apply this strategy at design-time. Specifically, checks are ordered at design-time based on their rejection rate and mean effort. This approach achieves some overprocessing reduction, but does not take into account the specificities of each case. This paper proposes an approach that further reduces overprocessing by incorporating the above strategy into a predictive process monitoring method. Specifically, the likelihood of each check leading to a positive outcome and the effort required by each check are estimated at runtime based on the available case data and machine learning models built from historical execution data. The checks are then ordered at runtime for the case at hand according to the estimated parameters.

The rest of the paper is organized as follows. Section 2 gives a more detailed definition of knockout checks and discusses related work. Section 3 presents the proposed knockout check reordering approach. Next, Sect. 4 discusses an empirical evaluation of the proposed approach versus design-time alternatives based on two datasets related to a loan origination process and an environmental permit process. Finally, Sect. 5 draws conclusions and outlines future work.

2   Background and Related Work

This paper is concerned with optimizing the order in which a set of knockout checks are performed in order to minimize overprocessing. The starting point for this optimization is a *knockout section*, defined as a set of *independent binary knockout* checks. By independent we mean that the knockout checks in the section can be performed in any order. By binary we mean that each check classifies the case into two classes, hereby called "accepted" and "rejected". And by knockout we mean that if the check classifies a case as "rejected", the case jumps to a designated point in the process (called an *anchor*) regardless of the outcome of all other checks in the section. An anchor can be any point in the process execution either before or after the knockout section. In the rest of the paper, we assume that the anchor point is an end event of the process, meaning that a case completes with a negative outcome as soon as one of the checks in the knockout section fails.

For example, a loan application process in a peer-to-peer lending marketplace typically includes several knockout checks. Later in this paper we will examine one such process containing three checks: identity check; credit worthiness check; and verification of submitted documents. Any of these checks can lead to rejection of the loan, thus the three checks constitute a knockout section.

The order of execution of checks in a knockout section can impact on over-processing waste. For example, in the above knockout section, if the identity check is completed first and succeeds and then the credit worthiness check is completed and leads to a rejection, then the identity check constitutes over-processing, as it did not contribute to the outcome of the case. Had the credit worthiness check been completed first, the identity check would not have been necessary.

Van der Aalst [3] outlines a set of heuristics to resequence the knockout checks according to the average processing time, rejection rate and setup time of each check. One heuristic is to execute the checks in descending order of rejection rate, meaning that the checks that are more likely to reject a case are executed first. A more refined heuristic is one where the checks are executed in descending order of the product of their rejection rate times their required effort. In other words, checks are ordered according to the principle of "least effort to reject" – checks that require less effort and are more likely to reject the case come first. This idea is identified as a redesign best practice by Reijers et al. [5] and called the "knockout principle" by Lohrmann and Reichert [6].

Pourshahid et al. [7] study the impact of applying the knockout principle in a healthcare case study. They find that the knockout pattern in combination with two other process redesign patterns improve some of the process KPIs, such as average approval turnaround time and average cost per application. Niedermann et al. [8] in the context of their study on process optimization patterns introduce the "early knockout" pattern. The idea of this latter pattern is moving the whole knockout section to the earliest possible point.

All of the above optimization approaches resequence the knockout checks at design time. In contrast, in this paper we investigate the idea of ordering the checks at runtime based on the characteristics of the current case. Specifically, we seek to exploit knowledge extracted from historical execution traces in order to predict the outcome of the knockout checks and to order them based on these predictions. In this respect, the present work can be seen as an application of *predictive process monitoring*.

Predictive process monitoring is a branch of process mining that seeks to exploit event logs in order to predict how one or multiple ongoing cases of a business process will unfold up to their completion [9]. A predictive monitoring approach relies on machine learning models trained on historical traces in order to make predictions at runtime for ongoing cases. Existing predictive process monitoring approaches can be classified based on the predicted output or on the type of information contained in the execution traces they take as input. In this respect, some approaches focus on the time perspective [10], others on the risk perspective [11]. Some of them take advantage only of a static snapshot of the data manipulated by the traces [9], while in others [12,13], traces are encoded as complex symbolic sequences, and hence the successive data values taken by each data attribute throughout the execution of a case are taken into account. This paper relies on the latter approach. The main difference between the present work and existing predictive monitoring approaches is that the goal is not to predict the outcome of the entire case, but rather to predict the outcome of individual activities in the case in order to re-sequence them.

The idea of using predictive monitoring to alter (or customize) a process at runtime is explored by Zeng et al. [14] in the specific context of an invoice-to-cash process. The authors train a machine learning model with historical payment behavior of customers, with the aim of predicting the outcome of a given invoice. This prediction is then used to customize the payment collection process in order to save time and maximize the chances of successfully cashing in the payment. In comparison, the proposal outlined in this paper is generally applicable to any knockout section and not tied to a specific application domain.

3   Approach

In this section we describe the proposed approach to resequencing knockout checks in order to minimize overprocessing. We first give an overview of the entire solution framework and then focus on the core parts of our approach.

3.1   Overview

Given a designated knockout section in a process, the goal of our approach is to determine how the checks in this section should be ordered at runtime in order to reduce overprocessing waste. Accordingly, our approach pre-supposes that any preexisting design-time ordering of the checks be relaxed, so that instead the checks can be ordered by a runtime component.

The runtime component responsible for ordering the checks in a knockout section relies on a predictive monitoring approach outlined in Fig. 1. This approach exploits historical execution traces in order to train two machine learning models for each check in the knockout section: one to predict the probability of the check to reject a given case, and the second to predict the *expected processing time* of the check. The former is a classification model while the latter is a regression model.

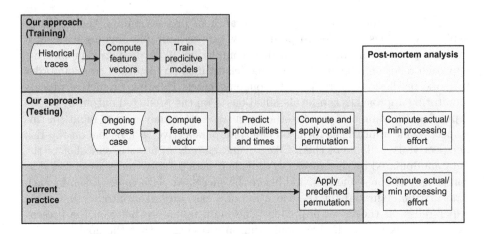

Fig. 1. Overview of the proposed approach.

To train these models, the traces of completed cases are first encoded as feature vectors and fed into conventional machine learning algorithms. The resulting models are then used at runtime by encoding the trace of an ongoing case as a feature vector and giving it as input to the models in order to estimate the *expected processing effort* of each allowed permutation of knockout checks and to select the one with the lowest expected effort. To validate the models, once the case has completed and the actual outcome of the checks is known, we compute the *actual processing effort* and compare it with the *minimum processing effort* required to either accept or knock out the case in question. The difference between the actual and the minimum effort is the overprocessing waste.

3.2   Estimation of Expected Processing Effort

As mentioned in the introduction, overprocessing results from the activities that add no value to the product or service. For example, if knockout activity rejects a case, then the case is typically terminated and the effort spent on the previous activities becomes overprocessing waste. Consequently, to minimize the overprocessing, we are interested in determining such a permutation σ of activities that the case will be knocked out as early as possible. In the best case, the first executed activity will knock out the case; in the worst case, none of them will knock out the case. Furthermore, among all activities that could knockout the case, the one with lowest effort represents the minimal possible processing effort W_{min} for a particular case to pass the knockout section. If none of the activities knocks out the case, there is no overprocessing.

Since the minimal possible processing effort is constant for a particular process case, minimizing overprocessing of a knockout section is essentially equivalent to minimizing overall processing effort W_σ, which is dependent on the actual number of performed activities M in the knockout section:

$$W_\sigma = \sum_{i=1}^{M} w_i = \sum_{i=1}^{M} T_i R_i, \quad 1 \le M \le N \tag{1}$$

where w_i is the effort of an individual activity, T_i is its expected processing time and R_i is the cost of a resource that performs the activity per unit of time, which is assumed constant and known.

At least one activity needs to be performed, and if it gives a negative result, we escape the knockout section. In the extreme case, if all activities are passed normally, we cannot skip any activity; therefore M varies from 1 to N.

However, the *actual* processing effort can only be known once the case has completed; therefore, we approximate it by estimating the *expected* processing effort $\widehat{W_\sigma}$ of a permutation σ of knockout checks. For that we introduce the notion of reject probability. The reject probability P_i^r of a check is the probability that the given check will yield a negative outcome, i.e. knock out the case. In other words, it is the percentage of cases that do not pass the check successfully.

Let us suppose we have a knockout section with three independent checks. Table 1 lists possible scenarios during the execution of the section depending on the outcome of the checks, as well as the probabilities of these scenarios and the actually spent effort.

Table 1. Possible outcomes of checks during the execution of a knockout section with three activities.

Outcome of checks	Probability of outcome	Actual effort spent
{failed}	P_1^r	w_1
{passed; failed}	$(1 - P_1^r)P_2^r$	$w_1 + w_2$
{passed; passed; failed}	$(1 - P_1^r)(1 - P_2^r)P_3^r$	$w_1 + w_2 + w_3$
{passed; passed; passed}	$(1 - P_1^r)(1 - P_2^r)(1 - P_3^r)$	$w_1 + w_2 + w_3$

Depending on the outcome of the last check, we are either leaving the knockout section proceeding with the case or terminating the case. In either situation, the processing effort would be the same. Thus, joining the last two scenarios, the *expected* effort to execute a knockout section of three checks would be:

$$\widehat{W_\sigma} = w_1 P_1^r + (w_1 + w_2)(1 - P_1^r)P_2^r + (w_1 + w_2 + w_3)(1 - P_1^r)(1 - P_2^r) \tag{2}$$

Generalizing, the *expected* processing effort of a knockout section with N activities can be computed as follows:

$$\widehat{W_\sigma} = \sum_{i=1}^{N-1} \left(\sum_{j=1}^{i} w_j \cdot P_i^r \prod_{k=1}^{i-1}(1 - P_k^r) \right) + \sum_{j=1}^{N} w_j \cdot \prod_{k=1}^{N-1}(1 - P_k^r). \tag{3}$$

To estimate the expected processing effort we propose constructing predictive models for reject probabilities P_i^r and processing times T_i (see Sect. 3.4).

Having found the expected processing effort for all possible permutations σ of knockout activities, in our approach we select the one with the lowest expected effort. To validate the results in terms of minimizing overprocessing, we need to compare the *actual* processing effort W_σ taken after following the selected ordering σ with W_{min}.

3.3   Feature-Encoding of Execution Traces

Business process execution traces are naturally modeled as complex symbolic sequences, i.e. sequences of events each carrying data payload consisting of event attributes. However, to make estimations of the reject probabilities and processing times of knockout checks, we first need to encode traces of completed process cases in the form of feature vectors for corresponding predictive models.

As a running example, let us consider the log in Table 2, pertaining to an environmental permit request process. Each case refers to a specific application for the permit and includes activities executed for that application. For example, the first case starts with the activity *T02*. Its data payload {*2015-01-10 9:13:00, R03*} corresponds to the data associated with the *Timestamp* and *Resource* attributes. These attributes are dynamic in the sense that they change for different events. In contrast, attributes like *Channel* and *Department* are the same for all the events in a case, i.e. they are static.

Table 2. Extract of an event log.

Case	Case attributes		Event attributes			
ID	Channel	Department	Task	Timestamp	Resource	...
1	Email	General	T02	2015-01-10 9:13:00	R03	...
1	Email	General	T06	2015-01-10 9:14:20	R12	...
2	Fax	Customer contact	T02	2015-01-10 9:18:03	R03	...
1	Email	General	T10	2015-01-10 9:13:45	R12	...
2	Fax	Customer contact	T05	2015-01-10 9:13:57	R12	...

To encode traces as feature vectors, we include both static information, coming from the case attributes and dynamic information, contained in the event payload. In general, for a case i with U case attributes $\{s_1, \ldots, s_U\}$ containing M events $\{e_1, \ldots, e_M\}$, each of them having an associated payload $\{d_1^1, \ldots, d_1^R\}, \ldots \{d_M^1, \ldots, d_M^R\}$ of length R, the resulting feature vector would be:

$$\boldsymbol{X_i} = (s_1, \ldots, s_U, e_1, \ldots, e_M, d_1^1, \ldots, d_1^R, \ldots d_M^1, \ldots, d_M^R) \qquad (4)$$

As an example, the first case in the log in Table 2 will be encoded as such:

$$\boldsymbol{X_1} = (\text{Email}, \text{General}, \text{T02}, \text{T06}, \text{T10}, \text{2015-01-10 9:13:00}, \text{R03}, \\ \text{2015-01-10 9:14:20}, \text{R12}, \text{2015-01-10 9:13:45}, \text{R12}) \qquad (5)$$

This kind of encoding, referred to as index-based encoding, is lossless since all data from the original log are retained. It achieves a relatively high accuracy and reliability when making early predictions of the process outcome [12,13].

3.4 Prediction of Reject Probability and Processing Time

To make online predictions on a running case, we apply pre-built (offline) models using prefixes of historical cases before entering the knockout section. For example, if a knockout section typically starts after the n-th event, as model features we can use case attributes and event attributes of up to $(n-1)$-th event. For predicting reject probabilities of knockout activities we train classification models, while for predicting processing times we need regression models. To train the models, in addition to historical case prefixes, we need labels associated with the outcome of a check (classification) and its processing time (regression). As a learning algorithm, we primarily use support vector machines (SVM), since they can handle unbalanced data in a robust way [15]. In addition, we fit decision trees and random forest models, for they have been used to address a wide range of predictive process monitoring problems [9,11,12,16].

To assess the predictive power of the classifiers, we use the area under receiver operator characteristic curve (AUC) measure [17]. AUC represents the probability that the binary classifier will score a randomly drawn positive sample higher than a randomly drawn negative sample. A value of AUC equal to 1 indicates a perfect ranking, where any positive sample is ranked higher than any negative sample. A value of AUC equal to 0.5 indicates the worst possible classifier that is not better than random guessing. Finally, a value of AUC equal to 0 indicates a reserved perfect classifier, where all positive samples get the lowest ranks.

As a baseline, instead of predicting the reject probabilities, we use *constant* values for them computed from the percentage of cases that do not pass the particular knockout activity in the log. Similarly, for processing times of activities, we take the average processing time for each activity across all completed cases. This roughly corresponds to the approach presented in [3]. Another, even simpler baseline, assumes executing knockout activities in a random order for each case, regardless of their reject probabilities and processing times.

4   Evaluation

We implemented the proposed overprocessing prediction approach as a set of scripts for the statistical software R, and applied them to two publicly available real-life logs. Below, we describe the characteristics of the datasets, we report on the accuracy of predictive models trained on these datasets, and we compare our approach against the two baselines discussed above in terms of overprocessing reduction. A package containing the R scripts, the datasets and the evaluation results is available at: http://apromore.org/platform/tools.

4.1   Datasets and Features

We used two datasets derived from real-life event logs. The first log records executions of the loan origination process of *Bondora* [18], an Estonian peer-to-peer lending marketplace; the second one originates from an environmental permit request process carried out by a Dutch municipality, available as part of the *CoSeLoG* project [19]. Table 3 reports the size of these two logs in terms of number of completed cases, and the rejection rate of each check. Each log has three checks, the details of which are provided next.

Table 3. Summary of datasets.

Dataset	Completed cases	Knockout checks	
		Name	Rejection rate
Bondora	40,062	*IdCancellation*	0.080
		CreditDecision	0.029
		PostFundingCancellation	0.045
Environmental permit	1,230	*T02*	0.005
		T06	0.013
		T10	0.646

Bondora Dataset. The Bondora dataset provides a snapshot of all loan data in the Bondora marketplace that is not covered by data protection laws. These data refers to two processes: the loan origination process and the loan repayment process. Only the first process features a knockout section, hence we filtered out the data related to the second process. When a customer applies for a loan, they fill in a loan application form providing information such as their personal data, income and liabilities, with supporting documents. The loan origination process starts upon the receipt of the application and involves (among other activities) three checks: the identity check (associated with event *IdCancellation* in the log); the credit worthiness assessment (associated to event *CreditDecision*); and the documentation verification (associated to event *PostFundingCancellation*). A negative outcome of any of these checks leads to rejection of a loan application.

Bondora's clerks perform these checks in various orders based on their experience and intuition of how to minimize work, but none of the checks requires data produced by the others, so they can be reordered. Over time, the checks have been performed in different orders. For example, during a period when listing loans into the marketplace was a priority due to high investor demand, loans were listed before all document verifications had been concluded, which explains why the third check is called *PostFundingCancellation*, even though in many cases this check is performed in parallel with the other checks.

In this log, the knockout section starts immediately after the case is lodged. Thus, the only features we can use to build our predictive models are the case attributes, i.e. the information provided by the borrower at the time of lodging the application. These features can be grouped into three categories. *Demographical* features include age of the loan borrower, their gender, country of residence, language, educational background, employment and marital status. *Financial* features describe the borrower's financial well-being and include information about their income, liabilities, debts, credit history, home ownership, etc. Finally, the third group includes *loan* features, such as amount of the applied loan, and its duration, maximum acceptable interest rate, purpose of the loan and the application type (timed funding or urgent funding). A more detailed description of each attribute is available from the Bondora Web site [18].

It should also be noted that in the Bondora log there is no information about the start time and the end time of each activity. Thus, we can only use it to estimate the reject probabilities, not the processing times.

Environmental Permit Dataset. The second dataset records the execution of the receiving phase of an environmental permit application process in a Dutch municipality [19]. The process discovered from the log has a knockout section (see Fig. 2) consisting of three activities: *T02*, to check confirmation of receipt, *T06*, to determine necessity of stop advice, and *T10*, to determine necessity to stop indication. In this scenario, the checks are not completely independent. Specifically, *T10* can only be done after either *T02* or *T06* has been performed – all permutations compatible with this constraint are possible.

Another special feature of this knockout section is that in a small number of cases some checks are repeated multiple times. If the first check in a case is repeated multiple times, and then the second check is executed (and the first check is not repeated anymore after that), we simply ignore the repetition,

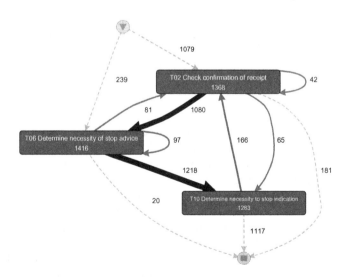

Fig. 2. Process map extracted from the environment permit log.

meaning that we treat the first check as not having been repeated by discarding all occurrences of this check except the last one. Similarly, we discarded incomplete cases as they did not allow us to assess the existence of overprocessing.

Each case in the log refers to a specific application for an environmental permit. The log contains both case attributes and event payload along with the standard XES attributes. Case attributes include channel by which the case has been lodged, department that is responsible for the case, responsible resource and its group. In addition to the case attributes, the predictive models can utilize attributes of events that precede the knockout section. Generally, there is only one such event, namely *Confirmation of receipt*, that includes attributes about the resource who performed it and its assigned group.

This log contains event completion timestamps but not event start timestamps. So also for this second log we do not have enough information to predict the processing time of each check, and we can only work with reject probabilities.

4.2   Predictive Accuracy

We split each dataset into a training set (80 % of cases) to train the models, and a test set (20 %) to evaluate the predictive power of the models built. As a learning algorithm we applied support vector machine (SVM) classification, trained using the e1071 package in R. This choice allows us to build a probability model which fits a logistic distribution using maximum likelihood to the decision values of all binary classifiers, and computes the a-posteriori class probabilities for the multi-class problem using quadratic optimization [20]. Therefore, it can output not only the class label, but the probability of each class. The probability of a zero class essentially gives us an estimation of the reject probability.

In both datasets the majority of cases pass all the checks successfully, thus the datasets are highly imbalanced with respect to the class labels. A naive algorithm that simply predicts all test examples as positive will have very low error, since the negative examples are so infrequent. One solution to this problem is to use a Poisson regression, which requires forming buckets of observations based on the independent attributes and modeling the aggregate response in these buckets as a Poisson random variable [21]. However, this requires discretization of all continuous independent attributes, which is not desirable in our case. A simpler and more robust solution would be to undersample positive cases. Weiss et al. [22] showed that for binary classification the optimal class proportion in the training set varies by domain and objective, but generally to produce probability estimates, a 50:50 distribution is a good option. Thus, we leave roughly as many positive examples as there are negative ones and discard the rest.

To ensure the consistency of the results we apply five-fold cross-validation. Figure 3 shows the average ROC curves, across all ten runs. the AUC varies from 0.812 (*PostFundingCancellation*) to 0.998 (*CreditDecision*) for the Bondora dataset, and from 0.527 (*T06*) to 0.645 (*T10*) for the Environmental dataset. The lower values in the latter dataset are due to the limited number of features that can be extracted (see Sect. 4.1), as well as by the fact that the dataset has

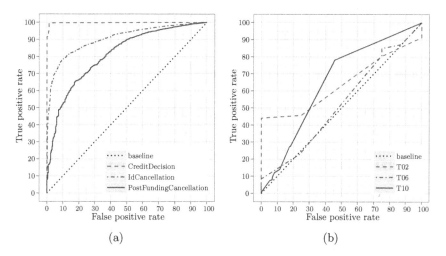

Fig. 3. ROC curves of predictive models for checks in *Bondora* (a) and *Environmental* (b) datasets.

much less completed cases for training (Table 3), which is further exacerbated by having to remove many positive samples after undersampling.

4.3   Overprocessing Reduction

As stated in Sect. 3.2, the *actual* processing effort is given by Formula 1. However, since the necessary timestamps are absent from our datasets, it is impossible to find the processing times T_i of the activities. Nor do we have data about the resource costs R_i. Therefore, we assume $T_i R_i = 1$ for all activities. Then the actual processing effort simply equals the number of performed activities in the knockout section. It can be shown that in this case the optimal permutation σ that minimizes the expected processing is equivalent to ordering the knockout activities by decreasing reject probabilities.

In Table 4 we report the average number of checks and percentage of overprocessing of our approach over the ten runs, against the two baselines (constant probabilities for each check and random ordering – see Sect. 3.4). We found that the actual number of performed checks in case of following our suggested ordering is less than the number of checks performed in either baseline. Specifically, for the Bondora dataset we are doing only 1.22 % more checks than minimally needed, which represents a 2.62 % points (pp) improvement over the baseline with constant probabilities and 4.51 pp improvement over the baseline with random ordering. However, for the environmental permit dataset the advantage of our approach over the constant probabilities baseline is very marginal. This can be explained by the skewed distribution of the knockout frequencies for the three checks in this dataset (the lowest knockout frequency being 0.5 % and the highest being 64.6 %). Thus, it is clear that the check with the lowest knockout frequency

Table 4. Average number of performed checks and overprocessing for test cases.

	Average # of checks		Average overprocessing, %	
	Bondora	Environmental	Bondora	Environmental
Optimal	21,563	416	0	0
Our approach	21,828	576	1.22	38.49
Constant P_i^r's	22,393	577	3.85	38.89
Random	22,800	657	5.74	58.16

Table 5. Distribution of number of checks across the test cases.

Ordering by	Bondora			Environmental		
	1	2	3	1	2	3
Optimal	1237	0	6775	163	0	83
Our approach	974	261	6777	2	158	86
Constant P_i^r's	642	359	7011	3	155	88
Random	413	410	7189	1	78	167

has to be executed at the end. Additionally, as mentioned in the Sect. 4.1, not all checks are independent in the second dataset. Therefore, the solution space for the optimal permutation is rather limited.

In addition, in Table 5 we report the number of cases with one, two or three knockout checks performed. As shown before, for a dataset with three checks the optimal number of checks is either one (if at least one check yields a negative outcome) or three (if all checks are passed). Therefore, in the cases with two checks, the second one should have been done first. In the Bondora dataset, such suboptimal choices are minimized; for the environmental dataset, again, our approach is just as good as the one that relies on constant probabilities.

4.4 Execution Times

Our approach involves some runtime overhead to find the optimal permutation as compared to the baseline scenario in which checks are performed in a predefined order. For real-time prediction it is crucial to output the results faster than the mean arrival rate of cases. Thus, we also measured the average runtime overhead of our approach. All experiments were conducted using R version 3.2.2 on a laptop with a 2.4 GHz Intel Core i5 quad core processor and 8 Gb of RAM. The runtime overhead generally depends on the length of the process cases and the number of possible permutations of the checks. For the Bondora dataset, it took around 70 s to construct the SVM classifiers (offline) for all the checks, using default training parameters. In contrast, for the Environmental dataset with much shorter feature vectors it took less than a second to train the classifier (see Table 6). At runtime, it takes less than 2 ms on average to find the

Table 6. Execution times of various components of our approach in milliseconds.

Component		Bondora		Environmental	
		Mean	St dev	Mean	St dev
Offline, overall	Learn classifier	75,000	9,000	150	20
Online, per case	Preprocess data	0.45	0.03	0.67	0.03
	Apply classifier	1.37	0.15	0.12	0.02
	Find optimal permutation	0.12	0	0.02	0

optimal permutation of knockout activities for an ongoing case for both datasets (including preprocessing of the data and application of the classifier). This shows that our approach performs within reasonable bounds for online applications.

4.5 Threats to Validity

Threats to external validity are the limited number and type of logs we used for the evaluation and the use of a single classifier. While we chose only two datasets from two distinct domains (financial and government), these two datasets represent real-life logs well. They exhibit substantial differences in the number of events, event classes and total number of traces, with one log being relatively large (over 40,000 cases) and the other relatively small (around 1,200 cases).

Both datasets used in this evaluation did not have the required start and end event timestamps to estimate the processing times of the knockout checks. Thus, we assigned a constant time to all checks. The inability to estimate processing time does not invalidate our approach. In fact, our approach would tend to further reduce the amount of overprocessing if processing times were known.

In the Bondora dataset, the three checks have been performed in different orders for different cases. When one of the checks leads to a negative outcome for a given case, the checks that were not yet completed at that stage of the case sometimes remain marked as negative, even if it might be the case that these checks would have led to positive outcomes should they have been completed. This issue may have an effect on the reported results, but we note that it affects both the reported performance of our approach and that of the baselines.

We reported the results with a single classified (SVM). With decision trees and random forests, we obtained qualitatively the same results, i.e. they all improved over the baselines. However, we decided to only retain SVM in the paper because this classifier yielded the highest classification accuracy among all classifiers we tested. However, our approach is independent of the classifier used. Thus, using a different classifier does not in principle invalidate the results. That said, we acknowledge that the goodness of the prediction, as in any classification problem, depends on the particular classifier employed. Hence, it is important to test multiple classifiers for a given dataset, and to apply hyperparameter tuning, in order to choose the most adequate classifier with the best configuration.

5 Conclusion and Future Work

We have presented an approach to reduce overprocessing by ordering knock-out checks at runtime based on their reject probabilities and processing times determined via predictive models. Experimental results show that the proposed runtime ordering approach outperforms a design-time ordering approach when the reject probabilities of the knockout checks are close to each other. In the dataset where one check had a considerably higher rejection rate than the other, the design-time and the runtime ordering approach yielded similar results.

The proposed approach is not without limitations. One limitation of scope is that the approach is applicable when the checks are independent (i.e. can be reordered) and every check is performed once within one execution of the knockout section. In particular, the approach is not applicable when some of the knockout checks can be repeated in case of a negative outcome. This is the case for example in a university admission process, where an eligibility check may initially lead to a rejection, but the applicant can ask the application to be re-considered (and thus the check to be repeated) after providing clarifications or additional information. In other words, the current approach is applicable when a negative outcome ("reject") is definite and cannot be revoked. Similarly, we assume that a check leading to a positive outcome is definite and cannot be reconsidered. Designing heuristics for cases where the outcomes of checks are revocable is a direction for future work.

Another limitation is that the approach is designed to minimize overprocessing only, without considering other performance dimensions such as cycle time (i.e. mean case duration). If we add cycle time into the equation, it becomes desirable to parallelize the checks rather than sequentializing them. In other words, rather than performing the checks in a knockout section in strict sequence, some or all of checks could be started in parallel, such that whenever the first check fails, the other parallel checks are cancelled. On the one hand this parallelization leads to higher overprocessing effort, since effort is spent in partially completed checks that are later cancelled. On the other hand, it reduces overall cycle time, particularly when some of the checks involve idle time during their execution. For example, in a university admission process when some documents are found to be missing, the checks involving these documents need to be put on hold until the missing documents arrive. If the goal is to minimize both overprocessing and cycle time, this waiting time can be effectively used to perform other checks.

The proposed approach relies on the accuracy of the reject probability estimates provided by the classification model. It is known however that the likelihood probabilities produced by classification methods (including random forests) are not always reliable. Methods for estimating the reliability of such likelihood probabilities have been proposed in the machine learning literature [23]. A possible enhancement of the proposed approach would be to integrate heuristics that take into account such reliability estimates.

Another avenue for future work is to apply predictive methods to reduce other types of waste, such as *defect waste* induced when a defective execution of an activity subsequently leads to part of the process having to be repeated in order to correct the defect (i.e. rework). The idea is that if a defective activity execution can be detected earlier, the effects of this defect can be minimized and corrected more efficiently. Predictive process monitoring can thus help us to detect defects earlier and to trigger corrective actions as soon as possible.

Acknowledgments. This research is funded by the Australian Research Council Discovery Project DP150103356 and the Estonian Research Council.

References

1. Wang, J.X.: Lean Manufacturing: Business Bottom-Line Based. CRC Press, London (2010)
2. Bauch, C.: Lean product development: making waste transparent. Master's thesis, Massachusetts Institute of Technology and Technical University of Munich (2004)
3. van der Aalst, W.M.P.: Re-engineering knock-out processes. Decis. Support Syst. **30**(4), 451–468 (2001)
4. Jansen-Vullers, M.H., Netjes, M., Reijers, H.A.: Business process redesign for effective e-commerce. In: Proceedings of the 6th International Conference on Electronic Commerce, pp. 382–391. ACM (2004)
5. Reijers, H.A., Mansar, S.L.: Best practices in business process redesign: an overview and qualitative evaluation of successful redesign heuristics. Omega **33**(4), 283–306 (2005)
6. Lohrmann, M., Reichert, M.: Effective application of process improvement patterns to business processes. Softw. Syst. Model. **15**, 353–375 (2014)
7. Pourshahid, A., Mussbacher, G., Amyot, D., Weiss, M.: An aspect-oriented framework for business process improvement. In: Babin, G., Kropf, P., Weiss, M. (eds.) E-Technologies: Innovation in an Open World. LNBIP, vol. 26, pp. 290–305. Springer, Heidelberg (2009)
8. Niedermann, F., Radeschütz, S., Mitschang, B.: Business process optimization using formalized optimization patterns. In: Abramowicz, W. (ed.) BIS 2011. LNBIP, vol. 87, pp. 123–135. Springer, Heidelberg (2011)
9. Maggi, F.M., Di Francescomarino, C., Dumas, M., Ghidini, C.: Predictive monitoring of business processes. In: Jarke, M., Mylopoulos, J., Quix, C., Rolland, C., Manolopoulos, Y., Mouratidis, H., Horkoff, J. (eds.) CAiSE 2014. LNCS, vol. 8484, pp. 457–472. Springer, Heidelberg (2014)
10. der Aalst, W.M.P., Schonenberg, M.H., Song, M.: Time prediction based on process mining. Inf. Syst. **36**(2), 450–475 (2011)
11. Conforti, R., de Leoni, M., La Rosa, M., van der Aalst, W.M.P., ter Hofstede, A.H.M.: A recommendation system for predicting risks across multiple business process instances. Decis. Support Syst. **69**, 1–19 (2015)
12. Leontjeva, A., Conforti, R., Di Francescomarino, C., Dumas, M., Maggi, F.M.: Complex symbolic sequence encodings for predictive monitoring of business processes. In: Motahari-Nezhad, H.R., Recker, J., Weidlich, M. (eds.) bpm 2015. LNCS, pp. 297–313. Springer, Cham (2015)
13. Verenich, I., Dumas, M., Rosa, M.L., Maggi, F.M., Francescomarino, C.D.: Complex symbolic sequence clustering and multiple classifiers for predictive process monitoring. In: BPI 2015 Workshop, pp. 1–12 (2016)

14. Zeng, S., Melville, P., Lang, C.A., Boier-Martin, I., Murphy, C.: Using predictive analysis to improve invoice-to-cash collection. In: Proceeding of the 14th ACM SIGKDD International Conference, KDD 2008, p. 1043 (2008)
15. Hwang, J.P., Park, S., Kim, E.: A new weighted approach to imbalanced data classification problem via support vector machine with quadratic cost function. Expert Syst. Appl. **38**(7), 8580–8585 (2011)
16. Grigori, D., Casati, F., Castellanos, M., Dayal, U., Sayal, M., Shan, M.C.: Business process intelligence. Comput. Ind. **53**(3), 321–343 (2004)
17. Bradley, A.P.: The use of the area under the ROC curve in the evaluation of machine learning algorithms. Pattern Recogn. **30**(7), 1145–1159 (1997)
18. Bondora: Loan Dataset. https://www.bondora.ee/en/invest/statistics/data_export. Accessed 23 Oct 2015
19. Buijs, J.: 3TU.DC Dataset: Receipt phase of an environmental permit applicationprocess (WABO). https://data.3tu.nl/repository/uuid:a07386a5-7be3-4367-9535-70bc9e77dbe6. Accessed 30 Oct 2015
20. Meyer, D., Dimitriadou, E., Hornik, K., Weingessel, A.: e1071: Misc Functions of the Department of Statistics, Probability Theory Group, TU Wien (2015)
21. Hill, S., Provost, F., Volinsky, C.: Network-Based Marketing: Identifying Likely Adopters via Consumer Networks. Stat. Sci. **21**(2), 256–276 (2006)
22. Weiss, G.M., Provost, F.: Learning when training data are costly: the effect of class distribution on tree induction. J. Artif. Intell. Res. **19**, 315–354 (2003)
23. Kull, M., Flach, P.A.: Reliability maps: a tool to enhance probability estimates and improve classification accuracy. In: Calders, T., Esposito, F., Hüllermeier, E., Meo, R. (eds.) ECML PKDD 2014, Part II. LNCS, vol. 8725, pp. 18–33. Springer, Heidelberg (2014)

Requirements Engineering

Formalizing and Modeling Enterprise Architecture (EA) Principles with Goal-Oriented Requirements Language (GRL)

Diana Marosin[1,2]([⊠]), Marc van Zee[3], and Sepideh Ghanavati[2]

[1] Luxembourg Institute of Science and Technology (LIST),
Esch-sur-Alzette, Luxembourg
diana.marosin@list.lu
[2] Radboud University Nijmegen, Nijmegen, The Netherlands
s.ghanavati@cs.ru.nl
[3] University of Luxembourg, Luxembourg, Luxembourg
marc.vanzee@uni.lu

Abstract. Enterprise Architecture (EA) principles are normally written in natural language which makes them informal, hard to evaluate and complicates tracing them to the actual goals of the organization. In this paper, we present a set of requirements for improving the clarity of definitions and develop a framework to formalize EA principles with a semi-formal language, namely the Goal-oriented Requirements Language (GRL). We introduce an extension of the language with the required constructs and establish modeling rules and constraints. This allows us to automatically reason about the soundness, completeness and consistency of a set of EA principles. We demonstrate our methodology with a case study from a governmental organization. Moreover, we extend an Eclipse-based tool.

Keywords: Enterprise architecture principles · Goal-oriented requirements language · OCL rules · Formalism · Analysis

1 Introduction

In practice, Enterprise Architecture (EA) is driven top-down by the business and/or IT strategies and bottom-up by projects and programs which are often owned and driven by the business units. These initiatives, programs and projects are often evaluated via EA principles. EA principles aim to ensure that current and new projects and programs are aligned with, and not deviating from, the business and IT strategies [18,22,26]. In this context, EA principles refer to either the engineering view on the EA (such as how the elements of the EA must be implemented or changed to provide a certain functionality and what business requirements are needed for this functionality), or the social view (such as the ones related to organization's culture or human aspects). For example, an EA principle "Be friendly with the client" can refer to both the social and

© Springer International Publishing Switzerland 2016
S. Nurcan et al. (Eds.): CAiSE 2016, LNCS 9694, pp. 205–220, 2016.
DOI: 10.1007/978-3-319-39696-5_13

engineering views. The social view of this principle could mean that the organization recommends its employees to be nice to the customers, which is an informal recommendation and cannot be enforced. Whereas, the engineering view of this principle could mean that the organization has a good IT infrastructure and intends to develop a user-friendly software experience. This latter engineering view can be formalized and enforced. In our work, we aim to focus on the engineering view of the EA principles that can be modeled, formalized and enforced.

Based on the experience with our industry partner, EA principles are usually written informally in a natural language format. This can cause ambiguities and lead to several interpretations. Moreover, there is no mechanism for consistency checking between various EA principles. In addition, the traceability between EA principles and the goals, objectives and strategies of the organizations are not fully documented. This lack of traceability can become problematic, particularly when the organizations' objectives and strategies change or a new project is introduced to it. It can also lead to difficulties in analyzing the impact of EA principles on the goals and objectives of organizations, as well as difficulties in performing trade-off analysis deciding to which EA principles adhere to.

A methodology for formal representation of EA principles together with a tool support can help organizations reduce the issues presented above. In recent years, much work has been done in other research fields such as regulatory compliance and goal-oriented requirements engineering in formalizing regulations and business rules (cf. Nómos3 [16] and LEGAL-URN [9] for analyzing regulatory compliance between laws, regulations and business rules and processes.) Furthermore, there are open-source tools such as jUCMNav [3] which support the representation and analysis of goal-oriented models. These approaches have shown that having a structured framework with tool-support can ensure that the organization's goals are aligned and in compliance with the current regulations and laws. Similarly, we look at EA principles from an engineering and normative perspective, noting that EA principles share similar characteristics with soft-laws [20]: semi-structured, represented in natural language and informal. Thus, a goal-oriented modeling approach could be suitable for formalizing, modeling and analyzing EA principles [21].

The identified issues with EA principles' formalism, as well as their resemblance with soft-laws and the previous work conducted in formalizing laws and business processes and analyzing of regulatory compliance, lead us to the following research question:

> How can we represent EA principles in a semi-formal structure with a goal-oriented modeling language? What are the needed language constructs? What are the modeling constraints?

We select Goal-oriented Requirements Language (GRL) [2] as the modeling language for formalizing EA principles. GRL is part of the User Requirements Notation (URN) [17] which is currently the only modeling language part of the ITU-T standard. Furthermore, URN has an open-source, Eclipse-based tool-support, called jUCMNav [3]. GRL supports different bottom-up and top-down *evaluation mechanisms* (e.g., qualitative, quantitative, hybrid) that allow analysis of goal satisfaction and trade-off analysis when choosing between different alternatives. New profiles can be created by annotating GRL intentional elements with stereotypes and incorporating constraint rules written in Object Constraint Language (OCL). The language can also be extended with the help of *Metadata* and *URN links*. To that end, we use and extend the jUCMNav plug-in with a principle-base set of stereotypes and OCL rules.

To answer our research question, we apply a design science methodology [14, 30] driven by practice. In our previous work, we analyzed the EA principles of the Schiphol group [21] and then mapped them to GRL intentional elements. In the current iteration, we conducted a more extensive literature study building on the work of Stezler [25] and Haki [12], analyzing the existing definitions of EA principles. In this paper, we provide guidelines on how to define EA principles in a more structured format and how to model them with GRL. We aim to improve the Principle-based GRL profile to capture various principle structures. We provide steps for modeling and we define means to verify the correctness and well-formedness of the GRL models. We validate our approach with a new case study within a governmental organization in Europe. We uploaded our GRL extension, together with the case study description, the resulted models and instructions to an online repository[1].

Following our methodology, we first introduce the related work in Sect. 2. We present the steps for modeling EA principles with GRL in Sect. 3. We evaluate our approach with a case study and present the case results in Sect. 4. We conclude and present directions for future work in Sect. 5.

2   Related Work

In EA, principles have been defined as guidelines and rationales for the design and evolution of technology plans [4, 10, 15, 24, 26]. In other words, EA principles can be seen as "rules of conduct" and can be made more precise and operational by formalization. The empirical studies conducted by Haki, Fischer and Winter (cf. [8, 12, 13, 32]) provide insights from a practitioners' point of view on the use of principles. According to them, one of the difficulties in the use and adoption of EA principles is caused by a lack of understanding of their impact. According to Winter [32], EA principles miss a methodology for the adoption and application guidelines and there are no regular checks for usefulness and consistency.

Efforts in formalizing EA principles were made by Chorus *et al.* [6] and Bommel *et al.* [27, 28]. The authors present a collection of EA principles from TOGAF and show the feasibility of formalization. The approach is done in two steps. The first step consists of interpreting the EA principles as defined in natural language. The authors identified a set of issues regarding the interpretation from natural language. The second step includes the representation of EA principles as an ORM/ORC expression[2]. Their approach has limitations since the EA principles are represented in isolation. They are not connected to either the

---

[1] https://github.com/RationalArchitecture/eGovernment.
[2] Object Role Modeling and Object-Role Calculus.

goals of the organization or other EA principles. Therefore this formalism does not support the impact analysis. Platianiotis *et al.* [23] proposed a conceptual framework for tracing the EA design decisions to their rationals, however the method does not provide any formalism for the EA principles. Additionally, the framework proposed by van Zee *et al.* [29] contains logic-based rules for verifying the integrity of EA decisions, but does not consider EA principles.

ARMOR [7], which is based on Goal-Oriented Requirements Engineering (GORE) approach aims to fill the gap for modeling motivation but it does not focus on formally modeling the principles. Moreover, ARMOR is not scalable and does not include automatic analysis mechanism and tool support. On the other hand, the motivational extension to ArchiMate [5] tries to help representing EA principles in terms of goals and rationales, but does not provide any formalism.

Focused on information systems, Akhigbe *et al.* [1] introduce an adaptive EA framework (BI-EAEA[3]), that allows one to pro-actively accommodate the changes that occur in evolving settings (e.g., how an enterprise responds to various changes, such as modification, deletion and addition of organizations' objectives). However, this method does not provide any formalization for EA principles and it only evaluates changes without considering the EA principles' impacts.

We previously introduced a framework called Principles-based GRL [21], in which we made the first steps towards formalizing EA principles and set grounds on checking compliance between EA principles and EA models [20]. In this paper, we aim to improve the GRL profile for principles and introduce constraints for modeling EA principles (i.e. OCL rules). Our approach aims to represent EA principles in terms of rationals, goals and operational actions. It also takes advantage of the GRL tool-support provided by using jUCMNav. jUCMNav allows users to break the model into hundreds of diagrams and intentional elements and perform GRL analysis for all of the models. This feature which helps scalability of GRL also solves the scalability issues mentioned in the literature.

3 Goal-Oriented Based Framework for EA Principles

In this section we aim to:

1. state the requirements for defining a set of EA principles
2. create a consistent definition of EA principles that enable us to analyze the EA principles in the Goal-oriented Requirements Language (GRL).
3. define modeling constraints (i.e. OCL rules) for ensuring the well-formedness of EA principles when represented in GRL.

3.1 Requirements for Defining a Set of EA Principles

Lindstrom [19] uses the characteristics of "good requirements, originating from requirements engineering" (e.g., IEEE Std 830-1998, Software Requirement

---

[3] Business Intelligence - Enabled Adaptive Enterprise Architecture.

Specification) to define the requirements for a good set of EA principles. The authors distinguish between syntax (the form of the principle) and semantics (the meaning and content of the principles). The criteria for assessing the quality of EA principles are as follows: verifiability, completeness, correctness, modifiability, unambiguity, consistency and stability. Similarly, TOGAF [26] lists five criteria that distinguish a set of good EA principles: understandable, robust, complete, consistent and stable.

Op 't Land and Proper [22] define two methodologies on how to create a SMART set of EA principles (e.g., specific, measurable, achievable, realistic, time-related). The authors introduce the notion of prioritizing the EA principles based on the key objectives (contrary to Lindstrom who intentionally left out these issues.) An important requirement is the completeness of the set of EA principles.

Based on the requirements given by TOGAF and Op 't Land, we define the following requirements for a set of EA principles.

1. **Understandable: Each principle should be sufficiently definitive and precise to be quickly grasped and understood by individuals and to support consistent decision making in complex, potentially controversial situations.** This definition is a result of combining the properties *Unambiguous*, *Robust* and *Specific*.

2. **Complete: Every potentially important principle governing the management of the organization is defined.** We intentionally left out the reference to IT and technology as defined in TOGAF [26] and created a more general requirement. Lindstrom [19] states that when validating if the principles are correct and complete the following questions must be asked: "Are the stated principles relevant to the organization?", "Are all necessary principles defined?"

3. **Consistent: Principles should not be contradictory to the point where adhering to one principle would violate the goal of the other.** Note that in practice, we have found conflicting EA principles. Multiple violations of one or another principle can result in a revision of the set of EA principles, until the set becomes consistent [21].

4. **Measurable: Both on long-term and short-term, over the future architecture and project portfolio.** Measurements are needed to assure that the organization's goals are achieved and to check if the EA principles are really followed and what is their impact on the organization [19].

5. **Stable: Principles should be enduring, yet able to accommodate change.** There is a need to establish a methodology for changing the set of principles and this should be triggered when (a) a strategy or goals of the organization change; (b) principles are conflicting; (c) principles are constantly violated.

3.2 Mapping EA Principles to Goal-Oriented Requirements Language Constructs

In this subsection, we

- summarize the definitions of EA principles as found both in the current academic literature and practice
- introduce the GRL constructs and the stereotypes needed to formalize the EA principles
- we present a mapping of EA principles to GRL constructs.

Goal-oriented Requirements Language (GRL), which is based on the i^* language, describes business concerns, goals satisfactions and stakeholders' beliefs and dependencies. It can be extended and become domain specific by using **stereotypes** attached to the basic constructs of the language. Introducing stereotypes allows us to first define a domain specific notation for the EA principles and then introduce restrictions for the modeling language to assure the well-formedness of the models.

We summarize the definitions of the existing constructive elements of EA principles as found both in the current academic literature and practice, and we annotate them with stereotypes as presented in Table 1. All stereotypes related to EA principle are grouped under the name $ST\_Principle$. An example of the mapping is shown in Fig. 3.

- **Name:** This field captures the essence of the principle and should be easy to remember [11,22,26]. EA principles are not part of the GRL language definition. In order to evaluate the impact of the EA principles on a goal (and *vice versa*), we introduce an element that explicitly refers to the EA principle itself and stereotyped it with the annotation ≪Principle≫ IE. For example, Principle 4 (*We prefer to communicate digitally with citizens and businesses* of Sect. 4 is annotated by ≪Principle≫ softgoal in GRL in Fig. 3.
- **Statement:** This field is a clear, unambiguous description of the principle [11,22,26]. The statement is in some sense a summary of the EA principle,

Table 1. Mapping EA principles constructs to GRL intentional elements

EA Principle Element	Stereotype Value	GRL Element
Name	≪Principle≫	Softgoal (⬭)
Statement	-	Comment
Added Value	≪AddedValue≫	Softgoal, Goal (⬭)
Impact/restrictions	-	The value of GRL links (e.g., quantitative impact (integer value between - 100 and 100) or a qualitative value, marked with the keywords {*make, help, some+, some-, hurt, break*}.
Key Actions	≪KeyAction≫	Task (⬭)
Preconditions	≪Precondition≫	Softgoal, Goal, Task, Resource (▭)
Architecture Domain	-	Actor (⬡)

very useful in human communication, but does not necessarily carry much semantics in a formal language. Therefore, it is stored as a comment that is attached to the EA ≪Principle≫ IE.

- **Added Value:** This field states clearly what is aimed to be achieved when applying the EA principle (e.g., goals/softgoals to which the principle contributes to, either positively or negatively). Different researchers have named this field differently such as *Motivation* [22,31] or *Rational* [8,26]. We found it in practice[4] [21] also under the names *Future situation* and *Goal*. We represent the added value in GRL as a softgoal or a goal, to which we attach ≪AddedValue≫ stereotype. In Fig. 3, *Fast and efficient communication* is one of the ≪AddedValue≫ of Principle 4.

- **Impact and Restrictions:** This field defines the impact of an EA principle on the design of other principles or elements of the architecture, as well as the restrictions caused by enforcing the principles [8]. In practice [21], it is also called *Constraints*. It can also be called *Implications* [19,22,24]. We chose to use the term *Impact*, as it is less ambiguous in this context. This is modeled in GRL by a contribution/correlation link (both with *positive* or *negative* values). Contribution links show the direct impact of one intentional element to the other while correlation links show the side-effect. Both links can have qualitative or values. The links between ≪Principle≫ and other intentional elements in Fig. 3 represent impact.

- **Key Actions:** This field states what the operational actions to be taken are so that the principle is realized. In practice [21], it is also called *Application*, *Key Actions*[8], *Assurance* [22] or *Implications* [15]. This element corresponds to *task* in GRL and it is annotated by ≪KeyAction≫ stereotype. *We offer supplementary possibilities to be contacted* is a ≪KeyAction≫ in Fig. 3.

- **Preconditions:** This field contains preconditions and requirements to be fulfilled before the principle can be applied. In practice, we found this field under the name *Implications*[5]. Hoogervorst [15] introduces the field *key actions for effectuating the architecture* to ensure that the principle can be followed. We introduce a new element in GRL ≪Precondition≫ IE. A precondition can be modeled as a *task, resource, softgoal* or *goal*. An example of a ≪Precondition≫ is *Clear view of the customer*.

- **Architecture Domain:** This field states to which part of the architecture the principle is applied (e.g., business, infrastructure, organization...) [4,15, 21]. We use the concept of "actor" for bounding in representation of the GRL intentional elements that constitute an EA principle. EA Principle 4 is an actor in Fig. 3 which includes Principle 4 and all of its intentional elements.

3.3 OCL Rules for Checking the Well-Formedness of EA Principles

The Object Constraint Language (OCL) is a declarative language for describing rules that apply to formal models. Due to its Eclipse OCL plug-ins that support rule definitions, checking, and explanation, OCL can be integrated with

---

[4] Schiphol airport case study.
[5] *eGovernmnet* case study.

jUCMNav. It is, therefore, possible to define and verify OCL rules for any GRL model. We provide ten OCL rules for checking the well-formedness of the EA principles. Given the space restrictions for this paper, we exemplify in Fig. 1 the implementation of one OCL rule[6].

1. **An EA principle must be modeled as a softgoal. (PrincipleAsSoft-Goal)** As stated before, the EA principles are seen as "rules of conduct" and cannot be fully enforced. Since the EA principles are high-level and somewhat vague in nature, we enforce modeling any element that has the stereotype ≪Principle≫ as a softgoal intentional element.

2. **A key action must be modeled as a task. (KeyActionAsTask)** By refining the EA principles to the level of tasks we ensure we operationalize the usage of EA principles.

3. **The added value must be modeled as a softgoal or as a goal. (AddedValueAsGoalOrSoftgoal)** EA principles should have an impact on the high level goals or softgoals of the organization. *Softgoals*, represent what a stakeholder wants to achieve. Contrary to goals, softgoals do not have quantifiable measurements. *Goals*, however, are more precise, have quantifiable measurements and can be clearly achieved.

4. **EA Principles, added values, preconditions, and key actions cannot be modeled as beliefs. (BeliefsNotStereoTyped)** This rule is required since beliefs in GRL are different entities from the intentional elements (i.e. goals, softgoals, resources, and tasks). *Beliefs* capture the rationales and justifications of GRL intentional elements and their links.

5. **Each EA principle must have at least one contribution from a key action. (KeyActionToPrinciple)** In order to operationalize the EA principles, we consider it necessary to refine their definition until we reach the tasks' level. This means that it is necessary to clearly define the key actions for realizing the EA principle. Therefore, each intentional element that has the stereotype ≪Principle≫ must be refined and have at least one contribution from an intentional element with the stereotype ≪KeyAction≫.

6. **If a precondition is introduced using a contribution link, the link must get the maximum value. (ContributionFromPreconditionIsMax)** In GRL, the evaluation algorithms depend on the values of the links. By giving the contribution the maximum value (e.g., 100 or *make*), we enforce that the precondition has at least high priority in the evaluation as the other intentional elements linked to the parent.

7. **If a precondition is introduced using a dependency link, the precondition must be modeled as source. (PreconditionAsSourceOfDependency)** In GRL notation, the dependency links are modeled as follows: **target** ➖ **source**. We introduce this OCL rule in order to assure that preconditions are modeled correctly in GRL notation. A dependency link shows a relationship between a dependent intentional element which

---

[6] The implementation of the rest of OCL rules is part of the Principle-based GRL framework and can be found at https://github.com/RationalArchitecture/eGovernment.

depends on a precondition intentional element. At the time of the evaluation, the intentional element dependent on a precondition receives the minimum value between its own evaluation and the evaluation of the precondition.

8. **Each EA principle must contribute to at least one (soft) goal** (here stereotyped ≪AddedValue≫) **of the organization. (PrincipleToGoal)** By introducing this rule we assure that we do not introduce an EA principle that has no real value for the goals of the organization.

9. **Each (soft) goal** (here stereotyped ≪AddedValue≫) **of the organization must have at least one contribution link from the set of EA principles. (GoalToPrinciple)** By introducing this rule, we assure that every goal of the organization is also addressed by at least one EA principle.

10. **The EA principles should not propagate a "conflict" satisfaction value for added value. (NoConflicts)** A set of two or more EA principles must not have contradictory contribution links on the same goal. If this happens and the goal gets "conflict" satisfaction value, a warning is triggered and the set of EA principles has to be revised in such a way that it is kept consistent.

```
── OCL Rule 8
context grl :: IntentionalElement
inv PrincipleToGoal
   self.getMetadata('ST_Principle') = 'Principle'
     implies
       self.linksSrc
       -> select(link | link.oclIsTypeOf(grl :: Contribution))
       -> collect(link | link.oclAsType(grl :: Contribution)).dest
       -> select(ie | ie.oclIsTypeOf(grl :: IntentionalElement))
       -> collect(ie | ie.oclAsType(grl :: IntentionalElement))
       -> select(ie | ie.getMetadata('ST_Principle')='AddedValue')
       -> size() > 0
```

Fig. 1. Implementation of OCL rule 8: **PrincipleToGoal**

3.4 Synthesis

In Sect. 3.1, we presented requirements for a set of good principles based on a summary of previous approaches found in the literature (e.g. [19, 22, 26]). Furthermore, in Sect. 3.2, we revised definitions of EA principles from literature (e.g. [15, 18, 26, 31, 32]) and practice (e.g. [21]) and created a unified structure for EA principles. We mapped these constitutive elements of EA principles to constitutive elements of GRL, creating a Principle-based GRL profile. In order to check the correctness of the GRL models for EA principles we defined ten OCL rules in Sect. 3.3. In Table 2, we check the properties of a good set of principles over the defined OCL rules.

Table 2. Verifying the requirements for a good set of EA principles over the EA principles' OCL rules

	PrincipleAsSoftGoal	KeyActionAsTask	AddedValueAsSoftGo..	BeliefsNotStereoTyped	KeyActionToPrinciple	ContributionFromPrec..	PreconditionAsSource..	PrincipleToGoal	GoalToPrinciple	NoConflicts
Understandable	✗	✗	✗							
Complete					✗			✗	✗	
Consistent	✗	✗	✗	✗		✗	✗			✗
Measurable	✗	✗	✗		✗			✗	✗	

4   Evaluation

In the previous sections, we presented our motivation for formalizing EA principles in GRL, along with the steps and requirements for this task. We evaluate our approach with a case study. We offer *a posteriori* rationalization and formalization of the EA principles used by a governmental organization whom for professional reasons wishes to remain anonymous, hereafter called *eGovernment*.

4.1   Case Study Presentation

eGovernment is the tax collection and customs administration of a European country. As part of the Ministry of Finance, *eGovernment* is responsible for supervising the import, export and transit of goods, detecting fiscal, economic and financial frauds, levying and collecting taxes, and paying out income-related benefits for child care, rent and health care.

The administration of *eGovernment* has discussed about how they envision their organization in 2020: an efficient governmental organization that achieves maximum compliance at minimum cost. Furthermore, an organization that is well in contact with citizens and businesses, interacts with them and adapts to their needs and behaviors. Changing circumstances, such as aging population, globalization and digitalization require *eGovernment* to transform itself. This emerging vision and the way *eGovernment* wants to be positioned into society was translated into nine design principles to guide their transformation.

We choose to analyze in detail a particular EA principle regarding the digitalization of *eGovernment*, as presented in Fig. 2.

4.2   Results: Formalization and Modeling of EA Principles in GRL

In this section, we first provide the extended definition of *eGovernment*'s EA Principle: *We prefer to communicate digitally with citizens and businesses*. Next, we analyze and interpret the statements and create the GRL model for the principle based on the mapping and OCL rules of Sect. 3. This definition has been translated from its original language to English. We tried to avoid any interpretation errors and kept the translation as close to the original meaning as possible.

Principle 4: **We prefer to communicate digitally with citizens and businesses** (1) Supplementary possibilities to contact us are only offered when these have additional values in the communication. If that is too much of the case, then we ensure that citizens and companies receive consistent information despite the channel from which they are served. (2)

- Digital communication is fast and efficient for both parties. (3)
- Since we aim for compliant behavior and due to the fact that digital communication does not contribute to that in all cases, we offer supplementary possibilities to contact us. (4)
- Since we are a governmental organization, we are obliged to make our services accessible to everybody, digitally experienced or not. (5)

This means that:

- We persuade citizens and companies to use Internet, the preferred medium. (6)
- We realize consistency in policy and execution over the different channels. (7)
- Information and transactions of citizens and companies is processed via different channels into a clear view of the customer. (8)
- We offer all electronic transaction services via two channels: a basic service via a portal and a system-to-system matching (as much as possible using *TechnologyX* via *Portal*) for the fiscal employees and entrepreneurs who use commercial software packages. (9)

Fig. 2. Original definition and translation of *eGovernment*'s EA principle: *We prefer to communicate digitally with citizens and businesses*

Originally the EA principles of *eGovernment* are represented in natural language using an adaptation of the EA principles' structure from TOGAF [26]: name, statement, rationale and implications. In this context, the term "Rationale" refers to the goals that are tackled by applying the principle and "Implications" refers to the requirements and preconditions that have to be fulfilled. In Fig. 2, the name is represented in **bold** text and the statement is composed of the following paragraph. The first set of bullet points represent the "Rationale" and those under "That means that" represent the "Implications". We observed that the natural language text yields additional information about the *Preconditions* and *Key Actions* for operationalization of the EA principle.

We reorganize the original representation of the EA principle in such a way that it follows the EA principles' definition presented in Sect. 3. We identified the following information in a tabular format: natural language description, NL Statement, (for which we marked in Fig. 2 each statement), the simplified GRL IE description, GRL Desc., the reference of the current GRL element, Ref., the type of the GRL intentional element and the stereotype when applicable, GRL Type, the element to which it is related, Linked to, the relation type, Rel. Type, and the link value, Link Val.. Additional information, such as the actor or comments regarding the modeling solution or difficulties in interpretation of the natural language description can also be included. We present a partial semi-formal tabular representation of *eGovernment*'s EA principle: *We prefer to communicate digitally with citizens and businesses* in Table 3.

One limitation for the *a posteriori* rationalization and the formalism is the challenge of evaluating the contribution links. In this example, we have introduced the values randomly. This step should be performed together with the architects and other involved stakeholders. A second challenge is raised by the interpretation of the natural language statements.

Table 3. Partial representation of *eGovernment*'s EA principle 4 in a semi-formal definition

Natural language statement	GRL description	Ref.	GRL IE Type	Linked to	Rel. Type	Link value
(1) We prefer to...	We prefer to communicate...	EAP4	Softgoal ≪Principle≫	AV1	Contrib	Help
(3) Digital communication is...	Fast and efficient communication	AV1	Softgoal ≪AddedValue≫	EAP4		
(5) Since we are a governmental..	Make our services accessible..	KA1	Task ≪KeyAction≫	EAP4	Contrib.	Some+
(7) We realize consistency over..	We realize consistency...	T1	Task	KA1	Contrib.	Make

Abbreviations: *EAP* = Enterprise Architecture Principle; *AV*= AddedValue; *KA* = KeyAction

4.3   Analysis of the EA Principles and GRL Models

In *eGovernment*, the EA principles (also originally called *Appointments*) were introduced with social aspects of the organization in mind. The EA principles were left ambiguous so that they could raise questions and bring people together for negotiations and finding solutions.

In our analysis, we identified and could confirm the following facts: EA principles are ambiguous. They have no traceability links to strategies, other principles, or activities of the organization. EA principles do not have a change management mechanism in place and have no formal mechanism for checking compliance. We also noticed that our formalism is more appropriate to the technology related EA principles. That is why we chose the EA principles related to technology, applications and infrastructure to formalize.

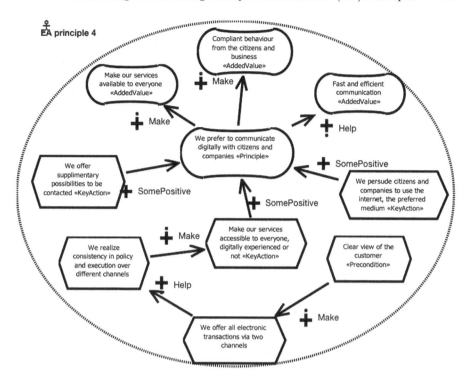

Fig. 3. GRL representation of *eGovernment*'s EA principle 4

4.4 Results: Evaluation from *eGovernment*'s Enterprise Architects

To ensure GRL models captured the essence of the EA principles correctly, we evaluated the models with two Enterprise Architects from *eGovernment*. The architects found the GRL models very useful in that they could visualize the principles and were easier for them to understand the links between the rationale, added value, actions and the goals of the principles. Furthermore, since the EA principles were linked to the high-level goals of the organization, it made them easier to justify and analyze. Also, we captured the traceability links between the related EA principles which helped the architects to document the links and verify the connections. The architects also informed us that assigning values for contribution links can be done at design time together with the architects.

We aim to extend our models to more principles and provide analysis of the principles with high-level goals as well as low-level operationalized activities of the organization.

5 Conclusions and Future Work

In this paper, we focused on how to formalize and represent EA principles in a goal oriented modeling-language. For this, we first presented five requirements for good sets of EA principles and how to create EA principles. We, then, introduced a Principle-based GRL profile by adding stereotypes to the intentional elements of GRL. The correctness of the models is assured by defining ten OCL rules. Our method was applied to a case study from a European governmental organization. We formalized their technology related EA principles in GRL and conducted interviews with the involved architects for evaluation.

In future work, we will focus on creating a formal change mechanism for revising the set of EA principles. This is a missing item for creating a "stable" set of EA principles. First, changes in the set of principles (e.g., addition, deletion or modification of principles) trigger consistency checks on the models and revision of the current landscape, second, analysis of the current situation (e.g., current objectives or current environment of the organization, as well as addition of new projects and programs) trigger changes in the set of principles, potentially making the principles outdated and create conflicts with the new goals, new situations and potential imposed regulations. In order to realize the second type of revision, good traceability links between EA principles and business processes and architecture are needed, therefore we will also focus on this stream of research.

Acknowledgements. The authors would like to thank Michiel Borgers and Saco Bekius, for providing fruitful insights on their work.

References

1. Akhigbe, O., Amyot, D., Richards, G.: A framework for a business intelligence-enabled adaptive enterprise architecture. In: Yu, E., Dobbie, G., Jarke, M., Purao, S. (eds.) ER 2014. LNCS, vol. 8824, pp. 393–406. Springer, Heidelberg (2014)
2. Amyot, D., et al.: Evaluating goal models within the goal-oriented requirement language. Int. J. Intell. Syst. **25**, 841–877 (2010)
3. Amyot, D., et al.: Towards advanced goal model analysis with jUCMNav. In: Castano, S., Vassiliadis, P., Lakshmanan, L.V.S., Lee, M.L. (eds.) ER 2012 Workshops 2012. LNCS, vol. 7518, pp. 201–210. Springer, Heidelberg (2012)
4. Armour, F.J., Kaisler, S.H., Liu, S.Y.: A big-picture look at enterprise architectures. IT Prof. **1**(1), 35–42 (1999)
5. Azevedo, C., et al.: An ontology-based semantics for the motivation extension to ArchiMate. In: EDOC 2011
6. Chorus, G., Janse, Y., Nellen, C., Hoppenbrouwers, S., Proper, H.A.: Formalizing architecture principles using object-role modelling. Via Nova Architectura (2007)
7. Engelsman, W., Wieringa, R.: Goal-oriented requirements engineering and enterprise architecture: two case studies and some lessons learned. In: Regnell, B., Damian, D. (eds.) REFSQ 2011. LNCS, vol. 7195, pp. 306–320. Springer, Heidelberg (2012)
8. Fischer, C., Winter, R., Aier, S.: What is an enterprise architecture principle? - towards a consolidated definition. In: Lee, R. (ed.) Computer and Information Science 2010. Studies in Computational Intelligence, vol. 317, pp. 193–205. Springer, Heidelberg (2010)

9. Ghanavati, S., Amyot, D., Rifaut, A.: Legal goal-oriented requirement language (Legal-GRL) for modeling regulations. In: MiSE @ICSE (2014)

10. Greefhorst, D., Proper, H.: Architecture Principles - The Cornerstones of Enterprise Architecture. EE Series. Springer, Heidelberg (2011)

11. Greefhorst, D., Proper, H.A., Plataniotis, G.: The dutch state of the practice of architecture principles. J. EA **4**, 20–25 (2013)

12. Haki, M.K., Legner, C.: New avenues for theoretical contributions in enterprise architecture principles - a literature review. In: Aier, S., Ekstedt, M., Matthes, F., Proper, E., Sanz, J.L. (eds.) PRET 2012 and TEAR 2012. LNBIP, vol. 131, pp. 182–197. Springer, Heidelberg (2012)

13. Haki, M.K., Legner, C.: Enterprise architecture principles in research and practice: insights from an exploratory analysis. In: ECIS, p. 204 (2013)

14. Hevner, A.R., March, S.T., Park, J., Ram, S.: Design science in information systems research. MIS Q. **28**(1), 75–105 (2004)

15. Hoogervorst, J.A.P.: Enterprise architecture: enabling integration, agility and change. Int. J. Coop. Inf. Syst. **13**(3), 213–233 (2004)

16. Ingolfo, S., Jureta, I., Siena, A., Perini, A., Susi, A.: Nomos 3: legal compliance of roles and requirements. In: ER 2014 (2014)

17. ITU-T. Recommendation Z.151 (11/08): User Requirements Notation (URN)-Language Definition (2008). http://www.itu.int/rec/T-REC-Z.151/en

18. Lankhorst, M., et al.: Enterprise Architecture at Work: Modelling, Communication and Analysis. Springer, Heidelberg (2005)

19. Lindström, Å.: On the syntax and semantics of architectural principles. In: Proceedings of HICSS-39, 4–7 January 2006, Kauai, HI, USA (2006)

20. Marosin, D., Ghanavati, S.: Measuring and managing the design restriction of enterprise architecture (EA) principles on EA models. In: Proceedings of 8th RELAW Workshop, 24–28 August 2015, Ottawa, Canada (2015)

21. Marosin, D., Ghanavati, S., van der Linden, D.: A principle-based goal-oriented requirements language (GRL) for enterprise architecture. In: Proceedings of the 7th International i* Workshop, Thessaloniki, Greece (2014)

22. Op 't Land, M., Proper, H.A.: Impact of principles on enterprise engineering. In: Österle, H., Schelp, J., Winter, R. (eds.) The 15th European Conference on Information Systems, pp. 1065–1076. University of St. Gallen, St. Gallen, Switzerland, June 2007

23. Plataniotis, G., De Kinderen, S., Ma, Q., Proper. E., A conceptual model for compliance checking support of enterprise architecture decisions. In: Proceedings of IEEE 17th Conference on Business Informatics (CBI), vol. 1, pp. 191–198, July 2015

24. Richardson, G.L., Jackson, B.M., Dickson, G.W.: A principles-based enterprise architecture: lessons from texaco and star enterprise. MIS Q. **14**(4), 385–403 (1990)

25. Stelzer, D.: Enterprise architecture principles: literature review and research directions. In: Dan, A., Gittler, F., Toumani, F. (eds.) ICSOC/ServiceWave 2009. LNCS, vol. 6275, pp. 12–21. Springer, Heidelberg (2010)

26. The Open Group. The Open Group - TOGAF Version 9. Van Haren Publishing, Zaltbommel (2009)

27. van Bommel, P., et al.: Architecture principles - a regulative perspective on enterprise architecture. In: EMISA (2007)

28. van Bommel, P., Hoppenbrouwers, S.J.B.A., Proper, H.A.E., van der Weide, T.P.: Giving meaning to enterprise architectures: architecture principles with ORM and ORC. In: Meersman, R., Tari, Z., Herrero, P. (eds.) OTM 2006 Workshops. LNCS, vol. 4278, pp. 1138–1147. Springer, Heidelberg (2006)

29. van Zee, M., Plataniotis, G., Marosin, D., van der Linden, D.: Formalizing enterprise architecture decision models using integrity constraints. In: 16h IEEE Conference on Business Informatics (CBI), May 2014

30. Wieringa, R.: Design science methodology: principles and practice. In: Proceedings of the 32nd ACM/IEEE International Conference on Software Engineering, ICSE 2010, vol. 2, pp. 493–494. ACM, New York (2010)

31. Wilkinson, M.: Designing an 'adaptive' enterprise architecture. BT Technol. J. **24**(4), 81–92 (2006)

32. Winter, R., Aier, S.: How are enterprise architecture design principles used? In: EDOCW, pp. 314–321. IEEE Computer Society (2011)

Engineering Requirements with *Desiree*: An Empirical Evaluation

Feng-Lin Li[1](✉), Jennifer Horkoff[2], Lin Liu[3], Alex Borgida[4],
Giancarlo Guizzardi[5], and John Mylopoulos[1]

[1] University of Trento, Trento, Italy
fenglin.Li@unitn.it
[2] City University, London, UK
[3] Tsinghua University, Beijing, China
[4] Rutgers University, New Brunswick, USA
[5] Federal University of Espirito Santo, Vitoria, Brazil

Abstract. The requirements elicited from stakeholders suffer from various afflictions, including informality, vagueness, incompleteness, ambiguity, inconsistencies, and more. It is the task of the requirements engineering process to derive from these a formal specification that truly captures stakeholder needs. The *Desiree* requirements engineering framework supports a rich collection of refinement operators through which an engineer can iteratively transform stakeholder requirements into a specification. The framework includes an ontology, a formal representation for requirements, as well as a tool and a systematic process for conducting requirements engineering. This paper reports the results of a series of empirical studies intended to evaluate the effectiveness of *Desiree*. The studies consist of three controlled experiments, where students were invited to conduct requirements analysis using textbook techniques or our framework. The results of the experiments offer strong evidence that with sufficient training, our framework indeed helps users conduct more effective requirements analysis.

Keywords: Requirements problem · Controlled experiment · Hypothesis testing · Effect size

1 Introduction

Upon elicitation, requirements are typically mere informal approximations of stakeholder needs that the system-to-be must fulfill. The core Requirements Engineering (RE) problem is to transform these requirements into a specification that describes formally and precisely the functions and qualities of the system-to-be. This problem has been elegantly characterized by Jackson and Zave [14] as finding the specification S that for certain domain assumptions DA entails given requirements R, and was formulated as $DA, S \models R$. Here DA circumscribes the domain where S constitutes a solution for R.

© Springer International Publishing Switzerland 2016
S. Nurcan et al. (Eds.): CAiSE 2016, LNCS 9694, pp. 221–238, 2016.
DOI: 10.1007/978-3-319-39696-5_14

The RE problem is compounded by the very nature of the requirements elicited from stakeholders. There is much evidence that stakeholder requirements (written in natural language) are often ambiguous, incomplete, unverifiable, conflicting, or just plain wrong [11,15]. More specifically, in our earlier studies on the PROMISE requirements dataset [22], we found that 3.84 % of the 625 (functional and non-functional) requirements are ambiguous [18], 25.22 % of the 370 non-functional requirements (NFRs) are vague, and 15.17 % of the NFRs are potentially unattainable (e.g., they implicitly or explicitly use universals like "*any*" as in "any time") [19].

Our *Desiree* framework tackles the RE problem in its full breadth and depth. In particular, it addresses issues of ambiguity (e.g., "notify users with email", where "*email*" may be a means or an attribute of user), incompleteness (e.g., "sort customers", in ascending or descending order?), unattainability (e.g., "the system shall remain operational at *all* times") and conflict (e.g., "high comfort" vs. "low cost"). The *Desiree* framework includes a modelling language for representing requirements (e.g., *DA*, *S*, and *R*), as well as a set of requirement operators that support the incremental transformation of requirements into a formal, consistent specification. The refinement and operationalization operators strengthen or weaken requirements to transform what stakeholders say they want into a realizable specification of functions and qualities.

Requirement operators provide an elegant way for going from informal to formal, from inconsistent/unattainable to consistent, also from complex to simple. To support incremental refinement, we have proposed a description-based representation for requirements [18,19]. Descriptions, inspired by AI frames and Description Logics (DL) [5], have the general form "*Concept* $<slot_1$: $D_1>$ ... $<slot_n$: $D_n>$", where D_i restricts $slot_i$; e.g., $R_1 :=$ "Backup <actor: {the_system}> <object: Data> <when: Weekday>". This form offers intuitive ways to strengthen or weaken requirements. For instance, R_1 can be strengthened into "Backup ... <object: Data> <when: {Mon, Wed, Fri}>", or weakened into "Backup ... <object: Data> <when: Weekday $\lor$ {Sat}>". Slot-description (*SlotD*) pairs "$< slot : D >$" allow nesting, hence "<object: Data>" can be strengthened to "<object: Data <associated_with: Student>>". In general, a requirement can be strengthened by adding slot-description pair(s), or by strengthening a description. Weakening is the converse of strengthening. The notion of strengthening or weakening requirements maps elegantly into the notion of subsumption in DL and is supported by off-the-shelf reasoners for a subset of our language.

Our main objective is to empirically evaluate *Desiree*, thereby answering the key question: Does *Desiree* improve the RE process? In particular, the paper presents three empirical studies involving upper-level software engineering students through controlled experiments. The results provide strong evidence that with a training time of two hours, *Desiree* can indeed help people to identify and address issues when refining stakeholder requirements. This work builds on our earlier publications that introduced our language for requirements and presented most of the operators [12,18,19].

The remainder of the paper is structured as follows. Section 2 introduces *Desiree*, Sect. 3 describes the three experiments, and Sect. 4 presents and discusses the results. Section 5 discusses related work, while Sect. 6 concludes, and sketches directions for further research.

2   The *Desiree* Framework

In this section, we present the *Desiree* framework [18], including a set of requirement concepts, a set of requirement operators, a description-based syntax for representing these concepts and operators, and a systematic methodology for transforming stakeholder requirements into a requirements specification.

2.1   Requirements Concepts

The core notions of *Desiree* are shown in Fig. 1 (shaded in the UML model). As in goal-oriented RE, we model stakeholder requirements as goals. We have 3 goal sub-kinds, 4 sub-kinds of specification elements (those with stereotype Specification Element), and domain assumptions, all of which are subclasses of Desiree Element. These concepts are derived from our experiences in analyzing the large PROMISE [22] requirements dataset. We use examples from this set to illustrate each of these concepts and relations.

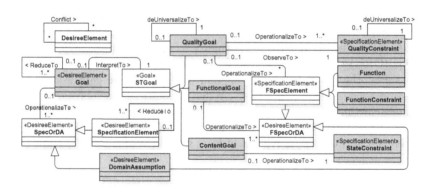

Fig. 1. The requirements ontology (adapted from [18])

There are three points to be noted. First, '>' and '<' are used to indicate the reading directions of the relations. Second, the relations (except "Conflict") are derived from applications of requirements operators (to be discussed in Sect. 2.2): if an operator is applied to an X object then the result will be $n..m$ Y objects; if that operator is not applied, then there is no relation (thus we have 0..1 as the lower bound). Third, "STGoal", "SpecOrDA", "FSpecOrDA" and "FSpecElement" are artificial concepts, used to represent the union of their sub-classes, e.g., "STGoal" represents the union of "FunctionalGoal", "QualityGoal" and

"ContentGoal". These classes are added to overcome the limitations of UML in representing inclusive (e.g., an operationalization of a functional goal) and exclusive (e.g., an interpretation of a goal) OR.

Functional Goal, Function and Functional Constraint. A functional goal (**FG**) represents a desired state, and can be operationalized by function(s), functional constraint(s), domain assumption(s), or a combination thereof. For example, the goal "student records be managed" specifies the desired state "managed". We capture the intention of something to be in a certain state (situation) by using the symbol ":<". So this example is modeled as an FG "Student_record :< Managed" (here "Managed" refers to an associated set of individuals that are in this specific state). This FG can be operationalized using functions such as "add", "update" and "remove" on student records.

When specifying a function (**F**), many pieces of information (e.g. actor, object, and trigger) can be associated with the desired capability. For example, "the system shall allow users to search products" will be captured as "F_0 := Search <subject: {the_system}><actor: User><object: Product>". A functional constraint (**FC**) constrains the situation under which a function can be manifested. As above, we specify intended situations using "$< s : D >$" pairs and constrain a function or an entity involved in a function description to be in such a situation using ":<". For example, "Only managers are able to activate debit cards" can be captured as "FC_1 := Activate <object: Debit_card> :< <actor: Manager>".

Quality Goal and Quality Constraint. We treat a quality as a mapping function that maps a subject to a value. A quality goal (**QG**) and quality constraint (**QC**) are requirements that require a quality to have value(s) in a desired quality region (QRG) [12]. In general, a QG/QC has the form "Q (SubjT) :: QRG". For instance, "the file search function shall be fast" will be captured as a QG "Processing_time (File_search) :: Fast". When the subject consists of one or more individuals (instances, in object-oriented terms), we use curly brackets to indicate a set, e.g., "{the_system}". Note that QGs and QCs have the same syntax, but different kinds of QRGs: regions of QGs are vague (e.g., "low") while those of QCs are measurable (e.g., "[0, 30]").

Content Goal and State Constraint. A content goal (**CTG**) often specifies a set of properties of an entity in the real word. To satisfy a CTG, a system needs to be in a certain state, which represents the desired world state. That is, concerned properties of real world entities should be captured as data in the system. We use a state constraint (**SC**) to specify the desired system state. For example, to satisfy the CTG "a student shall have Id, name and GPA", the student record database table of the system must include three columns: Id, name and GPA. This example can be captured as "CTG_1 := Student :< <has_id: ID> <has_name: Name> <has_gpa: GPA>" and a state constraint (**SC**), "SC_2 := Student_record :< <ID: String> <Name: String> <GPA: Float>".

Domain Assumption. A domain assumption (**DA**) is an assumption about the operational environment of a system. For instance, "the system will have a functioning power supply", which will be captured as "{the_system} :< <has_power: Power>". In *Desiree*, DAs are also used to capture domain knowledge, e.g., "Tomcat is a web server" will be captured as "Tomcat :< Web_server".

2.2 Requirements Operators

An overview of the requirements operators is shown in Table 1, where "#" indicates cardinality. As shown, *Desiree* includes two groups of operators (adapted from our previous work [18,19]): *refinement* and *operationalization*. In general, refinement operators refine goals to goals, or specification elements to specification elements, and operationalization operators map from goals to specification elements.

Table 1. An overview of the requirements operators

Requirements operators		#InputSet	#OutputSet
Refinement	Reduce (R_d)	1	1..*
	Interpret (I)	1	1
	deUniversalize (U)	1	1
	Resolve (R_s)	2..*	0..*
Operationalization	Operationalize (O_p)	1	1..*
	Observe (O_b)	1	1

Reduce (R_d). "Reduce" is used to refine a composite element (goal or specification element) to simple ones, or a high-level element to low-level ones. We allow making explicit domain assumptions when applying the "R_d" operator. For example, when reducing G_0 "pay for the book online" to G_1 "pay with credit card", one needs to assume DA_1 "having a credit card with enough credit". We capture this reduce refinement as "$R_d (G_0) = \{G_1, DA_3\}$".

Interpret (I). "Interpret" generalizes the original "Disambiguate" operator, and allows us to not only disambiguate a requirement by choosing the intended meaning, but also classify a requirement and encode it using descriptions. For example, a goal G_1 "notify users with email" can be interpreted as a functional goal FG_2 "User :< Notified <means: Email>". We denote this as "$I (G_1) = FG_2$".

deUniversalize (U). U applies to a QG/QC to weaken the requirement, such that it is no longer expected to hold universallly. For example, going from "(all) file searches shall be fast", captured as QG1-1 "$Processing\_time (File\_search) :: Fast$", to "(at least) 80 % of the searches shall be fast", captured as QG1-2 "$U(QG1-1, File\_search, 80\%)$". Here we revised the signature of U by explicitly specifying the set of individuals to which U will be applied ("File_search", in this case).

Resolve (R_s). In practice, some requirements will conflict with each other (i.e., they cannot be satisfied simultaneously). For example, the goal G_1 "use digital certificate" would conflict with G_2 "good usability" in a mobile payment scenario. We use a *"conflict"* relation to capture this phenomenon (*"Conflict* ($\{G_1, G_2\}$)"), and propose a new "Resolve" operator to address this conflict. In this example, we can replace G_2 by G_2' "acceptable usability" or drop G_1, which can be denoted as "R_s ($\{G_1, G_2\}$) = $\{G_1, G_2'\}$" or "R_s ($\{G_1, G_2\}$) = $\{G_2\}$", respectively.

Operationalize (O_p). The O_p operator is used to operationalize goals into specification elements. In general, O_p takes as input one goal, and outputs one or more specification elements. For instance, the operationalization of FG_1 "Products :< Paid" as F_2 "Pay <means: Credit_card>" and DA_3 "Credit_card :< Having_enough_credit" will be written as "O_p (G_1) = $\{F_2, DA_3\}$". One can use O_p to operationalize a QG as QC(s) to make it measurable, or as Fs and/or FCs to make it implementable. In addition, we can also operationalize a CTG as SC(s).

Observe (O_b). The O_b operator is derived from the original "Agreement" operator by separating de-universalization from it. It is employed to specify the means, measurement instruments or human used to measure the satisfaction of QGs/QCs, as the value of slot "*observed_by*". Consider "(at least) 80 % of the surveyed users shall report the interface is simple", which operationalizes and relaxes "the interface shall be simple". The original goal will be expressed as QG2-1 "*Style* ($\{the\_interface\}$) :: *Simple*". To capture the relaxation, we first use O_b, asking a set of surveyed users to observe QG2-1 and obtaining QC2-2 "O_b ($QG2-1$, $Surveyed\_user$)", and then use U, to require (at least) 80 % of the users to agree that QG2-1 hold, i.e., "U ($QC2-2$, $Surveyed\_user$, 80 %)".

2.3 A Transformation Methodology

The *Desiree* transformation process takes as input informal stakeholder requirements, and outputs a formal and consistent specification through incremental applications of the operators. We use a simple requirement "The system shall collect real time traffic info" to illustrate our three-staged *Desiree* method. The outputs of all stages are shown together in Fig. 2.

The informal stage. We first capture this requirement as a goal G_0. We then identify its concerns by asking "what does it concern?": a function "collect", a quality "timeliness" of collected traffic info, and a content concern "traffic info", and accordingly reduce G_0 to G_1, G_2 and G_3.

The interpretation stage. At this stage, we interpret G_1 to a functional goal FG_4, G_2 to a quality goal QG_7, G_3 to a content goal CTG_9, and encode the derived goals using our description-based syntax.

The smithing stage. At this stage, we operationalize the structured goals into specification elements. For example, we operationalize FG_4 "Traffic_info :< Collected" as a function "$Func_5$:= Collect <actor: $\{the\_system\}$> <object:

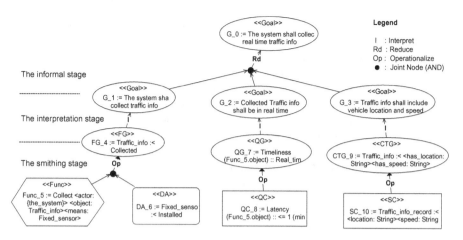

Fig. 2. An illustrative example for the *Desiree* method (with stereotypes on nodes)

Traffic_info> <means: Fixed_sensor>" and a domain assumption "$DA_6 :=$ Fixed_sensor :< Installed".

We have developed a prototype tool[1] to support the *Desiree* framework. Once we have derived a specification from stakeholder requirements, we can automatically translate it into a DL ontology using the prototype tool, and perform some useful reasoning tasks. For example, we can check which requirements are related to "Traffic_info" with the query "<relate_to: Traffic_info>".

Interested readers are referred to our previous work [18,19], where we have assessed the coverage of our requirements ontology by applying it to all the 625 requirements in the PROMISE dataset [22], evaluated the expressiveness of our description-based language by using it to rewrite all the 625 requirements in that dataset, and illustrated our methodology and available reasoning power by applying *Desiree* to a realistic *Meeting Scheduler* case study.

3   Experiments

In this section, we describe three controlled experiments, conducted to assess whether *Desiree* can indeed help people to conduct better requirement analysis. In the experiments, we compared *Desiree* with a *Vanilla* RE approach, where a participant uses the characteristics of a good software requirement specification (SRS) adapted from the IEEE standard 830 [8] and a set of guidelines for writing good requirements introduced in Wiegers et al. [23]. In the *Vanilla* method, participants manually go through and improve stakeholder requirements using these desirable characteristics and guidelines. This process approximates requirements walkthroughs using inspection checklists, and is used as a baseline representing how requirements are improved in practice.

---

[1] The tool is available at https://goo.gl/oeJ9Fi.

To prepare, we defined a set of requirements issues as in Table 2 by identifying the inverse of each characteristic introduced in the IEEE standard [8]. Our experiments check to see if people can identify more of these issues when refining stakeholder requirements with *Desiree* or with the *Vanilla* RE approach. We do not consider the "Ranked" characteristic, as *Desiree* currently does not support requirements prioritization. We also do not compare *Desiree* with the *Vanilla* method on "Traceability" because *Desiree* is a goal-oriented method, and as such it intrinsically supports requirements to requirements traceability (requirements to sources, and requirements to design traceability are out of scope for our experiments). In addition, we introduce "Unsatisfiable", which is practically important but missing in the IEEE standard.

Table 2. Requirements issues

Issue	Definition
Invalid	A requirement is invalid if it is not the one that stakeholders want
Incomplete	(1) incomplete requirement - a requirement is incomplete if necessary information is missing for implementation; (2) incomplete specification: an SRS is incomplete if any requirement is missing
Ambiguous	A requirement is ambiguous if it has more than one interpretation
Unverifiable	A requirement is unverifiable if it specifies unclear or imprecise value regions
Inconsistent	An SRS is inconsistent if there are: (1) conflicts between requirements; (2) terms are used in different ways in different places
Unmodifiable	An SRS is un-modifiable if its requirements are : (1) not structurally organized; (2) redundant; or (3) intermixing several requirements
Unsatisfiable	A requirement is practically unsatisfiable (attainable) if it is impossible or too costly to fulfill

3.1   Research Question

Our research question can be stated as: *compared with the Vanilla method, can Desiree help people to identify more requirements issues when transforming stakeholder requirements to specifications?*

We define the null hypothesis, H_0, as: there is no statistical difference in the number of requirements issues found when using *Desiree* (μ_D) vs. the *Vanilla* method (μ_V). The alternative hypothesis, H_1, is accordingly defined as: there is a positive statistical difference in the number of issues found using *Desiree* vs. the *Vanilla* method. These two hypotheses can be formulated as Eq. 1. Similarly, we can define the null and alternative hypotheses for all the 7 kind of issues defined in Table 2. Due to space limitation, we do not present them here.

$$H_0 : \mu_D - \mu_V = 0;$$
$$H_1 : \mu_D - \mu_V > 0;$$
(1)

3.2 Experiment Design

The experimental task was to transform a set of given stakeholder requirements into a specification through refinements. To evaluate the differences in their performance, each participant was required to perform the task twice: s/he uses the *Vanilla* method on a project X in the first session, and then uses *Desiree* on another project Y in the second session. In both sessions, the participants discussed with stakeholders to elicit necessary information for addressing identified issues (e.g., one probably needs further information to quantify "fast", which is vague), and submitted a refined specification. All experimental tasks were performed electronically and online.

The experiment was duplicated three times, the first at University of Trento, Italy, and the second and the third at Tsinghua University, China. In each experiment, we used two projects, *Meeting Scheduler* (MS) and *Realtor Buddy* (RB), which are selected from the PROMISE requirements set [22], for the experimental task. We chose 10 requirements, which cover some typical functionalities and qualities (e.g., search, usability), from each project, and identified a list of issues for both projects. We also added some issues that are newly identified by participants into the reference issue lists in each experiment. Roughly, each project has approximately 45 issues, and each issue type has around 5 instances (except incomplete, which accounts for nearly 50 % of the issues in each project). The statistics of these issues are available at https://goo.gl/oeJ9Fi.

In experiment one, we had 17 participants: Master's students at the Department of Information Engineering and Computer Science, University of Trento, taking the RE course at the spring term of 2015. We also had 4 Ph.D. students or postdocs in the research group of Software Engineering and Formal Methods playing the role of stakeholder. We assigned two stakeholders to a project, and randomly separated the students into two teams, RG1 and RG2. In the *Vanilla* session, we introduced the characteristics of a good SRS [8] and the textbook techniques [23] in 30 min, presented the domain knowledge of the two projects in 10 min, and tested in 90 min. In this session, RG1 worked on MS and RG2 worked on RB. In the *Desiree* session, we introduced the framework and its supporting tool in 40 min, and tested in 90 min. In this session, the teams were given the other project.

In experiment two, we had 18 volunteer participants: Master's students at the Institute of Information System and Engineering, School of Software, Tsinghua University. Compared with experiment one, a few changes were made to the experimental design. First, to improve the consistency of stakeholders' answers, we randomly separated the 18 participants into 6 small teams of size 2 − 4, and hired 1 constant stakeholder for all the 6 teams on the same project (the 6 teams conducted the experiment one by one, not concurrently). Second, based on our initial observations that the training time was too short, we increased the

Desiree training time from 40 min to 2 h, 1 h for the method and 1 h for the tool (we also increased the *Vanilla* training time to 1 h). In addition, we had updated the *Desiree* tool based on the feedback collected in experiment one, mainly on the usability aspect (e.g., copy and paste).

In experiment three, we had 30 participants[2]: Master's students at the School of Software, Tsinghua University, taking the RE course at the fall term of 2015. This experiment replicates the first, with the only change to *Desiree* training time: 45 min for the method, and 60 min for the tool (the *Vanilla* training time is 45 min). Also, we hired 6 students who have already participated experiment two as our stakeholders (7 in total, including the trainer). Similarly, stakeholders are randomly assigned to the two projects, and students are randomly separated into two teams. The two teams were given different projects in the two sessions.

4   Results

In this section, we report and discuss the experiment results. The data statistics collected from the three experiments are shown in Table 3. There are three points to be noted. First, in each session of the three experiments, participants were expected to discuss questions over the given requirements via text interface with stakeholders, and produce a refined textual requirements specification or a refined *Desiree* requirements model. Second, in each experiment, the output of the *Vanilla* session was only text while that of the *Desiree* session could be a mix of models and texts: if a participant cannot model all the given requirements using the *Desiree* syntax and tool within specified time, s/he was required to refine unmodelled requirements using natural language, but still following the *Desiree* method. In a few cases, participants submitted only models or only textual specifications in a *Desiree* session. Third, in the experiments, a few participants (e.g., 2 in the *Vanilla* session of experiment three) have refined the given requirements without discussing any questions with stakeholders.

Table 3. Statistics of collected data: conversations, requirements texts and models

Session	Experiment one		Experiment two		Experiment three	
	Vanilla	*Desiree*	*Vanilla*	*Desiree*	*Vanilla*	*Desiree*
Time (*min*)	63	89.5	74	94	62	97
Discussions	17	16	18	15	28	29
Textual requirement specifications	17	14	18	12	30	23
Desiree requirement models	-	11	-	15	-	29
Complete samples	16		15		29	

---

[2] We conducted experiment three at Tsinghua University again because: (1) the sample size of experiment two (15) is relatively small; (2) we had additional available participants at Tsinghua (one of the authors was teaching a RE class in the fall term there).

4.1 Descriptive Statistics

We carefully went through participants' discussions and refined requirements (both texts and models) to check how many issues they have identified in the experiments. We say a participant has identified an issue if either of the two conditions hold.

1. A participant has asked a corresponding question, e.g., we gave a count of identified unverifiable issue if someone has asked "how to measure fast?" to quantify "fast".
2. A participant has eliminated an issue in his/her refined requirements specification, either texts or models, although s/he did not ask any related question. E.g., a participant has eliminated a term inconsistency in RB by changing "the product" to "the system" without asking any questions.

To keep consistency, the trainer performed the evaluation for all the three experiments. We show the average percentage of identified issues of participants in Table 4, where positive results are in bold. We see that in experiment one, on average, a participant was able to find more issues with *Desiree* than with the *Vanilla* method (35.79 % vs. 30.08 %), but discovered fewer "Ambiguous" and "Unverifiable" issues. In experiment two, as the training time for *Desiree* increased from 40 min to 2 h, we can see that the participants performed better in general: they found more issues in total (46.27 % vs. 32.93 %). Experiment three has provided similar evidence as experiment two: with a training time of near 2 h, participants are able to find more issues with *Desiree* (39.98 % vs. 28.17 %). In addition, we have compared the performance of each participant on the two sample projects (MS and RB). The detailed statistics (including raw data and statistical calculations) are available at https://goo.gl/oeJ9Fi.

Table 4. Statistics of issues identified by participants in the three experiments

	Experiment one			Experiment two			Experiment three		
	Vanilla	*Desiree*	Diff	*Vanilla*	*Desiree*	Diff	*Vanilla*	*Desiree*	Diff
Incomplete	15.84 %	19.70 %	**3.86 %**	27.30 %	31.64 %	**4.34 %**	21.49 %	30.77 %	**9.28 %**
Ambiguous	24.22 %	20.31 %	−3.91 %	32.22 %	54.44 %	**22.22 %**	12.93 %	38.45 %	**25.52 %**
Inconsistent	10.42 %	15.62 %	**5.20 %**	6.67 %	8.89 %	**2.22 %**	16.09 %	16.38 %	**0.29 %**
Unverifiable	88.75 %	84.37 %	−4.38 %	81.33 %	92.67 %	**11.34 %**	79.37 %	90.27 %	**10.90 %**
Unmodifiable	20.83 %	47.92 %	**27.09 %**	9.44 %	43.33 %	**33.89 %**	3.45 %	47.41 %	**43.96 %**
Unsatisfiable	2.78 %	12.44 %	**9.66 %**	10.56 %	50.00 %	**39.44 %**	3.45 %	24.14 %	**20.69 %**
Total	30.08 %	35.79 %	**5.71 %**	32.93 %	46.27 %	**13.34 %**	28.17 %	39.98 %	**11.81 %**

4.2 Hypothesis Testing

We statistically analyzed the participants' differences in terms of identified issues when using *Desiree* vs. the *Vanilla* approach. Since we have far less than 30 participants in experiment one and two, and our Shapiro-Wilk Normality tests showed that the participants' differences in experiment three are not normally distributed on 3/7 of the issue indicators, we employed both *paired Student's t test* [2] and *Wilcoxon Signed-Rank* test (WSR) [3] for our one-tailed hypothesis testing. The paired T test assumes that the differences between pairs (repeated measurements on a sample, before and after a treatment) are normally distributed, and is robust to moderate violation of normality [21]. As a complement, the WSR test is a non-parametric alternative to the paired T test if the differences between pairs are severely non-normal [21].

Table 5. Statistical p-value for issues identified by participants

	Experiment one		Experiment two		Experiment three	
	Paired T	WSR	Paired T	WSR	Paired T	WSR
Incomplete	0.08331	**0.03717**	0.10593	0.1221	**0.00007**	**0.00021**
Ambiguous	0.71236	0.6753	**0.00144**	**0.00288**	**0.00069**	**0.00145**
Inconsistent	0.37845	0.37097	0.33507	0.30345	0.47585	0.66204
Unverifiable	0.92169	0.8449	**0.01428**	**0.02747**	**0.00396**	**0.00519**
Unmodifiable	**0.00269**	**0.003**	**0.00001**	**0.00052**	**<0.00001**	**<0.00001**
Unsatisfiable	**0.04449**	0.05155	**<0.00001**	**0.00032**	**0.00006**	**0.00013**
Total	0.076	0.06023	**<0.00001**	**0.00036**	**<0.00001**	**0.00001**

We report the p-values in Table 5. We can see that there is strong evidence that *Desiree* can help people to identify more issues in general (the last row): for both tests, p-value $\leq 0.00036 << \alpha = 0.05$ (the common confidence level) in experiment two and three, and p-value ≈ 0.05 in experiment one. Specifically, there are strong evidence that *Desiree* is able to help people to identify more "Incomplete", "Ambiguous", "Unverifiable", "'Unmodifiable', and "Unsatisfiable" issues (their p-values ≤ 0.05 in at least two experiments). We also see that there is no evidence that *Desiree* can help people to identify more "Inconsistent" issues (p-value $>> 0.05$) in all the three experiments.

To mitigate the potential risk of *accumulated type I error* (a false rejection of the null hypothesis due merely to random sampling variation) when running multiple tests [17], we applied the Bonferroni adjustment [1] to the p-values obtained in experiment three. We report the adjusted p-values and the related statistics (i.e., t values for the paired T tests, Z values for the WSR tests) in Table 6. The very small adjusted p-value (p-value $< 0.00001 << 0.05$) indicates a very strong evidence that the samples are not from the null distribution. We can hence reject the null hypothesis H_0 stated in Eq. 1 at the confidence level $\alpha = 0.05$, and accept the alternative hypothesis H_1.

We also analyzed the *effect sizes*, which are shown Table 6. Effect size is the magnitude of a treatment effect [6], i.e., it tells to what degree a treatment (e.g., the *Desiree* method) affects the participants. For example, according to Coe [6], an effect size of 0.8 means that the score of the average person in

Table 6. Analyzing experiment three: p-values, statistics, and effect

| | Paired T Test | | | | Wilcoxon Signed-Rank (WSR) | | | |
	p-value	Bonferroni	t(28)	Effect	P value	Bonferroni	Z value	Effect
Incomplete	0.00007	0.00046	4.4302	0.82266	0.00021	0.0015	3.52263	0.64314
Ambiguous	0.00069	0.0048	3.5536	0.6599	0.00145	0.01017	2.97754	0.54362
Inconsistent	0.47585	1	0.06111	0.01135	0.66204	1	−0.41805	−0.07633
Unverifiable	0.00396	0.02773	2.8598	0.53105	0.00519	0.03631	2.5631	0.46796
Unmodifiable	<0.00001	<0.00001	8.6828	1.61236	<0.00001	0.00002	4.57097	0.83454
Unsatisfiable	0.00006	0.00044	4.4458	0.82556	0.00013	0.00094	3.64313	0.66514
Total	<0.00001	<0.00001	6.5681	1.21967	0.00001	0.00008	4.24921	0.7758

the experimental group is 0.8 standard deviations above the average person in the control group, and hence exceeds the scores of 79 % of the control group. We checked the effect sizes in experiment three for each kind of requirements issue[3], and found that this interpretation matches very well with the actual situation. Using Cohen's conventional criteria of "small" (effect size from 0.2 to 0.3), "medium" (around 0.5), or "big" (0.8 to infinity) effect [7], the effect sizes for "Total", "Incomplete", "Ambiguous", "Unverifiable", "Unmodifiable" and "Unsatisfiable" issues in experiment three fall into the"medium" or "large" category.

4.3 Analysis

In general, the results meet our expectations.

Incomplete. In our observations, *Desiree* is helpful in identifying incomplete requirements issues mainly because: (1) the description-based syntax drives users to think about the kinds of properties that shall be associated with the capability when specifying a function; (2) the syntax facilitates the consideration of "which attributes shall be used to describe the description (filler)?" when specifying a slot-description pair. Take "the system shall be able to search meeting rooms records" as an example, with *Desiree*, many participants were able to find the following missing information: who can search? what kinds of search parameters shall be used? Further, more participants have asked "what kinds of information shall a meeting room record include?", identifying a missing content requirement.

Ambiguous. Desiree offers operational rules for identifying potential ambiguities: (1) checking the subject of a slot (property); (2) checking the cardinality of the restriction of a slot in a function description. These rules are shown to be useful in our experiments. For example, more participants have identified the ambiguity in the requirement "the system shall be able to download contact info for client": is "for client" attached to the function "download" or the entity "contact info"? More interestingly, for the requirement "the system shall allow privileged users to view meeting schedules in multiple reporting views", after addressing the

---

[3] The effect sizes in experiment one and two can be found at https://goo.gl/oeJ9Fi.

unverifiable issues of "privileged user" and "multiple", several participants have further asked "Shall these reporting views be opened simultaneously or not?", identifying an implicit ambiguity issue.

Unverifiable. We observed that the participants can easily find simple unverifiable issues in given requirements, but tend to miss "deep" vague issues in stakeholders' answers when using the *Vanilla* method. With *Desire*, the structuring of each requirement could remind them about implicit unverifiable issues. For example, most of the participants were able to justify "the product shall have good usability" as unverifiable, but few of them realized that "the product shall be easy to learn for realtors", which was given by stakeholders as a refinement of the previous requirement, is still vague. With *Desireee*, participants would keep asking "how to measure easy?". That is, when using the *Vanilla* method, participants were more likely to accept vague stakeholder answers, while using *Desiree*, they were more likely to notice and correct vague responses.

Un-modifiable. *Desiree* requires users to identify the concerns of a requirement, and separate them if there are several. This helps to avoid intermixed requirements. With *Desiree*, many participants were able to successfully decouple composite requirements into simple ones. For example, they decoupled "the system shall be able to generate a CMA (Comparative Market Analysis) report in acceptable time" into "generate a CMA report" (F_1 := Generate <object: CMA_report>) and "the generation shall be in acceptable time" (QG_2 := Processing_time (F_1) :: Acceptable). Further, they were able to capture interrelations between requirements by utilizing the *Desiree* tool. For example, in the above example, the two elements are interrelated through the use of F_1 as the subject of QG_2. This enables us to systematically identifying the requirements to be affected when updating a requirement.

Un-satisfiable. *Desiree* offers a "de-Universalize" operator for weakening requirements in order to make them practically satisfiable. The supporting tool also provides hints for relaxation when the "Observe" operator is applied. As such, the participants were able to identify more potentially un-satisfiable issues. For example, when operationalizing the QG "the search of meeting rooms shall be intuitive" by assigning surveyed users, many of them have asked "how many percentage of the surveyed users shall agree?"

Inconsistent. Our framework assumes that conflicts are explicitly defined by analysts and provides an "Resolve" operator to resolve them. As such, the framework does not as yet offer much help in identifying inconsistency issues.

We had some additional observations over experiment results. First, we omitted "Invalid" from our experiment results since there were no invalid issues in the two projects (it is hard to justify which requirement is not desired by original stakeholders who provided the requirements set). Second, the participants in experiment one had a poorer performance on identifying "Ambiguous" and "Unverifiable" issues mainly because the training time of 40 min is too short: many students have spent a lot of time struggling with the syntax and the tool, and did not have enough time to analyze the requirements themselves. Third, the learning of *Desiree* varies from individual to individual: in experiment three, 24 out of the 29 participants (82.76 %) have better performance when using the *Desiree* method while the rest (5/29, 17.24 %) have slightly poorer performance.

4.4   Feedback

We have conducted a survey on the two RE methods in each experiment. In general, the majority of the participants have reported that the *Desiree* framework is useful or very useful, but hard to learn. For example, among the 24 collected responses in the survey of experiment three, 20 out of 24 (20/24) have reported that *Desiree* is useful or very useful, and 11 out of them (11/24) have reported that *Desiree* is hard to learn. Specifically, the participants have pointed out that the framework is useful because it offers a structured way for classifying and representing requirements, and provides a systematic method for reducing complex requirements; it is hard to learn mainly because of its grammar. We have also got positive feedback from the participants in each experiment. Interested readers are referred to our survey reports available at https://goo.gl/oeJ9Fi.

1. "*Desiree* embodies correctness check. It enforces you to think if what you are doing is right, e.g., functional goals, quality goals ...."
2. "The method helps a lot when reducing the complex requirements and help with the standard representation of those items. Nothing is useless. The method makes the analysis process clearer more or less. "
3. "The tool makes me thinking in the structural and the mind is more MECE (Mutually Exclusive, Collectively Exhaustive)."

4.5   Threats to Validity

There are several threats to the validity of our evaluation.

Independence between participants. We have tried to minimize mutual interference between participants in each experiment by: (1) assuming an exam scenario and asking them to perform the experimental task individually; and (2) requiring them to use text to communicate with stakeholders instead of speaking aloud (we had only 4 face-to-face conversations in the *Vanilla* session of experiment three since these students did not bring their laptops).

Assessment. The experiment results were evaluated by only one person. We have used objective and consistent rules for making judgments, to minimize the impact of individual subjectivity.

The nature of participants. Most of the participants in our experiments are students. However, in experiment three, at least 8 participants (8/29) have more than 1 year work experience (5/8 specific to RE). Also, holding the studies in two different universities provides more confidence in the generalizability of our results. We could further minimize this threat by conducting experiments in an realistic industrial setting.

Order. Desiree is used after the *Vanilla* method in each experiment. Although each participant applied *Desiree* to a different project in the second task, s/he may have learned from the *Vanilla* application in her/his first task. We could have done counterbalancing: some groups apply *Vanilla* then *Desiree*, and others apply *Desiree* then *Vanilla*; however, this setup would have been difficult to implement as part of the course design, with alternating tutorials and exercises for different groups of students.

Sample size. The sample size of 29 in experiment three is sufficient to assume the normality for paired T test. Also, we have ran the Wilcoxon Signed-Rank test, which does not assume any distribution of the population, in each experiment. The threat of generalizing our conclusion is relative low.

Training. In our experiments, the *Desiree* framework was taught by the designer; and how the *Vanilla* RE method was taught may affect results. We have tried to be fair in teaching and not bias the results.

Projects. The *Desiree* method can be more or less successful for different types of projects, e.g., larger or more realistic. We have tried to mitigate this by using more than one project.

5   Related Work

In the RE literature, many empirical evaluations have been conducted to assess the utility of some languages or methods, but mainly on their expressiveness and effectiveness [10,13]. Al-Subaie et al. [4] have used a realistic case study to evaluate KAOS and its supporting tool, Objectiver, with regarding to a set of properties of requirements, introduced in Davis et al. [9] and the IEEE Std 830-1998 [8]. They reported that KAOS is helpful in detecting ambiguity and capture traceability, but the formalism of KAOS is only applicable to goals that are in enough detail and can be directly formalized.

Work by Matulevicius et al. [20] is quite relevant. In their evaluation, the authors have compared i^* and KAOS through experiments. Besides the quality of languages themselves, they also compared the models generated by using the two frameworks with regarding to a set of qualitative properties in the semiotic quality framework [16]. Their findings indicate a higher quality of the KAOS language (not significant), but a higher quality of the i^* models (the participants are not required to write formal specifications with KAOS). They also found that the goal models produced by both frameworks are evaluated low at several aspects, including verifiability, completeness and ambiguity.

These evaluations show that requirements initially captured in goal models are of low quality and error prone, and techniques for incrementally improving the quality of requirements captured in traditional goal models are needed. We have proposed *Desiree* for addressing such deficiencies [18,19], in this work we conducted three experiments to evaluate its effectiveness.

6 Conclusion

In this paper, we have presented a series of three controlled experiments that are conducted to evaluate the effectiveness of the *Desiree* framework. The evaluation results have provided strong evidence that given a training time around two hours, *Desiree* indeed can help people to perform better requirements analysis (e.g., less ambiguous, more complete, etc.) with a medium or big effect.

There are several directions can be further explored. First, the usability of the *Desiree* tool, and the accessibility of the tutorial for the *Desiree* approach (e.g., wiki, video, help manual) needs to be improved. Second, our *Desiree* framework currently does not have a built-in set of slots, and may result in different outputs when used by different users as they may use different words for the same relation (e.g., "belong to" vs. "associated with"). An interesting idea is "slot mining": statistically analyzing the requirements in specific application domains and eliciting a set of frequent slots.

Acknowledgements. This research has been funded by the ERC advanced grant 267856 "Lucretius: Foundations for Software Evolution" (April 2011–March 2016). It has also been supported by the Key Project of National Natural Science Foundation of China (no. 61432020), and the Key Project in the National Science & Technology Pillar Program during the Twelfth Five-year Plan Period (No. 2015BAH14F02). Jennifer is supported by an ERC Marie Skodowska-Curie Intra European Fellow-ship (PIEFGA - 2013 - 627489) and by a Natural Sciences and Engineering Research Council of Canada Postdoctoral Fellowship (September 2014–August 2016).

References

1. Bonferroni correction, November 2015. https://en.wikipedia.org/w/index.php?title=Bonferroni_correction&oldid=692500900
2. Student's t-test, October 2015. https://en.wikipedia.org/w/index.php?title=Student%27s_t-test&oldid=687517571
3. Wilcoxon signed-rank test, November 2015. https://en.wikipedia.org/w/index.php?title=Wilcoxon_signed-rank_test&oldid=690943842
4. Al-Subaie, H.S., Maibaum, T.S.: Evaluating the effectiveness of a goal-oriented requirements engineering method. In: CERE 2006, pp. 8–19. IEEE (2006)
5. Baader, F.: The Description Logic Handbook: Theory, Implementation, and Applications. Cambridge University Press, Cambridge (2003)
6. Coe, R.: It's the effect size, stupid: what effect size is and why it is important (2002)
7. Cohen, J.: Statistical Power Analysis for the Behavioral Sciences. Academic Press, New York (2013)
8. Committee, I., Board, I.S.S.: IEEE Recommended Practice for Software Requirements Specifications. IEEE (1998)
9. Davis, A.M.: Software Requirements: Objects, Functions, and States. Prentice-Hall, Inc., Englewood Cliffs (1993)
10. Estrada, H., Rebollar, A.M., Pastor, Ó., Mylopoulos, J.: An empirical evaluation of the i^* framework in a model-based software generation environment. In: Martinez, F.H., Pohl, K. (eds.) CAiSE 2006. LNCS, vol. 4001, pp. 513–527. Springer, Heidelberg (2006)

11. Fabbrini, F., Fusani, M., Gnesi, S., Lami, G.: The linguistic approach to the natural language requirements quality: benefit of the use of an automatic tool. In: IEEE/NASA SEW-26, pp. 97–105. IEEE (2001)
12. Guizzardi, R., Li, F.L., Borgida, A., Guizzardi, G., Horkoff, J., Mylopoulos, J.: An ontological interpretation of non-functional requirements. In: FOIS 2014, vol. 267, pp. 344–357. IOS Press (2014)
13. Horkoff, J., Aydemir, F.B., Li, F.-L., Li, T., Mylopoulos, J.: Evaluating modeling languages: an example from the requirements domain. In: Yu, E., Dobbie, G., Jarke, M., Purao, S. (eds.) ER 2014. LNCS, vol. 8824, pp. 260–274. Springer, Heidelberg (2014)
14. Jackson, M., Zave, P.: Deriving specifications from requirements: an example. In: ICSE 1995, pp. 15–24. ACM (1995)
15. Kamalrudin, M., Hosking, J., Grundy, J.: Improving requirements quality using essential use case interaction patterns. In: ICSE 2011, pp. 531–540. ACM (2011)
16. Krogstie, J.: A semiotic approach to quality in requirements specifications. In: Liu, K., Clarke, R.J., Andersen, P.B., Stamper, R.K., Abou-Zeid, E.-S. (eds.) Organizational Semiotics. IFIP, vol. 94, pp. 231–249. Springer, New York (2002)
17. LeBlanc, D.C.: Statistics: Concepts and Applications for Science, vol. 2. Jones & Bartlett Learning, Burlington (2004)
18. Li, F.-L., Horkoff, J., Borgida, A., Guizzardi, G., Liu, L., Mylopoulos, J.: From stakeholder requirements to formal specifications through refinement. In: Fricker, S.A., Schneider, K. (eds.) REFSQ 2015. LNCS, vol. 9013, pp. 164–180. Springer, Heidelberg (2015)
19. Li, F.L., Horkoff, J., Mylopoulos, J., Guizzardi, R.S., Guizzardi, G., Borgida, A., Liu, L.: Non-functional requirements as qualities, with a spice of ontology. In: RE 2014, pp. 293–302. IEEE (2014)
20. Matulevičius, R., Heymans, P.: Comparing goal modelling languages: an experiment. In: Sawyer, P., Heymans, P. (eds.) REFSQ 2007. LNCS, vol. 4542, pp. 18–32. Springer, Heidelberg (2007)
21. McDonald, J.H.: Handbook of Biological Statistics, vol. 2. Sparky House Publishing, Baltimore (2009)
22. Menzies, T., Caglayan, B., He, Z., Kocaguneli, E., Krall, J., Peters, F., Turhan, B.: The PROMISE Repository of empirical software engineering data, June 2012
23. Wiegers, K., Beatty, J.: Software Requirements. Pearson Education, Harlow (2013)

A Modelling Language for Transparency Requirements in Business Information Systems

Mahmood Hosseini$^{(\boxtimes)}$, Alimohammad Shahri, Keith Phalp, and Raian Ali

Bournemouth University, Poole, UK
{mhosseini,ashahri,kphalp,rali}@bournemouth.ac.uk

Abstract. Transparency is a requirement of businesses and their information systems. It is typically linked to positive ethical and economic attributes, such as trust and accountability. Despite its importance, transparency is often studied as a secondary concept and viewed through the lenses of adjacent concepts such as security, privacy and regulatory requirements. This has led to a reduced ability to manage transparency and deal with its peculiarities as a first-class requirement. Ad-hoc introduction of transparency may have adverse effects, such as information overload and reduced collaboration. We propose a modelling language for capturing and analysing transparency requirements amongst stakeholders in a business information system. Our language is based on four reference models which are, in turn, based on our extensive multi-disciplinary analysis of the literature on transparency. As a proof of concept, we apply our modelling language and the analysis enabled by it on a case study of marking exam papers.

Keywords: Transparency requirements · Transparency engineering · Transparency analysis · TranspLan modelling language

1 Introduction

Transparency, and transparent decision-making, is generally considered to be a requirement of democratic societies [15]. Recently, transparency has received a lot of attention, e.g., following the financial crisis of 2008 which was the result of the lack of transparency in financial environments [4], or the Ashley Madison incident which was the result of unnecessary, unwanted transparency [11]. The escalated attention to transparency is supported by the fact that the millennials and the younger generation live in a more transparent world [16] and demand even more transparency [10].

With transparency requirements on the rise, one expects to find a vast body of literature studying transparency, its causes and its effects. This is not far from the truth. The literature on transparency spans several fields of study, such as politics [3], sociology [1], and management [13]. In computer sciences, transparency has also been occasionally studied. For example, transparency is frequently observed as a requirement of various stakeholders within a business information system (BIS) which must be satisfied [6,7].

© Springer International Publishing Switzerland 2016
S. Nurcan et al. (Eds.): CAiSE 2016, LNCS 9694, pp. 239–254, 2016.
DOI: 10.1007/978-3-319-39696-5_15

However, the literature on transparency in general, and in computer sciences in particular, still lacks a critical focus, which is a systematic modelling of transparency. Without a rigorous and systematic model, several other problems cannot be duly addressed. The first problem is that a transparency model can facilitate a consistent method for eliciting transparency requirements of stakeholders. Second, a transparency model can provide methods for analysing transparency, which could be automated as well. Third, a rigorous transparency model can also make way for automated validation and evaluation of transparency. Such a model, however, does not still exist for transparency.

Based on our extensive multi-disciplinary literature study on transparency and our transparency facets [8], in this paper we propose *TranspLan*, a language for modelling and analysing of transparency requirements in a BIS. This language facilitates different aspects of transparency requirements elicitation, modelling and analysis. We define the *TranspLan* language mathematically, provide a graphical representation for it, and enrich it with two specification models.

The rest of the paper is structured as follows. In Sect. 2 we explain the background study for our transparency language. In Sect. 3 we introduce our transparency language, formally define it and provide its mathematical definition. In Sect. 4 we evaluate our language using a case study involving transparency requirements of different stakeholders in a coursework marking exam in a university. We conclude our work in Sect. 5.

2   Background

Few studies in the field of computer science have attempted to model transparency, mostly from a requirements perspective. [2] is amongst the first works on transparency modelling, which argues that NFR Framework [5] and i^* modelling [17] can manage transparency requirements. Interestingly, the paper concludes that i^* modelling is not the ultimate answer to transparency, and augmentations to this model might be needed for a more efficient management of transparency requirements. This work has also led to a more detailed work on transparency in [12], which discusses software transparency using Softgoal Interdependence Graph (SIG). This paper also proposes a transparency ladder, which contains five non-functional requirements that must be met in order to reach transparency. Finally, [14] proposes the use of Argumentation Frameworks to elicit transparency requirements of stakeholders.

We introduce three reference models for engineering transparency, based on transparency facets [8], advocating these models are needed alongside a fourth dimension, i.e., information quality [9]. These reference models are as follows:

1. Transparency Actors Wheel: This reference model discusses the stakeholders involved during transparency provision. Based on their position in information disclosure, these stakeholders are categorised as: (1) information provider, (2) information receiver, (3) information entity, and (4) information medium. A summary of this reference model can be viewed in Fig. 1.
2. Transparency Depth Pyramid: This reference model explains the level of transparency meaningfulness based on the content of disclosed information.

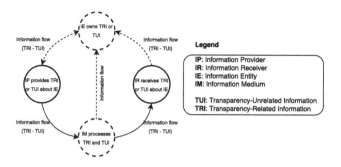

Fig. 1. Transparency actors wheel with transparency classifications

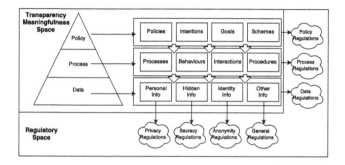

Fig. 2. Transparency depth pyramid (meaningful transparency)

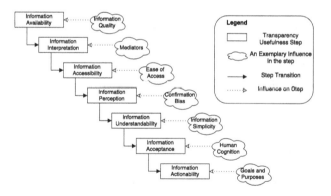

Fig. 3. Transparency achievement spectrum (useful transparency)

These levels are: (1) data transparency, (2) process transparency, and (3) policy transparency. A summary of this reference model can be viewed in Fig. 2.

3. Transparency Achievement Spectrum: This reference model describes the steps of reaching transparency usefulness based on stakeholders' ability to act upon the disclosed information in order to make informed decisions. These steps are: (1) information availability, (2) information interpretation,

(3) information accessibility, (4) information understandability, (5) information perception, (6) information acceptance, and (7) information actionability. A summary of this reference model can be viewed in Fig. 3.

3   TranspLan: A Transparency Modelling Language

Based on the proposed reference models for providing transparency, we introduce Transparency Modelling Language, or *TranspLan*, which helps a BIS in engineering their transparency requirements. *TranspLan* consists of StakeHolders' Information Exchange Layout Diagram (*Shield* diagram) for the visual representation of information exchanges amongst stakeholders and their transparency requirements. *TranspLan* is also accompanied by two descriptive specification models for information elements and stakeholders, called INFOrmation eLEment Transparency Specification (*Infolet* specification) and Stakeholders' Information Transparency REQuirements Specification (*Sitreq* specification), respectively. These specification models explain the information elements and the stakeholders with their elicited transparency requirements in the *Shield* diagram.

3.1   Modelling Constituents and Representations

The *TranspLan* language is mainly built based on three different constituents: *stakeholders*, *information elements*, and the *relationships* between stakeholders and information elements. Relationships can be decomposed using *decomposition relations*. An *information exchange* is a combination of all these constituents and illustrates the flow of information amongst different stakeholders. These constituents are described as follows.

- **Stakeholders** are the people, departments, organisations, etc., which are involved in providing, receiving, or requesting transparency in any information exchange amongst stakeholders. When categorising stakeholders, they are commonly represented as one entity, e.g., Student or Finance Department. However, the exchanged information within an information exchange system may concern all the stakeholders within that system, or it may even concern the public audience.
- **Information elements** are pieces of information exchanged amongst stakeholders. Stakeholders' transparency requirements affect the way information elements should be formed and presented to other stakeholders. Information elements have a type, which is related to their transparency meaningfulness. These types can be the *data* type, the *process* type, or the *policy* type.
- **Stakeholder-information relationships** exist between stakeholders and information elements, and they describe how the information element is associated with the stakeholder. The *production* relationship denotes that the stakeholder produces the information element for other stakeholders. The *obligation* relationship denotes that the stakeholder provides the information element based on coercive supply or requests the information element based on legal

demands. The *optionality* relationship denotes that the stakeholder provides the information element based on voluntary supply or requests the information element based on personal demands. The *restriction* relationship denotes that the information element should not be available to the stakeholder. The *undecidedness* relationship denotes that the relationship between the stakeholder and the information element is not known or decided yet.

- **Decomposition relations** exist between some relationships and can be one of the following: the *and* decomposition relation, the *or* decomposition relation, and the *xor* (exclusive or) decomposition relation.
- **Information exchanges** illustrate the flow of information from an information provider to an information receiver or requester. An information exchange system is a collection of all information exchanges in a BIS.

3.2   TranspLan Mathematical Definition

The *TranspLan* language and its constituents can be defined using the ordinary mathematical language as follows:

Definition 1 (Information element). *Let $IE = \{ie_1, ie_2, ..., ie_m\}$ be the set of information elements, and IE_Label and IE_Name be sets of unique labels and names respectively. Every $ie_i \in IE$ can be defined as follows:*

$$IE = \{ie | ie = (ietype, ielabel, iename, ieused) \land ietype \in IE\_type \land ielabel \in IE\_label \land iename \in IE\_name \land ieused \subset ielabel\}$$
$$IE\_type = \{data, process, policy\}$$

Definition 2 (Stakeholder). *Let $S = \{s_1, s_2, ..., s_n\}$ be the set of stakeholders, $IE = \{ie_1, ie_2, ..., ie_m\}$ be the set of information elements, and $R = \{r_1, r_2, ..., r_l\}$ be the set of stakeholder-information relationships. The set of stakeholders and two subsets of S, called PS and RS, can be defined as follows:*

$$S = \{s | s \text{ is a stakeholder}\}$$
$$PS = \{s | s \in S \land ie \in IE \land (s, ie, production) \in R\}$$
$$RS = \{s | s \in S \land ie \in IE \land rt \in \{obligatory, optional, restricted, undecided\} \land (s, ie, rt) \in R\}$$

Definition 3 (Stakeholder-information relationship). *Let $R = \{r_1, r_2, ..., r_l\}$ be the set of relationships where each relationship is between stakeholder $s_i \in S$ and information element $ie_j \in IE$. Every $r_i \in R$ can be defined as follows:*

$$R = \{r | r = (s, ie, rtype) \land s \in S \land ie \in IE \land rtype \in R\_type\}$$
$$R\_type = \{production, obligatory, optional, restricted, undecided\}$$

Definition 4 (Decomposition relation). *Let $Rel = \{rel_1, rel_2, ...rel_k\}$ be the set of relations where each relation is between two or more relationships $R_1, R_2, ..., R_j \in R$. Every $Rel_i \in Rel$ can be defined as follows:*

$$Rel = \{rel | rel = (r_1, r_2, .., r_j, reltype) \land r_1, r_2, .., r_j \in R \land reltype \in Rel\_type\}$$
$$Rel\_type = \{and, or, xor\}$$

Definition 5 (Information exchange). *Let* $IEX = \{iex_1, iex_2, ..., iex_t\}$ *be the set of information exchanges amongst stakeholders where one stakeholder* $s \in PS$ *produces some information elements* $IESet \subset IE$ *that is received or requested by a group of other stakeholders* $RSSet \subset RS$ *and* $s \notin RSSet$*. Every information exchange* iex_i *can be defined as follows:*

$$IEX = \{iex | iex = ((s_i, ie_i, r_i), (s_j, ie_i, r_j)) \wedge s_i \in PS \wedge s_j \in RS \wedge r_i = production \wedge (s_i, ie_i, r_i), (s_j, ie_i, r_j) \in R\}$$

3.3   Shield Diagram

The *Shield* diagram is the graphical representation of the *TranspLan* language. The constituents of the *TranspLan* language can be illustrated in the *Shield* diagram as follows.

Stakeholders are illustrated in one of the four following ways.

- One stakeholder can be illustrated by a circle with the stakeholder's name inside the circle.
- All stakeholders within an information exchange system can be shown by two nested circles, labelled *All*. This is mainly for the purpose of facilitating a more efficient, clutter-free visual design.
- The previous notion is further enriched by the *exclusion* notation, which uses brackets inside the two nested circles with an *All* label to refer to those stakeholders who are excluded from the information exchange. For example, two nested circles with the label '*All [Supervisor]*' will indicate that information is received by or requested by all stakeholders inside the information exchange system, except the supervisor.
- Three nested circles, labelled *Public*, are also utilised in this diagram to refer to the public, i.e., all stakeholders inside and outside the information exchange system under study.

Information elements are illustrated by a three-part rectangle. In the left-side part, the type of information element is written. This type shows the meaningfulness of the information element in the transparency setting, and can hold one of the following values, or it can be left empty if the nature of the information is unknown during the diagram design.

- *Data* illustrates an information element containing only data.
- *Process* illustrates an information element containing processes (and data).
- *Policy* illustrates an information element containing policies (and processes and data).

The middle part of the information element is used for the information element label and information element name. The label is a unique tag that can be used to identify the information element. The right-side part is used to list all the other information element tags which use, partly or completely, the current information element. This can be used to track how information travels and can also be used to check whether information is received by stakeholders who are not meant to receive it.

Stakeholder-information relationships are illustrated by either simple lines, dotted arrows, or double lines, and always connect stakeholders to information elements.

- *Simple lines* imply the production of information by a stakeholder.
- *Dotted arrows with a black head* show obligatory information flow that arises either from coercive information provision, or legal information requests.
- *Dotted arrows with a white head* denote optional information flow that is the result of voluntary information provision or personal information demands.
- *Dotted arrows with a circle head* illustrate information flows whose nature (i.e., obligatory, optional) is undecided at the time of diagram design.
- *Double lines* indicate that the information element is not meant for the specified stakeholder and must be hidden from them.

Arrows are intentionally chosen to be dotted in order to emphasise that such information flow may or may not serve its transparency purpose because its usefulness must be decided through complicated procedures and involvement with stakeholders which simply cannot be captured through such diagrams. For this reason, we use two specifications, as described in the next subsections.

Decomposition relations describe the relationship amongst relationships. Relationships of any kind can have the following relations amongst them.

- *And* relation is the default relation.
- *Or* relation is shown by a line amongst relationships.
- *Xor* (exclusive or) relation is shown by double lines amongst relationships.

Information exchange system is illustrated by a rectangle divided into four parts and is illustrated as follows.

- The top left part is reserved for the information exchange system name.
- The top right part is used to write extra notes regarding the information exchange system.
- The bottom left part is used to list all the stakeholders in the information exchange system, including two pre-defined *All* and *Public* stakeholders.
- The bottom right part is the main part and is used to draw the information exchange amongst the stakeholders, using the notation described above.

Figure 4 illustrates the summary of the aforementioned building blocks used in a *Shield* diagram.

3.4 Sitreq Specification

Every stakeholder in the *Shield* diagram is accompanied by Stakeholder's Information Transparency REQuirements Specification (*Sitreq*), as illustrated in Fig. 5. *Sitreq* is a descriptive tool for stakeholders and their transparency requirements in the *Shield* diagram. *Sitreq* explains how stakeholders are related to certain information elements, their transparency requirements on those information elements, and other stakeholders involved in the process.

3.5   Infolet Specification

Every information element in the *Shield* diagram is accompanied by a INFOr-mation eLEment Transparency Specification (*Infolet*), as illustrated in Fig. 6. *Infolet* is a descriptive tool for information exchanges in the *Shield* diagram. It describes each information element (IE) in the diagram, providing more in-depth information on them. *Infolet* is meant to capture all the four reference models of transparency, along with general modelling information required for each information element, as follows. The numbers on parentheses illustrate the corresponding segments in *Infolet*.

1. General modelling requirements (1, 2, 4, 5, 13)
2. Transparency depth pyramid (3)
3. Transparency actors wheel (6, 7, 8, 9, 10)
4. Transparency information quality (11)
5. Transparency achievement spectrum (12)

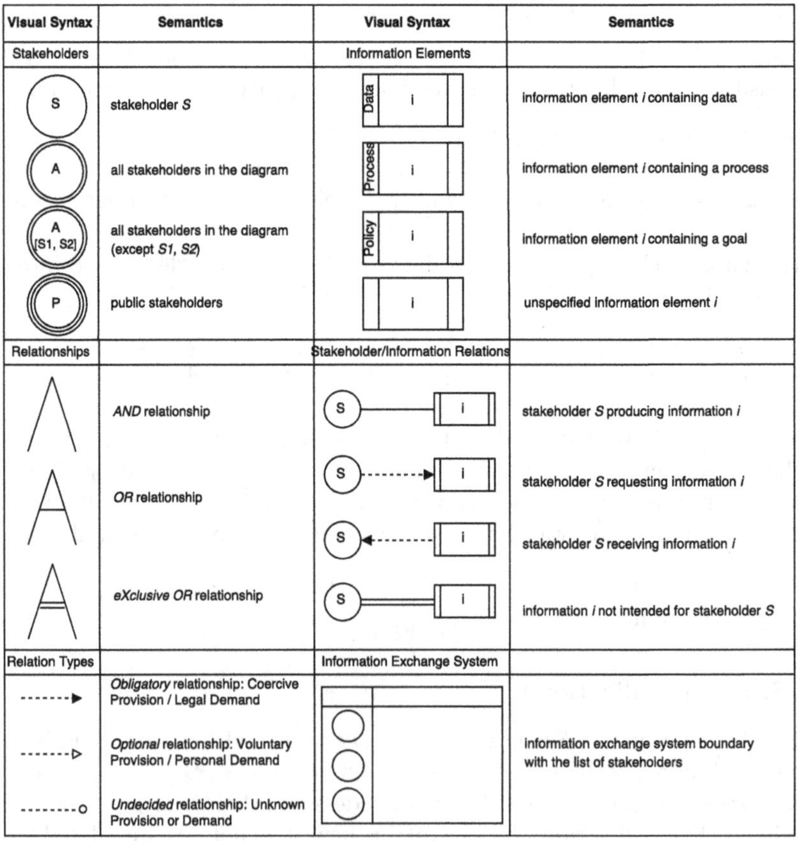

Fig. 4. Building blocks of *Shield* and their interpretations

Stakeholder's Information Transparency REQuirements Specification (Sitreq)						
Stakeholder's Name: *Stakeholder's Name*						
IE Label	IE Name	Relationship	Requirement Description	Transparency Requirement Type	Transparency Meaningfulness Type	Stakeholders Involved
IE label	*IE name*	*Relationship type*	*A brief description of the stakeholder's requirements regarding the IE*	*The transparency requirement of the stakeholder regarding the IE*	*The meaningfulness type requirement regarding the IE*	*List of stakeholders in this information exchange*

Fig. 5. Stakeholder's Information Transparency REQuirements Specification (*Sitreq*)

INFOrmation eLEment Transparency Specification (Infolet)		
Information Element Label, Name, Description, Inter-relations and Type (Transparency Meaningfulness)	① **Information Element Label** A unique label for IE identification	② **Information Element Name** A name selected for the IE	③ **Information Element Type** IE type can be selected from: {Data, Process, Policy}

④ **Information Element Description**

A brief description of IE and its content

⑤ **List of Other Information Elements Using This Information Element**

A list of IE labels and names which use part of all of the current IE

Information Element Stakeholders Classification and Their Information Provision/Request/Restriction Type (Transparency Stakeholders)

⑥ **Information Element Creator/Authority**

Information entity responsible for creating, producing, and rendering IE

⑦ **Information Element Provider**

Stakeholder who provides the information is listed.

⑧ **List of Stakeholders Receiving Information Element and Information Element Provision Type**

Stakeholders who receive the information are listed
IE provision type can be selected from: {Coercive, Voluntary}

⑨ **List of Stakeholders Requesting Information Element and Information Element Request Type**

Stakeholders who request the information are listed
IE request type can be selected from: {Legal, Personal}

⑩ **List of Stakeholders with Restricted Access to Information Element and Restriction Type**

Stakeholders who cannot access the information are listed
Restriction type can be selected from: {Secrecy, Privacy, Anonymity, Other}

Information Element Quality Control (Transparency Quality)

⑪ **Information Element Quality Control (Sound, Dependable, Useful, Usable)**

○ Free of Error   ○ Concise Rep.   ○ Completeness   ○ Consistent Rep.
○ Timeliness   ○ Security
○ App. Amount   ○ Relevancy   ○ Understandability   ○ Objectivity   ○ Interpretability
○ Accessibility   ○ Believability   ○ Ease of Manipulation   ○ Reputation   ○ Value-added

IE qualities are checked when these qualities are met.

Information Element Level of Achievement (Transparency Usefulness)

⑫ **Information Element Level of Achievement**
○ Information Availability (Information is made available to the stakeholders)
○ Information Interpretation (Information is appropriately interpreted for the stakeholders)
○ Information Accessibility (Information is easily accessible by the stakeholders)
○ Information Perception (Information is perceived credible by the stakeholders)
○ Information Understandability (Information is comprehended by the stakeholders)
○ Information Acceptance (Information is believed and accepted by the stakeholders)
○ Information Actionability (Information helps stakeholders in their informed decision-making)

IE level of achievement is checked.

Information Element Additional Data

⑬ **Information Element Notes**

Further notes about IE, samples, links, etc.

Fig. 6. INFOrmation eLEment Transparency Specification (*Infolet*)

3.6   Transparency Requirements Analysis

Our modelling language, *TranspLan*, and its components, the *Shield* diagram and *Sitreq* and *Infolet* specifications, provide a viable solution for addressing several problems that a BIS may encounter during transparency provision, because they enable automated transparency analysis and tool support. The automated analysis enables algorithmic investigation of transparency in order to identify issues such as transparency shortage or abundance [7] in an information exchange system and amongst stakeholders. In the following subsections, we provide two algorithms for the analysis of transparency requirements.

Transparency Meaningfulness Mismatch. Transparency meaningfulness mismatch happens when the level of meaningfulness provided by a stakeholder does not match with the level that is requested by another stakeholder. Failure in reaching the required transparency level (e.g., disclosing the actions without giving the rationale behind them) may reduce accountability, while exceeding the required transparency level (e.g., disclosing the reasons for a particular action when only the data obtained from the action is needed) may introduce information overload. The following algorithm finds and lists all information elements where there is a transparency meaningfulness mismatch.

---

foreach $iex((s_i , ie_i , r_i), (s_j , ie_j , r_j)) \in InformationExchange$ **do**
    $Open(s_i.Sitreq)$;
    $Open(s_j.Sitreq)$;
    $p\_tmt = s_i.ie_i.TransparencyMeaningfulnessType$;
    $r\_tmt = s_j.ie_i.TransparencyMeaningfulnessType$;
    if *(p_tmt=data and r_tmt !=data) or (p_tmt=process and r_tmt=policy)* **then**
        Print("Reaching the required transparency level failed!");
        ProduceError(Transparency_Mismatch_Error);
    end
    if *(p_tmt=policy and r_tmt!=policy) or (p_tmt=process and r_tmt=data)* **then**
        Print("The required transparency level is exceeded!");
        ProduceError(Transparency_Mismatch_Error);
    end
end

Algorithm 1. Transparency Mismatch Detection

Transparency Leakage. In this context, transparency leakage refers to the availability of information elements to stakeholders who initially were not meant to receive that information because of the restricted nature of other stakeholders' transparency requirements. Transparency leakage can produce several adverse effects, e.g., it can affect stakeholders' trust in the BIS negatively. The following algorithm finds and lists all the instances where transparency leakage has occurred.

---

foreach r (s , ie , $rtype$) $\in R$ **do**
   if $(r.rtype = restricted)$ **then**
      foreach $ielabel \in ie.ieused$ **do**
         if $(r$ (s , $ielabel$, $rtype).rtype$!= $restricted)$ **then**
            Print(s, "has restricted access in", i.e., "but unrestricted access in", ieused, "."));
            ProduceError(Transparency_Leakage_Error);
         end
      end
   end
end

Algorithm 2. Transparency Leakage Detection

---

4 Case Study: University Marking Scheme

As a proof of concept, we conducted a case study on an information exchange system, namely university marking scheme. The full evaluation process, the *Shield* diagram and all the *Sitreq* and *Infolet* specifications are available upon request of the readers and researchers.

4.1 University Marking Scheme Specification

For modelling and analysis of transparency requirements, we used the following marking scheme specification which concerns university students' examinations and assignments assessment and marking process. The specification was elicited from university officials involving unit leaders and framework leaders.

During and at the end of each semester, **students**' understanding of a unit is evaluated by a combination of coursework and exams, hereby called *assignment*. The *marking* is generally performed by two markers. The first marker is the **unit leader** by default, and the **second marker** performs marking for quality assurance purposes. The marking is performed using a *marking scheme* provided by the **university** as a general guideline. *Feedback on assignments* is also provided by the first marker to students. Besides, students may ask the first marker to give them *statistics about markings*. Sometimes, an **external examiner** is also involved in the marking process by marking the assignments in order to evaluate the quality of the marking performed by the first and second marker. The external examiner also provides *feedback on marking* of the first and second marker. Furthermore, a **teaching committee** is in charge of *reviewing all the markings* and *accepting* or *refusing* them.

If any inconsistencies arise between the two markers, or between the two markers and the external examiner, then an **exam board** will *review the markings* and decide the final marking. The exam board also investigates *students' complaints* about their marks, which must not be disclosed to the unit leader, and *investigates the marking refusal* if the teaching committee refuses the marking. The exam board decision on students' marking will be final.

4.2   Building the Transparency Model

Based on the university marking scheme specification, we identified seven stakeholders (marked in the specification as bold) and 14 information elements (marked in the specification as italics). We used the information about stakeholders, information elements, and the possible relationships amongst them to build the initial transparency model. We observed that the initial model suffers from several gaps related to transparency provision. For example, Some data regarding the nature of the information elements, and regarding the relationship amongst stakeholders and information elements was missing and needed to be elicited from the stakeholders. The transparency model also provided the starting point for our transparency requirements analysis.

4.3   Analysis of the Transparency Model

After building the initial transparency model, we identified several gaps and issues in transparency provision which was highlighted by our transparency model. These issues are as follows:

- The analysis of *Sitreq* specifications revealed that several transparency meaningfulness types were missing, i.e., the level of transparency meaningfulness (i.e., data, process, or policy) required by the stakeholders was unknown. Furthermore, some *Infolet* specifications missed the same information, meaning that the level of transparency some information elements provide was not investigated, irrespective of the stakeholders' requirements.
- The analysis of *Sitreq* specifications also showed that several transparency provision types were missing, i.e., whether the transparency is coercive or voluntary supply, or legal or personal demand, could not be identified.
- The use of *Infolet* specifications helped the detection of negligence in information quality checks for information elements.
- The use of *Infolet* specifications also facilitated the discovery of inattention to transparency usefulness.
- Running the first algorithmic analysis on transparency mismatch detection revealed some issues in transparency provision. For example, while the first marker's feedback on assignments contained the spotting and revealing of the mistakes students had made on their assignments (i.e., 'data'), students requested that the first marker also emphasises on why they think one solution is wrong and how these mistakes could be avoided (i.e., 'policy').

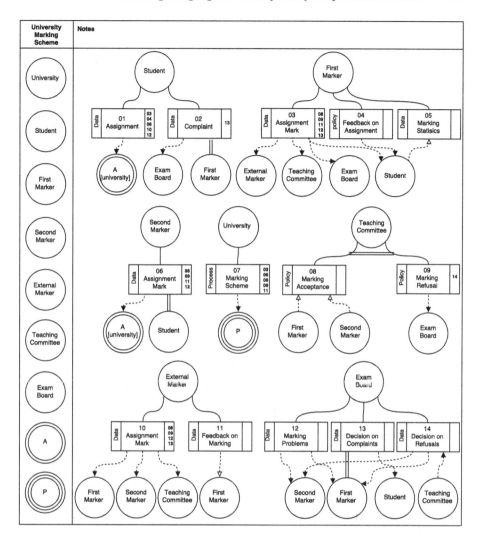

Fig. 7. The complete *Shield* diagram for the case study

- Running the second algorithmic analysis on transparency leakage detection revealed some problems in transparency provision. For example, the students did not want their complaints to be seen by the first marker. The exam board, however, provided the first marker with their decisions on complaints, literally revealing the complaints to the first marker. While this is not a privacy issue or a security problem, it can put pressure on students and probably discourage them from making further complaints.

			Stakeholder's Information Transparency REQuirements Specification (Sitreq)			
			Stakeholder's Name: Student			
IE Label	IE Name		Requirement Description	Transparency Requirement Type	Transparency Meaningfulness Type	Stakeholders Involved
01	Assignment	Producer	Assignment should be handled by different stakeholders	Coercive	Data	All except university
02	Complaint	Producer	Complaint is hidden from the first marker	Restricted	N/A	First marker
02	Complaint	Producer	Complaint should be handled by the exam board	Coercive	Data	Exam board
03	Assignment mark	Receiver	First marker provides the mark to the student	Coercive	Data	First marker
04	Feedback on assignment	Receiver	First marker sends feedback on marking	Coercive	Policy	First marker
05	Marking statistics	Requester	Student wants the statistical figures	Personal	Data	First marker
06	Assignment mark	Receiver	Second marker should not provide the mark to student	Restricted	N/A	
07	Marking scheme	Receiver	Student has public access to marking scheme	Legal	Process	University
13	Decision on Complaint	Receiver	Student gets exam board's decision on their complaint	Coercive	Data	Exam board

Fig. 8. A sample of *Sitreq* specification for the case study

INFOrmation eLEment Transparency Specification (Infolet)		
① Information Element (IE) Label 02	② Information Element (IE) Name Complaint	③ Information Element (IE) Type Data

④ **Information Element Description**
This information element contains data about students' complaints on their grades. The complaint uses an online form provided by the university on their unit's webpage, and can be accessed only by the exam board. The form is also available offline.

⑤ **List of Other Information Elements Using This Information Element**
13: Decision on Complaints

⑥ **Information Element Creator/Authority**
Student

⑦ **Information Element Provider**
Student

⑧ **List of Stakeholders Receiving Information Element and Information Element Provision Type**
Exam Board: Coercive

⑨ **List of Stakeholders Requesting Information Element and Information Element Request Type**
N/A

⑩ **List of Stakeholders with Restricted Access to Information Element and Restriction Type**
First Marker: Restricted

⑪ **Information Element Quality Control (Sound, Dependable, Useful, Usable)**

☑ Free of Error	○ Concise Rep.	☑ Completeness	☑ Consistent Rep.
☑ Timeliness	☑ Security		
☑ App. Amount	☑ Relevancy	☑ Understandability	○ Objectivity	☑ Interpretability
☑ Accessibility	☑ Believability	☑ Ease of Manipulation	☑ Reputation	☑ Value-added

⑫ **Information Element Level of Achievement**
☑ Information Availability (Information is made available to the stakeholders)
☑ Information Interpretation (Information is appropriately interpreted for the stakeholders)
☑ Information Accessibility (Information is easily accessible by the stakeholders)
☑ Information Perception (Information is perceived credible by the stakeholders)
☑ Information Understandability (Information is comprehended by the stakeholders)
☑ Information Acceptance (Information is believed and accepted by the stakeholders)
☑ Information Actionability (Information helps stakeholders in their informed decision-making)

⑬ **Information Element Notes**
The sample form for filing a complaint can be accessed on the following link.

Fig. 9. A sample of *Infolet* specification for the case study

These issues and gaps in the transparency model necessitated the clarification of transparency requirements by consulting with the stakeholders and filling in the missing information in our transparency model.

4.4   Updating the Transparency Model and Further Analysis

After consulting with the stakeholders and eliminating the gaps in transparency provision, the transparency model was updated and analysed once again to ensure no inconsistencies have remained. The updated *Shield* diagram is illustrated in Fig. 7, and an instance of *Sitreq* specification and an instance of *Infolet* specification are illustrated in Figs. 8 and 9, respectively.

5   Conclusion

In this paper, we proposed *TranspLan*, a language for modelling and analysis of transparency. *TranspLan* is based on our extensive literature study on transparency and our conceptual models of transparency. It uses a graphical language and provides several benefits for transparency engineering, including automated reasoning. Our case study, as a proof of concept, demonstrated the feasibility and potentials of *TranspLan* for modelling and analysis of transparency in a BIS.

Acknowledgements. The research is supported by an FP7 Marie Curie CIG grant (the SOCIAD project).

References

1. Bauhr, M., Grimes, M.: Indignation or resignation: the implications of transparency for societal accountability. Governance **27**(2), 291–320 (2014)
2. Cappelli, C., do Prado Leite, J.C.P., de Padua Albuquerque Oliveira, A.: Exploring business process transparency concepts. In: Proceedings of the 15th IEEE International Requirements Engineering Conference, pp. 389–390 (2007)
3. Casalino, N., Buonocore, F., Rossignoli, C., Ricciardi, F.: Transparency, openness and knowledge sharing for rebuilding and strengthening government institutions. In: Proceedings of the 10th IASTED International Conference on Web-Based Education (2013)
4. Castells, M.: End of Millennium: The Information Age: Economy, Society, and Culture. Wiley, Chichester (2010)
5. Chung, L., Nixon, B.A., Yu, E., Mylopoulos, J.: Non-functional Requirements in Software Engineering. Kluwer Academic Publishers, Boston (2000)
6. Cysneiros, L.M.: Using i* to elicit and model transparency in the presence of other non-functional requirements: a position paper. In: Proceedings of the 6th International i* Workshop, pp. 19–24 (2013)
7. Hosseini, M., Shahri, A., Phalp, K., Ali, R.: Towards engineering transparency as a requirement in socio-technical systems. In: Proceedings of the 23rd IEEE International Requirements Engineering Conference, pp. 268–273 (2015)

8. Hosseini, M., Shahri, A., Phalp, K., Ali, R.: Foundations for transparency requirements engineering. In: Requirements Engineering: Foundation for Software Quality. pp. 225–231. Springer International Publishing (2016)
9. Kahn, B.K., Strong, D.M., Wang, R.Y.: Information quality benchmarks: product and service performance. Commun. ACM **45**(4), 184–192 (2002)
10. Kemball-Cook, A.: Winning the trust of millennials. Global Coaching, p. 30 (2015)
11. Kim, M., Ly, K., Soman, D.: A behavioural lens on consumer privacy. Behavioural Economics in Action, Research Report Series (2015)
12. do Prado Leite, J.C.S., Cappelli, C.: Software transparency. Bus. Inf. Syst. Eng. **2**(3), 127–139 (2010)
13. Schnackenberg, A.K., Tomlinson, E.C.: Organizational transparency a new perspective on managing trust in organization-stakeholder relationships. J. Manag. (2014)
14. Serrano, M., do Prado Leite, J.C.S.: Capturing transparency-related requirements patterns through argumentation. In: Proceedings of the 1st International Workshop on Requirements Patterns, pp. 32–41 (2011)
15. Swank, O.H., Visser, B.: Is transparency to no avail? Scand. J. Econ. **115**(4), 967–994 (2013)
16. Weber, J.: Discovering the millennials' personal values orientation: a comparison to two managerial populations. J. Bus. Ethics, 1–13 (2015)
17. Yu, E.: Modelling Strategic Relationships for Process Reengineering. Ph.D. thesis, Graduate Department of Computer Science, University of Toronto (1994)

Process Mining

The ROAD from Sensor Data to Process Instances via Interaction Mining

Arik Senderovich[1]([✉]), Andreas Rogge-Solti[2], Avigdor Gal[1],
Jan Mendling[2], and Avishai Mandelbaum[1]

[1] Technion – Israel Institute of Technology, Haifa, Israel
sariks@tx.technion.ac.il, {avigal,avim}@ie.technion.ac.il
[2] Vienna University of Economics and Business, Vienna, Austria
{andreas.rogge-solti,jan.mendling}@wu.ac.at

Abstract. Process mining is a rapidly developing field that aims at automated modeling of business processes based on data coming from event logs. In recent years, advances in tracking technologies, e.g., Real-Time Locating Systems (RTLS), put forward the ability to log business process events as location sensor data. To apply process mining techniques to such sensor data, one needs to overcome an abstraction gap, because location data recordings do not relate to the process directly. In this work, we solve the problem of mapping sensor data to event logs based on process knowledge. Specifically, we propose *interactions* as an intermediate knowledge layer between the sensor data and the event log. We solve the mapping problem via optimal matching between interactions and process instances. An empirical evaluation of our approach shows its feasibility and provides insights into the relation between ambiguities and deviations from process knowledge, and accuracy of the resulting event log.

Keywords: RTLS data · Business processes · Optimal matching · Knowledge-driven

1 Introduction

Process mining is a rapidly developing field that aims at automated modeling of business processes based on data coming from event logs [1]. Most process mining techniques assume that the event logs are directly related to the underlying process and contain information on activities, resources, and durations. In recent years, advances in tracking technologies, using e.g., Real-Time Locating Systems (RTLS), put forward the ability to track entities that are involved in process executions such as customers, resources. Currently, these technologies are mainly used for monitoring location of entities. For example, in hospitals, nurses use a real-time map to track patients that are next to enter service. To apply process mining techniques to location data, one needs to overcome an abstraction gap, since sensor data recordings do not relate to the process directly.

© Springer International Publishing Switzerland 2016
S. Nurcan et al. (Eds.): CAiSE 2016, LNCS 9694, pp. 257–273, 2016.
DOI: 10.1007/978-3-319-39696-5_16

In this paper, we propose a *knowledge-driven* approach that facilitates process knowledge for accurately transforming raw sensor recordings that contain locations and timestamps of process entities into standardized event logs that comprise process instances. To this end, we define the notion of *interactions* as an intermediate knowledge layer. These interactions are mined from the sensor data as a set of recordings that contain entities that overlap in time and space. Assuming that interactions correspond to an activity instance, we formulate an *optimal matching* problem that maps interactions to activity labels. The problem is thus formulated as an Integer Linear Program with parameters encoded from existing process knowledge. The resulting interaction-to-activity mapping creates process instances, which completes the construction of an event log. We test our technique with controlled experiments on simulated data, inspired by a real-life healthcare process in an outpatient cancer hospital.

The remainder of the paper is structured as follows. Section 2 presents our data models and defines the ROAD problem. We outline the solution through interaction mining in Sect. 3. The optimal matching problem between interactions and activities is detailed in Sect. 4. We empirically evaluate our approach in Sect. 5. In Sect. 6, we discuss related work, followed by concluding remarks and future work in Sect. 7.

2   Data Models and Problem Statement

In this section we introduce our data models, and present the ROAD problem that leads from raw sensor data to business process instances. To motivate our work, we start with a running example of a real-life healthcare process.

Example 1 (DayHospital). Figure 1 presents a treatment process in DayHospital, a large outpatient cancer hospital. DayHospital treats cancer patients on an ambulatory basis. Specifically, approximately 1000 patients arrive every day and typically go through three activities: a blood draw, an examination, and a chemotherapy infusion. The hospital is equipped with nearly 900 Real-Time Locating System (RTLS) receivers that track all business entities involved in the process (e.g., patients, physicians, nurses) as well as some of the medical devices. The emitted data is recorded in a 3-s resolution, and is currently used only for real-time tracking of process entities and equipment. This example motivates the following data model definitions.

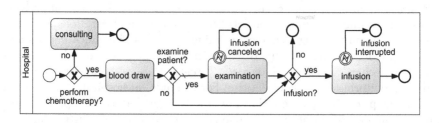

Fig. 1. The main process in an outpatient hospital.

Definition 1 (rO log). *Let B be a set of entity identifiers, $\mathcal{R}$ a set of receiver identifiers, and $\mathbb{TS}$ a set of timestamps. The* raw Observation *(rO) log is a set of triples $D_{raw} = \{(b, r, t)\}$ s.t. $b \in B$, $r \in \mathcal{R}$, and $t \in \mathbb{TS}$.*

Definition 1 formalizes a raw observation log, as captured by an RTLS system. Hereafter, we shall use the "dot" notation to represent elements of a tuple. Therefore, for $d = (b, r, t)$, we use $d.b$, $d.r$, and $d.t$ to denote the tuple's elements. We assume that an entity can be tracked by a single receiver at a time. As background knowledge we assume the existence of a mapping $\theta : B \to \mathcal{T}$ that assigns an entity type to an entity identifier. For example, badge identifier 'Bob111' is of type nurse. Entity types may be put into a taxonomy, e.g., an infusion nurse is a type of a nurse. Also, given a tuple $(b, r, t) \in D_{raw}$, we define a spatial function $S : \mathcal{R} \to \Lambda$, where $\mathcal{R}$ is a set of receiver identifiers as before and Λ is a set of locations that maps receivers into named spatial locations, e.g. Infusion Room 705C.

We next aggregate consecutive reads of the same entity and location as follows. Given an rO log D_{raw}, a *consecutive set of raw observations* is a set $d_{cons} \subseteq D_{raw}$ such that the following three (badge, space and time) continuity conditions hold:

C1: $\forall d = (b, r, t), d' = (b', r', t') \in d_{cons} : b = b' \wedge S(r) = S(r')$.
C2: $\forall d = (b, r, t), d' = (b', r', t') \in d_{cons} :$
$\quad \exists d'' = (b'', r'', t'') \in D_{raw}(b = b'', S(r) = S(r''), t < t' < t'') \to d'' \in d_{cons}$.
C3. $\forall d = (b, r, t), d' = (b', r', t') \in d_{cons} :$
$\quad \nexists d'' = (b'', r'', t'') \in D_{raw}(b = b'', S(r) \neq S(r''), t < t'' < t'$.

Condition C1 ensures that every d_{cons} consists of observations that share badge id, $d_{cons}.b$ and location $d_{cons}.l$. C2 states that if badge $d_{cons}.b$ was observed in location $d_{cons}.l$ in the time between two consecutive observations in d_{cons}, that observation also belongs to d_{cons}. Last, C3 ensures that badge $d_{cons}.b$ was not observed in location other than $d_{cons}.l$, in the time between two consecutive observations in d_{cons}. A consecutive set of raw observations d_{cons} is *maximal* if there is no $d'_{cons} \subseteq D_{raw}$ such that $d_{cons} \subset d'_{cons}$. We denote by $D_{cons}(D_{raw})$ (or D_{cons} when D_{raw} is clear from the context) the set of all maximal consecutive sets of raw observations.

Definition 2 (RO log). *Let D_{raw} be an rO log. The* aggRegated Observation *(RO) log over D_{cons} is a set of quadruples $D_{agg} = \{(b, l, s, c)\}$ s.t. $\forall d_{cons} \in D_{cons}, \exists d = (b, l, s, c) : b = d_{cons}.b \wedge l = d_{cons}.l \wedge s = \min_{d \in d_{cons}}(d.t) \wedge c = \max_{d \in d_{cons}}(d.t)$.*

The RO log creates a new log from the raw observations log, mapping a receiver identifier to a location and aggregating continuous observations of an entity in a location into intervals with start and end times being the minimum and maximum times over the aggregated raw observations per entity and location, respectively. For the hospital described in Example 1, the RO log is created automatically from a given rO log as a service of the RTLS vendor company.

Table 1. Aggregated hospital tracklog - Sample from Dec. 3rd, 2013.

b	$\theta(b)$	l	s	c
Anna555	Patient	Room 705C	10:00AM	10:30AM
Bob111	Nurse	Room 705C	10:10AM	10:20AM
Anna555	Patient	Room 907	11:50AM	12:17PM
Bob111	Nurse	Room 907	11:40AM	12:15PM
Jenna333	Physician	Room 907	12:00PM	12:20PM

Following Example 1, Table 1 provides a sample of the RO log (the second column associates an entity identifier with an entity type). Patient Anna enters an infusion room 705, chair C at 10:00AM to receive a chemotherapy treatment. She is followed by nurse Bob at 10:10AM, who starts the infusion and leaves the room at 10:20AM. Anna then continues to an examination room with nurse Bob and physician Jenna.

Clearly, the RO log does not contain the necessary information to understand high-level information such as activities, participating resources, and start/end times. For example, we are interested in log entries such as $\langle Anna555, Infusion, \{Bob111\}, InfusionRoom705C, 10:10AM, 10:20PM\rangle$, consisting of patient identifier, activity label, set of resource entities, location, and time interval.

Definition 3 (AD log). *Let B be a set of entity identifiers, A a set of activity labels, Λ a set of locations, and $\mathbb{TS}$ a set of timestamps. The* Activity Data *(AD) log is a set of tuples $L = \{(b, a, E, l, s, c)\}$ that correspond to activity instances s.t. $b \in B$ is the case identifier, $a \in A$ is the activity, $E \subseteq B$ is the set of participating resource entities, $l \in \Lambda$, and $s, c \in \mathbb{TS}$.*

Let $\mathcal{L}$ be the set of all possible AD logs. We define a similarity measure $\Delta : \mathcal{L} \times \mathcal{L} \longrightarrow [0][1]$ that quantifies the extent to which two AD logs differ. Such a similarity measure combines several aspects of the log. For example, when comparing activity labels between traces, we could use a string edit distance measure, while for comparing resource sets we may use Jaccard similarity. The concrete formulation of Δ depends on the requirements of the domain. For example, an organization might be most interested in resource accuracy, while another one might prioritize activity orderings.

Let L be an AD log of a real process, and let α be a mapping such that $\hat{L} = \alpha(D_{agg})$ transforms an RO log into an AD log. Because we do not know the real process, but only observe its RO log D_{agg}, the problem we aim at solving can be states as follows:

Problem 1 (aggRegated Observations to Activity Data (ROAD)). *The ROAD problem aims at finding a mapping α of the RO log, D_{agg} to an AD log $\hat{L} = \alpha(D_{agg})$ such that $\Delta(L, \hat{L})$ is minimized.*

3   The ROAD to Solution: Interaction Mining

Our solution to the ROAD problem is based on mining interactions between business entities from the RO log and mapping these interactions to activity instances. Figure 2 depicts our two-step solution to the ROAD problem, which results in a transformation α that maps an RO log to an AD log. While our proposed solution does not provide a formal guarantee of the minimality of Δ, our empirical evaluation verifies that the solution yields accurate results when comparing the AD log ($\alpha(D_{agg})$) with the 'real' event log. We first mine interactions from the RO log (Sect. 3.1). The second step of our approach involves creating an optimal matching between interactions and activities via process knowledge (Sect. 4). This matching results in an AD log.

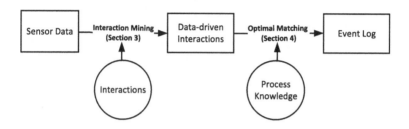

Fig. 2. The ROAD to solution.

To bridge the gap between the RO and the AD logs, we aim at using process knowledge that is readily available in many real-life scenarios, e.g., in the form of process models. However, it is unclear how to directly connect process knowledge and the RO log. For example, observing that a patient is in a certain location does not immediately indicate an ongoing activity. To resolve ambiguities, we create an intermediate knowledge layer, namely *interactions*. These interactions correspond to involvements of business entities, such as patients, nurses, and equipment in activities. To illustrate the notion of interactions, consider Fig. 3 that corresponds to the DayHospital data example from Table 1. Figure 3 depicts the hierarchy of data abstraction levels. Specifically, we assume that activity instances result in interactions, which in turn can be observed in the RO log. In our data example, nurse Bob and patient Anna share a location over time, indicating an interaction that belongs to a certain activity instance, e.g., a chemotherapy infusion.

3.1   Interaction Mining

In this section, we formally define the notion of interaction and propose a methodology for mining interactions from the RO log. The terminology we use follows the terminology of complex event processing (CEP) [2], where complex events are detected from streams of events while our approach operates on historical data logs.

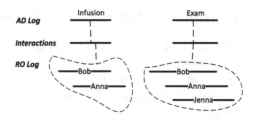

Fig. 3. Hierarchy of Instances: Activities, Interactions, and Raw Data.

Definition 4 (Interaction). *An interaction is a tuple $i = (E, l, s, c)$, where E is a set of interacting entities (badges), l is a location, and s and c stand for the interaction start and end times, respectively.*

Mining a set of interactions $\{(E, l, s, c)\}$ from an RO log requires four basic functions over the RO log, D_{agg}, namely *selection*, *grouping*, *filtering*, and *construction*. As a guiding example we consider the mining of *co-location interactions*, which are interactions that involve two or more entities in the same location over an overlapping timespan. In DayHospital, this a highly relevant interaction, since the execution of medical activities requires the presence of a patient and at least one of the resources.

We first define a selection function over the RO log, which enables us to consider only relevant tuples for interactions. For DayHospital, we are not interested in conference rooms, where doctors spend their time resting, as we are interested in clinical activities.

Definition 5 (Selection). *Let $\psi(\Sigma)$ be a logical predicate over the RO log D_{agg} with a set of external parameters, Σ. A selection function $\sigma(D_{agg}, \psi(\Sigma))$ returns a subset of D_{agg}, s.t. $\{d \in D_{agg} \mid \psi(\Sigma) = True\}$.*

For example, selection over the DayHospital log with location parameter $\lambda = Room705C$ would return all RO tuples in that location. We denote by D_{sel} the outcome of a selection over D_{agg}, which contains individual tuples of the RO log that satisfy the logical rule. However, interactions typically comprise several tuples (e.g. two doctors entering a room correspond to two tuples in the RO log). To this end, we group tuples of D_{sel} into sets by an operation that we refer to as grouping.

Definition 6 (Grouping). *Let $m, M \in \mathbb{N}$ be two natural numbers. A grouping function over D_{sel}, γ, returns the set $\{D \subseteq D_{sel} \mid m \leq |D| \leq M\}$.*

In other words, grouping returns the set of sets of D_{sel} having a minimal size of m, and a maximal size of M. Setting a lower and upper bound on the size of the sets reduces the number of tuple sets, since in the worst case of $m = 1, M = \infty$ one needs to consider all elements of $2^{D_{sel}}$ as interaction candidates. Returning to the co-location example, we are interested in interactions with two entities or more, thus we set $m = 2$, and $M = \infty$. Let D_{group} denote the grouped set of D_{sel}.

Having gathered all relevant sets of tuples into D_{group} we are interested in filtering out subsets of D_{group} that satisfy an interaction rule (e.g. co-location). For example, if a set in D_{group} contains only tuples that do not share the location, we shall not consider this set as an interaction candidate. To this end, we first define the interaction condition $\eta(D)$ over $D \in D_{group}$, which evaluates to true if D satisfies the condition for an interaction. The filtering function that returns only subsets of D_{group} that satisfy ϕ is defined as follows.

Definition 7 (Interaction Filter). *Let $\eta(D)$ be the interaction predicate over D. An interactions filter, ϕ, is a function that returns all subsets of D_{group} that satisfy the interaction condition, i.e., $\phi(D_{group}, \eta(D)) = \{D \in D_{group} \mid \eta(D) = True\}$.*

For the co-location interactions we define the condition:

$$\eta_{co\text{-}locate}(D) = \forall d, d' \in D \ \{(d'.s < d.c \ \wedge \ d'.c > d.s) \ \wedge \ d.l = d'.l\}. \quad (1)$$

with which we operate the filtering function on D_{group}, and obtain D_{filter}, filtered subsets of D_{group} that corresponds to an interaction. As a last step, every set D_{filter} needs to be converted into a set of interactions that correspond to Definition 4. For this last step we define an interaction constructor function.

Definition 8 (Interaction Constructor). *An interaction constructor is a mapping, ξ, which receives $D \in D_{filter}$, and returns a set of interaction tuples $\{(E, l, s, c)\}$.*

The set of interactions I that is mined from D_{agg} (through selection, grouping, and filtering) is defined as $I = \{\bigcup_{D \in D_{filter}} \xi(D)\}$. Note that ξ is a set to set mapping, since every set in D_{filter} may correspond to several interactions. For example, if $D \in D_{filter}$ contains co-location of doctor Bob, patient Anna and nurse Jenna. When doctor Bob enters, he may start a new interaction with the two entities (e.g., examination by physician and nurse). However, it may be that the doctor's entry is not related to the ongoing procedure. Since we need to consider all possible options, a single co-location set $D \in D_{filter}$ may correspond to several possible interactions.

To demonstrate the mining of the co-location interactions set $I_{co\text{-}locate}$ we return to Fig. 3 that corresponds to the RO log in Table 1, and focus on the interaction of the Exam activity (the rightmost interaction). We observe three time intervals in the RO log corresponding to nurse Bob, patient Anna and doctor Jenna, interacting in an examination room. According to our definition, while nurse Bob is alone in the room (at the beginning) and while doctor Jenna is alone in the room (at the end), there are no ongoing interactions. When patient Anna first enters the room, a possible interaction between nurse Bob and patient Anna is recorded. When Jenna enters the room, an interaction may start between either Bob and Jenna, or Anna and Jenna, or all three together; all three options are considered to be part of $I_{co\text{-}locate}$. Furthermore, the interaction between nurse Bob and patient Anna may continue, as Jenna could be visiting the room unrelated to the ongoing activity.

Formally, let D_{filter} be a set of the filtered sets that correspond to the co-location interaction. Then, the interaction set $I_{co\text{-}locate} = \{(E, l, s, c)\}$ is mined by applying an interaction condition $\xi_{co\text{-}location}$ to every $D \in D_{filter}$ with the condition being

$$\xi_{co\text{-}location}(D) = \{(E = \bigcup_{d \in D'} d.b, l = D'.l, s = \max_{d \in D'} d.s, c = \min_{d \in D'} d.c) \mid D' \subseteq D\},$$

(2)

and $D'.l$ being the shared location for every set $D' \in D$.

In the remainder of this work, we focus only on co-location interactions, since they are key indicators for service-oriented activities that require the presence of cases and resources. However, considering only the co-location interaction has the disadvantage of missing activities that do not require more than a single entity, such as a nurse examining blood results. To capture the latter, complementary interactions can be applied. For example, filtering interactions that involve special locations (e.g. blood laboratory), and certain types of entities (e.g. nurses).

4   Optimal Mapping of Interactions to Activities

In this part, we formulate an optimal matching problem (OMP) between the interaction set I and the activity set A. Specifically, we consider the interaction set $I_{co\text{-}locate}$, which we obtain by the mining technique proposed in Sect. 3.1. First, we write the matching problem as an Integer Linear Program (ILP). Then, we define process knowledge and demonstrate its encoding into the ILP. The solution to the OMP as an ILP results in a mapping between the RO log and the AD log, which is then easily transformed into an event log, hence solving the ROAD problem.

4.1   The Optimal Matching Problem

Let I be the interaction set (e.g., $I_{co\text{-}locate}$) and A be the set of activity labels. In this paper, we make a simplifying assumption that an interaction contains exactly one case. To ground the notion of a case in the process log we assume the existence of a case function $\tau : 2^B \to 2^B$ that returns the *case entities* (e.g., patients) from a set of entities E. For the matching problem, we consider only interactions with a single case:

$$I_c = \{i \in I \mid \exists b \in i.E \ (\tau(i.E) = \{b\}))\}.$$

(3)

Now, we turn to formulate the OMP problem as an Integer Linear Program, which consists of binary decision variables, a score function, and the constraints matrix [3].

Let $x_{i,a} \in \{0,1\}, i \in I_c, a \in A$ be binary decision variables that are assigned with the value 1 if interaction $i \in I_c$ is matched to activity label $a \in A$. Let $\mathbf{x}$ denote the vector of $x_{i,a}$, $g(\mathbf{x})$ be a linear score function, and B denote the constraint matrix of size $|I_c| \times |A|$. The ILP formulation of the matching problem is:

$$\underset{\mathbf{x}}{\text{maximize }} g(\mathbf{x}) \quad \text{subject to} \quad B^{\mathsf{T}}\mathbf{x} \leq 0 \tag{4}$$

The derivation of the AD log from the solution to the ILP is done by creating a tuple in the AD log for every $x_{i,a} = 1$ such that $(b, a, E, l, s, c) = (\tau(i.E), a, i.E \setminus \tau(i.E), i.l, i.s, i.c)$.

4.2 Encoding Process Knowledge into the ILP

We are now ready to demonstrate the instantiation of the ILP problem via an encoding of given process knowledge. We consider three types of process knowledge: (1) interaction knowledge (e.g., a doctor cannot be involved in two examinations simultaneously), (2) activity knowledge (e.g., the distributions of the infusion activity) and (3) behavioral knowledge (e.g., precedence constraints among activities for patients). These knowledge types can be derived from process-related documents, interviews with process experts, appointment books, and process models.

Interaction Knowledge – Pruning Alternative Co-locations: Interaction knowledge considers the activity dynamics of the underlying process. For example, one may decide that hallway interactions between patients are not process interactions and should not be considered as activity candidates. Such knowledge may reduce the size of I_c, therefore improving the performance of the ILP solver. To demonstrate how interaction knowledge may assist in pruning alternative interactions from I_c, we make the following assumptions:

A1 : An entity cannot be involved in two interactions at the same time.
A2 : An activity instance corresponds to at most a single interaction in I_c, and every interaction stems from at most a single activity instance.

From A1 we get that interactions that overlap in time and intersect in the set of involved entities cannot co-exist in the mapping. Clearly, this may not be the case in every business process: sometimes resources may participate in interactions with two case entities simultaneously. The second assumption, A2, prevents from mapping interactions to more than a single activity. Here, we assume that two interactions cannot stem from a single activity instance. This may not hold in processes where activities have a complex life cycle with interrupts.

We start by encoding assumption A1 into the ILP. As a preprocessing step, we mine an exclusion relation $I_X \subseteq I_c \times I_c$ from I_c such that $(i_1, i_2) \in I_X \iff i_1.E \cap i_2.E \neq \emptyset$, and i_1, i_2 overlap in time. For every pair of these interactions we add a constraint to the ILP allowing at most one interaction to be mapped to an activity, otherwise their joint mapping would be inconsistent:

$$\forall(i_1, i_2), \in I_X : \sum_{a \in A} x_{i_1,a} + \sum_{a \in A} x_{i_2,a} \leq 1. \tag{5}$$

Next, we demonstrate the encoding of assumption A2 into B. The interaction set I_c can be partitioned according to case entities, since every $i \in I_c$ contains exactly one case entity $\tau(i)$. Let I_c^j be the set of interactions that corresponds to case entity $j \in J$, with J being the set of case entities. Then, we write the constraints for A2 in a way that allows an interaction to be mapped to at most a single activity label:

$$\forall i \in I_c : \sum_{a \in A} x_{i,a} \leq 1; \quad \forall j \in J, \forall a \in A : \sum_{i \in I_c^j} x_{i,a} \leq 1. \tag{6}$$

Further pruning on the interaction level is possible. For example, one may consider interactions with durations only above a certain threshold, and allow for only a single interaction per each location at a time.

Activity Knowledge – Durations, Resources, and Locations: Here, we consider specific types of activity knowledge, namely durations, possible resource assignments, and possible locations of activity executions. Such knowledge is often available in historical patient records, appointment books and models. We take a stochastic perspective on activity knowledge, assuming components to be random. Formally, we define the activity knowledge components as random variables and specify their corresponding distribution functions. For every activity $a \in A$, let D_a, E_a, and L_a be the random durations, random sets of assigned resources, and random locations, respectively. We denote by f_{D_a}, f_{E_a}, and f_{L_a} the probability distribution functions (PDFs) for these random variables, respectively. Therefore, $f_{D_a}(d) = Pr\{D_a = d\}, f_{E_a}(E) = Pr\{E_a = E\}$, and $f_{L_a}(l) = Pr\{L_a = l\}$.

We assume that activity knowledge is shared among all instances. However, our model is general enough to consider instance-level knowledge (e.g., the distribution of patient Anna's infusion duration from her past visits). Below, we demonstrate the encoding of activity knowledge into the ILP score function $g(\mathbf{x})$. We attach a reward coefficient to each of the decision variable $x_{i,a}$, which is defined as:

$$w_{i,a} = Pr\{x_{i,a} = 1 \mid i = (E, l, s, c)\}. \tag{7}$$

The coefficient $w_{i,a}$ can be interpreted as the posterior probability that interaction i is mapped to activity a given that i has values (E, l, s, c). By applying Bayes theorem:

$$w_{i,a} = \frac{\pi_a Pr\{i = (E, l, s, c) \mid x_{i,a} = 1\}}{Pr\{i = (E, l, s, c)\}}, \tag{8}$$

with $\pi_a = Pr\{x_{i,a} = 1\}$ being the prior that any interaction maps to activity a, $Pr\{i = (E, l, s, c) \mid x_{i,a} = 1\}$ being the likelihood of interaction $i = (E, l, s, c)$ if it comes from activity a, and $Pr\{i = (E, l, s, c)\}$ being the probability to get the values (E, l, s, c) by randomly selecting an interaction from I_c. The denominator in Eq. 8 is a scaling factor that does not depend on the $x_{i,a}$ and can therefore be excluded from the score function. Further, we assume that the three knowledge components, D_a, E_a, and L_a are independent, which allows us to write the following multiplicative form for $w_{i,a}$:

$$w_{i,a} = \pi_a Pr\{i.E, i.l, i.c - i.s \mid x_{i,a} = 1\} = \pi_a f_{D_a}(i.c - i.s) f_{E_a}(i.E) f_{L_a}(i.l). \quad (9)$$

Thus, the score function can be written as:

$$g(\mathbf{x}) = \sum_{i \in I_c} \sum_{a \in A} w_{i,a} x_{i,a} = \sum_{i \in I_c} \sum_{a \in A} \pi_a f_{D_a}(i.c - i.s) f_{E_a}(i.E) f_{L_a}(i.l) x_{i,a}. \quad (10)$$

The assumption that we make in Eq. 10 is that the reward is additive for matching i to a, and is linear in the likelihood of i to be an interaction coming from activity a according to durations, resources and locations.

Table 2. Left-hand side – soft encoding; right-hand side – hard encoding.

Soft encoding	Hard encoding
$\forall (a,b) \in \prec_P, \forall i \in I_c$:	$\forall (a,b) \in \prec_P, \forall i \in I_c$:
$z_{i,a,b} \leq 1 - x_{i,b} + y_{i,a}$	$x_{i,b} \leq y_{i,a}$
$z_{i,a,b} \geq 1 - x_{i,b}$	
$z_{i,a,b} \geq y_{i,a}$	
$z_{i,a,b} \in \{0,1\}$	

Behavioral Knowledge – Precedence Order: Behavioral knowledge is a relation between activities in A, which can be obtained from various sources, e.g., by computing behavioral profiles from a given process model [4]. In DayHospital, one may use the schedule of patients to derive precedence constraints between activities. Here, we demonstrate the encoding of a precedence order between activities. Let $\prec_P \subseteq A \times A$ be the precedence relation, where $a \prec_P b$ if b's execution implies that $c_a \leq s_b$, with c_a being the completion time of a and s_b being the start time of b. Further, we assume that loops do not exist, and if an activity a is repeated it corresponds to a new activity label, a'.

As a preliminary phase to encoding precedence knowledge, let $P : I_c \rightarrow 2^{I_c}$ be the precedence function for interactions in I_c such that $P(i)$ returns the set all interactions that precede i, and have the same case entity (e.g. the same patient identifier): $\{j \in I_c \mid \tau(i) = \tau(j), i.c \leq j.s\}$. Let $y_{i,a} = \sum_{j \in P(i)} x_{j,a}$ denote the sum of mappings between $j \in I_c$ in precedence to $i \in I_c$ that map to a. $y_{i,a}$ indicates if an interaction that precedes i was mapped to a.

To encode $\prec_P$ into the ILP problem, we have the choice of adding hard constraints (into B), thus preventing violations in precedence order, or assigning smaller rewards for mappings that violate $\prec_P$. Table 2 summarizes the formulation of the two options. For hard encoding of the precedence constraints we add the constraints on the right-hand side of Table 2 into B. For soft encoding, we add additional variables $z_{i,a,b} \in \{0,1\}$ to the ILP and add constrains into B as stated on the left-hand side of Table 2. These constraints are equivalent to the logical predicate $x_{i,b} \rightarrow y_{i,a}$. Having defined $z_{i,a,b}$, we add these variables and their corresponding rewards into the score function of the ILP program. The size of the reward for a matching that does not violate precedence constraints is user-defined, and is set by default to the median of $w_{i,a}$, as defined in Eq. 7. These default values are used to scale precedence violation weights in correspondence with activity knowledge weights.

5   Evaluation

In this section, we present the evaluation of our ROAD solution via controlled experiments. Specifically, we introduce the experimental setting, present results, and discuss the main factors that influence the accuracy of our approach.

Experimental Setting. We implemented our solution to the ROAD problem in the ProM framework.[1] The design of our experiment is depicted in Fig. 4 and consists of five steps. In step 1, we generate a simulation ready stochastic Petri net (SPN) model based on knowledge from the healthcare process described in Example 1, and the process model in Fig. 1. Note that model parameters vary across three different scenarios that we use to test the sensitivity of our solution. In step 2, the SPN is simulated to create the ground truth AD log, denoted L. In step 3, the AD log is converted (by label removals) into the RO log, which contains time intervals involving sets of entities in different locations. In step 4, we use process knowledge and apply the ROAD approach to the RO log, which results in a reconstructed AD log, denoted $\hat{L}$. Step 5 computes a similarity measure that quantifies the difference between L and $\hat{L}$.

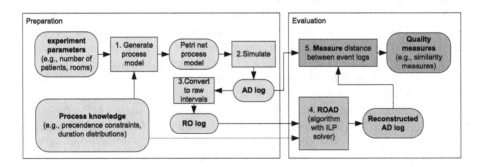

Fig. 4. Evaluation setting to test accuracy of the ROAD approach.

We use a multi-dimensional similarity measure that consists of four quantifiers. For reconstructing trace activity labels (including their order) we use the complementary of average Levenshtein distance measure between two traces [5]. For duration similarity we consider the complementary of the symmetric mean

---

[1] See **StochasticNet** package. http://www.promtools.org.

absolute percentage error (sMAPE) [6]. For comparing two resource sets we use the average Jaccard similarity, and for location similarity we use the average of an indicator that is set to 1 if the location was reconstructed correctly (and 0 otherwise).

To test the accuracy and sensitivity of our ROAD solution, we consider the following three scenarios. In *scenario 1*, we alter the level of entropy in process knowledge for resource assignments and activity locations, namely E_a and L_a. Specifically, we change the probability distributions, f_{E_a}, f_{L_a}, from deterministic (no entropy), to uniform distributions (maximal entropy). We expect that deterministic values will result in accurate discrimination between activities, while for maximal entropy, the performance of our solution will deteriorate. For example, it is more difficult to reconstruct activity instances for locations that are used for multiple activities, as opposed to locations that support a single activity.

In *scenario 2*, we introduce noise in the form of deviations in the execution of the process with respect to the existing process knowledge. For example, we insert swaps between activity instances in the simulated AD log such that precedence constraints are violated. Further, we allow for changes in location and assigned resource sets. We hypothesize that an increase in noise will cause a reduction in similarity measures.

Last, in *scenario 3*, we increase the number of activities that can occur in the same time and place. This, by definition of the co-location interactions, results in an exponential increase in the size the interaction set $I_{co\text{-}locate}$. We hypothesize that this exponential increase will result in an accuracy reduction, as well as in run-time deterioration. Note that in scenarios 2 and 3, the entropy level in the process knowledge corresponds to the realistic values coming from the real-life process described in Example 1.

Results. The results of our evaluation for the three scenarios are presented in Fig. 5a, b, and c, respectively. The vertical axes in these figures correspond to the four aforementioned similarity measures, and to the run-time performance of our approach (in seconds). The horizontal axes for the three scenarios correspond to the level of entropy in the process knowledge (Fig. 5a), the noise percentage (Fig. 5b), and the maximal number of overlapping activities per location (Fig. 5c). We omit the formal definition of entropy level and noise percentage due to space limitations. Figure 5a shows a steep decline in all four similarity measures as the level of entropy approaches its maximal value; the run-time shows a negligible increase across entropy levels. As for scenario 2 (Fig. 5b) we observe a linear decline in accuracy, i.e., the error is proportional to the noise inserted. For scenario 3 (Fig. 5c) a mild decrease in accuracy is evident, while we observe an exponential growth in run-time. It is worth noting that for scenarios 1 & 2, all similarity measures display an almost identical behavior, which means that any aggregated similarity measure would demonstrate the same pattern. For scenario 3, while we see a mild decrease for all measures, the shape of the decrease vary slightly.

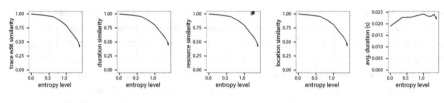

(a) Similarity with respect to increasing entropy in the mapping to activities.

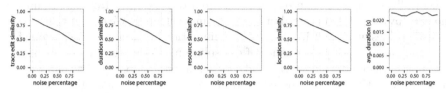

(b) Similarity with respect to increasing noise reflecting deviations from the process knowledge.

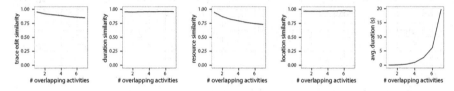

(c) Similarity with respect to increasing overlap in activities per location.

Fig. 5. Accuracy results assessing the ROAD solution.

Discussion. Our evaluation shows that the quality of process knowledge has most influence on the accuracy of the ROAD solution. Specifically, process knowledge becomes less informative as entropy increases, and cannot be applied to reconstruct the AD log. The second most relevant source for inaccuracies stems from deviations in process knowledge (i.e., the noise factor). Further, our definition for co-locating interactions leads to an exponential growth in the size of the considered interaction set, and may pose computational limitations. However, in real-life processes, we seldom observe multiple overlapping activities in a single location.

To conclude, the ability to go from RO to AD using our approach depends on both the informativeness of the process knowledge (for higher accuracy), and the definition of interactions (for lower run-time complexity).

6   Related Work

Our research is most closely related to automatic process discovery, process alignment, and activity recognition. Bridging the abstraction gap between raw events and activity data has been a subject of several recent works in process mining, c.f. [7] and the references within. In [7,8], a semi-automated approach was proposed where process knowledge is used to match raw events to process activities; the approach is extended to use constraint programming in [9]. Our work generalizes these approaches by optimally mapping raw data to activities, and by considering further dimensions (e.g. time, resources). In [10], classification and regression techniques are used to create process views from low-level multi-dimensional data, without assuming the existence of pre-defined activity labels. Their approach uses logs with process related raw events. Other approaches in process mining for connecting low-level events with activities include clustering [11], Expectation-Maximization based sequence mining [12]. These techniques focus on structural and behavioral aspects of the control-flow perspective, which our work extends towards a multi-perspective approach. None of the aforementioned works in process mining consider tracking data, but rather event logs that come from information systems executing the processes.

Our approach is also related to a multi-perspective conformance checking and alignment of event logs to process models, c.f. [13] and the references within. We propose an optimal matching between interactions and activities while considering event logs that are not semantically related to activities. In order to reduce the search space, we adopt techniques from process matching, where processes are matched according to structural and behavioral similarities [14]. Our approach includes behavioral matching according to precedence constraints, in the spirit of [4].

In our solution, we are also inspired by techniques for sensor-based *activity and event recognition*. The former is a well-established task in Artificial Intelligence [15]. Methods for activity recognition include two main approaches: data-driven and knowledge-driven activity recognition. Event recognition, a related task, is a well-studied problem in the field of complex event processing [16]. Similarly to our interaction mining technique, the idea behind these works is to use logical predicates to filter events. However, state-of-the-art event and activity recognition techniques do not assume a process perspective. In our work we take the knowledge-driven approach to activity recognition, based on logical predicates, in the spirit of [16,17], while introducing the context of processes, which in turn creates dependencies between activities. To conclude related work, we narrow the scope to literature on mining location data. A methodology for clustering RFID trajectories to reconstruct entity paths was proposed in [18]. Moreover, a probabilistic model for workflow discovery from RTLS data was applied in [19]. In contrast to our solution, the former work disregards the process perspective, while the latter assumes that locations correspond to activities in a one-to-one fashion.

7   Conclusion

In this work, we provided a transformation of sensor data (e.g. Real-Time Locating System data) into standard event logs, to enable the application of process mining techniques to raw location recordings. The transformation was based on the notion of interactions, which is an intermediate knowledge layer that bridges between raw sensor data, and process instances. After mining interactions from the raw data, we solved a matching problem that is based on process knowledge. The solution to the problem finds optimal correspondences between the interactions and activity labels, and creates activity instances, which comprise the target event log. We evaluated the approach with controlled experiments by using simulated event logs. The experiments show that the accuracy of our technique depends on the informativeness of process knowledge, while the complexity of the technique depends on the number of possible interactions.

In future work, we aim at a feature complete encoding of process models into the optimal matching setting. This requires a process model at hand, which can be obtained via process discovery. Such encoding would enable further automation of our ROAD solution. Moreover, we would like to test our solution on real-world processes that emit sensor data by cross-validating the resulting event log against information that comes from process-aware systems that accompany and execute the process.

Acknowledgment. This work was supported by the EU project SERAMIS (612052).

References

1. van der Aalst, W.: Process Mining: Discovery, Conformance and Enhancement of Business Processes. Springer, Heidelberg (2011)
2. Etzion, O., Niblett, P.: Event Processing in Action. Manning Publications Co., Greenwich (2010)
3. Schrijver, A.: Theory of Linear and Integer Programming. Wiley, Chichester (1998)
4. Leopold, H., Niepert, M., Weidlich, M., Mendling, J., Dijkman, R., Stuckenschmidt, H.: Probabilistic optimization of semantic process model matching. In: Barros, A., Gal, A., Kindler, E. (eds.) BPM 2012. LNCS, vol. 7481, pp. 319–334. Springer, Heidelberg (2012)
5. Wagner, R.A., Fischer, M.J.: The string-to-string correction problem. J. ACM **21**(1), 168–173 (1974)
6. Hyndman, R.J., Koehler, A.B.: Another look at measures of forecast accuracy. Int. J. Forecast. **22**(4), 679–688 (2006)
7. Baier, T., Mendling, J., Weske, M.: Bridging abstraction layers in process mining. Inf. Syst. **46**, 123–139 (2014)
8. Baier, T., Mendling, J.: Bridging abstraction layers in process mining by automated matching of events and activities. In: Daniel, F., Wang, J., Weber, B. (eds.) BPM 2013. LNCS, vol. 8094, pp. 17–32. Springer, Heidelberg (2013)
9. Baier, T., Rogge-Solti, A., Weske, M., Mendling, J.: Matching of events and activities - an approach based on constraint satisfaction. In: Frank, U., Loucopoulos, P., Pastor, Ó., Petrounias, I. (eds.) PoEM 2014. LNBIP, vol. 197, pp. 58–72. Springer, Heidelberg (2014)
10. Folino, F., Guarascio, M., Pontieri, L.: Mining predictive process models out of low-level multidimensional logs. In: Jarke, M., Mylopoulos, J., Quix, C., Rolland, C., Manolopoulos, Y., Mouratidis, H., Horkoff, J. (eds.) CAiSE 2014. LNCS, vol. 8484, pp. 533–547. Springer, Heidelberg (2014)

11. Günther, C.W., Rozinat, A., van der Aalst, W.M.P.: Activity mining by global trace segmentation. In: Rinderle-Ma, S., Sadiq, S., Leymann, F. (eds.) BPM 2009. LNBIP, vol. 43, pp. 128–139. Springer, Heidelberg (2010)
12. Ferreira, D.R., Szimanski, F., Ralha, C.G.: Mining the low-level behaviour of agents in high-level business processes. Int. J. Bus. Process Integr. Manag. 6(2), 146–166 (2013)
13. Mannhardt, F., de Leoni, M., Reijers, H., van der Aalst, W.: Balanced multi-perspective checking of process conformance. Computing 98(4), 407–437 (2016)
14. Dijkman, R., Dumas, M., Van Dongen, B., Käärik, R., Mendling, J.: Similarity of business process models: metrics and evaluation. Inf. Syst. 36(2), 498–516 (2011)
15. Chen, L., Hoey, J., Nugent, C.D., Cook, D.J., Yu, Z.: Sensor-based activity recognition. IEEE Trans. Syst. Man Cybern. B Cybern. 42(6), 790–808 (2012)
16. Artikis, A., Skarlatidis, A., Portet, F., Paliouras, G.: Logic-based event recognition. Knowl. Eng. Rev. 27(04), 469–506 (2012)
17. Azkune, G., Almeida, A., López-de Ipiña, D., Chen, L.: Extending knowledge-driven activity models through data-driven learning techniques. Expert Syst. Appl. 42(6), 3115–3128 (2015)
18. Han, Y., Tucker, C.S., Simpson, T.W., Davidson, E.: A data mining trajectory clustering methodology for modeling indoor design space utilization. In: ASME 2013 International Design Engineering Technical Conferences and Computers and Information in Engineering Conference, American Society of Mechanical Engineers V03BT03A017–V03BT03A028 (2013)
19. Liu, C., Ge, Y., Xiong, H., Xiao, K., Geng, W., Perkins, M.: Proactive workflow modeling by stochastic processes with application to healthcare operation and management. In: Proceedings of the 20th ACM SIGKDD International Conference on Knowledge Discovery and Data Mining, KDD 2014, pp. 1593–1602. ACM, New York (2014)

Correlating Unlabeled Events from Cyclic Business Processes Execution

Dina Bayomie$^{(\boxtimes)}$, Ahmed Awad, and Ehab Ezat

Information Systems Department, Faculty of Computers and Information,
Cairo University, Giza, Egypt
{dina.sayed,a.gaafar,e.ezat}@fci-cu.edu.eg

Abstract. Event logs are invaluable sources about the *actual* execution of processes. Most of process mining and postmortem analysis techniques depend on logs. All these techniques require the existence of the case ID to correlate the events. Real life logs are rarely originating from a centrally orchestrated process execution. Hence, *case ID* is missing, known as *unlabeled* logs. Correlating unlabeled events is a challenging problem that has received little attention in literature. Moreover, the few approaches addressing this challenge support acyclic business processes only. In this paper, we build on our previous work and propose an approach to *deduce* case ID for unlabeled event logs produced from cyclic business processes. As a result, a set of ranked labeled logs are generated. We evaluate our approach using real life logs.

Keywords: Unlabeled event log · Event correlation · Cyclic processes loops · Process mining

1 Introduction

Most of information systems produce event logs as an evidence of processes execution. An *event log* consists of a set of events. Each event represents an executed *activity* in a business process. An event has a *case identifier*, an execution *timestamp*, and may have other *context* data such as the human resources or life cycle transition etc.

Postmortem analysis techniques of event logs, e.g., conformance checking [1], Enhancement [2], and process performance analysis [14], require the existence of *case identifiers* associated with events. A case identifier is important to correlate the events of a process instance. However, case identifiers genuinely exist in event logs that are produced from a centrally orchestrated system, so called *labeled* event logs.

There are many reasons why execution of business processes may produce event logs with missing information or errors [5,7,12] such as: some events are collected and recorded by humans, as well as the lack of central orchestration systems that are aware of the process model. The latter case is the most common case in real life. It is called unmanaged execution of processes and represents the middle level of the event logs categories [2], as well as *level-4* or lower of logging information as in [5]. These logs do not contain *case identifiers* and are called *unlabeled* event logs.

The problem of *labeling* unlabeled logs has received little attention in the community of business process management [1]. The work in [5,6,12,16] has addressed the

© Springer International Publishing Switzerland 2016
S. Nurcan et al. (Eds.): CAiSE 2016, LNCS 9694, pp. 274–289, 2016.
DOI: 10.1007/978-3-319-39696-5_17

issue in the form of directly mining process models from unlabeled event logs. But these approaches do not support mining the logs generated from cyclic processes.

In a previous work [4], we introduced the Deduce Case IDs, *DCI*, approach which deduces the case identifiers of the unlabeled events, and generates a set of labeled event logs based on acyclic processes. In this paper, we extend DCI to support unlabeled events that are generated from cyclic processes. We call the extension DCIc. In DCIc, we introduce a preprocessing step for the process model to construct a relationship matrix that represents the relations among the activities considering the cyclic behavior in the model. Also we modify the deducing process to support the labeling possibilities based on the cyclic behavior. For our approach to work, in addition to the unlabeled log, we require as input the executed business process model and heuristic information about the execution duration time of the activities within the model. The output is a set of ranked labeled event logs. The ranking score indicates the degree of trust in the labeling of events within each log.

The remainder of this paper is organized as follows: preliminaries and foundational concepts are discussed in Sect. 2. The overview of the approach and a running example are presented in Sect. 3. In Sect. 4, we discuss the preparation and construction of the relationship matrix from the process model. In Sect. 5, we present the details of DCIc approach. Implementation details and experimental evaluation on real life logs are discussed in Sect. 6. Related work is discussed in Sect. 7. Finally, we conclude the paper in Sect. 8 with a critical discussion of our approach.

2   Preliminaries

In this section, we discuss the fundamental concepts that are used in our approach. In Sect. 2.1, we define the decision tree used in *DCIc*. In Sect. 2.2 we explain the behavioral profile used to construct the relationship matrix. In Sect. 2.3, we discuss *heuristic* data that are used by DCIc.

2.1   Decision Tree

In general, a decision tree represents the decisions and their possible consequences. Each node has a conditional probability to its parent which affects the decisions in the tree. In the context of our work [4], a decision tree is used to represent the *possible* labelings for each input *unlabeled* event. An unlabeled event can be represented with a set of different nodes in the tree based on the event possible labelings.

Definition 1 (Case Decision Tree). *A case decision tree is a tuple CTree=⟨Node, F, root, Leaves⟩*

- *Node is the set of nodes within a tree. Each node is further attributed by the caseId, timestamp, activity, event identifier and a probability,*
- *F ⊂ (Node × Node) is the relation between nodes,*
- *root ∈ Node is the root node of the tree, defined with caseId = 0,*
- *Leaves ⊂ Node is the set of leaf nodes in the tree.*

*A branch(n_i) σ in the tree is the sequence of nodes visited when traversing the tree from
the node n_i to the root. $\sigma = n_i, n_{i-1}, ...n_1, root|(root, n_1) \in F \wedge \forall_{i=2}^{j}(n_{i-1}, n_i) \in F$.*

Definition 1 describes the structure of the decision tree used in DCIc. Each child
of the *root* represents a case. The set of branches within the same case describe the
possible execution behavior for this case. Each node carries its conditional probability
w.r.t its parent node.

2.2   Behavioral Profile

A behavioral profile (BP) describes a business process model (BPM) in terms of relations between activities of the model [17].

Definition 2 (Behavioral Profile). *Let A be the set of activities within a process model
BPM. The behavioral profile is a function BP : $A \times A \rightarrow \{\perp, \leftsquigarrow, \rightsquigarrow, +, \|\}$ that for any
pair of activities defines the behavioral relation as none $\perp$, reverse $\leftsquigarrow$, sequence $\rightsquigarrow$,
exclusive + or parallel $\|$.*

A behavioral profile returns one of the relationships $\rightsquigarrow, \leftsquigarrow, +, \|$ or $\perp$ for any pair
of activities (a, b) that belong to the process model under investigation [4,17]. To
explain what these relations mean, imagine two traces on the form a, b, c, d and a, c, b, e.
The $BP(a, b)$ $=\rightsquigarrow$ because a was observed directly followed by b, so the relation
$BP(b, a)$ $=\leftsquigarrow$. $BP(b, c)$ $=\|$ because both b, c and c, b were observed. $BP(d, e)$ $= +$.
Finally, $BP(a, d)$ $= \perp$ because we never observe in any trace the sequence a, d nor
d, a and in the mean time they both appear in at least one trace. The $\|$ relation is identified between two activities a and b whenever two or more traces $..., a, b, ...$ and
$..., b, a, ...$ are observed. In terms of the process structure, such traces can be observed
whether tasks a and b are belonging to two concurrent branches or a and b are belonging to a cyclic component of the process. Within the context of this paper, behavioral
profiles are used to filter out the incorrect labelings of events. However, it is crucial
for correct labeling to distinguish between concurrent behavior and cyclic behavior. We
elaborate more on that in Sect. 4.

2.3   Activity Heuristics

Activity heuristics are some statistical data about the execution duration of each activity.
This duration is represented in the range [*min, max*], and an average (*avg*) value. This
information is useful in building the case decision tree, as with this extra data we are
able to deduce the labeling possibilities of an unlabeled event.

3   Approach Overview

Figure 1 shows the main components of DCI [4] and the proposed extension *DCIc*.
DCIc has three main inputs: the unlabeled event log (S), the heuristic data, and the
process model. Also, it has an optional input: the ranking-score threshold, to display
the labeled logs based on the user-specified value. As an output DCIc generates a set of

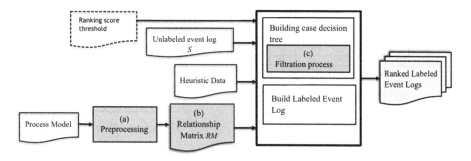

Fig. 1. Approach overview

ranked labeled event logs, as a result of the uncertainty in the labeling process of a single unlabeled event. As shown in Fig. 1, there is a preprocessing step to produce so-called the relationship matrix (*RM*) that describes the relations between the process model activities. The relationship matrix supports the representation of the cyclic behavior, which is one of the main contributions in this paper. Details about the preprocessing step of creating the relationship matrix are discussed in Sect. 4.

The case ID *deduction* process starts with the "Build Case Decision Tree" step. It uses the unlabeled event log to construct the *CTree*. During the CTree construction, the "Filtering process" step is applied using both the relationship matrix and the heuristic data to filter for the valid *labeling* possibilities. The last step in DCIc is "Build Event Logs", which is introduced in [4]. This step generates the different consistent combinations between the cases that are represented by CTree branches and writes each combination into a different labeled event log along with its ranking score, cf. [4]. Details about how DCIc works and the handling of cyclic behavior are presented in Sect. 5. The rest of this section discusses a running example to explain the inputs to DCIc.

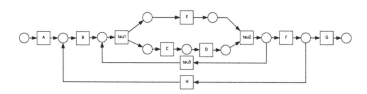

Fig. 2. Order business process

Our approach as described in Fig. 1 needs the following inputs:

(1) A process model, cf. Fig. 2. That is used later to produce the relationship matrix.
(2) An unlabeled event log *S* with activity and timestamp, where case ID is unknown. A sample unlabeled log is shown in Fig. 3a.
(3) Activity heuristics *heur*, are data about the execution duration of each activity. As discussed in [5], extra data about the execution behavior is required to be able to

Case Id	Activity	Timepstamp	Case Id	Activity	Timepstamp
-	A	1	-	H	18
-	A	2	-	D	19
-	B	4	-	B	20
-	B	5	-	F	22
-	C	8	-	G	24
-	E	9	-	E	25
-	D	11	-	E	30
-	E	12	-	F	32
-	C	15	-	G	34
-	F	16			

Activity	Min	Avg	Max
A	1	2	3
B	1	4	6
C	1	3	5
D	2	4	6
E	2	5	7
F	2	5	7
G	1	2	3
H	2	4	6

(a) Unlabeled Event Log (S)   (b) Heuristic Data

Fig. 3. Required input for example in Fig. 2

correlate the unlabeled events. DCIc requires heuristic execution data to be able to reduce the possibilities of case identifiers for the unlabeled events. Example values of these heuristics for activities of the process in Fig. 2 are shown in Fig. 3b.

(4) The threshold ranking-score (optional) is used to suppress generated labeled logs with a ranking score less than the threshold, by default all generated labeled logs are displayed e.g. threshold=0.

As shown in Fig. 1, the result of DCIc is a set of ranked labeled logs. These logs are categorized as either: (a) *Complete* logs that include all events existing in S. (b) *noisy* logs that contain logs with either model violation or inconsistent with heuristic execution data or under the user defined ranked threshold.

There are some *assumptions* that are considered for DCIc to work. First, There is no waiting time between the activities. Each event in S has a timestamp that represents the *completion* time of an activity and the start time of the next activity. If there would be consideration of waiting times, that would require explicit *start* and *complete* lifecycle transition events, which is not always the case for logs from unmanaged executions. The second assumption is that the input process model must be dead- and live-lock free. The third assumption is that there is exactly one start activity that is not contained in any loop, see $G3$ in [9].

4   Generating the Relationship Matrix

DCIc uses so-called the relationship matrix among activities to deduce case identifiers of unlabeled events. This matrix is based on the behavioral profile, cf. Sect. 2.2. However, a limitation of the behavioral profile, wrt this paper, is that a BP does not distinguish a concurrent execution of two activities from a cyclic execution. For example, cf. Figs. 2 and 6a, $BP(B, F) = \|$, the same as the relation $BP(E, D)$. However, when checking these relations in the acyclic form of the model, cf. Fig. 6b, $BP(B, F) = \leadsto$ whereas $BP(E, D) = \|$ as it is a result of a concurrent behavior not a cyclic behavior. We are interested in having that distinction. Thus, we generate the relationship matrix in a four-step approach. The first step is to obtain the behavioral profile of the original, possibly cyclic, input process model. The second step is to iteratively detect loops and remove the connecting branch from the exit to the entry nodes of the loop. These elements are maintained in a separate structure. The second step is repeated until all loops are

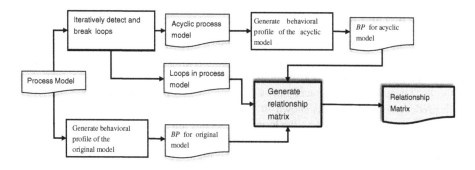

Fig. 4. Relationship matrix creation steps

removed. The repetition is intended to account for nested and unstructured/irreducible loops. The third step is to obtain the behavioral profile of the acyclic model. The fourth and the final step is to merge the two profiles from step one and step three to obtain the relationship matrix. Fig. 4 shows the steps of generating RM.

Definition 3 (Relationship Matrix). *Let A be the set of activities within a process model. The Relationship Matrix is a function $RM : A \times A \rightarrow \{\perp, \leftsquigarrow, \rightsquigarrow, +, \|\}$ that for any pair of activities defines the relation as none $\perp$, reverse $\leftsquigarrow$, sequence $\rightsquigarrow$, exclusive $+$ or parallel $\|$. We define some auxiliary functions:*

- *$Predecessors(b) = \{P : P \subset 2^A \wedge \forall a \in P \; BP(a,b) = \rightsquigarrow \wedge \forall a, c \in P \; BP(a,c) - \|$*
  $\wedge((\exists P' \in Predecessors(b) ; P \neq P') \; \flat \forall a \in P \forall a' \in P' \; BP(a,a') \neq \|)\}$
  $Loop(b)$ return the loops, that contains b, such that loop $= (Is, Ss, Es, Bs, IEs)$ where Is is the activities within loop, $Ss \subset Is$ represents the start activities, $Es \subset Is$ represents the ends activities, $Bs \subset Is$ contains the activities within the loop branch.
- *$StartActivities() = \{a : a \in A \wedge Predecessors(a) = \emptyset\}$*

The predecessors of an activity b, $Predecessors(b)$, is represented as a set of sets where the relation between members in the same set is *parallel* whereas the relation between members of different sets is not *parallel*. For example, in Fig. 2, $Predecessors(F) = \{\{E, D\}\}$, the predecessors of F are both activities E and D that are in $\|$ relation. The loops within the model are represented by a set of *loop* objects, cf. Fig. 6c. For example, in Fig. 2, as C is part of nested loops so $Loop(C) = \{L1 = (Is = \{B, C, D, E, F, H\}, Ss = \{B\}, Es = \{F\}, Bs = \{H\}), L2 = (Is = \{C, D, E\}, Ss = \{C, D\}, Es = \{D, E\}, Bs = \{\})\}$.

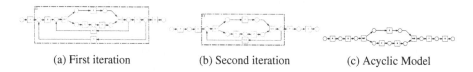

(a) First iteration   (b) Second iteration   (c) Acyclic Model

Fig. 5. Apply the second step of generating RM for the original model in Fig. 2

4.1 Detecting and Breaking Loops

We use *Tarjan's* algorithm [13] to identify the loops by detecting the strongly connected component with length ≥ 1. For each loop, we identify the start and end activities, and the *loop branch*. The loop branch is the back edge flow between the loop end activities, i.e. activities with successors $\notin$ loop, and the loop start activities, i.e. activities with predecessors $\notin$ loop. As shown in Fig. 5, this step is repeated until all loops are detected and removed by cutting the loop branch each time. So, if a loop is unstructured or irreducible, i.e. a loop with multiple entries, our approach is still able to handle it because in one step one of the branches will be removed and in a later step the other branch will be removed.

The results from the 'remove loops' are: (a) An *acyclic* model, cf. Fig. 5c (b) The *Loops*, cf. Fig. 6c. For *acyclic* input process models, the resulting model will be identical to the input and there will be no detected *loops*.

4.2 Generating the RM

This step generates the relationship matrix by merging the behavioral profiles of the original model BP, the acyclic model BP_a and the identified loops. The output of the generation process is the relationship matrix(RM), cf. Fig. 6d, as defined in Definition 3. RM is used later on as an input for *DCIc*. The 'Generate relationship matrix' step determines the relation between pairs of activities a, b as the following:

1. $BP(a,b) = \| \wedge (\exists L \in Loops : a,b \in L.Bs) \wedge a \in predecessors(b) \rightarrow RM(a,b) = \rightsquigarrow$
2. $BP(a,b) = \| \wedge (\exists L \in Loops : a,b \in L.Bs) \wedge b \in predecessors(a) \rightarrow RM(a,b) = \leftsquigarrow$
3. $BP(a,b) = \| \wedge (\exists L \in Loops : a \in L.Es \wedge b \in L.Bs \wedge a \in predecessors(b)) \rightarrow RM(a,b) = \rightsquigarrow$
4. $BP(a,b) = \| \wedge (\exists L \in Loops : a \in L.Bs \wedge b \in L.Ss \wedge a \in predecessors(b)) \rightarrow RM(a,b) = \rightsquigarrow$
5. $BP(a,b) = \| \wedge (\exists L \in Loops : a \in L.Es \wedge b \in L.Ss \wedge L.Bs = \emptyset) \rightarrow RM(a,b) = \rightsquigarrow$
6. $BP(a,b) = \| \wedge (\exists L \in Loops : a \in L.Ss \wedge b \in L.Es) \wedge a \in predecessors(b) \rightarrow RM(a,b) = \rightsquigarrow$
7. $BP(a,b) = \| \wedge (\exists L \in Loops : a,b \in L.Is \wedge ((a \vee b) \notin L.Es \cup L.Ss \cup L.Bs \vee a,b \in L.Ss \vee a,b \in L.Es)) \rightarrow RM(a,b) = BP_a(a,b)$
8. $BP(a,b) = \| \wedge (\forall L \in Loops : a,b \notin L.Is) \rightarrow RM(a,b) = BP(a,b)$
9. $BP(a,b) \neq \| \rightarrow RM(a,b) = BP(a,b)$

Items 1 to item 7 explain the conditions used for activities within loops. Items 1 and 2 handle the case when both a and b exist within the loop branch, and a is a predecessor of b. Then the relation in RM is sequence, otherwise it is reverse. In item 3, if a is part of the end nodes of the loop, b is one of the branch activities and a is a predecessor of b then the relation is sequence. For example, the relation between F and H, where $F \in L1.Es \wedge H \in L1.Bs$, so $RM(F, H) = \rightsquigarrow$, cf. Fig. 6. In item 4, if a is part of the branch, b is part of the loop start activities and a is a predecessor of b, then $RM(a, b) = \rightsquigarrow$, as the relation between H and B, where $H \in L1.Bs \wedge B \in L1.Ss \wedge H \in Predecessors(B)$, so $RM(H, B) = \rightsquigarrow$. In item 5, the relation between the loop end and loop start activities when there is no branch activities is sequence, as the relation between D and E where $D \in L2.Es \wedge E \in L2.Ss \wedge L2.Bs = \emptyset$. item 6 handles the case when a loop start activity is a predecessor of a loop end activity. In that case, the relation is sequence, as the relation between C and D where $C \in L2.Ss \wedge D \in L2.Es \wedge C \in Predecessors(D)$, then

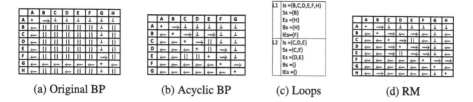

| (a) Original BP | (b) Acyclic BP | (c) Loops | (d) RM |

Fig. 6. The 'Generate relationship matrix' process input and output for the process model in Fig. 2

$RM(C, D) = \leadsto$. item 7 handles the loop default case, where either a or b only is part of the loop activities, or both belong to either the start or end activities of the loop. In such case, the relation is the same as the acyclic relation between the two activities. For example, the relation between D and F is $\leadsto$, also the C and E is *parallel* based on the acyclic relation. In item 8, If the relation between two activities is parallel and both are not included in any loop then the relation remains parallel. Last condition in generating RM is when the relation is not parallel, so the relation remains as the relation in the original model, cf. item 9.

5   Deducing Case IDs

In this section, we explain in details how DCIc works, cf. Fig. 1. The first step is to build the *CTree*, i.e. case decision tree, cf. Definition 1, for the unlabeled log S. During this step the filtering process takes place to avoid incorrect combinations based on the RM and the heuristics data, cf. Figs. 3, 6d and Definition 3 respectively. The second step is to generate the set of ranked labeled event logs, while ignoring redundant cases or events within the same log, cf. [4].

5.1   Building Case Decision Tree

The first step in generating labeled event logs is deducing the case identifier (*caseId*) for each unlabeled event in (S) by building the Case Decision Tree (*CTree*). Algorithm 5.1 builds the *CTree* based on the unlabeled event log S, the relationship matrix *RM*, and the heuristic data *Heur*, cf. Figs. 3, 6d. While building *CTree*, unlabeled *events* are allocated in their respective locations using a filtering process based on model and heuristic data. According to the results of the filtering process, i.e. possible parents, new nodes are defined for the event with different probabilities w.r.t each node's parent.

Algorithm 5.1, in line 5, the filtering process is applied to obtain the candidate parent nodes in the tree for each unlabeled event. The filtering process avoids invalid combinations w.r.t *RM*, and *out-of-range* execution time w.r.t heuristics data. The output of Algorithm 5.2 is a dictionary, i.e. *Parents*, that categorizes the *event* possible parents nodes w.r.t its heuristic range $\in$ ('avg','otherRanges'). In lines 6–15, for each possible parent, a new child node is created to represent the event in the tree. Lines 7–11 assign the *caseId* of the *event* based on its parent (*n.caseId*). If the parent is the *root*, i.e. *caseId* = 0, then the *event* represents the start of a new case.

Algorithm 5.1. Building Case Decision Tree

Input: *S*	//the unlabeled event log (Fig. 3a)
Input: *RM*	//the relationship matrix (Fig. 6d)
Input: *Heur*	//the heuristics about activity executions (Fig. 3b)
Output: *Tree*	// it represents a *CTree* in Definition 1

```
 1: Tree = new CTree()
 2: OutOfRangeEvents = newDict()
 3: labelCaseId = 1; eventId = 1
 4: for all (event ∈ S) do
 5:     Parents = Filteringprocess(event, RM, Heur, Tree, OutOfRangeEvents)   //see algorithm 5.2
 6:     for all (n ∈ (Parents[avg] ∪ Parents[otherRange])) do
 7:         caseId = n.caseId
 8:         if (caseId == 0) then          //n represents root
 9:             caseId = labelCaseId       //defines a new case
10:             labelCaseId+ = 1
11:         end if
12:         node = new Node(caseId, timestamp, activity, eventId)       // in Definition 1
13:         node.setProbability(heurDic); node.setParent(n)
14:         Tree.addNode(node);
15:     end for
16:     eventId+ = 1
17: end for
```

Filtering for candidate parents for unlabeled event is covered by Algorithm 5.2. First, it uses *RM* to filter for the permissible combinations by getting the relation between the leaves activities of *CTree* and the current event's activity. Second, it uses the heuristic data to check if each candidate parent from the model is in the execution range of the activity, cf. [4]. Finally the filtering process produces the possible parents as {'*avg*','*otherRanges*'}

Algorithm 5.2 starts with checking if the *activity* of the current *event* is a start activity in lines 2–4. In that situation, *event* represents a new case, i.e. a direct child of *root*. Otherwise, *Tree* is traversed from *leaves* till *root*, in lines 6–7, looking for possible parents. Line10, defines a set with the running loops within the branch by traversing from *node* till *root* and split the branch w.r.t *loop.S s* and *loop.Es*, cf. Definition 3. *cb* is begin from the last occurrence of any start activity of *RM.Loop(activity)* that is not followed by any of loop end activities. As *Loop(activity)* may result with set of loops contains event activity, so the branch can be spited into set of running loops. Line 12, uses *RM* to retrieve the relation between *activity* of the current *event* and the leaf *nodeactivity*. There are four types of relations:

- In case of none (⊥), lines 13–37 we ignore the branch and don't do any further investigation.
- In case of exclusive (+) or reverse (↞↝), lines 14–14, we traverse the tree upwards searching for labeling possibilities.
- In case of sequence (↝↝), lines 15–24. We get the nodes corresponding to the existed predecessors of the event activity within the *cb*, i.e. current branch, in line 16. Based on the results of predecessors nodes, the heuristic filtering step is performed.
  As *RM* represents the relation between *end* and *start* activities of a loop as sequence relation. So if the activity is part of a loop and the node is in the execution range of the event, then it traverses the branch to explore the other possibles based on cyclic behavior, in line 21.

Algorithm 5.2 Filtering process

Input: *event*   // object contains activity with its executed timestamp From S
Input: *RM*   //relationship matrix (see Definition 3 and Fig. 6d)
Input: *Heur*   //the heuristics about activity executions duration (Fig. 3b)
Input: *Tree*   // represents a *CTree* that defined in Algorithm 5.1
Input: *OutOfRangeEvents*   //Dict contains the activity and its max out of range events, that defined in Algorithm 5.1
Output: *possibleParents*   // represents {'avg': *avg*, 'otherRanges': *otherRanges*}
 1: *possibleParents = newDict(), avg = {}, otherRanges = {}*
 2: *activity = event.activity*
 3: **if** (*activity* ∈ *RM.StartActivities()*) **then**
 4:         *avg = avg* ∪ {*Tree.root*}
 5: **else**
 6:         **for all** (*node* ∈ *Tree.getLeaves()*) **do**
 7:                 **while** (*node!* = *Tree.root*) **do**
 8:                         **if** (*node.eventIdentifier* ∈ *OutOfRangeEvents*[*activity*]) **then** break
 9:                         **end if**
10:                         *currentBranches = getRunningLoops(Tree.Branch(node), RM.Loops(activity))*
11:                         **for all** (*cb* ∈ *currentBranches*) **do**
12:                                 *relation = RM(node.activity, activity)*
13:                                 **if** (*relation == ⊥*) **then** break
14:                                 **else if** (*relation == + || relation ==↜*) **then** *node = node.parent*
15:                                 **else if** (*relation ==↝*) **then**
16:   *predecessorNode = getExistedPredecessors(cb, RM.Predecessors(activity))*
17:   *outMaxRange = False*
18:   **if** (*predecessorNode ≠ ∅*) **then**
19:   *outMaxRange = HeuristicsFiltering(event, Heur, avg, otherRanges)*
20:   **end if**
21:   **if** (*RM.Loop(activity)! = null && !outMaxRange*) **then**
22:   *node = node.parent*
23:   **else** break //when relation is 'seq'
24:                                 **end if**
25:                                 **else if** (*relation == ||*) **then**
26:   *predecessorNode = getExistedPredecessors(cb, RM.Predecessors(activity))*
27:   **if** (*predecessorNode ≠ ∅*) **then**
28:   **if** (*activity* ∈ *currentBranch* & &*RM.Loop(activity)! = null*) **then**
29:   break
30:   **end if**
31:   *outMaxRange = False*
32:   *outMaxRange = HeuristicsFiltering(event, Heur, RMavg, otherRanges)*
33:   **end if**
34:   **if** (*!outMaxRange*) **then** *node = node.parent*
35:   **else** break
36:                                 **end if**
37:                         **end if**
38:                 **end for**
39:                 **end while**
40:         **end for**
41:         *possibleParents = {'avg' : avg, 'otherRanges' : otherRanges}*
42: **end if**

- In case of parallel (||), lines 25–36. As parallel activities executed in different order and behavior, we need to make sure that the event activity doesn't not exist in the current branch, i.e. *cb*. Whereas, if parallel activities are part of a loop then they can be repeated within the branch..In line 28, check the existence of the event activity within the current branch and if the event activity doesn't include in any loop, i.e. *Loop(activity) = ∅*, then the event can't be added on this branch. otherwise, get the nodes corresponding to the existed predecessors of the event activity within the *cb*, and proceed with the Heuristic filtering step, in line 32. After that check the execution duration if its in heuristic execution range of event activity, then it traverses the branch to explore the other possibles of both parallel and cyclic behavior.

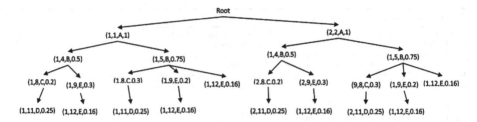

Fig. 7. Case Decision Tree

Figure 7 visualizes the output *CTree* of the Algorithm 5.1 for the inputs in Figs. 3, 6d. The tuple (id, ts, a, p) with each node defines the deduced case ID, the time stamp, the activity name and node *probability* respectively. As shown in Fig. 7, unlabeled event $(5, B)$ in S, cf. Fig. 3a, is represented in *CTree* by two nodes, case 1 includes one node with probability 0.75 for this event and the same for case 2 but with probability 0.25. Also note that the event $(12, E)$ is represented by six nodes, in case 1 it has three nodes with different parent nodes and the same for case 2. As shown in the model, cf. Fig. 2, activity E exists within two loops, and it considers as a part of the end and the start activities of the inner loop, so the relation between E and itself is ⤳, cf. Fig. 6d. Thats why DCIc considers the event $(9, E)$ as a parent event for $(12, E)$. The final result of applying DCIc is shown in Fig. 8.

```
(1, 'Ranking Score :', 0.1705992345698696)
1:1:A 2:2:A 2:4:B 1:5:B 2:8:C 1:9:E 2:11:D 1:12:E 1:15:C
2:16:F 2:18:H 1:19:D 2:20:B 1:22:F 1:24:G 2:25:E 2:30:E 2:32:F 2:34:G
----------------------------
(2, 'Ranking Score :', 0.1311242345698696)
1:1:A 2:2:A 1:4:B 2:5:B 1:8:C 2:9:E 1:11:D 2:12:E 2:15:C
1:16:F 1:18:H 2:19:D 1:20:B 2:22:F 2:24:G 1:25:E 1:30:E 1:32:F 1:34:G
----------------------------
other event logs
(3, 'Ranking Score :', 0.1450951149730726)
2:2:A 2:4:B 2:8:C 2:11:D 2:16:F 2:18:H 2:20:B 2:25:E 2:30:E 2:32:F 2:34:G
----------------------------
```

Fig. 8. Generated labeled logs by DCIc

6 Evaluation

We implemented a prototype[1] for *DCIc* and *Relationship Matrix* RM. We implemented DCIc in Python, and implemented RM in Java as it is based on the behavior profile implementation. We improved the performance of DCIc over DCI, cf. [4], by applying dynamic programming techniques in building CTree, and using the producer-consumer threading pattern to build the labeled logs while constructing the CTree.

Figure 9 shows the evaluation steps of DCIc with both synthetic and real life logs. To generate synthetic logs, we use the ProM [15] plug-in: "Perform a simple simulation of a (stochastic) Petri net". Then the simulated log is updated to reflect the heuristic data.

---

[1] Complete implementation in https://github.com/DinaBayomie/DCI-Cyclic.

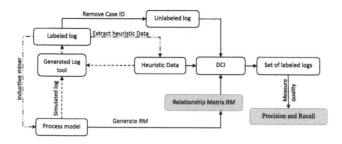

Fig. 9. Evaluation steps

For real life logs, we used the ProM plug-in: "Mine Petri net with Inductive Miner" for inductive mining technique [8] to obtain the process model. Then we extracted heuristic information from the real life log using a tool we built. In either case, we remove *caseId* from the labeled log to produce an unlabeled log. Also we build the relationship matrix for the process model. Finally, we measure the quality of our generated labeled logs by calculating the precision and recall with respect to the original labeled log. Precision measures the percentage of cases in the generated labeled logs that are correct i.e. also exists in the original labeled log, while recall measures the percentage of the correct cases that have been found, cf. Eq. 1.

$$precision = \frac{tp}{tp + fp} \ , \ recall = \frac{tp}{tp + fn} \tag{1}$$

In the above formulas, tp be the set of cases that exist in the generated labeled log and also in the original, fp is the set of cases that exist in the generated labeled log but do not exist in the original log, and fn is the set of cases that do not exist in the generated labeled log but exist in the original log.

We evaluated DCIc against different real and synthetic log, as shown in Table 1. We calculated the precision and recall using the top-most ranked generated labeled log against the given labeled log, cf. Eq. 1. The precision and recall of the BPI-2012 is lower

Table 1. DCIc results from different logs

	# of Cases	# of events	Precision	Recall	Execution time
CoseLog[a]	1403	8556	0.82	0.72	35 min
BPI 2012[b]	13087	262201	0.47	0.47	11 h
BPI 2013[c]	1487	6660	0.81	0.72	40 min
Synthetic Log	100	1979	0.80	0.80	60 min

[a]CoSeLoG, http://data.3tu.nl/repository/uuid:a07386a5-7be3-4367-9535-70bc9e77dbe6
[b]BPI 2012, http://data.3tu.nl/repository/uuid:3926db30-f712-4394-aebc-75976070e91f
[c]BPI 2013 http://data.3tu.nl/repository/uuid:c2c3b154-ab26-4b31-a0e8-8f2350ddac11

than the others as the mined model does not fit the log. So the quality of the generated logs is directly affected by the quality of the given model, because the deducing process is based on the model. If there is a deviation between the model and the log, i.e. activities exist in the log and do not exist in the model, that leads to consider the generated labeled logs as a *noisy* log.

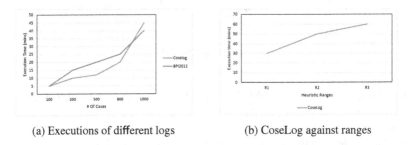

(a) Executions of different logs   (b) CoseLog against ranges

Fig. 10. Execution results

Figure 10 shows different execution times for DCIc. As shown in Fig. 10a, The number of events in the unlabeled log influences the execution time of DCIc. As the number of events affects both the breadth and depth of the CTree used in deducing case id for the unlabeled event. As shown in Table 1, the execution time of BPI-2012 log that has 262201 events is 11 h while the execution of the same log but with considering only 11388 events is around 30 min, cf. Fig. 10a. Also the execution time is affected by the number of the loops within the model, which influences the breadth and depth of the CTree, as for the synthetic log which takes 60 min, cf. Table 1. As shown in Fig. 10b, we deduce CoseLog using different heuristic ranges, which affects both the execution time and the labeled logs quality. Because DCIc depends on the heuristic range to eliminate and filter some of the possible labels that resulted from the model filtering process. So when the heuristic ranges are not accurate and not realistic that leads to produce a noisy labeled logs. Also when the ranges are too large this leads to filter only based on the model and no labeling possibilities will be eliminated based on the heuristic ranges.

7   Related Work

There are several process mining techniques that discover and conform the model from event logs. Most of these techniques need a labeled event log to proceed [1]. Also there are different performance analysis techniques that use labeled event logs to extract process performance indicators [14]. We see our work as intermediate step between low quality logs, according to [2], and those mining and analysis approaches.

In [3], authors address the problem of mapping of the process model activities and the executed event activity names. They introduce a semiautomated approach to map events to activities using declarative constraints that are extracted from the model and the labeled log. In common with our approach is the need for more information beyond the log, namely the process model whose execution should have generated the log. In contrast to our work, the approach in [3] addresses the problem of correlating a labeled event to a specific activity within a process instance whereas we address a challenge on an earlier step which is labeling the events in the log.

Handling event correlation problem within the web service environment is addressed in [5, 11]. In [5], authors discuss how to discover web service workflows and the difficulty of finding a rich log with specific information. The execution of web services has missing workflow case identifiers in order to analyze workflow execution log. They also discuss the need for extra information regarding execution time heuristics. In [11], the authors introduce a semiautomated approach to discover the set of process views based on finding correlation conditions. A process view is a representation of the process model from the process instance view. Common with our approach is the need for heuristic data to eliminate some correlation options. In contrast they correlate event using data from different layers, while we only requires the process model and heuristic information.

The handling of unlabeled log problem is also addressed in [6, 16]. In [6], an Expectation Maximization approach is introduced to estimate a Markov model from an unlabeled event log. It is a greedy algorithm that finds a single solution most often with a local maximum of the likelihood function. The building process of the Markov chain against the unlabeled event log is an ongoing process, it stops when the Markov chain stops changing. The main limitations of the approach are the lack of support for loops and that the existence of parallelism may lead to mislabeling some events in the unlabeled log. In [16], a sequence partitioning approach is introduced to produce set partitions that represent the minimum cover of the unlabeled log. The main limitations of the approach are the lack of support of loops and also the representation of parallelism as it will represent the execution of concurrent parts of the process into different partitions as if they are not related.

In [12], authors introduced Correlation Miner to discover the process model of the unlabeled logs, by using Integer linear programming to set the constraints to find the suitable model. In contrast to our approach, they mine the log to get process model, while we use the given process model to deduce the case id for the unlabeled event. A limitation of this approach is the lack of support for cyclic behavior.

In [10], authors used the redo logs and data model to construct labeled logs from the database. In common with our approach is the need from extra information to be used for correlating the events. In contrast with our approach is the type of the required data, also the source of the unlabeled events as they are extracted from redo logs.

8   Discussion

In this paper, we have shown an approach to label unlabeled event logs based on extending the deduce case IDs [4], DCIc. The extension is to allow labeling of unlabeled event logs from cyclic process execution. We use as input, in addition to the unlabeled event log, process model and heuristic data about activity execution in order to generate a set of labeled event logs with ranking scores. There is a preprocessing step to generate the relationship matrix, RM, to describe the relations between process model activities to handle cyclic behavior.

The quality of the output labeled logs is affected by the quality of the inputs. First, if the unlabeled log deviates from the process execution this is reflected in generation of noisy logs. If activities in the log appear in a control flow order other than implied by the model, the DCIc might fail to assign a label for an event and thus the labeled log will miss some events. Also, if the input log is originally missing some events this will lead to noisy logs. If activity heuristics were inaccurate, this will affect the overall score of the logs and might result in more noisy logs to be generated. In this regard, our approach can be seen as a conformance checking technique between unlabeled logs and process model.

We assumed that an event in the unlabeled log represents the *completion* event of an activity and the *start* of the next activity. A relaxation of this assumption would affect the runtime of the deduction algorithm as the CTree would contain more combinations. In this case, the accuracy of the activity heuristics will affect also the growth rate of the CTree as it will be used to correlate start and complete events for the same activity.

Other factors that affect the runtime of the deduction step are the size of the input log, the number of concurrent execution branches and the number of (nested) loops as all these factors contribute to the growth of the depth and the breadth of the CTree.

References

1. der Aalst, W.V.: Process Mining: Discovery Conformance and Enhancement of Business Processes. Springer, Heidelberg (2011)
2. van de Aalst, W., et al.: Process mining manifesto. In: Daniel, F., Barkaoui, K., Dustdar, S. (eds.) BPM Workshops 2011, Part I. LNBIP, vol. 99, pp. 169–194. Springer, Heidelberg (2012)
3. Baier, T., Di Ciccio, C., Mendling, J., Weske, M.: Matching of events and activities - an approach using declarative modeling constraints. In: Gaaloul, K., Schmidt, R., Nurcan, S., Guerreiro, S., Ma, Q. (eds.) BPMDS 2015 and EMMSAD 2015. LNBIP, vol. 214, pp. 119–134. Springer, Heidelberg (2015)
4. Bayomie, D., Helal, I.M.A., Awad, A., Ezat, E., ElBastawissi, A.: Deducing case IDs for unlabeled event logs. In: BPI workshop, BPM (2015)
5. Dustdar, S., Gombotz, R.: Discovering web service workflows using web services interaction mining. IJBPIM 1(4), 256 (2006)
6. Ferreira, D.R., Gillblad, D.: Discovering process models from unlabelled event logs. In: Dayal, U., Eder, J., Koehler, J., Reijers, H.A. (eds.) BPM 2009. LNCS, vol. 5701, pp. 143–158. Springer, Heidelberg (2009)
7. Herzberg, N., Kunze, M., Rogge-Solti, A.: Towards process evaluation in non-automated process execution environments. In: CEUR Workshop Proceedings on ZEUS, vol. 847, pp. 97–103 (2012). http://www.CEUR-WS.org
8. Leemans, S.J.J., Fahland, D., van der Aalst, W.M.P.: Discovering block-structured process models from event logs containing infrequent behaviour. In: Lohmann, N., Song, M., Wohed, P. (eds.) BPM 2013 Workshops. LNBIP, vol. 171, pp. 66–78. Springer, Heidelberg (2014)
9. Mendling, J., Reijers, H.A., van der Aalst, W.M.P.: Seven Process Modeling Guidelines (7PMG). Inf. Softw. Technol. 52(2), 127–136 (2010)
10. de Murillas, E.G.L., van der Aalst, W.M.P., Reijers, H.A.: Process mining on databases: unearthing historical data from redo logs. In: Motahari-Nezhad, H.R., Recker, J., Weidlich, M. (eds.) BPM. LNCS, vol. 9253, pp. 367–385. Springer, New York (2015)

11. Nezhad, H.R.M., Saint-Paul, R., Casati, F., Benatallah, B.: Event correlation for process discovery from web service interaction logs. VLDB J. **20**(3), 417–444 (2011)
12. Pourmirza, S., Dijkman, R., Grefen, P.: Correlation mining: mining process orchestrations without case identifiers. In: Barros, A., et al. (eds.) ICSOC 2015. LNCS, vol. 9435, pp. 237–252. Springer, Heidelberg (2015). doi:10.1007/978-3-662-48616-0_15
13. Rose, D.J., Tarjan, R.E.: Algorithmic aspects of vertex elimination. In: Proceedings of the 7th Annual ACM Symposium on Theory of Computing, pp. 245–254 (1975)
14. Suriadi, S., Ouyang, C., van der Aalst, W.M., ter Hofstede, A.H.: Event gap analysis: understanding why processes take time. Technical report, QUT: ePrints (2014)
15. Van Der Aalst, W.M.P., Van Dongen, B.F., Günther, C., Rozinat, A., Verbeek, H.M.W., Weijters, A.: Prom: the process mining toolkit. In: CEUR Workshop Proceedings, vol. 489 (2009). http://www.CEUR-WS.org
16. Walicki, M., Ferreira, D.R.: Sequence partitioning for process mining with unlabeled event logs. Data Knowl. Eng. **70**(10), 821–841 (2011)
17. Weidlich, M.: Behavioral profiles - a relational approach to behaviour consistency. Ph.D. thesis. University of Potsdam (2011)

Efficient and Customisable Declarative Process Mining with SQL

Stefan Schönig[1]([✉]), Andreas Rogge-Solti[1], Cristina Cabanillas[1],
Stefan Jablonski[2], and Jan Mendling[1]

[1] Vienna University of Economics and Business, Vienna, Austria
{stefan.schonig,andreas.rogge-solti,cristina.cabanillas,
jan.mendling}@wu.ac.at
[2] University of Bayreuth, Bayreuth, Germany
stefan.jablonski@uni-bayreuth.de

Abstract. Flexible business processes can often be modelled more easily using a declarative rather than a procedural modelling approach. Process mining aims at automating the discovery of business process models. Existing declarative process mining approaches either suffer from performance issues with real-life event logs or limit their expressiveness to a specific set of constaint types. Lately, RelationalXES, a relational database architecture for storing event log data, has been introduced. In this paper, we introduce a mining approach that directly works on relational event data by querying the log with conventional SQL. By leveraging database performance technology, the mining procedure is fast without limiting itself to detecting certain control-flow constraints. Queries can be customised and cover process perspectives beyond control flow, e.g., organisational aspects. We evaluated the performance and the capabilities of our approach with regard to several real-life event logs.

Keywords: Declarative process mining · Relational databases · SQL

1 Introduction

Process mining is the area of research that embraces the automated discovery, conformance checking and enhancement of process models. All involved techniques are evidence-based, as the input is event logs that comprise a collection of computer recorded information that track the executions of process instances.

Two different types of processes can be distinguished [1]: well-structured routine processes with exactly predescribed control flow and flexible processes whose control flow evolves at run time without being fully predefined a priori. Likewise, two different representational paradigms can be distinguished: procedural models describe which activities can be executed next and declarative

This work was funded by the European Unions Seventh Framework Programme (FP7/2007–2013) grant 612052 (SERAMIS) and the Austrian Research Promotion Agency (FFG) grant 845638 (SHAPE).

S. Nurcan et al. (Eds.): CAiSE 2016, LNCS 9694, pp. 290–305, 2016.
DOI: 10.1007/978-3-319-39696-5_18

models define execution constraints that the process has to satisfy. The more constraints we add to the model, the less possible execution alternatives remain. As flexible processes may not be completely known a priori, they can often be captured more easily using a declarative rather than a procedural modelling approach [2–4]. Declarative languages like *Declare* [5], *Dynamic Condition Response* (DCR) graphs [6] or *Declarative Process Intermediate Language* (DPIL) [7] can be used to represent these models, and tools like DeclareMiner [8], MINERful [9] or DPILMiner [10] offer capabilities to automatically discover such models from event logs. Existing declarative process mining approaches either suffer from performance issues with real-life event logs or limit their search space to a specific and fixed set of constraints to be able to cope with the size of real-life event logs. Both issues are highlighted in current literature, e.g., [9–12]. To the best of our knowledge an approach that is fast and customisable does not exist.

We fill this research gap by introducing a declarative mining approach that works on event data that is stored in relational databases by querying the log with conventional SQL. An overview of the approach is given in Fig. 1. Process mining by means of SQL queries turns out to be an integrated and language over-spanning solution to process discovery. By leveraging relational database performance technology, e.g., indexes on data columns, it is relatively fast without limiting itself to certain predefined constraints. Queries can be tailored to arbitrary aspects of a process, e.g., control flow as well as organisational issues. Furthermore, the results can be transformed to each of the mentioned process modelling languages. We evaluated the performance using several real-life event logs. Moreover, we demonstrate capabilities, expressiveness and additional insights of our approach by providing a list of queries for discovering commonly used process constraints. All queries are published in a technical report [13]. Further material as well as a screencast are accessible online at http://sqlminer.kppq.de. Summing up the contributions of this work, we introduce a *(i) customisable, (ii) language independent* and *(iii) performant* declarative process mining technique.

The remainder of this paper is structured as follows: Sect. 2 describes the input data, fundamentals of declarative process mining and related work. In Sect. 3 we introduce our approach to discover process constraints using SQL queries. The approach is evaluated in Sect. 4, and Sect. 5 concludes the paper.

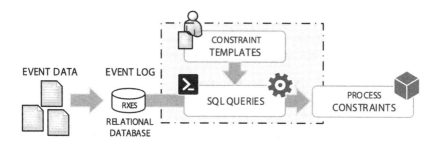

Fig. 1. Overview of the SQL-based process mining approach

2   Background and Related Work

Next, we describe the input data for our approach as well as fundamentals of declarative process modelling and automated discovery of models.

2.1   Storing Event Log Data in Relational Databases

Our process mining approach takes as input *(i) an event log*, i.e., a machine-readable file that reports on the execution of activities during the enactment of the instances of a given process, and optionally *(ii) organisational background knowledge*, i.e., prior knowledge about the roles, capabilities and the assignment of resources to organisational units. In an event log, every process instance corresponds to a sequence (*trace*) of recorded entries, namely, *events*. We require that events contain an explicit reference to the enacted activity. For discovering resource-related aspects we additionally require an explicit reference to the operating resource. Typically, these requirements are met when business processes are enacted by information systems [14].

The standardised, extensible storage format OpenXES was developed for the purpose of storing event data [15]. Lately, with *RelationalXES (RXES)* a relational database architecture for storing event log data has been introduced [16]. The RXES architecture uses a database to store the event log where traces and events are represented by tables with identifiers (IDs). RXES provides a full implementation of all OpenXES interfaces using the database as a backend. The database schema used in RXES allows for a significant reduction of redundancy by storing frequently occurring attributes only once rather than repeating them for every occurrence.

In this paper, we consider an event log to be available according to the RXES architecture and therefore to be stored in a conventional relational database. For readability we use a denormalised event log table like in Table 1, capturing only the attributes *EventID* (unique identifier for each recorded event), *TraceID* (unique identifier for the corresponding trace), *ActivityID* (name of the corresponding activity the event refers to), *Time* (date and time the event has occurred) as well as *Identity* (identifier of the performing resource or person). In the remainder of the paper, we will use the shorthand notation (a, id_x) for indicating an event of activity a that has been executed by an identity id_x. The given events are ordered temporally so that timestamps are not encoded explicitly. The following *example event log* contains four traces comprising events of four different activities and executed by five different resources:

$$\langle (a,id_1),(b,id_1),(c,id_2) \rangle, \ \langle (b,id_2),(c,id_2) \rangle, \ \langle (a,id_2),(d,id_4),(c,id_2) \rangle,$$
$$\langle (a,id_5),(a,id_5),(b,id_1),(c,id_3) \rangle.$$

In the case that correlations between process execution and resource characteristics should be examined, organisational background information, e.g., in form of an organisational model must also be given in a relational database table.

Table 1. Event log excerpt stored in a denormalized relational database table

Event ID	Trace ID	Activity ID	Time	Identity
1	1	a	2015-11-06 15:31:00	id_1
2	1	b	2015-11-06 15:35:00	id_1
3	1	c	2015-11-06 15:37:00	id_2
4	2	b	2015-11-06 16:22:00	id_2
5	2	c	2015-11-06 16:45:00	id_2
...				

We build upon the generic organisational meta-model defined in [17]. A Identity represents an individual person that can be directly assigned to activities. A Group describes several resources as a whole. A Relation represents the interplay between Identity and Group. For Relations, a RelationType specifies its interpretation. For instance, an organisation may have three Groups (Professor, Student, Admin), five Identities (id_1, id_2, id_3, id_4 and id_5) and the following four Relations of RelationType "role" describing the roles that are assigned to each resource:

(id_1,role,Student), (id_2,role,Professor), (id_3,role,Professor), (id_4,role,Admin), (id_5,role,Student).

This knowledge can help us to identify resource allocation rules as well as control flow rules that only apply to certain groups.

2.2 Fundamentals of Declarative Process Mining

In the following, we describe the basic aspects of declarative process modelling and the principle of automated discovery of such models from event log data.

Declarative Process Modelling Languages. During the last decade several declarative process modelling languages have been developed [5–7]. These languages are based on so-called *constraint templates*. A constraint template captures frequently occurring relations and defines a particular type of constraint. Templates have formal semantics specified through logical formulae and are equipped either with user-friendly graphical representations (e.g., in Declare [5]) or macros in textual languages (e.g., in DPIL [7]) that make the model easier to understand. A constraint template consists of placeholders, i.e., typed variables. It is instantiated by providing concrete values for these placeholders.

Concrete constraints are rules constraining, e.g., the execution of activities. For example, *Response(a,b)* of the Declare language is a constraint on the activities a and b, forcing b to be executed eventually if activity a was performed before. The *ChainResponse(a,b)* constraint is stronger and forces activity b to be executed *directly* after activity a was executed. Some languages allow in addition to control-flow aspects the definition of constraints concerning the assignment of certain resources to activites. *RoleBasedAllocation(a,r)* of the DPIL language is a constraint on activity a, demanding a, if executed, to be performed by a person in a specific role r.

As shown, constraint templates can be categorized into different groups depending on the process perspective they concern or their cardinality, i.e., the number of activities affected. For example, instances of the *Response(A,B)* template are pure control flow constraints that describe the temporal relation between two activities. On the other hand, the *RoleBasedAllocation(A,R)* template refers to the resource perspective and constrains the resources that are assigned to one certain activity.

Declarative Process Mining. For almost each declarative process modelling language a corresponding mining approach exists. The first approach to extract declarative constraints from event logs introduced by Maggi et al. is the *DeclareMiner* [8]. Here, the user can select from a set of predefined Declare constraint templates the ones to be discovered. The system then generates all possible constraints by instantiating the chosen set of constraint templates with all possible combinations of occurring process elements provided in the event log. For example, the *Response(A,B)* template consists of two placeholders for activities. Assuming that $|A|$ different activities occur in the event log, $|A|^2$ *constraint candidates* are generated. All the resulting candidates are subsequently checked w.r.t. the event log. Additional mining parameters like PoE (Percentage of Events) or PoI (Percentage of Instances) are used to distinguish between valid and non-valid constraint candidates. Maggi et al. propose an evaluation of this algorithm with the adoption of a two-phase approach [11]. During the first phase, frequent sets of correlated activities are identified. The candidate constraints are only generated on the basis of these activities. In the second phase, the candidates are then checked in the same way as in [8]. Additionally, there are post-processing approaches that aim at simplifying the resulting Declare models in terms of , a.o., redundancy elimination [9,18] and disambiguation [19]. In essence, the focus of these approaches is control flow with extensions to cover data dependencies [20]. The *DPILMiner* [10] proposes a declarative mining approach to incorporate the resource perspective and to mine for a set of predefined resource assignment constraints. All the mentioned approaches suffer from performance issues w.r.t. real-life event logs. Furthermore, the set of constraint templates to be analysed is predefined, i.e., cannot be customised by the user.

Efficient algorithms to discover Declare models are presented in [12,21]. Westergaard presents the *UnconstrainedMiner* [12], whose outstanding performance is obtained by constraint checking parallelisation and by relying on efficient data structures. The *MINERful* approach [9] that has been implemented [21] in the ProM framework has shown to be the most efficient algorithm to discover control-flow constraints using the Declare language. Both approaches, however, are limited to discover control-flow constraints of the Declare language.

Mining Metrics. Checking constraint candidates provides for every constraint candidate the number of satisfactions in the event log. The constraint *Response(a,b)*, e.g., is satisfied three times in the example event log since in three cases of an occurrence of *a*, *b* eventually follows in the same trace. Based on the number of satisfactions two metrics *Support* and *Confidence* are calculated that express the probability of a constraint to hold in the process. Constraints are considered valid, if their Support and Confidence measures are above a user defined threshold. In literature, there are two different definitions of support and confidence in the context of process mining. For our approach we adopt the most recent definition by Di Ciccio et al. [9] where the metrics are defined as follows:

- **Support:** It is the number of fulfilments of a constraint divided by the number of occurrences of the condition of a constraint. In the example log, the support of *Response(a,b)* is 0.75, as 3 *a*'s out of 4 fulfil the constraint. In case of constraints that do not depict implications like *Existence* constraints in Declare, the Support is defined as the number of fulfilments divided by the number of traces in the log.
- **Confidence:** It is the product of the support and the fraction of traces in the log where the condition (implications) or the constrained activity (not implications) occurs. The confidence of *Response(a,b)* is $0.75 \cdot 0.75 = 0.5625$, since condition *a* occurs in 3 traces out of 4.

The definitions above show that for discovering a certain constraint three different constraint specific values need to be extracted from event logs: *(i) the number of occurrences of the condition of the constraint, (ii) the number of fulfilments of the constraint*, and *(iii) the fraction of traces in the log where the condition holds.*

3 Declarative Process Mining with SQL

With RXES a standardised architecture for storing event log data in relational databases was introduced. In this section we show that it is possible to extract relevant process knowledge from event logs stored in relational tables by applying conventional database queries without any parsing or data conversion. The Structured Query Language (SQL) is a declarative language designed for managing data held in a relational database. It is based upon relational algebra. For space reasons we cannot explain language details and therefore refer to one of the available SQL handbooks [22].

In the following we introduce a procedure to map constraint templates from various declarative process modelling languages to SQL queries. First, we describe the general query assembly by means of the *Response* constraint template. Subsequently, we describe the mapping of a more complex control flow constraint template. Finally, we show that it is possible to map and discover customised constraints involving different process perspectives apart from control flow.

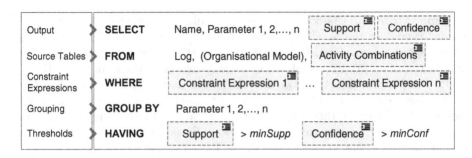

Fig. 2. SQL query assembly for querying declarative constraint templates

3.1   General Query Assembly

Figure 2 depicts the basic structure of an SQL query that discovers all constraints of a certain template under consideration of two thresholds *minSupp* and *min-Conf*. Here, subqueries are marked with a symbol on the upper right corner. We describe the different SQL directives in the order they get executed.

We show the approach with an example, namely, the *Response(A,B)* constraint template, which aims at discovering all the activity combinations (a,b) where b is forced to be executed if a was completed at some point before. As depicted in Fig. 2, the query for discovering *Response* constraints is organised as follows:

```
SELECT  'response', A, B, [Support], [Confidence]
FROM Log l1, [ActivityCombinations] c
l1.Activity = c.A
AND
EXISTS(SELECT *
       FROM Log l2
       WHERE l2.Activity = c.B AND l2.Instance = l1.Instance AND
             l2.Time > l1.Time)
GROUP BY c.A, c.B
HAVING [Support] > minSupp AND [Confidence] > minConf
```

FROM clause: Here, the data source tables are joined together, i.e., the table of the analysed event *Log* where every tuple depicts a single event and, if available, the table of the *OrganisationalModel*. Furthermore, the clause contains a subquery *ActivityCombinations* that provides a table with the activity combinations that should be checked. In case of constraints that comprise two activities like *Response*, this subquery looks as follows:

```
SELECT l1.Activity AS A, l2.Activity AS B
FROM Log l1, Log l2 WHERE l1.Activity != l2.Activity
GROUP BY l1.Activity, l2.Activity
```

Every source table gets an abbreviation assigned to be referable in other clauses, e.g., "l1" for the event log table or "c" for the combination table.

WHERE clause: This clause contains the different constraint expressions that have to hold for activities and their events, i.e., the constraint activation condition as well as their fulfilment requirements. If an expression cannot be derived directly, a corresponding subquery is used. For *Response* constraints the condition activation is any occurrence of an event of the currently selected activity *a*. In order to be fulfilled the constraint expression has to hold: activity *b* must occur in the same instance and it must occur eventually after *a*. Therefore, the WHERE clause for querying *Response* constraints contains a subquery:

```
l1.Activity = c.A
AND
EXISTS(SELECT *
       FROM Log l2
       WHERE l2.Activity = c.B AND l2.Instance = l1.Instance AND
             l2.Time > l1.Time)
```

It tests if at least one event of an activity *b* exists that is executed after the currently observed event of *a*. In case all logical terms in the clause evaluate to true, the currently observed tuple depicts one fulfilment of the constraint. The resulting set of tuples depicts all fulfilments of the analysed constraint template.

GROUP BY clause: After deriving the fulfilments, the tuples are grouped by the set of parameters of the constraint template. Hence, in the query to discover *Response* constraints, we group w.r.t. the two parameters referring to activities *A* and *B*.

HAVING clause: As described in Sect. 2.2 the number of fulfilments of each constraint needs to be computed in order to calculate the support and confidence values. After grouping, the number of tuples corresponding to a certain parameter combination can be extracted using the SQL aggregate function COUNT(*). In addition, a subquery computes the number of occurrences of the condition of the constraint. This way, the *Support* value of each constraint can be derived. In case of *Response* constraints the condition is depicted by the number of occurrences of the currently selected activity *a*. The SQL expression for calculating the *Support* of *Response* constraints is given as:

```
COUNT(*)  /  (SELECT COUNT(*) FROM Log WHERE Activity = A)
```

The *Confidence* of each parameter combination can be calculated in a similar way. Recall that *Confidence* is defined as the product of *Support* and the fraction of traces in the log where the condition occurs. Therefore, in case of *Response*, we calculate the fraction of the outcome of two subqueries to *(i)* extract the number of instances where *a* occurs at least once and *(ii)* to extract the number of traces in the log.

```
Support * ((SELECT COUNT(*) FROM
(SELECT Instance FROM Log WHERE Activity = A GROUP BY Instance) t ) /
(SELECT COUNT(*) FROM (SELECT Instance FROM Log GROUP BY Instance) t2 ))
```

Table 2. Result table of the *Response* query w.r.t. the example log

ID	Name	A	B	Support	Confidence
1	Response	a	b	0.75	0.5625
2	Response	a	c	1	0.75
3	Response	b	c	1	0.75
4	Response	d	c	1	0.25

The resulting values of both queries can then be filtered by user-defined thresholds.

SELECT clause: In the last step the query output is selected, i.e., the parameter combination and its corresponding *Support* and *Confidence* values. The result set contains tuples for each parameter combination that fulfils the constraint under consideration of the given thresholds. Table 2 results from applying the *Response* query to the example event log of Sect. 2.2 with the thresholds *minSupp=0.7* and *minConf=0.2*.

3.2 Mining Complex Control-Flow Constraints

More complex control flow constraint templates can be mapped to SQL queries by adding the additional constraint expressions of the constraint template to the WHERE-clause of the query. Consider for example the *ChainResponse(A,B)* constraint template of the Declare language which states that an activity *b* is always executed *directly* after an activity *a* has been completed. In addition to the fulfilment requirements of a *Response* constraint, a *ChainResponse* requires that *b* has to follow *a* without any other activity in-between. This additional requirement is implemented by adding another subquery to the WHERE-clause:

```
[Response Constraint Expressions Subquery]
AND
NOT EXISTS(SELECT * FROM Log 12, Log 13
           WHERE 13.Instance = 11.Instance AND 12.Instance = 11.Instance
           AND 12.Activity = c.B
           AND 13.Time > 11.Time AND 13.Time < 12.Time)
```

The subquery provides all events that temporally took place in-between the currently selected event of an activity *a* and any event of an activity *b* in the same instance. The constraint is only fulfilled for a certain activity combination *(a,b)*, if there exists no event of any activity between any occurrence of *a* and *b*. Other constraint templates of the Declare language, like *AlternateResponse*, *Precedence* or *NotSuccession* can be mapped in an analogous manner. Subsequently, the result set can be post-processed with existing pruning methods for declarative process mining, like pruning based on constraint hierarchies [23].

3.3   Customised Queries Including Additional Perspectives

In this section, we demonstrate how queries can be customised by adding aspects of further process perspectives. First, we focus on the organisational perspective, i.e., we describe how resource assignment contraints can be discovered by means of SQL queries. Second, we show how queries can be customised in order to analyse the interplay of different perspectives, specifically to discover the influence of resources on the control flow of the process [10]. We explain the functionality with example constraints.

Resource Assignment Constraints.   Resource assignment in business processes is extensively discussed by the workflow resource patterns. These patterns capture the various ways in which resources are represented and utilised in processes [24]. As an example, we explain the SQL query to extract role-based resource assignment constraints, i.e., that a certain activity can only be executed by resources assigned to a certain role. This constraint type is captured by the *RoleBasedAllocation(A,R)* template in the DPIL language and consists of parameters for activities A and roles R. Here, we assume organisational information to be available in a relational table *Relations*. Without loss of generality *Relations* has the attributes *Resource*, *RelationType* and *Group*. The FROM, WHERE and GROUP BY clauses of the query are then given as follows:

```
FROM Log l, Relations r1, [ActivityCombinations] c
WHERE l.Activity = c.A AND r1.RelationType = 'role'
AND l.Resource = r1.Resource AND
NOT EXISTS(SELECT * FROM Log l2, Relation r2
           WHERE l2.Resource = r2.Resource AND r2.RelationType = 'role'
           AND l2.Activity = l.Activity AND NOT r2.Group = r1.Group)
GROUP BY c.A, r1.Group
```

Table 3. Result table of the *RoleBasedAllocation* query w.r.t. the example log

ID	Name	A	Role	Support	Confidence
1	RoleBasedAllocation	d	Admin	1	0.25
2	RoleBasedAllocation	c	Professor	1	1

In addition to the event log and the activity combinations we also join the table with all relations according to the organisational model in the FROM clause. The constraint is only fulfilled for a certain event of an activity a if there exists no event of a that has been performed by a resource with a different role. The fulfilments are then grouped by every occurring activity and role combination. Since the condition of the constraint is like in case of the *Response* constraints the occurrence of activity a, the SELECT and HAVING clauses are identical. Applying the query with the thresholds *minSupp=0.7* and *minConf=0.2* to the example event log and organisational model described in Sect. 2.1 results in a set of two tuples as shown in Table 3. The constraints express that activity *d* has always been performed by a resource with role *Admin* and activity *c* by a resource with role *Professor*, respectively.

Cross-Perspective Constraints. Resource allocation can also have effects on the execution order of activities. These rules are called "cross-perspective" [10]. They can be found in different application areas, e.g., in cases where the execution order of certain process steps is bound to conditions that hold only for certain resources. A *RoleBasedResponse(A,B,R)* template, e.g., represents situations in which an activity must be executed after another one for specific organisational roles but not for others. These types of contraints cannot be discovered with pure control-flow mining approaches but require a customisation to combine the control flow and organisational perspectives. In order to extract control flow dependencies between activities that only hold for resources with a certain role, the subquery for calculating the *Support* value of *RoleBasedResponse* query needs to be given as follows:

```
COUNT(*)  /  (SELECT COUNT(*) FROM Log 12, Relation r2
WHERE r2.RelationType = 'role' AND 12.Resource = r2.Resource
AND Activity = c.A AND r2.Group = r1.Group)
```

Here, the number of fulfilments of the constraint is divided by the number of occurrences of events of activity *a* that have been performed by resources with a certain role. Applying the customised query with the thresholds *minSupp = 0.7* and *minConf=0.2* to the example event log and the organisational model of Sect. 2.1 the resulting constraints are given in Table 4. When comparing the discovered constraints with the *Response* constraints of Table 2, we can see that in general activity *b* does not have to be executed after *a* in every case (*Support=0.75*). However, when activity *a* has been performed by a Student, *b* followed eventually in every case (*Support=1*). The results of the customised query give a more fine-grained resolution of constraint satisfaction w.r.t. the roles of performing resources.

Note that the higher flexibility in the constraints (e.g., ternary versus binary constraints) increases the number of possible rule candidates exponentially in the number of parameters. This curse of dimensionality can lead to overfitting issues, i.e., the constraint model allows us to capture rules that reflect noise rather than real patterns. Nevertheless, this problem is mitigated by the use of a higher confidence threshold for the constraints. That way, we make sure that we do not incorporate rules that are only triggered a few times. Given enough data samples, however, these more precise constraints can also reach higher confidence levels and in the end yield a more accurate model.

4 Evaluation

The approach has been implemented and tested by means of conventional SQL and a relational database. Furthermore, we implemented a tool that imports

Table 4. Result table of the *RoleBasedResponse* query w.r.t. the example log

ID	Name	A	B	Role	Support	Confidence
1	RoleBasedResponse	a	b	Student	1	0.25
2	RoleBasedResponse	a	c	Professor	1	0.25
3	RoleBasedResponse	a	c	Student	1	0.25
4	RoleBasedResponse	a	d	Professor	1	0.25
5	RoleBasedResponse	b	c	Professor	1	0.25
6	RoleBasedResponse	b	c	Student	1	0.5
7	RoleBasedResponse	d	c	Admin	1	0.25

event logs given in the XML-based XES format to a relational database table. We evaluate our approach in two phases: first, we measure the performance with respect to publicly available real-life event logs. Second, we assess capabilities and expressiveness of SQL-based process mining (*SQLMiner*).

4.1   Performance Analysis

We measure the performance of the SQLMiner w.r.t. two real-life event logs from the financial[1] and healthcare[2] domains by means of control-flow contraints. Their characteristics are summarised in Table 5. The event logs have been imported into a Microsoft SQL Server 2008 R2 database. We compare the performance to the ProM implementations (Version 6.5.1) of state-of-the-art declarative process mining tools, namely, *DeclareMiner* [11], *MINERful* [21] and the *Unconstrained-Miner* [12]. For all tests we use the default settings of each tool.

  We execute the queries of eight commonly known Declare constraint templates: *AlternateReponse*, *Response*, *ChainResponse*, *AlternatePrecedence*, *Precedence*, *ChainPrecedence*, *RespondedExistence* and *NotSuccession*. Note that all these templates have as parameters two activities. Hence, the result tables have the same number and type of columns. Consequently, all the queries can be executed together by connecting them with the SQL UNION operator. All the computation times reported in this section are measured on a Core i7 CPU @ 2.80 GHz with 8 GB RAM. Table 5 shows the results of our performance tests. We can see that for both logs the *MINERful*[3] and *UnconstrainedMiner* tools reach an outstanding performance due to their efficient and specialised data structures. Nonetheless, the *SQLMiner* performs slower than these tools only within the range of seconds or a few minutes, respectively. The *DeclareMiner* takes for the analysis in both cases more than one, respectively three, hours. Recall that in contrast to the specialised Declare mining tools, SQL queries can be adapted to the analysts needs and refer to all the stored process information of different perspectives. Therefore, our approach depicts a trade-off between customisation and performance.

---

[1] doi:10.4121/uuid:3926db30-f712-4394-aebc-75976070e91f.
[2] doi:10.4121/d9769f3d-0ab0-4fb8-803b-0d1120ffcf54.
[3] The MINERful plugin does not allow to select certain templates to be analysed.

Table 5. Performance of SQL-based mining over real-life event logs

Source	Activities	Traces	Events	Total Time	Miner
Financial Log	24	13 087	262 200	01:03:47	Dec. Miner
				00:00:17	MINERful
				00:00:14	Unc. Miner
				00:01:08	SQLMiner
Hospital Log	624	1 143	150 291	03:11:12	Dec. Miner
				00:12:28	MINERful
				00:16:45	Unc. Miner
				00:19:30	SQLMiner

4.2   Capabilities and Expressiveness

For showing the capabilities of SQL-based process mining, we express commonly known process constraints of different perspectives to SQL queries and test them on real-life event logs. All queries are published in a technical report [13] and are additionally accessible online at http://sqlminer.kppq.de. For control flow related constraints, we map and test a list of fourteen frequently used Declare constraints, e.g., *Response* and *ChainResponse* among others defined in [9]. For resource-related aspects (i.e., the organisational perspective) we use the group of so-called *creation patterns* of the workflow resource patterns [24] including, a.o., role-based allocation and separation of duties. The SQLMiner is able to discover six creation patterns, similarly to the DPILMiner [10].

Furthermore, we show the additional insights in process data by applying *(i)* the traditional *Response* query and *(ii)* the cross-perspective *RoleBasedResponse* query to a real-life university business trip management event log[4]. The log contains 2104 events of 10 different activities related to the application and the approval of university business trips as well as the management of accommodations and transfers, i.e., booking hotels and buying transport tickets. The system has been used for 6 months by 10 university employees. In total, there are 128 business trip cases recorded in the log. We configured the queries with the thresholds $minSupp = 0.7$ and $minConf = 0.5$, respectively. The result set was composed of 29 *Response* and also 29 *RoleBasedResponse* constraints. The additional insights are explained by means of the following two extracted constraints that describe the temporal dependency between the activities *Apply for Trip* and *Book flight*:

– *Response, Apply for trip, Book flight, Supp=0.75, Conf=0.75*
– *RoleBasedResponse, Apply for trip, Book flight, Student, Supp=1, Conf=0.75*

---

[4] The event log is available for download at sqlminer.kppq.de.

We discovered the influence of resources on the execution order of the activities. Although employees usually applied for the trip before they booked the corresponding flight, it was apparently not mandatory. Nonetheless, there are cases in which certain employees already booked the flight without applying for the trip (*Support=0.75*). However, when analysing the ordering of tasks under consideration of performing resources, we extracted that resources with role *Student* always applied for the trip before they booked a flight (*Support=1*). While professors are free to book a flight without an approved application, students mandatorily have to stick to a certain order of tasks.

5   Conclusions and Future Work

In this paper, we introduced an SQL-based declarative process mining approach that analyses event log data stored in relational databases. While existing declarative process mining approaches either suffer from performance issues with real-life event logs or limit their search space to a specific and fixed set of constraints, the SQLMiner approach constitutes a trade-off between performance and customisation capabilities. We showed that it is possible to discover commonly used process constraints by means of conventional SQL queries. Leveraging relational database performance technology the approach is fast without limiting itself to certain predefined constraints. Queries can be customised and comprise process perspectives apart from control flow, such as organisational aspects. We evaluated the performance w r t several real life event logs. Moreover, we demonstrated capabilities and expressiveness by providing a list of queries for discovering commonly used process constraints.

The approach still has missing aspects, e.g., data-related constraints have not been integrated yet. As future work we plan to extend the SQLMiner to cover further process perspectives as well as to develop a publicly available query tool for declarative process mining on relational databases. Furthermore, understandability of queries will be enhanced by using SQL functions to represent common parts of different queries.

References

1. Jablonski, S.: MOBILE: a modular workflow model and architecture. In: Working Conference on Dynamic Modelling and Information Systems (1994)
2. van der Aalst, W., Pesic, M., Schonenberg, H.: Declarative workflows: balancing between flexibility and support. Comput. Sci. Res. Dev. **23**(2), 99–113 (2009)
3. Pichler, P., Weber, B., Zugal, S., Pinggera, J., Mendling, J., Reijers, H.: Imperative versus declarative process modeling languages: an empirical investigation. In: Daniel, F., Barkaoui, K., Dustdar, S. (eds.) Business Process Management Workshops. LNBIP, vol. 99, pp. 383–394. Springer, Heidelberg (2012)
4. Vaculín, R., Hull, R., Heath, T., Cochran, C., Nigam, A., Sukaviriya, P.: Declarative business artifact centric modeling of decision and knowledge intensive business processes. In: EDOC, pp. 151–160 (2011)

5. Pesic, M., van der Aalst, W.M.P.: A declarative approach for flexible business processes management. In: Eder, J., Dustdar, S. (eds.) BPM Workshops 2006. LNCS, vol. 4103, pp. 169–180. Springer, Heidelberg (2006)

6. Hildebrandt, T., Mukkamala, R.R., Slaats, T., Zanitti, F.: Contracts for cross-organizational workflows as timed dynamic condition response graphs. J. Logic Algebraic Program. **82**(5), 164–185 (2013)

7. Zeising, M., Schönig, S., Jablonski, S.: Towards a common platform for the support of routine, agile business processes. In: Collaborative Computing: Networking, Applications and Worksharing (2014)

8. Maggi, F.M., Mooij, A., van der Aalst, W.: User-guided discovery of declarative process models. In: CIDM, pp. 192–199 (2011)

9. Di Ciccio, C., Mecella, M.: On the discovery of declarative control flows for artful processes. ACM Trans. Manage. Inf. Syst. **5**(4), 24:1–24:37 (2015)

10. Schönig, S., Cabanillas, C., Jablonski, S., Mendling, J.: Mining the organisational perspective in agile business processes. In: Gaaloul, K., Schmidt, R., Nurcan, S., Guerreiro, S., Ma, Q. (eds.) BPMDS 2015 and EMMSAD 2015. LNBIP, vol. 214, pp. 37–52. Springer, Heidelberg (2015)

11. Maggi, F.M., Bose, R.P.J.C., van der Aalst, W.M.P.: Efficient discovery of understandable declarative process models from event logs. In: Ralyté, J., Franch, X., Brinkkemper, S., Wrycza, S. (eds.) CAiSE 2012. LNCS, vol. 7328, pp. 270–285. Springer, Heidelberg (2012)

12. Westergaard, M., Stahl, C., Reijers, H.: UnconstrainedMiner: efficient discovery of generalized declarative process models. BPM Center Report, No. BPM-13-28 (2013)

13. Schönig, S.: SQL Queries for Declarative Process Mining on Event Logs of Relational Databases. arXiv preprint. arXiv: 1512.00196 (2015)

14. van der Aalst, W.: Process Mining: Discovery, Conformance and Enhancement of Business Processes. Springer, Heidelberg (2011)

15. Verbeek, H.M.W., Buijs, J.C.A.M., van Dongen, B.F., van der Aalst, W.M.P.: XES, XESame, and ProM 6. In: Soffer, P., Proper, E. (eds.) CAiSE Forum 2010. LNBIP, vol. 72, pp. 60–75. Springer, Heidelberg (2011)

16. van Dongen, B.F., Shabani, S.: Relational XES: data management for process mining. In: CAiSE Forum, pp. 169–176 (2015)

17. Bussler, C.: Organisationsverwaltung in Workflow-Management-Systemen. Dt. Univ.-Verlag (1998)

18. Maggi, F.M., Bose, R.P.J.C., van der Aalst, W.M.P.: A knowledge-based integrated approach for discovering and repairing declare maps. In: Salinesi, C., Norrie, M.C., Pastor, Ó. (eds.) CAiSE 2013. LNCS, vol. 7908, pp. 433–448. Springer, Heidelberg (2013)

19. Bose, R.P.J.C., Maggi, F.M., van der Aalst, W.M.P.: Enhancing declare maps based on event correlations. In: Daniel, F., Wang, J., Weber, B. (eds.) BPM 2013. LNCS, vol. 8094, pp. 97–112. Springer, Heidelberg (2013)

20. Maggi, F.M., Dumas, M., García-Bañuelos, L., Montali, M.: Discovering data-aware declarative process models from event logs. In: Daniel, F., Wang, J., Weber, B. (eds.) BPM 2013. LNCS, vol. 8094, pp. 81–96. Springer, Heidelberg (2013)

21. Di Ciccio, C., Schouten, M.H.M., de Leoni, M., Mendling, J.: Declarative process discovery with minerful in prom. In: BPM Demos, pp. 60–64 (2015)

22. Bowman, J.S., Emerson, S.L., Darnovsky, M.: The Practical S.Q.L Handbook: Using Structured Query Language. Addison-Wesley Longman Publishing, Boston (1996)

23. Di Ciccio, C., Maggi, F.M., Montali, M., Mendling, J.: Ensuring model consistency in declarative process discovery. In: Motahari-Nezhad, H.R., Recker, J., Weidlich, M. (eds.) Business Process Management. LNCS, vol. 9253, pp. 144–159. Springer, Cham (2015)

24. Russell, N., van der Aalst, W.M.P., ter Hofstede, A.H.M., Edmond, D.: Workflow resource patterns: identification, representation and tool support. In: Pastor, Ó., Falcão e Cunha, J. (eds.) CAiSE 2005. LNCS, vol. 3520, pp. 216–232. Springer, Heidelberg (2005)

Conceptual Modeling

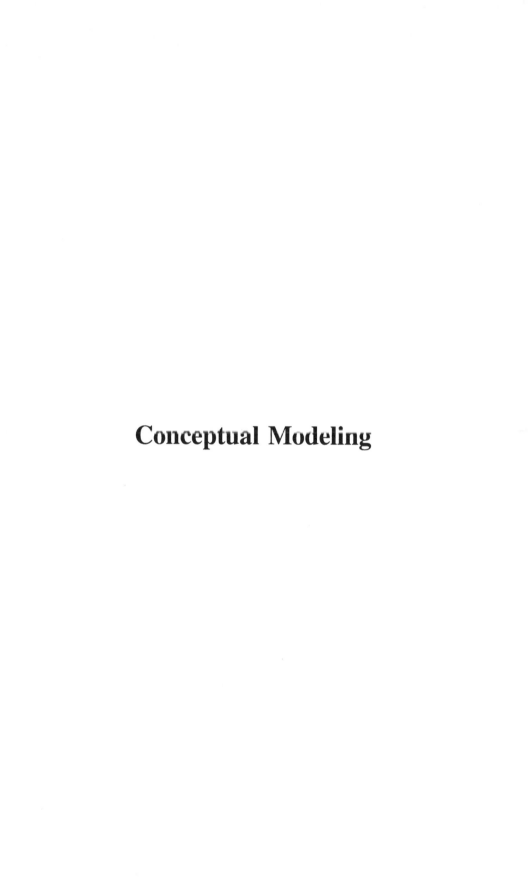

Using a Well-Founded Multi-level Theory to Support the Analysis and Representation of the Powertype Pattern in Conceptual Modeling

Victorio Albani Carvalho[1,2]([⊠]), João Paulo A. Almeida[1],
and Giancarlo Guizzardi[1]

[1] Ontology and Conceptual Modeling Research Group (NEMO),
Federal University of Espírito Santo (UFES), Vitória, ES, Brazil
victorio@ifes.edu.br, jpalmeida@ieee.org,
gguizzardi@inf.ufes.br
[2] Federal Institute of Espírito Santo (IFES), Colatina, ES, Brazil

Abstract. Multi-level conceptual modeling addresses the representation of subject domains dealing with multiple classification levels. In such domains, the occurrence of situations in which instances of a type are specializations of another type is recurrent. This recurrent phenomenon is known in the conceptual modeling community as the powertype pattern. The relevance of the powertype pattern has led to its adoption in many important modeling initiatives, including the UML. To address the challenge of multi-level modeling, we have proposed an axiomatic well-founded theory called MLT. In this paper, we demonstrate how MLT can be used as a reference theory for capturing a number of nuances related to the modeling of the powertype pattern in conceptual modeling. Moreover, we show how this theory can be used to analyze, expose limitations and redesign the UML support for modeling this pattern.

Keywords: Conceptual modeling · Multi-level modeling · Powertype · UML

1 Introduction

Three fundamental quality attributes that must be reinforced in all conceptual modeling languages are *expressivity, clarity* and *parsimony* [1]. The first refers to the ability of the language to capture all relevant aspects of the phenomena in reality it purports to represent; the second to how easy it is for the language users to unambiguously recognize which aspects of the underlying phenomena are represented; the third to how economic a language is in not forcing the modeler to represent more than it is necessary for a problem at hand. There is now a long tradition in conceptual modeling of using *Reference Theories* to evaluate and (re) design conceptual modeling languages according to these quality attributes [2]. Examples of fundamental conceptual modeling constructs that have been analyzed and re-designed following this strategy include types and taxonomic structures, part-whole relations, intrinsic and relational properties, roles, etc. [3]. In this paper, we address a fundamental conceptual modeling notion,

© Springer International Publishing Switzerland 2016
S. Nurcan et al. (Eds.): CAiSE 2016, LNCS 9694, pp. 309–324, 2016.
DOI: 10.1007/978-3-319-39696-5_19

which is recurrent in a multitude of application domains, namely, the notion of *multi-level classification*.

In several subject domains, the *categorization scheme* itself is part of the subject matter. In these subject domains, experts make use of *categories of categories* in their accounts. For instance, to describe the conceptualization underlying the software development domain, one needs to represent entities of different (but nonetheless related) classification levels, such as tasks (i.e., specific events occurring in time and space), types of tasks, and types of types of tasks. Other examples of multiple classi-fication levels come from domains such as biological taxonomy [4] and product types [5]. The need to support the representation of subject domains dealing with multiple classification levels has given rise to what has been referred to as multi-level modeling [5, 6]. Techniques for multi-level conceptual modeling must provide modeling concepts to deal with types in various classification levels and the relations that may occur between those types. The interest in multi-level modeling has led to a number of research initiatives in this subject (e.g. [5–9]).

In this paper, we address an early and important approach for multi-level modeling named the *powertype pattern* [8, 9]. This pattern is manifested when we have a case in which the instances of a type (the so-called "powertype") are specializations of a lower-level type (the so-called "base type"). Take, for instance, the case in which we want to express that the instances of the powertype *Bird Species* are types that spe-cialize the base type *Bird*, including the particular subtypes of bird *Golden Eagle* and *Emperor Penguin*. The powertype pattern is extensively used in many important modeling initiatives. An example is the ISO/IEC 24744 standard [10]. Moreover, this pattern can regularly be found in many catalogues of modeling best practices, in which it appears as an ingredient of other patterns (see, for instance, [11]). Finally, the relevance of this pattern has led to its adoption in the current version of the Unified Modeling Language (UML) [12], which allows modelers to specify a powertype in the context of a "generalization set".

Despite its intuitive characterization, there are many important and subtle aspects of the relation between the "powertype" and "base type" in the powertype pattern that are often neglected. For instance, when stating that the instances of Bird Species are subtypes of Bird, do we mean that all subtypes of Bird are instances of Bird Species? Do we mean that only subtypes of Bird are instances of Bird Species? Both? Moreover, if the powertype can have as instances the subtypes of the base type then it follows that the instances of the base type can be *instances of instances* of the powertype. But does that mean, for example, that all instances of Bird must be instances of at least one instance of Bird Species? Does that mean that the instances of Bird cannot be instances of more than one instance of Bird Species? Both?

In order to explore the semantic issues involving the powertype pattern, we employ here a multi-level modeling theory called MLT, which we have proposed originally in [13]. MLT is a formal axiomatic theory founded on the notion of (ontological) instantiation and is able to: (i) clarify and position conflicting definitions of powertype in the literature; and, (ii) enrich the expressivity of multi-level modeling primitives, by defining new structural relations for variants of the powertype pattern. So far, we have used MLT in order to provide conceptual foundations for dealing with types at different levels of classification in core [14] and foundational ontologies [15]. Here we apply MLT to analyze the UML support for modeling the powertype pattern.

UML is a *de facto* standard for conceptual modeling and information systems engineering. Moreover, it is the basis for ontology-driven conceptual modeling languages such as OntoUML [3], which in the past years have gained increasing adoption in the conceptual modeling and ontology engineering communities [16]. For this reason, we believe that providing precise and unambiguous semantics and advancing the UML support for modeling powertypes amounts to an important contribution for conceptual modeling, in general, and for ontology-driven conceptual modeling and ontology engineering, in particular.

By using MLT as a well-founded *reference theory*, we analyze and expose a number of limitations in the existing UML support for modeling the powertype pattern. In particular, we demonstrate that this support: (i) lacks *expressivity*, for example, for representing different definitions of powertype that exist in the literature [8, 9], each of which has relevant applications; (ii) that it lacks *clarity*, for example, because it confounds constraints that apply to powertype instantiation with those that apply to corresponding generalization sets; (iii) that it lacks *parsimony,* for example, because it forces the modeler to explicitly represent at least one instance of each powertype. By employing the results of this analysis, we propose a UML profile for addressing the exposed limitations. We use the distinctions put forth by MLT to devise this profile and we use the formal rules inherent to MLT to guide the development of the profile's syntactic constraints.

The remainder of this paper is structured as follows: Sect. 2 reviews briefly the MLT multi-level theory; Sect. 3 discusses UML's current support for powertypes, revealing its limitations in light of MLT; Sect. 4 presents our proposal to extend a fragment of UML reflecting the rules of MLT; Sect. 5 discusses related work and Sect. 6 presents concluding remarks.

2   MLT: A Theory for Multi-level Modeling

MLT is formally defined using first-order logic, quantifying over all possible entities (individuals and types). According to MLT, types are predicative entities that can possibly be applied to a multitude of entities (e.g. Person, Car, Student). If a type *t* applies to an entity *e* then it is said that *e is an instance of t*. In contrast, particular entities, that have no instances, are considered *individuals* (e.g. John, Lassie, my car).

The *instance of* relation is represented in this formal theory by a binary predicate *iof (e,t)* that holds if an entity *e is instance of* an entity *t* (denoting a type). MLT admits types having individuals as instances as well as types that have other types as instances. In order to accommodate these varieties of types, the notion of *type order* is used. Types having individuals as instances are called *first-order types*, types whose instances are first-order types are *second-order types* and so on.

The logic constant "Individual" is used to define the conditions for entities to be considered individuals: *an entity is an instance of "Individual" iff it does not have any possible instance* (Axiom A1 in Table 1). The constant "First-Order Type" (or shortly "1stOT") *characterizes the type that applies to all entities whose instances are instances of "Individual"* (A2 in Table 1). Analogously, each *entity whose possible extension contains exclusively instances of "1stOT" is an instance of "Second-Order Type"* (or shortly "2ndOT") (A3 in Table 1).

It follows from axioms A1, A2 and A3 that "Individual" is instance of "1stOT" which, in turn, is instance of "2ndOT". We call "Individual", "1stOT" and "2ndOT" the basic types of MLT. According to MLT, every possible entity must be instance of exactly one of its basic types (except the topmost type) (A4 in Table 1). For our purposes in this paper, first- and second-order types are enough. However, this scheme can be extended to consider as many orders as necessary [13].

Some structural relations to support conceptual modeling are defined in MLT. According to MLT, a type *t specializes* another type *t'* iff *all instances of t are also instances of t'* (see definition D1 in Table 1). Since the reflexivity of the *specialization* relation may be undesired in some contexts, we define in MLT the *proper specialization* relation as follows: *t proper specializes t' iff t specializes t' and t is different from t'* (see D2 in Table 1). The definitions presented thus far guarantee that both *specializations* and *proper specializations* may only hold between types of the same order.

From the axioms and definitions presented so far one can conclude that every type that is not one of MLT's basic types (e.g., a domain type) is an instance of one of the basic higher-order types (e.g., "1stOT", "2ndOT"), and, at the same time proper specializes the basic type at the immediately lower level (respectively, "Individual" and "1stOT") [13]. For example, consider a type "Person" that applies to all human beings. Since "Person" applies to individuals, it is an instance of "1stOT" and proper specializes "Individual". Further, consider a type named "Person Age Phase" whose instances are specializations of "Person" (thus, instances of "1stOT") that classify persons according to their age (e.g. "Child" and "Adult"). Thus, "Person Age Phase" is instance of "2ndOT" and proper specializes "1stOT".

MLT also defines relations that occur between types of adjacent orders, the so-called *cross-level structural relations*. These relations support an analysis of the notions of powertype in the literature.

One prominent notion of powertype was proposed by Cardelli [9]. According to Cardelli, the same way specializations are intuitively analogous to subsets, *powertypes* are intuitively analogous to powersets: "if A is a type, then Power(A) is the type whose elements are **all** the subtypes of A (including A)" [9]. Based on this notion, MLT defines a *powertype* relation between a higher-order type and a base type at a lower order as follows: *a type t is powertype of a base type t' iff all instances of t specialize t' and all possible specializations of t' are instances of t* (see D3). For example, consider a type called "Person Type" such that all possible specializations of "Person" are instances of it and, conversely, all its instances specialize "Person". In this case, "Person Type" is the powertype of "Person". Since "Person" *is instance of* "1stOT", "Person Type" *is instance of* "2ndOT" and *specializes* "1stOT". Note that it follows from the definition of powertype that "1stOT" *is powertype of* "Individual". Analogously, "2ndOT" *is powertype of* "1stOT", and so on. In other words, the notion of orders or levels in MLT can be seen as a result of the iterated application of Cardelli's notion of powertype to the basic types of MLT.

An important variant of the notion of powertype was discussed by Odell [8]. Odell defined *powertype* simply as a type whose instances are subtypes of another type (the *base type*), excluding the *base type* from the set of instances of the *powertype*. Based on Odell's definition for powertypes [8], MLT defines the *characterization* relation between types of adjacent levels: *a type t characterizes a type t' iff all instances of t are proper specializations of t'* (definition D4). The *characterization relation* occurs between a higher-order type t and a base type t' when *the instances of t specialize* t' according to a specific *classification criteria*. Thus, differently from the cases involving (Cardelli's) *is powertype of*, there may be specializations of the base type t' that are not instances of t. For example, we may define a type named "Person Role" (with instances "Employee" and "Client") that *characterizes* "Person", but is not a *powertype of* "Person" since there are specializations of "Person" that are not instances of "Person Role" (e.g. "Child" and "Adult").

Finally, MLT defines some refinements of the cross-level relation of characterization, which are useful to capture further constraints in multi-level models. We consider that *a type t completely characterizes t' iff t characterizes t' and every instance of t' is instance of, at least, an instance of t* (D5). Moreover, *iff t characterizes t' and every instance of t' is instance of, at most, one instance of t* it is said that *t disjointly characterizes t'* (D6). Finally, a common use for the notion of powertype in literature considers a second-order type that, simultaneously, completely and disjointly characterizes a first-order type. To capture this notion MLT defines the *partitions* relation. Thus, *t partitions t' iff each instance of the base type t' is an instance of exactly one instance of t* (D7). For example, we may consider a second-order type "Person Age Phase" (with instances "Child", "Adult" and "Elderly") that *partitions* "Person". A complete formalization of MLT in first-order logic can be found in [13].

Table 1. MLT axioms

A1	$\forall x \operatorname{iof}(x, \text{Individual}) \leftrightarrow \neg \exists y \operatorname{iof}(y, x)$
A2	$\forall t \operatorname{iof}(t, \text{1stOT}) \leftrightarrow (\exists y \operatorname{iof}(y, t) \wedge (\forall x \operatorname{iof}(x, t) \rightarrow \operatorname{iof}(x, \text{Individual})))$
A3	$\forall t \operatorname{iof}(t, \text{2ndOT}) \leftrightarrow (\exists y \operatorname{iof}(y, t) \wedge (\forall t' \operatorname{iof}(t', t) \rightarrow \operatorname{iof}(t', \text{1stOT})))$
A4	$\forall x (\operatorname{iof}(x, \text{Individual}) \vee \operatorname{iof}(x, \text{1stOT}) \vee \operatorname{iof}(x, \text{2ndOT})) \vee (x = \text{2ndOT})$
D1	$\forall t, t' \operatorname{specializes}(t, t') \leftrightarrow (\exists x \operatorname{iof}(x, t) \wedge \exists y \operatorname{iof}(y, t') \wedge (\forall e \operatorname{iof}(e, t) \rightarrow \operatorname{iof}(e, t')))$
D2	$\forall t, t' \operatorname{properSpecializes}(t, t') \leftrightarrow (\operatorname{specializes}(t, t') \wedge t \neq t')$
D3	$\forall t, t' \operatorname{isPowertypeOf}(t, t') \leftrightarrow (\exists x \operatorname{iof}(x, t) \wedge (\forall t'' \operatorname{iof}(t'', t) \leftrightarrow \operatorname{specializes}(t'', t)))$
D4	$\forall t, t' \operatorname{characterizes}(t, t') \leftrightarrow (\exists x \operatorname{iof}(x, t) \wedge (\forall t'' \operatorname{iof}(t'', t) \rightarrow \operatorname{properSpecializes}(t'', t')))$
D5	$\forall t, t' \operatorname{completelyCharacterizes}(t, t') \leftrightarrow (\operatorname{characterizes}(t, t') \wedge$ $(\forall e \operatorname{iof}(e, t') \rightarrow \exists t'' (\operatorname{iof}(e, t'') \wedge \operatorname{iof}(t'', t))))$
D6	$\forall t, t' \operatorname{disjointlyCharacterizes}(t, t') \leftrightarrow (\operatorname{characterizes}(t, t') \wedge$ $(\forall e, t'', t''' (\operatorname{iof}(t'', t) \wedge \operatorname{iof}(t''', t) \wedge \operatorname{iof}(e, t'') \wedge \operatorname{iof}(e, t''')) \rightarrow t'' = t'''))$
D7	$\forall t, t' \operatorname{partitions}(t, t') \leftrightarrow (\operatorname{completelyCharacterizes}(t, t') \wedge \operatorname{disjointlyCharacterizes}(t, t'))$

3 UML's Powertype Pattern Support in a Nutshell

The notion of *generalization set* is central to the UML's powertype pattern support. According to the UML 2.4.1 specification [12] each *generalization set* contains a particular set of *generalizations* that collectively describe the way a specific classifier (a class) is specialized into subclasses. To provide support to the powertype pattern, UML includes in its "powertypes" package a meta-association that relates a classifier (the so-called "powertype") to a generalization set that is composed by the generalizations that occur between the base classifier and the instances of the powertype [12]. The relation between the powertype and the generalization set is represented in the UML notation by placing the name of the classifier next to the generalization set preceded by a colon. For example, in Fig. 1 three specializations of "Tree" are defined, namely "Elm", "Apricot" and "Saguaro". The text ":Tree Species" denotes that the three subtypes enumerated in the generalization set are instances of "Tree Species" and that "Tree Species" is the "powertype" of the generalization set. Note that the term "powertype" as used in UML does not correspond to the notion of "powertype" as proposed by Cardelli. (This issue is discussed in Sect. 4.) The "disjoint" constraint means that the subtypes have no instances in common while the "incomplete" constraint means that there are instances of "Tree" that are not instances of "Elm", "Apricot" and "Saguaro". The relation between the powertype (e.g. "Tree Species") and the base type (e.g. "Tree") may be represented using a regular association with no special syntax and semantics.

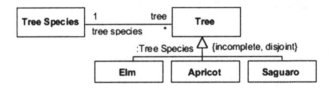

Fig. 1. The UML notation for the powertype pattern (adapted from [12]).

A key observation is that for a classifier to be considered a "powertype" in UML, it must be related to a generalization set. Thus, in UML, the powertype pattern can only be applied when specializations of the base type are explicitly modeled (otherwise there would be no generalization set). We consider this undesirable as it rules out simple models such as one defining "Tree Species" as a "powertype" of "Tree", without forcing the modeler to define specific instances for "Tree Species".

Furthermore, the only syntactic constraint defined in UML concerning powertypes is that "the classifier that maps to a generalization set may neither be a specific nor a general classifier in any of the generalization relationships defined for that generalization set" [12]. While this rule prevents the powertype from being involved in the generalization set defined to represent its own relation with the base type, this constraint is insufficient to rule out scenarios in which the powertype is incorrectly related by generalization with types of any other levels.

4   Applying MLT to Revisit the Powertype Support in UML

The application of MLT to revise the powertype support in UML leads to the formulation of modeling recommendations to ensure: (i) a precise interpretation for the UML constructs used to express the powertype pattern, (ii) a comprehensive support for the powertype pattern including its variants in the literature, and; (iii) a number of syntactic rules to prevent the construction of inconsistent models.

First of all, we should observe that the UML specification is silent with respect to whether Cardelli's notion of powertype can be adopted. However, given that a *generalization set* can be said to define the *classification criteria* used to specialize the general type, the UML notion of powertype seems to correspond to the *characterization relation* in MLT (not to the *is powertype of* relation), in particular as other generalization sets may co-exist defining other classification criteria for the subtypes. This interpretation is corroborated by statements in the specification that explain that the subtypes of a basetype are the instances of the "powertype" (excluding the basetype itself).

Our first recommendation is to mark the association between the base type and the higher order type with the «instantiation» stereotype, in order to distinguish it from other domain relations that do not have an instantiation semantics. An association stereotyped «instantiation» represents that instances of the target type are instantiated by instances of the source type and, thus, denote that there is a *characterization* relation between the involved types (regardless of possible generalization sets). For example, in Fig. 2 an association stereotyped «instantiation» having "Tree" as source and "Tree Species" as target type is used to represent that instances of "Tree" are instances of instances of "Tree Species" and, conversely, that instances of "Tree Species" have instances of "Tree" as instances. Therefore, in MLT terms, it denotes that "Tree Species" *characterizes* "Tree". Since this modeling structure does not rely on generalization sets, the modeler is not forced to represent instances of the powertype, which would have been required in the case of plain UML.

Fig. 2. Illustrating the use of «instantiation».

The multiplicities of the "target" side of an «instantiation» association can be used to distinguish between the different variations of characterization. Whenever the lower bound multiplicity of the target association end is set to one, each instance of the base type is instance of, at least one instance of the powertype. Thus, the higher order type completely characterizes the base type. In contrast, if the lower bound multiplicity of the target association end is set to zero, the inferred characterization relation is not a complete characterization. Analogously, if the upper bound multiplicity of the target association end is set to one, each instance of the base type is instance of, at most one instance of the higher order type. Thus, in this case, the higher order type disjointly characterizes the base type. In contrast, if the upper bound multiplicity of the target association end is set to many (*), the inferred characterization relation is not a disjoint characterization.

Table 2 summarizes the suggested interpretation in terms of MLT, considering different combinations of lower and upper bound multiplicities for the target association end. The combinations of multiplicities of the «instantiation» association with the values of the related generalization set attributes create additional challenges for modelers using the powertype pattern. These combinations are discussed in each of the following subsections, in which we expose some semantic issues.

Table 2. The influence of the multiplicities in the semantics of «instantiation» associations.

UML Notation	Semantics in terms of MLT
H «instantiation» B 1 ◄ 0..*	disjointlyCharacterizes (H, B) ∧ completelyCharacterizes(H, B) ≡ partitions(H, B)
H «instantiation» B 0..1 ◄ 0..*	disjointlyCharacterizes (H, B) ∧ ¬completelyCharacterizes(H, B)
H «instantiation» B 1..* ◄ 0..*	completelyCharacterizes(H, B) ∧ ¬disjointlyCharacterizes (H, B)
H «instantiation» B 0..* ◄ 0..*	characterizes(H, B) ∧ ¬completelyCharacterizes(H, B) ∧ ¬disjointlyCharacterizes(H, B)

Lower and upper bound multiplicities set to one. When both the lower and the upper bound multiplicities of an «instantiation» association are set to one, we have that the powertype simultaneously, *completely* and *disjointly characterizes* (i.e. *partitions*) the base type. For example, according to Fig. 2 "Tree Species" *partitions* "Tree" (i.e. each instance of "Tree" is instance of exactly one instance of "Tree Species"). If it is used in tandem with a *complete* generalization set it means that all the instances of the higher-order type are enumerated in the diagram. For example, the model in Fig. 3(a) represents that: (i) every instance of "Person" must be either an instance of "Man" or an instance of "Woman" and that (ii) "Man" and "Woman" are the only admissible instances of "Person Gender".

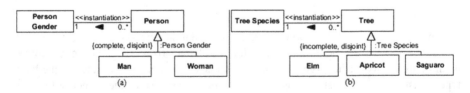

Fig. 3. Using «instantiation» to denote *partitions* relations.

At a first superficial inspection, one could consider that «instantiation» associations having the lower bound multiplicity (of the target association end) set to one could only be combined with a *complete* generalization set (as in Fig. 3(a)). However, this is not the case because the *"complete" constraint* represents whether all instances of the supertype are instances of one of the subtypes *in the generalization set*, and it is silent with respect to whether the higher-order type completely characterizes the base type. Thus, a combination of an «instantiation» association having both lower and upper multiplicities set to one in a pattern with an *incomplete* generalization set is admissible, and would mean that there are instances of the higher-order type that are not enumerated in the generalization set. For example, Fig. 3(b) represents that: (i) each instance of "Tree" is instance of exactly one instance of "Tree Species" (represented by the «instantiation» association), (ii) "Elm", "Apricot" and "Saguaro" are instances of "Tree Species" (see the generalization set name), (iii) there are instances of "Tree" that are not instances of "Elm", "Apricot" nor "Saguaro" (represented by the *incomplete* constraint). Given the semantics of the «instantiation» stereotype in tandem with the semantics of the incomplete generalization set we can infer that (iv) there are instances of "Tree Species" that are not represented in the diagram.

Since the upper bound multiplicity of an «instantiation» association set to one means that each instance of the base type is instance of <u>at most</u> one instance of the higher-order type, a model combining it in a pattern with an overlapping generalization set is inconsistent, and thus, deemed syntactically invalid.

Lower bound multiplicity set to zero and upper bound set to one. An association stereotyped «instantiation» having the lower multiplicity set to zero and the upper bound multiplicity set to one denotes that the target type *disjointly characterizes* but *does <u>not</u> completely characterize* (in MLT sense) the source type. For example, suppose that an organization defines a type of roles called "Management Role" such that an employee cannot play more than one role of such type and it is not the case that all employees play some "Management Role". This scenario is illustrated in Fig. 4(a), showing "Organization President" and "Department Dean" as examples of instances of "Management Role". The interpretation of the combination of an «instantiation» association having zero as the lower bound and one as the upper bound multiplicity with an incomplete generalization set is more subtle than the cases we have discussed so far. In order to analyze this combination, we should first note that: (i) there are instances of "Employee" which are not instances of any instance of "Management Role" (as a consequence of the semantics of the «instantiation» association); and (ii) there are instances of "Employee" which are neither "Organization President" nor "Department Dean" (as a consequence of the semantics of *incomplete* generalization sets). The model is still silent with respect to whether all instances of "Management Role" are enumerated in this generalization set. It is possible that there are no other instances of "Management Role", but an interpretation in which there are other management roles not mentioned in the model (e.g. "Division Head") is also admissible.

Since an «instantiation» association having zero as the lower bound multiplicity implies that there are instances of the base type that are not instances of any instance of the higher-order type, a model combining it in a pattern with a complete generalization set is deemed syntactically invalid. Further, as previously discussed, the combination of an «instantiation» association with upper bound multiplicity set to one in a pattern with an overlapping generalization set is also deemed syntactically invalid.

Lower bound multiplicity set to one and upper bound set to many. An «instantiation» association having the lower multiplicity set to one and the upper bound multiplicity set to "many" (*) denotes that the target type *completely characterizes* but *does not disjointly characterize* (in MLT sense) the source type. For example, suppose that the rules of an organization define a type of roles called "Business Role" (having instances as "Programmer", "DB Designer" and "Sw Designer") such that every employee must play one or more roles of such type.

Associations stereotyped «instantiation» with "one" as lower bound multiplicity and "many" as upper bound multiplicity can be combined with any generalization sets despite they are *complete or incomplete, disjoint or overlapping*. However, the generalization sets constraints influence the semantics of the diagrams. For example, in Fig. 4(b) the generalization set is *complete* and *disjoint* meaning each instance of "Employee" plays exactly one of the represented instances of "Business Role". Therefore, since the multiplicities of the «instantiation» association between "Business Role" and "Employee" denotes that the instances of the former are overlapping, we conclude that there are non-represented instances of "Business Role" such that some of these instances are overlapping between them or some of them are overlapping with the represented ones. If the generalization set of Fig. 4(b) were defined incomplete we could infer that there were non-represented instances of "Business Role" such that the whole set of instances of "Business Role" classifies all instances of "Employee" having some overlaps. Finally, considering the hypothesis in which the generalization set of Fig. 4(b) were defined complete and overlapping we would have two possible interpretations: (i) all instances of "Business Role" are represented in the model or (ii) there are non-represented instances of "Business Role" but the represented ones already classify all instances of "Employee" having overlaps between them.

Lower bound multiplicity set to zero and upper bound set to many. An «instantiation» association having the lower multiplicity set to zero and the upper bound multiplicity set to many (*) denotes that the target type *characterizes* (in MLT sense) the source type, however it is neither a *complete characterization* nor a *disjoint characterization*. Therefore, there may be instances of the base type that are instances of more than one instance of the higher-order type and there may be instances of the base type that are not instances of any instance of the higher-order type. For example, Fig. 5(a) consider a second-order type named "Social Role" whose instances represent roles that instances of "Person" may play in social relations, such as "Client", "Employee" and "Husband". Some instances of "Person" may play more than one "Social Role" and some other instances may play no social role.

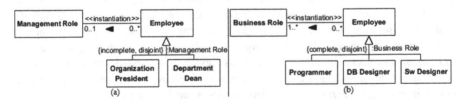

Fig. 4. Using «instantiation» with different multiplicities.

Table 3. Analyzing the combination of «instantiation» with generalization set constraints

Association multiplicities		Generalization sets constraints			
Lower	Upper	{disjoint}		{overlapping}	
		{complete}	{incomplete}	{complete}	{incomplete}
1	1	*enumerated*	*non enumerated*	*invalid*	*invalid*
0	1	*invalid*	*silent*	*invalid*	*invalid*
1	*	*non enumerated*	*non enumerated*	*silent*	*non enumerated*
0	*	*invalid*	*non enumerated*	*invalid*	*silent*

Note that it is not possible to infer whether all instances of "Social Role" are represented or not in Fig. 5(a): (i) they may all be enumerated, or (ii) there may be non-represented instances of "Social Role". If the generalization set of Fig. 5(a) were *disjoint*, the diagram would still be considered syntactically valid and we could infer that there were non-represented instances of "Social Role" such that the whole set of instances of "Social Role" have some overlaps. Finally, if the generalization set of Fig. 5(a) were *complete*, the diagram would be considered syntactically invalid since the whole set of instances of "Social Role" does not classify all instances of "Person".

Table 3 summarizes the semantics of the combinations of the multiplicities of «instantiation» associations with the possible constraints of generalization sets, classifying each possible combination as: (i) *enumerated* if one can infer that all instances of the higher-order type are represented in the diagram; (ii) *non enumerated* if one can infer that there are instances of the higher-order type not represented in the diagram; (iii) *silent:* if it is not possible to infer whether the instances of the higher-order type are enumerated or not; or (iv) *invalid* if the combination is syntactically invalid.

The «powerType» stereotype. Our second recommendation is to use the «power-Type» stereotype to represent Cardelli's notion of powertype [9]. If a class stereotyped «powerType» is the target of an «instantiation» association this means that this type *is powertype of* the source type, i.e. the source type and all its specializations are instances of the target element. For example, in Fig. 5(b), all types that (directly or indirectly) *specialize* "Person" are instances of "Person Type".

According to Cardelli's notion of powertype the base type itself is instance of the higher-order type. Thus, in these cases, the lower bound multiplicity of the «instantiation» association must be set to one and the upper bound to many (*). Moreover, models in which the «powerType» stereotype is applied to types (classifiers) that are not target of any «instantiation» association are deemed syntactically invalid.

Another important syntactic constraint involving «powerType» is that, since a powertype (in MLT) does not define a classification criteria to be applied to instances of the base type, there should be no generalization set anchored in types stereotyped «powerType» (i.e. *powertype* relations do not give rise to generalization sets). For example, considering the scenario illustrated in Fig. 5(b), a generalization set named ":Person Type" is not admissible. However, all subtypes of "Person", despite the generalization sets in which they are involved, are instances of "Person Type". Thus, all instances of "Person Gender" and "Social Role" are instances of "Person Type".

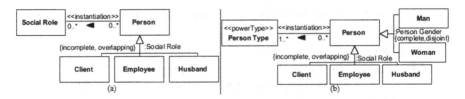

Fig. 5. Using «instantiation» (a) with unbounded multiplicities, and (b) with «powerType».

Syntactic constraints motivated by MLT rules. An important aspect of the proposed interpretation is that it allows us to leverage the axioms and theorems of the MLT formalization in order to guide the modelers in producing sound models. For instance, given the definition of the *is powertype of* relation of MLT, a type may not have more than one *powertype* and a higher order *type* may be a *powertype of* at most one other type. This suggests a clear syntactic constraint: a class stereotyped «powerType» can only be target of at most one «instantiation» association and a regular class can only be the source of at most one «instantiation» association having as target a class stereotyped «powerType». Further, the MLT theorem stating that if a type *t specializes* a type *t'* then the *powertype of t specializes* the *powertype of t'* may be used to check the syntax of powertype hierarchies, and to generate the powertypes hierarchy corresponding to the base types hierarchy. For example, in Fig. 6(a) the conjunction of the facts that: (i) "Employee" *specializes* "Person", (ii) "Person Type" *is powertype of* "Person" and (iii) "Employee Type" *is powertype of* "Employee" implies that "Employee Type" must *specialize* "Person Type".

Considering the MLT definitions of *powertype*, *characterization* and *proper specialization* we conclude that if a type *t'* is *powertype of* a type *t* and a type *t"* *characterizes* the same base type *t* then all instances of *t"* are also *instances of t'* and, thus, *t" proper specializes t'*. This theorem also suggests a syntactic constraint. For example, in Fig. 6(a) "Management Role" *characterizes* "Employee" and *specializes* "Employee Type", whereas "Person Gender" *characterizes* "Person" and *specializes* "Person Type". In this case, if the modeler fails to include any of the specializations between the higher-order types, it would be possible to infer them automatically.

Another MLT theorem states that if two types *t'* and *t"* both *partition* the same type *t* then it is not possible for *t'* to specialize *t"*. Again this suggests a clear syntactic constraint. For example, in Fig. 6(b), "Person Age Phase" *partitions* "Person" according to their age having "Child" and "Adult" (and other non-represented types) as instances. "Person Gender", in turn, *partitions* "Person" according to their gender having "Man" and "Woman" as instances. Thus, to be syntactically valid, the model may not include a specialization between "Person Age Phase" and "Person Gender".

Recall that the MLT cross-level relations (*characterization* and *is powertype of*) hold between a higher-order type and another type at one order lower. Thus, if two types are linked through an «instantiation» association the type at the source association end is at an order lower than the one in the target (e.g. in Fig. 6(b) "Person" is one order lower than "Person Age Phase"). Hence, cycles of associations stereotyped «instantiation» are not allowed. For example, suppose *A* is the target in an «instantiation» association in which *B* is the source while *B* is the target in another

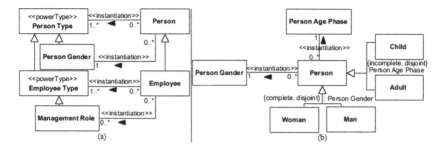

Fig. 6. Syntactical constraints concerning specializations types and the types order.

«instantiation» association in which A is the source. This scenario is absurd since A must be at one order lower than B and, simultaneously, B must be at one order lower than A.

Finally, we consider that all higher-order types represented in diagrams must have cross-level relations with other types. Thus, we can determine the order of a type considering the «instantiation» associations in which they are involved as target. Types that are not targets of any «instantiation» association are first-order types (e.g. "Person", "Man", "Woman", "Adult" and "Child" in Fig. 6(b)). Types that are target in «instantiation» associations in which the sources are first-order types are second-order types (e.g. "Person Gender" and "Person Age Phase" in Fig. 6(b)), and so on. The MLT axiom that states that each domain type must be instance of exactly one MLT basic type (being thus at only one order) can be syntactically verified in our models. Further, the MLT theorem that specialization relations may only hold between two types at the same order may also be syntactically verified. For example, in Fig. 6(b) there may not be specialization relations between a first-order type (i.e., "Person", "Man", "Woman", "Adult" or "Child") and a second-order type (i.e. "Person Gender" or "Person Age Phase"). Otherwise, the model would be considered syntactically invalid. A prototype plugin for the Visual Paradigm modeling tool that implements the proposed profile and performs syntactic verification of MLT rules is available at http://github.com/nemo-ufes/MLT-VP-plugin.

5 Related Work

An early attempt to address multi-level modeling by Odell [8] defined the concept of powertype informally using regular associations between the powertype and a base type. This differs from our approach because we use constructs having specialized semantics to denote the cross-level relations between types defined in MLT. This allows us to prescribe syntactic rules for the models that use these relations following the axioms in the formal theory.

Similarly to Odell [8], Gonzalez-Perez and Henderson-Sellers [7] use an association labeled "partitions" between a powertype and a base type (called a "partitioned type" in their terminology). The authors illustrate their technique with a diagram in which "partitions" is modeled as a many-to-one association between "Task" and

"TaskKind", meaning that every instance of the partitioned type ("Task") is linked to exactly one instance of the powertype ("TaskKind"). In the sequel, they discuss that the "*partitions* association possesses instantiation semantics", and that, because of this, "Task" is a special instance of "TaskKind" (the most generic kind of task). However, if "Task" itself is an instance of "TaskKind", then the lower bound multiplicity of the "partitions" association in the "TaskKind" end cannot be *one*. This is because all instances of subtypes of "Task" are also instances of "Task", and thus instances of at least *two* "TaskKinds" (one which is "Task" itself). This is an example of a mistake, which could be avoided with a richer language support for the powertype pattern and its variants, as we propose here.

The concept of powertype is founded on the notion that "instances of types can also be types" [8]. Motivated by a similar observation, Atkinson and Kühne [17] defined the notion of *clabject*, which is valuable to our approach. They discuss that every instantiable entity has both a type (or class) facet and an instance (or object) facet. In our approach, instances of higher-order types may be considered *clabjects*. For instance, considering the previous example all instances of "TaskKind" as well as all instances of "TaskPowertype" have their own instances being, thus, *clabjects*.

Atkinson and Kühne have also proposed a *deep instantiation based* approach [6], [18] as a means to provide for multiple levels of classification whereby an element at some level can describe features of elements at each level beneath that level. The authors consider the main benefit of deep instantiation is to support multi-level modeling without the need of introducing the required base type in the powertype pattern, which they consider superfluous [18]. For example, using this approach it is possible to define mobile phone models, such as "IPhone6" and "GalaxyS6", omitting the notion of "Mobile Phone" from the domain model. Important consequences of omitting base types are that the modeler become unable to express whether the instances of a higher-order type (mobile phone model in this example) are disjoint and/or covering types and we are also prevented from determining metaproperties (such as e.g., rigidity) of the base type (mobile phone in this case). It is worth noticing that the deep instantiation approach allows the modeler to represent the base type if it is deemed desirable. However, if the modeler decides to represent the base type, the approach does not provide constructs to represent the relation between it and the higher-order type, not distinguishing thus between the different possible kinds of cross-level relations. As a consequence, the approach does not provide mechanisms to check if the rules concerning these relations are respected, e.g., to guarantee that all instances of the higher-order type ("Mobile Phone Model") specialize the base type ("Mobile Phone").

Telos [19] is a knowledge representation language that supports the representation of types having other types as instances (i.e. *clabjects*). Roughly 30 axioms are defined to formalize Telos' principles for instantiation, specialization, object naming and attribute definition [19]. Although it supports multi-level modeling through its notion of type, it does not elaborate on the nature of cross-level relations between higher-order types and base types. Further, it does not employ systematically the powertype pattern, although we consider it would be possible to extend the Telos built-in support by using its features of user-defined constraints and rules to formally define the cross-level structural relations proposed in MLT.

6 Final Considerations

In this paper, we have addressed multi-level modeling from the perspective of the *powertype pattern*. We have used a well-founded reference theory to support the analysis and revision of the powertype support, demonstrating that the current support lacks *expressivity*, *clarity*, and *parsimony*. By employing the result of this analysis, we propose a UML extension to address the exposed limitations. We use the formal rules of MLT to systematically incorporate syntactic constraints in the profile thus guiding the modeler to produce sound multi-level models. Our approach is able to distinguish properties of the relation between higher-order and base types that cannot be expressed in UML and that are required to represent multi-level classification schemes.

In [3], one of us has evaluated a fragment of UML at light of the Unified Foundational Ontology (UFO). Based on this analysis, a UML extension for the purposes of conceptual modeling (dubbed OntoUML) has been proposed. The ontology was used as a theory to inform the definition of a profile with syntactic constraints that reflect the UFO axioms. In this paper, we have applied a similar approach to extend UML class diagrams using MLT as a theory to incorporate distinctions and constraints for multi-level modeling. In [15], we have already combined MLT and UFO in order to leverage both benefits of the foundational ontology and the multi-level modeling theory. A natural extension of this work is to enrich OntoUML with the support for the powertype pattern as discussed here. Finally, we aim at applying MLT to analyze and enrich the semantics of the so-called deep modeling approaches [5, 18].

Acknowledgments. This research is funded by the Brazilian Research Funding Agencies CNPq (grants number 311313/2014-0, 485368/2013-7, 312158/2015-7 and 461777/2014-2) and CAPES. The authors would like to thank Claudenir M. Fonseca for implementing the Visual Paradigm plugin for the UML profile presented here.

References

1. Halpin, T., Morgan, T.: Information Modeling and Relational Databases. Morgan Kaufmann, San Francisco (2008)
2. Recker, J., Rosemann, M., Green, P., Indulska, M.: Do ontological deficiencies in modeling grammars matter? MIS Q. **35**(1), 57–79 (2011)
3. Guizzardi, G.: Ontological foundations for structural conceptual models. University of Twente, Enschede, The Netherlands (2005)
4. Mayr, E.: The Growth of Biological Thought: Diversity, Evolution, and Inheritance. Belknap Press, Cambridge (1982)
5. Neumayr, B., Grün, K., Schrefl, M.: Multi-level domain modeling with m-objects and m-relationships. In: Proceedings of the 6th Asia-Pacific Conference on Conceptual Modeling, pp. 107–116 (2009)
6. Atkinson, C., Kühne, T.: The essence of multilevel modeling. In: Proceedings of the 4th International Conference on the Unified Modeling Language, pp. 19–33, Toronto, Canada (2001)

7. Gonzalez-Perez, C., Henderson-Sellers, B.: A powertype-based metamodelling framework. Softw. Syst. Model. **5**(1), 72–90 (2006)
8. Odell, J.: Powertypes. J. Object-Oriented Program. **7**(2), 8–12 (1994)
9. Cardelli, L.: Structural subtyping and the notion of powertype. In: Proceedings of the 15th ACM Symposium of Principles of Programming Languages, pp. 70–79 (1988)
10. ISO/IEC: ISO/IEC 24744: Software Engineering – Metamodel for Development Methodologies. ISO, Geneva (2007)
11. Fowler, M.: Analysis Patterns: Reusable Object Models. Addison-Wesley, Boston (1997)
12. OMG: UML Superstructure Specification – Version 2.4.1 (2011)
13. Carvalho, V.A., Almeida, J.P.A.: Towards a Well-Founded Theory for Multi-level Conceptual Modeling (2015, submitted). http://nemo.inf.ufes.br/mlt
14. Carvalho, V.A., Almeida, J.P.A.: A semantic foundation for organizational structures: a multi-level approach. In: 19th IEEE International Enterprise Distributed Object Computing Conference (EDOC 2015), pp. 50–59, Adelaide, Australia (2015)
15. Carvalho, V.A., Almeida, J.P.A., Fonseca, C.M., Guizzardi, G.: Extending the foundations of ontology-based conceptual modeling with a multi-level theory. In: Johannesson, P., et al. (eds.) ER 2015. LNCS, vol. 9381, pp. 119–133. Springer, Heidelberg (2015). doi:10.1007/978-3-319-25264-3_9
16. Guizzardi, G., et al.: Towards ontological foundation for conceptual modeling: the unified foundational ontology (UFO) story. Appl. Ontol. **10**, 259–271 (2015). IOS Press
17. Atkinson, C., Kühne, T.: Meta-level independent modeling. In: International Workshop on Model Engineering (in conjunction with ECOOP 2000), Cannes, France (2000)
18. Atkinson, C., Kühne, T.: Reducing accidental complexity in domain models. Softw. Syst. Model. **7**(3), 345–359 (2008). Springer
19. Jeusfeld, M.A.: Metamodeling and method engineering with conceptbase. In: Jeusfeld, M. A., Jarke, M., Mylopoulos, J. (eds.) Metamodeling for Method Engineering, pp. 89–168. MIT Press, Cambridge (2009)

Mutation Operators for UML Class Diagrams

Maria Fernanda Granda[1,3(✉)], Nelly Condori-Fernández[2],
Tanja E.J. Vos[3], and Oscar Pastor[3]

[1] Computer Science Department, University of Cuenca, Cuenca, Ecuador
fernanda.granda@ucuenca.edu.ec
[2] Vrije Universiteit van Amsterdam, Amsterdam, The Netherlands
n.condori-fernandez@vu.nl
[3] PROS Research Centre, Universitat Politècnica de València, Valencia, Spain
{fernanda.granda,tvos,opastor}@pros.upv.es

Abstract. Mutation Testing is a well-established technique for assessing the quality of test cases by checking how well they detect faults injected into a software artefact (mutant). Using this technique, the most critical activity is the adequate design of mutation operators so that they reflect typical defects of the artefact under test. This paper presents the design of a set of mutation operators for Conceptual Schemas (CS) based on UML Class Diagrams (CD). In this paper, the operators are defined in accordance with an existing defects classification for UML CS and relevant elements identified from the UML-CD meta-model. The operators are subsequently used to generate first order mutants for a CS under test. Finally, in order to analyse the usefulness of the mutation operators, we measure some basic characteristics of mutation operators with three different CSs under test.

Keywords: Mutation testing · Mutation operators · Test cases quality · Conceptual schemas · Class diagram mutation

1 Introduction

A conceptual schema (CS) defines the general knowledge required by an information system in order to perform its functions [1], so that an accurate representation of this information (following the requirements) is a key factor in the successful development of the system, especially in a Model-driven environment context [2]. The development of a conceptual schema is an iterative process involving evaluation of the CS, its accuracy and its improvement from the evaluation results. Testing is a well-established technique that helps to accomplish this task. It provides a level of confidence in the end product based on the coverage of the requirements achieved by the test cases.

In this context, we proposed an approach for testing-based validation of Object-Oriented Conceptual Schemas in a Model-driven environment [3, 4], where one group of engineers (e.g. requirements engineers) specifies requirement models (RM) from which the test scenarios with test cases (i.e. an executable concrete story of a user-system interaction and the expected result) are automatically generated. These test cases are then used to test the conceptual schemas in an early phase of software

© Springer International Publishing Switzerland 2016
S. Nurcan et al. (Eds.): CAiSE 2016, LNCS 9694, pp. 325–341, 2016.
DOI: 10.1007/978-3-319-39696-5_20

analysis and design. Since testing is performed to provide insight into the accuracy of a CS, we need to ensure the test suite quality (i.e. ability to reveal faults).

Mutation testing assesses the quality of a test suite [5] using mutation operators to introduce small modifications or mutations into the software artefact under test, e.g. CS. The artificial faults can be created using a set of mutation operators to change ("mutate") some parts of the software artefact. Mutants can be classified into two types: First Order Mutants (FOM) and Higher Order Mutants (HOM) [6]. FOMs are generated by applying mutation operators only once. HOMs are generated by applying mutation operators more than once [5]. Assuming that the software artefact being mutated is syntactically correct, a mutation operator must produce a mutant that is also syntactically correct. Each faulty artefact version, or mutant, is executed against the test suite. The ratio of detected mutants is known as the "mutation score" and indicates how effective the tests are in terms of fault detection. Approaches that employ mutation testing at higher levels of abstraction, especially on CS, are not common [5].

In Mutation testing the most critical activity is the adequate design of mutation operators so that they reflect the typical defects of the artefact under test. This paper presents the design of a set of mutation operators for Conceptual Schemas (CS) based on Unified Modelling Language (UML) Class Diagrams (CD) [7]. The main potential advantage of mutation operators is to describe precisely the mutants that can generate and thus support a well-defined, fault-injecting process [8]. The main contributions of this paper are:

- It provides a classification of 50 mutation operators for UML CD-based CS, which may be used in evaluating verification[1] and validation[2] approaches. The resulting operators are mainly based on a defects classification reported previously [9].
- It illustrates the application of an effective subset of 18 mutation operators, which generate only first order mutants. These mutation operators were applied to three UML CD-based CS with the aim of showing their usefulness in evaluating testing approaches.

The paper is organized as follows. Section 2 describes an UML CD-based CS. Section 3 reviews the defect types at the model level. Section 4 explains the design process of the mutation operators. Section 5 demonstrates the application of the operators in three CS. Section 6 summarizes related work. Finally Sect. 7 concludes.

2 UML CD-Based Conceptual Schemas

The aim of this work is to design mutation operators for evaluating the effectiveness of test cases in finding faults in a CS during the analysis and design of the software. The defects will be introduced by deliberately changing a UML CD-based CS, resulting in wrong behaviour possibly causing a failure.

---

[1] Verification is to check that the conceptual schema meets its stated functional and non-functional requirements (making the right product) [27].

[2] Validation is to ensure that the conceptual schema meets the customer's expectations (making the product right) [27].

The CS of a system should describe its structure and its behaviour (constraints). In this paper a UML-based class diagram is used to represent such a CS. A class diagram (see Fig. 1) is the UML's main building block that shows elements of the system at an abstract level (e.g. class, association class), their properties (ownedAttribute), relationships (e.g. association and generalization) and operations. In UML an operation is specified by defining pre- and post-conditions. Figure 1 shows an excerpt of the UML structure for a class diagram and highlights eight elements of interest for this work. Finally, mutation testing requires an executable CS for validating the behavioural aspects included in the CS structural elements. Therefore, we used the Action Language for Foundational UML (Alf [10]) and the virtual machine of Foundational UML (fUML [11]) as the execution environment for mutation testing.

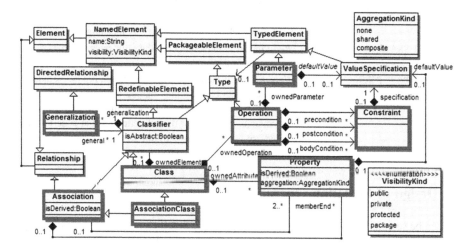

Fig. 1. Excerpt of the meta-model of an UML class diagram [7]

3   Defect Types in UML-Based Conceptual Schemas

An important aspect when applying mutation testing to a CS is that the injected defect should represent common modelling errors. In previous work [5] we classified UML model defects reported in the literature and related the types of the defects with the CS quality goals affected by them. Table 1 summarizes the defect types for CS.

Missing and unnecessary elements (i.e. redundant and extraneous) and incorrectly modelled requirements are the main causes of a design model inaccuracy that can be detected basing on requirement testing. Inconsistency defects require comparing CS versions in order to find them. Finally, ambiguous elements require of user (e.g. modeller, low-level designer) criteria for finding defects.

Table 1. Defect types in a UML-based model (excerpt taken from [9])

Defect cause	Sub modes
MISSING Something is absent that should be present.	
WRONG Something is incorrect, inconsistent or ambiguous	*Inconsistent*: There are contradictions in the models (1) vertical inconsistency (i.e. contradictions between model versions) and (2) horizontal inconsistency (i.e. contradictions between different model views)
	Incorrect: There is a misrepresentation of modelling concepts, their attributes and their relationships, as well as the violation of the rules by combining of these concepts at the time of building partial or complete models
	Ambiguous (wrong wording): The representation of a concept in the model is unclear, and could cause a user (e.g. modeller) to misinterpret its meaning
UNNECESSARY (Extra) Something is present that need not be	*Redundant*: If an element has the same meaning that other element in the model
	Extraneous: If there are items that should not be included in the model because they belong to another level of abstraction, e.g. details of implementation, which are decisions (e.g. type of data structure used at code level) that are left to be made by the developers, and is not specified at an earlier level (e.g. CS)

4 Design of Mutation Operators

As can be seen in Fig. 2, a CS mutant M_i is a faulty CS, which is generated by injecting defects (adding, deleting or changing elements) into modelling elements (see Fig. 1 in Sect. 2) of the original CS. A transformation rule that generates a mutant from the original model is known as a mutation operator. If the mutant is generated by applying only one mutation operator in the original CS, it is a first order mutant (e.g. CS with an added constraint), otherwise, it is a higher order mutant if it applies various changes in the CS by using nested operators. For example, a CS that has been mutated by deleting a class has also evidently deleted associations, properties, constraints, operations and parameters associated with the deleted class. During execution each CS mutant Mi will be run against a test case suite T. If the result of running Mi is different from the result of running CS for any test case in T, then the mutant Mi is said to be "killed", otherwise it is said to have "survived". A CS mutant may survive either because it is equivalent to the original model (i.e. it is semantically identical to the original model although syntactically different) or the test set is inadequate to kill the mutant.

To apply Mutation Analysis in the context of UML CD-based CS we need to formulate mutation operators for CS. Mutation is based on two fundamental hypotheses, namely, the Competent Programmer Hypothesis (CPH) and the Coupling Effect Hypothesis (CEH), both introduced by DeMillo et al. [13]. The CPH states that a program produced by a competent programmer is either correct or near the correct

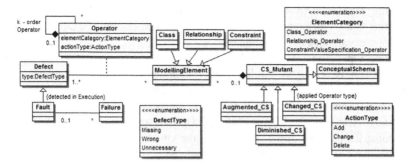

Fig. 2. Relationships among conceptual entities used in the mutant definition (adapted from [12])

version. The CEH states that complex (or higher-order) mutants are coupled to simple mutants in such a way that a test data set that detects all simple faults in a program will detect a high percentage of the complex faults [14]. Consequently, we use the following guiding principles [15]:

- Mutation categories should model potential faults.
- Only syntactically correct mutants should be generated
- Only first-order mutants should be generated.

4.1   Mutation Operators Categories

There are several elements of a CS that can be subject to faults. The defined mutation operator set takes the intrinsic characteristics of a UML CD-based CS into consideration, where some UML elements are composed by other elements. They are thus divided into seven categories: (1) constraint operators, (2) association operators, (3) generalization operators, (4) class operators, (5) attribute operators, (6) operation operators, and (7) parameters operators. Each element-based group is then sub classified according to the three defect types of UML models (i.e. unnecessary, wrong or missing) [9]. However, as our research focuses on defining mutation operators for evaluating testing approaches, the inconsistent and ambiguity defects are not addressed in this work because they generate a faulty CS that is detected without requiring execution (i.e. testing is not required). The faulty CS is not detected by comparing the model against the requirements. Inconsistency defects are detected by comparing models to detect contradictions between them. Ambiguity defect are detected by the modeller which finds that the representation of a concept in the model is unclear. So that twenty-one categories are obtained, such as Unnecessary Constraint (UCO), Wrong Constraint (WCO), Missing Constraint (MCO), Unnecessary Association (UAS), Wrong Association (WAS); Missing Association (MAS) and so on. Based on the UML meta-model (see Fig. 1) and the defects and faults reported in the literature [9, 16–18] we identified CD element features that can be mutated for their usefulness in evaluating testing approaches:

- Mutating Classes: The attributes isAbstract and visibility can be mutated.
- Mutating Class Attributes (i.e. Class Variables): The visibility, isDerived, and data type of the variables can be mutated.
- Mutating Operations: The visibility and returned value type when the operation isQuery can be changed. Additionally, swapping compatible parameters in the definition of an operation can be another operation mutant.
- Mutating Parameters: The data type can be mutated.
- Mutating Associations: The visibility, isDerived can be mutated. Additionally, swapping the member of the Association, the kind aggregation and multiplicity for the members of the Association can be mutated.
- Mutating Generalization: swapping the member of the Generalization.
- Mutating Constraints: Changes the constraints by mutating operators (arithmetic, conditional, and negation), references to class attributes, references to operations.

These categories and the main element features give rise to 50 mutation operators (see Table 4 in Appendix). Each of the 50 mutant operators is represented by a three-letter acronym of its category and a sequential number within its category if it is necessary. Some of these operators resulted in a CS that is determined to be faulty without

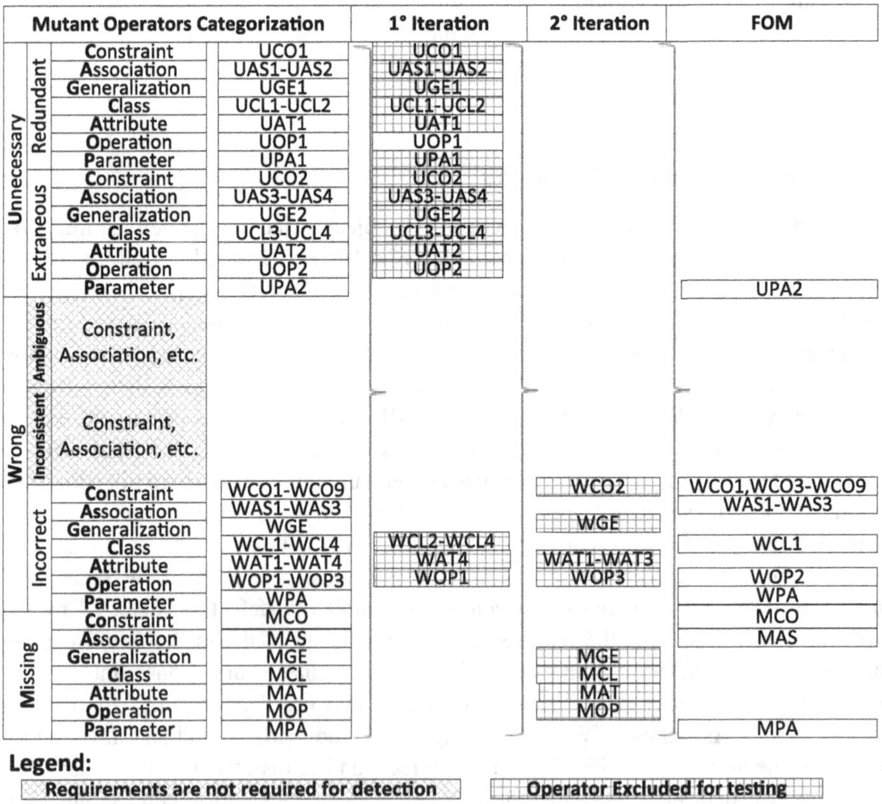

Mutant Operators Categorization			1° Iteration	2° Iteration	FOM
Unnecessary	Redundant	Constraint	UCO1	UCO1	
		Association	UAS1-UAS2	UAS1-UAS2	
		Generalization	UGE1	UGE1	
		Class	UCL1-UCL2	UCL1-UCL2	
		Attribute	UAT1	UAT1	
		Operation	UOP1	UOP1	
		Parameter	UPA1	UPA1	
	Extraneous	Constraint	UCO2	UCO2	
		Association	UAS3-UAS4	UAS3-UAS4	
		Generalization	UGE2	UGE2	
		Class	UCL3-UCL4	UCL3-UCL4	
		Attribute	UAT2	UAT2	
		Operation	UOP2	UOP2	
		Parameter	UPA2			UPA2
Wrong	Ambiguous	Constraint, Association, etc.			
	Inconsistent	Constraint, Association, etc.			
	Incorrect	Constraint	WCO1-WCO9		WCO2	WCO1,WCO3-WCO9
		Association	WAS1-WAS3			WAS1-WAS3
		Generalization	WGE		WGE	
		Class	WCL1-WCL4	WCL2-WCL4		WCL1
		Attribute	WAT1-WAT4	WAT4	WAT1-WAT3	
		Operation	WOP1-WOP3	WOP1	WOP3	WOP2
		Parameter	WPA			WPA
Missing		Constraint	MCO			MCO
		Association	MAS			MAS
		Generalization	MGE		MGE	
		Class	MCL		MCL	
		Attribute	MAT		MAT	
		Operation	MOP		MOP	
		Parameter	MPA			MPA

Legend:

Requirements are not required for detection   Operator Excluded for testing

Fig. 3. Selection process of the mutation operators used for evaluating testing approaches

requiring execution (i.e. testing is not required) and others resulted in behavioural faults (i.e. testing is required). Some of them generate FOM and others HOM. Since we only focus in FOM, 18 mutation operators (see the mutation operators marked with "*" in Table 4) that can generate FOM were obtained through two iterations, as follows (see Fig. 3).

First iteration (Exclude Equivalent and Non-valid Mutants). We obtained a detailed list of actions that involve applying each mutation operator, to obtain the rules for each mutation operator (see Table 4).

If the rule to generate the mutant is not followed, the mutant generated is a non-valid mutant, which can be detected at parser level. For example, the mutation operator MAS causes an association in a CS to be deleted, however, the constraints related with this association must be deleted in order to generate a valid mutant, otherwise this mutant will be detected by the parser and cannot be used for a testing process. We analysed the mutation operators that always generate a non-valid or equivalent mutant. These results are included in Table 4 as a restriction in the operator rule. These mutation operators are described as follows:

- Adding duplicated elements (i.e. UCO1, UAS1, UAS2, UGE1, UCL1, UCL2, UAT1, UOP1 and UPA1) within a scope (redundant type defect) is determined to be faulty without requiring model execution (i.e. testing is not required). Therefore, these operators are not considering in this work.
- A closer inspection of equivalent mutants generated by the WOP2 mutation operator (changes the visibility property of an operation) suggests that this operator generates an equivalent mutant when it is applied to a constructor operation because it only affects the access inherited by child classes (a private constructor of the super class is not inheritable). It is therefore impossible to detect this mutation operator when it is applied to a constructor operation. We therefore have to include this restriction in the rule of the WOP2 mutation operator to avoid generating this type of mutant.
- Changing a navigable association to a shared aggregation or vice versa (WAS2) generates an equivalent mutant because "aggregation = shared" has no semantic effect in a executable model using Alf [10]. Therefore, we only applied this operator changing from aggregation ="none" to aggregation="composite" or vice versa.
- Changing an Association Class to a Class with two associations or vice versa (WCL2 and WCL3). The association class effect can be equivalently modelled when the CS is expressed in Alf [11] (i.e. our execution environment).

The following operators could generate both and equivalent and non-valid mutants:

- Changing the visibility kind of an attribute (WAT4) generates both equivalent and invalid mutants, depending on whether the attribute is accessed internally by any member of the class (it is equivalent because everyone has access) or externally for any constraint that refers to this attribute through an association. In the last case, the mutant is non-valid and is detected by the parser.
- Changing a class abstract or vice versa (WCL4) when it does not result in a fault that the parser will detect when it tries to instantiate the class.

- Adding extraneous elements to CS (i.e. UCO2, UAS3, UAS4, UGE2, UCL3, UCL4, UAT2 and UOP2) generate equivalent mutants. Apparently, these operators did not inject a fault into a CS due to the nature of the test suite: only expected elements are tested. So, any additional element will remain untested. However, the operator that adds a Parameter to an Operation (UPA2) has to be considered because this affects a CS element (operation) that is tested by the test suite and so can be killed. These operators require a structural coverage analysis to be detected.

Finally, the operator that changes the order of the parameters in an operation (WOP1) generates a defect of inconsistency between the signatures of the CS operations and the operation calls from test cases. This defect affects the testing process more than the CS itself and also is detected by the parser. Therefore, this operator is not considered in this work. All the excluded operators generate mutants that require a static (without execution) technique for detecting.

Second Iteration (Exclude High Order Mutants). We next analysed each derivation rule and identified the mutation operators that generate FOM and those that can generate HOM (see in Table 4 the relations between operators). Needless to say, if no other nested elements exist, this mutation operator also generates a FOM. For example, applying an operator to delete an operation (MOP) which has no parameters or related constraints generates a FOM. According to the CEH, the HOM are coupled to simple mutants (FOM) in such a way that a test data set that detects all FOM will detect a high percentage of the HOM. The operators that generate HOM are the following: WCO2, MOP, WCL2, WCL3, WCL4, WAT1, WAT2, WAT3, WOP3, MCL, MGE, MOP and MAT. We added restrictions to several of these operators in order to generate only FOM. Table 4 shows the 18 operators that we used in this work (marked with "*"), which were obtained as products of the described iterations. Figure 4 shows a partial view of a CS in which five mutation operators have been applied. Four operators will generate valid mutants and the MPA operator will generate a non-valid FOM because there is a class attribute (i.e. product_name) that is related with the parameter (p_atr-product_name), therefore more changes (i.e. HOM) are required so as not to be detected by the parser. This CS is used in the literature to explain the development of a requirements model [19] which is used for our test case generation approach. This CS is included in our analysis in Sect. 5.

5   Application and Analysis of Mutation Operators

The quality of mutants depends first on how well they reflect real errors that modellers make and second on whether they can be injected into a CS in such a way that they can be used for mutation testing. In order to analyse the effectiveness of the mutation operators, we used three conceptual schemas and respective test suites, which are described below.

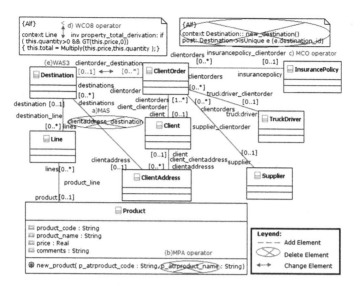

Fig. 4. Excerpt of a UML CD-based CS and the application of five mutation operators

5.1   Conceptual Schemas Under Test

We applied our mutation operators to three CS under test (CSUT) to evaluate the effectiveness of our mutation operators. These CS represent three kinds of systems: (i) the Super Stationery system (SS), which makes use of classes with attributes and derived attributes, associations and constraints but has no generalizations, (ii) an Expense Report management system (ER) that uses fewer classes and relations but more constraints, and lastly, (iii) the Sudoku Game (SG) system [20], which is more variant-rich than the other two CS including generalization relations, derived associations and aggregations. The size of each CSUT is shown in Table 2 in terms of model elements.

Table 2. Elements of the Conceptual Schemas Under Test

Element	Super stationery	Expense report	Sudoku game
Classes	9	7	11
Attributes	44	36	26
Derived attributes	1	6	6
Operations	32	24	19
Parameters	91	75	48
Associations	9	8	6
Derived associations	0	0	2
Composite aggregations	0	0	3
Constraints	12	21	19
Generalizations	0	0	4

5.2 Mutant Generation

We developed a mutation tool prototype [21] to generate and analyse FOMs by applying the 18 selected mutation operators. This tool is divided into three distinct parts: (a) calculate a mutants list, (b) generate the mutants previously calculated; and, (c) performing a syntactic analysis of the mutants. Figure 5 shows the number of valid and non-valid mutants generated by each mutation operator and CSUT.

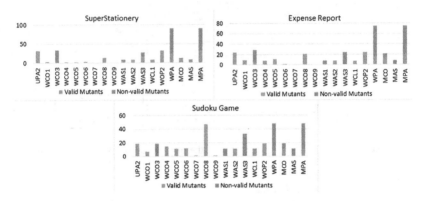

Fig. 5. Valid and non-valid mutants by each mutation operator.

The number of valid mutants produced by the WCO8 is the highest of the three CS (13, 21 and 47 respectively). Operators like UPA2, WCO1, WCO4, WCO5, WCO6, WCO7, WCO8, WCO9, WAS2, WCL1 and WOP2 generated only valid mutants for the CSUTs. However, the WCO7 and WCO9 operators generated only 1 mutant for the CSUT of the Sudoku Game system, giving a total 528 valid mutants (195, 159 and 174 respectively) and 495 non-valid mutants (171, 174, 150 respectively).

5.3 Mutation Testing Results

In this section, we assess the usefulness of the mutation operator for injecting faults in three CSUT. Test suites used in this study include tests checking all the CS class operations and constraints. Finally the data resulting from applying mutation analysis to the CS were collected by applying the following measures.

For a conceptual schema CS and test suite T, M_T let the total number of non-equivalent mutants generated for CS and M_K (T) be the number of mutants killed by T. Mutation score for a test suite (MS (T) = M_K (T)/M_T) is the main measure used in mutation to measure the test suite effectiveness to kill mutants generated by applying all mutation operators. Where, non-equivalent mutants (M_T) = killed mutants (M_K) + the surviving mutants. The following measures, reflecting basic characteristics of mutation operators, were defined to evaluate the usefulness of the mutation operators [18]. Table 3 summarizes results of these calculations.

Table 3. Results of mutation operator evaluation

CS OP	Super stationery			Expense report			Sudoku game		
	CF	MS	II	CF	MS	II	CF	MS	II
UPA2	0.16	1.00	0.080	0.14	1.00	0.064	0.10	1.00	0.119
WCO1	0.01	0.00	0.028	0.05	0.67	0.031	0.04	0.86	0.088
WCO3	0.01	0.50	0.037	0.03	0.80	0.040			
WCO4	0.01	1.00	0.042	0.05	0.75	0.036	0.07	0.54	0.063
WCO5	0.01	1.00	0.042	0.06	0.73	0.033	0.06	0.55	0.073
WCO6	0.01	1.00	0.038	0.01	1.00	0.043	0.06	0.36	0.057
WCO7							0.01	1.00	0.082
WCO8	0.06	0.69	0.034	0.11	1.00	0.054	0.22	0.68	0.058
WCO9							0.01	1.00	0.082
WAS1	0.03	1.00	0.046						
WAS2	0.04	0.00	0.004	0.05	0.0	0.000	0.06	0.00	0.038
WAS3	0.09	0.00	-0.035						
WCL1	0.04	1.00	0.050	0.04	1.00	0.047	0.06	1.00	0.101
WOP2	0.11	1.00	0.028	0.10	1.00	0.018	0.04	1.00	0.053
WPA	0.13	1.00	0.071	0.10	1.00	0.056	0.05	1.00	0.097
MCO	0.05	1.00	0.052	0.09	1.00	0.055	0.06	1.00	0.101
MAS	0.03	1.00	0.046						
MPA	0.16	1.00	0.080	0.13	1.00	0.063	0.06	1.00	0.101

- Contribution Factor of mutation operator MO (CF (MO) = M_T (MO)/M_T). It shows to what extend mutants generated by applying mutation operator MO contributes to the total number of mutants generated for CS.
- Mutation Score of a mutation operator MO (MS (MO, T) = M_K (MO, T)/M_T (MO)). It shows the degree of detection for mutants generated by applying MO.
- Impact Indicator of a mutation operator MO (II (MO, T) = MS (T)-((M_K (T)-M_K (MO, T))/(M_T-M_T (MO))). It shows how the mutation score obtained for T changes when operator MO was not applied.

For the SS, we ran 62 test cases. These test cases were executed against 206 mutated CS created by the mutation operators, killing 82 % of the mutants. In the case of the ER, we executed 88 test cases against 174 mutants created, killing 90 % of the mutants. For the case of the SG, we executed 90 test cases against 185 mutants, killing 74 %. Therefore 89 % of the mutation operators (16/18 operators) generate mutants that can detected by the test suites. More detailed information on the mutation results can be found at https://staq.dsic.upv.es/webstaq/mutuml/mutation_operators.htm.

5.4 Discussion

The results in Table 3 show that the behaviour of the mutation operators may depend on some characteristics of the CS they are applied to (such as complexity of constraints, the number and type of elements included in the CS). However, the results suggest that some of these operators UPA2, WCO7, WCO9, WAS1, WCL1, WOP2, WPA, MCO, MAS, and MPA generated mutants that were relatively easy to detect by the provided test suites (the test suites had mutation scores of 100 %). Moreover, all the operators had a "positive" impact (column value II > 0) in the test suite assessment results. This means that the test suite quality is overestimated when any of these operators is not used. An underestimation of test quality, especially when the test suite is under development, would force an improvement of the test suite, while its overestimation could compromise the quality of any testing performed by them. The mutation operators WCO1, WCO3, WCO4, WCO5, WCO6, WCO8, WAS2 and WAS3 all having a low mutation score, should always be applied because they generate hard to detect mutants and their application would stimulate selection of high quality tests. WAS2 and WAS3 mutation operators suggest that there is a lack of use (test) in the test suite of the CS elements affected by these operators.

Despite the mutation operator restrictions, all these mutation operators generated mutants in one or other of the three CS, these restrictions ensure that the mutants generated meet the condition "mutant has to be syntactically correct for mutation testing". Thus, these operators support a well-defined, fault-injecting process. Finally, mutation testing is computationally expensive, so it is important to use a technique that reduces the computational cost, the restrictions included in the mutation operator rules avoid generating non-valid mutants (495 in total in the three CS), which has practical benefits in the time saved in the mutation testing process. Additionally, the CEH states that complex (or higher-order) mutants are coupled to simple mutants (FOM) in such a way that a test data set that detects all FOM will detect a high percentage of the HOM.

6 Related Work

Mutation Testing has been widely studied since it was first proposed in the 1970s by Hamlet [22] and DeMillo et al. [13]. In 2010, Jia and Harman [5] made a good survey of mutation techniques and also created a repository containing many interesting papers on mutation testing (last updated in 2014). This survey stated that mutation testing is mainly applied at the software implementation level (i.e. more than 50 % of survey papers). But it has also been applied to models at the design level, for example to Finite State Machines [23], State Charts [24] and Activity Diagrams [25].

As far as we know, the idea of applying mutation testing to modify a UML CD-based CS and to assess the quality of test cases by checking how well they detect faults injected into a CS has not been explored to date in practice. However, some similarities can be found in Strug [18, 26] Dinh-Trong et al. [17] and Derezinska [16]. In the former [26], the author introduces nine mutation operators to apply manual mutations to the test suite provided for a UML/OCL-based design model instead of modifying the model, which is a different approach to that used in the present paper. In the latter [18], the author presents a classification of 16 mutation operators defined for constraints specified in OCL and used in UML/OCL-based design models. Constraints are among the CS elements covered by our approach. Dinh-Trong et al. [17] describe a set of mutation operators for a UML class diagram but do not include the restriction on generating valid mutants. Finally, Derezinska introduced a set of mutation operators which can be applied to the UML CD specification but which are evaluated at the code level (C ++) [16].

The present work is based on UML-based model defects classified in a previous work [9]. We also adapted some mutation operators proposed by Derezinska [16], Dinh-Trong et al. [17] and some operators for OCL constraints proposed by Strug [18]. Finally, in our approach the faults introduced include restrictions on generating only valid mutants for detecting in the CS at the analysis and design phases. This differs from current conventional mutation, in which the faults are introduced and detected at the code level.

7   Conclusions and Future Work

Mutation testing applied at the CS level can improve early development of high quality test suites (e.g. elements coverage) and can contribute to developing high quality systems (i.e. it meets requirements) especially in a model-driven context. In this paper we describe a mutation-testing based approach for UML CD-based CS level and report our recent work: (1) classifying a set initial of 50 mutation operators in the context of Conceptual Schemas based on a UML class diagram; (2) selecting and applying 18 mutation operators for FOM to evaluate the usefulness of the mutation operators in three CS. The main potential advantage of the defined mutation operators is that can support a well-defined, fault-injection process.

As opposed to code-based mutation, our mutation operators are based on the element characteristics of a UML CD-based CS and although some of the proposed operators perform syntactic changes at the constraints level, they are mainly focused (i.e. 41 of 50 operators) on the semantic changes of the high-level CD constructs. Our mutation operators are classified according to the element affected by the operator, injected defect type, and the action required by the mutation operator to generate valid mutants (syntactically correct). Since our purpose is to select mutation operators to be used to evaluate testing approaches, the selection process of mutation operators was divided into two iterations. In the first iteration, some operators were excluded because they generated only equivalent mutants (e.g. UCO2, UAS3, UAS4) and non-valid mutants, (e.g. WCL4, UCO1, UAS1), which require a static technique (without CS execution) for detecting (e.g. syntax analysis or structural coverage analysis), and so are not useful for mutation testing. In the second iteration, we aimed to analyse the dependencies between different operators and to reduce the cost of applying mutation testing by selecting 18 mutation operators that generate only first order mutants. Based on the results obtained by applying the mutation testing, 56% (10/18) of our mutant operators generated a high number of killed mutants (score mutation = 100%). These results suggest that these operators generated mutants that are relatively easy to detect by the provided test suites. In the other case 44% (8/18) of the operators related to characteristics of associations (i.e. multiplicity and aggregation type) and constraints generated hard to detect mutants and their application would stimulate selection of high quality tests. However, the behaviour of the mutation operators may depend on the characteristics of the CS they are applied to, such as the number, element type and complexity of constraints.

This study is a part of a more extensive research project, whose principal goal is to propose an approach for testing-based conceptual schema validation in a Model-Driven Environment. Future work will proceed to extend the test suite for stimulating the disabled behaviour detected in this mutation analysis. We hope to evaluate the use of HOMs and compare them with FOMs. Finally, the proposed mutation analysis will be performed on a significant number of CS.

Acknowledgments. This work has been developed with the financial support by SENESCYT of the Republic of Ecuador, European Commission (CaaS project) and Generalitat Valenciana (PROMETEOII/2014/039).

A Appendix

Table 4. Mutation operators defined for a UML CD-based CS

#	Code	Mutation operator rule and relation with other mutation operators
1	UCO1	Adds a redundant constraint to the CD
2	UCO2	Adds an extraneous constraint to the CD
3	UAS1	Adds a redundant association to the CD
4	UAS2	Adds a redundant derived association to the CD. **Relation:** UCO2
5	UAS3	Adds an extraneous association to the CD
6	UAS4	Adds an extraneous derived association to the CD. **Relation:** UCO2
7	UGE1	Adds a redundant generalization to the CD
8	UGE2	Adds an extraneous generalization to the CD
9	UCL1	Adds a redundant class to the CD
10	UCL2	Adds an extraneous class to the CD
11	UCL3	Adds a redundant association class to the CD
12	UCL4	Adds an extraneous association class to the CD
13	UAT1	Adds a redundant attribute to a Class
14	UAT2	Adds an extraneous attribute to a Class
15	UOP1	Adds a redundant operation to a Class
16	UOP2	Adds an extraneous operation to a Class
17	UPA1	Adds a redundant parameter to an Operation
18	UPA2*	Adds an extraneous Parameter to an Operation
19	WCO1*	Changes the constraint by deleting the references to a class Attribute
20	WCO2	Changes the Attribute data type in the constraint. **Relation:** WPA, WAT3
21	WCO3*	Change the constraint by deleting the calls to specific operation
22	WCO4*	Changes an arithmetic operator for another and supports binary operators: +, -, *, /
23	WCO5*	Changes the constraint by adding the conditional operator "not"

(Continued)

Table 4. (*Continued*)

#	Code	Mutation operator rule and relation with other mutation operators
24	WCO6*	Changes a conditional operator for another and supports operators: or, and
25	WCO7*	Changes the constraint by deleting the conditional operator "not"
26	WCO8*	Changes a relational operator for another operators: < , <=, > , >=, ==, !=
27	WCO9*	Changes a constraint by deleting a unary arithmetic operator (-)
28	WAS1*	Interchange the members (memberEnd) of an Association
29	WAS2*	Changes the association type (i.e. normal, composite)
30	WAS3*	Changes the memberEnd multiplicity of an Association (i.e. *-*, 0..1-0..1, *-0..1)
31	WGE	Changes the Generalization member ends. **Relation:** MPA, UPA
32	WCL1*	Changes visibility kind of the Class (i.e. private)
33	WCL2	Changes Class by an Association Class
34	WCL3	Changes Association Class for a Class
35	WCL4	Changes the Class feature "isAbstract "to true
36	WAT1	Changes the Attribute feature "Is Derived" to true. **Relation:** UCO2
37	WAT2	Changes the Attribute property "Is Derived" to false. **Relation:** MCO
38	WAT3	Changes the Attribute data type. **Relation:** WPA, WCO2
39	WAT4	Changes the Attribute visibility property
40	WOP1	Changes the order of the parameters
41	WOP2*	Changes the visibility kind of an operation. **Restriction**. WOP2 has to be applied to operations that are not related with any constraints. **Relation:** MCO
42	WOP3	Changes the data type returned by operation. **Relation:** WAT3
43	WPA*	Changes the Parameter data type (i.e. String, Integer, Boolean, Date, Real). **Restriction**. WPA has to be applied to parameters that are not related with attributes in a constructor operation. To reduce mutants only a change is counted
44	MCO*	Deletes a constraint (i.e. pre-condition, post-condition constraint, body constraint)
45	MAS*	Deletes an Association. **Restriction.** MAS has to be applied to associations that are not related with any constraints. **Relation:** MCO
46	MGE	Deletes a Generalization relation. **Relation:** MPA, UPA
47	MCL	Deletes the class (i.e. normal or association class). **Relation:** MCO, MAT, MOP, MGE
48	MAT	Deletes an Attribute. **Relation:** MPA, MCO
49	MOP	Deletes the operation. **Relation:** MPA, MCO, WCO3
50	MPA*	Deletes a Parameter from an Operation. **Restriction.** This mutation operator has to be applied to operations without related constraints. **Relation:** MCO

References

1. Olivé, A.: Conceptual Modeling of Information System. Springer, Heidelberg (2007)
2. Pastor, O., Molina, J.C.: Model-Driven Architecture in Practice. Springer, Berlin Heidelberg, Cambridge (2007)
3. Granda, M.F.: Testing-based conceptual schema validation in a model-driven environment. In: CAiSE 2013 Doctoral Consortium, Valencia (2013)
4. Granda, M.F., Condori-Fernandez, N., Vos, T.E.J., Pastor, O.: Towards the automated generation of abstract test cases from requirements models. In: 1st International Workshop on Requirements Engineering and Testing, pp. 39–46. IEEE, Karlskrona, Sweden (2014)
5. Jia, Y., Harman, M.: An analysis and survey of the development of mutation testing. Softw. Eng. IEEE Trans. **37**, 1–31 (2011)
6. Jia, Y., Harman, M.: Higher order mutation testing. Inf. Softw. Technol. **51**, 1379–1393 (2009)
7. Object Management Group: Unified Modeling Language (UML) (2015)
8. Andrews, J.H., Briand, L.C., Labiche, Y.: Is mutation an appropriate tool for testing experiments? In: Proceedings of 27th International Conference on Software Engineering, ICSE, pp. 402–411 (2005)
9. Granda, M.F., Condori-fernández, N., Vos, T.E.J., Pastor, O.: What do we know about the defect types detected in conceptual models? In: IEEE 9th International Conference on Research Challenges in Information Science (RCIS), pp. 96–107. IEEE, Athens, Greece (2015)
10. Object Management Group: Action Language for Foundational UML (ALF) (2013)
11. Object Management Group: Semantics of a Foundational Subset for Executable UML Models (fUML) (2012)
12. IEEE: IEEE Standard Classification for Software Anomalies (2010)
13. DeMillo, R., Lipton, R., Sayward, F.G.: Hints on test data selection: help for the practicing programmer. Comput. (Long. Beach. Calif.) **11**, 34–41 (1978)
14. Offutt, J.: Investigations of the software testing coupling effect. ACM Trans. Softw. Eng. Methodol. **1**, 5–20 (1992)
15. Woodward, M.R.: Errors in algebraic specifications and an experimental mutation testing tool. Softw. Eng. J. **4**, 211–224 (1993)
16. Derezińska, A.: Object-oriented mutation to assess the quality of tests. In: Proceedings of Conference on EUROMICRO, pp. 417–420 (2003)
17. Dinh-Trong, T., Ghosh, S., France, R.: A taxonomy of faults for UML designs. In: 2nd MoDeVa workshop - in Conjunction with MoDELS (2005)
18. Strug, J.: Classification of mutation operators applied to design models. Adv. Des. Manuf. **572**, 539–542 (2014)
19. España, S., González, A., Pastor, Ó., Ruiz, M.: Technical Report Communication Analysis and the OO-Method: Manual Derivation of the Conceptual Model the SuperStationery Co. Lab Demo, Valencia (2011)
20. Tort, A., Olivé, A.: Case study: conceptual modeling of basic sudoku. http://guifre.lsi.upc.edu/Sudoku.pdf
21. MutUML Tool. https://staq.dsic.upv.es/webstaq/mutuml.html
22. Hamlet, R.G.: Testing programs with the aid of a compiler. IEEE Trans. Softw. Eng. **SE-3**, 279–290 (1977)
23. Fabbri, S.C., Maldonado, J.C., Masiero, P.C., Delamaro, M.E.: Mutation analysis testing for finite state machines. In: 5th International Symposium Soft Reliability Engineering, pp. 220–229 (1994)

24. Ferraz, S., Maldonado, J.C., Sugeta, T., Masiero, P.: Mutation testing applied to validate specifications based on statecharts. In: Proceedings 10th International Symposium on Software Reliability Engineering, pp. 210–219. IEEE, Boca Raton, FL (1999)
25. Farooq, U., Lam, C.P.: Mutation analysis for the evaluation of AD models. In: International Conference on Computer Intelligent Model Control Automation CIMCA, pp. 296–301 (2008)
26. Strug, J.: Mutation testing approach to evaluation of design models. Adv. Des. Manuf. **572**, 543–546 (2014)
27. Sommerville, I.: Software Engineering. Addison-Wesley, Boston (2011)

Automated Clustering of Metamodel Repositories

Francesco Basciani[1], Juri Di Rocco[1], Davide Di Ruscio[1(✉)], Ludovico Iovino[2],
and Alfonso Pierantonio[1]

[1] Department of Information Engineering, Computer Science and Mathematics,
Università degli Studi dell'Aquila, L'Aquila, Italy
`francesco.basciani@graduate.univaq.it`, {`juri.dirocco,davide.diruscio,`
`alfonso.pierantonio`}`@univaq.it`
[2] Gran Sasso Science Institute, L'Aquila, Italy
`ludovico.iovino@gssi.infn.it`

Abstract. Over the last years, several model repositories have been proposed in response to the need of the MDE community for advanced systems supporting the reuse of modeling artifacts. Modelers can interact with MDE repositories with different intents ranging from merely repository browsing, to searching specific artifacts satisfying precise requirements. The organization and browsing facilities provided by current repositories is limited since they do not produce structured overviews of the contained artifacts, and the ategorization mechanisms (if any) are based on manual activities. When dealing with large numbers of modeling artifacts, such limitations increase the effort for managing and reusing artifacts stored in model repositories. By focusing on metamodel repositories, in this paper we propose the application of clustering techniques to automatically organize stored metamodels and to provide users with overviews of the application domains covered by the available metamodels. The approach has been implemented in the MDEForge repository.

Keywords: Model Driven Engineering · Model repositories · Metamodel clustering · MDEForge

1 Introduction

The increasing adoption of Model-Driven Engineering (MDE) [1] in business organizations led to the need for gathering artifacts in model repositories [2]. Several model repositories (see [3–6] just to mention a few) have been introduced in the past decade. Among them *metamodel zoos* (as for instance the Ecore Zoo[1]) hold metamodels, which are typically categorized to improve search and/or browse operations. However, locating relevant information in a vast repository is intrinsically difficult, because it requires domain experts to manually annotate *all* metamodels in the repository with accurate metadata [7]: an activity that is

---

[1] ATLAS Ecore Zoo: http://www.emn.fr/z-info/atlanmod/index.php/Zoos.

© Springer International Publishing Switzerland 2016
S. Nurcan et al. (Eds.): CAiSE 2016, LNCS 9694, pp. 342–358, 2016.
DOI: 10.1007/978-3-319-39696-5_21

time consuming and prone to errors and omissions. In fact, acquiring knowledge about a software artifact is a challenging task: it is estimated that up to 60 % of software maintenance is spent on comprehension [8].

Software clustering [9] is a well-established discipline, which has found numerous applications in reverse engineering and software maintenance. It promotes the automated categorization of software artifacts (like functions, classes, or files) into high-level structures based on their similarity distance [10]. Software clustering is applied, for instance, to detect misplaced software artifacts [11].

In this paper, in order to mitigate the difficulties related to the manual categorization of metamodels, we propose the application of clustering techniques for metamodel repositories able to automatically organize metamodels into clusters. Mutually similar metamodels are grouped together depending on a proximity measure, whose definition can be given according to specific search and browsing requirements. The approach is based on agglomerative hierarchical clustering [12] (see Sect. 3) and explores well-known proximity measures as well as metamodel-specific ones, each providing different browsing characteristics. The method has been already implemented in the MDEForge repository [13] and it is available online[2]. Furthermore, an evaluation has been conducted by considering different similarity measures, each characterized by specific accuracy and performance indexes. The evaluation permitted also to identify the application domains represented by the metamodels stored in an arbitrary repository.

This paper is structured as follows. In Sect. 2 we illustrate the main characteristics of modeling repositories. Section 3 provides an overview about clustering techniques. In Sect. 4, we present our approach and show how it is able to automatically categorize metamodel repositories. In the next section, the approach is evaluated by applying it to a corpus of about 300 metamodels. A discussion about the results is provided in Sect. 6. In Sect. 7 related work is discussed and finally, in Sect. 8, we conclude and outline future plans.

2 Repositories of Modeling Artifacts in MDE

Modelers can interact with model repositories for several purposes. For instance, as in the case of source code repositories, users can be interested in acquiring knowledge from already developed modeling artifacts that might represent precious know-how to be conveyed to new modelers. Users that have clear requirements about the desired modeling artifacts, can use model repositories with the aim of finding the modeling artifacts that best fit the user needs. Whatever the modeler intents, repositories should provide users with a dedicated support for properly organizing the contained artifacts, and to effectively search and retrieve them. Especially in the case of large repositories, the potential benefits related to the availability of reusable artifacts might be missed if they cannot be suitably discovered. By considering the ways artifacts are organized, and thus the provided searching and browsing functionalities, it is possible to identify different kinds of repositories as discussed below.

---

[2] MDEForge site: http://www.mdeforge.org.

Flat Repositories: They are not structured in the sense that contained artifacts are not categorized, and searching and browsing functionalities are not available. With this kind of repositories we refer to any publicly available collection of artifacts that are stored in a file-system like manner. For instance, it's plenty of GitHub repositories containing modeling artifacts. Modelers are obliged to download and inspect such models in order to gain some insights about them and to check if they might satisfy their requirements.

Manually Classified Repositories Without *Searching and Browsing Functionalities:* Artifacts are manually categorized, and searching and browsing functionalities are not available. For instance, the Ecore Zoo repository consists of an organized list of metamodels. For each metamodel, different attributes are given including a short description about it, and a list of domains where the metamodel can be applied. To search for a specific metamodel in the repository, modelers have to rely on the in-page search facility of the used Web browser. Thus, when searching for specific words, modelers have to manually check where they occur (e.g., in the description, or in the domain attributes). For instance, in the case of the Ecore Zoo, different metamodels are available for supporting the management of projects in organizations, e.g., how to assign tasks and resources. Such metamodels can be identified by searching the string *"project management"* in the Ecore Zoo web page. In addition, also the Maven[3] metamodel is found, as the searched string occurs in its description, although Maven is a building tool thus it refers to a different domain.

Manually Classified Repositories with *Searching and Browsing Functionalities:* Artifacts are manually categorized, searching and browsing functionalities are available. Similarly to repositories like Ecore Zoo, artifacts are manually classified according to a predefined set of labels. The available searching facility permits to give search strings as input and match them against the description field of the available artifacts (e.g., see [2]).

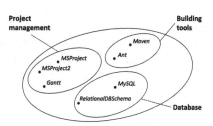

Fig. 1. Example of classified metamodels

Most of the potential benefits of such repositories remain unexploited especially when hundreds or even thousands of modeling artifacts have to be managed. In particular, by focusing on the provided functionalities for organizing, browsing, and searching *metamodels*, all the available repositories are affected by the following challenges:

C1. they do not provide the means to automatically produce structured overviews of the contained metamodels, which are typically shown as merely lists of stored elements, and which are consequently difficult to browse. Organizations like the one shown in Fig. 1 would permit to have an overview of the metamodels stored in the considered repository, e.g., with respect to the covered application domains;

[3] http://maven.apache.org/.

C2. all the available repositories do not provide mechanisms to automatically categorize the stored artifacts, by making the interaction with the repositories complex. Even users that want to contribute with additional artifacts have to manually annotate and classify them during the creation phase. This activity is subject to errors and inaccuracies especially for large repositories, and can compromise the searchability of artifacts. By considering the example shown in Fig. 1, it would be extremely relevant having a mechanism able to automatically assign the metamodel being added to one of the currently available categories (e.g., *building tools*, *database*, and *project management*) or even create a new one if none of them are appropriate.

In the next sections we propose techniques and tools to address these challenges by focusing on the management of metamodels stored in publicly available repositories. We propose the application of an unsupervised metamodel clustering mechanism, which permits to automatically organize unstructured metamodel repositories, and provides the users with overviews of the available metamodels. Thus *manually annotating metamodels is no longer necessary*, since the provided approach is able to automatically catogorize metamodels according to their content and structure.

3 Overview of Clustering Techniques

Clustering is one of the techniques for doing data mining and can be defined as the *process of organizing objects into groups of similar objects* [14]. A cluster is therefore a collection of objects, which are similar between them and are dissimilar to the objects belonging to other clusters [12]. Clustering is also known as *unsupervised classification* since we do not know a priori neither the number of classes nor their attributes. Clustering techniques are applied in a wide spectrum of areas including *biology* to classify plants and animals according to their properties, and *geology* to classify observed earthquake epicenters and thus to identify dangerous zones. Clustering has found numerous applications to *software* as well [9], where it is used in reverse engineering and software maintenance for categorizing software artifacts in many respects. Over the years several clustering methods have been developed like the hierarchical and partitional ones [12]. In the remainder of the section we focus on the hierarchical clustering technique since it underpins the approach proposed in the next section.

Hierarchical clustering produces a nested set of groups based on a criterion for merging or splitting clusters based on similarity. The nested grouping and similarity levels obtained by means of hierarchical algorithms are typically represented by means of *dendrograms* like the one in Fig. 2b.

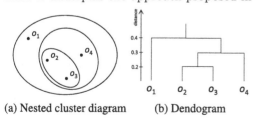

(a) Nested cluster diagram   (b) Dendogram

Fig. 2. Explanatory hierarchical clustering example

By cutting the dendrogram at a desired distance *threshold,* a clustering of the data objects into disjoint groups is obtained. For instance, by considering the example in Fig. 2 if we choose as distance threshold the value 0.25 we obtain three clusters, i.e., $\{o_1, \{o_2,o_3\}, \{o_4\}\}$. With the threshold value 0.35 the obtained clusters are $\{o_1, \{o_2,o_3,o_4\}\}$. Hierarchical clustering methods can be *agglomerative* or *divisive.* The former starts with one object clusters and recursively merges two or more of the most similar clusters. The latter starts with a single cluster consisting of all the elements in the source data set and recursively split the clusters according to some criterion for obtaining at the end of the process a partition of one object clusters (named singleton clusters hereafter) [14].

Algorithm 1. Basic agglomerative hierarchical clustering algorithm

---

1: Compute the proximity graph;
2: Merge the closest (most similar) two clusters;
3: Update the proximity matrix to reflect the proximity between the new cluster and the original clusters;
4: Repeat steps 3 and 4 until only a single cluster remains;

All the existing clustering methods share the fact that they can be applied when it is possible to specify a *proximity (or distance) measure* that permits to assess if elements to be clustered are mutually similar or dissimilar. The basic idea is that the *similarity level of two elements is inversely proportional to their distance.* The definition of the proximity measure plays a key role in any clustering method and it depends on many factors including the considered application domain, available data, and goals. Once the proximity measure is defined, it is possible to produce a proximity matrix, which is an n by n matrix (where n is the number of objects to be clustered) containing all the pairwise similarities or dissimilarities between the considered objects. For instance, by considering a simple data set O consisting of the objects o_1, o_2, o_3, and o_4, a corresponding proximity matrix based on a sample similarity function $s : O \rightarrow [0,1]$ can be given like the one shown in Fig. 3a.

	o_1	o_2	o_3	o_4
o_1	1	0.65	0.43	0.45
o_2	0.65	1	0.2	0.6
o_3	0.43	0.2	1	0.3
o_4	0.45	0.6	0.3	1

(a) Proximity matrix

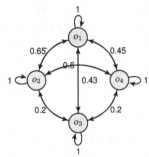

(b) Proximity graph

Fig. 3. Sample proximity matrix and graph

A proximity matrix induces the definition of a weighted graph (like the one shown in Fig. 3b) where nodes are the objects being clustered, and weighted edges represent the similarities between the connected objects. The availability of proximity graphs permits to see the clustering problem from a graph point of view as that of breaking the graph into connected components, one for each cluster [15]. By focusing on the *agglomerative hierarchical clustering,* a basic algorithm would use the proximity graph as shown in Algorithm 1 borrowed from [16]:

It is worth noting that to execute such a clustering algorithm a notion of *cluster proximity* is necessary to execute the second step of the algorithm. To this end, three different definitions of cluster distance can be used, namely *single link*, *complete link*, and *group average* [16]. With the single (complete) link definition, the proximity of two clusters is defined as the minimum (maximum) distance between any two objects in the considered clusters. Whereas, with the group average technique, the proximity of two clusters is the average pairwise proximities of all pairs of objects from the considered clusters.

In the next section we discuss how the traditional clustering concepts previously outlined can be employed in the context of metamodel repositories.

4   Proposed Metamodel Clustering Approach

In order to deal with the issues discussed in Sect. 2 in this section we show how to apply clustering techniques in the domain of model-driven engineering. The proposed approach is able to automatically organize metamodels stored in a given repository by analysing their content and not their metadata that might be erroneous or misplaced. An overview of the approach is given in Sect. 4.1, its implementation is presented in Sect. 4.2.

4.1   Overview

The main functionalities of the proposed clustering approach are shown in Fig. 4. It is important to remark that the figure shows only the functionalities strictly related to the automated classification of metamodels. For an overview about the typically provided functionalities of existing model repositories, interested readers can refer to [17]. As shown in Fig. 4, two different user roles are involved in the proposed clustering approach namely the *Repository Maintainer* and the *Repository User* discussed in the following.

Repository Maintainer: The application of the whole metamodel clustering approach is performed by the maintainer of the repository who can have access to the functionalities described below.

Apply Metamodel Clustering: It represents the key functionality of the proposed clustering approach. It consists of calculating the proximity matrix (as shown in Sect. 3) representing the similarities of all the metamodels available in the repository, and then applying the clustering algorithm in Algorithm 1.

Manage Singleton Clusters: When a new metamodel is being added to the repository, it may happen that according to the used proximity measure it does not fit in any of the existing clusters and consequently it induces the creation

Fig. 4. Actors and use cases of the proposed approach

of a singleton cluster, i.e., a cluster consisting of only one element. The repository maintainer can periodically consider the available singleton clusters and verify if they have been created, e.g., because the used proximity measure has to be refined.

Refine the Proximity Measure: The proximity measure plays a key role in the whole clustering approach, and consequently its definition is an iterative process, aiming at increasing the accuracy of the automatically obtained metamodel clusters. The refinement process relies on the availability of reference data, which are typically obtained by manual activities. Such data must be approximated by the automated clustering procedure as discussed in the next section.

Repository User: Similarly to what happens in the case of open source software, the availability of public model repositories can give place to multitudes of users and developers that are willing to share their modeling artifacts. In this respect, by focusing on the metamodel clustering aspects, the proposed approach provides the users with the functionalities discussed below.

Add New Metamodel: In contrast with existing metamodel archives, users that add new metamodels in the repository can omit the specification of corresponding metadata. Even in such cases, the provided approach is able to automatically classify the new metamodels. In fact the appropriate clusters are identified by considering the content of the metamodels without the need for additional user input. However, as previously mentioned, it might happen that newly added metamodels do not fit in any of the existing clusters. Then, the repository maintainer takes care of such situations by means of the functionality *Manage Singleton Clusters* shown in Fig. 4.

Visualize Metamodel Clusters: The approach produces overviews of the automatically produced metamodel clusters. Thus in addition to the list of available metamodels, the system is able to generate graphical representations of the available metamodel clusters, and gives also the means to navigate them and to retrieve detailed information about their content if requested by the user.

4.2 Supporting Tool

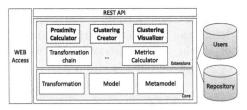

Fig. 5. MDEForge architecture

The proposed clustering method has been implemented as extensions in the MDEForge platform. In particular, as shown in Fig. 5, MDEForge consists of *core* services that are provided to enable the management of modeling artifacts, namely transformations, models, and metamodels. Atop of such core services, *extensions* can be developed to add new functionalities. For instance, in [18] we propose a service to automatically compose model transformations according to user requirements. We have also developed extensions to calculate several metrics on stored artifacts, and to support the understanding of metamodel and transformation characteristics [19,20].

In the remainder of the section, we give details about the extensions that are shown in Fig. 5 in bold and that we have developed to support the proposed clustering approach. Concerning the other services of MDEForge the reader can refer to [13,17].

Proximity Calculator: It plays a key role in the proposed clustering approach since it is responsible of calculating the mutual similarities between all the metamodels and thus create a corresponding proximity matrix like the one shown in Fig. 3a. Such calculations rely on the definition of a given similarity measure. As discussed in Sect. 3 identifying the appropriate similarity measure is a difficult task that might depend on the available data set, on the considered application domain, on the goal of the analysis being performed, etc. [12]. Consequently, from an architectural point of view, the proximity calculator has been designed in terms of an interface consisting of a method `calculateSimilarity(Metamodel` mm_1, `Metamodel` mm_1), and then different concrete implementations can be provided. So far we have developed different similarity measures already available in the system even though we plan to experiment and provide additional ones. In particular, several similarity measures have been proposed in literature [14]. Among those typically applied to text documents we have considered the *cosine similarity* [14] and the *Dice's coefficient* [21] with the aim of relating the similarity of two metamodels on the terms used therein and consequently on the corresponding application domains. In particular:

- *Cosine similarity:* given two documents represented as term vectors, the similarity of the input documents corresponds to the correlation between the derived vectors. Such a correlation is calculated as the cosine of the angle between vectors [14]. In order to apply such a similarity measure on metamodels, for each of them we derive the corresponding string by borrowing the serialization mechanisms available in EMF-REST[4];
- *Dice's coefficient:* it is defined as twice the number of common bigrams (i.e., pairs of adjacent letters in the string) in the compared strings divided by the total number of terms in both strings [21]. Similarly to the application of the cosine similarity, to calculate the Dice's coefficient between two metamodels, we first derive a string serialization of them.

We have developed also two additional similarity functions specifically conceived for modeling artifacts. Both of them rely on the matching model calculated by means of EMFCompare[5]:

- *Match-based similarity:* it is defined as the total number of matched elements identified by EMFCompare divided by the total number of elements contained in the analysed couple of metamodels;
- *Containment-based similarity:* the previous index does not perform well when one of the input metamodels is contained in the other one. As an example we

---

[4] http://emf-rest.com/.

[5] http://www.eclipse.org/emf/compare/.

can consider the full specification of UML and the UML Class Diagrams. In such cases the match-based similarity value would be very low since the total number of matched elements would be much lesser than the total number of elements contained in the two metamodels. In order to deal with such cases, the containment-based similarity is defined as the total number of matched elements divided by the lesser of the total elements in the two input metamodels.

The application on a concrete data set of the measures used by the proximity calculator is in-depth discussed in the next section.

Clustering Creator: By using the proximity calculator previously discussed, it creates clusters of metamodels by applying the agglomerative hierarchical clustering algorithm shown in Algorithm 1. As to the cluster proximity calculation, which is performed during each iteration of the algorithm, it is possible to specify the distance to be used, i.e., single link, complete link, and group average (see Sect. 3).

Cluster Visualizer: It creates graphical and tabular representations of the calculated metamodel clusters. The user can explore the available metamodels by specifying the similarity measure to be applied, and the threshold value used to filter the identified metamodels pairs and show only those that have a similarity value greater than the given threshold. The left hand side of Fig. 6 shows the cluster visualizer at work. In particular, the shown connected graphs represent the identified clusters and the thickness of the edges is proportional to the proximity value of the connected metamodels represented as nodes in the graph. For each cluster, the system permits to retrieve additional information as shown in the upper right-hand side of Fig. 6. In particular, given a cluster all the contained metamodels are listed together with additional information like

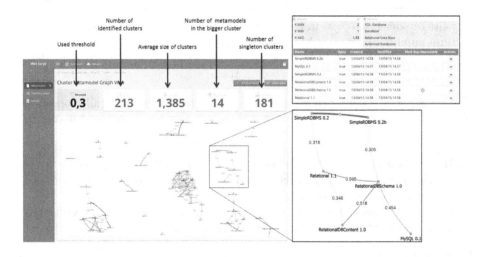

Fig. 6. Sample visualizations of automatically created metamodel clusters

the most representative metamodel, i.e., the one most connected with the other ones in the cluster. Additionally, metamodels can be downloaded or even viewed by means of an integrated tree-based editor.

It is important to remark that the platform is modular in the sense that interested developers can extend or even substitute the provided services, for instance, to refine the proximity measures if the proposed ones do not properly meet their requirements.

5   Evaluation of the Proposed Metamodel Clustering Approach

In this section we discuss the application of the clustering approach on a concrete data set consisting of 295 metamodels retrieved from the Ecore Zoo. The main goal of this section is to discuss the ability of the clustering method *(i)* to automate the creation of metamodel groups according to different similarity measures, and *(ii)* to provide the user with organized and interactive views of the metamodel repository. We have applied the clustering technique by using the four similarity functions discussed in the previous section and by specifying different thresholds.

In order to evaluate the calculated clusters we have applied a clustering validation technique based on *external criteria* [22]: the final goal is to validate the results of the employed clustering technique comparing them with the manually pre-specified clusters.

Experimental Setting and Dataset. We have downloaded all the metamodels from the Ecore Zoo and we have manually grouped them with respect to their content and the domain descriptions when available. Thus, we have individually analysed the metamodels and incrementally defined the metamodel clusters. At the end of this manual process, that took about two working days of one senior researcher with a consolidated expertise in metamodeling and model-driven engineering, we identified 90 groups, including 43 singleton[6]. Each group represents a specific application domain, e.g., database management, project management, building tools, and model transformation languages. Subsequently, we have applied on the downloaded metamodels the proposed clustering approach by using the four similarity functions previously discussed and by shifting the thresholds from the value of 0.1 to 1.0 with 0.05 steps. Clearly, a too low threshold corresponds to consider the repository population almost undistinguished, whilst a too high threshold returns too many clusters with too few elements. The manually identified clusters and those automatically created are analysed as discussed later on this section.

---

[6] All the manipulated data are reported in the spreadsheet publicly available at https://goo.gl/aogGqs.

Table 1. Calculated metamodel clusters

(a) Cosine similarity

Thrsd	#clst	Avg. clst size	Max clst size	#non-sing clst	Corr. with IM
0.1	14	21.071	282	1	0.16
0.15	25	11.800	264	4	0.23
0.2	48	6.146	224	7	0.31
0.25	86	3.430	186	8	0.39
0.3	113	2.218	127	15	0.45
0.35	170	1.735	63	24	0.48
0.4	201	1.468	31	29	**0.49**
0.45	215	1.372	22	28	**0.49**
0.5	227	1.300	15	24	**0.49**
0.55	236	1.250	14	20	**0.49**
0.6	245	1.204	14	17	0.48
0.65	249	1.850	14	15	0.46
0.7	250	1.180	14	16	0.45
0.75	256	1.152	13	13	0.44
0.8	261	1.130	12	13	0.42
0.85	264	1.117	11	14	0.40
0.9	271	1.089	8	12	0.39
0.95	283	1.042	4	9	0.37

(b) Dice's coefficient

Thrsd	#clst	Avg. clst size	Max clst size	#non-sing clst	Corr. with IM
0.1	1	295	295	1	0.00
0.15	1	295	295	1	0.02
0.2	1	295	295	1	0.03
0.25	1	295	295	1	0.04
0.3	1	295	295	1	0.05
0.35	2	147.5	294	1	0.06
0.4	2	147.5	294	1	0.08
0.45	2	147.5	294	1	0.10
0.5	7	42.143	289	1	0.14
0.55	17	17.353	279	1	0.20
0.6	55	5.364	230	7	0.28
0.65	146	2.021	91	25	0.41
0.7	207	1.425	47	22	0.48
0.75	230	1.283	14	24	**0.49**
0.8	242	1.219	14	23	0.47
0.85	254	1.161	14	16	0.44
0.9	263	1.122	8	15	0.41
0.95	273	1.081	8	12	0.38

(c) Match-based similarity

Thrsd	#clst	Avg. clst size	Max clst size	#non-sing clst	Corr. with IM
0.1	45	6.555	228	8	0.26
0.15	96	3.072	152	20	0.41
0.2	157	1.878	72	28	0.50
0.25	192	1.536	19	32	**0.52**
0.3	214	1.378	14	32	0.50
0.35	227	1.299	14	26	0.48
0.4	234	1.260	14	24	0.47
0.45	238	1.239	14	25	0.46
0.5	245	1.204	14	21	0.45
0.55	250	1.180	13	18	0.44
0.6	256	1.152	12	15	0.43
0.65	257	1.148	12	15	0.42
0.7	259	1.139	12	16	0.41
0.75	263	1.122	8	17	0.40
0.8	268	1.101	6	16	0.39
0.85	272	1.085	4	14	0.38
0.9	280	1.054	4	12	0.37
0.95	288	1.024	3	6	0.35

(d) Containment-based similarity

Thrsd	#clst	Avg. clst size	Max clst size	#non-sing clst	Corr. with IM
0.1	2	147.5	294	1	0.08
0.15	2	147.5	294	1	0.09
0.2	2	147.5	294	1	0.12
0.25	4	73.75	292	1	0.16
0.3	11	26.818	284	2	0.20
0.35	15	19.667	275	3	0.24
0.4	18	16.389	273	2	0.29
0.45	40	7.375	241	6	0.36
0.5	66	4.470	213	6	0.40
0.55	73	4.041	204	7	0.41
0.6	144	2.049	121	18	0.47
0.65	167	1.766	72	23	0.49
0.7	189	1.561	21	30	0.49
0.75	215	1.372	16	28	0.50
0.8	223	1.323	16	24	**0.51**
0.85	228	1.294	16	22	**0.51**
0.9	233	1.266	14	21	**0.51**
0.95	239	1.243	14	17	0.50

(e) Execution time

Cosine similarity	Dice's coefficient	Match-based similarity	Containment-based similarity
≈ 10min	≈5min	≈4 hours	

Evaluation Metrics. The manually defined clusters are used to generate the incidence matrix I defined as follows:

$$I(i,j) = \begin{cases} 1 & \text{if } mm_i \text{ and } mm_j \text{ are grouped in the same cluster} \\ 0 & \text{otherwise} \end{cases} \quad (1)$$

where $i, j = 1, \ldots, n$, and mm_i and mm_j are metamodels in the data set manually processed. Moreover, for each selected threshold and similarity function we binarized the calculated similarity matrix. The basic idea of binarization consists in the introduction of binary values associated to the similarity values. Each binary value is 1 if the numerical value to which it is associated has a value above a certain *threshold*, 0 otherwise. More formally, a similarity matrix S is binarized in $B(S)$ as follow:

$$B(S(i,j)) = \begin{cases} 1 & \text{if } Sim(mm_i, mm_j) \geq threshold \\ 0 & \text{otherwise} \end{cases} \tag{2}$$

where $i, j = 1, \ldots, n$, and mm_i and mm_j are metamodels in the corpus, and Sim is the considered similarity measure.

Inspired by the external validation technique discussed in [22], we have validated the metamodel clustering approach by measuring the similarity between the incidence matrix I, and the binarized similarity matrix $B(S)$ induced by the adopted similarity measure and threshold. Intuitively, the more similar the incidence matrix I and $B(S)$ are the better is the considered clustering technique. To this end we have applied the MATLAB `corr2` function[7] that returns the correlation coefficient in the range of -1.00 (perfect negative correlation) and +1.00 (perfect positive correlation) between two matrices or vectors of the same size. A correlation with value 0 indicates that the two considered elements are not correlated.

Data Analysis. The outcomes of the performed experiments are reported in Table 1. In particular, for each similarity function and threshold (denoted with *Thrsd* in the table) the following data are shown:

- *#clst*: the number of identified clusters;
- *Avg. clst size*: the average number of metamodels in each cluster;
- *Max clst size*: the number of metamodels in the bigger cluster;
- *#non-sing clst*: the number of clusters consisting of more than one metamodel;
- *Corr. with IM*: it indicates the correlation index between the automatically calculated clusters and the one manually identified.

It is worth noting that the data reported in the tables can be reproduced by interacting with the cluster visualizer component discussed in the previous section, which permits to select the similarity measure and the preferred similarity threshold. The graphical representation of the retrieved clusters is updated in real time accordingly.

According to the calculated correlations shown in the last column of Table 1(a–d), the match-based similarity with 0.25 as threshold value optimally approximates the metamodel clusters that we have manually defined. However, according to Table 1e the match-based similarity is also one of the most time consuming measure like the containment-based similarity one. The text-based similarity measures take less time than that required by the structural-based similarities. This result depends on the matching function of EMFCompare, that

---

[7] http://it.mathworks.com/help/images/ref/corr2.html.

is exponential and depends on the number of all the elements contained in all the possible metamodels couples. This is not the case of text-based similarities that instead are based on the textual distance between the vectors encoding as strings the metamodels being analysed.

6   Discussion

The main strengths of the approach proposed in this paper are related to the advantages of classifying metamodels in repositories in an automated way instead of using manual techniques that are strongly correlated to the maintainer background. This permits to relieve maintainers and contributors of the responsibility of annotating metamodels, which is beneficial for the accuracy of core functionalities such as searching and browsing. Nevertheless, the approach as proposed in this paper can be enhanced in different directions as discussed below.

Similarity Measure: The generation of metamodel clusters strongly depends on the adopted similarity measure. Depending on the purpose of the desired clustering, a corresponding measure has to be properly selected from existing ones in literature or even defined from scratch. As we have presented in Sect. 4, besides using two similarity measures that are commonly applied to text documents, we have developed two additional similarity measures (namely match-based and containment-based) that are model specific (in fact, they rely on the match models calculated by EMFCompare). However, even if we restrict our focus on metamodels, it is unlikely to define a similarity measure that meets the requirement of any modeler. This justifies the decision of conceiving an extensible proximity calculator that can be enriched by adding the implementation of further similarity measures that the user can then select and play with from the front-end of the application.

Performance: The complexity of hierarchical agglomerative algorithms is $O(n^2 \ log \ n)$ [12] with n the number of elements in the considered data set. Consequently, for very large data sets the adoption of alternative algorithms is suggested. The hierarchical agglomerative clustering technique used in this work is only one of the many possible ones. Moreover, the developed supporting tool is agnostic of the clustering technique. It is important to remark that the developed system nightly updates all the proximity matrices in order to consider in the clustering calculation also newly added metamodels. Thus users do not experiment performance issues when playing with the cluster visualizer since all the required data are already pre-calculated.

Cluster Characterizations: In the current version of the approach each metamodel is assigned to exactly one cluster only. However, in some cases a given metamodel might belong to different clusters simultaneously. Moreover, by exploiting the content of the considered metamodels and the corresponding descriptions, when available, it can be possible to create cluster labels automatically. Supporting such characterizations represents a relevant improvement that we intent to investigate in the future.

Experimentation and Evaluation: The implementation of the approach has been applied by considering the metamodels available in the Ecore Zoo. However, to better assess the validity of the approach and of the optimal parameters presented in the previous section, and to obtain more extensive feedback, it is necessary to consider an extended data set consisting of additional metamodels that can be retrieved from further repositories like ReMoDD.

7 Related Work

Clustering techniques have been used in several applications including software and data comprehension, data migration, and reverse engineering.

In [23] authors use clustering techniques and Model-Driven Reverse Engineering principles for software comprehension. In particular, authors start by extracting data from source code for the input data matrix construction. For the code extraction, they consider the paragraph as the smallest atomic unit and their cluster analysis is based on the hypothesis that record fields existing in the same paragraphs can be grouped. For the data matrix the chosen distance of similarity for the cluster identification is the Euclidean distance. In [24] authors propose a software automatic categorization system called MUDABlue, based on Latent Semantic Analysis (LSA), which is a method to extract and represent the usage of words in texts by means of statistical computations. Similarly to our approach, [23, 24] propose techniques able to automatically categorize set of similar objects. Whereas they focus on software comprehension, our approach specifically focuses on metamodels stored in repositories.

In [25] authors present a methodology for handling the problem of database migration. The approach uses semantic clustering to facilitate the translation of extended entity relationship schema into complex objects schema. They start from an Extended Entity Relationships (EER) schema to create a set of clustered schemata such that each clustered schema corresponds to a level of abstraction and grouping of the initial schema. By iteratively shrinking portions of EER diagram into complex entities, the approach creates a schema of entities by adding a layer of abstraction. The user can select a level of clustering to show components at some degree of detail exactly like we do in our approach.

In [26] authors present an approach to support the visualization of large-scale diagrams, which are decomposed into clusters of model elements. Graph clustering techniques are employed by defining the node similarity in terms of node distance. Differently to our approach, in [26] authors apply clustering techniques to create sub-models whereas in our approach we categorize metamodels without splitting their contents.

The work in [27] presents a technique, which is based on metamodeling, Petri nets, and Facets for the analysis and clustering of requirements diagrams. Intuitively, the approach is able to obtain the domain description in terms of the relations and dependencies of modeled services. Then the analysis and the clustering of requirements are automatically calculated accordingly. The work in [28] presents a semi-automatic technique for the construction of feature models based on requirements clustering. This approach automates the activities of feature identification and reorganization using clustering techniques. Starting from an existing system, the main idea is that tight-related individual functional requirements are clustered into features, and functional features are organized into an application feature model, which is then merged into a domain feature model. Differently to our approach, [27,28] are specifically conceived for the management of functional requirements, and clustering techniques are employed at model level.

8   Conclusion and Future Work

In this paper, we studied the problem of the automated categorization of metamodel repositories. The proposed approach adopted an agglomerative hierarchical clustering algorithm, which according to different similarity metrics (some of them specifically devised for metamodels) detects the application domains represented in an arbitrary repository. The effect of these similarity metrics is evaluated over a corpus of metamodels: while metamodel-specific similarities perform better at the price of a high execution-time, generic text-based similarities still offer acceptable accuracy with much better execution-time.

Future plans include a more systematic experimentation of the available similarity metrics to provide repository maintainers with tools, which can offer to the user a multi-dimensional browsing experience. In addition, we are interested in understanding how to use the variance between the incidence matrix and the experimental data as a feedback to improve similarity measures. We plan to experiment the application of clustering techniques also on other sets of modeling artifacts, like models and model transformations. In particular, we want to investigate to what extent it is possible to substitute model transformations that have source and/or target metamodels in common belonging to the same clusters. Positive results in such direction might be beneficial for enhancing the reuse of model transformations.

References

1. Schmidt, D.C.: Guest editor's introduction: model-driven engineering. Computer **39**, 25–31 (2006)
2. France, R.B., Bieman, J.M., Mandalaparty, S.P., Cheng, B.H.C., Jensen, A.: Repository for Model Driven Development (ReMoDD). In: Proceedings of 34th International Conference on Software Engineering (ICSE), pp. 1471–1472. IEEE (2012)
3. Hein, C., Ritter, T., Wagner, M.: Model-driven tool integration with modelbus. In: Workshop Future Trends of Model-Driven Development at International Conference on Enterprise Information Systems (ICEIS), pp. 50–52 (2009)
4. Karasneh, B., Chaudron, M.R.V.: Online Img2UML repository: an online repository for UML models. In: Proceedings of the 3rd International Workshop on Experiences and Empirical Studies in Software Modeling at MoDELS, pp. 61–66 (2013)
5. Koegel, M., Helming, J.: EMFStore: a model repository for EMF models. In: Proceedings of the 32nd ACM/IEEE International Conference on Software Engineering, ICSE 2010, pp. 307–308. ACM (2010)

6. Kutsche, R., Milanovic, N., Bauhoff, G., Baum, T., Cartsburg, M., Kumpe, D., Widiker, J.: BIZYCLE: model-based interoperability platform for software and data integration. In: Proceedings of MDTPI at ECMDA (2008)

7. Bislimovska, B., Bozzon, A., Brambilla, M., Fraternali, P.: Textual and content-based search in repositories of web application models. ACM Trans. Web **8**, 11:1–11:47 (2014)

8. Bourque, P., Dupuis, R., Abran, A., Moore, J.W., Tripp, L.L.: The guide to the software engineering body of knowledge. IEEE Softw. **16**, 35–44 (1999)

9. Anquetil, N., Fourrier, C., Lethbridge, T.C.: Experiments with clustering as a software remodularization method. In: Proceedings of the Sixth Working Confernce on Reverse Engineering, WCRE 1999, pp. 235–255. IEEE Computer Society (1999)

10. Beck, F., Diehl, S.: On the impact of software evolution on software clustering. Empirical Softw. Eng. **18**, 970–1004 (2012)

11. Vanya, A., Holland, L., Klusener, S., van de Laar, P., van Vliet, H.: Assessing software archives with evolutionary clusters. In: 16th International Conference on Program Comprehension, pp. 192–201. IEEE (2008)

12. Jain, A.K., Murty, M.N., Flynn, P.J.: Data clustering: a review. ACM Comput. Surv. (CSUR) **31**, 264–323 (1999)

13. Basciani, F., Di Rocco, J., Di Ruscio, D., Di Salle, A., Iovino, L., Pierantonio, A.: MDEForge: an extensible web-based modeling platform. In: Proceedings of CloudMDE at MoDELS, pp. 66–75(2014)

14. Berkhin, P.: A survey of clustering data mining techniques. In: Kogan, J., Nicholas, C., Teboulle, M. (eds.) Grouping Multidimensional Data, pp. 25–71. Springer, Heidleberg (2006)

15. Steinbach, M., Ertöz, L., Kumar, V.: The challenges of clustering high dimensional data. In: Wille, L.T. (ed.) New Directions in Statistical Physics, pp. 273–309. Springer, Heidelberg (2004)

16. Tan, P.N., Steinbach, M., Kumar, V.: Introduction to Data Mining. Pearson Education, London (2006). Chapter 8

17. Di Rocco, J., Di Ruscio, D., Iovino, L., Pierantonio, A.: Collaborative repositories in model-driven engineering. IEEE Softw. **32**(3), 28–34 (2015)

18. Gomes, C., Barroca, B., Amaral, V.: Classification of model transformation tools: pattern matching techniques. In: Dingel, J., Schulte, W., Ramos, I., Abrahão, S., Insfran, E. (eds.) MODELS 2014. LNCS, vol. 8767, pp. 619–635. Springer, Heidelberg (2014)

19. Di Rocco, J., Di Ruscio, D., Iovino, L., Pierantonio, A.: Mining correlations of ATL model transformation and metamodel metrics. In: Proceedings of the Seventh International Workshop on Modeling in Software Engineering, MiSE 2015 - ICSE, pp. 54–59. IEEE Press (2015)

20. Di Rocco, J., Di Ruscio, D., Iovino, L., Pierantonio, A.: Mining metrics for understanding metamodel characteristics. In: 6th International Workshop on Modeling in Software Engineering, MiSE 2014 - ICSE, Hyderabad, India, 2–3 June 2014, pp. 55–60 (2014)

21. Dice, L.R.: Measures of the amount of ecologic association between species. Ecology **26**, 297–302 (1945)

22. Halkidi, M., Batistakis, Y., Vazirgiannis, M.: On clustering validation techniques. J. Intell. Inf. Syst. **17**, 107–145 (2001)

23. El Beggar, O., Bousetta, B., Taoufiq, G.: Comparative study between clustering and model driven reverse engineering approaches. Lect. Notes Softw. Eng. **1**(2) (2013)

24. Kawaguchi, S., Garg, P.K., Matsushita, M., Inoue, K.: Mudablue: an automatic categorization system for open source repositories. J. Syst. Softw. **79**, 939–953 (2006)
25. Missaoui, R., Godin, R., Sahraoui, H.: Migrating to an object-oriented database using semantic clustering and transformation rules. Data Knowl. Eng. **27**, 97–113 (1998)
26. Strüber, D., Selter, M., Taentzer, G.: Tool support for clustering large meta-models. In: Proceedings of the Workshop on Scalability in Model Driven Engineering, BigMDE 2013 at STAF, pp. 7: 1–7: 4. ACM (2013)
27. Lopez, O., Laguna, M.A., Garcia, F.J.: Reuse based analysis and clustering of requirements diagrams. In: Eighth International Workshop on Requirements Engineering: Foundation for Software Quality (REFSQ02), pp. 71–82 (2002)
28. Chen, K., Zhang, W., Zhao, H., Mei, H.: An approach to constructing feature models based on requirements clustering. In: Proceedings of 13th IEEE International Conference on Requirements Engineering, pp. 31–40 (2005)

Mining and Decision Support

Predictive Business Process Monitoring Framework with Hyperparameter Optimization

Chiara Di Francescomarino[2(✉)], Marlon Dumas[1], Marco Federici[3],
Chiara Ghidini[2], Fabrizio Maria Maggi[1], and Williams Rizzi[3]

[1] University of Tartu, Liivi 2, 50409 Tartu, Estonia
{marlon.dumas,fmmaggi}@ut.ee
[2] FBK-IRST, Via Sommarive 18, 38050 Trento, Italy
{dfmchiara,ghidini}@fbk.eu
[3] University of Trento, Via Sommarive 9, 38123 Trento, Italy
{marco.federici,williams.rizzi}@studenti.unitn.it

Abstract. Predictive business process monitoring exploits event logs to predict how ongoing (uncompleted) traces will unfold up to their completion. A predictive process monitoring framework collects a range of techniques that allow users to get accurate predictions about the achievement of a goal for a given ongoing trace. These techniques can be combined and their parameters configured in different framework instances. Unfortunately, a unique framework instance that is general enough to outperform others for every dataset, goal or type of prediction is elusive. Thus, the selection and configuration of a framework instance needs to be done for a given dataset. This paper presents a predictive process monitoring framework armed with a hyperparameter optimization method to select a suitable framework instance for a given dataset.

Keywords: Predictive process monitoring · Hyperparameter optimization · Linear temporal logic

1 Introduction

Predictive Business Process Monitoring. [10] is a family of techniques that exploits event logs extracted from information systems in order to predict how current (uncompleted) traces of a process will unfold up to their completion. Based on the analysis of event logs, a runtime component continuously provides the user with estimations of the likelihood that a goal will be achieved upon completion of any given running trace of the process.

In previous work [4,10], we presented a customizable predictive process monitoring framework comprising a set of techniques to construct models to predict whether or not an ongoing trace will ultimately satisfy a given classification function based both on: (i) the sequence of events executed in the given trace; and (ii) the values of data attributes associated to the events. The latter is important as, for example, in a patient treatment process, doctors may decide whether to

© Springer International Publishing Switzerland 2016
S. Nurcan et al. (Eds.): CAiSE 2016, LNCS 9694, pp. 361–376, 2016.
DOI: 10.1007/978-3-319-39696-5_22

perform a surgery or not based on the age of the patient, while in a sales process, a discount may be applied only for premium customers.

Incorporating in a single framework a range of techniques that can be combined and configured in different framework instances is a necessary step in building a tool that supports predictive business process monitoring. The construction and selection of the appropriate framework instance, indeed, can greatly impact the performance of the resulting predictions [9]. Constructing an effective instance of a predictive monitoring framework, able to maximize the performance of the underlying techniques for a given dataset, is, however, non-trivial. For example, this construction may imply a choice among different classification techniques (e.g., decision trees or random forests) and clustering algorithms (e.g., k-means, agglomerative clustering or dbscan), as well as the hyperparameters that these techniques require have to be tuned according to the specific dataset and prediction problem. While these choices may be challenging even for experts, for non-experts they often result in arbitrary (or default-case) choices [17].

The conventional way to face this problem is combining manual and exhaustive search [19]. We also adopt this approach and, in particular, we perform two specific steps: first, we run different configurations of the techniques on an appropriate dataset used for training and validating and, second, we compare the outcomes of the different configurations to select the one that outperforms the others for the given domain.

While this overall strategy has the potential to ease the construction of an effective instance of the predictive monitoring framework, its concrete realization poses two challenges that may hamper its practical adoption. A first challenge is given by the computational burden of running different configurations for different combinations of techniques. A second challenge is related to the complexity of comparing different configurations and then select the best one for a business analyst/process owner.

The framework presented in this paper provides a predictive process monitoring environment armed with a hyperparameter optimization method able to address the two challenges emphasized above. First, it enables to run an exhaustive combination of different technique settings on a given dataset in an efficient and scalable manner. This is realized through a meta-layer built on top of the predictive process monitoring framework. Such a layer is responsible of invoking the framework on different framework instances and to provide, for each of them, a number of aggregated metrics (on a set of validation traces). The meta-layer is optimized to schedule and parallelize the processing of the configurations across different threads and reuse as much as possible the pre-processed data structures. Second, it provides user support for the comparison of the results, thus enabling to easily select a suitable framework instance for a given dataset. This is done by providing the user with a set of aggregated metrics (measuring different dimensions) for each configuration. These metrics can be used for opportunely ranking the configurations according to the user's needs and hence for supporting the user in the parameter tuning.

After an introductory background section (Sect. 2), Sects. 3 and 4 introduce two motivating scenarios and the overall approach, respectively. The overall architecture is then detailed in Sect. 5, and an evaluation presented in Sect. 6. Sections 7 and 8 conclude with related and future works.

2 Background

In this section, we provide background notions useful in the rest of the paper.

Predictive Process Monitoring. The execution of business processes is generally subject to internal policies, norms, best practices, regulations, and laws. For example, a doctor may only perform a certain type of surgery, if a pre-operational screening is carried out beforehand. Meanwhile, in a sales process, an order can be archived only after the customer has confirmed the receipt of all ordered items. Based on an analysis of past execution traces, the idea of *Predictive Process Monitoring* [10] is to continuously provide the user with estimations of the likelihood of achieving a user-specified *business goal* in an ongoing trace.[1] Such predictions generally depend both on: (i) the sequence of events executed in the ongoing trace; and (ii) the values of data attributes associated to the events.

Linear Temporal Logic. In our approach, a business goal can be formulated in terms of Linear Temporal Logic (LTL) rules. LTL [14] is a modal logic with modalities devoted to describe time aspects. Classically, LTL is defined for infinite traces. However, when focusing on the compliance of business processes, we use a variant of LTL defined for finite traces (since business process are supposed to complete eventually). We assume that events occurring during the process execution fall in the set of atomic propositions. LTL rules are constructed from these atoms by applying the temporal operators $\mathbf{X}$ (next), $\mathbf{F}$ (future), $\mathbf{G}$ (globally), and $\mathbf{U}$ (until) in addition to the usual boolean connectives. Given a formula φ, $\mathbf{X}\varphi$ means that the next time instant exists and φ is true in the next time instant (strong next). $\mathbf{F}\varphi$ indicates that φ is true sometimes in the future. $\mathbf{G}\varphi$ means that φ is true always in the future. $\varphi\mathbf{U}\psi$ indicates that φ has to hold at least until ψ holds and ψ must hold in the current or in a future time instant.

Hyperparameter Optimization. Traditionally, machine learning techniques are characterized by model parameters and by *hyperparameters*. While model parameters are learned during the training phase so as to fit the data, hyperparameters are set outside the training procedure and used for controlling how flexible the model is in fitting the data. For example, the number of clusters in the k-means clustering procedure is a hyperparameter of the clustering technique. The impact of hyperparameter values on the accuracy of the predictions can be huge. Optimizing their value is hence important but it can differ based on the dataset. The simplest approaches for hyperparameter optimization are grid

---

[1] In line with the forward-looking nature of predictive monitoring, we use the term *business goal* rather than *business constraint* to refer to the monitored properties.

search and random search. The former builds a grid of hyperparameter values, evaluates each of them by exploring the whole search space, and returns the one that provides the best result. The latter, instead of exhaustively exploring the search space, selects a sample of values to be evaluated. Several smarter techniques have been recently developed for the hyperparameter optimization. For example, Sequential Model based Optimization (SMBO) [7] is an iterative approach that constructs explicit regression models to describe the dependence of target algorithm performance on hyperparameter settings.

3   Two Motivating Scenarios

We aim at addressing the problem of easing the task of predictive process monitoring, by enabling users to easily select and configure a specific predictive process monitoring scenario to the needs of a specific dataset. In this section, we introduce two motivating scenarios that will be used also as a basis for the evaluation of the *Predictive Process Monitoring Framework* in Sect. 6.

Scenario 1. Predicting Patient History. Let *Bob* be a medical director of an oncology department of an important Hospital who is interested in predicting the type of exams a patient, *Alice*, will perform. In particular, he is interested in knowing, given the clinical record of *Alice* whether: (a) she will need two specific exams named *tumor marker CA* − 19.9 and *ca* − 125 *using meia*, and when; and (b) the occurrence of a particular exam (*CEA* − *tumor marker using meia*) will be followed by another exam for the diagnosis of *squamous cell carcinoma*. Since his department has started an innovative project aiming at using predictive process monitoring techniques based on the analysis of event logs related to the patient history, his Hospital owns a number of relevant datasets to enable the usage of a predictive process monitoring framework. However, when ready to use the framework, he finds out that: (i) he needs to select a number of techniques to create an instance of the framework; (ii) for each of these techniques, he has to set a number of hyperparameters needed for their configuration. However, being a medical doctor he does not have the necessary knowledge to understand which technique is better to use and the parameters to set. His knowledge only enables him to select the predicate he wants to predict and the dataset of similar traces relevant for the prediction. Thus, a way for helping him in understanding which configuration works best for his dataset and specific prediction is needed.

Scenario 2. Predicting Problems in Building Permit Applications. Let *John* be a clerk handling building permit applications of a Municipality. The majority of regular building permit applications required for building, modifying or demolishing houses must be accompanied with the necessary fees and documentation, including design plans, photos and pertinent reports. They are, therefore, often unsuccessfully checked for completeness, and the applicant has to be contacted again for sending the missing documents. This implies extra work for *John* and for the building permit applications office. In addition, many of the permit applications also require an environmental license (WABO) and getting the WABO license can either be fast or demand for a long extension of the building permit procedure. This would require a rescheduling of the work of the building permit applications office. *John* is, therefore, interested in knowing whether: (a) the 4 applications he has just received and for which he has acknowledged receipt will undergo a series of actions required to retrieve missing data; and (b) these applications will require the environmental license. As in *Scenario 1*, the Municipality where *John* works stores all the necessary datasets to enable the usage of a predictive process monitoring framework, but the difficulty in choosing the right technique and the need of configuring parameters may seriously hamper his ability to use the framework. Thus, a way for helping him to set up the correct configuration which works best for his dataset and specific prediction is needed also in this scenario.

4   Approach

In this section, we describe the approach to provide users with a predictive process monitoring framework equipped with methods to support them in the selection of the framework instance that is most suitable for the dataset and the prediction they are interested in.

The approach is based on two main components: the *Predictive Process Monitoring Framework*, in charge of making predictions on an ongoing trace, and the *Technique and Hyperparameter Tuner*, responsible of the invocation of the *Predictive Process Monitoring Framework* with different configurations (framework instances). Figure 1 shows the conceptual architecture of the framework. The *Predictive Process Monitoring Framework* takes as input a training set, a prediction problem and an ongoing trace, and returns as output a prediction related to the input prediction problem for the ongoing trace. The *Technique and Hyperparameter Tuner* acts as a meta-layer on top of the *Predictive Process Monitoring Framework*. As well as the training set and the prediction problem, the *Technique and Hyperparameter Tuner* takes as input a set of traces (*validation set*) and uses them to feed the *Predictive Process Monitoring Framework* on a set of potentially interesting framework instances. Specifically, for each considered framework instance, the traces of the validation set are replayed and

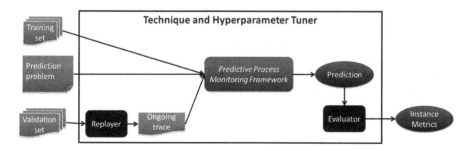

Fig. 1. *Tuning-enhanced Predictive Process Monitoring Framework* architecture

passed as a stream of events to the *Predictive Process Monitoring Framework*. Once a new trace is processed by the *Predictive Process Monitoring Framework* and a predicted value returned, it is compared with the actual value of the trace in the validation set. Based on this comparison and other characteristics of the prediction (e.g., how early along the current trace the prediction has reached a sufficient confidence level), a set of aggregated performance metrics (e.g., the accuracy or the failure rate) is computed. Once the set of all the interesting framework instances has been processed, the user can compare them along the performance dimensions.

5   Architecture

In this section, we describe in detail the two layers of the *Tuning-enhanced Predictive Process Monitoring Framework*. We first introduce the *Predictive Process Monitoring Framework*, by providing an overview of its modules and of the techniques that are currently plugged in each of them, and we then present the tuner layer that supports users in the selection of the framework instance that best suites with their dataset and prediction problem.

5.1   *Predictive Process Monitoring Framework*

As shown in Fig. 1, the *Predictive Process Monitoring Framework* requires as input a set of past executions of the process. Based on the information extracted from such execution traces, it tries to predict how current ongoing executions will develop in the future. To this aim, before the process execution, a pre-processing phase is carried out. In such a phase, state-of-the-art approaches for clustering and classification are applied to the historical data in order to (i) identify and group historical trace prefixes with a similar control flow, i.e., to delimit the search space on the control flow base (clustering from a control flow perspective); and (ii) get a precise classification in terms of data of traces with similar control flow (data-based classification). The data-structures (e.g., clusters and classifiers) computed at the different stages of the pre-processing phase are stored. At runtime, the classification of the historical trace prefixes is used to classify new traces during their execution and predict how they will behave in the future. In particular, the new trace is matched to a cluster, and the corresponding classifier is used to estimate the (class) probability for the trace to achieve a certain outcome and the corresponding (class) support (that also gives a measure of the reliability of classification algorithm outcomes). The overall picture of the framework is illustrated in Fig. 2. Within such a framework, we can identify three main modules: the *encoding*, the *clustering* and the *supervised classification learning* module. Each of them can be instantiated with different techniques. Figure 3 shows an overview of possible framework instances.

For example, for the trace encoding a *frequency based* and a *sequence based* approach have been plugged in the framework. The former is realized encoding each execution trace as a vector of event occurrences (on the alphabet of

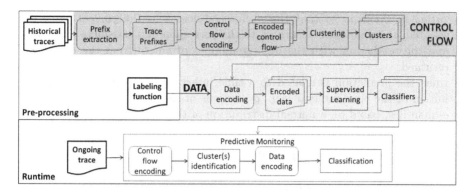

Fig. 2. *Predictive Process Monitoring Framework*

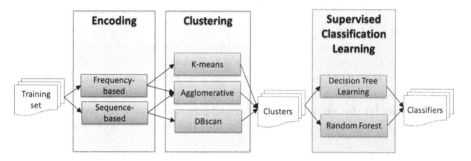

Fig. 3. Framework instances overview

the events), while, in the latter, the trace is encoded as a sequence of events. These encodings can then be passed to the clustering techniques available in the framework: the *dbscan clustering*, the *k-means clustering* and the *agglomerative clustering* algorithms. For example, the *euclidean* distance, used by the *k-means clustering*, is computed starting from the *frequency based* encoding, while the *edit* distance, used by the *dbscan clustering*, is computed starting from the *sequence based* encoding of the traces. Within the supervised learning module, *decision tree* and *random forest* learning techniques have been implemented.

Each of these techniques requires, in turn, a number of hyperparameters (specific for the technique) to be configured. Specifically, k-means and agglomerative clustering take as input the number of clusters, while the dbscan technique requires two parameters: the minimum number of points in a cluster and the minimum cluster ray.

Moreover, the framework also allows for configuring other parameters, such as:

- size of prefixes of historical traces to be grouped in clusters and used for training the classifiers;

- *voting mechanism*, so that the p clusters closest to the current trace are selected, the prediction according to the corresponding classifiers estimated, and the prediction with the highest number of votes (from the classifiers) returned;
- when the prediction is related to a time interval, a mechanism for the definition of the time interval (e.g., q intervals of the same duration, based on q-quantiles, based on a normal distribution of the time).

The framework has been implemented as an Operational Support (OS) provider of the OS Service 2.0 [11,18] of the ProM toolset. Specifically, an OS service is able to interact with external workflow engines by receiving at runtime streams of events and passing them to the OS providers.

5.2   Technique and Hyperparameter Tuning

The *Tuning-enhanced Predictive Process Monitoring Framework* has been designed as a client-server architecture, where the *Predictive Process Monitoring Framework* is the server, and the client is a toolset that can either be used (i) for "replaying" a stream of events coming from a workflow engine and invoke the server to get predictions on a specific problem; or (ii) for evaluation purposes and, in particular, for supporting users in tuning the framework techniques and hyperparameters according to the dataset and the input prediction problem.

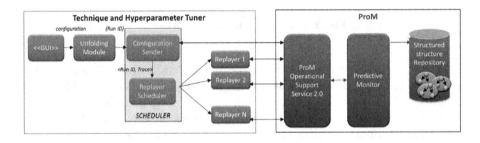

Fig. 4. Logical architecture

When used for evaluation purposes, the client (the *Technique and Hyperparameter Tuner*) evaluates the *Predictive Process Monitoring Framework* for each of the techniques and hyperparameter configurations. Specifically, for each of them, the client replays each trace of the validation set and invokes the *Predictive Process Monitoring Framework* for getting a prediction (and the associated class probability) at different points of the trace (*evaluation points*). As soon as the class probability and support of the returned prediction are above a certain threshold, the prediction is considered reliable enough and kept as the *Predictive Process Monitoring Framework* prediction at the specific evaluation point. The final predicted value is then compared with the actual one. With this information for each trace, the client is finally able to provide the users with few aggregated metrics about the performance of the framework instance. In detail, the following three *evaluation dimensions* (and corresponding metrics) are computed:

- *Accuracy*, which intuitively represents the proportion of correctly classified results (both positive and negative); it is defined as:

$$accuracy = \frac{T_P + T_N}{T_P + F_P + T_N + F_N}. \tag{1}$$

  Accuracy ranges between 0 and 1. High values of accuracy are preferred to low ones.
- *Failure rate*, which is the percentage of traces for which a reliable prediction cannot be given. Failure rate ranges between 0 and 1. In this case low values are preferred to high ones.
- *Earliness*, which is the ratio between the index indicating the position of the last evaluation point (the one corresponding to the reliable prediction) and the size of the trace under examination. Earliness ranges as well between 0 and 1 and a low value of earliness indicates early predictions along the traces.

In order to speed-up the above time-consuming procedure, the client application implements a scheduling mechanism that distributes the prediction computations across 2 or more parallel replayer threads. In addition, in the pre-processing phase, the data structures are stored for reuse purposes. However, only some of them can be reused. Each choice of technique (and hyperparameter) in the configuration can indeed affect the *Predictive Process Monitoring Framework* flow at different stages. For example, the choice of the encoding type affects the clusters built from the historical traces; the choice of the classification learning technique does not affect the clusters but it does affect the classifiers built on top of them. Only the data structures of previous choices that are not affected by the current choice can be reused.

Figure 4 shows the logical architecture of the client application (left part) and its interactions with the OS Service. It is composed of three main parts: the *Unfolding Module*, the *Scheduler Module* and the *Replayers*.

The *Unfolding Module* combines the sets of techniques (and their hyperparameters) provided by the user through an intuitive GUI into a set of different configuration runs. Each configuration run is associated with an ID (*Run ID*), which is used to refer such a configuration. Once the list of the interesting configurations has been created, the *Configuration Sender* sequentially sends each configuration to the server that uses it to encode the traces, as well as to compute clusters and classifiers for that specific configuration. Once the server has done with the pre-processing, the *Configuration Sender* starts sending the traces to the *Replayer Scheduler* in charge of optimizing the distribution of the traces among different replayers on different threads. Each replayer sends the trace (and the reference to the specific configuration Run ID) to the server and waits for the results. As soon as the results are provided by the OS Service, they are progressively visualized in the result interface (Fig. 5). Each tab of the result interface refers to a specific configuration run, while the summary tab reports a summary of all the configuration runs with the corresponding evaluation metrics. From this interface, the user can easily sort the configurations based on one or more evaluation metrics.

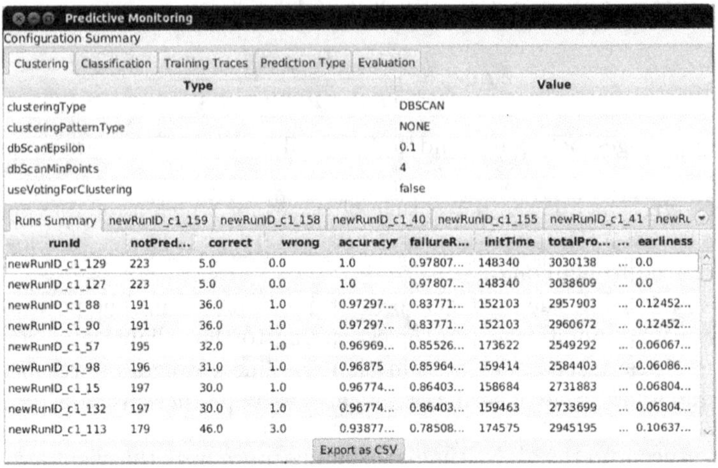

Fig. 5. Result interface

6   Evaluation

In this section, we provide an evaluation of the *Tuning-enhanced Predictive Process Monitoring Framework*. In detail, we would like to investigate if it can be used in practice to support users in selecting a suitable configuration for their prediction problem. Specifically, we want to see whether: (i) the *Tuning-enhanced Predictive Process Monitoring Framework* is effective in returning a set of configurations suitable for the specific dataset and prediction problem; (ii) the configuration suggested by the *Tuning-enhanced Predictive Process Monitoring Framework* actually provides accurate results for the specific prediction problem; (iii) the framework does it in a reasonable amount of time.

6.1   Datasets

For the tool evaluation, we used two datasets provided for the BPI Challenges 2011 [1] and 2015 [5], respectively.

The first event log pertains to the treatment of patients diagnosed with cancer in a large Dutch Academic Hospital. It contains 1,140 traces, 149,730 events referring to 623 different activities. In this case, we used our framework to predict the information that, for example, *Bob* is interested to know about the *Alice*'s case (see *Scenario 1* in Sect. 3). More formally, we used our framework to predict the compliance of a trace with respect to the following two LTL rules:

- $\varphi_{11} = \mathbf{F}(\text{"}tumor\ marker\ CA-19.9\text{"}) \vee \mathbf{F}(\text{"}ca-125\ using\ meia\text{"})$,
- $\varphi_{12} = \mathbf{G}(\text{"}CEA-tumor\ marker\ using\ meia\text{"} \rightarrow \mathbf{F}(\text{"}squamous\ cell\ carcinoma\ using\ eia\text{"}))$.

The second log was provided by a Dutch Municipality. The log is composed of 1,199 traces, 52,217 events and 398 event classes. The data contains all building permit applications over a period of approximately four years. It contains several activities, denoted by both codes and labels, both in Dutch and in English. In this case, we used the *Tuning-enhanced Predictive Process Monitoring Framework* to investigate the configurations that are more suitable with respect to the *John's* problem (see *Scenario 2* in Sect. 3). Formally, we investigate the following two LTL rules:

- $\varphi_{21} = (\mathbf{F}(\text{"}start\ WABO\ procedure\text{"}) \wedge \mathbf{F}(\text{"}extend\ procedure\ term\text{"}))$,
- $\varphi_{22} = (\mathbf{G}(\text{"}send\ confirmation\ receipt\text{"}) \rightarrow \mathbf{F}(\text{"}retrieve\ missing\ data\text{"}))$.

6.2 Experimental Procedure

In order to evaluate the technique and hyperparameter tuning of the *Tuning-enhanced Predictive Process Monitoring Framework*, we adopted the following procedure.

1. We divided both our datasets in three parts: (i) training set: 70 % of the whole dataset; (ii) validation set: 20 % of the whole dataset; (iii) testing set: 10 % of the whole dataset.
2. For both the analyzed scenarios, we used the training and the validation sets for identifying the most suitable (according to one or more evaluation dimensions) *Predictive Process Monitoring Framework* configurations for the specific dataset and prediction problem. Moreover, we computed the time required for tuning the parameters with and without reuse of data structures and with and without replayers working in parallel.
3. We evaluated the identified configurations on the testing set.

6.3 Experimental Results

As described in Sect. 5, the *Tuning-enhanced Predictive Process Monitoring Framework* explores all the configurations of a finite set and computes for each of them, three evaluation metrics: accuracy, failure rate and earliness. Table 1 reports, for each formula of each scenario, the descriptive statistics of these metrics on a set of 160 different configurations, obtained by combining two algorithms for the clustering step (dbscan and k-means), two algorithms for the classifier learning step (decision tree and random forest) and varying a number of hyperparameters (e.g., the number of clusters for k-means or the number of trees in the random forest).

By looking at the table, we can get an idea of the distribution of the configuration settings in the space of the evaluation metrics. We can observe that such a distribution is not the same for all the rules. For example, for the rules in the first scenario, the configurations produce values for all the three evaluation metrics that are widely distributed (e.g., the failure rate for φ_{11} ranges from 0 to 0.98).

Table 1. Descriptive Statistics related to the tuning phase

Rule	Accuracy				Failure rate				Earliness				Computation
	Min	Max	Avg	Std. dev	Min	Max	Avg	Std. dev	Min	Max	Avg	Std. dev	Time (h)
φ_{11}	0.43	1	0.73	0.15	0	0.98	0.42	0.31	0	0.48	0.13	0.13	42.68
φ_{12}	0.55	0.91	0.73	0.08	0	0.93	0.27	0.3	0	0.43	0.07	0.09	32.05
φ_{21}	0.87	0.91	0.87	0.006	0	0.29	0.02	0.05	0	0.09	0.008	0.02	1.87
φ_{22}	0.77	1	0.95	0.06	0	0.76	0.09	0.17	0	0.35	0.06	0.08	2.93

When, like in this case, the results obtained by running different configurations are distributed, the configuration that best fits with the user needs can be identified in the tuning phase (for example, the user could prefer earliness more than accuracy). On the other hand, for the other two rules, and, in particular for φ_{21}, the performance of the different tested configurations do not vary significantly. In this case, the different configuration settings are mostly restricted within a limited area of the space of the three evaluation metrics, thus making the results of the prediction less dependent on the choice of the configuration.

Table 2. Results related to the tuning evaluation

Rule	Conf. ID	Choice criterion	Tuning			Evaluation		
			Accuracy	Failure rate	Earliness	Accuracy	Failure rate	Earliness
φ_{11}	109	accuracy	0.92	0.46	0.074	0.86	0.57	0.056
	4	fail. rate	0.6	0	0.02	0.86	0	0.009
	50	earliness	0.73	0.06	0.004	0.62	0.05	0.003
	108	balance	0.85	0.18	0.096	0.84	0.26	0.107
φ_{12}	108	accuracy	0.89	0.43	0.016	0.95	0.46	0.129
	76	fail. rate	0.75	0	0.03	0.73	0.02	0.026
	149	earliness	0.64	0	0.001	0.69	0	0
	154	balance	0.77	0.1	0.016	0.87	0.05	0.028
φ_{21}	17	accuracy	0.91	0.29	0.033	0.92	0.12	0.013
	86	fail. rate	0.87	0	0.004	0.91	0	0.002
	65	earliness	0.87	0	0	0.91	0	0
	65	balance	0.87	0	0	0.91	0	0
φ_{22}	22	accuracy	1	0.12	0.246	1	0.26	0.335
	136	fail. rate	0.98	0	0.021	1	0	0
	127	earliness	0.98	0.04	0.001	1	0	0
	25	balance	0.99	0.03	0.12	0.96	0.06	0.18

Among the configurations in the set, we picked the ones that a user could be interested in a typical scenario like the ones considered in this evaluation. We selected as choice *criteria* the performance of the configuration with respect to each of the evaluation dimensions and the performance of the configuration with respect to all the evaluation dimensions. Specifically, we selected, for each evaluation dimension, the configuration that scores best (with respect to that dimension), provided that the other two dimensions do not significantly underperform. Furthermore, we manually selected a fourth configuration that balances the performance of the three evaluation dimensions. Table 2 (*Tuning* column) shows, for each rule, the best (in terms of accuracy, failure rate, earliness and a mix of the three) configurations and the corresponding performance. The identified configurations differ one from another not only for the hyperparameter values but also for the selected algorithms. For example, in configuration 109 for rule φ_{11}, identified as the one with the best accuracy, the clustering algorithm is dbscan, while in configuration 22, i.e., the one with the best accuracy for rule φ_{22}, the clustering algorithm is k-means.

In order to evaluate whether the identified configurations could actually answer the prediction problem in the specific domain, we evaluated them on the testing set. Table 2 (*Evaluation* column) shows the results obtained in terms of accuracy, failure rate and earliness. By comparing the results obtained with the ones obtained in the tuning phase, we can observe that, according to our expectations, they are aligned. Moreover, by further inspecting the table, we have a confirmation of the trend that we observed by looking at the descriptive statistics of the data related to the tuning phase (Table 1). The values of the three metrics along the four selected configurations are quite similar for the rules in *Scenario 2*, whereas they differ for the rules in *Scenario 1*. In the latter, hence, the user (e.g., *Bob*) has the possibility to choose the configuration based on his needs. If, for example, he is more interested in getting accurate predictions, he would choose configuration 109 for φ_{11} and 108 for φ_{12}. If, he is more interested in obtaining a prediction, taking the risk that it could also be inaccurate, then he would choose configurations 4 and 76 for the two rules, respectively. Similarly for early predictions and predictions balancing all the three dimensions.

Finally, we looked at the time required by the *Tuning-enhanced Predictive Process Monitoring Framework* for processing the configurations for each of the four rules. The last column of Table 1 reports the overall time spent to this purpose. Here, we can notice a difference in the computation time required by the two datasets. This difference can be due to the difference in the length of the traces in the two datasets. Indeed, the traces of the dataset related to the Dutch Academic Hospital are on average longer than the ones in the Dutch Municipality dataset. Moreover, in order to investigate the time saved with the reuse of data structures, we performed a run in which all the data structures had already been computed and stored in the server and we observed a time reduction of about 20 %. Finally, we performed a further run with 8 replayers rather than with a single replayer and we observed a further time reduction of about 13.1 %.

Threats to Validity. Three main external threats to validity affect the results of the evaluation: (i) the subjectivity introduced by the user; (ii) the potential overfitting introduced during the tuning phase; and (iii) the limited number of analyzed scenarios. Concerning the first threat, the user is involved in the process (and hence in the evaluation) both in the initial definition of the configurations and in the selection of the configuration. The results of the experiment could hence be influenced by the human subjectivity in these choices. We tried to mitigate the impact of this threat by analyzing what a user would do in "typical" scenarios. As for the second threat, the construction of the configuration parameters would have benefit of a cross-validation procedure, which would have increased the stability of the results. Finally, although we only limited our evaluation to two datasets and to four specific rules, we defined realistic scenarios and used real-life logs.

7 Related Work

In the literature, there are two main branches of works related to this paper: those concerning predictive monitoring and those related to hyperparameter optimization.

As for the first branch, there are works dealing with approaches for the generation of predictions, during process execution, focused on the time perspective. In [2], the authors present a set of approaches in which annotated transition systems, containing time information extracted from event logs, are used to: (i) check time conformance; (ii) predict the remaining processing time; and (iii) recommend appropriate activities to end users to improve the process performance. In [6], a predictive clustering approach is presented, in which context-related execution scenarios are discovered and modeled through state-aware performance predictors. In [15], the authors use stochastic Petri nets to predict the remaining execution time of a process. Another group of works, in the literature, focuses on approaches that generate predictions and recommendations to reduce risks. For example, in [3], the authors present a technique to support process participants in making risk-informed decisions with the aim of reducing the process risks. In [13], the authors make predictions about time-related process risks by identifying and exploiting statistical indicators that highlight the possibility of transgressing deadlines. In [16], an approach for Root Cause Analysis through classification algorithms is presented.

A key difference between these approaches and the *Tuning-enhanced Predictive Process Monitoring Framework* approach is that they either rely on the control-flow or on the data perspective for making predictions at runtime, whereas the predictive process monitoring framework [4,10] takes both perspectives into consideration. In addition, we provide a general, customizable framework for predictive process monitoring, which is flexible and can be implemented in different variants with different sets of techniques, and which supports users in the tuning phase.

As for the second branch of works, several approaches in machine learning have been proposed for the selection of learning techniques [12], for the tuning of hyperparameters [7], and for the combined optimization of both techniques and hyperparameters [8,17].

The problem that we address is to tune both the machine learning technique and hyperparameter values. One of the first works that falls in this group of approaches is Auto-WEKA [17]. The idea of this work is to map the problem of algorithm selection to that of hyperparameter optimization and to approach this problem based on sequential model-based optimization and a random forest regression model. MLbase [8] also addresses the same problem as Auto-WEKA and approaches it using distributed data mining algorithms. Differently from these approaches, the problem that we face in this work is more complex. In our case, we have more than one machine learning (sub-)problem (e.g., clustering and classification) and these sub-problems depend on each other. Hence, the algorithm (and hyperparameter) optimization for a (sub-)problem cannot be defined independently of the other sub-problems. This is why the solution we propose combines manual and exhaustive search.

8   Conclusion

The contribution of this paper is a predictive process monitoring framework incorporating a hyperparameter optimization method that supports users in the selection of the techniques and in the tuning of the hyperparameters according to the specific dataset and prediction problem under analysis. We evaluated the approach on two datasets and we found that the *Tuning-enhanced Predictive Process Monitoring Framework* provides users with interesting sets of tunable configurations in a reasonable time. This allows users to adopt configurations that generate accurate predictions for the specific dataset and prediction problem.

In the future, we plan to further investigate: (i) how to increase the user support; (ii) how to optimize the exhaustive search. Concerning the former, we would like to provide users with an automatic heuristic-based approach for the exploration of the search space. This would allow us to go beyond the exhaustive analysis of a limited search space of the configurations by exploiting an objective function to explore a larger search space. For example, we could use as objective function each of the evaluation metrics considered in this work or we could use a multi-objective function for the optimization of all three of them. As for the latter, we would like to borrow state-of-the-art techniques for algorithm selection and hyperparameter tuning and, if possible, to customize them for our problem.

Finally, a further interesting direction is to extend our framework to support prescriptive process monitoring. The idea is to provide recommendations to the user to achieve a certain goal in a given ongoing trace. Recommendations would allow users not only to know whether a goal will be achieved but also what to do for increasing the chances of achieving it.

Acknowledgments. This research is funded by the EU FP7 Programme under grant agreement 609190 (Subject-Orientation for People-Centred Production) and by the Estonian Research Council (grant IUT20-55).

References

1. 3TU Data Center: BPI Challenge 2011 Event Log (2011)
2. van der Aalst, W.M.P., Schonenberg, M.H., Song, M.: Time prediction based on process mining. Inf. Syst. **36**(2), 450–475 (2011)

3. Conforti, R., de Leoni, M., La Rosa, M., van der Aalst, W.M.P.: Supporting risk-informed decisions during business process execution. In: Salinesi, C., Norrie, M.C., Pastor, Ó. (eds.) CAiSE 2013. LNCS, vol. 7908, pp. 116–132. Springer, Heidelberg (2013)

4. Di Francescomarino, C., Dumas, M., Maggi, F.M., Teinemaa, I.: Clustering-Based Predictive Process Monitoring. arXiv preprint (2015)

5. van   Dongen;   B.:   Bpi   challenge   (2015).   doi:10.4121/uuid:a0addfda-2044-4541-a450-fdcc9fe16d17

6. Folino, F., Guarascio, M., Pontieri, L.: Discovering context-aware models for predicting business process performances. In: Meersman, R., Panetto, H., Dillon, T., Rinderle-Ma, S., Dadam, P., Zhou, X., Pearson, S., Ferscha, A., Bergamaschi, S., Cruz, I.F. (eds.) OTM 2012, Part I. LNCS, vol. 7565, pp. 287–304. Springer, Heidelberg (2012)

7. Hutter, F., Hoos, H.H., Leyton-Brown, K.: Sequential model-based optimization for general algorithm configuration. In: Coello, C.A.C. (ed.) LION 2011. LNCS, vol. 6683, pp. 507–523. Springer, Heidelberg (2011)

8. Kraska, T., Talwalkar, A., Duchi, J.C., Griffith, R., Franklin, M.J., Jordan, M.I.: Mlbase: A distributed machine-learning system. In: CIDR (2013). www.cidrdb.org

9. Luo, G.: Mlbcd: a machine learning tool for big clinical data. Health Inf. Sci. Syst. 3(1), 1–19 (2015)

10. Maggi, F.M., Di Francescomarino, C., Dumas, M., Ghidini, C.: Predictive monitoring of business processes. In: Jarke, M., Mylopoulos, J., Quix, C., Rolland, C., Manolopoulos, Y., Mouratidis, H., Horkoff, J. (eds.) CAiSE 2014. LNCS, vol. 8484, pp. 457–472. Springer, Heidelberg (2014)

11. Maggi, F.M., Westergaard, M.: Designing software for operational decision support through coloured Petri nets. Enterprise Information Systems, 1–21 (2015)

12. Pfahringer, B., Bensusan, H., Giraud-Carrier, C.: Meta-learning by landmarking various learning algorithms. In: ICML, pp. 743–750 (2000)

13. Pika, A., Aalst, W., Fidge, C., Hofstede, A., Wynn, M.: Predicting deadline transgressions using event logs. In: La Rosa, M., Soffer, P. (eds.) BPM Workshops, pp. 211–216. Springer, Heidelberg (2013)

14. Pnueli, A.: The temporal logic of programs. In: 18th Annual Symposium on Foundations of Computer Science, pp. 46–57 (1977)

15. Rogge-Solti, A., Weske, M.: Prediction of remaining service execution time using stochastic petri nets with arbitrary firing delays. In: Basu, S., Pautasso, C., Zhang, L., Fu, X. (eds.) ICSOC 2013. LNCS, vol. 8274, pp. 389–403. Springer, Heidelberg (2013)

16. Suriadi, S., Ouyang, C., Aalst, W., Hofstede, A.: Root cause analysis with enriched process logs. In: La Rosa, M., Soffer, P. (eds.) BPM Workshops, pp. 174–186. Springer, Heidelberg (2013)

17. Thornton, C., Hutter, F., Hoos, H.H., Leyton-Brown, K.: Auto-WEKA: combined selection and hyperparameter optimization of classification algorithms. In: Proceedings of KDD-2013, pp. 847–855 (2013)

18. Westergaard, M., Maggi, F.M.: Modeling and verification of a protocol for operational support using coloured petri nets. In: Kristensen, L.M., Petrucci, L. (eds.) PETRI NETS 2011. LNCS, vol. 6709, pp. 169–188. Springer, Heidelberg (2011)

19. Wistuba, M., Schilling, N., Schmidt-Thieme, L.: Hyperparameter search space pruning – a new component for sequential model-based hyperparameter optimization. In: Appice, A., Rodrigues, P.P., Santos Costa, V., Gama, J., Jorge, A., Soares, C. (eds.) ECML PKDD 2015. LNCS, vol. 9285, pp. 104–119. Springer, Heidelberg (2015)

Decision Mining Revisited - Discovering Overlapping Rules

Felix Mannhardt[1,2(✉)], Massimiliano de Leoni[1], Hajo A. Reijers[1,3],
and Wil M.P. van der Aalst[1]

[1] Eindhoven University of Technology, Eindhoven, The Netherlands
{f.mannhardt,m.d.leoni,h.a.reijers,w.m.p.v.d.aalst}@tue.nl
[2] Lexmark Enterprise Software, Naarden, The Netherlands
[3] Vrije Universiteit Amsterdam, Amsterdam, The Netherlands

Abstract. Decision mining enriches process models with rules underlying decisions in processes using historical process execution data. Choices between multiple activities are specified through rules defined over process data. Existing decision mining methods focus on discovering mutually-exclusive rules, which only allow one out of multiple activities to be performed. These methods assume that decision making is fully deterministic, and all factors influencing decisions are recorded. In case the underlying decision rules are overlapping due to non-determinism or incomplete information, the rules returned by existing methods do not fit the recorded data well. This paper proposes a new technique to discover overlapping decision rules, which fit the recorded data better at the expense of precision, using decision tree learning techniques. An evaluation of the method on two real-life data sets confirms this trade off. Moreover, it shows that the method returns rules with better fitness and precision in under certain conditions.

Keywords: Decision mining · Process mining · Overlapping rules

1 Introduction

Organizations use process models representing their business processes for multiple reasons. Process models are used, for example, to document, specify, and analyze processes [1]. Generally, process models depict activities (i.e., units of work) and their dependencies in a graph representation, which specifies the order of activities in the process execution. During the execution of non-trivial processes, next to the ordering of activities, *decisions* between multiple alternative activities needs to be made. Those choices are explicitly modeled in process models as so-called *decision points*. A decision point specifies the alternatives available. An important challenge when using process models is to understand the decision that need to be made in a process, and the conditions under which certain alternative activities are performed. Awareness that modeling and analyzing decisions is key in process management is increasing. See for

---

The work of Dr. de Leoni has received funding from the European Community's Seventh Framework Program FP7 under grant agreement num. 603993 (CORE).

S. Nurcan et al. (Eds.): CAiSE 2016, LNCS 9694, pp. 377–392, 2016.
DOI: 10.1007/978-3-319-39696-5_23

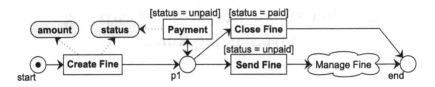

Fig. 1. Fragment of a process model taken from a road traffic fine management process with overlapping rules governing an exclusive choice based on the payment of the fine.

example the interest in the Decision Model and Notation (DMN) standard [2] supported by vendors such as Signavio and Camunda.

Process mining methods are able to discover process models with decision points by using event logs. Event logs contain information on performed activities (i.e., sequences of events) and are available in today's information systems [1]. *Decision mining* aims to discover the rules that are underlying those decisions. Those rules are determined using data recorded by information systems that support the process [3,4]. Events in event logs used for decision mining need to contain process data, which was available when the activity was performed (i.e., attributes). Take, for instance, the process model fragment depicted in Fig. 1, which shows a simplified fragment of a road-traffic fine management process [5]. After creating a fine notice (Create Fine) and recording the amount (amount), an exclusive choice between three alternatives has to be made. Either a payment is received (Payment), possibly in multiple installments, the fine is closed (Close Fine), or the police sends a fine notice (Send Fine) and the process continues with further management of the fine. Please note, that only one out of these three alternatives can be taken, which is different to an inclusive choice that allows the execution of multiple alternatives. The rules depicted in Fig. 1 drive this choice. Activity Close Fine can only be executed if the value of attribute status is *paid*. Thus, the process can only finish directly if the fine has been paid in a timely manner. Rules defined over the process data are an integral part of this process. Traditionally, decision mining methods [3,4,6] use decision tree learning techniques such as C4.5 [7] to determine rules governing the process execution based on event logs. For example, attribute values recorded for status and amount are used as *feature*, while the choice between Payment, Send Fine, Close Fine is used as *target class*. Then, mutually exclusive rules for each activity are built using the obtained decision tree, thus, the choice at the decision point is completely determined by the values of status and amount.

Existing decision mining techniques for exclusive choices rely on the strong assumption that the rules attached to the alternative activities of a exclusive choice need to be *mutually exclusive*. However, business rules are often non-deterministic and this *"cannot be solved until the business rule is instantiated in a particular situation"* [8]. This ambiguity can occur due to conflicting rules or missing contextual information [8]. For example, decisions taken by process workers may depend on contextual factors, which are not encoded in the system and, thus, not available in event logs. Moreover, even if those factors are encoded in the system event logs are often incomplete [9]. Without complete information in the event log the mutually exclusive rules underlying decision-making cannot be discovered. Hence, this assumption is typically not met in reality. For example, the process model shown in Fig. 1, which is taken from a real-life process, contains overlapping rules for an exclusive choice. This means that on a decision point more than one of multiple activities may be executed under the same condition, i.e., when the same attribute values have been observed beforehand. In case the payment status is *unpaid*, the choice between Payment and Send Fine is deferred, i.e., an unpaid fine can be either paid directly or a notification is sent to the offender. The actual decision between either of those activities is not specified. It might depend on an unavailable contextual factor, e.g., some fines can be paid on-the-spot depending on the context. Please note that an exclusive choice with overlapping rules is different to an inclusive choice, which, for certain process executions, prescribes multiple alternatives activities to be executed. For example, in case of an inclusive choice, if status is *unpaid*, both payment and send fine are prescribed to occur. State of the art techniques [3,4,6] only use decision trees, and, hence, cannot discover overlapping rules on exclusive choices. For instance, current techniques fail to discover the rule in Fig. 1.

This paper proposes a technique that discovers *overlapping rules* in those cases that the underlying observations are characterized better by such rules. The technique is able to deliberately trade the precision of mutually-exclusive rules, i.e., only one alternative is possible, against fitness, i.e., the overlapping rules that are less often violated. In short, as in [3,4,6], our technique builds an initial decision tree based on observations from the event log. Then, for each decision tree leaf, the wrongly classified instances are used to learn a new decision tree leading to new rules. These new rules are used in disjunction with the initial rules yielding overlapping rules of the form $rule_1 \vee rule_2$. We evaluate our technique on two real-life data sets: an event log taken from a road traffic fine management process and an event log with pathways of patients in a hospital. The evaluation shows that our technique discovers overlapping rules in real-life data, and that those rules provide a better balance in terms of fitness and precision. For example, our technique discovers overlapping rules similar to the ones depicted in Fig. 1, whereas traditional method fail, e.g., to discover a rule for activity Payment.

As to the structure of this paper, we introduce necessary formalisms for process models and event logs (Sect. 2). Then, we present our discovery technique for process models with overlapping rules (Sect. 3). We evaluate our technique based on real-life event logs (Sect. 4). We discuss related work (Sect. 5), and conclude with a summary and sketched future work (Sect. 6).

2   Background

We present necessary preliminaries such as the formalism we use to represent process models and event logs, and criteria used to determine the quality of decision rules.

2.1   Process Model

Generally, our decision mining technique is independent of the formalism used to model the process, e.g., BPMN, UML-activity diagrams, EPCs or YAWL. We choose Data Petri Nets (DPN) [4] as modeling language because it has simple and clear semantics.

A **DPN** is a Petri net [10] that is extended with variables (i.e., data attributes). A Petri net consists of a set of **places**, a set of **transitions** and the flow relations that describe the bipartite graph between places and transitions. Transitions correspond to activities in the process. The state of a Petri net is defined by its marking. The marking of a Petri net assigns a number of tokens to each place. Executing a transition consumes one token from each of its input places and produces one token on each of its output places. We denote with output transitions of a place the set of transitions for which there is a directed edge from the place to those transitions. A transition can only can be executed (fired) when there is at least one token in every input place.

A DPN is a Petri net with additional components: a set of **variables** defined over a universe of possible values; a set of **write operations** for each transition; a **guard expression** (guard) for each transition. Transitions update the values of variables through write operations. Furthermore, guards defined over the variables of the DPN further constrain when transitions may be executed. A transition in a DPN can be executed only if all its input places contain at least one token and the guard is satisfied by the current variable assignment. Unless specified otherwise we assume the guard true for each transition, i.e., the transition can fire regardless of the current variable assignment. The state of a DPN is defined by both the marking and the current values of all its variables. The behavior of a DPN corresponds to all sequences of transition firings starting from an initial state to any final state. The initial state is made of the initial marking, i.e., the initial number of tokens in each place and an empty set of variable values. Final states are all final markings. For sake of space we refer to [5] for a comprehensive introduction to DPNs.

Example 1. Figure 1 shows a simplified process in the DPN notation. The process starts with executing transition `Create Fine`, which writes attribute `status`. When executing transition `Create Fine` a token is removed from the place *source* and a new token is put in place p_1. Now, a choice between the output transitions of p_1, `Payment`, `Send Fine`, and `Close Fine`, has to be made. Therefore, place p_1 is called *decision point*. As there are guards placed on all three transitions their enablement depends on the current assignment of attribute `status`. For example, both transitions `Send Fine` and `Payment` can only be executed when `status` is *unpaid*. As the guards of `Send Fine` and `Payment` overlap, the choice between both transitions is non-deterministic. Assuming transition `Create Fine` assigned the value *paid* to `status`, i.e., the fine has been paid directly, then, only transition `Close Fine` can be executed and the process ends by reaching the final marking of the DPN.

2.2   Event Log

An event log stores information about the executed activities in a process [1]. Given a set of transitions, variables, and variable values, we define an **event log** $\mathscr{E}$ as a collection of unique **events** [1, 11]. Each event $e \in \mathscr{E}$ is associated with a set *values(e)* containing the latest values of all attributes recorded before the event occurred starting with an initial value. Moreover, each event refers to the execution of a transition *trans(e)* and the set of variables that are written by event e is obtained by *writes(e)*. Table 1 shows an event log for the process model introduced in Fig. 1. Each row represents a unique

Table 1. Event Log $\mathscr{E}$ with data attributes **status** and **amount**

Id	Case	Activity	Status	Amount		Id	Case	Activity	Status	Amount
e_1	1	Create Fine	unpaid	30		e_6	3	Create Fine	unpaid	30
e_2	1	Payment	unpaid	-		e_7	3	Payment	paid	-
e_3	1	Send Fine	-	-		e_8	3	Close Fine	-	-
e_4	2	Create Fine	unpaid	30		… … …			…	
e_5	2	Send Fine	-	-						

recorded activity execution (i.e., event) together with the produced data (i.e., attributes). Special attributes like an **id**, the case identifier **case**, and the activity name **activity** are recorded for each event. The location of an event in the case, i.e., the order in which the events occurred, is uniquely identified through the **id** attribute.

Example 2. For the example event log in Table 1 we can determine the transition corresponding to event e_2 as $trans(e_2) = $ Payment. Moreover, we can obtain the value of all attributes at the moment when e_2 occurred as $values(e_2) = (($status $= unpaid)$, ($amount $= 30))$. Finally, the variables written by e_2 are $writes(e_2) = \{$status$\}$.

2.3   Quality Criteria - Fitness and Precision

We use two criteria to determine the quality of the guards defined on the output transitions of place p of a DPN given an event log $\mathscr{E}$: place fitness and place precision. We denote the set of events for transitions in the output transition of a place p with $\mathscr{E}_p$, i.e., $e \in \mathscr{E}$ iff $trans(e)$ is an output transition of p. We define the **place fitness** of a place based on the number of events in $\mathscr{E}_p$ for which the guard is violated:

$$fitness_{\mathscr{E},p} = 1 - \frac{\left|\{e \in \mathscr{E}_p \mid \text{Guard of } trans(e) \text{ is violated}\}\right|}{|\mathscr{E}_p|}$$

The place fitness linearly decreases with an increase of the fraction of output transitions that fire violating the respective guard. The **place precision** of a place p is defined as is based on the possible behavior at p defined by the DPN, and actual behavior observed in $\mathscr{E}_p$. We use functions $pos_p : \mathscr{E} \to \mathbb{N}$ and $obs_p : \mathscr{E} \to \mathbb{N}$ returning the possible and observed executions of output transitions of place p before event e occurred. Work [12] describes how to obtain values for pos_p and obs_p given an event log and a DPN. Using pos_p and obs_p, we define the place precision as:

$$precision_{\mathscr{E},p} = \frac{\sum_{e \in \mathscr{E}_p} |obs_p(e)|}{\sum_{e \in \mathscr{E}_p} |pos_p(e)|}$$

Given a data set that allows for precise disjunctive guards, the place precision gets lower when guards on the output transitions are more overlapping.

3   Discovery of DPN with Overlapping Decision Rules

Given an event log containing information about process executions and a process model, the problem of decision mining can be regarded as that of discovering a DPN that characterizes the process: given a Petri net, we aim to discover the variables, write operations and guards of a DPN. Without loss of generality, we assume that event log $\mathcal{E}$ is defined over the same transitions, variables and universe of values as the DPN.

Furthermore, we make four assumptions on the input event log $\mathcal{E}$. First, we assume that ignoring the variables, all recorded process instances are *compliant* with regard to the process represented by the Petri net. Second, for each event $e \in \mathcal{E}$ the executed transition can be uniquely determined, i.e., there are no unobservable transitions and each event can be uniquely mapped onto a single transition of the model. Third, we assume that events write attributes consistently, i.e., if an event writes an attribute v then all other events corresponding to the same transition also write attribute v. Fourth, we assume an initial value for each attribute. We show later in Sect. 3.3 that any event log can be transformed to an event log fulfilling these assumptions.

We discover the write operations of the DPN as follows. For each transition t of the Petri net, variable v is written by transition t if there exists an event $e \in \mathcal{E} : trans(e) = t$ that assigns a value to variable v (i.e., $v \in writes(e)$). We discover the guards for each transition t as described the next Sect. 3.1.

3.1   Overall Discovery Procedure

For each decision point p (i.e., places with more than two output transitions) we construct a set of observation instances related to p to be used to discover the guards. Given a set X, we denote the set of all multi-sets over a set X with $\mathbb{B}(X)$. Moreover, we use notation $X = [a^2, b]$ as short-hand notation to denote the multi-set $X = [a, a, b]$. Finally, we use $\uplus$ to denote the sum of two multi-sets, i.e., $X \uplus [b, c] = [a^2, b^2, c]$.

Definition 1 (Observation Instances). *Let V be a set of variables and let U be a universe of possible values. Let P be the set of places of a Petri net and let $p \in P$ be a decision point. We denote with $p^\bullet = \{t_1, \ldots, t_m\}$ the output transitions of p. Function $I \in P \to \mathbb{B}((V \to U) \times T)$ returns the multi-set of observation instances for p:*

$$I(p) = \biguplus_{e \in \mathcal{E}, trans(e) \in p^\bullet} [(values(e), trans(e))]$$

For each event $e \in \mathcal{E}$ that refers to an output transition of p, i.e., $trans(e) \in p^\bullet$, the set of observation instances of p contains an instance $(\boldsymbol{x}, t) \in I(p)$, with $x \in (V \to U)$ being the observed values of the attributes, and t the observed transition. The values of $\boldsymbol{x}$ are obtained by taking the latest observed value for the attributes in preceding events.

Example 3. Given the process model introduced in Example 1 and the event log $\mathcal{E}$ introduced in Example 2 the multiset of observation instances for place p_1 is $I(p_1) = [((\text{status} = unpaid, \text{amount} = 30), \text{Payment})^2, ((\text{status} = unpaid, \text{amount} = 30), \text{Send Fine})^2, ((\text{status} = paid, \text{amount} = 30), \text{Close Fine})]$.

Algorithm 1. discoverGuards

Input: Petri net (Places P, Transitions T), Compliant Event Log ($\mathscr{E}$), Minimum Instances (v), Merge Ratio (ε)
Result: Guards of the DPN G

1   **foreach** $p \in P$ *s.t.* $|p^\bullet| > 1$ **do** $\psi_p \leftarrow$ buildEstimator$(p,I,v \cdot |I(p)|,\varepsilon)$
2   **foreach** $t \in T$ **do**
3      $G(t) \leftarrow$ true
4   **foreach** $p \in {}^\bullet t$ **do** $G(t) \leftarrow G(t) \wedge \psi_p(t)$
5   **end**
6   **return** G

Algorithm 1 describes the overall discovery method for the entire Petri net. Using the observation instances I_p, we build the guard function ψ_p for each decision point $p \in P$ through function buildEstimator. Having obtained the guard function, we assign each transition the conjunction of all rules obtained from their input places [4]. Function buildEstimator is described in the next Sect. 3.2.

3.2 Discovering Overlapping Rules

Whereas the construction of the observation instances $I(p)$ and the overall discovery procedure share similarities with the previous work [4], our technique considerably differs in how the actual rules are obtained through function buildEstimator. Our contribution is a new algorithm that discovers guards that may be partially overlapping, i.e., two or more transitions may be enabled for some state reachable in the DPN. We now describe how to compute function buildEstimator, which discovers overlapping guards for place p given the observation instances $I(p)$ and two user-defined parameters, the minimum number of instances n and the merge ratio ε. As our approach makes use of decision trees, we introduce the concept of decision tree builder.

Definition 2 (C4.5 Decision Tree Builder). *Let T be a set of transitions. Let $O = \mathbb{B}((V \to U) \times T)$ be a multi-set of observation instances over a set V of variables with values U. Let $n \in \mathbb{N}$ be the minimum number of instances on a leaf for the splitting criterion in the decision tree induction. Let $\mathscr{F}(V)$ be the universe of formulas over variable V. Function* buildTree$_n(O) \in 2^{\mathscr{F}(V) \times T}$ *returns the leaves of a C4.5 decision tree built using the supplied set of instances. A leaf $(expr,t) \in$ buildTree$_n(O)$ predicts transition $t \in T$ under condition $expr \in \mathscr{F}(V)$.*

The rule for a leaf of the decision tree is obtained by taking the conjunction of all conditions represented by those nodes that are encountered on a path from the leaf up to the root node [4]. As in [4], a **base decision tree** $baseTree =$ buildTree$_n(I(p))$ is first built. We obtain the initial guard of transition t by taking the disjunction of all rules predicting t:

$$\psi(t) \leftarrow \begin{cases} \bigvee_{(expr,t) \in baseTree}(expr) & \text{if } \exists\, expr' \text{ s.t. } (expr',t) \in baseTree \\ \text{false} & \text{otherwise} \end{cases}$$

For each leaf $l = (expr,t)$ of the base decision tree, we extract those instances $\bar{I}_l$ that have been wrongly classified by the base classifier: $\bar{I}_l$ contains all those instances

$(x,t') \in I(p)$ such that the predicted transition t' is different from the transition t in leaf l, i.e., $t' \neq t$. Next, we build an **new decision tree** *subTree* based on $\bar{I}_l$ for each leaf, i.e., *subTree* $=$ buildTree$_{n'}(\bar{I}_l)$. Since the size of $\bar{I}_l$ can be significantly smaller than that of I, we scale down the parameter n to $n' = n \cdot |\bar{I}_l| / |I|$. The idea is that the second decision tree *subTree$_l$* can *further discriminate* between the observed transitions among the wrongly classified instances, thus, possibly introducing partial overlap with the existing rule. There are two possible cases:

1. a decision tree with more than one leaf is found: $|subTree_l| > 1$;
2. a single-node decision tree with a single leaf $(\mathtt{true}, t')$: $subTree_l = (\mathtt{true}, t')$

In the **first case**, we build rules for each leaf $l' = (subExpr, t') \in subTree_l$ by taking the conjunction of the rule *expr* from leaf l of tree *baseTree* and the newly discovered rule *subExpr*. We obtain the new guard of transitions t' by adding newly discovered rules in disjunction to the existing ones:

$$\psi(t') \leftarrow \psi(t') \vee \bigvee_{(subExpr, t') \in subTree_l} (expr \wedge subExpr).$$

In the **second case** the decision tree represents a majority vote, i.e., the transition that was most often observed within the wrong instances is predicted. In this case we add rule *expr* to the existing guard $\psi(t')$, i.e., $\psi(t') \leftarrow \psi(t') \vee (expr)$, but only if two conditions are met that avoid overfitting the data. First, $|\bar{I}_l| > n$, and, second, the fraction of observation instance in $\bar{I}_l$ referring to t' is larger than the user-specified merge ratio ε. Finally, we assume that all transitions for which no rule could be found are always enabled. For a formal discussion of our algorithm refer to the technical report [13].

Fig. 2. Two decision trees that are discovered on the example data set. The number of instances is written in the root node (rectangle). The number of wrongly and correctly predicted instances is written next to leaf nodes (circle)

Example 4. Given the multi-set of observations for place p_1 obtained from the events given in Table 1, we build the guard estimation functions for each output transition of p_1. First an initial decision tree is built. Assume that this initial decision tree consists of two leafs $l_1 = (\mathtt{status} = \mathit{paid}, \mathtt{Close\ Fine})$ and $l_2 = (\mathtt{status} = \mathit{unpaid}, \mathtt{Send\ Fine})$ as shown in Fig. 2. Ten of the 30 instances classified as Close Fine are wrongly classified. In all those instances transition Payment was observed. Those wrongly classified instances give evidence that also transition Payment is performed when status is *unpaid*. As depicted on the right-hand side of Fig. 2 an additional decision tree is built for those 10 instances. As the set of wrong observation instances $\bar{I}_{l_2}$ only contains instances for transition Payment, the additional decision tree only consists of one leaf that always predicts transition Payment by majority vote. If the user-defined threshold n is below the number of wrongly classified instances $|\bar{I}_{l_2}| = 10$, then, the condition status = *unpaid* will be added to the guard function of Payment. The same rule as shown in Fig. 1 is then discovered. Please note that this example is deliberately simplified. In a real-life setting event logs contain more than two attribute and, therefore, the additional decision would consist of multiple leafs.

3.3 Dealing with Real-Life Event Logs

In Sect. 3 we have made several assumptions to explain the key idea: the event log fits the Petri net perfectly, the set of attributes written by an event is consistent throughout the log, and every attribute value is initialized in the event corresponding to the first transition. Generally, real-life event logs do not satisfy this requirement. However, we can deal with these issues as shown next.

Non-compliant Event Log and Duplicate Transitions. An event log might contain events that cannot be matched reliably to a single transition in the DPN (e.g., in presence of noise or duplicate transitions). Similarly, for some transitions that are required according to the model no event has been recorded (e.g., when the recording is incomplete or for invisible routing transitions). Therefore, it might not be possible to determine *trans(e)* for every event $e \in \mathcal{E}$. Using *alignment-based* techniques such as [5, 11] we can determine a closest corresponding **process trace**, i.e., the sequence of transition executions leading to a final state of the DPN, for each *log trace*. Work [4] uses the same technique to deal with non compliant event logs and shows that for reasonably compliant event logs the error introduced by such an alignment is negligible.

Inconsistent Attributes. In Sect. 3, we restricted the set of write operations for a transition to those variables that are consistently given a value by every event e in *trans(e)*. In real-life logs attribute values can be missing due to temporary recording errors leading to an inconsistent recording of attributes for some transitions. Moreover, the *alignment-based* techniques might need to introduce artificial events with missing attribute values. Therefore we introduce a user-defined threshold K like in [4], but add a way to deal with missing values to it. A variable v is added to the set of write operations of a transition t when the variable is observed to be given a value by $K\%$ of the events e of t (i.e., *trans(e)* = t). As a result, attributes might be missing from the set of attributes written for an event $e \in \mathcal{E}$. Every time an event e does not assign a value to variable v even though it should, we assume its value *values(e)(v)* to be $\diamond$. Symbol $\diamond$ indicates that the value is *missing*. The C4.5 algorithm can deal with such missing values.

Unassigned Attributes. Decision trees cannot deal with uninitialized attributes (similar to NULL values in databases). In real-life event logs, attributes might be uninitialized if some of the first events of the log's traces do not assign a value to all attributes. This issue can be mitigated by defining default values that are used when attribute have not taken on values yet. As an example, let us assume an attribute APPROVAL with two literal values assigned by events: No and Yes. As default value, we can introduce a third possible value Unknown, make it possible to discover rules APPROVAL = Unknown.

4   Evaluation

We evaluate our technique using two real-life data sets, and compare the obtained results to standard methods like decision tree induction algorithms. An implementation of our technique is available in the *MultiPerspectiveExplorer* [14] package of the open-source process mining framework ProM.

4.1   Evaluation Setup

Approaches. We compared the performance of our approach expressed in terms of place fitness and place precision with three other methods. We choose two methods at the extreme ends of the respective measure, and one method that naïvely introduces overlap. In total, we compared the following four approaches:

WO. The model without rules, i.e., the guard `true` is used for all transitions. This results in a perfect place fitness, no guard is violated.

DTF. The model with rules discovered by a decision tree as in work [4] using `false` as guard for transitions that are not observed in the tree. This method will always result in a perfect place precision as there is only one enabled transition.

DTT. The model with rules discovered by a decision tree as in work [4] using `true` as guard for transitions not observed in the tree. This method naïvely introduces overlap by enabling all those transitions.

DTO. The model with rules discovered by the approach reported on in this paper as described in Sect. 3.1.

The DTF and WO methods are at the extreme ends of the respective measures. Our approach aims at providing better place fitness (i.e., less violated guards) at the expense of some place precision (i.e., multiple enabled transitions). Therefore, our approach should provide better place fitness than the DTF method together with better place precision than the a model without rules (WO). Method DTT is included to investigate whether our approach improves over a naïve method to introduce overlap.

Event Logs and Process Models. We used two anonymized real-life data sets: *road fines* and *sepsis*. The road fines event log was taken from an information system handling road-traffic fines by an Italian local police force [15]. The road fines log contains more than 150,000 cases with approximately 500,000 events. There are 9 data attributes recorded including the fine amount and the payment amount. The sepsis event log contains events about the pathways of patients within a hospital that have a suspicion for sepsis, a life threatening condition typically caused by an infection. This event log contains data recorded during a full year resulting in 1056 cases with about 15,000 events. There are 39 data attributes recorded, e.g., the results of blood tests and information about the patient from checklists filled in by nurses. For both event logs, we obtained a normative process model of the control-flow, thus, without any guards. We used the control-flow of the process model presented in [5] for the road fines data set. For the sepsis data set, we created a model with help of domain experts from the hospital. Both models allow for most the behavior observed in the logs, but are lacking precision.

We checked this using the fitness measure defined for DPNs in work [5] (road fines: 99.7 %, sepsis: 98.6 %) and the precision measure for DPNs proposed by [12] (road fines: 63.9 % , sepsis: 16.5 %). Therefore, both models are good candidates for adding precision through discovered rules.

Experimental Design. We performed experiments for every decision point for the road-fines and sepsis models, with the exception of four decision points of the sepsis model for which no technique was able to discover rules. We use the C4.5 implementation of the WEKA toolkit with the pruning feature activated; the merge ratio ε was set to 0.5 in all experiments. For each technique, we used 10 different values of *minimum number of instances* (`minInstances`) parameter that were equally distributed within a certain interval, which is determined as follows. The smallest value of the interval was chosen such that the discovered guards were not composed by more than 7 atoms. This choice was based on the assumption that guards with more than 7 atoms are too complex and humanly unreadable and, hence, of no business value. The upper bound of the interval was the smallest value that could still return a rule, i.e. larger values would return no rules. In fact, a too large value of the `minInstances` parameter would constrain the decision tree to be representative of so many instances that no reliable rule can be returned. It is worth observing that the interval potentially changed with varying the decision point and the technique (DTO, DTT and DTF) being considered.

4.2   Results and Discussion

We conducted the experiments and recorded the obtained place fitness and place precision for 15 places and 10 parameter settings[1]. The boxplot in Fig. 3 shows the results. In the following paragraphs, we compare our method to the three other approaches.

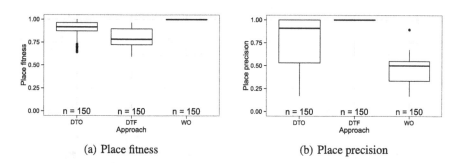

(a) Place fitness   (b) Place precision

Fig. 3. Place fitness and local precision achieved by the proposed method (DTO) compared to the standard decision tree classifier (DTF), and the model without guards (WO)

---

[1] The data used for the evaluation is available under http://purl.tue.nl/844997340832257. For confidentiality reasons we cannot share the sepsis event log.

DTO vs. WO. Compared to WO, the results from our experiment (Fig. 3(b)) show clearly that DTO provides rules that increase the place precision against the process model without guards. The large spread of the obtained place precision indicates that, for some decision points and some parameter settings, our approach deliberately trades precision to obtain better fitting guards. This result is in line with the expectation that our approach returns overlapping rules that lose some precision for a better fitness.

DTO vs. DTF. The experimental results show that DTO discovers decision rules that lead to a better place fitness than the rules discovered by DTF (Fig. 3(a)) with, on average, a limited trade-off for lower precision. The outliers for DTO in Fig. 3(a) deserve some discussion. We inspected them and found that for some combinations of parameter settings and places, our approach failed to discover overlapping guards. It discovers the exact same rules as returned by DTT. Mostly, this happens for decision points with only two outgoing transitions and high settings of the `minInstances` parameter. This can be expected, as for decision trees with instances from two classes $\{A,B\}$ the wrong instances on a leaf $l = (expr,A)$ predicting transition A can only belong to the other transition B. Therefore, our approach will not discover a second decision tree with leafs predicting B, but rather use rule *expr* from leaf l for the majority vote transition B. Our approach only allows this if the number of instances for B is above the setting of the `minInstances` parameter. Therefore, for high settings of `minInstances` and decision points with two outgoing transitions our approach is unlikely to improve over the normal decision tree classifier approach.

DTO vs. DTT. We also compare DTO against DTT, which naïvely assumes the guard `true` for transitions that are not predicted by the decision tree. For this comparison, we compare the results for decision points with more than two outgoing transitions, $|p^\bullet| > 2$, as the results obtained through DTT differ from the results of DTF only for those decision points. Figure 4(b) shows the fitness and precision for those places averaged over 10 parameter settings as discussed in Sect. 4.1. Each place is given a name for reference. The results in Fig. 4(b) show that DTO is able to discover overlapping guards that fit the observations better: for all of the considered decision points, the decision

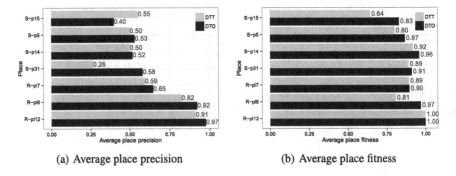

(a) Average place precision   (b) Average place fitness

Fig. 4. Average place fitness and place precision achieved by the DTO method compared to the DTT method. Only decision points with more than two choices are shown.

rules returned by our approach increase the place fitness against those rules returned by DTT. Furthermore, the results show that for all except one decision point our app-roach discovers rules with higher place precision. In other words, it discovers more precise guards without loosing fitness. In fact, for decision point S-p31 our approach obtained an average place precision of 0.58 whereas the rule returned by the DTT app-roach scores only 0.26. Our approach discovers guards for all six outgoing transitions whereas DTT only discovers guards for three transitions. On the remaining three DTT uses `true` as a guard, i.e., always enabled. The only decision point for which DTO obtains a worse precision score than DTT is S-p15. Our approach discovers guards that correspond to `true` for all three alternatives. However, this is not necessarily a bad rep-resentation of the observed data. In fact, the guards discovered by DTT cause the lowest place fitness in our experiment 0.65, i.e., the discovered guards are wrong in one third of the cases.

Example. Figure 5 shows a part of the DPN that we used for the sepsis data set. Table 2 shows the guards discovered by DTF, DTT and DTO, the approach presented in this paper, for the three alternative activities on decision point S-p5. All rules are based on two attributes: `Lactate` (L) and `Hypotensie` (H). DTF discovers the rule that patients with a lactate measurement (i.e., $L > 0$) are generally admitted to normal care and patients without lactate measurement ($L \leq 0$) leave the hospital. The guard for the admission to intensive care is returned as `false`. This leads to the situation where patients are never admitted to intensive care even if it is part of the model and observed. Obviously, this cannot be correct. DTF is unable to find a mutually-exclusive rule that includes this alternative activity given the information recorded in the event log. DTT discovers the same rules but naïvely assumes the guard `true` for admission to inten-sive care. Clearly, the DTT results are not satisfying as DTT would convey no rules about the admission of patients to intensive care. Our approach - DTO - discovers that patients with a lactate measurement ($L > 0$) can always be admitted to normal care. As an alternative to normal care, if attribute $H = $ `true` then patients can also be admitted to intensive care; otherwise, if $H = $ `false` patients leave the hospital. The guards for the activities overlap and the final decision is likely to be made on the basis of contextual factors, which are not encoded in the event log.

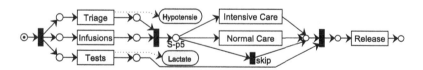

Fig. 5. Fragment of the process model used for the sepsis data set. After a triage form is filled, infusions are given and blood tests are taken patients are admitted to normal care, intensive care, or not admitted (skip). Two relevant attributes are recorded: `Lactat` (L) and `Hypotensie` (H).

Limitations and Threats to Validity. The results show that our technique is successful in uncovering overlapping rules in processes from event logs, and that these rules pro-vide in some cases a much better characterization of the observed behavior. Still, the

Table 2. Guards discovered by the compared approaches at decision point S-p5

Approach	Normale care	Intensive care	Not admitted
DTF	$L > 0$	`false`	$L \leq 0$
DTT	$L > 0$	`true`	$L \leq 0$
DTO	$L > 0$	$L > 0 \wedge H = \texttt{true}$	$(L > 0 \wedge H = \texttt{false}) \vee L \leq 0$

proposed technique has some limitations and we evaluated our technique using only two real-life event logs. More experimental validation using event logs from different settings is required. An inherent limitation of our approach is that it can only use the majority vote to introduce overlapping guards for a decision point with two output transitions. This might cause the guard of one transition to be turned into the rule `true`, e.g. when the initial guards were based on a single condition. Our approach tends to discover guards that are more complex: Guard may become unreadable if algorithm's parameters are not carefully chosen.

5   Related Work

There are several approaches for decision mining given an event log with historical data about the process [1,3,4,6,16–21]. In all of these approaches, the decision-mining problem is translated into a classification problem, and solved using classification analysis techniques such as C4.5 [7]. However, every approach only discovers mutually-exclusive rules. Most related from the traditional classification field to our approach is work about multi-label classification [22,23]. In a multi-label classification problem classes are not mutually exclusive, instances can be labeled with multiple classes, and the goal is to find the correct set of classes for unseen instances. Our setting is still different as we deal with instances that are only associated with one class, i.e., the executed transition. So, there is no work about discovering overlapping rules in the context of process models. Classifier chains methods are the closest to our work. They decompose the problem into multiple binary classification problems, one for each label [24]. This method assumes that instances are labeled with multiple classes. Also related to our work are methods for association rule mining [25]. The main problem of association-rule mining is that a potentially large set of rules is usually returned, failing to provide insights that are easy to interpret.

6   Conclusion

We propose a new technique for the discovery of overlapping rules in process models using event data. Existing techniques only return rules that assume completely deterministic decisions. This assumption rarely holds in reality. Our technique is the *first proposal* of a discovery technique that introduces overlapping rules. The technique aims to create process models that trade the precision of mutually-exclusive rules for the fitness of overlapping rules when the observed behavior gives evidence to such rules.

The evaluation using several real data sets shows that our technique is able to produce models with overlapping rules that fit the observed behavior better without loosing too much precision. For some decision points, with more than 2 alternative activities, our technique returns rules that are both more fitting and more precise than the existing method [4]. As future work, we aim to investigate the application of other machine-learning techniques to decision mining. Moreover, we want to address limitations of decision mining techniques for data sets with imbalanced distributions of classes. We found that our technique helps to reveal rules when one transition is only observed for a small fraction of the cases, but a more thorough investigation of this phenomenon is needed.

References

1. van der Aalst, W.M.P.: Process Mining - Discovery, Conformance and Enhancement of Business Processes. Springer, Heidelberg (2011)
2. Object Management Group (OMG): Decision Model And Notation (DMN) Version 1.0, formal/2015-09-01 (2015)
3. Rozinat, A., van der Aalst, W.M.P.: Decision mining in ProM. In: Dustdar, S., Fiadeiro, J.L., Sheth, A.P. (eds.) BPM 2006. LNCS, vol. 4102, pp. 420–425. Springer, Heidelberg (2006)
4. de Leoni, M., van der Aalst, W.M.P.: Data-aware process mining: discovering decisions in processes using alignments. In: SAC 2013, pp. 1454–1461. ACM (2013)
5. Mannhardt, F., de Leoni, M., Reijers, H.A., van der Aalst, W.M.P.: Balanced multi-perspective checking of process conformance. Computing **98**(4), 407–437 (2016)
6. Grigori, D., Casati, F., Castellanos, M., Dayal, U., Sayal, M., Shan, M.C.: Business process intelligence. Comput. Ind. **53**(3), 321–343 (2004)
7. Quinlan, J.R.: C4.5: Programs for Machine Learning. Morgan Kaufmann Publishers Inc., San Francisco (1993)
8. Rosca, D., Wild, C.: Towards a flexible deployment of business rules. Expert Syst. Appl. **23**(4), 385–394 (2002)
9. Bose, R.P.J.C., Mans, R.S., van der Aalst, W.M.P.: Wanna improve process mining results? In: IEEE Symposium on Computational Intelligence and Data Mining, pp. 127–134 (2013)
10. Desel, J., Esparza, J.: Free Choice Petri Nets. Cambridge University Press, New York (1995)
11. van der Aalst, W.M.P., Adriansyah, A., van Dongen, B.F.: Replaying history on process models for conformance checking and performance analysis. Wiley Interdiscip. Rev. Data Min. Knowl. Discov. **2**(2), 182–192 (2012)
12. Mannhardt, F., de Leoni, M., Reijers, H.A., van der Aalst, W.M.P.: Measuring the precision of multi-perspective process models. In: Business Process Management Workshops - BPM 2015 (2015, to appear)
13. Mannhardt, F., de Leoni, M., Reijers, H.A., van der Aalst, W.M.P.: Decision mining revisited - discovering overlapping rules. Technical report, BPMcenter.org, BPM Center Report BPM-01-06 (2016)
14. Mannhardt, F., de Leoni, M., Reijers, H.A.: The multi-perspective process explorer. In: BPM Demo Session 2015, vol. 1418, pp. 130–134. CEUR-WS.org (2015)
15. de Leoni, M., Mannhardt, F.: Road traffic fine management process. Eindhoven University ofTechnology. Dataset (2015). doi:10.4121/uuid:270fd440-1057-4fb9-89a9-b699b47990f5
16. Jareevongpiboon, W., Janecek, P.: Ontological approach to enhance results of business process mining and analysis. Bus. Process. Manag. J. **19**(3), 459–476 (2013)

17. Catalkaya, S., Knuplesch, D., Chiao, C., Reichert, M.: Enriching business process models with decision rules. In: Lohmann, N., Song, M., Wohed, P. (eds.) BPM 2013 Workshops. LNBIP, vol. 171, pp. 198–211. Springer, Heidelberg (2014)
18. Ghattas, J., Soffer, P., Peleg, M.: Improving business process decision making based on past experience. Decis. Support Syst. **59**, 93–107 (2014)
19. Bazhenova, E., Weske, M.: Deriving decision models from process models by enhanced decision mining. In: Business Process Management Workshops - BPM 2015 (2015, to appear)
20. Dunkl, R., Rinderle-Ma, S., Grossmann, W., Anton Fröschl, K.: A method for analyzing time series data in process mining: application and extension of decision point analysis. In: Nurcan, S., Pimenidis, E. (eds.) CAiSE Forum 2014. LNBIP, vol. 204, pp. 68–84. Springer, Heidelberg (2015)
21. de Leoni, M., Dumas, M., García-Bañuelos, L.: Discovering branching conditions from business process execution logs. In: Cortellessa, V., Varró, D. (eds.) FASE 2013 (ETAPS 2013). LNCS, vol. 7793, pp. 114–129. Springer, Heidelberg (2013)
22. Boutell, M.R., Luo, J., Shen, X., Brown, C.M.: Learning multi-label scene classification. Pattern Recogn. **37**(9), 1757–1771 (2004)
23. Tsoumakas, G., Katakis, I.: Multi-label classification: an overview. Int. J. Data Warehouse. Min. **2007**, 1–13 (2007)
24. Read, J., Pfahringer, B., Holmes, G., Frank, E.: Classifier chains for multi-label classification. Mach. Learn. **85**(3), 333–359 (2011)
25. Agrawal, R., Imieliński, T., Swami, A.: Mining association rules between sets of items in large databases. SIGMOD Rec. **22**(2), 207–216 (1993)

An Adaptability-Driven Model and Tool for Analysis of Service Profitability

Ouh Eng Lieh[1(✉)] and Stan Jarzabek[2]

[1] Institute of Systems Science, National University of Singapore,
25, Heng Mui Keng Terrace, Singapore 119615, Singapore
englieh@nus.edu.sg
[2] Faculty of Computer Science, Bialystok University of Technology, Bialystok, Poland
s.jarzabek@pb.edu.pl

Abstract. Profitability of adopting Software-as-a-Service (SaaS) solutions for existing applications is currently analyzed mostly in informal way. Informal analysis is unreliable because of the many conflicting factors that affect costs and benefits of offering applications on the cloud. We propose a quantitative economic model for evaluating profitability of migrating to SaaS that enables potential service providers to evaluate costs and benefits of various migration strategies and choices of target service architectures. In previous work, we presented a rudimentary conceptual SaaS economic model enumerating factors that have to do with service profitability, and defining qualitative relations among them. A quantitative economic model presented in this paper extends the conceptual model with equations that quantify these relations, enabling more precise reasoning about profitability of various SaaS implementation strategies, helping potential service providers to select the most suitable strategy for their business situation.

Keywords: Service provider · Service profitability · Service architecture · Service variability · Service engineering

1 Introduction

Cloud computing paradigm promises service providers to reach large customer base, selling software at cheaper price (which benefits customers). Still, cloud computing, and Software-as-a-Service (SaaS) in particular is not for all businesses, nor for all software applications. The question whether or not a service solution will be profitable is not easy to answer. The following sample illustrates why informal analysis of SaaS profitability is difficult:

Service profitability depends on the cost of engineering a service for a given customer base, on service provisioning cost, and on the revenue gained from selling the service to that customer base. The customer base depends on the level of service adaptability, i.e., on Service Provider's ability to vary service requirements to meet requirements of various customers. The cost of engineering a service for adaptability depends on selected service architecture. A service architecture that minimizes provisioning cost at the same

© Springer International Publishing Switzerland 2016
S. Nurcan et al. (Eds.): CAiSE 2016, LNCS 9694, pp. 393–408, 2016.
DOI: 10.1007/978-3-319-39696-5_24

time limits service adaptability, which in turn decreases the customer base and profit. The cost of engineering a service further depends on the required level of service adaptability, and whether we build service from scratch or by modernizing the legacy code. In the latter case, the cost depends on availability of modernization methods that aid and automate the migration process.

SaaS profitability is determined by a complex web of inter-related and often conflicting forces that make manual analysis unreliable. Service profitability has been widely discussed primarily in the context of novel service business and pricing models, engineering and provisioning methods (covered in Sect. 6) however no formal treatment of the subject taking into account the many factors has been proposed. These existing works take into account only a small subset of these factors, giving a potentially incomplete analysis of service profitability especially without considering the trade-offs among these factors. In this paper, we fill this gap by proposing a quantitative economic model of service profitability.

In our previous works [1, 2], we set a rudimentary formal ground for analysis of service profitability. We identified factors that affect service profitability, and built a qualitative conceptual model formalizing dependencies among those factors. Our conceptual model shows how decisions regarding the choices of service architecture, dynamic (at service runtime) versus static (at the service construction-time) service adaptation techniques, or the size of the tenant base affect service profitability. The conceptual model built so far allows us to do qualitative analysis of service profitability. It helps a Service Provider to spot the decisions regarding service architecture and provisioning that are relevant in her situation, but it does not allow her to reason about the impact of those decisions on profitability in any rigorous way.

The contribution of this paper is a quantitative economic model of service profitability that we built on top of the conceptual model. This extended model assigns weights to various decisions and captures the impact of those decisions as formulas, in quantitative way. In particular, our economic model allows Service Providers to reason about profitability under various assumptions and answer questions such as: "To what degree does the selection of service architecture impact service profitability?"

Our economic model can help Service Providers to evaluate the impact of various decisions and SaaS strategies in a more systematic way than the conceptual model alone, but is difficult to use manually. Therefore, we also implemented a tool that automates model calculations and guides Service Provider in exploring migration strategies to SaaS and their expected profits. Section 2 documents our proposed Service Profitability Model. We introduce a process method and tool to evaluate for service profitability in Sects. 3 and 4. Experiments and analysis are in Sect. 5, followed by related work in Sect. 6. Conclusions and future works are in Sect. 7.

2   Service Profitability Model

The concept map shown in Fig. 1 summarizes our model concepts. In our earlier paper, we described how this concept map can be applied to address key service profitability questions that are of interest to Service Providers. In this paper, we extends the conceptual model with definitions and equations that quantify the relationships among the factors in the concept map.

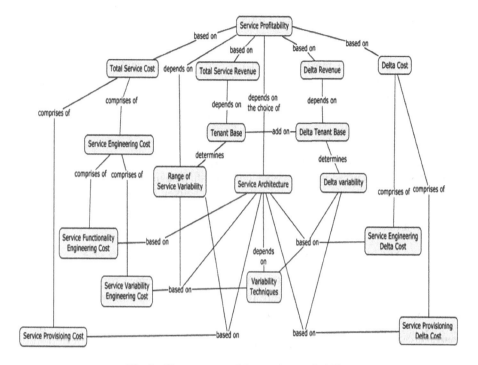

Fig. 1. Concept map of the service profitability

2.1 Preliminary Concepts and Definitions

Definition 1 (Tenant Base). The initial Tenant Base (*TB*) comprises of the initial tenants of a given service. Delta Tenant Base (*DTB*) comprises of the tenants a Service Provider expects to on-board in a specific time frame in the future.

Service Provider needs to address two sets of tenants' requirements for a given service: the initial tenant base (*TB*) and the delta tenant base (*DTB*). A Service Provider may already have the need to provide the service to a set of initial tenants. On the other hand during service period, new tenants may request to use the service and these tenants form the delta tenant base.

Definition 2 (Range of Service Variability). The Range of Service Variability (*RSV*) is the extent to which a Service can be adapted to varying service requirements of different tenants.

The bigger range the service can accommodate, more tenants can be on-boarded and higher revenue for the Service Provider. To on-board a tenant, the Service must be able to meet the requirements of that tenant. As *RSV* reflects the Service Provider's ability to customize the Service, *RSV* determines the *TB* that can be supported. On the other hand for business strategic reasons, the Service Provider may have some target tenants in mind and engineer the *RSV* to meet the varying requirements of the target *TB*. Service Provider's dream is always to engineer a service where *RSV* fulfills the varying requirements of the *TB*, maximizing service profits.

Definition 3 (Service Engineering Costs). Service Engineering Costs (*SEC*) are incurred to engineer the functionality of the Service and to engineer the Service to support a given *RSV* on a given Service Architecture (*SA*). We termed this as Service Functionality Engineering Cost (*SFEC*) and Service Variability Engineering Cost (*SVEC*) respectively, collectively termed as the Service Engineering Costs (*SEC*).

Service Variability Engineering Cost (*SVEC*) is the cost of engineering Service based on the selected Variability Techniques (*VT*) to support a given *RSV* on a given *SA*, defined as a function of < *SA, RSV, VT*>. The relevant variability techniques to support a given *RSV* are discussed in [1]. Service Functionality Engineering Cost (*SFEC*) is the cost of engineering Service functionality to support a given *RSV* on a given *SA*. Service Engineering Cost (*SEC*) is the cost of engineering the Service for a given *SA* and *RSV* defined as a function of < *SA, RSV, VT*>.

$$SEC <SA, RSV, VT> = SFEC <SA> + SVEC <SA, RSV, VT>$$

Definition 4 (Service Provisioning Costs). Service Provisioning Cost (*SPC*) is the cost to provide hardware and infrastructure resources to provision a Service to support a given *RSV* on a given *SA*. *SPC* is defined as a function of < *SA, RSV*>. *SPC* can be incurred upfront independent of number of tenants termed as $SPC_{Upfront}$ or during operation based on the number of tenants termed as SPC_{Op}.

Definition 5 (Total Service Costs). Total Service Costs (*TSC*) is the total service costs of engineering (*SEC*) and provisioning (*SPC*) the Service on a given service *SA* to a given *TB*.

$$TSC < SA, RSV, VT > = SEC < SA, RSV, VT > + SPC < SA, RSV >$$

Definition 6 (Total Service Revenue). Total Service Revenue (*TSR*) is the total revenue from selling the Service on a given service *SA* to a given *TB*.

Definition 7 (Delta Variability). Delta Variability (*DV*) is the changes to existing Service requirements required to on-board a given *DTB*. The degree of engineering changes due to *DV* is termed as $DV_{engineering}$ and the degree of provisioning changes due to *DV* is termed as $DV_{provisioning}$.

Definition 8 (Delta Cost). Delta Cost (*DC*) is the engineering and provisioning costs to implement *DV* for a given *DTB* on a given *SA*.

Service Engineering Delta Cost (*SEDC*) is the cost to engineer the *DV* of a given *DTB* for Service on a given *SA* defined as a function of < *SA, DV, VT* >. Service Provisioning Delta Cost (*SPDC*) is the cost to provide hardware and infrastructure resources to support the *DV* of a given *DTB* on a given *SA*, defined as a function of < *SA, DV*>.

DC comprises of Service Engineering Delta Cost (*SEDC*) and Service Provisioning Delta Cost (*SPDC*) and is defined as a function of < *SA, DV, VT* >.

$$DC < SA, DV, VT > = SEDC < SA, DV, VT > + SPDC < SA, DV >$$

Definition 9 (Delta Revenue). Delta Revenue (*DR*) is the revenue from selling a Service to a given *DTB*.

Definition 10 (Service Profits). Service Profits (*SP*) is the profits from selling a Service to a given *TB* and *DTB* defined as a function of < *TSC, TSR, DC, DR* >.

2.2 Service Profitability

Service Profits (*SP*) are the monetary benefits from selling the service, taking into account the cost and revenue of both the tenant base and the delta tenant base: Providing services for multi-tenants is typically a multi-year project for the Service Providers. As such, we take into account the present value of money over time for economic analysis and use the net present value, expanding on existing literature studies [3, 4] for the analysis of service profitability. The net present value takes into account the engineering and provisioning costs and the revenue gained for both the tenant and delta tenants over an investment cycle. Given an investment cycle Y referring to the expected duration of the investment measured in number of years and discount rate d referring to the time value of money, typically range between 0.1 and 0.2, *SP* can be measured as given by:

$$SP = -(SEC + SPC_{Upfront}) + \sum_{y \in Y}^{Y} \frac{TSR_{(y)} - SPC_{Op(y)} + DR_{(y)} - DC_{(y)}}{(1+d)^y} \tag{1}$$

Intuitively, the overall profits are based on the service costs incurred (fixed costs) regardless of the number of on-boarded tenants and the yearly profits (taking into account the value of money over time) with the tenant and delta tenant base. The expected return on investment (*ROI*) takes into account service profits over the total service and delta costs for a specified number of investment years and can be measured by:

$$ROI = \frac{SP}{\left(SEC + SPC_{Upfront}\right)} \tag{2}$$

Dividing the above *ROI* value by the number of investment years would yield the annualized *ROI*.

3 Analysis of Service Profitability

In this section, we introduce a process to analyze service profitability. The steps of the process are primarily composed of tenant management, service cost management, service delta cost management and service profitability shown in Fig. 2. In each step, the Service Provider enters estimations to characterize her situation.

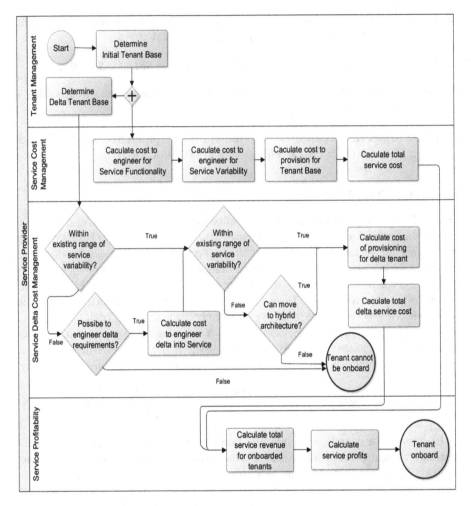

Fig. 2. Process to analyze service profitability

3.1 Tenant Management

This process step allows the Service Provider to specify or make their assumptions on the initial and delta set of tenants' requirements. These requirements can be in terms of the number of tenants, number of users per tenant and their requirements. The Service Provider should be able to specify or assume (e.g. based on variability distributions) the tenant's requirements. These inputs and assumptions is essential for the subsequent computations of the costs, revenue and profits. The Service Provider can modify these inputs to model different possible set of initial and delta tenants.

3.2 Service Cost Management

In our previous study [2], we introduced five types of service architectures. Fully-Shared (SA_{FS}), Partially-Shared (SA_{PS}), Non-Shared (SA_{NS}) and Hybrids (SA_{FSPS} and SA_{FSPSNS}). To manage the variability of tenant's requirements for SA_{FS}, we can design using service oriented architecture (SOA) technique for dynamic binding of the service components.

For SA_{NS}, we can design using product-line variability management technique [5] for static binding of the service components. Similar techniques can be used to manage variability for SA_{PS}, SA_{FSPS} and SA_{FSPSNS}. For analysis of service profitability, Service Provider estimates the costs to engineer both the service functionality and service variability of a given service for the initial tenant base. In order to engineer the service for varying requirements of the tenants, the Service Provider needs to adopt variability techniques of which the costs can differ substantially. These service costs can also differ if the Service Provider decides to migrate from existing application or develop the service from scratch. Cost estimation for both service engineering and service variability engineering can be calculated using existing effort cost estimation models such as COCOMO II. Based on a given service architecture, Service Provider also has to incur cost to provision the service for the tenants. These provisioning costs can differ if the Service Provider decides to lease from external cloud providers, hosting as private cloud or adopt hybrid cloud. Cost estimation for the service provisioning on the cloud can be calculated by using available data from existing cloud providers (e.g. Amazon EC2).

3.3 Service Delta Cost Management

Besides calculating the cost for the initial tenant base, it is also important for the Service Provider to analysis the potential delta tenant base for a more complete service profitability analysis. For each of the delta tenant, a Service Provider need to estimate the effort and cost to engineer the service and service variability for the varying requirements of the tenant. Based on the range of service variability supported by a given service architecture, the Service Provider may need to decide whether to incur additional engineering to address the delta variability as required by the new tenant. The Service Provider may choose to incur the additional cost to engineer the requirements or choose not to on-board the new tenant (e.g. due to shortage of resources).

The Service Provider also has to provision the service for the delta tenant based on the given service architecture. If the given service architecture cannot support the delta tenant's provisioning requirements (e.g. high isolation requirements on a given fully-shared service architecture), the Service Provider can consider to move to hybrid service architecture or choose not to on-board the new tenant. Cost estimation for the delta service engineering and service provisioning can be calculated using the same models as in service cost management.

3.4 Service Profitability

The services costs, service delta costs and revenue gained from on-boarded tenant collectively determined the service profits. Service revenue from the tenant can vary based on the type of pricing models such as pay-per-use, subscription-based. Together with service costs, service delta costs and revenue, service profits and *ROI* can be calculated over a pre-determined service period. The *ROI* can be further annualized based on the number of investment years. The Service Provider can evaluate the outcomes of the service profitability based on different inputs and decisions made.

4   Tooling for Service Profitability Analysis

It is a Service Provider's challenge to design a service for profitability considering multiple factors affecting costs and gains. When designing and provisioning a service, Service Provider may also have various goals for profitability analysis or constraints regarding tenant base or service costs. We implemented a Service Profitability Analyzer (SPA) tool to allow Service Provider to analyze service profitability under various strategies for service design and deployment. SPA implements the concepts and equations defined in the Profitability Model to carry out the analysis under required assumptions. The user interface of SPA is shown in Fig. 3.

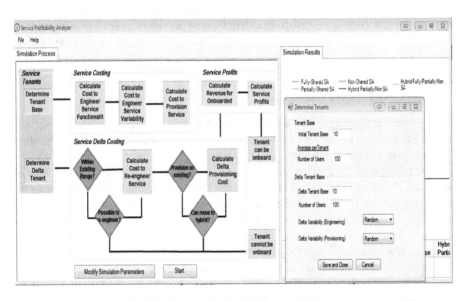

Fig. 3. Service profitability analyzer

A typical scenario is that Service Provider wants to know which service architecture to adopt to maximize profits. To analyze that, Service Provider inputs Service Costing values for the service to SPA. Based on COCOMO II, Service Provider can compute the service functionality and service variability engineering costs. The effort estimation of COCOMO II is based on the following formula where EAF is the effort adjustment Factor derived from the software cost drivers E is an exponent derived from the five software scale drivers.

$$Effort\ Estimation = 2.94 * EAF * (KSLOC)^E \tag{3}$$

One model to calculate provisioning costs is based on Amazon Web Services (AWS). The tool allows for cost inputs for the key web services provided by Amazon; Amazon Elastic Compute Cloud (EC2), Simple Storage Service (S3), Relational Database Service (RDS), DynamoDB, Route 53 and CloudFront. Amazon EC2 provides resizable compute capacity while Amazon S3 provides the fully redundant data storage infrastructure for storing and retrieving any amount of data. Amazon RDS makes it easy to set up, operate, and scale a relational database (e.g. MySQL, Oracle, SQL Server) in the cloud while Amazon DynamoDB is a fast and flexible NoSQL database service for all applications that need consistent, single-digit millisecond latency at any scale. In terms of networking and content delivery, Amazon Route 53 is a highly available and scalable Domain Name System (DNS) web service and Amazon CloudFront provides an easy way to distribute content to end users with low latency and high data transfer speeds. The calculations of the Amazon services are based on the publicly accessible pricing calculator [6].

To capture the demand parameters of the service, the tool enables Service Provider to input the service tenant's requirements in terms of the number of users and tenants for the initial tenant base. In addition, Service Provider can also provide the expected number of delta tenants and the estimated variability ranges of these delta tenants for both the engineering and provisioning requirements as shown in Fig. 3. The possible delta variability values are low, high and random. A low delta variability value indicates a high proportion of the delta tenants require minimum changes required to existing service and a high delta variability value indicates a high proportion of the delta tenants require substantial changes to existing service. A random delta variability value allows the tool to simulate based on a random distribution of the tenants' delta variability.

With these demand inputs, the tool simulates the number of tenants of a given delta variability values for a specified number of investment years. Each tenant along with their delta variability (DV) values are used to calculate the delta engineering $(SEDC)$ and provisioning cost $(SPDC)$ for that tenant as follows.

$$SEDC = DV_{engineering} * SEC * \alpha_{SA,VT} \tag{4}$$

$$SPDC = DV_{provisioning} * SPC * \beta_{SA} \tag{5}$$

α and β are weighted cost coefficients, denoting the impact to the engineering and provisioning costs with a given service architecture and applied variability technique. The higher the value of these cost coefficients, the higher the cost incurred. With the Eqs. 1–5, the overall profits and ROI can be calculated.

We implemented SPA using Visual Basic .Net to compute the equations defined in the Service Profitability Model and allow for dynamic user interactivity. The design of the tool is modular and allow Service Provider to plug-in her own model to calculate estimates of the engineering and provisioning costs. These plug-ins are implemented as dynamic link libraries (DLLs) using .Net. The tool uses .Net reflection to dynamically load the DLLs during runtime. A Service Provider may have more cost factors. For example, branding or marketing costs which impact service profits. The SPA tool can be further adapted with plugins to include such factors.

5 Experiments and Analysis

5.1 Experiments Overview

We conducted experiments using the SPA tool to analyze service profitability of adopting five service architectures for Apache OfBiz (OfBiz) [7]. OfBiz is an open source Java Enterprise Edition (J2EE) package used for enterprise resource planning. In our study we focus on four OfBiz existing services (eCommerceStoreService, Order-Service, CatalogService and PartyService) to be migrated to support multiple tenants. These services comprises of 136 Java classes with close to 48 K lines of code, 61 Groovy files, 127 Freemarker templates and 24 XML Widgets.

To capture the demand parameters of the service, we set the 8 initial tenant base and 30 delta tenants over a 5 year investment period. For the service costs calculation of each service architecture, we first capture the engineering provisioning costs for SA_{FS} and then extrapolate for the rest of the architectures. We estimate the engineering costs by measuring the five major components; external inputs, external outputs, external inquiries, internal logical files and external interface files to obtain 394 unadjusted function points. We use these unadjusted function points value to calculate the effort of engineering the functionality of the service ($SFEC$) based on the COCOMO II model. The COCOMO parameters "required software reliability", "architecture/risk resolution" and "platform" are set to high and the "parameter developed for reusability" is set to very high, the rest of the parameters are set to nominal. We extrapolate service variability engineering costs ($SVEC$) for SA_{PS} by 20 % more than SA_{FS}, based on an earlier study by Poulin and Himler [8] showing that building components for an SOA requires an approximate of 20 % additional cost over development for one-time use. For SA_{NS} using static binding variability technique based on our experiences with the adaptive reuse technique and the study of cost estimation in Software Product Lines [9], we assumed an additional 30 % more in $SVEC$ than SA_{FS} to account for more extensive reuse effort to adopt product line techniques and development the product line assets. For SA_{PS}, SA_{PSNS} and SA_{FSPSNS}, we estimated another additional 10 % over SA_{NS} in engineering cost to manage variability using both SOA and product-line techniques.

For service engineering delta costs α, α_{NS} is lower than α_{FS} to account for greater flexibility in static binding [9] used in SA_{NS} over dynamic binding used in SA_{FS}. α_{PS} of SA_{PS} is higher than α_{NS} or α_{FS} based on the reasoning that additional effort is required to maintain both static and dynamic bindings. The values of α_{PS+NS}, $\alpha_{FS+PS+NS}$ are also set higher to account for the effort to maintain the hybrid service architectures. Based on the above reasoning, we make the assumption of $\alpha_{NS} < \alpha_{FS} < \alpha_{PS} < \alpha_{PSNS}$, α_{FSPSNS}. The weighted cost coefficient α values used in our experiments are as follows. These α values are configurable on the tool and sensitivity of these values are also discussed in Sect. 5.3.

$$\alpha_{NS}(SA_{NS}) = 0.2, \alpha_{FS}(SA_{FS}) = 0.3, \alpha_{PS}(SA_{PS}) = 0.4$$

$$\alpha_{PSNS}\left(SA_{PSNS}\right) = 0.5, \alpha_{FSPSNS}\left(SA_{FSPSNS}\right) = 0.5$$

For service provisioning cost (SPC), we based our estimates on Amazon AWS pricing calculator [6], using the recommended deployment architecture of a large web application (all instances on demand). The estimated costs to provision for the initial tenant base of SA_{FS} is based on the configuration of 10 m1.medium, 10 m1.large and 10 m1.large Amazon EC2 instances for web, application and database Servers respectively, shared by all tenants. For SA_{NS}, SA_{PS}, SA_{PSNS}, dedicated instances of 1 m1.medium, 1 m1.large and 1 m1.large Amazon EC2 instances for web, application and database Servers respectively are allocated to each of the 10 initial tenants. For SA_{FSPSNS}, we start with the same provisioning configuration as SA_{FS}.

For service provisioning delta costs β, β_{FS} is set lower to account for the sharing of resources while β_{NS} is set to 1 to denote the additional isolated resources required. β_{PS} is set between β_{FS} and β_{NS} to denote partial sharing of resources. The cost coefficient β_{PSNS}, β_{FSPSNS} are set to either 0.2, 0.5 or 1 depending on the adopted service architecture for that tenant. To capture the service revenue earned by the Service Provider, we use the subscription-based strategy. Each tenant pays a price depending on her requirements. Based on the above reasoning, we assumed that $\beta_{FS} < \beta_{PS} < \beta_{NS}$. The weighted cost coefficient β values used in our experiments are as follows. These β values are configurable on the tool and sensitivity of these values are also discussed in Sect. 5.3.

$$\beta_{FS}\left(SA_{FS}\right) = 0.2, \beta_{PS}\left(SA_{PS}\right) = 0.5, \beta_{NS}\left(SA_{NS}\right) = 1$$

$$\beta_{PSNS}\left(SA_{PSNS}\right) = 0.5 \text{ or } 1, \beta_{FSPSNS}\left(SA_{FSPSNS}\right) = 0.2, 0.5 \text{ or } 1$$

In summary, the assumptions made in the conduct of our experiments are (i) (SVEC) for SA_{PS} < (SVEC) for SA_{NS} < (SVEC) for $(SA_{PS}, SA_{PSNS}$ and $SA_{FSPSNS})$ (ii) $\alpha_{NS} < \alpha_{FS} < \alpha_{PS} < \alpha_{PSNS}$, α_{FSPSNS} and (iii) $\alpha_{FS} < \beta_{PS} < \beta_{NS}$. The actual values of SVEC, α and β are configurable on the tool user interface. In Sect. 5.3, we further evaluate the threat to validity due to the possible sensitivities of the actual values used for α, β and the extrapolation of SVEC.

In the initial case when fixed costs are incurred for engineering functionality and variability, assuming no upfront provisioning costs and no on-boarded tenants, the model returns the following values as shown in Fig. 4. These values are also manually calculated for verification using the functionality engineering cost and functionality variability engineering costs for each type of architecture. Note that the negative profits are the same for partially-shared and hybrids due to our same assumptions of calculating the service variability engineering cost (SVEC) for these architectures.

SA	Fully Shared	Partially Shared	Non Shared	Hybrid Partially/Non	Hybrid Fully/ Partially/Non
Service Profits	($257,998)	($283,798)	($279,498)	($283,798)	($283,798)

Fig. 4. Service profits (no tenant)

We further conduct three experiments with delta variability low, high and random. We executed each simulation 100 times recording the *ROI* and annualized *ROI* of the service profits for all the five service architectures.

5.2 Analysis

For the case of low delta variability as shown in Fig. 5, service profits of SA_{FS} ($1,112k) and annualized *ROI* of 86 % is the highest among the service architectures as expected. The maximum sharing of service components reduces the overall cost, while still being able to fulfill the tenant's low variation of requirements maximize the service profits.

Number of Simulations : 100		Number of Investment Years : 5			
Delta Variability (Engineering) : Low		Delta Variability (Provisioning) : Low			

SA	Fully Shared	Partially Shared	Non Shared	Hybrid Partially/Non	Hybrid Fully/ Partially/Non
Service Profits	$1,112,070	$835,913	$858,450	$840,052	$926,574
Expected ROI	431%	295%	307%	296%	326%
Annualized ROI	86%	59%	61%	59%	65%

Fig. 5. Low delta variability

However in the case of high proportion of new tenants with high delta variability as shown in Fig. 6 adopting SA_{FS} becomes the unwise decision in terms of service profits and *ROI* as some tenants cannot be on-board without significant architecture changes, resulting in reduced revenue to cover the initial engineering costs incurred. Adopting SA_{NS} is the best decision in this case that maximizes the annualized *ROI* (61 %) and service profits ($858k). Service Provider needs to think carefully if the assumption of supporting tenants with high variability of requirements holds or not as the profitability is entirely opposite if not. This insight also highlights the importance of Service Provider to evaluate more factors (e.g. tenant's variability) for service profitability in addition to reducing cost by sharing resources.

| Number of Simulations : 100 | | | | Number of Investment Years : 5 | |
| Delta Variability (Engineering) : High | | | | Delta Variability (Provisioning) : High | |

SA	Fully Shared	Partially Shared	Non Shared	Hybrid Partially/Non	Hybrid Fully/ Partially/Non
Service Profits	$301,832	$674,543	$858,561	$762,837	$781,171
Expected ROI	117%	238%	307%	269%	275%
Annualized ROI	23%	48%	61%	54%	55%

Fig. 6. High delta variability

SPA output also contains results of tenants of random delta variability as shown in Fig. 7. In this case, adopting either SA_{NS} with service profits ($857k) and annualized ROI (61 %) or the hybrids achieved good results as adopting these service architectures allow for more tenants to be on-boarded easily though there are higher initial engineering costs. Service Provider if unsure about the variability of tenant base should base their decision on this analysis instead. In this case, Service Provider is likely to achieve better ROI and service profits with using SA_{NS} or SA_{FSPSNS}. This also relates well with the fact that although managing variability incurs early high cost, the benefits is substantial over the long run.

| Number of Simulations : 100 | | | | Number of Investment Years : 5 | |
| Delta Variability (Engineering) : Random | | | | Delta Variability (Provisioning) : Random | |

SA	Fully Shared	Partially Shared	Non Shared	Hybrid Partially/Non	Hybrid Fully/ Partially/Non
Service Profits	$645,602	$743,446	$857,870	$793,718	$842,720
Expected ROI	250%	262%	307%	280%	297%
Annualized ROI	50%	52%	61%	56%	59%

Fig. 7. Random delta variability

5.3 Threats to Validity

The sensitivity of the parameters potentially impacts the simulation results. We did further simulations varying $SVEC$, α and β values, while keeping to the assumptions of (i) ($SVEC$) for SA_{PS} < ($SVEC$) for SA_{NS} < ($SVEC$) for SA_{PS}, SA_{PSNS} and SA_{FSPSNS}, (ii) α_{NS} < α_{FS} < α_{PS} < α_{PSNS}, α_{FSPSNS} and (iii) β_{FS} < β_{PS} < β_{NS}. For each assumption, we generate 100 sets of random values within the assumption constraints and conduct the experiments separately again. We observe similar trends as per our analysis and observations with the original values of these parameters. However, we noted that the possible ranges of *SVEC*, α and β values are extensive and complete validation of these values is considered as part of our future validation work.

These experiments are based on service costs of one case study of an open source package and the use of existing cost estimation models such as COCOMO II also have its own level of confidence. To further validate the model and tool, we acknowledge the need for more case studies with actual values should be compared with the simulated values.

6   Related Works

Analysis of service profitability is an area that attracts much interest. Service profitability is one key economic benefit for Service Providers and can be analyzed from multiple perspectives.

One perspective of analyzing service profitability are the area of new/novel business and pricing models that maximize revenue. Ma [10] proposes an analytical SaaS business model which analyzes user's fit and exit costs that help Service Providers to increase SaaS competitive ability. Ma and Seidmann [11] propose a pricing strategy analysis for SaaS business model to study the competition between the SaaS and the traditional COTS (Commercial off-the shelf) software. Gabriella and Arto [12] analyzes the relationship between architectural practices different pricing models to maximize revenue. Xu and Li [13] analyzes service profitability in terms of dynamic pricing mechanisms and formulate revenue maximization problem with dynamic pricing as a stochastic dynamic program.

Another perspective of analyzing service profitability focuses on effective service adaptation of multiple tenants, placement of tenants and resource allocation to minimize costs and maximize service profitability. Bikram and Abhik [14] discuss engineering issues that can impact service profitability and propose for a more tenant-driven evolution of a SaaS where a vendor can accommodate changes to a SaaS to meet tenant needs, within reasonable limits. Ju [15] proposes a formal model as a bi-objective optimization problem that attempts to maximize vendor profit and tenant functional commonality. Mietzner et al. [16, 17] propose to adopt variability techniques to enable more flexible late binding of service variants, customization of BPEL process with variability descriptors and Morin et al. [18] propose to use aspect techniques to weave aspects for variability management. Kwok and Ajay [19] proposes a method for optimal placement of tenants and instances based on their proposed multi-tenant placement model without violating any SLA requirements of all tenants in a set of servers.

For this study, our analysis of service profitability takes into account existing works in service pricing, engineering and provisioning and other factors to provide a more complete perspective and tradeoffs in quantitative analysis of service profitability.

7   Conclusions and Future Works

Our proposed economic model of service profitability formalizes the interplay of multiple factors that influence service profitability. We augmented a conceptual model of service profitability with impact and effort formulas to conduct both qualitative and quantitative analysis of how multiple service implementation scenarios affect service profits. A tool interprets the model helping the Service Provider to explore a space of decisions that affect service profitability. Our economic model accounts for factors such as the tenant base, delta tenant base to be on-boarded in the future, tenant's variability, cost estimations models, service architecture and the use of variability techniques. Our model shows how these factors affect service cost, revenue, profits and *ROI*. We illustrated the usage of our profitability model and supporting tool with experiments conducted on an open source package. The evaluation results provide quantitative insight to the benefit of incurring initial cost to address variability for higher long-term profitability. We believe this work is useful to Service Providers to make more informed decision and help in building a business case that maximize service profitability.

In our future work, we will explore application of scientifically proven negotiating decision and optimization models to provide a formal ground for economic models of service profitability, suitable for evaluating in quantitative terms the impact of decisions involved in planning SaaS adoption strategies.

References

1. Ouh, E.L., Jarzabek, S.: Understanding service variability for profitable software as a service - service provider's perspective. In: 26th International Conference on Advanced Information Systems Engineering (CAiSE) (2014)
2. Ouh, E.L., Jarzabek, S.: A conceptual model to evaluate decisions for service profitability. In: 7th International Conferences on Advanced Service Computing (2015)
3. Mili, A., Chmiel, S.F.o., Gottumukkala, R., Zhang, L.: An integrated cost model for software reuse. In: 22nd International Conference on Software Engineering (ICSE) (2000)
4. Frakes, W., Terry, C.: Software reuse - metrics and models. J. ACM Comput. Surv. (CSUR) **28**(2), 415–435 (1996)
5. Jarzabek, S., Daniel, D.: Adaptive reuse technique. http://art.comp.nus.edu.sg
6. Amazon Web Services, 3-Tier Auto-scalable Web Application Solution. http://calculator.s3.amazonaws.com/index.html#key=calc-LargeWebApp-140323. Accessed Aug 2015
7. Apache, Apache OFBiz. https://ofbiz.apache.org/. Accessed Aug 2015
8. Poulin, J., Himler, A.: The ROI of SOA based on traditional component reuse, 2006. http://semanticommunity.info/@api/deki/files/2729/=ROI_of_SOA.pdf
9. Nolan, A.J., Abrahão, S.: Dealing with cost estimation in software product lines: experiences and future directions. In: Bosch, J., Lee, J. (eds.) SPLC 2010. LNCS, vol. 6287, pp. 121–135. Springer, Heidelberg (2010)
10. Ma, D.: The business model of "Software-as-a-Service". In: IEEE International Conference on Services Computing (SCC) (2007)
11. Ma, D., Seidmann, A.: The pricing strategy analysis for the "Software-as-a-Service" business model. In: Altmann, J., Neumann, D., Fahringer, T. (eds.) GECON 2008. LNCS, vol. 5206, pp. 103–112. Springer, Heidelberg (2008)

12. Gabriella, L., Ojala, A.: SaaS architecture and pricing models. In: IEEE International Conference on Services Computing (SCC) (2014)
13. Xu, H., Li, B.: Dynamic cloud pricing for revenue maximization. In: IEEE Transactions on Cloud Computing (2013)
14. Sengupta, B. Roychoudhury, A.: Engineering multi-tenant software-as-a-service systems. In: 3rd International Workshop on Principles of Engineering Service-Oriented Systems. ACM (2011)
15. Ju, L., Sengupta, B.: Tenant Onboarding in Evolving Multi-tenant Software-as-a-Service Systems. In: 19th International Conference on Web Services (ICWS) (2012)
16. Mietzner, R., Metzger, A., Leymann, F., Pohl, K.: Variability modeling to support customization and deployment of multi-tenant-aware software as a service applications. In: ICSE Workshop on Principles of Engineering Service Oriented Systems (PESOS) (2009)
17. Mietzner, R., Leymann, F.: Generation of BPEL customization processes for SaaS applications from variability descriptors. In: International Conference of Services Computing (SCC) IEEE (2008)
18. Morin, B., Barais, O., Jézéquel, J.-M.: Weaving aspect configurations for managing system variability. In: 2nd International Workshop on Variability Modelling of Software-Intensive Systems (VaMoS) (2008)
19. Kwok, T., Mohindra, A.: Resource calculations with constraints, and placement of tenants and instances for multi-tenant SaaS applications. In: Bouguettaya, A., Krueger, I., Margaria, T. (eds.) ICSOC 2008. LNCS, vol. 5364, pp. 633–648. Springer, Heidelberg (2008)
20. Zhang, Y., Wang, Z., Bo, G.: An effective heuristic for on-line tenant placement problem in SaaS. In: International Conference on Web Services (ICWS) IEEE (2010)

Cloud and Services

Optimizing Monitorability of Multi-cloud Applications

Edoardo Fadda[1], Pierluigi Plebani[2(✉)], and Monica Vitali[2]

[1] Politecnico di Torino, Corso Duca degli Abruzzi 24, 10129 Torino, Italy
edoardo.fadda@polito.it
[2] Politecnico di Milano, Piazza Leonardo da Vinci 32, 20133 Milano, Italy
{pierluigi.plebani,monica.vitali}@polimi.it

Abstract. When adopting a multi-cloud strategy, the selection of cloud providers where to deploy VMs is a crucial task for ensuring a good behaviour for the developed application. This selection is usually focused on the general information about performances and capabilities offered by the cloud providers. Less attention has been paid to the monitoring services although, for the application developer, is fundamental to understand how the application behaves while it is running. In this paper we propose an approach based on a multi-objective mixed integer linear optimization problem for supporting the selection of the cloud providers able to satisfy constraints on monitoring dimensions associated to VMs. The balance between the quality of data monitored and the cost for obtaining these data is considered, as well as the possibility for the cloud provider to enrich the set of monitored metrics through data analysis.

Keywords: Optimized deployment · Monitoring requirements · Metric accuracy

1 Introduction

A multi-cloud application implies the availability of a set of cloud providers, not necessarily coordinated with each other, offering the capabilities to host and run resources and services that compose the application [12]. According to the Infrastructure as a Service (IaaS) provisioning model, these resources are Virtual Machines (VMs) and a multi-cloud application can rely on several VMs living on an infrastructure offered by several providers. In this context, for the application developer is important to figure out how to match VMs and cloud providers, ensuring an effective and efficient execution of the application.

In the recent years, several approaches have been proposed to find the optimal deployment of VMs among the different IaaS providers, mainly focusing on performance optimization [3] or energy consumption reduction [8]. This work integrates these important aspects with the perspective of application monitorability: the possibility to measure and assess the performances of the provided application. Instead of looking for a cloud provider able to sell VMs

S. Nurcan et al. (Eds.): CAiSE 2016, LNCS 9694, pp. 411–426, 2016.
DOI: 10.1007/978-3-319-39696-5_25

with some functional (e.g., size of VM) or non-functional (e.g., VM availability) characteristics, the application developer wants cloud providers able to measure those characteristics in order to know how the application using the VM behaves.

Goal of this paper is to propose a deployment optimization method based on the maximization of the quality of the monitoring system, with respect to the developer needs, and the cost of the monitoring. Here, we assume that a Cloud Broker receives the requests for deployment including the monitorability requirements. Exploiting a knowledge base, managed by the broker, the developer can easily express the monitorability requirements without entering into the technical details. The adopted multi-objective mixed integer linear optimization problem (MILP) can found the deployment solutions maximizing the quality of monitored data while minimizing the costs. To extend the possible matches, a Bayesian Network (BN) is adopted to make possible for a cloud provider to estimate the values for a dimension - that is not able to measure - based on the dependencies with other dimensions - which is actually able to measure.

The paper is structured as follows. Section 2 introduces the overall approach identifying the main stakeholders and the basic steps of the mechanism. Section 3 provides a formal definition of the optimization problem specifying the way in which the accuracy of monitored data is computed. Section 4 validates the approach discussing the performance and the limitations. Section 5 provides an overview of the current approaches related to the monitoring match-making in a cloud scenario. Finally, Sect. 6 concludes the work also outlining future extensions.

2   Overall Approach

The stakeholders considered in this approach are a developer and a set of cloud providers. The developer is interested in finding out where to instantiate the VMs needed to run a cloud-based application. The cloud providers offer the facilities to host and manage VMs. The selection of the best site where to instantiate a VM is usually based on both the services offered by the cloud providers and the quality of these services. VM customization, VM migration, VM monitoring are possible services offered by cloud providers to the developers. At the same time, these services can be differentiated with respect to their quality of service (QoS): time required to instantiate a new VM, availability of the VM, availability of the entire site, and costs are example of QoS dimensions considered.

In this paper we focus on the monitoring capabilities. Cloud providers express their offerings, while the developer defines its requests according to the models discussed in the following paragraphs. The proposed match-maker is based on the implementation of a MILP model to offer to the developer a set of admissible VMs instantiation plans able to satisfy all the constraints while maximizing the quality of the monitoring data and minimizing the costs.

2.1   Cloud Provider Monitoring Offering Model

Cloud infrastructures are equipped with monitoring systems able to measure aspects like availability of VMs, CPU load, memory usage, and so on. Not all

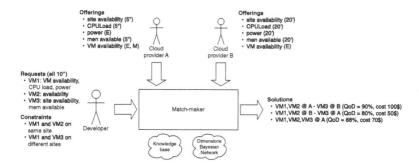

Fig. 1. Overall approach.

the cloud providers offer the same set of monitored properties with the same quality. Moreover, even the same cloud provider offer different levels of monitoring service based on different costs and the same property can be monitored differently in terms of sampling time, precision, or adopted unit of measure. For instance, Amazon CloudWatch[1] offers a basic monitoring service where preselected metrics are made available at five-minute frequency with no additional cost, and a detailed monitoring where the set of metrics is the same but at one-minute frequency and with an additional cost. Yet Paraleap CloudMonix (formerly known as AzureWatch)[2] offers the possibility to monitor an unlimited set of metrics but at ten-minutes frequency, with no additional cost, or at one-minute frequency with a fee. Based on this scenario, we can say that an offering of a cloud provider can include (see Fig. 1):

– Monitored dimensions directly usable by the provider specified by their sampling time and cost for usage (not reported in the figure).
– Monitored dimensions which are not directly measured but their trends are estimated exploiting the existing dependencies among metrics [18]. A Bayesian Network is adopted to express the likelihood of a metric to increase or decrease its value when the value of another metric increases or decreases. The mark *(E)*, i.e., estimate, is used to distinguish these dimensions. Sampling time and cost are provided, where the sampling time depend on the sampling time of the dimensions used to estimate the value, while the cost can be zero as the effort required by the cloud provider to estimate this value could be negligible. With this approach, each cloud provider can extend the set of monitored dimensions to be offered to the developer, declaring the reduced quality of the monitored data.
– Monitored dimensions which are not currently measured but the cloud provider is open to install probes able to measure them. The mark (M), i.e., make, is used to distinguish these dimensions. Cost in this case could be significantly higher than the estimate, as more effort is required to the cloud provider.

---

[1] https://aws.amazon.com/it/cloudwatch/.
[2] http://cloudmonix.com.

2.2   Developer Monitoring Request Model

For each of the VMs composing the application, the developer specifies the desired monitoring features in terms of dimensions of interest and sampling time. In the example shown in Fig. 1 we assume that all the dimensions need to be sampled every 10 s. It is also possible to specify a different sampling time for each dimension. The developer can define a maximum cost admissible for the solution (not reported in the figure).

The request model might also include constraints about the structure of the application. The developer can impose that the final deployment plan places groups of VMs in the same site. This could be required as the communication among those VMs is frequent and putting them on the same site can improve the performances. Other constraints can be related to the data locality or legal issues that may impose that a VM must be located (or not located) in specific countries.

As request definition can become a complex task, especially if the developer is not aware of all the possible dimensions, our approach assumes the existence of a knowledge base. In the next section, relations between dimensions, metrics, and metric measurements are defined to allow the developers to derive low-level requirements (e.g., VM Mem free, VM availability) starting from high-level requirements (e.g., VM status or VM performance).

3   Problem Statement

Before introducing a formalization of a cloud provider offering and a developer request, we formalize the common elements of our framework: i.e., *dimensions*, *metrics*, and *metric measurements*.

Definition 1. *A dimension is one of the perspectives of the application that the developer is willing to quantify (e.g. "performance", "sustainability"). It is usually an high level requirement that can not be directly measured. It is defined by its name and a set of metrics used to evaluate the dimension:*

$$d_i \in \mathcal{D} =< name, \{m_j\} >$$

Definition 2. *A metric defines how to assess a dimension by measuring some phenomenon. For instance, "response time" and "availability" are metrics related to the dimension "performance".*

$$m_j \in \mathcal{M} =< name, f(mm_k) >$$

where name is the name of the metric and $f(mm_k)$ is the function used to compute the metric based on some measurements of the environment. They correspond to low level requirements.

Definition 3. *A metric measurement is a measurement of the monitoring system used to compose the value of a metric. It is defined as:*

$$mm_k =< name, type, samplingTime >$$

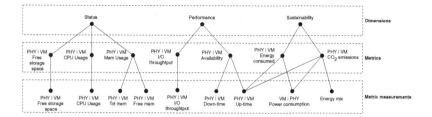

Fig. 2. Example of knowledge base.

As different cloud monitoring services can adopt different names to identify the same metric (e.g., as a basic example *CPUUtil* instead of *CPUUtilization*), in this paper we assume that both developers and cloud providers share the same vocabulary, thus no misunderstanding can occur in the match-making process. Anyway, the Cloud Broker can overcome such a limitation implementing existing techniques [14] for identifying similarities in names based on text analysis and domain-specific ontologies.

The set of relations between dimensions, metrics, and metric measurements constitutes a knowledge base shared by the developers and the cloud providers (Fig. 2). It provides information on how dimensions are defined: i.e., status (of both VM and physical servers PHY) can be assessed by CPU Usage, Mem Usage, and so on, while sustainability by the power consumed or the CO_2 emissions. For some metrics the computation requires more than one measurements (e.g. CO_2 emissions depend on the energy mix[3]), whereas for other metrics a direct measurement is possible (e.g., CPU Usage). Both cloud providers and developers browse the knowledge base to understand what to offer and what to request, but these two actors differ in the way they use it to express the requests and the offerings:

- Cloud providers, evaluating the leaves of the knowledge base, realize the coverage of the metric measurements given the installed monitoring infrastructure. Moreover, for each dimension (the roots) the provider is able to know which are the covered metrics and so to define the offerings. The knowledge base also provides a tool for providers to know the gap of their offerings with respect to a complete monitoring support.
- Developers use the knowledge base to select the dimensions or the metrics to be monitored. By working on the higher levels of the tree, it is not needed for the developer to know the details of the monitoring systems (i.e., the monitoring measurements). In this way, a developer can simply express in the request the need for measuring, for instance, the status of a VM. This implies that all the metrics linked to these dimensions should be supported. Alternatively, the developer could select only a subset of these metrics.

---

[3] Energy mix is defined as the proportion of the different power generation technologies, including fossil fuels, nuclear power, and renewable sources. Variation on this proportion has impact on the CO_2 emissions.

The knowledge base represents a common knowledge among the several parties involved in the match-making. It can be really implemented if a more formal agreement is required, or it can be considered as a tacit knowledge.

Definition 4. *A cloud provider offering for a site PO^s is composed of a collection of probes $\{p_l\}$ supported by the monitoring infrastructure offered by a provider s. Each sensor is defined as:*

$$p_l = \{\langle name, type, samplingTime, cost \rangle\}$$

The type of the sensor is a set of one or more of the three values $[A|M|E]$ that indicates: (A) the availability of the metric on the monitoring system; (M) the possibility to modify the monitoring system to also support the measurement of the metric; (E); the possibility to estimate the trend without modifying the monitoring system. The sampling time provides information about the frequency at which the measurement is collected. The cost associated to the metric provisioning is also specified.

The cost for a metric depends on the business model adopted by the cloud provider. Some may put the cost as 0 for sensors made already available by the monitoring system as its cost is included in the overall subscription. To have a fair comparison among the different offers, we assume that the cost of monitoring a metric is explicitly stated in the offering. It is also reasonable to assume that the cost for modifying the monitoring system to offer a metric (option M) implies a higher cost than the evaluation (option E).

Definition 5. *A developer request*

$$DR^d = \langle \bigvee_r mc_r^d, \bigvee_s cc_s^d[, cost] \rangle$$

is defined by a set of metric requests, a list of constraints, and, optionally, a maximum budget. Metric requests and constraints are expressed using the Disjunctive Normal Form (DNF). Each minterm represents an alternative, so that the request includes R admissible configurations for metrics and S configurations for constraints.

A metric configuration $mc_r^d = \bigwedge(\langle VM_{id}, m_t, samplingTime \rangle)$ includes the set of T metrics requested. Each of them specifies the VM to which it refers and the sampling time.

A constraint configuration $cc_s^d = \bigwedge(\langle VM_{id}, P_{id} \rangle)$ specifies where the VMs can be deployed. If a configuration does not include a VM then no constraints are imposed.

Formalization of the request and constraints in the offering using the DNF make the identification of the different valid alternatives easier as, by construction, only one minterm is true at the same time. For instance, assuming to have two cloud providers, i.e., P1 and P2, the constraints in the offering in Fig. 1 can be expressed as:

$$(\langle VM1, P1 \rangle \wedge \langle VM2, P1 \rangle \wedge \langle VM3, P2 \rangle) \vee (\langle VM1, P2 \rangle \wedge \langle VM2, P2 \rangle \wedge \langle VM3, P1 \rangle)$$

3.1   Optimization Problem Formulation

The mathematical model of our problem is described using the following sets:

- $\mathcal{V}$ is the set of all VMs. The cardinality of this set is V.
- $\mathcal{S}$ is the set of all sites. The cardinality of this set is S.
- $\mathcal{M}$ is the set of all metric measurements. The cardinality of this set is M.
- $\mathcal{MP}$ is the partition[4] induced by the set of all metrics in M. The cardinality of this set is MP.
- $\mathcal{SS}$ is the set of couples of VMs (v_0, v_1) such that VM v_0 must be deployed in the same site of v_1. The cardinality of this set is SS.
- $\mathcal{DS}$ is the set of couples of activities (v_2, v_3) such that VM v_2 must be deployed in a different site of v_3. The cardinality of this set is DS.
- $\mathcal{SR} \subseteq \mathcal{V} \times 2^{\mathcal{S}}$ is the set of couples $(v, \{s_0, \ldots, s_n\})$ such that VM v must be deployed in one of the sites $s_0, \ldots, s_n$.
- $\mathcal{MR} \subseteq \mathcal{V} \times \mathcal{M}$ is the set of all couples (v, m) such that we want to measure the metric measurement m for VM v.
- $\mathcal{S}(k) \subseteq \mathcal{S}$ is the set of all sites s such that we have a measure of metric measurement m.

For the parameters we will use the following notation:

- F_s cost of measuring from site s,
- $CI_{m,s}$ is the cost for implementing a probe for metric measurement m in site s,
- $CE_{m,s}$ is the cost for estimating a probe for metric measurement m in site s,
- $a_{m,s,v}^{(A)} \in [0,1]$ is the accuracy of metric measurement m for VM v in site s,
- $\Delta a_{m,s,v}^{(E)} \in [-1,1]$ is the variation of accuracy for VM v if we decide to evaluate a metric measurement m in site s,
- $\Delta a_{m,s}^{(MP)} \in [-1,1]$ is the variation of accuracy for VM v if we decide to implement a probe related to metric measurement m in site s,
- β is the budget, i.e., maximum amount of money that we want to pay.
- α is the minimum accuracy that we ask.

We will use the following variables:

- w_s, binary variable, true if site s is used;
- x_{vs}, binary variable, true if VM v is deployed in site s;
- y_{ms}, binary variable, true if metric measurement m in site s is made because not available (option M);
- z_{ms}, binary variable, true if metric measurement m in site s is estimated because not available (option E);
- l, measuring how much we violate the budget constraint that we fix.

---

[4] This may not be trivial, e.g. in Fig. 2 we have the metric measurement up-time that contributes to two metrics. In this case, we consider *uptime* to be in the set defined by the metric with more value for the user.

Our problem[5] is then:

$$\text{maximize} \sum_{m \in MP_1} (\sum_{s=1}^{S}(\sum_{v=1}^{V}(a_{m,s,v}^{(A)} x_{v,s}) + \sum_{v=1}^{V}(\Delta a_{m,s,v}^{(E)}) z_{m,s} + \sum_{v=1}^{V}(\Delta a_{m,s,v}^{(M)}) y_{m,s})), \cdots$$

$$\text{maximize} \sum_{m \in MP_M} (\sum_{s=1}^{S}(\sum_{v=1}^{V}(a_{m,s,v}^{(A)} x_{v,s}) + \sum_{v=1}^{V}(\Delta a_{m,s,v}^{(E)}) z_{m,s} + \sum_{v=1}^{V}(\Delta a_{m,s,v}^{(M)}) y_{m,s})),$$

$$\text{minimize } l$$

subject to:

$$w_s \geq x_{v,s} \quad \forall \; v \in V, \; s \in S \quad (1) \qquad\qquad \sum_{s=1}^{S} x_{v,s} = 1 \quad \forall \; v \in V \quad (2)$$

$$y_{m,s} \leq \sum_{v=1}^{V} x_{v,s} \quad \forall \; s \in S, \; m \in M \quad (3) \qquad a_{m,s,v} \leq 1 - z_{m,s} \quad \forall \, v \in V, \; s \in S, \; m \in M \quad (4)$$

$$z_{m,s} \leq \sum_{v=1}^{V} x_{v,s} \quad \forall \; s \in S, \; m \in S \quad (5) \qquad x_{v_0,s} = x_{v_1,s} \quad \forall \; s, (v_0, v_1) \in SS \quad (6)$$

$$x_{v_0,s} + x_{v_1,s} \leq 1 \; \forall \; s, (v_0, v_1) \in DS \quad (7) \qquad \sum_{s \in (v,\{s\}) \in SR} x_{v,s} = 1 \; \forall \; v, (v, \{s\}) \in SR \quad (8)$$

$$\sum_{s=1}^{S} F_s w_s + \sum_{m=1}^{M} \sum_{s=1}^{S} CE_{m,s} z_{m,s} + \sum_{m=1}^{M} \sum_{s=1}^{S} CI_{m,s} y_{m,s} = \beta + l \quad (9)$$

$$\max_s \left[a_{m,s,v}^{(A)} x_{v,s} + \Delta a_{m,s,v}^{(E)} z_{m,s} + \Delta a_{m,s,v}^{(M)} y_{m,s} \right] \geq \alpha \quad \forall \; (v, m) \in MR \quad (10)$$

$$w_s \in \{0,1\} \quad \forall \; s; \quad x_{v,s} \in \{0,1\} \quad \forall \; v, s; \quad y_{m,s} \in \{0,1\} \quad \forall \; m, s$$

$$z_{m,s} \in \{0,1\} \quad \forall \; m, s; \quad l \in \mathbb{R}$$

The constraints have the following meaning:

1. If we deploy VM v in site s then we use site s.
2. All VMs must be deployed.
3. We can implement a probe relative to metric measurement m in site s only if we have a VM in that site.
4. We can estimate a metric measurements only if we don't have the measure.
5. We can ask for an evaluation of the metric measurement m in site s only if we have a VM in that site.
6. Some VMs must be deployed on the same site.
7. Some VMs must be deployed on different sites.

---

[5] The proposed problem formulation assumes that the utility of the decision maker can be well approximated by a linear function as it is reasonable to think that the second order iterations between the accuracy of different metric measurements is negligible.

Algorithm 1. Accuracy Computation (A)

Input: mm_m: the metric measurement to evaluate
Input: PO^s: the monitoring infrastructure offered in site s
Output: $a_{m,s,v}^{(A)}$: the accuracy of the measurement of mm_m in the site s
1: $a_{m,s,v}^{(A)} = 0$
2: **for** $p_l \in PO^s$ **do**   ▷ *Find the probe in PO^s measuring mm_m*
3:     **if** $mm_m.name == p_l.name$ & $(A) \in p_l.type$ **then** ▷ *the sensor provides a measured value*
4:         $a_{m,s,v}^{(A)} = min(1, \frac{p_l.samplingTime}{mm_m.samplingTime})$
5:     **end if**
6: **end for**

8. Some VMs must be deployed on a fixed set of sites.
9. We don't want to spend too much money.
10. We must measure some metric measurements for some VMs.

In order to have a MILP, we have to change (10) with other linear constraints. For the discussion we consider m, v fixed. Constraint (10) is equivalent to:

$$a_{m,1,v}^{(A)} x_{v,1} + \Delta a_{m,1,v}^{(E)} z_{m,1} + \Delta a_{m,1,v}^{(M)} y_{m,1} \geq \alpha \ \vee \ a_{m,2,v}^{(A)} x_{v,2} + \Delta a_{m,2,v}^{(E)} z_{m,2} + \Delta a_{m,2,v}^{(M)} y_{m,2} \geq \alpha \ \vee \cdots$$

$$a_{m,S,v}^{(A)} x_{v,S} + \Delta a_{m,S,v}^{(E)} z_{m,S} + \Delta a_{m,S,v}^{(M)} y_{m,S} \geq \alpha$$

this can be translate using linear expressions by introducing:

$$u_s = \begin{cases} 1, & \text{if } a_{m,s,v}^{(A)} x_{v,s} + \Delta a_{m,s,v}^{(E)} z_{m,s} + \Delta a(M)_{m,s,v} y_{m,s} - \alpha \geq 0 \\ 0, & \text{otherwise} \end{cases}.$$

that must satisfy $\sum_{s=1}^{U} u_s \geq 1$. Hence in order to fix the conditions about the behaviour of u_s we have to add the following constraints:

$$a_{m,s,v}^{(A)} x_{v,s} + \Delta a_{m,s,v}^{(E)} z_{m,s} + \Delta a_{m,s,v}^{(M)} y_{m,s} - \alpha \leq u_s$$

$$\alpha - a_{m,s,v}^{(A)} x_{v,s} - \Delta a_{m,s,v}^{(M)} z_{m,s} - \Delta a_{m,s,v}^{(M)} y_{m,s} \leq 1 - u_s$$

In the following paragraph we describe how the metrics accuracy and their variations needed for running the optimization algorithm are estimated using a probabilistic approach supported by a Bayesian network.

3.2   Quality of Data Computation

The optimization is based on the accuracy of the measurability of each of the selected metrics $a_{m,s,v}^{(A)}$ that depends from several factors. Each metric is derived from the composition of several metric measurements, which can be available in the considered site, estimated, or implementable at a given cost. In case all the metric measurements related to a metric are available, the accuracy of the metric depends from the discrepancy between the required quality in terms of sampling time of the metric and the one required. In this case, the lower sampling time between all of the metric measurements is considered in the evaluation (worst case), as described in Algorithm 1.

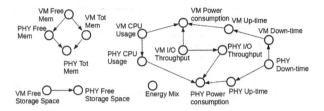

Fig. 3. Bayesian Network for metric measurement estimation

The same approach can be used in case the implementation of a metric measurement is required (M), since the cloud provider declares the accuracy that will be provided. In this case, the gain in implementing a new sensor is $\Delta a_{m,s,v}^{(M)} = a_{m,s,v}^{(M)} - a_{m,s,v}^{(A)}$, which is convenient only if a physical sensor is not yet implemented.

An additional level of abstraction is needed for the computation of the accuracy of an estimated metric measurement $(a_{m,s,v}^{(E)})$. In some condition, the collection of the data required by the developer can be not available without an additional cost that could bring the total amount of cost higher than the specified budget. However, in some cases, the cost of the implementation does not worth the benefit obtained, since for some metric the developer can be interested in trends more than in precise values. In such cases, an estimation is possible by modelling correlations through a Bayesian Network. The set of data used for its generation is obtained from the monitoring of all the sites in the multi-cloud environment, in order to derive general relations between metric measurements. The BN is composed of: (i) nodes, each one represents a metric measurement; (ii) edges, directed links that connect two nodes expressing a dependency between a parent and a child; (iii) Conditional Probability Tables (CPTs) associated to each node in the BN, quantifying the influence of the parents on the node. The CPT usually expresses conditional probabilities between each of the possible states of the child variable knowing the values of the parents. In this case we consider binary values, expressing the likelihood that a given metric measurement will increase given the trends of its parent set. An example of BN structure is shown in Fig. 3, using the metric measurements illustrated in Fig. 1. The BN is computed using the techniques described in [18]. It is created from the analysis of the correlation values between the metric measurements collected in all the sites and refined using the Max-Min Hill Climbing Algorithm [17] for links orientation. This inter-site BN enables making predictions about the trends even in sites where the specific measurement is not provided.

The accuracy of the estimated metric measurement can be obtained by combining the accuracy of the metric measurements from which it is derived and a likelihood value expressing the reliability of the dependency obtained by the CPT of the node. The accuracy computation of estimated metric measurements is described in Algorithm 2.

Algorithm 2. Accuracy Estimation (E)

Input: mm_m: the metric measurement to estimate
Input: PO^s: the monitoring infrastructure offered in site s
Input: BN: the correlation existing between the metric measurements
Output: $\Delta a_{m,s,v}^{(E)}$: the accuracy of the estimation of mm_m in the site s

1: $a_{m,s,v}^{(E)} = 0$
2: **for** $p_l \in PO^s$ **do**   ▷ *Find the probe in PO^s measuring mm_m*
3:     **if** $mm_m.name == p_l.name$ & $(E) \in p_l.type$ **then**   ▷ *the probe provides an estimated value*
4:         $ST = 0$
5:         **for** $mm_x \in BN.Parents(mm_m)$ **do**
6:             $ST = max(ST, mm_x.samplingTime)$
7:         **end for**
8:         $rel = p(mm_m | BN.Parents(mm_m))$
9:         $a_{m,s,v}^{(E)} = min(1, rel \cdot \frac{min(ST}{mm_m.samplingTime})$
10:    **end if**
11: **end for**
12: $\Delta a_{m,s,v}^{(E)} = a_{m,s,v}^{(E)} - a_{m,s,v}^{(A)}$

---

4 Validation

The optimization problem formulated in Sect. 3 has been implemented in C++ using the commercial solver Gurobi[6] for the solution of the MILP[7]. The main limitation coming from this choice is that we cannot modify the algorithm in order to use characteristic of the problem that can improve the speed. Nevertheless, this software is good enough to deal with the real instances and, for this reason, we do not implement our own algorithm. The optimizer has been executed on an Intel® Core™ i7-5500U CPU @2.40 Ghz with 8 GB RAM and Microsoft® Windows™ 10 Home installed. To obtain reliable results, all the tests described in the following have been conducted 30 times.

As the optimization problem is NP-hard (complexity $\mathcal{O}(2^{max[VS,MS]})$) the goal of this validation is to figure out how much the response time of the optimizer increases when varying the number of VMs (i.e., V) and the number of metrics (i.e., M). Due to the nature of the problem, a reasonable variation of the number of sites, i.e., S, does not affect strongly the response time as adding more sites means not only to add constraints and variables but also to increase the feasible space (the more sites available the more possible solutions). The case in which we have a high variation of the number of sites will be considered in future work as a more efficient algorithm is required (e.g. imposing a very good initial solution derived from the use of a proper heuristic).

Figure 4 reports the response time of the optimizer varying the number of metric measurements included in the requests (from a min of 1 to a max of 17 according to the knowledge base presented in Fig. 2). Each curve corresponds to the response time required to obtain a solution with different set of VMs, each of them specifying a set of metric measurements in their request.

---

[6] http://www.gurobi.com.

[7] Due to page restrictions we are not able to specify all the elements of the problem in this article. If interested, the reader can find all the problem specifications and the code for running the application at https://github.com/monicavit164/requirementMeasurementMILP.

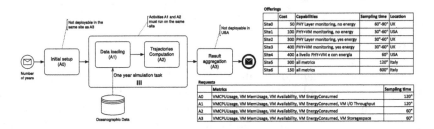

Fig. 4. Optimizer response time.   Fig. 5. Pareto front of Fig. 6 app.

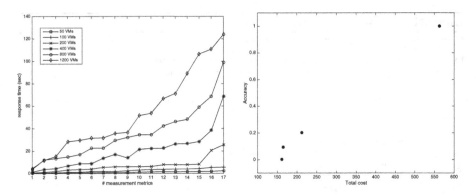

Fig. 6. Running example.

It is worth noting that the optimizer will be used at design time, when the developer wants to deploy the application. For this reason, a result is not necessarily required in seconds. Some minutes is also an acceptable response time. Anyway, the chart shows that the optmizer returns a solution in around 5 s in case of 100 VMs with 17 metric measurements. In the worst case, two minutes are enough to compute a solution with 1200 VMs with the same number of metric measurements.

We also considered a real HPC application in the ecology domain [11] shown with a BPMN in Fig. 6. Without entering into the details, the application starts with an initial setup (activity A0). The work is then split into several instances composed of two activities: data loading (A1) and computation (A2). Once all the instances terminate, the partial results are aggregated (A3) to provide the result to the final user. We assume that one VM is required for A0 and A3, while for A1 and A2 the number of VMs may change according to the number of iteration required. Based on this example, Fig. 6 also includes the requests and offerings tables. The former reflects the requirements in terms of monitoring for each of the VMs composing the application. The latter reports the capabilities of the 7 cloud providers where the VMs can be deployed. For the sake of simplicity, the offering table does not report the detailed list of the supported metric measurements, but a high level description (e.g., PHY layer monitoring means all the metric measurements at PHY level). For the sampling time we assumed that for the majority of the metric measurements the sampling time is equal.

Figure 5 shows the Pareto front calculated with 4 VMs, 7 sites, and 7 metric measurements which took 19.2 s. The curve has very few points as we have to fulfil some requests related to the metric measurements that we have to register hence we cannot go below some given price. Furthermore once that we have implemented all the probes we cannot improve more our solution. The discontinuous front derives from the adoption of a MILP. In order to compute the response time in Fig. 4 we have considered, for each point, ten random points in the Pareto Front by using several weighted sums of the M+1 objectives. The front in Fig. 5 considered 2 objectives and we compute point solution for a uniform grid of 10^4 points in the square $[0, 10]^2$. The choice of the square is related to the characteristic of the values of the two objective functions.

5   Related Work

Current approaches for monitoring applications distributed in different cloud infrastructures are usually provider-centric and focus on solutions to hide the heterogeneity of the adopted monitoring platforms [2, 19] through a common interface. As in this paper we follow a multi-cloud approach, the perspective is client-centric and, in particular, the end-user is the application that coordinates the access and utilization of different cloud providers to meet the application requirements [16]. Here, the role of the Cloud Broker, as seen by the NIST [10], can provide intermediation services to facilitate the relationships between the cloud providers and the application (that holds the role of cloud consumer). In our case, the cloud broker enhances the deployment strategy of the cloud consumer making easier to find the cloud providers able to support the monitoring capabilities as needed by the application.

Some work in the state of the art has investigated the issue of modelling and in some cases discovering the relations between different metrics that can give a hint about the value of a missing metric, allowing the owner of the application to reason about the metric even if the real value is not directly provided by the monitoring system. The framework proposed in [9] looks for influential factors between metrics, represented in a dependency tree learned using machine learning techniques. The influential factors existing among indicators are statically and manually defined by the user. A study conducted by Google [5] employs a neural network framework that learns from monitored data to model and predict the outcome of some modifications over the monitored variables. A more complex and comprehensive approach has been proposed in [18]. Here, relations between the information collected at several levels of abstraction (monitored information and complex metrics) is represented in a Bayesian Network built automatically from the analysis of historical data, and kept updated through a continuous refinement. Even if in [18] the modelled relations are about satisfaction and dissatisfaction of constraints among metric values, this can be adapted to model relations about trends observed in the collected data provided by the monitoring system. In this work we applied a modification of this approach to provide a prediction about missing metrics to the user.

The optimized deployment of VMs in a cloud environment can depend on several factors. In [6] a multi-objective algorithm is employed for VM placement in a cloud system. The algorithm minimize total resource wastage and power consumption providing a Pareto set of solutions. In [7], a greedy allocation algorithm is used to optimize the cloud provider's profit, considering energy efficiency, virtualization overheads, and SLA violation penalties as decision variables. In these approaches a single cloud provider is considered, thus measurability is not a relevant issue for the authors.

The relevance of the problem addressed in this paper is witnessed by the existence of several cloud platforms which differ in terms of set of metrics, sampling times, costs, and flexibility. About the possibility to extend, on user demand, the monitored metrics, in addition to the already mentioned Amazon CloudWatch and Paraleap CloudMonix, different monitoring solutions like Nagios, PCMONS, and Sensus, support the extensibility of the monitoring metrics[8][1].

Moving to the knowledge base, semantic technologies are gaining more and more attention also in the cloud computing [15]. Focusing on the monitoring system, in [13] linked data are used to handle the heterogeneity of the collected data, whereas [4] provides a semantic meta-model for classifying dimensions and metrics.

6   Conclusion

In this paper, we have proposed an approach for supporting the deployment of multi-cloud applications where monitoring capabilities are taken into account. With a MILP problem, a cloud broker can figure out which is the best association among VMs composing the application and can make a request for some monitoring features, and for a cloud infrastructures providing some monitoring capabilities. A peculiar aspect of our approach relies on the possibility to extend the measurable metrics or to estimate the trends of metrics that are not supported by relying on other metrics. Estimation is based on a Bayesian Network able to infer how a metric changes with respect to other metrics. The deployment strategy proposed in this work balances between the cost for monitoring the application and the quality of the monitored data. The cost usually increases when the site offers a complete set of measurable metrics, thus with high quality of measured data. Conversely, the cost decreases for sites with limited set of measurable metrics that require an estimation of monitoring data, affecting the quality. The conducted experiments demonstrated the feasibility of the approach and, given the low response time, our optimizer can be adopted to facilitate the deployment of multi-cloud applications also composed of hundreds of VMs.

At this stage, the work focused on the IaaS multi-cloud provisioning model. Metrics considered in this work mainly refer to the physical and the virtualization layers. A complete set of metrics covering also the PaaS and SaaS provisioning models needs to be addressed in the future.

---

[8] https://www.nagios.org; https://code.google.com/p/pcmons; https://sensuapp.org.

References

1. Aceto, G., Botta, A., de Donato, W., Pescap, A.: Cloud monitoring: a survey. Comput. Netw. **57**(9), 2093–2115 (2013)
2. Alcaraz Calero, J.M., Knig, B., Kirschnick, J.: Using cross-layertechniques for communication systems, chap. In: Cross-Layer Monitoring in Cloud Computing. IGI Global, Hershey (2012)
3. Dai, W., Chen, H., Wang, W., Chen, X.: RMORM: a framework of multi-objective optimization resource management in clouds. Proceedings of IEEE Services, pp. 488–494 (2013)
4. Funika, W., Godowski, P., Pegiel, P., Król, D.: Semantic-oriented performance monitoring of distributed applications. Comput. Inf. **31**(2), 427–446 (2012)
5. Gao, J.: Machine learning applications for data center optimization. Technical report, Google (2014)
6. Gao, Y., Guan, H., Qi, Z., Hou, Y., Liu, L.: A multi-objective ant colony system algorithm for virtual machine placement in cloud computing. J. Comput. Syst. Sci. **79**(8), 1230–1242 (2013)
7. Goiri, Í., Berral, J.L., Fitó, J.O., Julià, F., Nou, R., Guitart, J., Gavaldà, R., Torres, J.: Energy-efficient and multifaceted resource management for profit-driven virtualized data centers. Future Gener. Comput. Syst. **28**(5), 718–731 (2012)
8. Kaur, T., Chana, I.: Energy efficiency techniques in cloud computing: a survey and taxonomy. ACM Comput. Surv. **48**(2), 22:1–22:46 (2015)
9. Kazhamiakin, R., Wetzstein, B., Karastoyanova, D., Pistore, M., Leymann, F.: Adaptation of service-based applications based on process uality factor analysis. In: Dan, A., Gittler, F., Toumani, F. (eds.) ICSOC/ServiceWave 2009. LNCS, vol. 6275, pp. 395–404. Springer, Heidelberg (2010)
10. Liu, F., et al.: NIST Cloud Computing Reference Architecture: Recommendations of the National Institute of Standards and Technology (Special Publication 500–292). CreateSpace Independent Publishing Platform, USA (2012)
11. Melià, P., Schiavina, M., Gatto, M., Bonaventura, L., Masina, S., Casagrande, R.: Integrating field data into individual-based models of the migration of european eel larvae. Marine Ecol. Prog. Ser. **487**, 135–149 (2013)
12. Petcu, D.: Multi-cloud: expectations and current approaches. In: Proceedings of the 2013 International Workshop on Multi-cloud Applications and Federated Clouds, MultiCloud 2013, NY, USA, pp. 1–6. ACM, New York (2013)
13. Portosa, A., Rafique, M., Kotoulas, S., Foschini, L., Corradi, A.: Heterogeneous cloud systems monitoring using semantic and linked data technologies. In: IFIP/IEEE International Symposium on Integrated Network Management, pp. 497–503, May 2015
14. Seco, N., Veale, T., Hayes, J.: An intrinsic information content metric for semantic similarity in Wordnet. In: Proceedings of Eureopean Conference on Artificial Intelligence (ECAI 2004), Valencia, Spain, 22–27 August 2004, pp. 1089–1090. IOS Press (2004)
15. Sheth, A., Ranabahu, A.: Semantic modeling for cloud computing, part 1. IEEE Internet Comput. **14**(3), 81–83 (2010)
16. Toosi, A.N., Calheiros, R.N., Buyya, R.: Interconnected cloud computing environments: challenges, taxonomy, and survey. ACM Comp. Surv. **47**(1), 1–47 (2014)
17. Tsamardinos, I., Brown, L.E., Aliferis, C.F.: The max-min hill-climbing bayesian network structure learning algorithm. Mach. Learn. **65**(1), 31–78 (2006)

18. Vitali, M., Pernici, B., O'Reilly, U.M.: Learning a goal-oriented model for energy efficient adaptive applications in data centers. Inf. Sci. **319**, 152–170 (2015)
19. Zeginis, C., Kritikos, K., Garefalakis, P., Konsolaki, K., Magoutis, K., Plexousakis, D.: Towards cross-layer monitoring of multi-cloud service-based applications. In: Lau, K.-K., Lamersdorf, W., Pimentel, E. (eds.) ESOCC 2013. LNCS, vol. 8135, pp. 188–195. Springer, Heidelberg (2013)

CloudMap: A Visual Notation for Representing and Managing Cloud Resources

Denis Weerasiri[1(✉)], Moshe Chai Barukh[1], Boualem Benatallah[1],
and Cao Jian[2]

[1] University of New South Wales, Sydney, Australia
{denisw,mosheb,boualem}@cse.unsw.edu.au
[2] Shanghai Jiaotong University, Shanghai, China
cao-jian@cs.sjtu.edu.cn

Abstract. With the vast proliferation of cloud computing technologies, DevOps are inevitably faced with managing large amounts of complex cloud resource configurations. This involves being able to proficiently understand and analyze cloud resource attributes and relationships, and make decisions on demand. However, a majority of cloud tools encode resource descriptions and monitoring and control scripts in tedious textual formats. This presents complex and overwhelming challenges for DevOps to manually read, and iteratively build a mental representation especially when it involves a large number of cloud resources. To alleviate these frustrations we propose a model-driven notation to visually represent, monitor and control cloud resource configurations; managed underneath by existing cloud resource orchestration tools such as *Docker*. We propose a *mindmap*-based interface and set of visualization patterns. We have employed an extensive user-study to base design decisions, and validate our work based on experimentation with real-world scenarios. The results show significant productivity and efficiency improvements.

Keywords: Cloud resource management · DevOps · Visual notations

1 Introduction

Cloud computing is rapidly evolving in public, private and hybrid cloud networks [1]. The many benefits include enabling virtualization capabilities as well as outsourcing strategies – the cloud will be a firm priority for productivity and economic development. It is estimated by 2016, growth in cloud computing will consume the bulk of IT spend[1]. There are however crucial gaps in the cloud-enabled endeavor [1]. Modern resource configuration management systems like *Puppet, Ubuntu Juju, Ansible, Amazon OpsWorks* and *Chef* provide scripting-based languages over cloud services [4]. This implies even sophisticated programmers and administrators are forced to understand different low-level cloud service Application Programming Interfaces (APIs), command-line syntax, and

---

[1] http://www.gartner.com/newsroom/id/2613015.

© Springer International Publishing Switzerland 2016
S. Nurcan et al. (Eds.): CAiSE 2016, LNCS 9694, pp. 427–443, 2016.
DOI: 10.1007/978-3-319-39696-5_26

programming constructs, to create and maintain complex cloud resource configurations. Moreover, this problem worsens as the variety of cloud services and the variations of application resource requirements and constraints increase.

Inevitably, typical cloud-based organizations are finding it difficult to productively utilize their very large repositories ladened with textual cloud resource description and management artifacts, [1]. For example, simple management tasks commonly involve: analyzing resource descriptions; understanding the inter-relationships between resources; and aggregating monitoring data. However, until now DevOps (i.e., developers and operation personnel who are collectively involved in designing, developing, deploying and managing cloud applications) are required to manually and iteratively read several low-level files and use command-line tools to extract monitoring information. In fact, it has been confirmed that DevOps dedicate the majority of their time to understand existing artifacts instead of creating new ones, updating and/or testing them [6].

To overcome these challenges, we present *CloudMap*. Leveraging the old-age dictum of *"a picture tells a thousand words!"*, we develop visual notations to simplify representing and managing cloud resources. We argue this novel approach will enable DevOps to invest more on creating, configuring and managing cloud resources, instead of the frustrations and time spent to understand them. Since we are at the foundational stage, we have specialized our framework to *Docker* [10]; albeit in future it can easily be extended with other orchestration tools (e.g., *JuJu* or *Ansible*). *Docker* is an open-source and widely-praised industry standard initiative. Its Container-based virtualization technique offers a lightweight and portable resource isolation alternative to Virtual Machines (VMs). This technique emerged to simplify and accelerate the configuration and management of cloud resources. More specifically, for composite service-based cloud resources that depend on multiple service middleware for their operations, container-based virtualizations enable accelerated and efficient deployment of optimally configured, scalable and lightweight middleware instances. However, since to the best of our knowledge current tools merely leverage textual resource representations, it does not do justice to improving the productivity and efficiency of DevOps. Accordingly, this paper makes the following main contributions:

Expert User-Study. Based on an extensive survey of 21 participants (system administrators and software engineers with 3–10 years experience), we discover gaps and challenges in current solutions. We form a strong understanding of the requirements, and derive key design decisions for our novel solution.

Visual Notation for Representing & Managing Cloud Resources. We formulate the necessary notational constructs (i.e., *Entities* and *Links*) and define the semantics for each. We also propose novel auxiliary features called *Probes* and *Control Actions*, that can be "tagged" to entities.

Cloud Visualization Patterns. We identify common visualization patterns for cloud resource configuration. Existing architectural patterns are high-level and mostly suitable for solution architects or IT directors [5]. In contrast, we believe DevOps require more fine-grained visual abstractions for understanding, navigating, monitoring and controlling complex cloud resources. Resultantly, we present three patterns and describe their benefits via practical scenarios.

The rest of this paper is organized as follows: In Sect. 2, we position this work with respect to our previous work; and explain how our visual notation is applied within the cloud resource lifecycle. Furthermore, we present the results of our user-study. In Sect. 3, we detail our visual notation and its semantics, and present three organizational patterns. We employ a mind-map interface, and illustrate how they could be used over various use-cases which span across selection, configuration, deployment, monitoring and controlling of cloud resources. In Sects. 4, we present our implementation and GUI; evaluation in Sect. 5; then related-work, and conclusions in Sect. 6.

2 Background

2.1 Motivating Example

Cloud resources management typically involves: (i) An initially **sequential** stage of consisting of: *Select, Configure* and *Deploy*; (ii) Followed by an **iterative** phase consisting of: *Monitor* and *Control*.

As a running example, consider the 3-tier system illustrated in Fig. 1. We begin by *selecting* the required resources. In this case, business logic is executed using *Business Process Execution Language (BPEL)*, with state data stored on a *MySQL DB*. For scaling purposes, we introduce a *Nginx Load Balancer* that propagates requests to a cluster of *Apache Orchestration Director Engine (ODE) Servers*. To *configure* and *deploy*, DevOps determine the relationships between components and write configuration and deployment scripts, that describes the attributes (e.g., no. of BPEL engines, CPU allocation). Subsequently, DevOps also collect and analyze events to *monitor* and apply *control* actions if necessary.

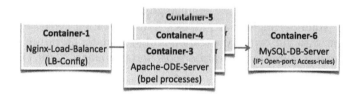

Fig. 1. Resource diagram of the typical 3-tier (BPEL-based) application

2.2 Requirements for Cloud Resources Visual Notation

To articulate the requirements of our novel solution, we sought to gain insight about the gaps and challenges in current strategies. We conducted a user-study over 21 experts with 3–10 years of working experience: 9 server administrators and 12 software engineers (e.g., cloud-based application developers).

Research Questions and Results. Three main areas of investigation were sought. Techniques to: (a) navigate and understand cloud resource attributes and relationships; and (b) monitor and control cloud resources. In addition, (c) we sought to discover how the above increased in complexity when the number of managed resources increased. Responses were automatically recorded in an online spreadsheet, and the raw results summarized in Fig. 2.

Navigating and Understanding Cloud-Resource Attributes & Relationships:						
1 How do you navigate cloud resources to understand their properties and relationships?	Command Line Tools (71.4%)	Simple GUI (52.4%)	Memorizing (42.9%)	Reading Scripts (38.1%)	I don't! (4.8%)	Other (9.5%)
2 How do you search for cloud resources deployed over different providers?	Search Indexes (57.1%)	Memorizing (38.1%)	Command Line Tools (47.6%)	Viz. Tools (42.9%)	Reading Scripts (23.8%)	Other (19%)
Monitor & Control Cloud-Resource:						
3 What are some of the techniques you follow to monitor deployed cloud resources?	SMS/Email Notifications (81%)	Log Files (76.2%)	I'm a Developer and not responsible (4.8%)		I notify others (9.5%)	Other (9.5%)
4 What are the techniques you adopt to control (e.g., scale-up, migrate, configure firewall)?	Command Line Tools (85%)	GUIs (38%)	API/SDKs (e.g. AWS REST, AWS Java SDK) (65%)		I don't! (0%)	Other (10%)
5 Do you have to switch between multiple tools to monitor and control multiple resources?	Yes! (100%)				No! (0%)	
Complexity of Cloud-Resource Information & Networks:						
6 On average, how many cloud resources do you manage?	Less than 10 (42.9%)		Between 10-10 0 (28.6%)		Over 100 (28.6%)	
7 On average, how many cloud resources providers (e.g., AWS, VMWare) do you have to rely	Only 1 (23.8%)		Between 1-5 (76.2%)		Over 5 (0%)	

Fig. 2. Survey questions and results

Survey Analysis. While a more detailed discussion of the analysis is largely outside the scope of this paper, we summarize our findings below and derive the fundamental requirements for our proposed visual notation. This was also done in conjunction with our own investigation and systematic literature review[2] on a range of cloud resource orchestration tools and techniques [2,10,11].

- The majority (71.4 %) of DevOps rely on command line tools to navigate cloud resources and discover their properties and relationships. While nearly half (38.1 %) has resorted to manual and error-prone techniques (e.g., reading and memorizing configuration files). This was primarily due to that fact most of simple GUIs were limited to resource *attributes* only. Accordingly, we have sought to extend visual techniques for displaying not only attributes, but types of resources and important directional links between resources.
- A large majority (76.2–81%) admitted they rely on log files and notifications (e.g., emails, SMS) to *monitor* cloud resources. While regarding *control* and

---

[2] Internal Report prepared and impending Journal to be submitted: *"D. Weerasiri et al. A taxonomy and survey of cloud resource orchestration techniques"*.

(re-)configuration, most DevOps use command-line tools, APIs and/or SDKs (65–85%). Participants also complained about the inconvenience of switching between multiple tools to monitor and control cloud resources. Accordingly, our work sought to integrate visual *probe* and *control* elements to facilitate not only monitoring, but (re-)actions and control of cloud resources.

– Overall, the need for simplifying all aspects of cloud resource management (i.e., navigation and understanding configured resources; monitoring and control), was widely championed by participants. This was because a wide majority (71.5 %) of DevOps manage large numbers (approx. <100) of cloud resources. Matters also exasperate when many (76.3 %) have to simultaneously manage multiple cloud resource providers (e.g., AWS, VMWare).

3   *CloudMap:* Visual Notation for Cloud Resource Management

CloudMap offers a refreshing "visual" attempt at simplifying the way DevOps can navigate and understand cloud resource configurations, as well as monitor and control such resources. The concepts of *CloudMap* are associated with both

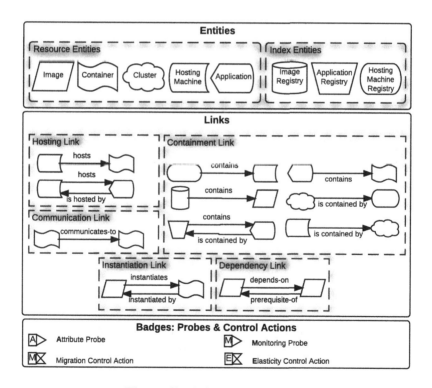

Fig. 3. *CloudMap* visual notations

a visual notation and an underlying textual JSON syntax. The textual syntax provides the context in which visual primates can be specified and executed.

The constructs of the notation are specified as the following: (i) ***Structural model*** represents primitive cloud resource entities and their attributes. Attributes have string name with one or a set of string values. (ii) ***Navigation Model*** represents the topology of links between entities. Links are directional with a single string label. The set of valid links are domain-specific; (we will explain in Sect. 4 how *CloudMap* depends upon our previous work *CloudBase* to determine domain context). (iii) ***Badges*** are an auxiliary feature to the fundamental constructs mentioned above. A badge represents a special entity that may be "tagged" to another entity. Visually, a badge is realized as a single or set of widgets, which may be used to monitor and/or control tagged entities. The data model of a badge specifies which entity-type it applies to.

Figure 3 illustrates the graphical notation, while Fig. 4 the syntactical schema of the underlying JSON model. Below we explain each of these constructs.

```
(a){
    "name": "Entity",
    "description": "string",
    "properties": {
        "name": {"type": "string"},
        "schema": {"type": "string"},
        "optional-attributes": [...] }
}
```

```
(b){
    "name": "Link",
    "description": "string",
    "properties": {
        "name": {"type": "string"},
        "schema": {"type": "string"},
        "source-participant": {"type": "string"},
        "target-participant": {"type": "string"},
        "optional-attributes": [...] }
}
```

```
(c){
    "name": "Badge",
    "description": "string",
    "properties": {
        "name": {"type": "string"},
        "schema": {"type": "string"},
        "type": {"type": "enum['probe','control-action']"},
        "tool-tip-description": {"type": "string"},
        "icon": {"type": "string"},
        "applies-to": {"type": "array"}, // entity it applies to
        "related-widgets": {"type": "array"} }
}
```

```
(d){
    "name": "Widget",
    "description": "Represent a Widget in CloudMap",
    "properties": {
        "display-name": {"type": "string"},
        "schema": {"type": "string"},
        "applies-to": {"type": "string"},
            // describe how to retrieve data via relevant DSM and Connector
        "dsm-config": {"name": "...", "monitored-events": ['...', '...']},
            //describe how to visualize retrieved data
        "visualization-config": {"type": "enum['bar-chart','list','pie-chart']"},
        "optional-attributes": [...] }
}
```

Fig. 4. *CloudMap* syntactical schema of constructs

3.1 Structural Model: Entities

An *entity* is a single cloud resource, referred to as a *Resource Entity*; or collection thereof, referred to as a *Index Entity*. Syntactically, an entity as shown in Fig. 4(a) contains a string `name` and `description` and set of `properties`. The overall structure for each entity type is in accordance with the Domain-Specific `schema`[3].

[3] See our previous work: ftp://ftp.cse.unsw.edu.au/pub/doc/papers/UNSW/201514.pdf.

Resource Entities. We have identified 5 resource entities types: *(1) Containers* represents a virtualized software container (e.g., Linux and OpenVZ[4] containers) where an application or a component of an application (e.g., an Apache ODE Server installed on Ubuntu OS) is deployed. *(2) Hosting Machines* represents a computer system where *Containers* are hosted (e.g., Virtual Machine (VM) or a physical machine). *(3) Clusters* represents a set of *Hosting Machines*. This reduces the overhead of dynamically managing multiple machines. For example, the *Cluster* may automatically decide which *Hosting Machine* will be chosen to deploy the given container based on an optimization algorithm [7]. *(4) Applications* represents a logical entity that includes a collection of related *Containers*. Each *Container* constitutes a component of the *Application*. *(5) Images* represents the deployment description of a *Container*, that is fed to the runtime of the orchestration tool in order to instantiate the *Container*.

Index Entities. Similarly, we have identified 3 index entity types: *(1) Hosting Machine Registry* is a logical entity that contains a set of *Hosting Machines* and *Clusters*. *(2) Application Registry* represents a repository of *Applications*. DevOps organize and discover all deployed cloud applications within the Registry. *(3) Image Registry* represents a repository of *Images* where DevOps may organize, curate and share resource deployment knowledge.

3.2 Navigation Model: Links

The relationship between entities are represented as links and enable navigation. Syntactically, links have a string `name` and `description`. They also define the `source` and `target` participants. Additional `attributes` may also be defined.

We have identified 5 different groups of links, as categorized below: *(1) Communication Links* are defined between two *Containers* that interact or exchange data. For example, an Apache ODE (BPEL) server communicates with a MySQL database server, about a BPEL instances. *(2) Containment Links* defines the hierarchical organization of entities. In practice, they may also be also used to simultaneously control a set of related resources (e.g., control actions on a parent automatically triggers actions on all children). The valid set of containment links are defined in the links' schema (also as illustrated in Fig. 3). *(3) Hosting Links* defines a relationship between a *Hosting Machine* and *Container* or an *Application*. For example, between a PHP application engine and a VM where the PHP application engine is deployed. *(4) Dependency Links* defines a relationship between two *Images*, where the attributes of a particular resource depend upon the other resource. *(5) Instantiation Links* defines a relationship between an *Image* and *Container*, when the latter may be produced from the former. For example, a *Conteiner* may instantiate an *Image*.

3.3 Badges: Probes and Control-Actions

A *badge* represents an auxiliary feature to the fundamental constructs of *entities* and *links*. Syntactically, they define a string `name` and `description`, and may

---

[4] http://openvz.org/.

only be applied to certain entity types, defined in the `applies-to` property. When *tagged* to some entity, they apply some behavioral function, depending on the `type` of badge: either a *probe* (used for monitoring) or *control action* (used for performing some action). Visually, when a badge is tagged to an entity, it renders a widget; a badge thus also contains a pointer to one or a set of `widgets`.

Probes. At present, we have developed 2 *probes*: *(1) Attribute Probe* displays the name and values of attributes for a given entity. For example, a VM in AWS-EC2 contains attributes about the number of CPU cores, storage and memory capacity, OS and access rules. *(2) Monitoring Probe* continuously monitor runtime data of deployed cloud resources. For example, if an *Application*, a *Container* or a *Hosting Machine* is tagged by the "monitoring probe", an appropriate widget becomes available to graphically analyze the underlying resource consumption statistics (e.g., memory usage, network I/O, CPU usage). Monitoring probes may also be attached on several resources at the same time, and the associated widget aggregates, summarizes and provides a visual technique to compare the performance of multiple cloud resources.

Control Actions. Actions can be both manual or automated. Manual actions are self-prompted by dragging specific badges onto entities. For example, *(1) Elasticity Control* applies to a *Container* or *Hosting Machine* to scale up or down (e.g., no. of CPUs or memory); and (2) *Migration Control* to migrate a container across VMs. Automated actions are inputed as ECA-rules (see Sect. 4), via a dedicated universal badge that renders a rule-input widget.

3.4   Visualization Patterns for Cloud Resource Configurations

We consolidate the above by identifying 3 organizational patterns commonly found within cloud resource management. We describe the benefits of these via practical scenarios and accompanying illustrations.

Image Map. An *Image Map* visualizes the recursive dependency of *Images* within a *Registry*. In general, cloud resource descriptions, deployment and/or

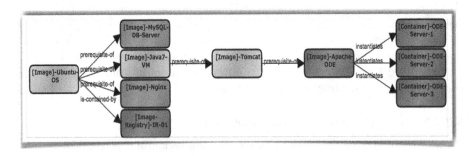

Fig. 5. Image Map

control scripts typically have inter-relationships among them. Understanding this is essential during deployment; it also assists to avoid errors in updating and creating new deployment artifacts. Ordinarily, DevOps would have to manually examine and comparing deployment artifacts to extract such inter-relationships.

Example. Figure 5 depicts an *Image Map* focused on "Ubuntu-OS". Consider we want to extend the "Apache-ODE" *Image* with an additional feature (e.g., BPEL4People). We are required to know all existing dependencies (e.g., Java-VM version) recursively up until the root Image. Thus the *Image Map* provides an indispensable visual technique to easily discover whether the "Apache-ODE" *Image* is dependent upon a particular version of "Java-VM" (e.g., Java7-VM). It is also useful as DevOps can identify, customize and reuse existing resources.

Application Map. An *Application Map* visualizes the organization and inter-action of *Hosting Machines* and/or *Containers* of an *Application.* Deployed resources usually depend on other cloud resources to provide and consume services. Thus understanding their runtime interactions proves extremely important, particularly when applying modifications (e.g., reconfiguring, scaling, shutting down). This could otherwise lead to Service-Level-Agreement (SLA) violations, or catastrophic disruptions to the complete resource infrastructure[5].

Example. Figure 6 depicts an Application Map focused on the "BPEL-App". Consider a DevOp may wish to scale-up the "Apache-ODE-Server". This requires creating a new "Apache-ODE-Server" and the communication links with any related *Containers* (e.g., "MySQL-DB-Server" and "Nginx-LB"). DevOps hence need to understand: (a) what are the existing *Containers* of an *Application*; (b) how each are related to one another; and (c) what *Image* is to be used to instantiate the new *Container.* Using the *Application Map* in conjunction with the *Image Map*, DevOps can easily determine which image would be needed, and the related containers to setup the communication links.

Another use-case is understanding the communication links between *Containers.* Traditionally, this is achieved via command-line tools, which only returns details about a single container. DevOps would thus iteratively discover information about each *Container* to derive a global view. Command-line tools are also only suitable for sophisticated administrators. Monitoring details and control actions are represented in textual forms which are hard to memorize and understand compared to visual forms.

Example. To optimize the overall performance of an *Application* we may minimize data communication across different *Hosting Machines.* One such technique is to detect inter-communicating *Containers* and migrate into one *Hosting Machine* to reduce network latencies.

---

[5] http://aws.amazon.com/message/65648/.

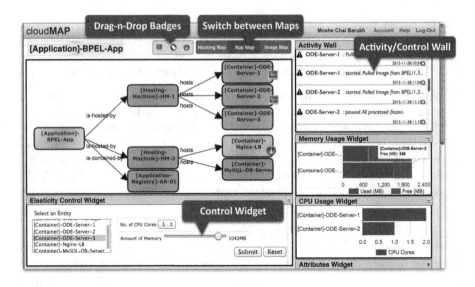

Fig. 6. Application Map

Hosting-Machine Map. A *Hosting-Machine Map* visualizes the organization of *Containers* and *Applications* within a specific *Hosting Machine*. This is useful for DevOps who manage a complete cloud environment; as opposed to the Application Map which only shows the Containers for a specific Application.

Example. Figure 7 shows the set of *Containers* deployed on a *Hosting Machine* "HM-1". DevOps are constantly responsible to check for optimization strategies: identifying under- or over- used machines. Suppose "HM1" can host a maximum of five *Containers*. We can use the map to determine there are only three running *Containers* (i.e., ODE-Server 1, 2 and 3). Thus it is possible to deploy two new *Containers* or migrate two existing ones. On the other hand, DevOps may delete *Hosting Machines* which are not currently hosting any *Containers*.

Furthermore, in conjunction with the *Monitoring Probe*, DevOps may observe data such as memory and storage utilization, as well as the existence of any exhausted machines. Actions may then be taken to avoid potential memory overflows and crashes of *Containers*. For instance, scaling-up the *Hosting Machines* to increase their underlying resources; or notify the owners to take any necessary actions (e.g., migrate *Containers* to a non-exhausted machines).

4   Implementation

We leverage our previous work *CloudBase* [14] to simplify the interactions between underlying orchestration tools. With our proposed *Domain Specific Model (DSM)*, high-level resource configurations can be supplied which are then automatically translated into their native language using *Connectors*. Layered above this as shown in Fig. 8, *CloudMap* implements: (i) An interactive mindmap visualization for navigating cloud resources; (ii) Detecting and displays

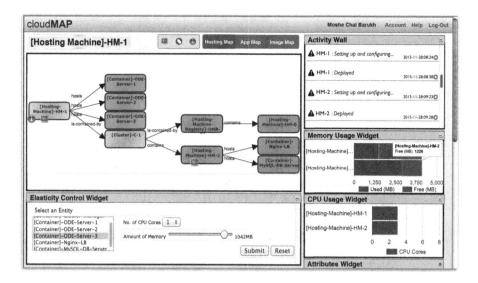

Fig. 7. Hosting Machine Map

events for monitoring; and (iii) allowing to perform both manual and automated actions.

Mind-Map Generation. The knowledge needed to generated the mind-maps are serialized from a supplied `CloudMap JSON` file. This is typically written by DevOps for a desired cloud configuration using the *CloudMap Notation* we presented in Sect. 3. As mentioned, constructs that pertain to some orchestration tool (e.g., *Docker*), must abide by the DSM's schema. For example, the *BPEL-App* entity abides by the `docker.rest.Application` schema, as shown in Fig. 8. When this is the case, behind the scenes the *CloudBase* engine is able to interpret complex and heterogeneous configurations and seamlessly connect to the underlying orchestration tool. This means, when a configuration file is written it is automatically translated into the low-level tool-specific language/API and deployed. The graphical mind-maps is rendered via the JS InfoVis Toolkit[6].

Event Management System. Upon loading a `CloudMap JSON` file, we also use *CloudBase* to determine the type of events that can be detected. For example, the *BPEL-App* includes events such as: @Created, @Stopped, @Pasued, @Running, etc. Thereby, the *Event Processor* component sets up the necessary, polling, processing and aggregating of event data. Once again, we leverage the `Connectors` implemented in *CloudBase* to help extract monitoring data from the low-level API (e.g., Docker Remote API[7]); and we assume access credentials are supplied in advance by the user. `Connectors` leverage Apache Camel[8] for event subscription. Events are then archived and indexed in a single MySQL

---

[6] http://philogb.github.io/jit/.
[7] http://docs.docker.com/reference/api/docker_remote_api/.
[8] http://camel.apache.org/.

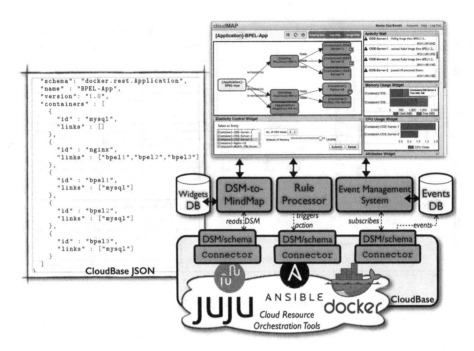

Fig. 8. CloudMap system architecture

database table, the *Monitoring Events DB*. Each table entry includes the ID of the Resource, timestamp, data-type (e.g., CPU or memory usage) and data-value.

Rule Processor. To enable automation, DevOps may also supply simple reactive rules. For example, *if* @Stopped *then* #notify, which implies if the BPEL-App stopped perform some notification action. To greatly simplify the way rules can be defined, we reuse a simple rule-definition language adapted from our previous work [9]. In that previous work, we assumed a *"Knowledge-driven"* approach, which means APIs and their constituents (i.e., operations, input/output types) of the orchestration tools are loaded in a knowledge-base. This makes it possible to write high-level rule definitions and translate into concrete actions.

Activity/Control Wall. To enable interactivity, we have implemented a contextualized dashboard and control wall. For example, when either a *Probe* or *Control* badge is drag-n-dropped onto a mind map entity, an appropriate widget is displayed. Activity events are also posted. Badges may also be attached to multiple nodes to formulate an aggregated visualization. For example, Figs. 6 and 7 compares absolute memory consumption statistics of each *Container* and *Hosting Machine*. Similarly, control actions widgets allow DevOps to "manually" perform actions to modify the resource configurations. Widgets are implemented in HTML/JS and leverages Google Chart Library[9]; we assume the requisite widgets are pre-built and curated in the *Widgets Base*. Realtime updates to the widget is also achieved by triggers on the *Monitoring Events DB* that notify the affected widget when new event entries are received in the DB.

5   Evaluation

5.1   Experimental Setup

We conducted a user-study to evaluate the following hypotheses: ***H1,*** *CloudMap* increases the efficiency to accurately understand and navigate attributes and relationships of deployed cloud resources; ***H2,*** increases the efficiency to accurately perform monitor and control actions; and ***H3,*** the key features offered are useful and comprehensible. We measured *efficiency* as the time taken to complete the tasks; and *accuracy* was determined using a set of questions (see below). The total time to complete the tasks was until all questions were answered accurately.

Evaluation Task & Questionnaire. The task consisted of both a *practical* and *written* component. Written feedback was provided via a questionnaire divided into four main parts: (a) Background; (b) Functionality; (c) Usability; and (d) Insights and Improvements. The *Background* questions sought to discover the participants' familiarity with existing cloud resource orchestration techniques (i.e., Docker). The *Functionality* questions provided the necessary instructions and to determine the accuracy in completing the tasks. Questions[10] targeted different features and were related to the given tools, such as understanding attributes; navigating relationships; and performing control actions.

Participant Selection & Grouping. Participants were sourced with diverse levels of technical expertise. For the sake of analysis, we classified a total of 12 participants into 2 main groups: (I) *Experts (7 participants)* with sophisticated understanding of cloud orchestration tools with 2–8 years of experience. And (II) *Generalists (5 participants)* who have average knowledge of cloud orchestration tool for day-to-day requirements, with around 1–5 years of experience.

5.2   Experiment Results and Analysis

Evaluation of *H*1 and *H*2. The hypotheses $H1$ and $H2$ were evaluated based on the *time* taken to perform the tasks and provide *accurate* responses to the questionnaire. Alternatively, we sought to disprove the null hypotheses $H1_0$ and $H2_0$. Both hypotheses were examined by conducting a t-test with a probability threshold of 5 %, and assuming unequal variance.

As shown in Fig. 9, it was pleasantly surprising that even generalists demonstrated a significant increase in efficiency (and reduction in time). The comparative experiment focused on one third-party tool only, *Shipyard*[11]. Due to the

---

[9] http://developers.google.com/chart/.

[10] See mosheb.web.cse.unsw.edu.au/CloudMapQns.html for a complete list of questions.

[11] https://shipyard-project.com/.

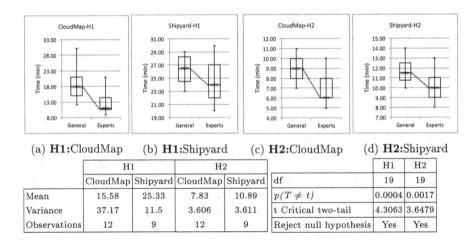

(a) **H1:CloudMap**   (b) **H1:Shipyard**   (c) **H2:CloudMap**   (d) **H2:Shipyard**

	H1		H2				H1	H2
	CloudMap	Shipyard	CloudMap	Shipyard	df		19	19
Mean	15.58	25.33	7.83	10.89	$p(T \neq t)$		0.0004	0.0017
Variance	37.17	11.5	3.606	3.611	t Critical two-tail		4.3063	3.6479
Observations	12	9	12	9	Reject null hypothesis		Yes	Yes

Fig. 9. Time results (grouped by expertise) to complete the tasks; and below t-test Results for H1 and H2

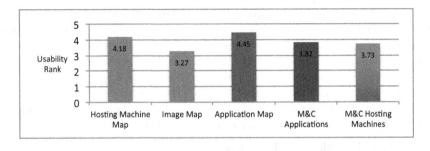

Fig. 10. Rate of usability of the main features of CloudMap

high number of existing cloud management tools, as well as project-based constraints, a more exhaustive comparative experiment was outside the scope. However, given the stark differences in times (means of 15.58 mins against 25.33 mins for $H1$; and means of 7.83 mins against 10.89 mins for $H2$), we postulate that it is unlikely to observe fundamental differences when comparing with any other tools similar to Shipyard. Accordingly, given our observations the likelihood of both $H1_0$ and $H2_0$ (equal mean modeling time) was around 5 %. Therefore, we could safely reject these null hypotheses, and imply the truth of $H1$ and $H2$.

Evaluation of $H3$. We evaluated this hypothesis through the *Usability* section of the questionnaire, and by asking participants to rate the usability for each feature (scale 0–5). We examined basic features such as the *Application, Image* and *Hosting Map*. As well as advanced features such as using badges and widgets to monitor and control (M&C) applications and hosting machines. We observed that the mean score for all features in Fig. 10 is above the neutral value of 3.

5.3 Discussion

Overall participants found that Mind-Map visualization a new but familiar concept. It was also impressive that *CloudMap* had a considerably fast learning-curve rate. Participants also championed the explicit visualization of cloud resource relationships as it is very useful for navigating through complex cloud resources. Similarly for the widgets that enabled seamless monitoring, analysis and control. Participants also suggested potential extensions such as widgets for: (a) cost visualization; (b) sorting and filtering based on the geographical region and role; (c) cost comparison; (d) scheduling orchestration tasks; and (e) generating recommendations to recover from error conditions.

6 Related Work and Concluding Remarks

Orchestrations tools (e.g., *AWS OpsWorks, Juju* or *Docker*) provide languages to represent and manage resources over cloud environments [10,11]. These languages can either be textual, visual or hybrid (i.e., a mixture of both textual and visual notations). The visual paradigm often simplify the manner of understanding compared to textual notations. While such visual techniques can be applied over most of the cloud resource lifecycle, we scope this paper on: navigation, understanding, discovery, monitoring and control concerns of cloud resources.

Discovery, Navigation, Understanding and Selection. Tools and research initiatives such as *AWS Management Console, OpenTOSCA,* and *CA AppLogic* provide visual features to facilitate discovery, navigation, understanding and selection of cloud resources [2]. However, these tools provide a flat view (e.g., catalogs) of cloud resources with sorting and filtering features. DevOps may select a particular resource to analyze their attributes, albeit they do not explicitly visualize relationships, dependencies and memberships between cloud resources. This implies DevOps would need to manually mine relationship details via textual descriptions. In contrast to the above, we contribute an extensible framework (i.e., in future additional Entities, Links, Badges and/or Widgets can be curated) for visualizing cloud resources via the familiar notion of mind-maps.

Deployment, Monitoring and Controlling. Tools such as *Juju GUI, OpenTOSCA* and *VisualOps* provide visual abstractions to describe deployment workflows and resource topologies [2,11,12]. Cloud resource monitoring tools such as *Nagios* and *CloudFielder* allow DevOps to define Service Level Agreement (SLA), detect anomalies and notify about SLA violations. *AWS Management Console, VisualOps, CA AppLogic* and other cloud resource management tools provide control features such as restarting, scaling and migration [12]. Ordinarily, DevOps would have to switch between multiple tools for different aspects of the cloud resource management lifecycle, this is time-consuming and cumbersome. In contrast, our tool greatly compliments this work, as we can integrate these features as pluggable widgets to seamlessly and centrally manage cloud resources.

Visual Notations in Other Domains. Visual notations are adopted in other closely related domains, such as Object-oriented programming, and Business Process modeling. Existing visual notations for service orchestration such as Business Process Modeling Notation (BPMN), focus primarily on the application layer. However, orchestrating cloud resources requires rich abstractions to reason about application resource requirements and constraints; support troubleshooting; and flexible and efficient scheduling of resources. *Architexa* [8] visualizes Java-based source codes and execution aspects in terms of hierarchical trees and UML sequence diagrams. WebML introduces a visual notation to model Web sites [3]. All these visual notations or languages adopt Entity-Relationship (ER) models (e.g., graphs, trees, UML class diagrams), which served as our motivation. *Eden* [15] is a visual notation for network management that proposed the concept of *Badges* to associate security and access policies with network devices. Similarly, we were inspired to propose the concept of *Badges* which can be attached to cloud resources to enable *Probes* and *Control Actions* functions.

Summary. Visual techniques provide a refreshing approach in contrast with existing largely text-based solutions. With the vast proliferation of cloud computing and large amount of complex configurations DevOps are faced with, this work provides a timely contribution. Our design was based on a detailed survey comprising 21 experts, where we aggregated, analyzed and applied our findings to propose a visual notation for cloud resource management. We further proposed the notion of *Badges* via drag-n-drop to enable monitoring and control features. To support the effectiveness of our approach, we also identified 3 common visualization patterns. We evaluated our work with a user-study of 12 participants, and our approach yielded significantly promising results with 33.29 % improved efficiency. We are therefore confident our work provides an innovative approach to a new way of cloud management. As future work, we plan to integrate visual notations to specify cloud resource deployment and reconfiguration workflows, also based on our previous work [13]. Moreover, we endeavor to provide high-level monitoring features such as cost estimation and comparison of cloud-based solutions across multiple providers (e.g., *AWS EC2* and *Google Cloud*).

References

1. Armbrust, M., et al.: A view of cloud computing. Commun. ACM **53**(4), 50–58 (2010)
2. Binz, T., Breitenbücher, U., Haupt, F., Kopp, O., Leymann, F., Nowak, A., Wagner, S.: OpenTOSCA – a runtime for TOSCA-based cloud applications. In: Basu, S., Pautasso, C., Zhang, L., Fu, X. (eds.) ICSOC 2013. LNCS, vol. 8274, pp. 692–695. Springer, Heidelberg (2013)
3. Ceri, S., Fraternali, P., Bongio, A.: Web modeling language (WebMI): a modeling language for designing web sites. Comput. Netw. **33**(1), 137–157 (2000)
4. Delaet, T., Joosen, W., Vanbrabant, B.: A survey of system configuration tools. In: 24th International Conference on LISA, pp. 1–8. USENIX Association (2010)
5. Fehling, C., Leymann, F., Retter, R., Schupeck, W., Arbitter, P.: Cloud Computing Patterns. Springer, Wien (2014)

6. Pigoski, T.M.: Practical Software Maintenance: Best Practices for Managing Your Software Investment. Wiley, New York (1996)
7. Schulte, S., Janiesch, C., Venugopal, S., Weber, I., Hoenisch, P.: Elastic business process management: state of the art and open challenges for bpm in the cloud. Future Gener. Comput. Syst. **46**, 36–50 (2015)
8. Sinha, V., et al.: Understanding code architectures via interactive exploration and layout of layered diagrams. In: Companion to the 23rd ACM SIGPLAN Conference on OOPSLA, OOPSLA Companion 2008, pp. 745–746. ACM (2008)
9. Sun, Y.-J.J., Barukh, M.C., Benatallah, B., Beheshti, S.-M.-R.: Scalable SaaS-based process customization with casewalls. In: Barros, A., Grigori, D., Narendra, N.C., Dam, H.K. (eds.) ICSOC 2015. LNCS, vol. 9435, pp. 218–233. Springer, Heidelberg (2015). doi:10.1007/978-3-662-48616-0_14
10. Turnbull, J.: The Docker Book: Containerization is the new virtualization (2014)
11. Ubuntu: Juju (2013). http://www.ubuntu.com/cloud/tools/juju
12. VisualOps: Visualops - wysiwyg for your cloud (2015). http://docs.visualops.io/
13. Weerasiri, D., Benatallah, B., Barukh, M.C.: Process-driven configuration of federated cloud resources. In: Renz, M., Shahabi, C., Zhou, X., Cheema, M.A. (eds.) DASFAA 2015. LNCS, vol. 9049, pp. 334–350. Springer, Heidelberg (2015)
14. Weerasiri, D., et al.: A model-driven framework for interoperable cloud resources management. Technical report UNSW-CSE-TR-201514, UNSW (2015)
15. Yang, J., Edwards, W.K., Haslem, D.: Eden: supporting home network management through interactive visual tools. In: Proceedings of the 23nd Annual ACM Symposium on User Interface Software and Technology, pp. 109–118. ACM (2010)

Keep Calm and Wait for the Spike! Insights on the Evolution of Amazon Services

Apostolos V. Zarras, Panos Vassiliadis[✉], and Ioannis Dinos

Department of Computer Science and Engineering,
University of Ioannina, Ioannina, Greece
{zarras,pvassil,idinos}@cs.uoi.gr

Abstract. Web services are black box dependency magnets. Hence, studying how they evolve is both important and challenging. In this paper, we focus on one of the most successful stories of the service-oriented paradigm in industry, i.e., the Amazon services. We perform a principled empirical study, that detects evolution patterns and regularities, based on Lehman's laws of software evolution. Our findings indicate that service evolution comes with spikes of change, followed by calm periods where the service is internally enhanced. Although spikes come with unpredictable volume, developers can count in the near certainty of the calm periods following them to allow their absorption. As deletions rarely occur, both the complexity and the exported functionality of a service increase over time (in fact, predictably). Based on the above findings, we provide recommendations that can be used by the developers of Web service applications for service selection and application maintenance.

Keywords: Software evolution · Web services · Lehman's laws

1 Introduction

Web services expose their functionalities through the Web, via application programming interfaces (APIs), which can be invoked by the client applications. Concerning software evolution, Web services are *black box dependency magnets*[1]. As application developers have no access to the internals of the services they use, they are clearly dealing with software modules of a black box nature. At the same time, even a small change in a Web service can reflect to a vast number of applications that use it. In particular, when a conventional API changes, the developers of the dependent applications can avoid dealing with the changes by sticking with an older version of the API. On the contrary, when a Web service changes, the evolution typically comes with a strict time plan, within which the developers of the dependent applications must migrate to the new version [4].

Understanding the evolution of Web services is therefore both difficult and important for application developers who need to know whether they can depend

---

[1] The term dependency magnet refers to a software module that is used by many others [13].

© Springer International Publishing Switzerland 2016
S. Nurcan et al. (Eds.): CAiSE 2016, LNCS 9694, pp. 444–458, 2016.
DOI: 10.1007/978-3-319-39696-5_27

on the stability of the services they use and whether there are patterns and regularities concerning their evolution. Unfortunately, although existing research [5,15] has provided valuable information on the statistical breakdown of the changes occurring to the services' interfaces, the understanding of regularities and patterns during the lifetime of services has not been investigated yet.

In this paper, *we focus on one of the most successful stories of the service-oriented paradigm in industry, i.e., the Amazon Web Services (AWS)*[2]. In this context, *we perform a principled empirical study that detects evolution patterns and regularities, based on Lehman's laws of software evolution* [3,11]. Our findings indicate that *service evolution typically comes with spikes of change, during which operations are added or updated, followed by longer or shorter "calm" periods* that focus on internal improvements of service correctness, performance and security and allow the developers of Web service applications to absorb the changes. Typically, *the provided functionality increases in a predictable manner*, whereas, unfortunately, its *incremental growth is not predicable*. Based on our findings, we provide recommendations that can be used by the developers of Web service applications for service selection and application maintenance. In particular, evolution histories with calm periods between spikes are a desirable feature in service selection, as it allows the absorbtion of change. Thus, the study of the change history and functionality expansion can be used to attest on the suitability of a service during service selection. Concerning maintenance, functionality expansion can be predicted. At the same time, as the heartbeat of change itself is unpredictable, resources and time must be allocated to keep the applications up to date.

The rest of this paper is structured as follows: Sect. 2 discusses related work on software evolution; Sect. 3 provides the basic concepts of our approach, along with the setup of the empirical study; Sect. 4 details our method and findings; Sect. 5 discusses the practical implications of the study for the developers of Web service applications; Sect. 6 concerns threats to validity; finally, Sect. 7 summarizes our contribution and discusses future work.

2 Lehman's Laws and Related Studies

To come up with patterns and detailed insights in the evolution of Web services, we resort to traditional tools from the area of software evolution. Back in the 70's, Meir Lehman and his colleagues initiated their study on the evolution of software systems [3] and continued to refine and extend it for the next 40 years (e.g., [11,12]). Lehman's laws concentrate on the evolution of *E-type systems*, i.e., software systems that solve a problem, or address an application in the real world. The essence of Lehman's laws is that *the evolution of an E-type system is a controlled process that follows the behavior of a feedback-based mechanism*. More specifically, the evolution process is driven by *positive feedback* that reflects the need to adapt to the changing environment, by *adding functionalities* to the evolving system. The growth of the system is constrained by *negative feedback*

---
[2] aws.amazon.com/.

that reflects the need to perform *maintenance activities*, so as to prevent the deterioration of the system's quality. In [9], the authors provide a detailed historical survey of the evolution of Lehmans's laws. Further studies revealed the diverse behavior of software concerning the validity of Lehman's laws. In [16], for instance, the authors found evidence that commercial software is typically more faithful to the laws than academic and research software. A number of studies focused on open source software (e.g., [7,8,10,18]), while in [17], we employed Lehman's laws to investigate the evolution of open-source databases; the common ground in all these studies is that they found support for the laws of continuing change and growth.

So far, the efforts that concern the evolution of Web services focus on classifications of changes, compatibility checks, version control and so on [1,5,6,15]. [5,15] provide a first valuable insight on the evolution of real-world services. In both of these works the authors observed that the changes occurring to the services' interfaces are mostly additions and updates, while the deletions were relatively few. Another interesting empirical study on Web service evolution is reported in [4]. In this study the authors interview the developers of Web service applications to investigate the problems they encounter, due to the evolution of the services they use. Moreover, they investigate the evolution policies employed by the service providers. The findings of this study showed that different providers follow different practices and essential features like versioning are sometimes neglected. Moreover, the providers force changes upon the developers of Web service applications, so as to co-evolve with the services.

Going beyond the state of the art, in this paper we perform, for the first time in the related literature, a principled empirical study that exploits Lehman's laws of software evolution to provide detailed insights on the evolution of Amazon services. Based on our findings we further provide recommendations that can be used by the developers of Web service applications for service selection and application maintenance.

3   Basic Concepts and Setup

In this section, we discuss the basic concepts and the overall setting of our study.

3.1   Basic Concepts

We study the evolution of services that follow the standard Web services architecture[3] and expose their functionalities via WSDL specifications. The core concept of the data model that we employ in our study is the *service evolution history*, which provides information about the way that a service evolves.

Definition 1. *Service evolution history* - *The evolution history for a service, s, is a list, $H_s = \{r_1^s, r_2^s, \ldots, r_N^s\}$, that consists of the different releases of s. The elements of H_s are totally ordered with respect to the their corresponding release dates.*

---

[3] www.w3.org/TR/ws-arch/.

Definition 2. *Service release* - *A service release that belongs to the evolution history, H_s, of a service, s, is a tuple, $r_i^s = (ID, date, Size, Change)$ that consists of the following elements:*

- *ID is the release identifier that reflects the order of r_i^s in H_s.*
- *date, is the release date of r_i^s.*
- *Size, is a tuple of basic size metrics that concern different parts of the WSDL specification of r_i^s. Specifically, $Size[Interfaces]$, $Size[Opers]$, $Size[Types]$, denote the number of interfaces, operations, and XML types, respectively.*
- *Change, is a tuple of basic change metrics that concern the transition from r_{i-1}^s to r_i^s. In particular, $Change[Adds]$, $Change[Dels]$, and $Change[Upds]$, denote the number of operation additions, removals, and updates, respectively[4]. For the purpose of our study, we consider operations as composite elements, whose updates involve (a) changes in their own structure (e.g., attributes, annotations), or (b) updates in the structure of their constituents (e.g., messages, XML types).*

3.2 Amazon Web Services

Amazon is a major service provider that provides a variety of services, hosted on the AWS infrastructure. AWS is very popular, having customers such as NASA, NASDAQ, Netflix, Facebook, Adobe, D-Link, etc.[5]. In our study, we selected 6 Web services, for which it was possible to recover their detailed evolution history. Following, we provide further details regarding the functionalities of the examined services, while Table 1 gives information concerning the service releases that we considered.

Table 1. Description of the data-sets.

Dataset	Releases	URL
EC2	73	aws.amazon.com/ec2
ELB	14	aws.amazon.com/elasticloadbalancing/
AS	12	aws.amazon.com/autoscaling/
SQS	16	aws.amazon.com/sqs/
RDS	41	aws.amazon.com/rds/
MTurk	20	aws.amazon.com/mturk/

Elastic Compute Cloud (EC2) allows to reuse computational resources, via the allocation and management of virtual servers, deployed on the AWS

---

[4] We empirically observed that bindings and ports rarely change, while changes to XML types and messages are very strongly correlated with changes to operations (Spearman's correlation is typically close to 1). For lack of space, we omit these findings.

[5] aws.amazon.com/solutions/case-studies/all/.

infrastructure. Elastic Load Balancing (ELB) can be used together with EC2, to balance the load that is handled by a set of virtual servers, which have been allocated, via EC2. Auto Scaling (AS) provides means for scaling up, or down, a set of virtual servers that have been allocated via EC2. Simple Queue Service (SQS) allows message-based communication via queues. Relational Database Service (RDS) provides means for managing and using relational databases, over the AWS infrastructure. Mechanical Turk (MTurk) provides access to a scalable workforce, via an interface that offers operations for the creation of tasks, the qualification/selection of workers who are going to perform the tasks, the retrieval/approval of the work done, the payment of the workers, etc.

3.3   Release History Extraction and Assessment Method

To proceed with our study we calculated the evolution history for each one of the examined Web services. To this end, we exploited the public service release notes and the WSDL specifications that are available in the service provider's Web portal. To automate the evolution history extraction we used Membrane SOA[6] which allows to parse and compare WSDL specifications. We exported the evolution histories in the form of an Excel spreadsheet, from which we produced more advanced metrics and graphical representations of the data, which facilitated the assessment of Lehman's laws in our context (Sects. 4 and 5). In our deliberations, we consider the latest definitions of Lehman's laws that are given in [11]. At a glance, the steps that constitute our assessment method are summarized below.

- For each law, we identify the criteria for the validation of the law in the context of Web services.
- Then, we evaluate these criteria in the case of Amazon services.
- We conclude on the validity of the law.
- Finally, we draw conclusions on what practitioners should conclude.

4   Findings

Due to the limited space it is practically impossible to provide all the data in detail[7]. Therefore, for each law, we discuss the main findings and we provide indicative graphical representations of the data for the most interesting cases.

4.1   Continuing Change (Law I)

"An E-type system must be continually adapted, or else it becomes less satisfactory in use" [11]. The intuition behind the first law is that as time goes by, both the operational environment and the users' needs change, causing the need

---

[6] http://www.membrane-soa.org/soa-model/.

[7] An extended report with all the results can be found at: www.cs.uoi.gr/~zarras/LehmanWS_WEB/LehmanWS.html.

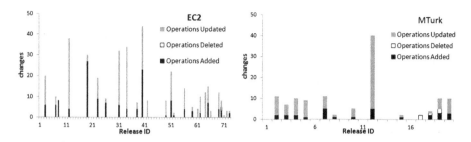

Fig. 1. Distribution of operation changes per release ID (releases with zero change also included).

for the system to change too [11]. In the service-oriented paradigm, as the services are publicly available through the Web, the number of the applications that depend upon them and their diversity is potentially unlimited. Hence, the potentials for the emergence of new requirements and the need for changing the services can be very high. In our study, we assess the first law based on *the heartbeat of changes* that have been performed during the service evolution history.

The Case of Amazon Services. The study of the heartbeat of changes in the case of Amazon services reveals two main observations. The first one is that *for a large number of service releases, the service interface remains unchanged* (Fig. 1). According to the service release logs, in these releases most of the activity concerns bug fixing, documentation, security and performance improvements, deployment extensions, provision of client side APIs for specific programming languages and environments. The second observation, which is inline with prior studies on the evolution of services [5,15], is that *the overwhelming majority of changes concern additions and updates*; there are very few cases of deletions. Overall, *the essence of the law holds* for the examined services. Notable properties are that *changes are mostly internal and involve the structure of the exported operations less frequently; when they do, they involve mostly updates and additions.*

4.2 Increasing Complexity (Law II)

"As an E-type system is changed its complexity increases and becomes more difficult to evolve, unless work is done to maintain or reduce the complexity" [11]. Software complexity is a vast concept that involves several aspects (Lehman et al. [11] refer to requirements and specification complexity, architecture complexity, design and implementation complexity, structural complexity, etc.) and metrics widely discussed in the literature (see e.g., [18] for a large number of complexity metrics). Addressing all these aspects in one study is simply not possible. Complexity from the viewpoint of the developers of Web service applications is mostly related to the effort required for (a) understanding, using and testing the functionalities of the interfaces exposed by the employed services [14], and,

(b) keeping the client applications up to date [2]. Regarding these aspects of service complexity, in the empirical study that we performed in [2], we found that the developers of Web service applications suggest the decomposition of fat interfaces, as they find them hard to understand and use. Based on this finding, in this paper we assess the second law with respect to the ratio of interfaces to operations. We consider that a particular service release is hard to understand, use and test if the provided interfaces consist of many operations. Following, we formally define the metric that we employ, with respect to the concept of service evolution history.

Definition 3. *Interface Complexity* - *For a service release r_i^s that belongs to the evolution history, H_s, of a service, s, we assess interface complexity in terms of the complement of the ratio of the provided interfaces to the operations offered by these interfaces, i.e., $C(r_i^s) = 1 - \frac{r_i^s.Size[Interfaces]}{r_i^s.Size[Opers]}$.*

The Case of Amazon Services. Regarding the second law, in all cases we observed that the value of $C(r_i^s)$ is generally high, which means that the interfaces of the examined services are composed of many operations (Fig. 2). This holds, even for the initial releases of the services, where the value of $C(r_i^s)$ is typically higher than 0.9 for all datasets (except SQS). *As time passes, the value of $C(r_i^s)$ increases smoothly with a slow logarithmic trend.* To further validate this observation we performed a logarithmic regression analysis. In all cases except for SQS (Fig. 2), the R^2 values that we obtained are high (from 0.576 to 0.928, 0.83 on average), indicating the logarithmic trend that we observed. *Notably, there is no evidence of the existence of a control mechanism for the aspect of complexity that we assess.* As we discussed in the case of the first law, the deletions of operations are very rare. Interface decomposition would be another possible way to reduce complexity (e.g., [2]). Nevertheless, for the examined services the number of provided interfaces is typically constant during the evolution history of the services. To sum up, *we conclude that the second law holds.* Specifically, the results brought out the following properties: *Interface complexity, measured in terms of the ratio of interfaces to operations, is high; it smoothly increases over time; usually the increase is logarithmic.*

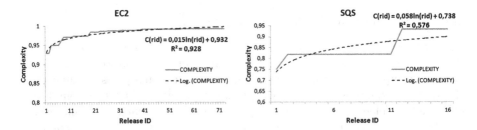

Fig. 2. Interface complexity - measured in terms of the ratio of interfaces to operations - per release ID.

4.3   Self Regulation (Law III)

"Global E-type system evolution is feedback regulated" [11]. The term regulation is used in the third law to emphasize that the system evolves in a controlled way, guided by (a) positive feedback activities that cause the system's functional capacity to grow, and, (b) negative feedback maintenance activities that resist to the unrestrained growth.

The validity of the third law is typically demonstrated by the existence of patterns in the incremental growth of a system [11,17,18]. Specifically, Lehman and his colleagues, observed ripples, which reflect the existence of a stabilization mechanism. Spikes indicate releases where the positive feedback activities that grow the functional capacity of the system dominate, while valleys indicate releases of small or even negative growth, where most of the effort is spent for negative feedback maintenance activities. Further studies report similar observations in open source software [18] and database schemas [17]. In the aforementioned studies, the incremental growth of the system is measured as the size difference between two subsequent releases. The size of the system is typically measured with respect to the system implementation (e.g., number of modules, number of schema tables). To assess the third law, in the case of services we follow a similar track, by looking for patterns in the incremental growth of a service. In our study, we measure the incremental growth of a service in terms of the difference in the number of operations provided by subsequent service releases, as this is the actual increase in the functional capacity of the service that is perceived by the developers of Web service applications.

Definition 4. *Incremental growth* - *For a pair of subsequent service releases r_i^s, r_{i+1}^s that belong to the evolution history, H_s, of a service, s, the operations' incremental growth $IG_{op}(r_i^s, r_{i+1}^s)$ is the difference in the number of operations defined in the specification of r_{i+1}^s and r_i^s, i.e., $IG_{op}(r_i^s, r_{i+1}^s) = r_{i+1}^s.Size[Opers] - r_i^s.Size[Opers]$.*

The Case of Amazon Services. As the case of typical E-type systems, *in the incremental growth of Amazon services we also have spikes*. However, an interesting *difference* is that the *spikes* are usually sparse interrupted by *periods of calmness*, where the functional capacity of the Web service does not grow. MTurk appears to be an exception with consequent spikes, and only one short calmness period. In traditional E-type systems, negative feedback is concerned with correction actions, documentation improvement, dead code elimination, structural cleanups and restructurings, aiming to restrict uncontrolled change and its side effects. In the case of Amazon services, although we do not observe significant restructuring activities that are externally visible (resulting in an increased structural complexity – Law II), we can however claim that the growth that results from the positive feedback is not uncontrolled or continuous: on the contrary, we frequently see occasions where documentation improvements, bug fixing, security patching and extension of programming facilities take place (see Law I). In conclusion, *there is evidence that the third law holds*. Although

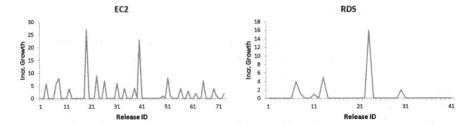

Fig. 3. Incremental growth –difference between the number of operations in subsequent service releases– per release ID.

there are no visible restructurings and consolidations, we observe *two patterns of incremental growth, specifically, spikes and calmness periods, which together indicate the existence of a stabilization mechanism.*

4.4   Conservation of Organizational Stability (Law IV)

"The work rate of an organization evolving an E-type system tends to be constant over the operational lifetime of that system, or phases of that lifetime" [11]. In practice, a constant work rate, along with the patterns that control the self-regulated evolution of the E-type system, facilitate the planning of resources that are needed for the E-type system's evolution activities. Unfortunately, though, the assessment of the law has been problematic early on (see e.g., [12] or [18]), as the available information on indicators like personnel time dedicated to software evolution is typically unavailable and inaccurate. An approximation suggested by Lehman et al. [12] involves measuring number of changes performed per release.

The Case of Amazon Services. In all cases we observed that *the amount of changes is not invariant* during the lifetime of the Amazon services; on the contrary, *it may vary a lot* (Fig. 1). Also, it is not possible to speak about phases in which the amount of changes remains constant. On the other hand, it is not possible to know precisely the work done behind the scenes (e.g., refactorings, repairs, etc.). Therefore, based on our results *we can not confirm or disprove the fourth law of software evolution.*

4.5   Conservation of Familiarity (Law V)

"The incremental growth of E-type systems is constrained by the need to maintain familiarity" [11]. Based on the observations of Lehman and his colleagues [12], the validity of the law is demonstrated by two factors that relate with incremental growth. The first one (which is more related to the wording of the law) is that releases characterized by high incremental growth are followed by releases with lower incremental growth, thus, smoothening the process of understanding and mastering the performed changes. The second factor is that in the long term there is a declining trend in the incremental growth of the system, due to the increasing complexity of the system, which hardens the understanding of the changed context.

The Case of Amazon Services. We do not observe a clear declining trend in the incremental growth of the operations that are provided by the examined services (Fig. 3). However, as pointed out in the case of the third law (Sect. 4.3), spikes in the incremental growth of the operations are typically followed by calmness periods of zero growth. Overall, we conclude that *the essence of the fifth law holds.* Specifically, the property that comes out from the results is that *releases characterized by non-zero incremental growth, tend to be followed by releases of zero incremental growth.*

4.6   Continuing Growth (Law VI)

"The functional capability of E-type systems must be continually enhanced to maintain user satisfaction over system lifetime" [11]. As discussed in detail in [11] the sixth law reflects the addition of new functionalities, while the first law generally concerns functional and behavioral changes. Based on the exact wordings of the law, its validity for a particular system involves the existence of a continuous increasing trend in the growth of the system. To assess the law in the case of Web services, we employ a metric typically used in the related literature [11,18], the functionality growth. In our study, we measure the growth of the service as the number of operations provided by a particular service release. More formally, we employ the following metric.

Definition 5. *Growth* - *The growth of the operations $G_{op}(r_i^s)$ for a service release r_i^s that belongs to the evolution history, H_s, of a service, s, is defined as the number of operations provided by r_i^s, i.e., $G_{op}(r_i^s) - r_i^s.Size[Opers]$.*

The Case of Amazon Services. In all of the Amazon services we observed *an increasing trend in the growth of the service operations.* However, the periods of growth are *interrupted by periods of calmness,* consisting of subsequent service releases that offer the same number of operations (in Fig. 4, the solid lines depict the actual growth, while the dashed and the dotted lines give growth predictions, discussed later in law VIII). Hence, *the results that we obtained indicate that the sixth law holds.* Nevertheless, the services *do not grow exactly as originally stated in the law; their functional capacity increases, but the increase is not continuous.*

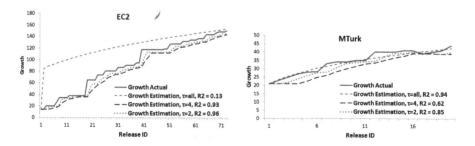

Fig. 4. Growth –number of operations– per release ID, and inverse square model predictions.

4.7   Declining Quality (Law VII)

"The quality of an E-type system will appear to be declining, unless rigorously maintained and adapted to operational environment changes" [11].

As discussed in [11] this law is closely related with the first and the sixth law, in the sense that the system must be adapted and extended, with respect to the evolving operational environment. Otherwise, it is likely that the provided functionalities will not be satisfactory for the users and the overall perceived quality of the system will downgrade. Regarding the assessment of the the seventh law, Lehman and his colleagues do not provide a concrete definition of quality. On the contrary, in [11] they state that the quality of an E-type system is a function of many factors, whose definition, modeling, measurement and monitoring depend on several aspects, which may include organization, product, process properties and goals. In the case of Web services, the main problem concerning the assessment of the seventh law is that the required data are typically not publicly available to the developer of Web service applications. Nevertheless, in [11,12], Lehman and his colleagues discuss a more general strategy to support the seventh law, which can be used in the case of Web services. Their strategy relies on logical induction, in the sense that the decline of the system quality, logically follows from the growth of the system's functional capacity (law VI), and from the increasing complexity that comes along with functionality growth (law II).

The Case of Amazon Services. So far, in our study we have evidence of the growing functional capacity of the examined services (Fig. 4) that confirm the validity of the sixth law (Sect. 4.6). Moreover, we have some evidence of the increasing interface structural complexity of the examined services (Fig. 2) that support the validity of the second law (Sect. 4.2). Therefore, by following the general strategy suggested by Lehman and his colleagues in [11,12], we have indications that the seventh law holds for the examined services. However, given that the publicly available specifications of the examined services are not accompanied by concrete qualitative evaluations, *we cannot confirm or disprove the law, based on indisputable objective measurements.*

4.8   Feedback System (Law VIII)

"E-type evolution processes are multi-level multi-loop, multi-agent feedback systems" [11]. According to Lehman, the last law is a concise summary of the other seven. In the literature, the main evidence for the validity of the law is to show that the actual growth of the system adheres to the inverse square (IS) model, which provides a *feedback-based growth prediction formula* [11,17,18]. In our study we also rely on this strategy. Following, we adapt the IS growth prediction formula, with respect to the definition of growth that we provided in Sect. 4.6.

Definition 6. *IS model for services* - *According to the IS model, the predicted operations' growth, $\widehat{G_{op}}(r_i^s)$, for a service release r_i^s that belongs to the evolution history, H_s, of a service, s, is:* $\widehat{G_{op}}(r_i^s) = \widehat{G_{op}}(r_{i-1}^s) + \dfrac{\overline{E}}{\widehat{G_{op}}(r_{i-1}^s)^2}$, *where* $\widehat{G_{op}}(r_{i-1}^s)$ *is the estimated operations' growth for the previous service release,* r_{i-1}^s, *and* $\overline{E}$ *estimates effort. More specifically,* $\overline{E}$ *is the average of individual* E_j, *calculated for the service release history* H_s, *as follows:* $E_j = (G_{op}(r_j^s) - G_{op}(r_{j-1}^s)) * G_{op}(r_{j-1}^s)^2$, *where* $G_{op}(r_j^s)$ *refers to the actual operations' growth for a service release* r_j^s, *and* $G_{op}(r_{j-1}^s)$ *refers to the actual operations' growth for the previous service release* r_{j-1}^s.

The Case of Amazon Services. To assess the eighth law we calculated the estimated values of the operations' growth, with respect to the IS model, and compared them with the respective actual values, derived from the evolution histories of the Amazon services. Specifically, we considered 3 variants of the model. The first variant, denoted by $\tau = all$, corresponds to the original IS model employed by Lehman in [12], where $\overline{E}$ is computed over the entire evolution history. The other two variants (inspired from [17]), compute an average effort taking only the recent past into consideration. Specifically, in $\tau = 2$ and $\tau = 4$, $\overline{E}$ is computed for every release r_i^s, over the previous 2 and 4 releases, respectively. To assess the quality of the estimated values, compared to the actual ones, we further calculated the values of the R^2 statistic for the IS model variants. Based on the results, we observed that $\tau = 2$ gives quite good estimations (R^2 ranges from 0.60 to 0.96, 0.78 on average). In fact, $\tau = 2$ gives the best estimations in all cases, but MTurk where $\tau = all$ outperforms the other two variants (Fig. 4). So, overall, *we have evidence that the eighth law holds*; specifically, we can safely state that *the growth of the examined Web services can be accurately estimated via a feedback-based formula that exploits changes in previous service releases*.

5   Practical Implications and Recommendations

Our study revealed that Amazon services live quite normal lives. Although their loyalty to Lehman's laws can not be fully confirmed, the Amazon services are popular and constitute an integral part of a successful platform. Therefore, we consider the evolution patterns that we observed in our findings, as a baseline for a list of recommendations that target the developers of Web service applications and concern service selection and usage.

How can I tell if this service lives a healthy life? Check the change heartbeat of the service; calm lives consisting of frequent periods of calmness, where the functional capacity of a service does not change, interrupted by spikes of change that involve mostly additions and updates, indicate a normal life. During the calm periods, the service is typically enhanced in terms of correctness, documentation, security, performance and usability, showing that the service provider takes perfective maintenance seriously, performs bug fixing and improvements. Check the incremental growth of the service; again, the existence of spikes and calmness periods indicates that the service evolves normally, with respect to an underlying stabilization mechanism.

Will I have time to absorb changes? Check the incremental growth of the service; if you observe that releases of non-zero incremental growth, tend to be followed by releases of zero incremental growth, it means that there will be ample time to absorb the changes that take place.

Is the heartbeat of changes predictable in some way? Even for healthy services, it may not really be possible to forecast the heartbeat of changes that occur over time. Thus, you have to accommodate for resources for the worst case.

Will I have time to learn about new functionalities? Check the growth of the service; typically there is an increasing trend in the growth of the service operations. If you observe that the increase is not continuous, you can count on the interval for the understanding of the new features.

Is the amount of new functionalities predictable in some way? It is likely that you could coarsely predict the expansion of the offered operations and plan accordingly; try to do this via a feedback-based regression formula that is based on Lehman's IS model.

Will the complexity of the service be a problem for service usage? Even for healthy services, complexity could be an issue. You have to assess the specific aspects of complexity that concern you (e.g., specification, architectural, structural, etc.). The complexity could be quite high and it may increase over time. However, if the increase is smooth and predictable, you do not have to worry too much. In any case, you will have to anticipate the need to allocate time and resources for understanding and using the service.

Will the quality of the service improve, decline, remain as is? Most likely you wont be able to tell, based on available information; first you will have to determine the aspects of quality that concern you, then you you will have to assess them by yourself. Anticipate the need to allocate time and resources for QoS evaluation.

6   Threats to Validity

Regarding *external validity*, our study focused on the in-depth analysis of Amazon services. We studied the evolution of Amazon services that provide various functionalities. The population of the examined services is reasonable, with respect to similar studies [5,15,17,18]. More importantly, we considered services that have already made a notable impact in industry. Hence, we are confident that our findings are representative of the overall population of Amazon services and that they are of interest to a broad community of developers. Nevertheless, the reader should be careful not to overgeneralize the results to the overall population of existing Web services. At the same time, our approach for the assessment of Web service evolution is general and can be used to perform further similar studies. Also, the recommendations that we provide for service selection and usage are general and concern the overall population of Web services.

When it comes to *construct validity*, we used Membrane SOA, a well-known open-source API, for the accurate construction of evolution histories. Moreover, we manually inspected random samples of the collected data. *Internal validity*, is not a major issue in our study as we do not attempt to establish any particular cause-effect relationships. Regarding *conclusion validity*, we validated the observed relations and trends with well-known statistic methods.

7 Conclusion

From a broader perspective, we believe that the success of the service-oriented development paradigm strongly depends on whether services live a normal life. Understanding the patterns and regularities that rule the evolution of services is a key factor for increasing the developers' confidence on the services that they use, or intend to use. In this paper, we studied the evolution of Amazon services. To perform our study we followed a principled approach that is based on Lehman's laws of software evolution. Although our findings showed that Amazon services are healthy, this cannot be taken for granted for all services. To this end, developers of Web service applications can exploit our principled approach, to assess the health of the services they are interested in. Based on our study, we further derived a list of practical recommendations that target the developers of Web service applications and concern service selection and application maintenance.

Regarding the future directions of this line of research, two open issues of significant practical importance are the forecasting of service evolution, and the study of the relationship between the evolution of services (e.g., number, size, frequency of spikes) and the applications that use them (e.g., number of clients, usage profile).Metrics for service complexity and growth that account for more factors (e.g., input/output parameters) is also a research issue that deserves to be further investigated. Finally, another interesting challenge is to introduce a principled patterns-based method that allows the developers of Web service applications to assess the healthiness of the Web services' that they use.

Acknowledgments. We would like to thank the reviewers of the paper for their helpful comments. This work was supported from the European Community's FP7/2007-2013 under grant agreement number 257178 (project CHOReOS).

References

1. Andrikopoulos, V., Benbernou, S., Papazoglou, M.P.: On the evolution of services. IEEE Trans. Softw. Eng. **38**(3), 609–628 (2012)
2. Athanasopoulos, D., Zarras, A., Miskos, G., Issarny, V., Vassiliadis, P.: Cohesion-driven decomposition of service interfaces without access to source code. IEEE Trans. Serv. Comput. **8**(4), 550–562 (2015)
3. Belady, L.A., Lehman, M.M.: A model of large program development. IBM Syst. J. **15**(3), 225–252 (1976)
4. Espinha, T., Zaidman, A., Gross, H.G.: Web API growing pains: loosely coupled yet strongly tied. J. Syst. Softw. **100**, 27–43 (2015)

5. Fokaefs, M., Mikhaiel, R., Tsantalis, N., Stroulia, E., Lau, A.: An empirical study on web service evolution. In: Proceedings of the 18th IEEE International Conference on Web Services (ICWS), pp. 49–56 (2011)

6. Fokaefs, M., Stroulia, E.: Using WADL specifications to develop and maintain REST client applications. In: Proceedings of the 22nd IEEE International Conference on Web Services (ICWS), pp. 81–88 (2015)

7. Godfrey, M.W., Tu, Q.: Evolution in open source software: a case study. In: Proceedings of the 16th IEEE International Conference on Software Maintenance (ICSM), pp. 131–142 (2000)

8. Herraiz, I., Robles, G., Gonzalez-Barahona, J.M., Capiluppi, A., Ramil, J.F.: Comparison between SLOCs and number of files as size metrics for software evolution analysis. In: Proceedings of the 10th IEEE European Conference on Software Maintenance and Reengineering (CSMR), pp. 206–213 (2006)

9. Herraiz, I., Rodriguez, D., Robles, G., Gonzalez-Barahona, J.M.: The evolution of the laws of software evolution: a discussion based on a systematic literature review. ACM Comput. Surv. **46**(2), 1–28 (2013)

10. Koch, S.: Software evolution in open source projects: a large-scale investigation. J. Softw. Maint. Evol. **19**(6), 361–382 (2007)

11. Lehman, M.M., Fernandez-Ramil, J.C.: Rules and tools for software evolution planning and management. In: Madhavji, N., Fernandez-Ramil, J.C., Perry, D. (eds.) Software Evolution and Feedback: Theory and Practice. Wiley, New York (2006)

12. Lehman, M.M., Fernandez-Ramil, J.C., Perry, D.E.: On evidence supporting the FEAST hypothesis and the laws of software evolution. In: Proceedings of the 5th IEEE International Software Metrics Symposium (METRICS), pp. 84–88 (1998)

13. Martin, R.C.: Clean Code. Prentice Hall, Upper Saddle River (2009)

14. Perepletchikov, M., Ryan, C., Tari, Z.: The impact of service cohesion on the analyzability of service-oriented software. IEEE Trans. Serv. Comput. **3**(2), 89–103 (2010)

15. Romano, D., Pinzger, M.: Analyzing the evolution of web services using fine-grained changes. In: Proceedings of the 19th IEEE International Conference on Web Services (ICWS), pp. 392–399 (2012)

16. Siebel, N.T., Cook, S., Satpathy, M., Rodríguez, D.: Latitudinal and longitudinal process diversity. J. Softw. Maint. **15**(1), 9–25 (2003)

17. Skoulis, I., Vassiliadis, P., Zarras, A.: Open-source databases: within, outside, or beyond Lehman's laws of software evolution? In: Jarke, M., Mylopoulos, J., Quix, C., Rolland, C., Manolopoulos, Y., Mouratidis, H., Horkoff, J. (eds.) CAiSE 2014. LNCS, vol. 8484, pp. 379–393. Springer, Heidelberg (2014)

18. Xie, G., Chen, J., Neamtiu, I.: Towards a better understanding of software evolution: an empirical study on open source software. In: Proceedings of the 25th IEEE International Conference on Software Maintenance (ICSM), pp. 51–60 (2009)

Variability and Configuration

Comprehensive Variability Analysis
of Requirements and Testing Artifacts

Michal Steinberger and Iris Reinhartz-Berger[(⊠)]

Department of Information Systems, University of Haifa, Haifa, Israel
mnachm04@campus.haifa.ac.il, iris@is.haifa.ac.il

Abstract. Analyzing variability of software artifacts is important for increasing reuse and improving development of similar software products, as is the case in the area of Software Product Line Engineering (SPLE). Current approaches suggest analyzing the variability of certain types of artifacts, most notably requirements. However, as the specification of requirements may be incomplete or generalized, capturing the differences between the intended software behaviors may be limited, neglecting essential parts, such as behavior preconditions. Thus, we suggest in this paper utilizing testing artifacts in order to comprehensively analyze the variability of the corresponding requirements. The suggested approach, named SOVA R-TC, which is based on Bunge's ontological model, uses the information stored and managed in Application Lifecycle Management (ALM) environments. It extracts the behavior transformations from the requirements and the test cases and presents them in the form of initial states (preconditions) and final states (post-conditions or expected results). It further compares the behavior transformations of different software products and proposes how to analyze their variability based on cross-phase artifacts.

Keywords: Variability analysis · Ontology · Software reuse · Software product lines · Application lifecycle management

1 Introduction

Variability analysis deals with determining the degree of similarity of different software artifacts, commonly in order to improve the effectiveness and efficiency of their development and maintenance through increase of reuse [7]. Variability analysis is extensively studied in the field of Software Product Line Engineering (SPLE) [11, 21], where *variability* is considered "an assumption about how members of a family may differ from each other" [28]. Variability analysis is known as time consuming and error-prone. Thus, various studies have suggested automatizing variability analysis using different software development artifacts. Many of these studies concentrate on analyzing the differences of requirements (e.g., [2, 12, 15]), perceiving reuse of requirements very important since requirements are essential in all development approaches and elicited and specified early in the software development lifecycle [11]. These studies frequently apply semantic, syntactic, metric-based, or graph-based similarity measurements and utilize clustering algorithms. The result is presented in a form of variability models, most notably feature diagrams [14]. Other types of

© Springer International Publishing Switzerland 2016
S. Nurcan et al. (Eds.): CAiSE 2016, LNCS 9694, pp. 461–475, 2016.
DOI: 10.1007/978-3-319-39696-5_28

software artifacts are also utilized in order to analyze variability, e.g., architecture [1] and code [3]. In contrast, testing artifacts seem to attract less attention in variability analysis [10]. This may be due to their reliance on other development artifacts (i.e., the requirements that they aim to test) or their description of specific scenarios (that sometimes include particular values or conditions). Moreover, to the best of our knowledge, utilizing different types of development artifacts in order to coherently analyze variability has not been studied. We claim that analyzing artifacts from different, but related, development phases may result in more comprehensive variability analysis outcomes that better represent the similarities and differences among software products and may consequentially increase reuse and improve software development and maintenance.

To this end, we propose in this paper to utilize information stored and managed on requirements and testing artifacts in existing software development tools. These kinds of artifacts are highly related in most development approaches and refer to software behaviors rather than to concrete implementations. Particularly, we explore Application Lifecycle Management (ALM) environments whose aim is to plan, govern, and coordinate the software lifecycle tasks. Although ALM environments are geared towards development of single products, we propose here to utilize them in order to analyze the variability of different software products managed in their repository. Particularly, we introduce a method, named Semantic and Ontological Variability Analysis based on Requirements and Test cases (or SOVA R-TC for short), that extracts software behaviors from requirements and testing artifacts, enables their comparison to other behaviors at different level of abstraction, and identifies variants of similar behaviors. Those variants set the ground for comprehensive variability analysis.

The rest of the paper is structured as follows: Sect. 2 reviews the background and related work, motivating the need to analyze variability of both requirements and testing artifacts. Section 3 elaborates on the suggested approach, while Sect. 4 presents insights from preliminary analysis of the approach outcomes. Finally, Sect. 5 concludes and provides directions for future research.

2 Background and Literature Review

2.1 Application Lifecycle Management (ALM)

Application Lifecycle Management (ALM) environments [15, 16] aim to support the development of software products from their initial planning through retirement. Their main advantages are: (1) maintaining high level of traceability between artifacts produced in different development phases, e.g., requirements and testing artifacts; (2) reporting on the development progress in real time to different stakeholders; and (3) improving stakeholders' communication across development tasks, e.g., developers can easily access the complete information about the failure of a test case and its results which led to finding defects (bugs). Due to those benefits, different frameworks and implementations of ALM can be found in the industry. Most of them support software requirements definition and management, software change and configuration management (SCM), software project planning, quality management (testing), and defect management. The first generation of environments, called ALM 1.0, integrates a few individual tools for helping stakeholders perform their tasks. The next generation, called ALM 2.0, proposes a holistic platform (rather than a collection of tools) for coordinating and managing development activities [15].

Although ALM environments typically relate to development of single products, BigLever [6] – a leading vendor of product line solutions – has already suggested *multi-phase* as one of three dimensions in their SPLE framework (the other two dimensions are *multi-baseline* referring to evolution of artifacts over time and *multi-product* referring to the diversity of products in the same software product line). The multi-phase dimension directly refers to the development lifecycle phases. It concerns consistency and traceability among asset variations in different lifecycle phases. Yet, this dimension addresses the development of single software products.

A recent industrial survey [5] reveals that SPLE is commonly adopted extractively (i.e., existing product artifacts are re-engineered into a software product line) or reactively (i.e., one or several products are built before the core assets are developed). In those scenarios the information stored in ALM environments for different software products can be utilized to analyze their variability.

Although no study suggests utilizing ALM environments for analyzing variability, different methods have been suggested for analyzing variability of different types of software artifacts stored in ALM environments, most notably requirements [10]. Next we review relevant studies on variability analysis at different development phases, concentrating of requirements engineering and testing artifacts.

2.2   Variability Analysis at Different Development Phases

Recently, Bakar et al. [4] conducted a systematic literature review on feature extraction from requirements expressed in a natural language. The main conclusions of this review is that most studies use Software Requirements Specifications (SRS) as inputs, but product descriptions, brochures, and user comments are also used due to practical reasons. The outputs of the suggested methods are commonly feature diagrams [14], clustered requirements, keywords or direct objects. Moreover, the extraction process can be divided into four phases: (1) requirements assessment, (2) terms extraction (using different techniques, such as algebraic models, similarity metrics, and natural language processing tools), (3) features identification, and (4) feature diagram (or variability model) formation. Most studies automatize the second phase of terms extraction, while the other phases are commonly done manually. A work that addresses the automatization of phases 3 and 4 in addition to that of phase 2 is SOVA (Semantic and Ontological Variability Analysis) which analyzes requirements variability based on ontological and semantic considerations [20, 22]. Due to the high relevance of SOVA to this work, we elaborate on it in Sect. 2.3.

In contrast to requirements, testing artifacts seem to attract less attention in variability management [10]. According to [10], only FAST – Family-Oriented Abstraction, Specification and Translation – can be considered covering the full lifecycle phases, from requirements engineering to testing. However, this approach concentrates on documentation and representation of variability and not on its analysis.

Other development artifacts, e.g., design artifacts [1, 17] and code [24], have also been analyzed to find differences between software products. A few approaches, e.g., [1, 25], further propose utilizing several distinct sources of information for analyzing variability. However, these sources commonly belong to the same lifecycle phase (e.g., textual feature descriptions and feature dependencies belonging to the requirements engineering phase; or software architecture and plugin dependencies belonging to the design phase). In our work, we aim to explore how analyzing the variability of artifacts from different lifecycle phases, particularly, requirements engineering and testing, can contribute to understanding the differences between various software products.

2.3   Semantic and Ontological Variability Analysis (SOVA)

SOVA aims to analyze variability among different software products based on their textual requirements. Feature identification relies on software behaviors extraction [20, 22]. For each behavior, the initial states (pre-conditions), the external events (triggers), and the final states (post-conditions) are identified. This is done by parsing the requirement text utilizing the Semantic Role Labeling (SRL) technique [13]. Six roles that have special importance to functionality are used in SOVA: (1) Agent – Who performs?; (2) Action – What is performed?; (3) Object – On what objects is it performed?; (4) Instrument – How is it performed?; (5) Temporal modifier – When is it performed?; And (6) Adverbial modifier – In what conditions is it preformed?

Based on these roles, the different phrases of the requirements (called vectors) are classified into initial states, external events, and final states. *External events* are: (1) Action vectors (i.e., vectors identified by verbs) whose *agents* are *external* and their *actions* are *active*, or (2) Action vectors whose *agents* are *internal* and their *actions* are *passive*. Oppositely, states are: (1) Action vectors whose *agents* are *internal* and *actions* are *active*, or (2) Action vectors whose *agents* are *external* and *actions* are *passive*. The decision whether a vector is classified as an initial state or a final state is done according to the place of the vector with respect to other vectors classified as external events. Particularly, *initial states* are: (1) Action vectors classified as states that appear *before* the *first* external events in the requirements, or (2) Non-action vectors (identified by temporal or adverbial modifiers) that appear *before* the *first* external events in the requirements. Conversely, *final states* are action vectors classified as states that appear *after* the *last* external event in the requirements.

As an example, consider Fig. 1 which presents SOVA's parsing outcome for the requirement: *When a borrower returns a book copy, the system updates the number of available copies of the book*. In this case, no initial state is extracted; the external event is returning a book copy by a borrower; and the final state is derived from updating the number of available copies of the book.

#	Agent	Action	Object	Instrument	Modifier	Ontological Class
1	a borrower	return	a book copy		AM-TMP: When	[Event]
2	the system	update	the number of available copies of the book			[Final]

Fig. 1. An example of SOVA's parsing outcome

After parsing the requirements and classifying their parts into initial states, external events, and final states, SOVA enables comparison of requirements, belonging to different software products, based on different perspectives. In [20], two perspectives are mainly discussed: structural – in which focus is put (through controlling weights) on differences in the initial and final states – and functional – which concentrates on differences in the external events. The final outcomes of SOVA are feature diagrams organized according to selected perspectives.

Despite the benefits of SOVA to analyze the commonality and variability of software behaviors [22], its success heavily depends on the level of details of the requirements and especially on their ability to express the initial state, external event, and final state. From practice, it is known that requirements are not always complete and particularly do not explicitly specify all pre-conditions and post-conditions. Hence, we aim to overcome this limitation by using the corresponding testing artifacts. To motivate the need, consider the following two requirements which may appear in different library management systems to describe book return functionality:

1. When a borrower returns a copy of a book that can be pre-ordered by other borrowers, the system sends a message to the borrower who is waiting for this book.
2. When a borrower returns a book copy, the system updates the number of available copies of the book.

The requirements are similar since they both handle returning a book copy. However, they differ in their pre- and post-conditions. While the post-conditions are specified in the requirements ("the system sends a message to the borrower who is waiting for this book" for the first requirement and "the system updates the number of available copies of the book" for the second requirement), the preconditions in this example are not explicitly specified. Specifically, in the first case, the precondition that there is a borrower waiting for the returned book is not mentioned. As a result, the similarity of these requirements will not reflect the difference in their preconditions and the variability analysis will be negatively affected. As we claim next, utilizing test artifacts associated with those requirements may improve variability analysis (increasing or decreasing the similarity of the corresponding requirements).

3   The Suggested Approach – SOVA R-TC

Our working hypothesis is that what commonly matters to stakeholders involved in different development lifecycle phases, including requirement engineers and testers, is the expected behavior of the implemented software. This premise is manifested by concepts such as functional requirements or functional testing. Therefore, the suggested approach, called SOVA R-TC, concentrates on functional requirements (hereafter requirements, for short) and the test cases associated to them. SOVA R-TC employs a view of a software product as a set of intended changes in a given application domain. We term such changes software behaviors. The approach uses an ontological model of behaviors based on concepts from Bunge's work [8, 9]. This model is described in Sect. 3.1. We further develop an ALM metamodel that concentrates on requirements and testing artifacts (Sect. 3.2) and use it for identifying variants based on the ontological model (Sect. 3.3).

3.1 The Ontological Model of Bunge

Bunge's work [8, 9] describes the world as made of things that possess *properties*. Properties are known via *attributes*, which are characteristics assigned to *things* by humans. Software products can be considered things.

To define or represent things and compare them, we have to define the point of view from which we wish to conduct the analysis. For example, libraries and car rental agencies may be perceived differently, since the first one deals with borrowing books that are different in terms of structure and functionality from cars, the focus of the second thing. However, these things can be perceived as very similar if we conduct the analysis from the point of view of checking out of items: both libraries and car rental agencies handle checking out of physical items (either books or cars).

To define the point of view, we use Bunge's notion of a *state variable* – a function which assigns a value to an attribute of a thing at a given time. The *state* of a thing is the vector of state variables' values at a particular point in time. The abstraction level of states can be controlled by selecting different sets of state variables, e.g., ISBN of a book and the license number of a car vs. an item identity. An *event* is a change of a state of a thing and can be external or internal: an *external event* is a change in the state of a thing as a result of an action of another thing (e.g., borrowing a book by a person or renting a car by a client), whereas an *internal event* arises due to an internal transformation in the thing (e.g., operations triggered by the library itself or the car rental agency). Correspondingly, a state can be stable or unstable: a *stable state* can be changed only by an external event while an *unstable state* may be changed by an internal event.

Bunge's ontological concepts have been widely adapted to conceptual modeling in the context of systems analysis and design [26, 27]. In [23], Bunge's ontological model is suggested to define software behavior as a triplet of an initial state describing the stable state the system is in before the behavior occurs, a sequence of external events that trigger the behavior, and a final state specifying the stable state the system reaches after the behavior terminates. Both initial and final states are described with respect to relevant state variables, allowing for variability analysis in different granularity levels. Formally expressed:

Definition 1 (Behavior). Given a stable state s_1 and a sequence of external events $<e_i>$, *a behavior* is a triplet $(s_1, <e_i>, s^*)$, where s^* is the first stable state the thing reaches when it is in state s_1 and the sequence of external events $<e_i>$ occurs. s_1 is termed the *initial state* of the behavior and s^* – the *final state* of the behavior. s_1 and s^* are defined over a set of state variables $SV = \{x_1...x_n\}$, namely, s_1 and s^* are assignments to $x_1...x_n$.

3.2 An ALM Metamodel

In order to use Bunge's concepts as a basis for comprehensively analyzing variability of software products, we turn now to the introduction of a partial ALM metamodel that depicts the characteristics of requirements and testing artifacts, as well as their relations. Exploring IBM's Collaborative Lifecycle Management (CLM) solution[1], which is one of the leading ALM environments [29], and different ISO standards, most notably, ISO/IEC/IEEE 29119-3 on software testing documentation [19], we drafted the metamodel in Fig. 2. A requirement exhibits just a textual description (in a natural language), besides some identification. The testing artifacts are described via test cases. According to [19], a test case is a set of "preconditions, inputs (including actions, where applicable), and expected results, developed to drive the execution of a test item to meet test objectives, including correct implementation, error identification, checking quality, and other valued information". A test case precondition describes "the required state of the test environment and any special constraints pertaining to the execution of the test case," whereas inputs are the "data information used to drive test execution." An expected result is "observable predicted behavior of the test item under specified conditions based on its specification or another source." Later in the standard, inputs are defined as actions "required to bring the test item into a state where the expected result can be compared to the actual results." This is in-line with the realization of inputs in existing ALM environments as fields named actions or test steps.

The mapping of the test case related elements to Bunge's terminology is quite straightforward: the preconditions define the initial state of the behavior (test case scenario), but also some technical constraints (e.g., regarding the environment); the inputs are the events that trigger ("drive") the behavior ("execution"); and the expected results partially[2] define the final states of the behavior.

Considering the two requirements mentioned earlier, Table 1 depicts a possible test case for each one of them. Generally, a single requirement may be validated by several test cases, e.g., a test case that validates the main scenario and test cases for different exceptions. Similarly, a single test case can validate more than one requirement, e.g., a test case that validates an exception common to different behaviors (requirements). Thus, the relations between requirements and test cases are many-to-many.

Given the suggested metamodel, a requirement or a test case is represented by the parts of the behavior they represent. For a requirement s_1, $<e>$, $s*$ are extracted using SOVA, while for a test case s_1 is the set of preconditions, $<e>$ is the sequence of inputs, and $s*$ is the set of expected results.

Definition 2 (A Requirement). A *requirement*[3] R is represented by R = (rs_1, $<re>$, $rs*$), where rs_1 is the initial state of the behavior described in the requirement, $<re>$ is the sequence of events triggering that behavior, and $rs*$ is the final state of that behavior.

---

[1] http://www-03.ibm.com/software/products/en/ratlclm.

[2] The reason why the expected results only partially define the final state is that expected results concentrated on "observable predicted behavior of the test item," and not necessarily refer to internal changes.

[3] Remember we refer here only to functional requirements.

Table 1. Examples of test cases in the form of preconditions, inputs, and expected results

Requirement	Preconditions	Inputs	Expected results
When a borrower returns a copy of a book that can be pre-ordered by other borrowers, the system sends a message to the borrower who is waiting for this book	- The book can be pre-ordered by other borrowers - A borrower is waiting for the book to be returned	A borrower returns a book copy	The system sends a message to the borrower who is waiting for this book
When a borrower returns a book copy, the system updates the number of available copies of the book	——	A borrower returns a book copy	The system updates the number of available copies of the book

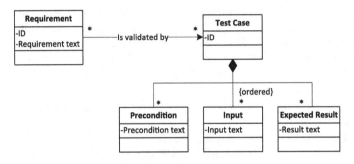

Fig. 2. A metamodel specifying the information on requirements and test cases

Definition 3 (A Test Case). A *test case* TC is represented by TC = (pre, <inp>, rst), where pre is the set of the preconditions of the behavior tested in the test case, <inp> is an ordered set of inputs, and rst is a set of expected results of the tested behavior.

In this paper, we assume that the test case inputs are actually realizations of the requirement external events (describing how the external events are captured by the system) and therefore we concentrate on the state of the system before the behavior occurs (as specified both in the initial states of the requirements and the preconditions of the test cases) and the state of the system after the behavior occurs (as specified both in the final states of the requirements and the expected results of the test cases). Note that these two parts of the behavior (s_1 and s^*) represent states and hence can be perceived as defined by possible assignments to state variables. Returning to the examples in Table 1, the precondition of the first test case refers to two assignments of state variables – the book can be pre-ordered (book = can_be_preordered) and a borrower is waiting for the book (borrower = is_waiting_for_the_book). Each of the post-conditions of the two test cases refers to an assignment to a state variable: sending a message (message_to_the_borrower = sent) for the first test case and updating the number of available copies (number_of_available_copies = increased_by_1) for the second test case. Next we formally define states (e.g., rs_1, rs^*, pre, and rst) as sets of pairs describing assignments to state variables.

Definition 4 (States). Let $SV = \{x_1, \ldots x_n\}$ be a set of state variables, such that Dom $(x_i) = \{v_{i1}, v_{i2}, \ldots\}$ is the possible values (domain) of x_i. A *state* s is defined as $s = \{(x_i, v_{ij}) \mid x_i \in SV \text{ and } v_{ij} \in Dom(x_i)\}$.

Since the suggested method assumes descriptions of behavior in a natural language (in the form of requirements and test cases), the extraction of state variables and assignments uses a natural language processing technique. Particularly, using the Semantic Role Labeling (SRL) technique mentioned in Sect. 2.3, the state variables are extracted from the object parts of the phrases, while the assignments are extracted from the action parts. The examples above follow these rules.

3.3 Behavior Transformations Deduced from Requirements and Test Cases

Using Bunge's ontological model and the metamodel introduced above, we aim to explore the relations between a requirement and its associated test cases in order to improve variability analysis. Particularly, SOVA R-TC compares the different parts of behaviors as specified in the requirements and their associated test cases.

While requirements describe what the system should do, namely, specify the high level functionality of the system, test cases detail how the functionality should be tested. Therefore, the initial state of a requirement may be different from the preconditions of the test cases associated to it. Particularly, the initial state of the requirement may be missing or the preconditions of the test cases may refine the initial state of the requirement. Similarly, the expected results of the test cases may differ (at least in the level of details) from the final state of the requirements. We do not refer to these differences as inconsistencies, but as differences in scope or in level of specification. Moreover, a single requirement may be associated to different test cases, each of which describes a different scenario to be tested. We thus consider the intersection of these scenarios (which describes the characteristics of the behavior rather than of a particular scenario/test case) and unify this intersection with the requirement in order to enrich the specification of the initial and final states. This is expressed through the notion of behavior transformation defined next.

Definition 5 (Behavior Transformation). Given a requirement $R = (s_1, <e>, s^*)$ and a set of test cases $\{TC_1, \ldots TC_n\}$ associated to it, such that $TC_i = (<pre_i>, <inp_i>, <rst_i>)$, we define the *behavior transformation* bt as (uis, ufs), where uis $= s_1 \cup _{i=1..n}pre_i$ is the unified initial state of the behavior and ufs $= s^* \cup _{i=1..n}rst_i$ is its unified final state.

For exemplifying behavior transformations, consider Table 2 which refers to a single requirement with two associated test cases. The initial state of behavior does not explicitly appear in the requirement and thus SOVA does not extract it. The final state generally refers to update of a certain variable (the number of available copies of the book). Using the two test cases associated to this requirement, we learn on two possible scenarios: one in which "no borrower pre-ordered the book" and the other in which "at least one borrower is waiting for the book." In both scenarios it is assumed that "the book was borrowed" and thus we can conclude that this assignment of the state variable (book_status) characterizes the behavior rather than provides technical conditions of specific test cases. As a result the unified initial state of the behavior transformation is "the book was borrowed." For similar reasons, the expected result of notifying the first borrower who is waiting for the book about the arrival is considered scenario-specific and hence the unified final state of the behavior transformation refers only to the state variable "number of available copies of the book." Here both requirement and test cases refer to this state variable, but slightly differently: the requirement generally refers to the need to update this state variable, while the test cases refer to how this state variable needs to be updated – increase by 1. Assuming that test cases are more detailed than requirements and refer to state variables in a higher level of details, we adopt the assignment proposed to a state variable by test cases. In other words, if the same state variable appears both in the requirements and in the test cases with different proposed assignments, the unified final state adopts the assignment suggested to the state variable in the test cases. Hence, in our case the unified final state of the behavior transformation is "the system increases the number of available copies of the book by 1."

Table 2. Examples of a requirement and two possible associated test cases

	s_1 (rs_1 or pre)	$<e>$ ($<re>$ or $<inp>$)	rs^* or post (rs_1 or pre)
Requirement		a borrower returns a book copy	the system updates the number of available copies of the book
Test case 1	- The book was borrowed - No borrower pre-ordered the book	a borrower returns a book copy	- The system increases the number of available copies of the book by 1
Test case 2	- The book was borrowed - At least one borrower is waiting for the book	a borrower returns a book copy	- The system increases the number of available copies of the book by 1 - The first borrower who waits for the book is notified about the arrival
Behavior transformation	- The book was borrowed		- The system increases the number of available copies of the book by 1

3.4 Calculating the Similarity of Requirements Considering Their Associated Test Cases

The basis for analyzing variability in SOVA R-TC is identifying variants of similar behaviors. Thus, given a set of software products, each represented by requirements and their associated test cases, we calculate the similarity of behaviors as follows.

Definition 6 (Behavior Similarity). Given two requirements R_1 and R_2, their associated transformation behaviors $bt_1 = (uis_1, ufs_1)$ and $bt_2 = (uis_2, ufs_2)$, respectively, and a semantic similarity sim, the *behavior similarity*, $Sim_{R\text{-}TC}$, is the weighted average of the pair-wise semantic similarities of their unified initial and final states. Formally expressed:

$$Sim_{R-TC}(R_1, R_2)$$
$$= w_{uis} \cdot \frac{\sum_{x_i \in uis_1} max_{x_j uis_2} sim(x_i, x_j) + \sum_{x_j \in uis_2} max_{x_j uis_1} sim(x_i, x_j)}{|uis_1| + |uis_2|}$$
$$+ w_{ufs} \cdot \frac{\sum_{x_i \in ufs_1} max_{x_j ufs_2} sim(x_i, x_j) + \sum_{x_j \in ufs_2} max_{x_j ufs_1} sim(x_i, x_j)}{|ufs_1| + |ufs_2|}$$

Where:

- w_{uis} and w_{ufs} are the weights of the unified initial and final states, respectively; $w_{uis} + w_{ufs} = 1$.
- $sim(x_i, x_j)$ is the semantic similarity of x_i and x_j – assignments to state variables in the unified initial or final states of a requirement.
- $|uis_1|, |uis_2|, |ufs_1|, |ufs_2|$ are the numbers of assignments in the unified initial states of the two requirements and in the unified final states of the two requirements, respectively.

Simplifying this definition, behavior similarity is calculated by matching the most similar assignments both in the unified initial and final states of the compared behaviors. To this end, different semantic similarity measures can be used. Those measures are commonly classified as corpus based or knowledge based [18]. Corpus-based measures identify the degree of similarity based on information derived from large corpora, while knowledge-based measures use information drawn from semantic networks. Combining corpus- and knowledge-based semantic approaches, the measure suggested by Mihalcea et al. (MSC) [18] calculates sentence similarity by finding the most similar words in the same part of speech class. The derived word similarity scores are weighted with the inverse document frequency scores that belong to the corresponding word.

We made the calculation of behavior similarity flexible by introducing weights of the unified initial and final states. Basically, we could assume $w_{uis} = w_{ufs} = 0.5$, however, we wanted to enable the analysts to fine tune the calculation, based on observations they may have, e.g., regarding the accuracy and completeness of the unified initial states vs. the unified final states of the compared software products.

As an example to the benefits of calculating requirements taking into consideration their associated test cases, consider Fig. 3. The two requirements, taken from different products, are similar in the sense that they handle borrowing books. However, the similarity value of SOVA is 0.5 and the similarity value of MCS is 0.6, pointing on medium similarity. Calculating the behavior similarity of these requirements in SOVA R-TC, using the same basic semantic metric (MCS), we get a higher value of 0.7 which better depicts the expected conclusion that the behaviors can be considered variants of each other.

4 Implications and Discussion

We developed a tool supporting SOVA R-TC and analyzed a set of requirements and their associated test cases. Based on these examples we extracted patterns that worth further discussion and explorations. Note that although we are interested in the differences between analyzing the variability based only on requirements (the output of SOVA) and additionally utilizing test cases (the output of SOVA R-TC), the patterns are presented and explained based on the relations between the requirements and the test cases in the compared behaviors. Particularly, we refer to the requirement using the

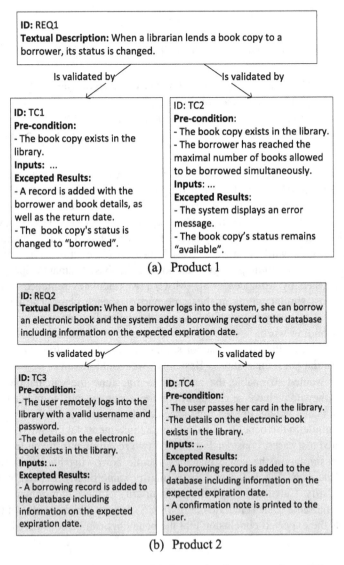

(a) Product 1

(b) Product 2

Fig. 3. An example of requirements and their associated test cases from different products

notation of rs_1 and rs^*, and to the intersection of test cases via the notation of $tcs_1 =$ and $tcs^* = \cap_{i=1..n} rst_i$. Remember that $s_1 = rs_1 \cup tcs_1$ and $s^* = rs^* \cup tcs^*$. Analyzing the four intersection possibilities between sets, Table 3 summarizes eight patterns, their characteristics, and implications on requirements similarity (and consequently on their variability analysis). Those patterns can be used in the future to study the impact of utilizing different types of software artifacts on the comprehensiveness of the variability analysis of their corresponding software products.

5 Summary and Future Research

Perceiving requirements as essential artifacts in software development, we advocate for utilizing test cases in order to better understand the similarity, and consequently the variability, of software products. Analyzing the similarity of requirements not just from their textual descriptions but also from their associated artifacts (test cases in our research), may improve understanding the requirements context and improve their reuse. This is especially important when the requirements are known to be incomplete

Table 3. Patterns of similarity in requirements

#	Name	Characteristics	Implications on similarity[a]	Explanations
1	Initial state refinement	$rs_1 \subseteq tcs_1$	↑ ↓	The requirements may become more or less similar, depending on the similarity of the added information (tcs_1-rs_1 or tcs^*-rs^*)
2	Final state refinement	$rs^* \subseteq tcs^*$	↑ ↓	
3	Initial state consolidation	$tcs_1 \subseteq rs_1$	—	The similarity of the requirements are unchanged as $s_1 = rs_1$ or $s^* = rs^*$
4	Final state consolidation	$tcs^* \subseteq rs^*$	—	
5	Initial state exceptions	$rs_1- tcs_1 \neq \varnothing$ $\wedge$ $tcs_1- rs_1 \neq \varnothing$	↑ ↓	This can happen due to specification of exceptions in the test cases. The core characteristics of the requirements appear also in the test cases. The exceptions may increase or decrease requirements similarity
6	Final state exceptions	$rs^*- tcs^* \neq \varnothing$ $\wedge$ $tcs^*- rs^* \neq \varnothing$	↑ ↓	
7	Initial state conflict	$tcs_1 \cap rs_1 = \varnothing$	unexpectedly	This can happen due to reuse of generic test cases that are not directly related to the examined requirements. As a result the requirements similarity can unexpectedly be changed (increased or decreased)
8	Final state conflict	$tcs^* \cap rs^* = \varnothing$	unexpectedly	

[a] ↑↓ = similarity changes (increases or decreases), — similarity unchanged.

or less detailed (e.g., in agile development approaches). The relevant information to do that is already stored and managed in Application Lifecycle Management (ALM) environments that are commonly used in software development. We suggest SOVA R-TC which utilizes ALM environments in order to extract the unified initial and final states of the behavior transformations and calculate the similarity of requirements considering the associated test cases. Based on this analysis, decisions on SPLE adoption (in extractive and reactive scenarios) can evidentially be taken.

In the future, we plan to further explore the patterns and evaluate their existence and potential meanings in different case studies. The evaluation will be done in comparison to existing methods and interviewing developers. We also intend to explore combination of patterns and examine similarity and variability of events (inputs) and how they impact requirements reuse, potentially adding patterns. Moreover, we plan to explore the impact of different types of relations between requirements and test cases (e.g., main scenarios vs. exceptions) on requirements similarity and variability.

References

1. Acher, M., Cleve, A., Collet, P., Merle, P., Duchien, L., Lahire, P.: Extraction and evolution of architectural variability models in plugin-based systems. Soft. Syst. Model. (SoSyM) **13** (4), 1367–1394 (2013)
2. Acher, M., Cleve, A., Perrouin, G., Heymans, P., Vanbeneden, C., Collet, P., Lahire, P.: On extracting feature models from product descriptions. In: Proceedings of the 6th International Workshop on Variability Modeling of Software-Intensive Systems, pp. 45–54 (2012)
3. Alves, V., Matos Jr., P., Cole, L., Borba, P., Ramalho, G.L.: Extracting and evolving mobile games product lines. In: Obbink, H., Pohl, K. (eds.) SPLC 2005. LNCS, vol. 3714, pp. 70–81. Springer, Heidelberg (2005)
4. Bakar, N.H., Kasirun, Z.M., Salleh, N.: Feature extraction approaches from natural language requirements for reuse in software product lines: a systematic literature review. J. Syst. Soft. **106**, 132–149 (2015)
5. Berger, T., Rublack, R., Nair, D., Atlee, J.M., Becker, M., Czarnecki, K., Wąsowski, A.: A survey of variability modeling in industrial practice. In: Proceedings of the Seventh International Workshop on Variability Modeling of Software-Intensive Systems, pp. 7:1–7:8. ACM (2013)
6. BigLever: The systems and software product line engineering lifecycle framework (2013). http://www.biglever.com/extras/PLE_LifecycleFramework.pdf
7. Böckle, G., van der Linden, F.J.: Software Product Line Engineering: Foundations, Principles and Techniques. Springer Science & Business Media, Heidelberg (2005). Pohl, K. (ed.)
8. Bunge, M.: Treatise on Basic Philosophy, Ontology I: The Furniture of the World, vol. 3. Reidel, Boston (1977)
9. Bunge, M.: Treatise on Basic Philosophy, Ontology II: A World of Systems, vol. 4. Reidel, Boston (1979)
10. Chen, L., Ali Babar, M., Ali, N.: Variability management in software product lines: a systematic review. In: Proceedings of the 13th International Software Product Line Conference (SPLC 2009), pp. 81–90 (2009)
11. Clements, P., Northrop, L.: Software Product Lines: Practices and Patterns. Addison Wesley, Boston (2001)

12. Davril, J.M., Delfosse, E., Hariri, N., Acher, M., Cleland-Huang, J., Heymans, P.: Feature model extraction from large collections of informal product descriptions. In: Proceedings of the 9th Joint Meeting on Foundations of Software Engineering, pp. 290–300 (2013)
13. Gildea, D., Jurafsky, D.: Automatic labeling of semantic roles. Comput. Linguist. **28**(3), 245–288 (2002)
14. Kang, K.C., Cohen, S.G., Hess, J.A., Novak, W.E., Peterson, A.S.: Feature-oriented domain analysis (FODA) feasibility study. Technical report (1990)
15. Kim, J.A., Choi, S.Y., Hwang, S.M.: Process & evidence enable to automate ALM (Application Lifecycle Management). In: 9th IEEE International Symposium on Parallel and Distributed Processing with Applications Workshops (ISPAW 2011), pp. 348–351 (2011)
16. Lacheiner, H., Ramler, R.: Application lifecycle management as infrastructure for software process improvement and evolution: experience and insights from industry. In: 37th EUROMICRO Conference on Software Engineering and Advanced Applications (SEAA 2011), pp. 286–293 (2011)
17. Losavio, F., Ordaz, O., Levy, N., Baiotto, A.: Graph modelling of a refactoring process for product line architecture design. In: Computing Conference (CLEI) XXXIX Latin American, pp. 1–12 (2013)
18. Mihalcea, R., Corley, C., Strapparava, C.: Corpus-based and knowledge-based measures of text semantic similarity. In: The 21st National Conference on Artificial Intelligence (AAAI 2006), vol. 1, pp. 775–780 (2006)
19. ISO/IEC/IEEE 29119-3: Software and systems engineering—software testing—part 3: test documentation. International Organization for Standardization (2013)
20. Itzik, N., Reinhartz-Berger, I., Wand, Y.: Variability analysis of requirements: considering behavioral differences and reflecting stakeholders perspectives. IEEE Trans. Soft. Eng. (2016). doi:10.1109/TSE.2015.2512599
21. Pohl, K., Böckle, G., van der Linden, F.: Software Product-Line Engineering: Foundations, Principles, and Techniques. Springer, Heidelberg (2005)
22. Reinhartz-Berger, I., Itzik, N., Wand, Y.: Analyzing variability of software product lines using semantic and ontological considerations. In: Jarke, M., Mylopoulos, J., Quix, C., Rolland, C., Manolopoulos, Y., Mouratidis, H., Horkoff, J. (eds.) CAiSE 2014. LNCS, vol. 8484, pp. 150–164. Springer, Heidelberg (2014)
23. Reinhartz-Berger, I., Sturm, A., Wand, Y.: External variability of software: classification and ontological foundations. In: Jeusfeld, M., Delcambre, L., Ling, T.-W. (eds.) ER 2011. LNCS, vol. 6998, pp. 275–289. Springer, Heidelberg (2011)
24. Roy, C.K., Cordy, J.R.: A survey on software clone detection research (2007). http://maveric0.uwaterloo.ca/~migod/846/papers/roy-CloningSurveyTech Report.pdf
25. She, S., Lotufo, R., Berger, T., Wasowski, A., Czarnecki, K.: Reverse engineering feature models. In: Proceedings of the 33rd International Conference on Software Engineering (ICSE 2011), pp. 461–470 (2011)
26. Wand, Y., Weber, R.: On the deep structure of information systems. J. Inf. Syst. **5**(3), 203–223 (1995)
27. Wand, Y., Weber, R.: An ontological model of an information system. IEEE Trans. Soft. Eng. **16**, 1282–1292 (1990)
28. Weiss, D.M., Lai, C.T.R.: Software Product-Line Engineering: A Family-Based Software Development Process. Addison-Wesley, Boston (1999)
29. Wilson, N., Duggan, J., Murphy, T.E., Sobejana, M., Herschmann, J.: Magic quadrant for application development life cycle management. Gartner report (2015). http://www.gartner.com/technology/reprints.do?id=1-2A61Y68&ct=150218&st=sb

Comprehensibility of Variability in Model Fragments for Product Configuration

Jorge Echeverría[1(✉)], Francisca Pérez[1], Carlos Cetina[1], and Óscar Pastor[2]

[1] SVIT Research Group, Universidad San Jorge,
Autovía A-23 Zaragoza-Huesca Km.299, 50830 Zaragoza, Spain
{jecheverria,mfperez,ccetina}@usj.es
[2] Centro de Investigación en Métodos de Producción de Software,
Universitat Politècnica de València, Camino de Vera, s/n, 46022 Valencia, Spain
opastor@pros.upv.es

Abstract. The ability to manage variability in software has become crucial to overcome the complexity and variety of systems. To this end, a comprehensible representation of variability is important. Nevertheless, in previous works, difficulties have been detected to understand variability in an industrial environment. Specifically, domain experts had difficulty understanding variability in model fragments to produce the software for their products. Hence, the aim of this paper is to further investigate these difficulties by conducting an experiment in which participants deal with variability in order to achieve their desired product configurations. Our results show new insights into product configuration which suggest next steps to improve general variability modeling approaches, and therefore promoting the adoption of these approaches in industry.

Keywords: Variability modeling · Software product line engineering ·
Model comprehension · Product configuration

1 Introduction

Since software artifacts have become essential and more complex, a fundamental challenge in almost any business is how to manage their software variability to optimize the development process (i.e., improve code reuse). Variability is extensively studied in the field of Software Product Line Engineering [3,16] to support the development and maintenance of families of software products.

General variability modeling approaches (that are independent of the language in which the software products are specified) include Feature-Oriented Domain Analysis (FODA) [9], Orthogonal Variability Model (OVM) [16] and Common Variability Language (CVL) [5]. FODA is widely used for variability management by describing characteristics (features). OVM is a language and a methodology for superimposing variability over any software development artifact without interfering into its contents. CVL is recommended for adoption as

© Springer International Publishing Switzerland 2016
S. Nurcan et al. (Eds.): CAiSE 2016, LNCS 9694, pp. 476–490, 2016.
DOI: 10.1007/978-3-319-39696-5_29

a standard by the Architectural Board of the Object Management Group to manage variability. These approaches can manage variability of product models by describing features in terms of model fragments.

In previous work [7], we detected that the domain experts of our industrial partner (BSH group) had difficulty understanding variability in model fragments to produce the software for the myriad of induction hob models that they produce (under the Bosch and Siemens brands among others). Since the ability to manage variability in models using a comprehensible representation is crucial [19], we further seek to investigate difficulties in understanding the variability of model fragments. Hence, the aim of this paper is to examine difficulties in comprehending variability in model fragments for product configuration.

To do this, we conducted an experiment in which variations points were expressed in models of a Domain-Specific Language (DSL). Using these models, the participants had to perform model fragment substitutions in order to reach a target product configuration.

Our results show four main findings that are relevant for general variability modeling approaches (FODA, OVM and CVL). First, our previous research [7] considered that using the concrete syntax of model fragments as configuration criterion was a source of incorrect solutions, but this experiment reveals that it is possible to harness this criterion to significantly reduce the time required to configure products. Second, the participants intuitively combine model fragments before performing product configuration. This operation turns out to improve the efficiency of product configurations. However, general variability modeling approaches do not support these fragment combinations. Third, the participants obtained the worst results in those fragments substitutions that involve recursive model fragments. Nevertheless, research on product configuration have neglected recursive model fragments. Finally, participants perform redundant configuration steps because they believe that they must perform model fragment substitutions for each variation point even though it already holds the elements of target configuration. Available training materials of general variability approaches lack instructions to avoid these redundant configuration steps. These findings provide insights into product configuration which suggest next steps to improve general variability modeling approaches.

The remainder of the paper is structured as follows: Sect. 2 provides the required background on product model configuration. Section 3 presents the experiment design and procedure. Section 4 presents the analysis procedure and results. Section 5 presents a discussion of the results. Section 6 describes the threats to validity. Section 7 reviews the related work, and Sect. 8 concludes the paper.

2   Background on Product Model Configuration

This section illustrates the relationship between the variability specification and model fragments. In addition, this section shows examples of model fragment substitutions to reach a desired product model configuration.

The upper half of Fig. 1 shows a hierarchy of features that represent the variability specification of a induction hob product using the three different general modeling approaches (FODA, OVM and CVL). These approaches follow the idea of superimposed variants [6] in which each feature is related to a model fragment that is expressed in the same terms of the product instances. The lower half of Fig. 1 shows a model fragment for each feature, which is expressed using the Induction Hob DSL. The superimposition of a feature in a model fragment could represent a variation point (see the *Hotplate* feature of Fig. 1), or an available option to set the configuration of a variation point (see the *Triple Inductor* and *Quad Inductor* features of Fig. 1 in which one of them can be selected to configure the *Hotplate* feature).

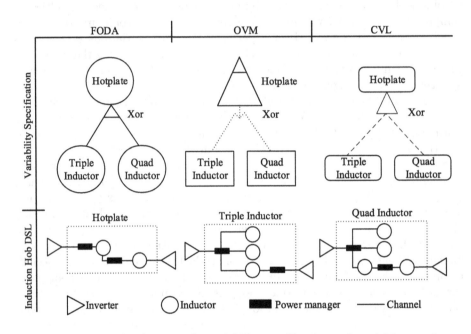

Fig. 1. Relationship between the variability specification and model fragments

After the superimposition of features in model fragments, these model fragments may not share any element (**isolated fragments**) as the upper-left part of Fig. 2 shows. By contrast, it is also possible that after the superimposition some elements are shared (**crossing fragments**) as the upper-middle part of Fig. 2 shows. Furthermore, all the elements of a model fragment can be shared with another model fragment (**recursive fragments**) as the upper-right part of Fig. 2 depicts.

In order to reach a target product configuration (e.g., the middle part of Fig. 2 shows a target induction hob configuration), model fragment substitutions are performed. A model fragment substitution is an operation that may substitute any model fragment (a set of arbitrary model elements and the references among them) with any other model fragment described in the same DSL according to the variability specification. For example, the variability specification that is

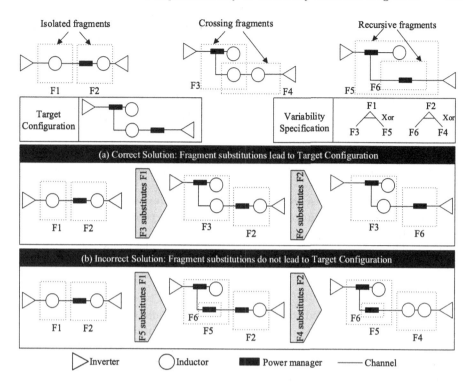

Fig. 2. Examples of correct and incorrect product configurations

shown in the middle part of Fig. 2 indicates that the model fragment F1 can be substituted with the content of either model fragment F3 or F5.

The lower part of Fig. 2 shows two examples of model fragment substitutions. On the one hand, Fig. 2(a) shows an example that reaches a **correct solution** since the product model obtained after the fragment substitutions corresponds with the target product configuration. This correct solution encompasses two model fragment substitutions as follows: first the F3 model fragment substitutes the content of the F1 model fragment, and second the F6 model fragment substitutes the content of the F2 model fragment. On the other hand, the example that is shown in Fig. 2(b) illustrates an **incorrect solution** because the target product configuration is not reached after the fragments substitutions.

A video showing product configuration of induction hobs by means of model fragments substitutions in an industrial environment can be found at: http://svit.usj.es/variabilitytool.htm.

3   Experiment Design and Procedure

3.1   Research Goal and Questions

The main goal of this research is to determine whether there are difficulties in comprehension of variability in model fragments for product configuration, and whether there are differences in comprehension of isolated, crossing, and recursive model fragments for product configuration. In relation to the above goal, we seek to answer the following research questions:

RQ1: Are there difficulties in comprehending variability in model fragments for product configuration?
RQ2: Are there differences in comprehension of isolated model fragments, crossing model fragments, and recursive model fragments for product configuration?

To our knowledge, there are no cognitive theories about variability in model fragments for product configuration. For this reason, we have not created a hypothesis related to this research question [13].

To answer the above research questions, we used a experimental design. The main dependent variables in our research design were comprehension score (as the percentage of correct product configurations), time spent, and the self-rated difficulty. The independent variable was the type of model fragments.

3.2 Procedure

The participants were asked to fill out a prequestionnaire and to sign a consent form to process the given data. The prequestionnaire obtained general information about the participants and their background, including age, gender, degree and subject of studies, background as software developers, background in software engineering, knowledge about software modeling, knowledge about variability specifications, and knowledge about DSLs.

After filling out the prequestionnaire, an instructor (using slides) explained the Induction Hob DSL used in the exercises. The participants got hard copies of the slides, which the participants could consult while answering the questions.

During the experiment, the participants were provided with exercises to perform product configurations. Each exercise has a target model configuration, a DSL model, and a set of model fragments. To do each exercise, the participants were asked to configure the DSL model by means of fragment substitutions. After the product configuration the resulting model must match the target model of the exercise in order to achieve the correct solution as the example shown in Fig. 2.

The exercises were divided into three groups based on the type of fragments produced by the superimposition of the features on the DSL model. First, isolated exercises denote exercises where the superimposition of the features produced isolated models fragments. Second, crossing exercises denote exercises where the superimposition of the features produced crossing models fragments. Finally, recursive exercises denote exercises where the superimposition of the features produced recursive models fragments. For each target configuration, there was an isolated exercise and a crossing exercise and a recursive exercise to reach that target configuration. Specifically, the experiment included three target configurations and three exercises for each configuration, which makes a total of nine exercises.

No rigid time constraints were imposed on the participants and the time spent on each question was saved. Once the participants had performed an exercise, they could not modify their response. Then, participants had to answer a subjective question about the perceived difficulty for every exercise, before beginning the next one. The answers ranged from 1=very easy to 7=very difficult [11]. Finally, the participants answered an open question in order to obtain their opinion about the exercise. After the exercises, a focus group interview [12] was performed. In this interview, the participants expressed their opinions about the solutions to the exercises.

The materials used in this experiment (the consent to process the data, the prequestionnarie, the training material, the exercises, the open questions and the notes of the focus group interview) are available at http://svit.usj.es/productconfigurationexperiment.

3.3   Participants

The participants were undergraduate students from Computer Engineering at San Jorge University of Zaragoza (Spain) and practitioners from Software Development Companies of Zaragoza. There were 20 students and 12 practitioners. Of the total, 27 were male (84 %) and 5 were female (16 %). The mean age was 24.2 years.

In the pre-questionnaire, all students stated that they had never worked as software developers or as software engineers. On the other hand, all practitioners stated that they had knowledge about software modeling, knowledge about feature diagrams, and familiarity with domain-specific languages. Furthermore, all the practitioners had developed software (with a mean of 6.5 years).

4   Analysis Procedure and Results

To analyze the results, we used the dependent variables: the comprehension score (as the percentage of exercises performed correctly), the time needed to perform the exercises and the participants' perceived difficulty. According to a Shapiro-Wilk test [22], the comprehension score, and time to perform the exercise follow a normal distribution.

Prior to our analysis, we checked whether the control variable 'type of participant', i.e. student or practitioner, had an influence on comprehension score and on time to perform the tasks. Since 'type of participant' did not have an influence on the comprehension score and the on time results, we decided to drop it from the final statistical tests we report.

(a) Comprehension score. An ANOVA test [4] was conducted to compare the comprehension score for the different model fragments. There was a significant effect of the model fragments on the comprehension score at $p<0.05$ for isolated fragments, crossing fragments, and recursive fragments [$F(2,93) = 22.729$, $p = 0.000$]. Figure 3(a) shows that the exercises related to isolated fragments were the easiest to comprehend and correctly answer (82.29 %), followed by exercises

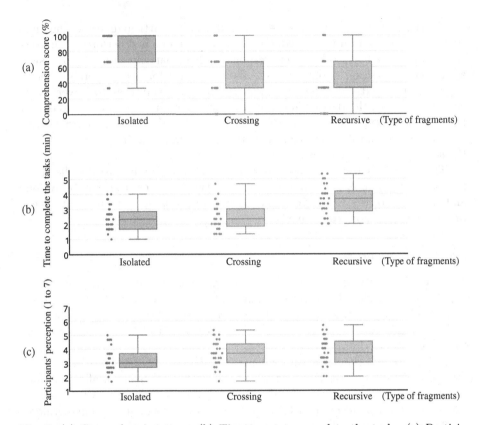

Fig. 3. (a) Comprehension score. (b) Time spent to complete the tasks. (c) Participants' perceived difficulty.

related to crossing fragments (51.04 %) and recursive fragments (40.62 %). We performed t-tests to find out differences between model fragment types in terms of comprehensibility. The differences between the comprehension score for isolated fragments and the scores for crossing and recursive fragments were significant. However, there were no significant differences between the comprehension score for crossing fragments and recursive fragments.

(b) Time spent to complete the tasks. We analyzed the time needed to complete the exercises with an ANOVA test. The results showed that there was a significant effect of the different model fragments on the time needed to perform the exercises [F(2,93) = 17.512, p = 0.000]. Figure 3(b) shows that the participants needed more time to perform the exercises related to recursive fragments (a mean of 3.55 min); the exercises related to isolated fragments and crossing fragments were performed by the participants in the same amount of time (a mean of 2.41 min). We performed t-tests to find out which model fragment types significantly differed from each other in terms of time. The t-test showed that there were no significant differences between the isolated fragments and the crossing fragments. In contrast, the differences between the recursive fragment exercises and the others exercises were significant.

(c) Participants' perceived difficulty. An ANOVA test was conducted to analyze the participants' perceived difficulty for different model fragments. There was a significant effect of the model fragments on the perceived difficulty at p<0.05 for isolated fragments, crossing fragments and recursive fragments [$F(2,93) = 3.561$, $p = 0.032$]. Figure 3(c) shows that the exercises with recursive fragments (3.79) and crossing fragments (3.70) were more difficult to understand than the exercises with isolated fragments (3.23). We performed t-tests to find out the users' perception of which model fragments significantly differed from each other. The differences between the users' perception for isolated fragments and both crossing and recursive fragments were significant.

The analysis of the data enables to answer the Research Questions as follows. *RQ1: Are there difficulties in comprehending variability in model fragments for product configuration?* As shown by Fig. 3(a), not all product configuration exercises were correctly solved. Specifically, 42.01 % of the exercises failed to perform a product configuration that matches the target configuration. *RQ2: Are there differences in comprehension of isolated model fragments, crossing model fragments, and recursive model fragments for product configuration?* Only exercises that include isolated model fragments for product configuration were comprehended by the majority (82.29 %). By contrast, exercises that include crossing model fragments or recursive model fragments obtained the worst results (51.04 % and 40.62 % respectively). Next section discusses these results and highlights our findings.

5   Discussion

Some participants (6.25 %) reported that the geometric shape of the model fragments seemed to be significantly important for product configuration. Specifically, these participants considered a model fragment as valid option whether its geometric shape fits with the geometric shape of a variation point. This is especially important because these participants gave to the geometric shape more priority than to the variability specification, which became shape criterion in a source of errors. Shape criterion produced incorrect configurations in the 27.5 % of the exercises in which it has been used. The concrete syntax of model fragments misleading product configurations matches with our previous research [7].

Although this geometric shape criterion was a source of errors, we also measured in this experiment the time spent in the exercises. We detected that the exercises, which both applied the geometric shape criterion and obtained a correct solution (72.5 %), reduced the time spent in the product configuration a 38 %. It turns out that we previously considered the geometric shape criterion as a source of incorrect solutions only, but this experiment reveals that this criterion could also significantly reduce the time required to configure products. These results suggest general variability modeling approaches should devise a mechanism to align geometric shape and variability specification in order to take advantage of the time improvement.

The participants also mentioned that they intuitively combined model fragments (creating a new model fragment) in order to inject the combination in a variation point. The participants said that these combinations of model fragments helped them to solve easier the exercises. The results reveal that the participants, who combined model fragments (34.4 % of participants), reduced both the number of fragment substitutions (an average of 33.18 %) to reach the target product configuration, and the number of errors (an average of 14 %) with regard to the participants who did not combined model fragments. Nevertheless, this operation is not supported in general variability modeling approaches (FODA, OVM and CVL). As our results reveal that this operation for combining model fragments is a positive complement for product configuration, new versions of general variability modeling approaches should consider the inclusion of this operation.

The results also show that participants obtained the highest percentage of correct solutions in the isolated model fragments (the mean of correct solutions is 82.29 %). This result matches with previous research works [18], which used isolated model fragments to perform product configurations. Crossing model fragments obtained a mean of 51.04 % of the correct solutions. The scientific community is already aware that crossing model fragments are difficult to understand [15, 23, 24], which is also confirmed in this experiment. Recursive model fragments obtained the worst results (a mean of 40.62 % correct solutions). Overall, the participants got a incorrect solution when they deepened the levels of recursion to reach the target configuration. To the best of our knowledge, recursive model fragments are neglected by the scientific community. The results of this experiment suggest that recursive model fragments are the major source of incorrect solutions to reach a target product configuration. Therefore, new experiments need to be performed in order to further investigate recursive model fragments in product configurations.

We found that participants made redundant fragment substitutions because they thought that variation points have to be always substituted with one of its available options. They considered this substitution mandatory even though the variation point already holds the model elements of the target product configuration. According to the participants, the tree layout of the variability specification (e.g., the variability specification that the upper half of Fig. 1 shows) reinforces the participants' idea that they should choose an option for each variation point. The results show that the 5.9 % of exercises included redundant fragment substitutions, which increase in a 6.93 % the necessary fragment substitutions to reach the target product configuration. It is important to highlight that we did not find instructions to avoid this redundancy in the materials [5, 9, 16] of the general variability modeling approaches, which were used in this experiment to train the participants. Hence, the results of this experiment suggest that the training materials of the variability modeling approaches should be extended to explicitly avoid this redundancy.

Table 1 summarizes the main findings of this work that are relevant for general variability modeling approaches. Each finding is tagged as type Confirms (the finding confirms results of previous research works) or type New (new finding revealed by this work). Finally, the table also summarizes the next steps for variability modeling approaches that we suggest taking into account the findings.

Table 1. Summary of findings

#	Finding	Type	Next Step
1	Concrete syntax of model fragments misleads product configuration	Confirms [7]	New versions of concrete syntax of model fragments should align geometric shape and variability specification in order to take advantage of the time improvement
2	Geometric shape criterion reduces the time required (38 % less time) to perform product configurations	New	
3	Model fragment combination improves the efficiency (33.18 % less steps) of product configurations and reduce the incorrect solutions (14 %)	New	General variability modeling approaches should consider the inclusion of the combination operation as a complement for product configuration
4	Highest percentage of correct solutions in the isolated model fragments (82.29 % of correct solutions)	Confirms [18]	Specific experiments need to be conducted to further investigate recursive model fragments in product configurations
5	Crossing model fragments are difficult to understand (51.04 % of correct solutions)	Confirms [15, 23, 24]	
6	Recursive model fragments are the major source of incorrect solutions (40.62 % of correct solutions)	New	
7	Redundant configuration steps are produced by misunderstanding variation points as mandatory substitutions.	New	Training materials of the variability modeling approaches should be extended to explicitly avoid this redundancy

6 Threats to Validity

We use the classification of threats to validity of [21, 25], which distinguishes four aspects of validity to acknowledge the limitations of our experiment.

Construct validity: This aspect of validity reflects the extent to which the operational measures that are studied represent what the researchers have in mind and what is investigated based on the research questions. In this work, the proposed exercises do not have a true/false answer. Therefore, it is very difficult for users to answers correctly if they do not understand the question.

Furthermore, to minimize this threat exercises and the responses were designed by two variability modeling experts. These experts have developed industrial variability modeling tools (in the induction hob domain and train control software domain). Their participation was limited to the design of the exercises and they were not involved in this paper.

Finally, the measures used in our research are the percentage of correct solutions, the time spent, and a self-rated difficulty. These measures are widely accepted in the software engineering research community [18, 19].

Internal validity: This aspect of validity is of concern when causal relations are examined. There is a risk that the factor being investigated may be affected by other neglected factors. In this work, we explained the DSL to the participants. The slides used in that explanation were given to the participants, so that lack of comprehension of DSL would not be a problem in performing the exercises.

External validity: This aspect of validity is concerned with to what extent it is possible to generalize the finding, and to what extent the findings are of relevance for other cases. The experiment was performed by students and practitioners, and this students' participation can be a source of weakness. However, using students as subjects instead of software engineers is not a major issue [10, 20] as long as the research questions are not specifically focused on experts. We considered that the variability modeling concepts under study are also relevant to students.

In the analysis procedure we have used a confidence interval $p < 0.05$ where conclusions are 95 % representative. This means that if they followed a normal distribution, the results would be true 95 % of the times.

Since the DSL used in this study is a very simple language in a specific domain, we think that the generalizability of findings should be undertaken with caution. The selected DSL is appropriate for easy comprehension by the participants. However, other experiments with other DSLs should be performed to validate our findings.

Reliability: This aspect is concerned with to what extent the data and the analysis are dependent on the specific researchers. To reduce this threat, two variability modeling experts who were not involved in the research designed both the exercises and the correct answers. We also performed this research using methods that are widely accepted by the software engineering community.

7   Related Work

There are research studies in the literature that analyze difficulties in model fragments for product configuration. In [24], Vasilevskiy and Haugen identify the problems generated after the superimposition of features in crossing model fragments. In [15], Oldevik et al. analyze confluence and conflict properties of multiple variation points. In [23], Svendsen et al. identify difficulties in crossing model fragments when the DSL models are modified. In our work, we have not only found that crossing model fragments are difficult to understand (which confirms the finding of the previous works) but also we analyzed isolated and recursive model fragments, the necessary time to reach a product configuration and the participants' perceived difficulty. This enables us to obtain new findings about the geometric shape of model fragments, combinations of model fragments, the major source of incorrect solutions, and redundant configuration steps.

There are research efforts in the literature regarding the comprehension of variability modeling. In [19], Reinhartz-Berger et al. present a study for comprehending feature models by performing an experiment with participants who are familiar with feature modeling and participants who are not familiar with it. Furthermore, Reinhartz-Berger and Figl [18] present an approach that investigates the comprehensibility of orthogonal variability modeling languages. Specifically, they conducted an experiment to examine potential comprehension problems in two orthogonal variability modeling languages: CVL and OVM. In [20], Reinhartz-Berger and Tsoury present a comparative analysis for managing variability using Feature-oriented and UML-based modeling methods. Nevertheless, these works do not analyze the differences in comprehensibility using isolated, crossing and recursive model fragments to reach a desired product configuration as our work does.

Medeiros et al. [14] perform interviews with developers about the use of the Č preprocessor to handle variability since developers use conditional directives to provide optional features or to select between alternative implementations. Berger et al. [1] present an exploratory case study of three companies that apply variability modeling to research about practices, characteristics, benefits and challenges of variability modeling. Even though these works provide empirical data on variability management in industrial application, they do not investigate difficulties in understanding product configuration when features are superimposed to a realization model.

There are also works that facilitate the comprehension of variability modeling by end users. For instance, Grünbacher et al. present a Configurable Product Line tool that enable customization by end users [8]. The authors abstract the technical issues of this customization to help end users understand the implications of the decisions that they make. Furthermore, Rabiser et al. [17] present an end-user oriented tool that can support diverse end-users such as project managers, salespeople, or engineers. Botterweck et al. present a metamodel and a tool that employs visualization techniques to support users in the process of product configuration [2]. These works focus on augmenting the capabilities of variability modeling tools to improve the feedback that the tools provide to their users. By contrast, our work does not address variability tool support an we focus on general variability modeling languages.

In [7], we performed a usability evaluation of a variability modeling tool in which we detected that the domain experts of our industrial partner (BSH group) had difficulty understanding variability due to the concrete syntax of model fragments. The work that this paper presents confirms that the concrete syntax of model fragments misleads participants during product configurations but this paper reveals that it is possible to harness concrete syntax to significantly reduce the time required to configure products. This paper also obtains new findings about combinations of model fragments, the major source of incorrect solutions, and redundant configuration steps.

8 Conclusions

In previous work [7], we detected that the domain experts of BSH group had difficulty understanding variability to configure the firmware of their products (induction hobs under the Bosch and Siemens brands). Specifically, domain experts had difficulty understanding variability in the model fragments that results of superimposing features [6], of the variability specification, on a DSL model.

In this work, we conducted an experiment in which participants deal with variability in model fragments to achieve their desired product configurations. The exercises were divided into three groups based on the type of fragments produced by the superimposition of the features on the DSL model: isolated model fragments, crossing model fragments and recursive model fragments. We measured comprehension score, time spent, and the self-rated difficulty. In addition, we obtained participants' opinion about the exercises by means of open questions and a focus group interview.

Our results show findings that are relevant for general variability modeling approaches (FODA, OVM and CVL). Specifically, results show four new findings revealed by this work:

- Geometric shape criterion reduces the time required to perform product configurations.
- Model fragment combination improves the efficiency of product configurations and reduce the incorrect solutions.
- Recursive model fragments are the major source of incorrect solutions.
- Redundant configuration steps are produced by misunderstanding variation points as mandatory substitutions.

And three findings that confirm results of previous research works:

- Concrete syntax of model fragments misleads product configuration.
- Highest percentage of correct solutions in the isolated model fragments.
- Crossing model fragments are difficult to understand.

Taking into account the above findings, we suggested next steps for variability modeling approaches that cover (1) new concrete syntax of model fragments, (2) the inclusion of the model fragment combination operation, (3) further investigation of recursive model fragments in product configurations and

(4) clarification of training materials of the variability modeling approaches. These next steps would contribute to promote the adoption of variability management approaches in industry.

Acknowledgments. This work has been partially supported by the Ministry of Economy and Competitiveness (MINECO), through the Spanish National R+D+i Plan and ERDF funds under The project Model-Driven Variability Extraction for Software Product Lines Adoption (TIN2015-64397-R).

References

1. Berger, T., Nair, D., Rublack, R., Atlee, J.M., Czarnecki, K., Wąsowski, A.: Three cases of feature-based variability modeling in industry. In: ACM/IEEE 17th International Conference on Model Driven Engineering Languages and Systems (MODELS) (2014)
2. Botterweck, G., Thiel, S., Nestor, D., bin Abid, S., Cawley, C.: Visual tool support for configuring and understanding software product lines. In: 12th International Conference on Software Product Line, SPLC 2008, pp. 77–86, September 2008
3. Clements, P., Northrop, L.: Software Product Lines: Practices and Patterns. Addison-Wesley Longman Publishing Co. Inc, Boston (2001)
4. Condori-Fernández, N., Panach, J.I., Baars, A.I., Vos, T.E.J., Pastor, O.: An empirical approach for evaluating the usability of model-driven tools. Sci. Comput. Program. **78**(11), 2245–2258 (2013)
5. CVL Submission Team. Common variability language (CVL), OMG revised submission (2012). http://www.omgwiki.org/variability/lib/exe/fetch.php?id=start& cache=cache&media=cvl-revised-submission.pdf
6. Czarnecki, K., Antkiewicz, M.: Mapping features to models: a template approach based on superimposed variants. In: Glück, R., Lowry, M. (eds.) GPCE 2005. LNCS, vol. 3676, pp. 422–437. Springer, Heidelberg (2005)
7. Echeverría, J., Font, J., Cetina, C., Pastor, O.: Usability evaluation of variability modeling by means of common variability language. In: Proceedings of the CAiSE 2015 Forum at the 27th International Conference on Advanced Information Systems Engineering co-located with 27th International Conference on Advanced Information Systems Engineering (CAiSE 2015), Stockholm, Sweden, 10 June 2015, pp. 105–112 (2015)
8. Grünbacher, P., Rabiser, R., Dhungana, D.: Product line tools are product lines too: lessons learned from developing a tool suite. In: 23rd IEEE/ACM International Conference on Automated Software Engineering, pp. 351–354, September 2008
9. Kang, K.C., Cohen, S.G., Hess, J.A., Novak, W.E., Peterson, A.S.: Feature-oriented domain analysis (FODA) feasibility study. Technical report, Carnegie-Mellon University Software Engineering Institute, November 1990
10. Kitchenham, B.A., Pfleeger, S.L., Pickard, L.M., Jones, P.W., Hoaglin, D.C., Emam, K.E., Rosenberg, J.: Preliminary guidelines for empirical research in software engineering. IEEE Trans. Softw. Eng. **28**(8), 721–734 (2002)
11. Krosnick, J.A., Presser, S.: Question and questionnaire design. In: Handbook of Survey Research, 2nd edn., pp. 263–314 (2010)
12. Krueger, R.A., Casey, M.A.: Designing and conducting focus group interviews. In: Krueger, RA., Casey, M.A., Donner, J., Kirsch, S., Maack, J.N. (eds.) Social Analysis, Selected Tools and Techniques, pp. 4–23 (2002)

13. Kumar, S., Karoli, V.: Handbook of Business Research Methods. Thakur Publishers, Lucknow (2011)
14. Medeiros, F., Kästner, C., Ribeiro, M., Nadi, S., Gheyi, R.: The love, hate relationship with the C preprocessor: an interview study (artifact). DARTS 1(1), 07:1–07:32 (2015)
15. Oldevik, J., Haugen, Ø., Møller-Pedersen, B.: Confluence in domain-independent product line transformations. In: Chechik, M., Wirsing, M. (eds.) FASE 2009. LNCS, vol. 5503, pp. 34–48. Springer, Heidelberg (2009)
16. Pohl, K., Böckle, G., van der Linden, F.: Software Product Line Engineering: Foundations Principles and Techniques. Springer, New York (2005)
17. Rabiser, R., Dhungana, D., Heider, W., Grünbacher, P.: Flexibility and end-user support in model-based product line tools. In: 35th Euromicro Conference on Software Engineering and Advanced Applications, SEAA 2009, pp. 508–511 (2009)
18. Reinhartz-Berger, I., Figl, K.: Comprehensibility of orthogonal variability modeling languages: the cases of CVL and OVM. In: Proceedings of the 18th International Software Product Line Conference SPLC 2014, New York, NY, USA, vol. 1, pp. 42–51. ACM (2014)
19. Reinhartz-Berger, I., Figl, K., Haugen, Ø.: Comprehending feature models expressed in CVL. In: Dingel, J., Schulte, W., Ramos, I., Abrahão, S., Insfran, E. (eds.) MODELS 2014. LNCS, vol. 8767, pp. 501–517. Springer, Heidelberg (2014)
20. Reinhartz-Berger, I., Tsoury, A.: Experimenting with the comprehension of feature-oriented and UML-based core assets. In: Halpin, T., Nurcan, S., Krogstie, J., Soffer, P., Proper, E., Schmidt, R., Bider, I. (eds.) BPMDS 2011 and EMMSAD 2011. LNBIP, vol. 81, pp. 468–482. Springer, Heidelberg (2011)
21. Runeson, P., Höst, M.: Guidelines for conducting and reporting case study research in software engineering. Empirical Softw. Eng. 14(2), 131–164 (2009)
22. Shapiro, S.S., Wilk, M.B.: An analysis of variance test for normality (complete samples). Biometrika 52(3/4), 591–611 (1965)
23. Svendsen, A., Zhang, X., Haugen, Ø., Møller-Pedersen, B.: Towards evolution of generic variability models. In: Kienzle, J. (ed.) MODELS 2011. LNCS, vol. 7167, pp. 53–67. Springer, Heidelberg (2012)
24. Vasilevskiy, A., Haugen, Ø.: Resolution of interfering product fragments in software product line engineering. In: Dingel, J., Schulte, W., Ramos, I., Abrahão, S., Insfran, E. (eds.) MODELS 2014. LNCS, vol. 8767, pp. 467–483. Springer, Heidelberg (2014)
25. Wohlin, C., Runeson, P., Höst, M., Ohlsson, M.C., Regnell, B., Wesslén, A.: Experimentation in Software Engineering: An Introduction. Kluwer Academic Publishers, Norwell (2000)

Static Analysis of Dynamic Database Usage in Java Systems

Loup Meurice[✉], Csaba Nagy, and Anthony Cleve

PReCISE Research Center, University of Namur, Namur, Belgium
loup.meurice@unamur.be

Abstract. Understanding the links between application programs and their database is useful in various contexts such as migrating information systems towards a new database platform, evolving the database schema, or assessing the overall system quality. In the case of Java systems, identifying which portion of the source code accesses which portion of the database may prove challenging. Indeed, Java programs typically access their database in a dynamic way. The queries they send to the database server are built at runtime, through String concatenations, or Object-Relational Mapping frameworks like Hibernate and JPA. This paper presents a static analysis approach to program-database links recovery, specifically designed for Java systems. The approach allows developers to automatically identify the source code locations accessing given database tables and columns. It focuses on the combined analysis of JDBC, Hibernate and JPA invocations. We report on the use of our approach to analyse three real-life Java systems.

Keywords: Database access recovery · Static analysis · Java · ORM

1 Introduction

In various maintenance and evolution scenarios, developers have to determine which portion of the source code of their applications accesses (a given fragment of) the database. Let us consider, among others, the cases of database reverse engineering, database refactoring, database platform migration, service identification, quality assessment or impact analysis for database schema change. In the context of each of these processes, one needs to identify and analyze all the database queries executed by the application programs.

In the case of systems written in Java, the most popular programming language today [1], database manipulation has become increasingly complex in recent years. Indeed, a large-scale empirical study, carried out by Goeminne et al. [8], reveals that a wide range of dynamic database access technologies are used by Java systems to manipulate their database. Those access mechanisms partly or fully hide the actual SQL queries executed by the programs [6]. Those queries are *generated* at run time before they are sent to the database server.

A. Cleve—This research is supported by the F.R.S.-FNRS via the DISSE project.

S. Nurcan et al. (Eds.): CAiSE 2016, LNCS 9694, pp. 491–506, 2016.
DOI: 10.1007/978-3-319-39696-5_30

In this paper, we address this problem of recovering the traceability links between Java programs and their database in presence of such a level of dynamicity. We propose a static analysis approach allowing developers to identify the source code locations where database queries are executed, and to extract the set of actual SQL queries that could be executed at each location. The approach is based on algorithms that operate on the call graph of the application and the intra-procedural control-flow of the methods. It considers three of the most popular database access technologies used in Java systems, according to [8], namely JDBC, Hibernate, and JPA. We evaluated our approach based on three real-life open-source systems with size ranging from 250 to 2,054 kLOC accessing 88 – 480 tables in the database. We could extract queries for 71.5 % – 99 % of database accesses with 87.9 % – 100 % of valid queries.

The paper is organized as follows. Section 2 introduces the three database access technologies considered by our approach. Section 3 presents our approach and illustrates it through examples. Section 4 reports on the use of our approach to analyze real-life Java systems. A related work discussion is provided in Sect. 5. Concluding remarks are given in Sect. 6.

2   Java Database Access Technologies

Below we briefly introduce JDBC, Hibernate and JPA, by illustrating their underlying database access mechanisms.

JDBC. The JDBC API is the industry standard for database-independent connectivity between the Java programming language and relational databases. It provides a call-level API for SQL-based database access, and offers the developer a set of methods for querying the database, for instance, methods from `Statement` and `PreparedStatement` classes (see Fig. 1).

```
1   public class ProviderMgr {
2       private Statement st;
3       private ResultSet rs;
4       private boolean ordering;
5
6       public void executeQuery(String x, String y){
7           String sql = getQueryStr(x);
8           if(ordering)
9               sql += " order by " + y;
10          rs = st.execute(sql);
11      }
12      public String getQueryStr(String str){
13          return "select * from " + str;
14      }
15      public Provider[] getAllProviders(){
16          String tableName = "Provider";
17          String columnName = (...) ? "provider_id" : "provider_name";
18          executeQuery(tableName, columnName);
19          ...
20      }}
```

Fig. 1. Java code fragment using the JDBC API to execute a SQL query (line 10).

Hibernate. Hibernate is an Object-Relational Mapping (ORM) library for Java, providing a framework for mapping an object-oriented domain model to a traditional relational database. Its primary feature is to map Java classes to database tables (and Java data types to SQL data types). Hibernate provides also an SQL-inspired language called *Hibernate Query Language* (HQL) which allows to write SQL-like queries using the mappings defined before. Figure 2 (1) provides an example of an HQL query execution (line 13). In addition, *Criteria Queries* are provided as an object-oriented alternative to HQL, where one can construct a query by simple method invocations. See Fig. 2 (2) for a sample usage of a Criteria Query. Hibernate also provides a way to perform *CRUD operations* (Create, Read, Update, and Delete) on the instances of the mapped entity classes. Figure 2 (3) illustrates a sample record insertion in the database.

(1) Java code executing a HQL query (line 13). Product selection according to its category

```
1    public class ProductDaoImpl implements ProductDao {
2
3        private SessionFactory sessionFactory;
4
5        public void setSessionFactory(SessionFactory sessionFactory) {
6            this.sessionFactory = sessionFactory;
7        }
8
9        public Collection loadProductsByCategory(String category) {
10           return this.sessionFactory.getCurrentSession()
11               .createQuery("from Product product where category=?")
12               .setParameter(0, category)
13               .list();
14       }}
```

(2) Java code executing a Criteria query. Customer selection restricted on the name and city

```
1    List cats = sess.createCriteria(Customer.class)
2        .add( Restrictions.eq("name", "Smith") )
3        .add( Restrictions.in( "city", new String[] { "New York", "Houston
         ", "Washington DC" } )
4        .list(),
```

(3) Hibernate operation on a mapped entity class instance. Insertion of a new customer

```
1    private static Session session;
2    ...
3
4    public static void saveCustomer(Customer myCustomer){
5        saveObject(myCustomer));
6    }
7
8    public static void saveObject(Object o){
9        session.save(o);}
```

Fig. 2. Samples of hibernate accesses.

Java Persistence API. JPA is a Java API specification to describe the management of relational data in applications. Just like Hibernate, JPA also provides a higher level of abstraction based on the mapping between Java classes and database tables permitting operations on objects, attributes and relationships instead of tables and columns. It offers the developers several ways to access the database. One of them is the *Java Persistence Query Language* (JPQL), a platform-independent object-oriented query language which is defined as part of the JPA API specification. JPQL is used to make queries against entities stored in a relational database. Like HQL, it is inspired by SQL, but it operates on JPA entity objects rather than on database tables. Figure 3 (1) shows an example of JPQL query execution. JPA also provides a way to perform CRUD operations

(1) Sample JPQL query. Customer selection according to a given id

```
1  EntityManagerFactory emf = ...;
2  EntityManager em = emf.createEntityManager();
3  Order order = ...;
4  Integer cust_id = order.getCustomerId();
5  Customer cust = (Customer)em.createQuery("SELECT c FROM Customer c
       WHERE c.cust_id=:cust_id")
6    .setParameter("cust_id", cust_id).getSingleResult();
```

(2) JPA operation on a mapped entity class instance. Creation and insertion of a new order

```
1  EntityManager entityManager = entityManagerFactory.createEntityManager
       ();
2  entityManager.getTransaction().begin();
3  Order order= createNewOrder();
4  entityManager.persist( order );
5  entityManager.getTransaction().commit();
6  entityManager.close();
```

Fig. 3. Samples of JPA accesses.

on the instances of mapped entity classes. For instance, Fig. 3 (2) illustrates the creation and insertion of a new order in the database.

3   Approach

Figure 4 presents an overview of our approach which combines three different analyses: the JDBC, Hibernate and JPA analyses. The output of the full process is a set of database access locations and the database objects (tables and columns) impacted/accessed by a given access. Those database objects are detected based on the actual database schema.

3.1   Initial Analysis

Call Graph Extraction. The complete recovery of a query executed in a given Java method is a complex process. In most cases, a SQL query (a database access in general) is constructed using some of the input parameters of the given method. For instance, the **executeQuery** method in Fig. 1 uses its parameters for constructing the SQL query. Consequently, the local recovery of the query is not sufficient and the exploration of the call graph of that given method is

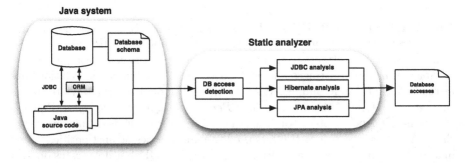

Fig. 4. Overview of the proposed approach.

necessary for determining the different possible values of the needed parameters. We designed an approach based on inter-procedural analysis in order to deal with the call graph reconstruction and the extraction of every possible value of the parameters used in the query construction.

Database Access Detection. The database access detection step aims to detect all the source code locations querying the database by means of a JDBC/Hibernate/JPA method. Our Java analyzer constructs an abstract syntax tree and uses a visitor to navigate through the different Java nodes and expressions. We defined an exhaustive list of JDBC, Hibernate and JPA methods accessing the database (based on the documentation of each technology). Our detection is designed to detect the calls of those methods and to send them to the corresponding analysis (JDBC, Hibernate or JPA analysis).

3.2 JDBC Analysis

Our JDBC analysis focuses on the database accesses using the JDBC API, where we follow a two-phase process. As illustrated in Sect. 2, a JDBC access recovery can be seen as a String expression recovery. Once our analyzer has detected a JDBC access, it will then recover the corresponding SQL query. Finally, our SQL parser constructs the abstract syntax tree of the SQL query and identifies which part of the database schema is involved in that access; that is, the parser identifies the database tables and columns accessed with it. This identification relies on the actual database schema.

Algorithm 1 formalizes the first phase allowing the recovery of all the possible string values of an expression (a more detailed description of the used procedures is given in Algorithm 2). First, we *locally* resolve the expression and then we deal with the call graph extraction, when it is necessary. Let us apply Algorithm 1 on the sample code in Fig. 1. This algorithm gets executed when the *Database Access Detection* finds a JDBC-based data access, i.e., st.execute(sql). Here, sql is the String expression which will be recovered by the algorithm and which is located in the method executeQuery(String x, String y). These two elements will be the inputs of the algorithm. First, the algorithm extracts the possible local values of sql, i.e., 'select * from x' and 'select * from x order by y' (line 2). Then it deals with the x and y input parameters by extracting the call graph first. Analyzing the call graph allows us to recover the possible values of the parameters. We illustrate this step for each possible value.

Let $value =$ 'select * from x'; x is the only parameter of the executeQuery method (line 4). The algorithm explores the code for retrieving the expressions invoking the executeQuery method (line 8). It returns only one call expression, namely executeQuery(tableName, columnName). The next step is to retrieve *tableName* (line 10), the input expression corresponding to x. For this step, we recursively resolve the expression *tableName* (line 13); the result is 'Provider'. Then, we replace all the input parameters with their corresponding values obtained earlier (line 15). In this example, we merely replace x with 'Provider' and thus, the resulting value for the query string is 'select * from Provider'.

Procedure recoverExpr(*Expression expr, Method method*)
Input: a Java expression representing a String value and the Java method where the
    expression is located.
Output: the list of every possible String values corresponding to this expression.
1   Expr[] result = initialize()
    // **Locally extracting the values of the given expression**
2   Expr[] values = getLocalValues(expr, method)
3   **for** *value* ∈ *values* **do**
        //**Extracting the used input parameters from the current value**
4   Variable[] inputs = getInputParams(method, value)
5   **if** *inputs* = *null* **then**
6   result.add(value)
7   **else**
            //**Extracting the call graph of the given method in order to recover**
            the value of each used input
8   MethodCallExpr[] callGraph = callGraph(method)
9   **for** *call* ∈ *callGraph* **do**
                //**Extracting the input values from the current call**
10   Expr[] inputExprs = extractParamValues(method, call, inputs)
11   Expr[][] inputValues = initialize()
12   **for** *inputExpr* ∈ *inputExprs* **do**
                    //**Recursive call for each input**
13   inputValues.add(**recoverExpr**(inputExpr, inputExpr.method()))
14   **end**
                //**Replacing each input by the obtained values**
15   Expr[] product = replaceInput(value, inputs, inputValues)
16   **for** *e* ∈ *product* **do**
17   result.add(e)
18   **end**
19   **end**
20   **end**
21   **end**
22   **return** result

Algorithm 1. Algorithm for recovering the string values of a given Java
expression.

Let *value* = 'select * from *x* order by *y*'; the process is slightly different. In this case there are two input parameters: *x* and *y*. The result for *x* is
the same as above ('Provider'), but *y*, reduced to *columnName*, may correspond to two different values: 'provider_id' and 'provider_name'. The algorithm returns two possible values (line 15): 'select * from Provider order
by provider_id' and 'select * from Provider order by provider_name'.

The final result of the algorithm will be 3 different string values for the
sql expression: 'select * from Provider', 'select * from Provider order
by provider_id', and 'select * from Provider order by provider_name'.
In the end of the process, the SQL parsing phase will point to the Provider
table and its provider_id and provider_name columns as the accessed objects.

3.3   Hibernate Analysis

Similarly to the JDBC API, Hibernate provides the developer multiple database access/query mechanisms. The aim of the Hibernate analysis is to identify
the source code locations accessing the database through Hibernate. While it
partly relies on the JDBC analysis and its algorithm of string value recovery,
the Hibernate analysis is more sophisticated due to the ORM complexity.

Procedure getLocalValues(*Expr expr, Method method*)
Input: A Java expression representing a String value and the Java method where the
expression is located
Output: All the possible values of the given expression by only exploring the given local
method.
Procedure getInputParams(*Method method, Expr expr*)
Input: A Java method declaration and a Java expression.
Output: The input parameters of the given method which are part of the given expression
Example:
  - method = public static void printCustomer(Connection con, Integer id)
  - expr = "select * from Customer where *cust_id* =" + id
  - res = [id]
Procedure callGraph(*Method method*)
Input: A Java method declaration.
Output: The Java expressions invoking the given method.
Procedure extractParamValues(*Method method, MethodCallExpr mce, Variable[] inputs*)
Input: A Java method declaration, a Java expression invoking the given method and a set of
input parameters of the given method.
Output: The corresponding value of each parameter.
Example:
  - method = public static void printCustomer(Connection con, Integer id)
  - mce = printCustomer(myConnection, 201456)
  - inputs = [id]
  - res = [201456]
Procedure replaceInput(*Expr expr, Variable[] inputs, Expr[][] inputValues*)
Input: A Java expression, a list of variables used by the given expression, the possible values
of each variable
Output: Replacing the variables part of the given expression by their corresponding values
Example:
  - expr = "select * from Customer where *first_name* =" + firstName + "and *last_name*
=" + lastName
  - inputs = [firstName, lastName]
  - inputValues = [['James', 'John'], ['Smith']]
  - res = [select * from Customer where *first_name* = 'James' and *last_name* = 'Smith',
select * from Customer where *first_name* = 'John' and *last_name* = 'Smith']

Algorithm 2. Description of the procedures used in Algorithm 1

Like the JDBC API, Hibernate also proposes different Java methods to execute either native SQL queries or HQL queries. The extraction process of those queries is similar to the JDBC analysis process (Algorithm 1). However, our HQL parser is slightly different from the parser of the JDBC analysis. Indeed, at this point we cannot just extract a SQL query string. Thus, we implemented a feature to be able to translate an HQL query into the corresponding SQL query. This translation is processed by invoking the internal HQL to SQL compiler of Hibernate (`org.hibernate.hql.QueryTranslator`) with the same context that would be used for execution. Once we obtained the corresponding translated SQL query, we are able to parse it and extract the involved objects.

Furthermore, as previously described, Hibernate also offers a set of methods operating on instances of mapped entity classes, e.g., Fig. 2 (3). This way of accessing the database cannot be reduced to a mere string recovery process. Instead, the purpose is to determine the Java class of the object. The proposed solution consists in firstly determining the entity class(es) of the input object and then, detecting the corresponding mapped database objects. This last phase analyzes the Hibernate mapping files of the system. These mapping files instruct Hibernate how to map the defined class or classes to the database tables. We did not present our algorithm allowing to determine the entity class of an input Java object because it uses the same logic (but simplified) that Algorithm 1. Instead, we illustrate the use of that algorithm on Fig. 2 (3). The Database Access Detection detects `session.save(o)` as a database access. *o* is the expression to resolve and it is located in `saveObject(Object o)`. *o* is identified as an input parameter of the method *saveObject*. Then, the algorithm explores the code to retrieve the expressions invoking the *saveObject* method (call graph extraction). Only one call expression is returned, namely `saveObject(myCustomer)`. Next, we recursively resolve the *myCustomer* expression. *myCustomer* is also a parameter of the `saveCustomer` method, however, there is no call expression for it (empty call graph). Thus, we resolve *myCustomer* locally: by exploring the `saveCustomer` method, we detect that *myCustomer* is an instance of the `Customer` class. This step will, therefore, return the `Customer` class as the only solution for the *o* expression. Finally, our solver will detect the mapping between the `Customer` class and its corresponding database table.

3.4 JPA Analysis

The JPA analysis concentrates on the database accesses by means of JPA. Like Hibernate, JPA proposes Java methods to execute either native SQL queries or JPQL queries. The extraction process of those queries is similar to the Hibernate analysis: we rebuild the query value by means of Algorithm 1 and then we parse the JPQL query. The JPQL parser uses the same approach as for HQL, by invoking the internal HQL to SQL compiler of Hibernate.

Like Hibernate, JPA also permits accessing the database by operating on Java instances of mapped entity classes, e.g., Fig. 3 (2). We use the same approach to address that problem. However, instead of using the Hibernate mapping files for establishing the mapping between the entity classes and the database tables, the DB Mapper will consider the JPA annotations which define this mapping.

3.5 Process Output

The output of the full process is the set of the database accesses detected by our static analysis as well as the code location of each access and the database tables and columns involved in it. The code location of a given access is expressed by the minimal *program path* necessary for creating and executing the database access. The below example shows sample information gathered for a database access where a SQL query is executed at line 124 in `DatabaseUtil.java`. The current method in which the query execution occurs is called by `CheckDrug OrderUnit.java` at line 56. The database objects involved in this query are the *drug_order* table and *units*, one of its columns.

```
JDBC access: 'SELECT DISTINCT units FROM drug_order WHERE units is NOT NULL'
Program path: [CheckDrugOrderUnit.java, line=56] → [DatabaseUtil.java, line=124]
Database schema objects:
    ↪ Database Tables: [ drug_order ]
    ↪ Database Columns: [ drug_order.units ]
```

4 Evaluation

In this section we evaluate our approach on three real-life systems. The detailed results of this evaluation are available as an online appendix[1].

4.1 Evaluation Environment

Table 1 presents an overview of the main characteristics of the target systems. Oscar (oscar-emr.com) is an open-source information system that is widely used in the healthcare industry in Canada. The source code comprises approximately two million lines of code. OSCAR combines JDBC, Hibernate and JPA to access the database. OpenMRS (openmrs.org) is a collaborative open-source project to develop software to support the delivery of health care in developing countries (mainly in Africa). OpenMRS uses a MySQL database accessed via Hibernate and dynamic SQL (JDBC). Broadleaf Commerce (broadleafcommerce.org) is an open-source, e-commerce framework written entirely in Java on top of the Spring framework. Broadleaf uses a relational database accessed via JPA.

Table 2 contains the results of the process of identifying database accesses applied to the three systems. For each system and technology supported, it presents the total number of locations accessing the database.

Table 1. Size metrics of the systems

System	Description	LOC	Tables	Columns
Oscar	Medical record system	2 054 940	480	13 822
OpenMRS	Medical record system	301 232	88	951
Broadleaf	E-commerce framework	254 027	179	965

Table 2. Number of database access locations per technology

System	Database accesses		
	JDBC	Hib	JPA
Oscar	123 661	727	31 729
OpenMRS	77	687	0
Broadleaf	0	0	930

Table 3. Complexity of database access recovery

	JDBC		Hib		JPA	
	$\bar{x}$	max	$\bar{x}$	max	$\bar{x}$	max
Oscar	4	8	1.5	3	3.8	7
OpenMRS	1.2	3	1	2	–	–
Broadleaf	–	–	–	–	1	1

Figure 5 shows the set of tables and columns accessible by the different technologies. In the Oscar system, we notice that JDBC remains the most widely used technology regarding the number of different columns accessed (10,350 columns accessed from 123,661 source code locations). Concerning OpenMRS, the biggest database part is accessed by Hibernate (713 columns for 687 locations) whereas JPA is the only used mechanism in Broadleaf (431 columns for 930 locations).

---

[1] https://staff.info.unamur.be/lme/CAISE16/.

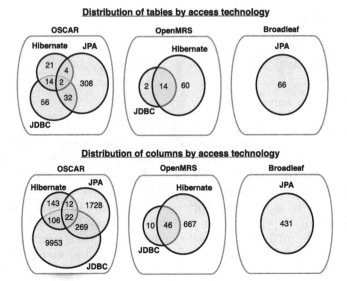

Fig. 5. Distribution of *tables and columns* by access technology

Table 3 depicts, for each system, the algorithmic complexity in terms of the number of recursive calls needed for completely recovering a code location accessing the database, i.e., the number of recursive calls in Algorithm 1. In Oscar, one can notice that 4 recursive calls are required, on average, to fully reconstruct a database access via JDBC, while the *most complex* detected accesses require 8 recursive calls. By comparing with the other systems in Table 3, we note that Oscar is the most complex, recursive calls being often necessary to recover the database accesses. In contrast, we can observe that in OpenMRS and Broadleaf, most database accesses are built within the same method.

4.2 Successfully Extracted Queries

The Oracle. To evaluate the effectiveness of our approach in extracting database accesses, we assess whether we can identify most of the database accesses and also the noise of the technique. First we need to have a ground truth, i.e., the *actual* set of queries that are sent to the database with their corresponding source code locations. Once we have this set of queries, we can compare them to our extracted set of queries. However, the availability of a complete ground truth is not a realistic working assumption in the context of large legacy systems.

The *oracle* that we used for assessing our approach is the set of unit tests of each software system. That is, we systematically collected all the database accesses (JDBC, Hibernate and JPA) produced by the execution of the test suites. We gathered this query set by analyzing trace logs of the execution of the unit tests of each system. To do so, we used our modified version of *log4jdbc*[2] to

---

[2] http://code.google.com/p/log4jdbc/.

Table 4. Coverage values of the unit tests

System	Test LOC	Test Runs	Covered classes HIB/JPA	Covered classes JDBC	Covered locations HIB/JPA	Covered locations JDBC
Oscar	49 086	1 311	65.00 %	1.05 %	56.79 %	0.28 %
OpenMRS	76 960	3 258	69.57 %	16.00 %	58.16 %	13.56 %
Broadleaf	17 633	255	33.96 %	-	19.10 %	-

collect trace logs containing the exact string values of all of the queries sent to the database and their corresponding stack traces.

Table 4 presents statistics about the unit tests of the systems under question. We count the number of test runs reported by the build system and show the total lines of Java code in the testing directories. In addition to the test classes, there are functional tests (e.g., Broadleaf uses Groovy tests), resulting that the number of executed test cases are larger than the number of test classes. In general, all the systems are well tested with unit tests, and developers do not just test core functionality of their systems, but the testing of DAO classes is also one of their main goals. All the systems have test databases and hundreds of test cases for testing database usage. Thus, it is reasonable to consider as oracle the data accesses collected through the execution of the unit tests.

The queries that we identify with the help of *log4jdbc* are filtered based on their stack traces, in order to distinguish between queries sent to the database directly through JDBC or Hibernate. Also, this filtering keeps queries generated by Hibernate explicitly for HQL or JPA queries and filters those implicit queries, which are generated for caching or lazy data fetching purposes, for instance.

Table 4 shows what percentages of the classes and locations (that we extracted as data accesses) are covered by the unit tests. For Oscar and Open-MRS, the two largest systems that we analyzed, this coverage value is 65 % for the classes where we found Hibernate or JPA queries. The coverage value of JDBC data accesses is, however, quite low for all systems. The reason for this is that these systems implement main features using ORM technologies, and it mostly happens out of the scope of the main features where they use JDBC to accesses the database, e.g., in utility classes for upgrading the database, or in classes to prepare test databases. These parts of the code are usually not tested by unit tests, resulting in low coverage for our analysis.

Percentages of Successfully Extracted Queries. Conceptually, the number of possible queries is infinite (i.e., when a part of a query depends on user input, its value could be anything). However, to assess if we were able to identify most of the database accesses or not, we calculate the percentages of *successfully extracted* and *unextracted* queries. We consider a query of the oracle (a query logged in the execution traces of the unit tests) *successfully extracted* if we could also extract it from the source code. Otherwise, we consider it *unextracted*. In other words, successfully extracted queries are the true positive queries, while the unextracted ones are the false negatives. To determine if a query in the oracle

Table 5. Percentage of successfully extracted queries for each system

System	Technologies		Total
	JDBC	HIB/JPA	
Oscar	1681/2038	892/1558	71,5 %
OpenMRS	31/41	268/322	82,4 %
Broadleaf	–	94/95	99 %

Table 6. Percentage of valid queries for each system

System	Technologies		Total
	JDBC	Hib/JPA	
Oscar	14/17	656/689	94.9 %
OpenMRS	8/8	86/99	87.9 %
Broadleaf	–	29/29	100 %

was successfully extracted or not, we compare the stack trace of all of these queries to the 'program paths' (see Sect. 3.5) of the extracted queries. Moreover, we compare the string values of the SQL queries.

Table 5 shows the percentages of the successfully extracted queries. For assessing the JDBC analysis on Oscar, we found 2,038 queries in the trace logs, among which our approach successfully extracts 1,681. Regarding the Hibernate/JPA analysis, we identified 892 queries out of 1,558. In general, we identified 71.5 % of the queries. In the case of OpenMRS, for the JDBC analysis, we identified 31 queries out of 41, while we identified 268 Hibernate/JPA accesses out of 322. In total, we identify 82.4 % of the queries. For Broadleaf, the percentage of successfully extracted queries is 99 % (94 JPA accesses out of 95).

Percentage of Valid Queries. It is possible that we extract a query, and we report it as valid, but it is never constructed in the code. Hence it is *invalid*. It can happen when our static technique fails to deal with constructs in the code which would require additional information that we cannot extract statically, e.g., evaluating conditional statements (see Sect. 4.3). We consider these queries as the noise of our approach. In other words, these queries are the false positive queries reported by our technique.

We limit the assessment to those database access points that are covered by the unit tests. If the tests cover an access point, we can make the assumption that the possibly valid queries on that location were sent to the database and traced by our dynamic analysis. All the queries that were reported for these locations, and are not in the oracle, are thus considered as invalid (false positives).

Results are presented in Table 6. In the case of Oscar, with the JDBC analysis we obtain 14 valid out of 17 queries and 656 valid out of 689 for the Hibernate/JPA analysis. The percentage of the valid queries value is 94.9 %. For OpenMRS, we obtain a percentage of 87.9 % with 8 true positive out of 8 for the JDBC analysis and 86 true positives out of 99 for the Hibernate/JPA analysis. Finally, for Broadleaf there are no invalid queries (29 true positives out of 29).

4.3   Limitations

As we have seen, our approach reached good results when applied to real-life Java systems. However, we identified some limitations of our approach that are mainly due to its static nature. Below, we give an overview of those limitations that may cause failures in the automated extraction of (valid) SQL queries.

String Manipulation Classes. The standard Java API provides developers with classes to manipulate String objects, such as StringBuilder and String-Buffer. The main operations of those classes are the *append* and *insert* methods, which are overloaded so as to accept data of any type. In particular, a String-Builder/StringBuffer may be used for creating a database access (e.g., a SQL query). The current version of our analysis does not handle the use of those classes in the string value recovery process. This is one reason for some unsuccessfully extracted queries. As we manually investigated it for the OpenMRS system, among the 54 Hibernate/JPA accesses not extracted by our parser (see Table 5), 49 are due to the use of StringBuilder objects for creating the query value. This obviously affects the percentage of successfully extracted queries[3].

User-Given Inputs. Similarly, executed SQL queries sometimes include input values given by the application users. This is the case in highly dynamic applications that allow users to query the database by selecting columns and/or tables in the user interface. In such a situation, which we did not encounter in our evaluation environment, our approach can still detect the database access location but the static recovery of the associated SQL queries may be incomplete.

Boolean Conditions. Another limitation we observed relates to the conditions in *if-then, while, for,* and *case* statements. Our parser is designed to rebuild all the possible string values for the SQL query. Thus, it considers all the possible program paths. Since our *static* analyzer is unable to resolve a boolean condition (a *dynamic* analysis would be preferable), these cases generate some noise (false positive queries). In the three subjects systems, a total of 12 invalid queries were extracted by our approach due to boolean conditions[4].

5   Related Work

The key novelty of our approach relies on the static reconstruction of SQL queries from Java source code in the presence of Object-Relational Mapping frameworks such as Hibernate and JPA. In particular, we are not aware of another approach supporting such a task in the case of *hybrid* database access mechanisms, where JDBC, Hibernate, and JPA accesses *co-exist* in the same information system.

Several previous papers identify database accesses by extracting dynamically constructed SQL queries (e.g., for JDBC-based database accesses). The purpose of these approaches ranges from error checking [4,9,15,17], SQL fault localization [5], fault diagnosis [10] to impact analysis for database schema changes [11,16]. A pioneer work was published by Christensen *et al.* [4], who propose a static string analysis technique that translates a given Java program into a flow graph, and then analyzes the flow graph to generate a finite-state automaton. They evaluate their approach on Java classes with at most 4 kLOC.

---

[3] Example of the use of *StringBuilder* to create a SQL query: http://bit.ly/1XNeL4e.

[4] Example of invalid extracted query: *"from Concept as concept left join concept.names as names where names.conceptNameType ='FULLY_SPECIFIED' and concept.retired = false order by concept.conceptId asc"*. http://bit.ly/1Y0TJAT.

Gould *et al.* propose a technique close to a pointer analysis, based on an interprocedural data-flow analysis [9,17]. Maule *et al.* use a similar k-CFA algorithm and a software dependence graph to identify the impact of relational database schema changes upon object-oriented applications [11]. van den Brink *et al.* present a quality assessment approach for SQL statements embedded in PL/SQL, COBOL and Visual Basic code [2]. The initial phase of their method consists in extracting the SQL statements from the source code using control and data-flow analysis techniques. They evaluate their method on COBOL programs with at most 4 kLOC. Ngo and Tan [14] make use of symbolic execution to extract database interaction points from web applications. Through a case study of PHP applications with sizes ranging 2 – 584 kLOC, they show that their method is able to extract about 80 % of such interactions.

Compared to the above previous approaches [2,4,9,11,14,17], our SQL extraction technique does not require an expensive data-flow analysis nor symbolic execution. Its input is the abstract syntax tree, and it relies on the intraprocedural control flow of the methods associated with their call graph. This makes the approach applicable to large-scale Java applications, as shown in this paper. In addition, the above approaches are not directly applicable to ORM-based Java systems.

There are only a few studies targeting applications using ORM frameworks, particularly Java applications using Hibernate. Goeminne *et al.* [7] study the co-evolution between code-related and database-related activities in data-intensive systems combining several ways to access the database (native SQL queries and Object-Relational Mapping). Their analysis remains at the granularity level of source code files, and does not involve the fine-grained inspection of the ORM queries. Chen *et al.* [3] propose an automated framework for detecting, flagging and prioritizing database-related performance anti-patterns in applications that use object-relational mapping. In this context, the authors identify database-accessing code paths through control-flow and data-flow analysis, but they do not reconstruct statically the SQL queries that correspond to the identified ORM code fragments. Instead, they execute the applications and rely on *log4jdbc* to log the SQL queries that are executed. The above papers study the peculiarities of ORM code, but they do not contribute to database usage analysis in general, nor to query reconstruction in particular. Our approach is, therefore, the first static analysis technique able to identify database accesses in Java systems that rely on an ORM framework and to translate them to queries sent to the database.

In our recent work, we applied an *earlier* version of our approach to two usage scenarios. First, we were able to elicit implicit foreign keys in a Java system [12], based on the analysis of JDBC invocations. We analyzed both the database schema and the schema recovered from the source code, but the Hibernate and JPA analysis was only limited to the analysis of the schema mapping files and annotations, used as heuristics. Second, in [13], we conducted a study on locating the source code origin of a SQL query executed on the database side. While this short paper relies on our query extraction approach, it focuses on the algorithm for matching *one* concrete SQL query against others. In this paper, we significantly extend our query extraction technique towards a *hybrid* approach by complementing it with the Hibernate and JPA analyses, and we perform an experimental evaluation of its accuracy based on real-life information systems.

6 Conclusions and Future Directions

We presented a static analysis approach that allows developers to identify and analyze database access locations from highly dynamic Java systems. Our approach is able to handle Java systems that combine JDBC-based data accesses with the usage of Hibernate and/or JPA as popular object-relational mapping technologies. The evaluation shows that the proposed approach can successfully extract queries for 71.5 % – 99 % of database accesses with 87.9 % – 100 % of valid queries. Although we identified some limitations (as we presented above), we argue that our approach is applicable in practice to real-life Java projects, and can achieve useful results for further analyzes.

In our future work, we plan to extend our results to other programming languages and database platforms. We also intend to empirically analyse database usage evolution practices, and to study program-database co-evolution patterns. Our ultimate goal is to support developers in the context of software evolution scenarios such as database schema change and database platform migration.

References

1. Tiobe programming community index. Accessed 01-02-2016. http://www.tiobe.com/index.php/content/paperinfo/tpci/index.html
2. Brink, H.V.D., Leek, R.V.D., Visser, J.: Quality assessment for embedded SQL. In: SCAM 2007, pp. 163–170. IEEE Computer Society (2007)
3. Chen, T.H., Shang, W., Jiang, Z.M., Hassan, A.E., Nasser, M., Flora, P.: Detecting performance anti-patterns for applications developed using object-relational mapping. In: ICSE 2014, pp. 1001–1012. ACM (2014)
4. Christensen, A.S., Møller, A., Schwartzbach, M.I.: Precise analysis of string expressions. In: Cousot, R. (ed.) SAS 2003. LNCS, vol. 2694, pp. 1–18. Springer, Heidelberg (2003)
5. Clark, S.R., Cobb, J., Kapfhammer, G.M., Jones, J.A., Harrold, M.J.: Localizing SQL faults in database applications. In: ASE 2011, p. 213. IEEE (2011)
6. Cleve, A., Mens, T., Hainaut, J.L.: Data-intensive system evolution. IEEE Comput. **43**(8), 110–112 (2010)
7. Goeminne, M., Decan, A., Mens, T.: Co-evolving code-related and database-related changes in a data-intensive software system. In: CSMR-WCRE 2014, pp. 353–357 (2014)
8. Goeminne, M., Mens, T.: Towards a survival analysis of database framework usage in Java projects. In: ICSME 2015 (2015)
9. Gould, C., Su, Z., Devanbu, P.: Static checking of dynamically generated queries in database applications. In: ICSE 2004, pp. 645–654. IEEE (2004)
10. Javid, M.A., Embury, S.M.: Diagnosing faults in embedded queries in database applications. In: EDBT/ICDT 2012 Workshops, pp. 239–244. ACM (2012)

11. Maule, A., Emmerich, W., Rosenblum, D.S.: Impact analysis of database schema changes. In: ICSE 2008, pp. 451–460. ACM (2008)
12. Meurice, L., Bermudez, J., Weber, J., Cleve, A.: Establishing referential integrity in legacy information systems: reality bites!. In: ICSM 2014. IEEE (2014)
13. Nagy, C., Meurice, L., Cleve, A.: Where was this SQL query executed?: a static concept location approach. In: SANER 2015, ERA Track. IEEE (2015)
14. Ngo, M.N., Tan, H.B.K.: Applying static analysis for automated extraction of database interactions in web applications. Inf. Softw. Technol. **50**(3), 160 (2008)
15. Sonoda, M., Matsuda, T., Koizumi, D., Hirasawa, S.: On automatic detection of SQL injection attacks by the feature extraction of the single character. In: SIN 2011, pp. 81–86. ACM (2011)
16. Wang, X., Lo, D., Cheng, J., Zhang, L., Mei, H., Yu, J.X.: Matching dependence-related queries in the system dependence graph. In: ASE 2010, pp. 457–466. ACM (2010)
17. Wassermann, G., Gould, C., Su, Z., Devanbu, P.: Static checking of dynamically generated queries in database applications. ACM ToSEM **16**(4), 308–339 (2007)

Open Source Software

A Longitudinal Study of Community-Oriented Open Source Software Development

Kateryna Neulinger[1]([✉]), Anna Hannemann[1], Ralf Klamma[1],
and Matthias Jarke[1,2]

[1] Advanced Community Information Systems (ACIS) Group,
RWTH Aachen University, Ahornstr. 55, 52056 Aachen, Germany
{neulinger,hannemann,klamma}@dbis.rwth-aachen.de
[2] Fraunhofer FIT, Birlinghoven Castle, Sankt Augustin, Germany
jarke@dbis.rwth-aachen.de
http://dbis.rwth-aachen.de

Abstract. End-users are often argued to be the source of innovation in Open Source Software (OSS). However, most of the existing empirical studies about OSS projects have been restricted to developer sub-communities only. In this paper, we address the question, if and under which conditions the requirements and ideas from end-users indeed influence the development processes in OSS. We present an approach for automated requirements elicitation process discovery in OSS communities. The empirical basis are three large-scale interdisciplinary OSS projects in bioinformatics, focusing on communication in the mailing lists and source code histories over ten years. Our study results in preliminary guidelines for the organization of community-oriented software development.

Keywords: Requirements engineering · End-user development · Open source software

1 Introduction

Recent communication infrastructures like Web 2.0 open up new opportunities for requirements engineering. Experts as well amateurs can easily contribute their knowledge to requirements engineering processes. By collecting external ideas, companies get access to a worldwide spread knowledge. Therefore, many companies already provide environments for community building of end-users (e.g. XEROX[1], SAP[2]). We call such software development concepts community-oriented. OSS projects represent a successful example of community-oriented development. OSS communities usually exhibit hierarchical structures with a core layer (core communities) supported by peripheral layers (peripheral communities) [34,37]. Histories of OSS projects can be used as a source to study

---

[1] http://open.xerox.com/.
[2] http://scn.sap.com/community/coil.

© Springer International Publishing Switzerland 2016
S. Nurcan et al. (Eds.): CAiSE 2016, LNCS 9694, pp. 509–523, 2016.
DOI: 10.1007/978-3-319-39696-5_31

a possible organization of end-user community integration in the requirements elicitation process. Community needs are posed through informal means and negotiated within community discourses. This kind of requirements elicitation (RE) can then be the starting point for a requirements engineering process in which these needs are formulated as requirements, and then specified and implemented in a current or later release of the OSS system. Despite a great number of OSS studies [12] and a novel research in "just-in-time" requirements engineering [2], an approach for automated requirements elicitation within OSS is seldom if ever addressed [8,35].

In this paper, we present a methodology for RE process discovery that incorporates a combination of knowledge mining techniques for community-generated content. In order to address the end user roles, we follow the observation of many papers [34,37] that OSS communities often expose a separation into core developers and a periphery. Our mining techniques are specifically geared to understand this periphery with their structure and contributions as well as the impact and evolution of these aspects over the history of an OSS community. Specifically, we pursue three research questions:

RQ1 Is there a difference of requirements contribution to the OSS community from core and peripheral members?

RQ2 To what extent do requirements correlate with general development activity?

RQ3 Does the level of participation in RE influence the level of satisfaction of peripheral project members?

Given the great variance of communities, and the early stage of this kind of research, we decided to choose for our empirical context of our technology initially three OSS communities that have at least some common properties, so that any differences we could identify can be expected not to be totally based on differences e.g. in domain, user competencies, and the like. Moreover, we wanted to conduct a long-term study over many years, and this obviously implied a certain bias towards relatively successful communities that even had such longevity. As a consequence, we focus this paper on three long-lived communities in the bioinformatics sector, for which we could mine rich, if heterogeneous data for a longitudinal study over eleven years. The rest of the paper is organized as follows. Section 2 gives an overview of existing concepts for end-user integration in the RE process and the organization of RE process in OSS. Section 3 presents a methodology for the RE process discovery in OSS. The methodology is later applied to the data shown in Sect. 4. The results of our study are described in Sect. 5. Section 6 concludes the paper with advices for the organization of community-oriented software development.

2   Related Work

Requirements elicitation (RE) process has evolved from a generally technical to an end-user oriented process [1]. In order to facilitate the requirements negotiation with end-users, different approaches are proposed: mobile technologies [30], scenario-based RE process [33], group support systems [3]. Additionally, conceptual paradigms for end-user integration vary. Whilst von Hippel [13] suggests to identify the lead users (experts among product users) and collect their needs, Chesbrough [4] proposes to collect innovative ideas from the masses. Maiden et al. [21] advise to apply creative problem solving for innovative idea finding. Yet, the question remains - which tools and paradigms are robust to overcome challenges of community-oriented RE process?

In the following, different analysis methods relevant for the RE process exploration in OSS projects are presented.

2.1   Community Clustering

Over the past decade OSS projects have been investigated in numerous research studies [12,29]. OSS communities represent multi-layer hierarchical structures [6,7,38]. Despite various layer definitions proposed by OSS researchers, we can generalize that the core of the OSS community is a small group of developers, surrounded by a much bigger periphery. The requirements in OSS projects are traditionally based on the personal experience and the knowledge of the core developers. However, questions and suggestions from peripheral users trigger significant modifications in the OSS product [14,25].

In order to investigate the role of requirements coming from core and peripheral communities, they have to be separated. In [7] three different approaches to the identification of the core in OSS communities are compared, based on (1) information on the project Website or other resources; (2) the contribution frequencies; (3) the hierarchical clustering of the social characteristics. In case of the first method, the data on the project Website might be not up-to-date. As for the second method, the contribution log of a project does not always reflect a complete picture of personal efforts. In many projects, only a very small group of developers have the right to commit changes. Therefore, a committer is not necessary the author of the code she/he commits. Finally, the hierarchical clustering makes use of the expected properties of the core to be more dense and cohesive than the periphery. Especially in the context of non-predefined social structures, hierarchical clustering of OSS communities is the most suitable method.

2.2   Requirements Detection

The whole OSS project management takes place in publicly available open access infrastructures. Although the composition of the OSS project infrastructure varies significantly from project to project, most projects include at least mailing lists, a project page and/or wikipage, and a code repository. Requirements in OSS are continuously emerging within communication and development processes 'just-in-time' [8]. Requirements in the form of ideas, complaints, posthoc description and others are spread among the artifacts created by the OSS community members within the project infrastructures [28].

OSS communities and projects are evolving structures [38]. Thus, OSS processes undergo continuous change and need to be approached as dynamic systems. To perform dynamic analyses of OSS repositories, some researchers divide data in periods of fixed size [26], while others use time points of releases as a cutting criterion [36]. Considering the mechanics of OSS projects, their rhythms and iterations, a continuous cycle of design-analysis-development can be identified. At some point in time during the development process, a current branch is frozen for the next release. From that time on, only bug fixes are allowed. After the code is released, only hotfixes - small code updates which address specific problems in the last release - are possible. Hence, a period (t_j, t_{j+1}) between two releases j and $j + 1$ can be considered as a logical step for the dynamic analysis. This approach is consistent with the metrics and laws of software evolution [19].

2.3 Sentiment Analysis

The integration of end-users in the development process aims not only to get the access to the domain knowledge, but also to better the end-users attitude towards the end product. Thus, by measuring the mood within the community, we estimate the level of satisfaction among users. The mood of a user can be implicitly estimated based on opinionated documents generated by the user. Methods of sentiment analysis (SA) assign each user document (e.g. mailing list posting) either to a positive or to a negative class. Methods of SA are often applied to measure the mood of community-generated artifacts, for example blogposts [22]. Within the OSS knowledge mining domain, Jensen et al. [16] analyze the sentiment of OSS mail postings manually.

3 Methods: Requirements Engineering Framework for Process Discovery in OSS

In this section, we describe a method framework for RE process discovery from OSS process history data. Our approach combines several mining techniques which typically should be applied in the following sequence (with possible backtracks as usual):

- A community structure analysis separates core from one or more periphery layers, as we expect these layers to influence the OSS development process in different ways, and our special interest is more the periphery than the already well-understood core of such communities. In this structural analysis for long-lived communities, a special demand is the identification of change and evolution both in the product (OSS) and in the community structure. Here, we propose a release-based rather than a real-time based temporal structuring, and present techniques for its implementation.
- Adapted text mining techniques are employed to detect user requirements among the many messages, in our case studies mostly mail postings, found in the community logs.

- Last not least, we adapt sentiment analysis technologies in order to measure the degree of satisfaction within the different community layers in the different time periods of the community life, as one of the possible outcome measures.

In all phases, noise in the history data (ranging from system-generated messages to external spam, to discussions on topics outside the actual OSS tasks etc.) has proven a major impediment, so data cleaning is a challenge in all three major steps above; space is not sufficient to describe all techniques in detail here, but we shall at least mention the most important ones.

3.1 Structural Analysis of OSS Communities' Evolution

Prior to the mailing lists analysis, multiple aliases of the same individuals are detected and consolidated. Communications created by automated notification services like Bugzilla, Redmine and Nightly Build are excluded from the analysis. Next, for each period between two releases j and $j+1$, an OSS community under study is mapped to a social network graph structure: community members are represented by nodes, their interaction by edges. Thus, for the OSS project with k releases, we generate a sequence of k project graphs:

$$\{graph_{(0,1)}; graph_{(1;2)}; \ldots graph_{(j;j+1)}; \ldots graph_{(k+1;k)}\} \tag{1}$$

Edges are defined as follows. If at least one thread exists, in which two project participants have submitted at least one mail posting in a mailing list, a link between them is added to the project graph. To simplify the further analysis, the edges are unweighted. As previously stated, we assume that core and periphery of the OSS communities participate differently in the RE process. Hierarchical clustering is used in order to separate these two community layers. The method is based on social network properties of community members. In this study, we cluster communities based on degree centrality (the number of edges incident upon a node). The primary approach behind this method is shown in Algorithm 1. In order to track the evolution of periphery and core over time, periphery is separated from core in period between two releases j and $j + 1$ in the corresponding social network $graph_{(j;j+1)}$.

3.2 Requirements Detection Within the OSS Mailing Lists

In order to automatically extract postings from the OSS mailing lists which contain requirements, adapted text mining algorithms are applied. First, irrelevant (or even distorting) posts such as quotations, Spam, auto-generated bug reports and announcements are deleted [9]. After this data cleaning, the OSS mailing list postings are considered as bags of words: one posting - one document. Each document is modeled as a vector of features which correspond to terms in the corpus vocabulary.

For the classification tasks, the Naïve Bayes algorithm is applied. The Naïve Bayes technique is one of the most efficient classification learning algorithms [39].

Algorithm 1. Divide social network in two hierarchical layers $C_{periphery}$ and C_{core}

```
Require: Graph G = (V, E) with |V| = N nodes
    Calculate out-degree kᵢ for node i ∀i, 0 ≤ i ≤ N − 1
    Sort all nodes based on out-degree kᵢ in ascending order
Ensure: k_min < kᵢ ∀i, 0 ≤ i ≤ n − 1
    k = k_min; j = 0;
    while j ≤ N do
        Calculate out-degree of the vⱼ ∈ V node kⱼ
        if kⱼ < k then
            kⱼ = k
        else
            k = kⱼ
            Remove vⱼ : V = V/vⱼ and its edges
        end if
    end while
    Determine (vₕ; vₗ) with the largest |kₕ − kₗ|
    j=0;
    while j ≤ N do
        if kₕ ≥ kⱼ then
            Add vⱼ to C_core
        else
            Add vⱼ to C_periphery
        end if
    end while
```

It is based on a probabilistic generative model. In order to assign documents (=postings) either to **requirement** or to **non-requirement** groups based on their content, a domain specific lexicon optimized to the jargon of bioinformatics OSS projects is created and presented in the Table 1. In this context, the Bayes rule is defined as follows:

$$Pr(req|words) = \frac{Pr(words|req)Pr(req)}{Pr(words)} \qquad (2)$$

where $Pr(req|words)$ is the probability that a document classified to the class **requirements** contains certain **words** which identify this class. The number of requirements is calculated and normalized for each period between two releases $REQ(t_j, t_{j+1})$. To perform classification tasks, the open-source data mining framework RapidMiner is used [18].

3.3 Sentiment Within the OSS Communities

To measure the "mood" within the OSS layers, a proportion of postings with positive sentiment to the overall number of postings is monitored. We expect positive mood among peripheral OSS project participants to reflect the satisfaction with the system and in turn the success of the RE process. In order to

Table 1. Segment of domain specific lexicon for detecting requirements

leak	crack	enhancement	bug	defect
shortcoming	change	adjustments	alter	modify
shift	transform	complain	protest	disagree
mistake	slip	exception	anomaly	deviation
unsuccessful	breakdown	break	crash	fault
insufficiency	misconception	feature	characteristic	highlight
restore	settle	flag	signal	idea
virus	replace	inaccuracy	fail	incompleteness
hypothesis	inspiration	intention	opinion	incorrect
improvement	adjustment	contribution	correction	flow
enrichment	recovery	insufficient	lacking	missing
absent	non-existing	wanting	miss	necessary
mandatory	need	require	vital	want

estimate the polarity of mailing lists' postings, we created a classification model for our data set. We selected a Support Vector Machine (SVM) algorithm as a classification approach, because it showed the most convincing results in the sentiment analysis [24]. A basic SVM classifier applied upon a set of input data classifies each given input into one of two possible classes: POS and NEG. Initially, the training set has to be provided, in order to infer some general correspondence between the input data and classification groups. Following a particular training set of labeled examples, the learning algorithm constructs a decision rule which can then be used to predict the labels of new unlabeled examples. The decision rule is based on the linear distance function [20].

A sentiment classifier was trained on the polarity data set used by [23] to assign POS and NEG polarities to the mailing list posts. A training data set adapted to the OSS domain was used to improve model performance. The proportion of positive sentiment to the total amount of postings is calculated for each period between two releases j and $j + 1$:

$$\frac{|POS(Postings_{j;j+1})|}{|(Postings_{j;j+1})|} \tag{3}$$

Despite the fact that the training data set, adapted for the OSS domain, consists of 100 entries, the results were improved compared to the initial classification model.

4   Data

Our framework for the RE process discovery is applied to the three large-scale bioinformatics OSS projects: BioJava [15], Biopython [5] and BioPerl [32].

Hereafter, Bio* refers to the three OSS projects. Bioinformatics represents an interdisciplinary research field: innovative computer science technologies and algorithms are developed in order to answer current research questions of computational biology. Interdisciplinary development is indispensable. In the Bioinformatics OSS peripheral project participants are expected to be mainly biologists, who make their first steps towards software development. Thus, generally speaking such OSS also represent a rich approximation for end-user integration in general. The Bio* projects provide open-source bioinformatics frameworks for the manipulation of biological sequences and structures. The frameworks of Bio* projects are based on Java, Python or Perl respectively.

BioJava and Biopython started in 1999, while BioPerl has been already developed since 1996. The infrastructures of the projects include wikipages, developer and general discussion mailing lists, bug management systems and GIT repositories for code management. Table 2 summarizes the status of each project.

Table 2. Bio* OSS overview (on January 1, 2011)

Project	Messages	Users in mailing lists	Commits	Developers
BioJava	11951	2208	8267	94
Biopython	16108	1138	16868	29
BioPerl	31755	2824	12848	139

Beside conceptual similarity, the projects have a long history of over thirteen years, which provides an ideal basis not only for comparative but also comprehensive longitudinal analysis. The entire data set amounts to ca. 60 000 postings from the Bio* mailing lists in the period of eleven years (January 2000–January 2011). In the following section the co-evolution of community, requirements, development and sentiment within the bioinformatics OSS projects is presented. By taking a look at all four dimensions of results, our goal is to relate the changes in RE to the correct historical events in the OSS projects lifetime.

5   Results

To perform a release-based dynamic analysis, all releases in every project under study are identified. Our investigations show, that in eleven years there were 8 releases in BioJava, 26 in Biopython and 18 in BioPerl.

5.1   Structural Analysis of the OSS Projects

Our study shows that the core members in the Bio* projects are responsible for creating the majority of messages in the mailing lists and of the contributions to the code repositories. Furthermore, the core communities in Bio* projects consist of two to three permanent leaders who play a significant role in the project.

An additional two to three developers from the peripheral communities join the core groups temporarily. Hence, the core groups experience continuous change. Despite similarity in the average size of the core communities (six members), the total number of the project members considerably differs. This results in different proportions of the core size to the total community. The core ratio in the total community in Biopython is 12 %. In BioJava, the ratio is about 6 %, while in BioPerl, it is about 4 %.

BioPerl managed to cultivate the biggest periphery among the three projects under study. More detailed investigation on the Bio* communities shows that the BioPerl community has evolved to a complex structure: the highly active core of creators, the long-tail of lurkers with a very low activity, and the intermediate layer of contributors. This social distribution can be related to "90-9-1" structure from crowdsourcing.[3]

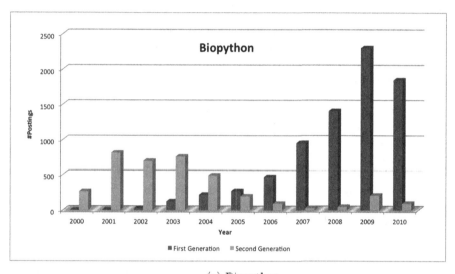

(a) Biopython

Fig. 1. Generation change in the Biopython project

In our study [11] we reported that we detected two generations in each of the Bio* projects. The central members of "first generation" were active near the first five years of the project. They also linked to all other project participants active during that period of time. During the next five years, new leaders together with other user layers formed a second community (= "second generation"). As an example, Fig. 1 presents the sum of postings written by the core of each generation year per year in the Biopython project. Due to their private, preferential or personal issues, people spend different amounts of time and

---

[3] http://www.nngroup.com/articles/participation-inequality/. For example, only 1 % of people create wikipedia-articles and 9 % modify and adjust them, the rest 90 % of wikipedia-users just use the content without any contribution.

effort for an OSS project. The displayed bar chart makes the generation switch obvious. Similar generation switch we observe in BioJava and BioPerl projects.

The generation switch introduces automatically detected changes in terms of sentiment within communities, development progress, requirements production/communication level/requirements creation in an OSS project. For instance, the substitution of the main contributors *Jeffrey C.* and *Brad C.* by *Peter C.* and *Michael H.* in Biopython led to a fivefold increase of releases and threefold increase of commits per year. The modification of the main concepts can induce people to leave an OSS community. The period of change of the core leaders is marked by the decrease of the development activity, especially in case of non-overlapping substitution. Interestingly, the generation switch happens around 2005 in all three projects.

5.2   Co-evolution of Requirements and Development

In the next stage of the RE process discovery framework, the explored social structures are connected to requirement creation and development progress. The amount of submitted software requirements from each sub-community (*core* and *periphery*) for each period (t_j, t_{j+1}) between two releases j and $j+1$ in every Bio* project is identified. An example of identified mail with requirement in the header text: *'Problems runing BLAST; blastall does not exist at blastcmd; New: Bug in PHYLIPFileBuilder with protein sequences.'* An example of identified mail with requirement in the content text: *"Looks like a good time to do the release. Yup, seems good. I guess there is only one request I have before release: Can we fix the tests that are failing? I think it would be nice if people could install biopython and not have tests failing on them. It seems like just some minor adjustments are all we need to do. Brad, how do you make the documentation? Do you have time to do that, or should I try and muddle through it?"* In order to get an approximate insight, if the detected requirements have influenced the project development, the correlation with general development activity is estimated during the release-periods.

In BioPerl, we observe the highest correlation coefficients for both core and periphery. Hence, the more requirements were submitted within the project, the more lines of code were implemented. In BioJava, again both core and periphery show the correlation. However, in this case the coefficients are much smaller indicating weaker influence of the requirements on the development progress. In Biopython, a small correlation could be identified only for the core sub-community. This may be linked to the fact that Biopython has the highest core/periphery ratio compared with other two projects. Due to the small periphery, the development of the Biopython project is perhaps driven by the core. This observation emphasizes the important role of the periphery and supports empirically the claim, that "OSS projects depend on the increase of the size of this user community" [31].

5.3   Sentiment Within the OSS Communities

End-user integration in the requirements negotiation is believed to improve the end-user attitude towards the developing system. To analyze whether the level of end-user participation in the requirements generation process influences the mood of peripheral community, sentiment analysis is applied to the mailing list postings. Our findings indicate that the general mood within Bio* projects is positive. In all three cases, approximately 60 % of mails from each project are classified to the POS group. However, there are several remarkable mood shifts, relevant to further investigation. Due to the space constraint, we provide an example of one community: Biopython. In this community a significant decrease in the number of positively marked messages from the periphery can be observed during period 29 to 37 This period correlates with a significant decrease in requirements fraction from peripheral project members. At the same time, the substitution of core leaders in Biopython happened. Biopython new core leaders, namely *Peter C.* and *Michiel H.* introduced new organizational principles: much shorter release iterations and continuous contribution of a high amount of changes to the code repository. The amount of submitted requirements from the periphery decreased compared to the core and the sentiment together with a great drop in activity within the peripheral community.

Such behavior is likely to be explained by negatively influenced sentiment. Negatively influenced sentiment in its turn can be caused by the fact that the development was mainly centered around the tasks that the community leaders found particularly useful for their own work. Despite not having positive attitude from the periphery, the development process intensively continued by a small group of active contributors from the core. This observation supports the leading role of core members in OSS development.

In BioJava, a decrease of sentiment in the peripheral community is observed during period 5. A more detailed analysis of this period shows that a very high amount of SPAM messages was submitted to the mailing lists [9]. For instance, out of 164 messages only 16 were not SPAM in the BioJava for the period of November, 2004. In the SPAM-free data set, we observe the negative mood within the project periphery. Enormous amount of SPAM annoys people subscribed to the project mailing lists. In [10], we detected the highest user outflow from the BioJava project in the period of the highest SPAM level in the project history. This further supports our assumption that high level of SPAM results in dissatisfaction within the community. During hotfix detection [10], we also discover an extremely large release within the BioJava project (33.5 times more edited lines of code than in most other releases). A manual analysis has shown, that this release was the result of complete restructuring of the project code base. The modification was executed in period 9. Although no sentiment reaction can be detected in the period-oriented view a more fine-granular overview (with a month as a step) shows that the modifications were first met with a negative reaction among peripheral project participants. After some time, the mood within the periphery became more positive again. Big reengineering and restructuring of a project usually has a long-term benefit while in the short run, peripheral members do not appropriate any changes. Restructuring of the project could mean for the peripheral members a need to rewrite their own programs, and therefore presents a short-term disadvantage.

BioPerl proved to be an example of an OSS project with the most "healthy" community and steady project development. Accordingly, the attitude towards the project by core and periphery is stable, both communities have more or less constant mood. The amount of submitted requirements from core and periphery are rather similar. The project development is triggered by the needs from the periphery and the core to the same extent.

6   Discussion and Conclusion

In this paper we proposed a framework for the requirements elicitation (RE) process discovery within OSS projects. The approach was successfully applied to the three bioinformatics OSS communities. Our study shows, that the communication in general and specifically the requirements stated within the community communication resources, give rise to the development process. However, when the core/periphery ratio exceeds 10 %, the development is mainly driven by requirements from the core leaders (**RQ2**). Hence, we do find a difference between the requirements contribution from the core and from the peripheral project participants (**RQ1**). For example, in BioPerl the periphery generates 58 % of requirements, while in BioJava and Biopython the peripheral requirements fraction is only 40 %.

The overall mood within the OSS communities is quite positive. Periods, when the periphery has almost no influence on the project, are marked by a decreasing level of satisfaction among the periphery (**RQ3**). Further, the mood of periphery gets more negative as a reaction to: (1) technical problems within project organization (e.g. high level of SPAM) and (2) major restructuring of the project. The organization of the RE process is mainly defined by the core leaders. The change of core leaders could be a stress factor for the community. In the most-established OSS projects within our study, the requirements from both core and periphery influence the development to a high extent. A stabilizing factor appears to be an intermediate layer of contributors coming from peripheral users. Based on the observed practices within the OSS communities, we hypothesize the following advices how to foster community building of end-users:

- Project managers and/or core developers, who will hold and lead the community need to be set. The management core should consists of 2–3 permanent project participants.
- Detect arising experts among the peripheral participants and motivate (provide special rewards) them to form an interlayer between the project managers and the community long-tail.
- Listen to the community needs, otherwise it will result in a negative mood and community shrinkage.
- Take care of the technology used for community management. Errors and disturbances within the community tools can chase the users away.
- In case of serious project restructuring, take time to explain the reasons for and advantages of the planned changes. Otherwise, it could cause some resistance of peripheral project participants.

Our findings are consistent with the few existing results of evolution studies achieved by other researchers. For example, [27] conducted a quantitative study of the evolution of the Debian community. The authors found out that the volunteer teams are dynamic and changeable over time, while their efforts are stable and reliable.

6.1 Threats to Validity

First, the quality of text and sentiment mining strongly depends on the quality of training data sets used for the classification models. These data sets have to be adapted for the OSS domain. Moreover, bioinformatics OSS projects are mostly driven by bioinformatics scientists and, therefore, presents an exploration-oriented [38] OSS. It is interesting further investigate Bio* communities in order to detect other sub-communities and their influence to development process. As also, further studies with domains outside bioinformatics are needed to achieve truly generalizable results.

Moreover, the quality of any data mining analysis is as good as the data. It can always happen, that some important decisions or negotiations take place privately. Cross examination of our automatically achieved results with other data acquisition methods such as interviews would thus be helpful to further validate our results. Within this work Bayes and SVM algorithms were used as the base for the requirements detection and opinion mining models. Those can be effectively extended by considering new achievements in the text mining discipline. For example, one of the possible ways to improve our sentiment classification model is to use the method based on Part-of-Speech (POS) tagging. Last but not least, in OSS mailing lists the same requirement can be described within various artifacts. Differently formulated identical ideas currently are classified as distinct requirements. The clustering model based on latent semantic analysis (LSA) can be used in order to identify similar requirements even if they do not share any common words.

References

1. Alexander, I.: Migrating towards co-operative requirements engineering. Comput. Control Eng. J. **10**(1), 17–22 (1999)
2. Bhowmik, T., Reddivari, S.: Resolution trend of just-in-time requirements in open source software development. In: Just In Time RE Workshop, Canada (2015)
3. Boehm, B., Grünbacher, P., Briggs, R.: Developing groupware for requirements negotiation: lessons learned. IEEE Softw. **18**(3), 46–55 (2001)
4. Chesbrough, W.: Open Innovation: The New Imperative for Creating and Profiting from Technology. Harvard Business School Press, Boston (2003)
5. Cock, P., Antao, T., Chang, J., Chapman, B., Cox, C., Dalke, A., Friedberg, I., Hamelryck, T., Kauff, F., Wilczynski, B., de Hoon, M.: Biopython: freely available python tools for computational molecular biology and bioinformatics. Bioinformatics **25**(11), 1422–1423 (2009)
6. Crowston, K., Howison, J.: Hierarchy and centralization in free and open source software team communications. Knowl. Technol. Policy **18**, 65–85 (2006)

7. Crowston, K., Wei, K., Li, Q., Howison, J.: Core and periphery in free/libre and open source software team communications. In: Proceedings of the 39th Annual Hawaii International Conference on System Sciences, HICSS 2006. IEEE Computer Society, Washington, D.C. (2006)
8. Ernst, A., Murphy, C.: Case studies in just-in-time requirements analysis. In: Proceedings of the Second IEEE International Workshop on Empirical Requirements Engineering (EmpiRE), pp. 25–32 (2012)
9. Hannemann, A., Hackstein, M., Klamma, R., Jarke, M.: An adaptive filter-framework for the quality improvement of open-source software analysis. In: Kowalewski, S., Rumpe, B. (eds.) Software Engineering. LNI, vol. 213, pp. 143–156. GI (2013)
10. Hannemann, A., Klamma, R.: Community dynamics in open source software projects: aging and social reshaping. In: Petrinja, E., Succi, G., El Ioini, N., Sillitti, A. (eds.) OSS 2013. IFIP AICT, vol. 404, pp. 80–96. Springer, Heidelberg (2013)
11. Hannemann, A., Klamma, R., Jarke, M.: Soziale Interaktion in OSS. Praxis der Wirtschaftsinformatik (2012)
12. Hauge, O., Ayala, C., Conradi, R.: Adoption of open source software in software-intensive organizations - a systematic literature review. Inf. Softw. Technol. 52(11), 1133–1154 (2010)
13. Hippel, E.: Lead users: a source of novel product concepts. Manag. Sci. 32(7), 791–805 (1986)
14. Hippel, E., Krogh, G.: Open source software and the "private-collective" innovation model: Issues for organization science. J. Organ. Sci. 14(2), 208–223 (2003)
15. Holland, R., Down, T., Pocock, M., Prlić, A., Huen, D., James, K., Foisy, S., Dräger, A., Yates, A., Heuer, M., Schreiber, M.J.: Biojava: an open-source framework for bioinformatics. Bioinformatics 24(18), 2096–2097 (2008)
16. Jensen, C., King, S., Kuechler, V.: Joining free/open source software communities: an analysis of newbies' first interactions on project mailing lists. In: Proceedings of the 44th Hawaii International Conference on System Sciences (HICSS), pp. 1–10 (2011)
17. Klamma, R., Spaniol, M., Cao, Y.: MPEG-7 compliant community hosting. J. Univ. Knowl. Manag. 1(1), 36–44 (2006)
18. Land, S., Fischer, S.: Rapid Miner in Academic Use (2012)
19. Lehman, M., Ramil, F., Wernick, D., Perry, E., Turski, M.: Metrics and laws of software evolution - the nineties view. In: Proceedings of the Fourth International Software Metrics Symposium, pp. 20–32 (1997)
20. Lovell, C., Walder, C.: Support vector machines for business applications. In: Voges, K., Pope, N. (eds.) Business Applications and Computational Intelligence, pp. 267–290. IGI Global, Hershey (2006)
21. Maiden, N., Jones, S., Karlsen, K., Neill, R., Zachos, K., Milne, A.: Requirements engineering as creative problem solving: a research agenda for idea finding. In: Proceedings of the 18th IEEE International Requirements Engineering Conference, pp. 57–66 (2010)
22. Melville, P., Gryc, W., Lawrence, D.: Sentiment analysis of blogs by combining lexical knowledge with text classification. In: Proceedings of the 15th ACM SIGKDD International Conference on Knowledge Discovery and Data Mining, KDD 2009, pp. 1275–1284. ACM, New York (2009)
23. Pang, B., Lee, L.: Opinion mining and sentiment analysis. Found. Trends Inf. Retrieval 2(1–2), 1–135 (2008)

24. Pang, B., Lee, L., Vaithyanathan, S.: Thumbs up?: Sentiment classification using machine learning techniques. In: Proceedings of the ACL-02 Conference on Empirical Methods in Natural Language Processing, EMNLP 2002, vol. 10, pp. 79–86. Association for Computational Linguistics, Stroudsburg (2002)

25. Raymond, E.: The Cathedral and the Bazaar. O'Reilly Media, New York (1999)

26. Robles, G., Gonzalez-Barahona, J.M.: Contributor turnover in libre software projects. In: Damiani, E., Fitzgerald, B., Scacchi, W., Scotto, M., Succi, G. (eds.) Open Source Systems, vol. 203, pp. 273–286. Springer, Boston (2006)

27. Robles, G., Gonzalez-Barahona, J.M., Michlmayr, M.: Evolution of volunteer participation in libre software projects: evidence from debian. In: Scotto, M., Succi, G. (eds.) Proceedings of the First International Conference on Open Source Systems, pp. 100–107 (2005)

28. Scacchi, W.: Understanding requirements for open source software. In: Lyytinen, K., Loucopoulos, P., Mylopoulos, J., Robinson, B. (eds.) Design Requirements Engineering. LNBIP, vol. 14, pp. 467–494. Springer, Heidelberg (2009)

29. Scacchi, W.: The future research in free/open source software development. In: Proceedings of ACM Workshop on the Future of Software Engineering Research (FoSER), Santa Fe, NM, pp. 315–319 (2010)

30. Seyff, N., Graf, F., Maiden, N.: Using mobile re tools to give end-users their own voice. In: Proceedings of the 18th IEEE International Requirements Engineering Conference, pp. 37–46 (2010)

31. Sowe, S.K.: Emerging Free and Open Source Software Practices. IGI Publishing, Hershey (2007)

32. Stajich, E., Block, D., Boulez, K., Brenner, E., Chervitz, A., Dagdigian, C., Fuellen, G., Gilbert, J., Korf, I., Lapp, H., Lehvaslaiho, H., Matsalla, C., Mungall, C., Osborne, B., Pocock, M., Schattner, P., Senger, M., Stein, L., Stupka, E., Wilkinson, M., Birney, E.: The bioperl toolkit: Perl modules for the life sciences. Genome Res. **12**(10), 1611–1618 (2002)

33. Sutcliffe, A.: Scenario-based requirements engineering. In: Proceedings of the 11th IEEE International Conference on Requirements Engineering, RE 2003, pp. 320–329. IEEE Computer Society, Washington, D.C. (2003)

34. Sutcliffe, A.: Evaluating the costs and benefits of end-user development. SIGSOFT Softw. Eng. Notes **30**(4), 1–4 (2005)

35. Vlas, R., Robinson, W.N.: A rule-based natural language technique for requirements discovery and classification in open-source software development projects. In: Proceedings of the 44th Hawaii International Conference on System Sciences (2011)

36. Wiggins, A., Howison, J., Crowston, K.: Heartbeat: measuring active user base and potential user interest in FLOSS projects. In: Boldyreff, C., Crowston, K., Lundell, B., Wasserman, A.I. (eds.) OSS 2009. IFIP AICT, vol. 299, pp. 94–104. Springer, Heidelberg (2009)

37. Wulf, V., Jarke, M.: The economics of end-user development: tools that empower users to create their own software solutions. Commun. ACM **47**(9), 41–42 (2004)

38. Ye, Y., Nakakoji, K., Yamamoto, Y., Kishida, K.: The co-evolution of systems and communities in free and open source software development. In: Koch, S. (ed.) Free/Open Source Software Development, pp. 59–82. Idea Group Publishing, Hershey (2004)

39. Zhang, H.: The optimality of naive bayes. In: Barr, V., Markov, Z. (eds.) FLAIRS Conference, pp. 562–567. AAAI Press, Miami Beach (2004)

OSSAP – A Situational Method for Defining Open Source Software Adoption Processes

Lidia López[1(✉)], Dolors Costal[1], Jolita Ralyté[2], Xavier Franch[1],
Lucía Méndez[1], and Maria Carmela Annosi[3]

[1] Universitat Politècnica de Catalunya (UPC), Barcelona, Spain
{llopez,dolors,franch}@essi.upc.edu,
emendez@lsi.upc.edu
[2] University of Geneva, Institute of Information Services Science,
Geneva, Switzerland
jolita.ralyte@unige.ch
[3] Ericsson Telecomunicazioni, Pagani, Italy
mariacarmela.annosi@ericsson.com

Abstract. Organizations are increasingly becoming Open Source Software
(OSS) adopters, either as a result of a strategic decision or just as a consequence
of technological choices. The strategy followed to adopt OSS shapes organizations' businesses; therefore methods to assess such impact are needed. In this
paper, we propose OSSAP, a method for defining **OSS A**doption business
Processes, built using a Situational Method Engineering (SME) approach. We
use SME to combine two well-known modelling methods, namely goal-oriented
models (using *i**) and business process models (using BPMN), with a
pre-existing catalogue of goal-oriented OSS adoption strategy models. First, we
define a repository of reusable method chunks, including the guidelines to apply
them. Then, we define OSSAP as a composition of those method chunks to help
organizations to improve their business processes in order to integrate the best
fitting OSS adoption strategy. We illustrate it with an example of application in a
telecommunications company.

Keywords: Situational method engineering · Open source software · i-Star

1 Introduction

Open Source Software (OSS) has become a driver for business in various sectors,
namely the primary and secondary IT sector. Organizations are increasingly becoming
OSS adopters, either as a result of a strategic decision or because it is almost
unavoidable nowadays, given the fact that most commercial software also relies at
some extent on OSS infrastructure: estimates exist that in 2016, a 95 % of all commercial software packages will include OSS components [1]. OSS adoption impacts far
beyond technology, because it requires a change in the organizational culture and
reshaping IT decision-makers mindset. Hence, the way in which organizations adopt
OSS shapes their business processes. In this context, methods for defining business
processes that tailor organizations to OSS adoption consequences are needed.

© Springer International Publishing Switzerland 2016
S. Nurcan et al. (Eds.): CAiSE 2016, LNCS 9694, pp. 524–539, 2016.
DOI: 10.1007/978-3-319-39696-5_32

In this paper, we propose OSSAP, a method for defining **OSS A**doption business Processes. The objective of OSSAP is to model the business processes that an organization needs in order to adopt OSS according to its strategic needs. In order to consider the variability of these strategic needs and the multiplicity of organizational situations to be taken into account, we use Situational Method Engineering (SME) [2] as approach to design our method as a composition of method chunks. In particular, we use the assembly-based SME approach that allows us to combine two well-known modelling frameworks, namely goal-oriented models (using $i*$ [3]) and business process models (using BPMN [4]) together with guidelines that focus on the OSS adoption strategies and its business processes. As a preliminary step, we will identify and define a set of method chunks to be used in this assembly-based approach.

The rest of the paper is organized as follows. Section 2 provides the background and general methodology of the paper. Section 3 describes the creation of the method chunks needed in our approach while Sect. 4 presents the design of the complete OSSAP method. Section 5 details an example of the application of the new method. Finally, Sects. 6 and 7 present discussion, conclusions and future work.

2   Background on SME and OSS Adoption

2.1   Situational Method Engineering

The discipline of Situational Method Engineering (SME) [2] promotes modularization and formalization of method knowledge in the form of autonomous and interoperable method components, and their composition into new methods taking into account the specific situation of the organization/project at hand. Such a modular definition of methods allows to achieve a better flexibility in method application and to ensure that the method takes all engineering situations into account and provides the best fitting guidance for each of them.

A detailed state of the art of the SME domain reveals various formalisations of method components as well as their assembly techniques [6]. For constructing the OSSAP method we apply the *assembly-based SME approach* [7] that supports new method construction as well as method extension by applying three steps: method requirements specification, method chunks selection and assembly of the selected chunks. Method chunks are reusable method components. A method chunk combines method process (i.e., the guidelines provided by the method chunk) and its related product knowledge (i.e., the formalisation of concepts and artefacts used by the method chunk). A method chunk also includes the situation in which it can be applied (i.e., the required input artefacts) and the intention (i.e. the engineering goal) to be reached.

Method chunks can be identified and defined in different ways. For instance, they can be created by reengineering existing methods into sets of reusable method chunks organized as strategic process models [8]. This reengineering variant (hereafter *reengineering SME*) is founded on the Map process modelling formalism [9], which allows to express methods in terms of intentions, and strategies to reach the intentions, instead of fixed steps and activities. Since many strategies can be defined for achieving an intention, Map allows to represent complex, flexible and situation-driven process models including multiple ways to achieve method intentions. Every section (i.e. a triplet <source intention, strategy, target intention>) in the process map is then assessed whether it represents autonomous and reusable method knowledge and in this case it is formalised as method chunk. If some map sections are not considered as such, the method map should be refined (e.g. by merging some intentions). Identified method chunks can be atomic or aggregate.

When no method exists, the *ad-hoc SME approach* [10] is more appropriate. In the ad-hoc approach, a method chunk is discovered as a means to satisfy some specific modelling purpose: the specific modelling domain must be analysed and method requirements supporting the engineering of this domain must be identified.

2.2   OSS Adoption

OSSAP builds upon a previous work [5] that we name *the DKE-approach* (after its publication venue) where we proposed a catalogue of $i*$ models to represent different OSS adoption strategies. These strategies were formulated by assigning in different ways the concepts of an OSS ontology into two actors that belong to an OSS ecosystem: the adopter organization and the OSS community that delivers the software.

The catalogue of adoption strategies is described in [5]. In short: (1) *OSS acquisition* consists in using existing OSS code without contributing to the underlying OSS project/community; (2) *OSS integration* implies the active participation of an organization in an OSS community with the purpose to share and co-create OSS in order to benefit from the commonly created OSS components; (3) *OSS initiative* consists in initiating an OSS project and establishing a community around it over which control is exercised; (4) *OSS takeover* means to take over an existing OSS project/community and to control it; (5) *OSS fork* consists in creating an own independent version of the software that is available from an existing OSS project or community; (6) *OSS release* implies that the organization releases bespoke software as OSS but does not care whether an OSS community forms around it.

2.3   Overall Strategy for Designing the OSSAP Method

As commented above, we will use the assembly-based SME approach to deliver the OSSAP method; this will be explained in detail in Sect. 4. Since the second step of assembly-based SME requires the selection of existing method chunks, in Sect. 3 we will construct such a catalogue in the basis of the needs of our method: some chunks for OSS adoption and some for process models:

- For the first subset, we will apply reengineering SME to the DKE-approach. The resulting subset supports the business analysts during the process of obtaining an $i*$ model for OSS adoption tailored to the strategic needs of a specific organization.
- For the second subset we will apply the ad-hoc SME approach. These new method chunks guide the analysts to obtain the BPMN business processes that implement the strategic goals from such $i*$ model.

3   A Catalogue of Method Chunks for the OSSAP Method

In this section we describe the creation of the method chunks that are used as starting point to design the OSSAP method that will be presented in Sect. 4. First, we focus on the method chunks for obtaining the OSS adoption strategies and then on those for obtaining the OSS business processes to implement them.

3.1   Method Chunks for Defining OSS Adoption Strategies

We have applied the re-engineering SME method [8] on the DKE-approach [5]. As explained in Sect. 2.1, the reengineering SME recommends to redefine first the process model of the existing method by using the Map formalism. Then the process map sections are formalised as method chunks. We develop next these two steps.

Step 1: OSS Adoption Process Map Construction. The DKE-approach is described in detail in [5]. Its process map is shown in Fig. 1. The initial intention is to document the organization business and its strategic goals (I1). As suggested by the DKE-approach, this intention is achieved by using $i*$ goal-oriented modelling as strategy (S1). Then, the DKE-approach proposes a two-step process with intentions: selecting the appropriate OSS adoption strategy from a predefined set of candidates (I2) and upgrading the organizational goal model with the goals defined in the selected strategy model (I3). To satisfy intention I2, the DKE-approach proposes (S2) the catalogue of OSS adoption $i*$ models described in Sect. 2.2 and a set of coverage metrics that measure the similarity of each of them with the organizational model. I3 is achieved by merging the organizational goal model with that of the selected strategy (S3).

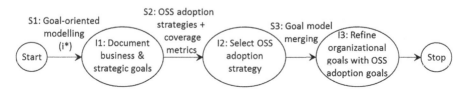

Fig. 1. Process map for defining OSS adoption strategies

Step 2: Method Chunks Identification and Construction. As explained in Sect. 2.1, the identification of method chunks is based on the analysis of the process map sections. The process map resulting from Step 1 is composed of three sections: <Start, S1, I1>, <I1, S2, I2>, <I2, S3, I3>. We consider each of these map sections as reusable method knowledge and accordingly we identify three method chunks:

- MC1: Goal modelling with $i*$. It corresponds to the $i*$ modelling framework [3].
- MC2: OSS adoption strategy selection. Provides the guidelines to select OSS adoption strategies as described in the DKE-approach [5]. Since these guidelines include a catalogue of candidate models (see Sect. 2.2), MC2 can be considered as

an aggregate method chunk and each of the six OSS adoption strategy models as a sub-chunk, MC2.1-MC2.6 (e.g., MC2.1 is OSS Acquisition adoption strategy).

- MC3: $i*$ model merging. Provides the guidelines to merge goal models as described in the DKE-approach [5].

We present three of the identified method chunks using a tabular representation based on the method chunk metamodel [8]. The process and product parts are presented in an abridged form. Table 1 describes the MC2 aggregate method chunk. Its process part guides the business analyst to select the adoption strategy which best covers the organizational goals. For each adoption strategy there is a corresponding sub-chunk.

Table 1. Method chunk for selecting an OSS adoption strategy

Identifier	MC2: OSS adoption strategy selection
Situation	Goal model representing organizational goals using the $i*$ framework
Intention	Select an OSS adoption strategy by using coverage metrics
Process part	*Product part*
1. Evaluate the coverage metrics using the organizational goal model and each of the following method chunks: "OSS Acquisition adoption strategy", "OSS Integration adoption strategy", "OSS Initiative adoption strategy", "OSS Takeover adoption strategy", "OSS Fork adoption strategy" and "OSS Release adoption strategy". 2. Select the most suitable adoption strategy according to the resulting measures. Some qualitative evaluation among similar coverage results can be needed.	• $i*$ model corresponding to the selected OSS adoption strategy (defined in the corresponding sub-chunk). • Definition of the coverage metrics provided by the DKE-approach (see [5], Sect. 6.1).

Table 2 presents the sub-chunk MC2.1 for the OSS Acquisition adoption strategy. All the sub-chunks for adoption strategies share a similar structure: situation: represents the decision to adopt the strategy; intention: documenting the goals related to the strategy; process: application of the proposed model; product: the $i*$ model representing the strategy. The Acquisition strategy implies to use OSS without contributing to the supporting OSS community. The product model shows how the OSS adopter only obtains and uses the component from the OSS community and does not give back any return to it. Therefore, only outgoing dependencies stem from the adopter actor and it depends on the community to obtain the OSS component and its documentation.

Finally, Table 3 describes the method chunk to refine organizational goals with the goals of an adoption strategy (MC3). Its process part consists in the application of guidelines to merge goal models. This method chunk is described in a way that can be applied to any context that requires merging two $i*$ models, making it highly reusable.

3.2   Method Chunks for Defining OSS Business Processes

In this section we describe the creation of method chunks for obtaining the OSS business processes that an organization should implement to attain the goals of its selected OSS adoption strategy. To our knowledge there are not existing proposals to define business process models for OSS adoption, so the reengineering SME method applied in Sect. 3.1 is not applicable. Instead, we have applied the ad-hoc approach in which the method chunk construction is made from scratch (see Sect. 2.1) [10].

Table 2. Method chunk for the OSS Acquisition adoption strategy

Identifier	MC2.1: OSS Acquisition adoption strategy
Situation	Decision to acquire OSS
Intention	Documenting goals related to the OSS Acquisition adoption strategy

Process part: use the proposed goal model for documenting organization's goals.
Product part:

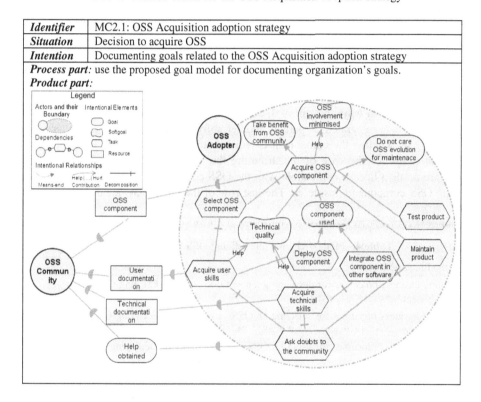

Method Chunk Identification. We have elicited the goals that represent requirements that the adopter organization must fulfil to apply each strategy from the adoption strategy *i** models (one shown in Table 2 and the rest available in [5]). These goals have led to the identification of method chunks for defining a specific OSS business process aimed at their satisfaction. In Table 4, we list those goals as method requirements together with their associated method chunks. For instance, the goal *OSS component used* from the OSS Acquisition strategy (see Table 2) has yield to the requirement *Defining business processes for using an OSS component* (third row in

Table 3. Method chunk for merging two *i** goal models

Identifier	MC3: *i** model merging
Situation	Two goal models which are conceptually overlapping
Intention	Merge two related goal models into a more general one, by unifying intentional elements that are shared in both of them

Process part	*Product part*
1. Merge both models applying a semantic similarity notion (see the DKE-approach as example [5]). 2. Making the necessary adjustments to the resulting model in order to resolve any possible inconsistency or ambiguity.	• Two *i** models with some conceptual overlap. • Definition of the merge rules provided by the DKE-approach (see [5], Sect. 6.2).

Table 4). There are three method chunks for it because the adoption strategy *i** models [5] include different ways to achieve it, depending on whether the component is simply deployed or it is integrated as part of another software artefact or, in the latter case, depending on whether the component is redistributed or not (i.e., OSS licenses define different rights for the case of redistributing the software [11] since the distributed software needs a license compatible with the OSS component license and the licenses of the OSS components inside it). The last row of the table provides the requirement

Table 4. Method chunks for Defining OSS business processes

Method requirement	Method chunk identified
Defining business processes for developing a new OSS component	MC4: Creating OSS
Defining business processes for selecting an OSS component	MC5: Selecting OSS
Defining business processes for using an OSS component	MC6: Deploying OSS
	MC7: Integrating and redistributing OSS
	MC8: Integrating OSS without redistributing it
Defining business processes for contributing to an OSS community	MC9: Reporting bugs about OSS
	MC10: Patching OSS
	MC11: Supporting OSS Community
Defining business processes for exercising the leadership of an OSS community	MC12: Leading OSS Community
Defining business processes for creating a community around an OSS component	MC13: Creating OSS Community
Defining business processes for OSS adoption	MC14: Defining OSS Adoption Business Processes

Defining business processes for OSS adoption which embraces all the previous ones and leads to the identification of a method chunk which is the aggregation of all the rest which can be seen as its sub-chunks.

Method Chunk Construction. When constructing new method chunks from scratch, theory plus best practice facilitates the initial definition of chunks [6]. Therefore, we have based our method chunk construction on the allocation of OSS adoption activities and resources from the OSS RISCOSS ontology [5, 12] (partially based on OFLOSSC [13]) to the method chunks; in other words, the business processes related to the method chunks should include the allocated activities and resources. The allocation has been based on the RISCOSS ontology definitions together with the expert knowledge from the RISCOSS EU-funded project industrial partners (www.riscoss.eu). Table 5 provides this allocation for one of the method chunks that we have identified, namely *MC10: Patching OSS*. According to the ontology, patching OSS refers to the development of a patch to correct some bug or add some new feature to an OSS component.

Table 6 describes the *Patching OSS* method chunk. Its situation reflects that it must be applied when an organization has as part of its adoption strategy the goal of providing patches to an OSS community. Its product part consists in a BPMN diagram with the activities and resources allocated to the chunk organized in a process.

Table 5. Allocation of activities and resources from the RISCOSS ontology

Method chunk	Activities	Resources
Patching OSS	Develop Patch, Test, Discuss Solutions, Commit Code, Send Patches, Acquire Legal Skills, Acquire Technical Skills, Acquire Management Skills	Patch, Solution Message, OSS License, Administrator Manual, API Documentation, Defect List, Developer Manual, Release Note, User Manual, Governance Documentation

This chunk has activities devoted to acquire the needed skills to develop patches for OSS, activities needed to develop the patch and reporting it to the OSS community and, in case the adopter organization is allowed to do it, the commit to incorporate the patch to the OSS component. All these activities come from the RISCOSS ontology except for: (1) *Acquire Community Practice Skills* and *Acquire Technical Quality Knowledge* which, actually, specialise an activity from the ontology, *Acquire Management Skills*, because only the part of the governance documentation related to community practices and quality policies is needed by the adopter to know how to develop the patching process and (2) *Report Patches* which is a specialization of *Discuss solutions*. All resources come from the RISCOSS ontology although the resource *Governance documentation* has been split into three: *Licensing Policies, Quality Policies and Community Practices* in order to distinguish the different parts of the governance documentation that are needed for different activities.

Table 6. Description of the patching OSS method chunk

Identifier	MC10: Patching OSS
Situation	Patching OSS is an organizational goal
Intention	Defining OSS adoption business processes by contributing to an OSS community

Process part: use the proposed process model.

Product part:

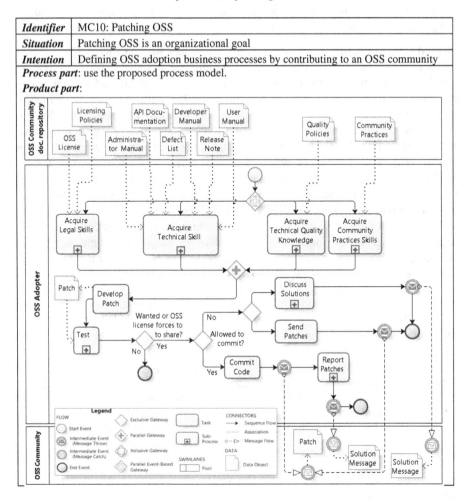

Table 7 describes the aggregate method chunk *MC14: Defining OSS Adoption Business Processes*. Its process part provides the criteria to discriminate which of the chunks for defining OSS business processes (MC4 – MC13) must be applied in a specific case according to the strategic goals of an organization.

4   OSSAP Method Design

To design the OSSAP method we apply the assembly-based approach outlined in Sect. 2.1 [7] using the method chunks identified in Sect. 3.

Table 7. Defining OSS adoption business processes method chunk

Name	MC14: Defining OSS adoption business processes
Situation	Goal model representing organizational goals
Intention	Defining business processes for OSS adoption
Process part: 1. For each chunk with intention *Defining OSS adoption business processes* (MC4 – MC13), check if the organizational goals include a goal matching with the situation of the method chunk. 2. If there is such a goal apply the method chunk.	*Product part:* BPMN diagrams imple-menting the OSS adoption strategic goals of the organization.

4.1 OSSAP Method Requirements Specification

The purpose of the OSSAP method is, first, to help organizations to refine their organizational goal models following an adequate OSS adoption strategy and, then, complement this with the OSS business processes describing the activities that the organization should undertake to implement the adoption strategy selected. In fact this is quite close to the intentions uncovered in Sect. 3.1 for the DKE-approach, therefore we decide to extend its process map (see Fig. 1) with the intention of obtaining OSS-aware business processes.

The final process map of the OSSAP method is illustrated in Fig. 2; plain lines indicate the intentions and strategies inherited from the DKE-approach, while dashed lines represent the new requirements. Only one new intention has been elicited: *Define OSS-aware business processes* (I4), and two new strategies: *Goal-elicitation techniques by reuse* (S1b), complementing the existing goal-oriented method to achieve I1; and *Process modelling (BPMN)* (S4) to achieve the new intention I4. The next sub section describes the chunk selection for these new strategies.

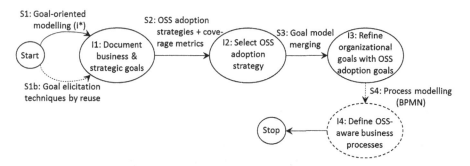

Fig. 2. Process map of the OSSAP method

4.2   OSSAP Method Chunks Selection

For the *Goal-elicitation techniques by reuse* strategy, we have selected to use as method chunk the set of *Business & OSS goals catalogues* (MC15) presented in [14]. OSSAP uses two of such catalogues: (1) the generic business goals catalogue, related to the external environment and the strategic organizational components (e.g., to consolidate market position); (2) the generic OSS goals catalogue, related to OSS adoption goals that any organization might want to achieve independently from the adoption strategy chosen (e.g., to avoid vendor/consultant lock-in).

For achieving the new intention I4 of defining OSS business processes, we use the new chunks created for this purpose described in Sect. 3.2 which already use BPMN as process modelling technique.

4.3   OSSAP Method Chunks Assembly

In the assembly-based SME approach, there are two assembly strategies: *association* and *integration* [7]. Association is used when the method chunks to assemble do not overlap in terms of intention to achieve and product to construct, for example when the results of one chunk are used as an input in the other. Integration is used when the chunks have similar engineering goals and their product models overlap.

The existing *MC1: Goal modelling with i** (see Sect. 3.1) and the new *MC15: Business & OSS goals catalogues* (see Sect. 4.2) are the method chunks selected for the strategies that reach I1. They share the same engineering goal, namely eliciting organizational goals; in addition, since the process of elicitation and documenting goals can be an iterative process, both can be combined and used in indistinct order. In this context, the integration strategy has to be used because both chunks contain the concept of goal (in the product part) and goals in the catalogues can be used in the *i** models as goals (or softgoals). It consists in simple merging of the common concepts; no naming problems have been identified.

On the other hand, the method chunks MC1 – MC3 selected for the strategies that attain the first three intentions (I1, I2 and I3) produce *i** goal models while the method chunks MC4 – MC14 selected to attain I4 produce BPMN models. Hence, we have two kinds of models: *i** and BPMN focusing on different, complementary aspects of an organization. These method chunks deal with complementary engineering goals and the simple association strategy is sufficient to assembly them, which consist in identifying links between concepts of different method chunks and ordering method chunks application. In OSSAP we consider that all the processes in business process modelling are defined to achieve a specific goal. Therefore, we need to create an association between process and goal concepts to establish the link between the selected OSS business process and the corresponding goal in the *i** model.

5   OSSAP Application: The TEI Case

We present the application of the OSSAP method to Ericsson Telecomunicazioni Italy (TEI). TEI is a division of Ericsson, one of the world's leading telecommunication corporations. One of TEI's roles within the Ericsson ecosystem is providing knowledge and expertise on OSS alternative to support efficient third party product handling. All organizational processes in TEI are defined in a detailed way and thus the rigour of OSSAP is well-suited to the company. OSSAP can help TEI in being aware about which processes they need to embrace according to their strategic needs when using an OSS component instead of proprietary software.

According to the OSSAP process map (Fig. 2), the application to the TEI case has been divided on the achievement of the four intentions reported below. The first three are only briefly described since they have been presented in detail in [5]; still we include them to make the paper self-contained.

- **Intention 1. Document TEI business and strategic goals**. We apply the method chunk *MC1: Goal modelling with i** in order to obtain the TEI organizational model as starting point. A significant except of this model appears in [5].
- **Intention 2. Select the TEI OSS adoption strategy**. We apply the method chunk *MC2: OSS adoption strategy selection*. From its sub-chunks, TEI selects *MC2.2: OSS integration adoption strategy*. [4] presents the full implementation of this chunk, applying the coverage metrics defined therein.
- **Intention 3. Refine TEI organizational goals model with the selected strategy.** We apply the method chunk *MC3: i* model merging* in order to refine the documentation of the TEI organizational goal model. Figure 3 shows a significant excerpt of this model (different from the one presented in [5]).
- **Intention 4. Define the OSS-aware TEI business processes.** We apply the aggregate method chunk *MC14: Defining OSS Adoption Business Processes* to select the adequate sub-chunks. In Table 8 we list the goals in the refined TEI organizational model that have led to a selection together with the chunks selected.

For instance, one of the intentional elements of the TEI organizational model was *Integrate* as a means to use an OSS component integrating it in a software product (G3 in Table 8 and also one of the intentional elements appearing in Fig. 3). This goal matches the situation of two different chunks that provide business processes for two cases of implementing OSS integration: *Integrating and redistributing OSS* and *Integrating without redistributing it*. The business processes for these two cases are different because there are legal implications regarding OSS licenses that must be dealt differently when the adopter wants to redistribute the software. If the software is not redistributed, license compliances issues may not have to be checked. Actually, depending on the contextual information and business scenario, TEI applies any of the chunks related to using an OSS component (goal *OSS component used* in TEI goal model): sometimes they need to supply an OSS operating system (*Deploying OSS* chunk), or use OSS libraries to be included in their software systems (*Integrating and redistributing OSS* chunk), or use some OSS components to be integrated in the software they use internally (*Integrating OSS without redistributing it*). Another intentional element in TEI organizational model was *Develop patches* (G5 in Table 8 and also one of the intentional elements appearing in Fig. 3) because it is a means to contribute to the OSS community that helps the OSS component evolve towards the features desired by TEI. It matches the *Patching OSS* method chunk (described in detail in Sect. 3). The effect of this method chunk application will be that the Table 6 business process diagram will be incorporated to TEI business processes in order to

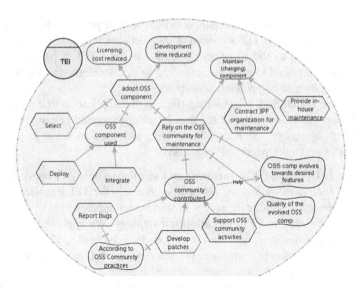

Fig. 3. Excerpt of TEI's organizational model adhering to the OSS integration adoption strategy

Table 8. Application of defining OSS adoption business processes (MC14) to the TEI case

Goal	Method chunks selected
G1: Select	MC5: Selecting OSS
G2: Deploy	MC6: Deploying OSS
G3: Integrate	MC7: Integrating and redistributing OSS
	MC8: Integrating OSS without redistributing it
G4: Report bugs	MC9: Reporting bugs about OSS
G5: Develop patches	MC10: Patching OSS
G6: Support OSS community activities	MC11: Supporting OSS community

implement the *Develop patches* intention. When TEI implements the *Patching OSS* process (see Table 6), since they are not interested on making public their code, they always go through the activity *Discuss solution* in the process defined by the chunk.

6 Discussion

In this section we analyze the relationships existing between the new method chunks for obtaining OSS business processes and the six OSS adoption strategies from the DKE-approach [5]. Since the method chunks have been identified from the goals of the OSS adoption strategies (see Sect. 3.2), clear relationships exist between them as can be seen in Table 9. Columns correspond to adoption strategies and rows to OSS business process method chunks. A dark cell means that the method chunk is mandatory to implement one of the goals of the adoption strategy (e.g. a fork strategy implies creating an OSS community in all cases). A grey cell means that the adoption

Table 9. Method chunks for OSS adoption strategies (black cell: mandatory, grey: optional).

Method chunks for defining OSS business processes	Acqui-sition	Inte-gration	Initia-tive	Takeo-ver	Fork	Rele-ase
MC4: Creating OSS			■		■	
MC5: Selecting OSS	■	■		■	■	▨
MC6: Deploying OSS	▨	▨	▨	▨	▨	
MC7: Integrating and redistributing OSS	▨	▨	▨	▨	▨	
MC8: Integrating OSS without redistributing it	▨	▨	▨	▨	▨	
MC9: Reporting bugs about OSS		■	■	■	■	
MC10: Patching OSS		▨	■	■	■	
MC11: Supporting OSS Community		▨	■	▨	▨	
MC12: Leading OSS Community					▨	
MC13: Creating OSS Community			■		■	

strategy may require or not that method chunk (e.g. an integration strategy may require patching OSS or not). This optionality comes from the fact that, for some adoption goals, there are several business processes that can be used to achieve them.

Beyond pure engineering aspects, it is also worth mentioning the conceptual difference between the DKE-approach and the OSSAP method. Whilst the DKE-approach assumed that the OSS adoption strategies behaved as a kind of high level patterns to be applied in all organizational contexts, the situational nature of OSSAP recognizes the fundamental diversity that may exist in each and every OSS adopter organization. As Table 9 shows, too many aspects exist that are configurable in every strategy. This is why we consider OSSAP a step beyond the real context in OSS adoption. Still, the work done while designing the DKE-approach has been crucial to generate OSSAP. We may sense that the formulation of OSSAP starts a second cycle in a design science approach [15] after the validation done in practice of the former DKE-approach.

7 Conclusions and Future Work

In this paper we have proposed a method for defining OSS Adoption business Processes (OSSAP). It has been designed using the assembly-based situational method engineering (SME) approach. Applying SME allows us to reuse the existing method presented in [5] (DKE-approach) and complementing it with a set of new chunks defining business process in BPMN related to OSS adoption. The process model of OSSAP is formalised using the Map formalism. This map proposes four intentions and several strategies to achieve them. The first three intentions embody the selection of the OSS adoption strategy that best fits with the organization's goals, and the last one aims to identify business processes to fulfil them. The main contributions of this work are:

(1) The OSSAP method, which allows us to derive OSS-aware business process models from the combination of the starting organizational model and the OSS adoption strategy chosen and (2) A set of method chunks that can be reused in contexts other than OSSAP. They are general-purpose, e.g. the $i*$ framework method chunk, or domain-specific, as the set of method chunks for the adoption strategies.

Using SME for building OSSAP facilitates its extension. If new strategies for OSS adoption emerge, OSSAP could integrate them as new method chunks. In addition, OSSAP addresses the definition of business processes related to OSS adoption but the approach could be generalized to other kinds of processes, e.g., quality assurance.

To our knowledge, in spite of the huge OSS body of knowledge, this is the first attempt to systematically embody the consequences of OSS adoption into organizational business processes. Other approaches that analyse OSS adoption as for instance Chang et al.'s [16], Daffara's [17] and Dornan's [18] provide classification criteria for OSS business models that rely on the concrete way in which OSS components are adopted in the organization. However, they do not make any attempt to systematically describe the business processes implied by these adoption strategies (they are discursive papers) and do not link these processes to intentions or goals.

The TEI example of application has been used as a preliminary validation of the applicability of OSSAP. As it was mentioned in [5] related to the first part of the method (selecting the OSS adoption strategy), independently of the complexity of the organizational models, the portion of these models involved in the selection of the OSS adoption strategy are not expected to grow in a way that they will be unmanageable. On the other side, the number of identified business processes is quite small, allowing us to keep the level of complexity of their selection low. Of course, further validation or this statement is required.

Future work addresses the validation of OSSAP in other OSS adopter organizations in order to properly finalize this design cycle. Also we will analyse the possibility of making the process maps more abstract in order to explore other possible strategies for implementing their intentions. Therefore, we could substitute the selection of techniques in the strategies ($i*$, BPMN and reuse-based elicitation) and leave room for other method chunks as KAOS [19], SPEM [20] or GRAM [21], respectively.

Acknowledgments. This work is a result of the RISCOSS project, funded by the EC 7th Framework Programme FP7/2007-2013, agreement number 318249. It was also supported by the Spanish project EOSSAC (TIN2013-44641-P).

References

1. Driver, M.: Hype cycle for open-source software. Technical report, Gartner (2013)
2. Henderson-Sellers, B., Ralyté, J., Ågerfalk, P., Rossi, M.: Situational Method Engineering. Springer, Heidelberg (2014)
3. Yu, E.: Modelling strategic relationships for process reengineering. Ph.D. thesis, University of Toronto, Toronto, Ontario, Canada (1995)
4. Object Management Group (OMG): Business process model and notation (BPMN), version 2.0. Technical report, January 2011

5. López, L., Costal, D., Ayala, C.P., Franch, X., Annosi, M.C., Glott, R., Haaland, K.: Adoption of OSS components: a goal-oriented approach. Data Knowl. Eng. **99**, 17–38 (2015)

6. Henderson-Sellers, B., Ralyté, J.: Situational method engineering: state-of-the-art review. J. Univers. Comput. Sci. **16**(3), 424–478 (2010)

7. Ralyté, J., Rolland, C.: An assembly process model for method engineering. In: Dittrich, K.R., Geppert, A., Norrie, M. (eds.) CAiSE 2001. LNCS, vol. 2068, pp. 267–283. Springer, Heidelberg (2001)

8. Ralyté, J., Rolland, C.: An approach for method reengineering. In: Kunii, H.S., Jajodia, S., Sølvberg, A. (eds.) ER 2001. LNCS, vol. 2224, pp. 471–484. Springer, Heidelberg (2001)

9. Rolland, C., Prakash, N., Benjamen, A.: A multi-model view of process modelling. Requirements Eng. J. **4**(4), 169–187 (1999)

10. Ralyté, J.: Towards situational methods for information systems development: engineering reusable method chunks. In: Proceedings of the International Conference on Information Systems Development (ISD 2004), pp. 271–282 (2004)

11. Rosen, L.: Open Source Licensing. Prentice Hall, Upper Saddle River (2004)

12. Ayala, C., Costal, D., Franch, X, Franco, O.H., López, L., Morandini, M., Siena, A.: D1.3 Modelling support (Consolidated Version). Technical report, RISCOSS FP7 project (2014)

13. Mirbel, I.: OFLOSSC, an ontology for supporting open source development Communities. In: Proceedings of the 11th International Conference on Enterprise Information Systems (ICEIS 2009), SAIC, pp. 47–52 (2009)

14. Tapia, L.M., López, L., Ayala, C.P., Annosi, M.C.: Towards an OSS adoption business impact assessment. In: Ralyté, J., et al. (eds.) PoEM 2015. LNBIP, vol. 235, pp. 289–305. Springer, Heidelberg (2015). doi:10.1007/978-3-319-25897-3_19

15. Wieringa, R.: Design Science Methodology for Information Systems and Software Engineering. Springer, Heidelberg (2014)

16. Chang, V., Mills, H., Newhouse, S.: From open source to long-term sustainability: review of business models and case studies. In: Proceedings of All Hands Meeting, OMII-UK Workshop (2007)

17. Daffara, C.: Business models in FLOSS-based companies. In: Proceedings of the Open-Source Software in Economic and Managerial Perspective Workshop (OSSEMP 2007) (2007)

18. Dornan, A.: The five open source business models. Information Week (2008)

19. Dardenne, A., van Lamsweerde, A., Fickas, S.: Goal-directed requirements acquisition. Sci. Comput. Program. **20**(1–2), 3–50 (1993)

20. Object Management Group (OMG): Software & systems process engineering meta-model specification (SPEM), version 2.0. Technical report, April 2008

21. Antón, A., Potts, C.: The use of goals to surface requirements for evolving systems. In: IEEE Proceedings of the 20th International Conference on Software Engineering (ICSE 1998), pp. 157–166 (1998)

Business Process Management

Narrowing the Business-IT Gap in Process Performance Measurement

Han van der Aa[1]([✉]), Adela del-Río-Ortega[2], Manuel Resinas[2],
Henrik Leopold[1], Antonio Ruiz-Cortés[2], Jan Mendling[3], and Hajo A. Reijers[1,4]

[1] Department of Computer Sciences, VU University Amsterdam,
Amsterdam, The Netherlands
`j.h.vander.aa@vu.nl`
[2] Dpto. de Lenguajes y Sistemas Informticos, University of Seville, Seville, Spain
[3] Institute for Information Business, WU, Vienna, Austria
[4] Department of Mathematics and Computer Science,
Eindhoven University of Technology, Eindhoven, The Netherlands

Abstract. To determine whether strategic goals are met, organizations must monitor how their business processes perform. Process Performance Indicators (PPIs) are used to specify relevant performance requirements. The formulation of PPIs is typically a managerial concern. Therefore, considerable effort has to be invested to relate PPIs, described by management, to the exact operational and technical characteristics of business processes. This work presents an approach to support this task, which would otherwise be a laborious and time-consuming endeavor. The presented approach can automatically establish links between PPIs, as formulated in natural language, with operational details, as described in process models. To do so, we employ machine learning and natural language processing techniques. A quantitative evaluation on the basis of a collection of 173 real-world PPIs demonstrates that the proposed approach works well.

Keywords: Performance measurement · Process performance indicators · Model alignment · Natural language processing

1 Introduction

Process Performance indicators (PPIs) play an important role in monitoring the performance of a process [12]. Defining and measuring suitable PPIs are key tasks for aligning strategic business objectives with the operational implementation of a process [22]. A major problem in this regard is that the formulation of

H.A. Reijers—This work has received funding from the European Commission (FEDER), the European Unionś Horizon 2020 research and innovation programme under the Marie Sklodowska-Curie grant agreement No 645751 (RISE_BPM), the Spanish and the Andalusian R&D&I programmes (grants TIN2012–32273 (TAPAS), TIC–5906 (THEOS) and COPAS (P12–TIC-1867)).

© Springer International Publishing Switzerland 2016
S. Nurcan et al. (Eds.): CAiSE 2016, LNCS 9694, pp. 543–557, 2016.
DOI: 10.1007/978-3-319-39696-5_33

PPIs is typically a *managerial* concern, while the monitoring of PPIs requires a *technical* perspective on a process [26]. The resultant gap, representative of the well-known *Business-IT-Gap* (cf. [11,14]), leads to a mismatch between the definitions of PPIs on the one hand and the process models that describe the actual implementation of processes on the other. This mismatch can result in PPI descriptions that refer to concepts of managerial interests that do not appear in the technical process definition.

The monitoring of process performance is furthermore hindered by the fact that managers frequently start out to provide relevant indicators in the form of unstructured natural language descriptions [24,26]. In order to compute values for these PPIs, the concepts contained in these textual PPI descriptions must be linked to their corresponding process model elements [23]. Currently, the only way to obtain these links is through manual identification. The effort associated with such a manual identification is considerable and, in many cases, hardly manageable due to the vast number of process models and accompanying PPIs that exist in organizations. Specifically, manual alignment actions do not scale with business process model repositories that contain hundreds or even thousands of process models [25], each of which may be accompanied by up to a dozen PPIs. These observations call for an effective and efficient means of automated support.

The goal of the presented research is to provide the necessary support for the establishment of links between textual PPI descriptions and process model elements. To this end, we introduce an approach that automatically relates a textual PPI description to the relevant parts of a process model. We shall refer to this relation as an *alignment*, following the terminology used to describe relations between concepts from different artifacts in contexts such as schema matching [5] and process model matching [4]. An alignment consists of a number of pair-wise *correspondences* between the PPI and process model elements. To obtain this alignment, we combine machine learning and natural language processing techniques in a novel manner. A quantitative evaluation with a set of 173 PPIs obtained from industry and industrial reference frameworks, demonstrates that our automated approach produces satisfying results. The vast majority of the automatically identified correspondences is in line with how people would manually align them. The approach thereby successfully supports what would otherwise be a laborious manual endeavor.

The remainder of this paper is structured as follows. Section 2 illustrates the problem of aligning unstructured textual PPI descriptions to process model elements. Section 3 describes the proposed approach to automatically generate alignments. The quality of the generated alignments is evaluated in Sect. 4. Section 5 discusses related work on both the problem and solution domains. Finally, we conclude the paper and discuss future research directions in Sect. 6.

2   Problem Illustration

We illustrate the challenges associated with the automated alignment of process model elements to a PPI using the process model depicted in Fig. 1. The process model describes the *request for change* process as implemented by the IT Department of the Andalusian Health Service.[1] The process starts when a requester submits a request for change (RFC). Then, the planning & quality manager analyzes the request in order to make a decision on its approval. Based on several factors, including the availability of required resources, expected costs, and the nature of the requested changes, the RFC will be either approved, canceled, or the decision will be elevated to further analysis by a committee. In the latter case, the RFC will return for a final decision to the planning & quality manager, after an in-depth consideration by the committee.

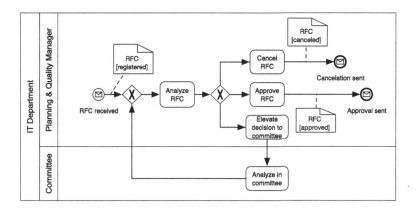

Fig. 1. Process model for the request for change example (simplified)

Table 1 presents six exemplary PPIs related to the request for change process. We will use the examples to illustrate that PPIs can have different measure types. Based on the classification from [24], we distinguish four such types: time, count, data, and derived measures. *Time* measures consider the duration between two instants during the execution of process instances. For instance, PPI1 measures the average time between the receipt of an RFC and its approval. The start and end points of time measures can also relate to the same activity, as can be seen for PPI3. PPI3, namely, measures the time between the start and end of the *"Analyze in committee"* activity. A *count* PPI measures the number of times something happens, for instance the number of times an RFC is registered in the process. *Data* measures consider the attribute values of data objects. PPI5, for example, sums the *"cost"* attribute of all approved RFCs. Lastly, we consider *derived* measures, which involve mathematical functions over one or more other measures. Because *fraction* measures represent the most common kind of derived measures, we consider these as an explicit sub-class of derived measures. Fraction measures divide the value of one measure by another, as seen for PPI6: it divides the number of canceled RFCs by the number of registered RFCs.

---

[1] The interested reader is referred to [24] for an extensive description of the process.

Table 1. PPIs for the request for change example

ID	Description	Measure	Model elements
PPI1	Average time between receipt and approval of an RFC	Time	RFC received, Approve RFC
PPI2	Average lifetime of approved RFCs	Time	RFC received, Approve RFC
PPI3	Average duration of a committee decision	Time	Analyze in committee
PPI4	Number of registered RFCs	Count	RFC [registered]
PPI5	Estimated costs of approved RFCs	Data	RFC [approved]
PPI6	% of rejected RFCs from all registered RFCs	Fraction	RFC [canceled], RFC [registered]

The exemplary PPIs and their related model elements specified in Table 1 illustrate that the type of a PPI affects the *kind* and *number* of process elements to be included in an alignment. For instance, though most measure types can relate to activities, events, and data objects, data-based measures exclusively relate to the latter. Furthermore, count and data-based measures, by definition, relate to a single process model element, whereas a fraction requires at least one element as a numerator and one as a denominator. Due to the differences that exist among the various measure types, the first challenge is, therefore, to ensure that generated alignments are well-defined, i.e. in accordance with the semantics of a PPI's measure type. To create an alignment, an automated approach must furthermore deal with the inherently ambiguous nature of natural language. In particular, a second challenge to overcome is the ability of natural language to express the same semantic concepts through a variety of syntactic patterns [3]. PPI1 and PPI2, for instance, both refer to the time duration between the "*RFC received*" event and the completion of the "*Approve RFC*" activity. However, the two descriptions are clearly distinct. PPI2 just refers to "*the lifetime of approved RFCs*", whereas PPI1 explicitly specifies start and end points of the measure. To overcome this challenge, an automated approach must be able to deal with the flexible and informal language preferred by human users [15]. Third, an alignment approach must handle differences between the terminology used to define PPIs and those used for the process model. For instance, PPI6 refers to "*rejected* RFCs", whereas the process model describes these as "*cancelled*". Such differences are particularly relevant because PPIs and process model are generally defined by different organizational stakeholders, with different perspectives (i.e. managerial versus operational). The alignment approach presented in Sect. 3 addresses these challenges in order to automatically generate alignments between PPIs and process model elements.

3   Alignment Approach

Figure 2 presents an overview of the proposed alignment approach. The approach takes a textual PPI description and a process model to which the PPI relates as input. Given this input, the approach generates an alignment in three steps. In the *type classification* step, we determine the measure type of a PPI based on its textual contents. In the *PPI parsing* step, we parse the textual PPI description in order to extract a set of phrases that specifically relate to parts of the considered process. Both of these steps build on a *decision tree classifier*. For the former step, this classifier provides the classification of a PPI's measure type. For the latter, we use a set of *type indicators* $\mathcal{T}$, automatically learned during the training of the decision tree, to support the parsing of a PPI's description. In the third and final step, we combine the results of the previous steps to generate an alignment between the extracted phrases and elements of the process model. In the following sections, we describe each step in detail.

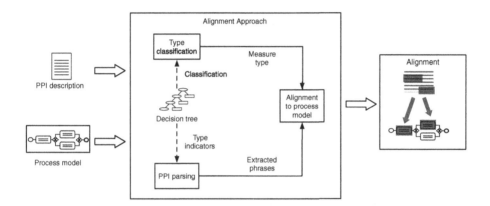

Fig. 2. Outline of the approach

3.1 Type Classification

The measure type of a PPI affects the number and kind of process model elements that such a PPI can or should be aligned to. It is, therefore, important to correctly determine the type of a given PPI. Without a correct type identification, an approach can yield nonsensical alignments, such as a data-based measure aligned to an activity, or a fraction without a denominator. To avoid such issues, we infer the type of a PPI based on the terms in its textual description. We achieve this by employing a *decision tree classifier*.

Classifiers are means to determine to which category of a pre-defined set a previously unseen data point most likely belongs. In the context of our approach, we specifically employ a decision tree classifier to determine if a PPI has a *time*, *count*, *data*, *derived*, or *fraction* type of measure. A decision tree is a type of classifier which models the classification process as a series of data-based choices, represented as the nodes of a tree. The choice for a decision tree is driven by their particular suitability to identify keywords that discriminate among the different measure types. For example, the occurrence of the term *"percentage"* in a PPI description is a good indicator that this PPI describes a fractional measure. We identify these discriminatory terms, which in the remainder we shall refer to as *type indicators*, by training a decision tree on the bag-of-words representations of previously categorized PPI descriptions. Figure 3 presents a fragment of a decision tree obtained in this manner. At each node, the presence or absence of a given term in the description is checked. Based on the outcome of this check, a branch is chosen from several alternatives. The process continues alongside this branch until a leaf node is reached. This node then represents the measure type predicted for the PPI.

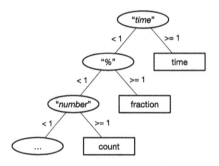

Fig. 3. Fragment of a decision tree

The purpose of the decision tree classifier is two-fold. First, we obtain a classifier as a means to classify the measure type of PPI in order to improve the quality of the alignments our approach generates. Second, we obtain a collection of type indicators $\mathcal{T}$, which are those terms that are used as nodes in the decision tree to distinguish between different measure types. We use these indicators to support the parsing of PPI descriptions, as described in Sect. 3.2.

3.2 PPI Parsing

In order to align a PPI to a process model's elements, we extract the phrases of a PPI description that relate to specific parts of a process. To achieve this, we first split a PPI description into a number of phrases. Afterwards, we filter out those phrases that relate to the computation of a PPI's value rather than to elements of the process itself. In this section, we will use PPI6, *"% of rejected RFCs from all registered RFCs"* as a running example.

Phrase Extraction. We first divide a PPI description into constituent groups of words or *phrases*. To achieve this, we make use of the *Stanford Parser* [8], a widely employed natural language processing tool. The parser generates a *parse tree*, which captures the syntactic structure of a text in a hierarchical manner.

Figure 4 provides an example of this for PPI6. A parse tree contains different types of phrases, e.g. prepositional phrases (denoted as PP), and noun phrases (NP), in a hierarchical structure. For the purposes of our alignment approach, we extract phrases that contain at most one (nested) noun phrase in its main clause. These phrases have a level of granularity similar to the granularity most commonly used in process models, where elements also generally contain a single noun [16]. For instance, most activity labels have a single noun in the form of a business object (e.g. an "RFC") on which an action (e.g. "approve") is performed. We augment the extracted main clauses with dependent clauses, if any, in order to capture information on resources that perform activities or on execution conditions. The latter is, for example, important if the computation of a PPI should only consider RFCs that have been rejected for a specific reason. For PPI6, the extraction step results in the following set of phrases P: { "%", "rejected RFCs", "from all registered RFCs"}.

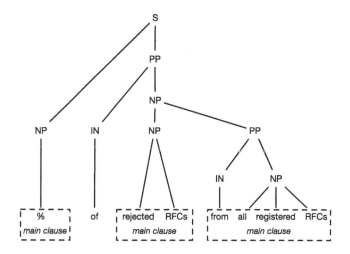

Fig. 4. Simplified parse tree for of PPI6

Phrase Filtering. Next, we filter out those phrases in P that relate to the calculation of a PPI's value rather than to parts of the process. These, for example, include the phrase "*average lifetime*" in PPI2 and "*%*" in PPI6. We identify these phrases by considering the type indicators T obtained while training the decision tree used in the previously described step. These indicators represents keywords that exclusively relate to the computation of PPI values for a certain measure type. Therefore, we identify a phrase that contains one or more of the terms in T as a phrase that relates to the calculation of a PPI. We thereby recognize that phrases such as "*%*" or "*average time*" do not relate to the process itself and as such should be excluded from consideration when creating an alignment. This approach has the great advantage that we filter phrases based on the automatically learned set of indicators $\mathcal{T}$, rather than depending on a manually defined catalog of keywords. For PPI6, this leaves the filtered set of phrases P_F as the outcome of this step: { "rejected RFCs", "from all registered RFCs" }.

3.3   Alignment to Process Model

In the final step of our approach, we generate an alignment between the extracted phrases P_F and the set of process model elements M. An alignment σ consists of a number of pair-wise correspondences, each between a phrase $p \in P_F$ and a process model element $m \in M$, denoted as $p \sim m$. Our approach sets out to find an optimal alignment $\hat{\sigma}$ between P_F and M, which we define as the alignment which (i) has the highest semantic similarity for its correspondences, and (ii) abides to constraints imposed based on the semantics of a PPI's measure type.

Semantic Similarity. To quantify the semantic similarity between a phrase p and a model element m, we compare the *bag-of-words* representations of p and the textual label of m. To obtain this representation, we first apply a *tokenization* function on the plain texts. This function splits a text into its individual terms, filters out stop words like "*the*", "*if*", "*from*", and lemmatizes the remaining terms. This last step transforms all terms to their grammatical base form or *lemma*, e.g. "*is*" and "*been*" are both transformed into "*be*". We next compare the resultant bags-of-words, ω_m and ω_p, using a semantic similarity measure.

The usage of specific terminology from business settings, commonly contained in PPI descriptions and process models, poses an important challenge here. To overcome this challenge, we make use of a similarity method called *second order similarity* [7]. This method is based on the statistical analysis of co-occurrences in large text collections. It therefore has the great advantage that it can deal with context-specific terms, often not fully captured by other natural language processing tools suchs as WordNet [18]. To compute the similarity score between ω_p and ω_m, we make use of a metric introduced in [17], which combines second order similarity scores and the inverse document frequency (idf) of terms. By incorporating idf, the metric assigns higher scores to terms that have a high discriminatory power in a given process context. For instance, in the context of the request for change example, the rarely occurring term "*registered*" has a much higher discriminatory power than the frequently occurring term "*RFC*".

Alignment Constraints. To generate an alignment in line with the semantics of PPIs, we impose constraints on the correspondences included in the alignment through a constraint function Γ. Specifically, we use Γ to capture constraints on three characteristics: (i) the classes of process model elements to be included in σ, (ii) the number of correspondences or *cardinality* of σ, and (iii) the possible overlap among correspondences in σ.

We instantiate the constraints for each type in accordance with their semantics, as specified in [24]. Table 2 provides an overview of the specific constraints

Table 2. Constraints imposed on alignments per measure type

Measure type	Model elements	Cardinality	Overlap
Count	Flow elements, data objects	1	n/a
Data	Data objects	1	n/a
Time	Flow elements, data objects	2	depends on $|P_F|$
Derived	Flow elements, data objects	$|P_F|$	yes
Fraction	Flow elements, data objects	2	no

imposed per measure type. The alignments generated for *count* and *data* measures are the least complex. Alignments of these types contain only a single correspondence between a phrase and model element in σ. For data measures, these elements can only include data objects, because these measures exclusively relate to attribute values of data objects. All other measure types can also relate to *flow elements*. These elements depict the steps executed in a process. For the BPMN notation, the most common flow elements include *activities* and *events*. The alignments for *time* and *derived* measures are more complex, because they can include multiple correspondences.

Time measures require start and end points. These two points may refer to the same model element, e.g. an activity, in order to describe a measure that computes the duration between the start and end of an activity. This is for instance seen for PPI3: *"The average duration of a committee decision"*. We can identify these cases through the number of phrases extracted from the PPI description, i.e. $|P_F|$. If the description contains only a single phrase related to the elements of a process, we expect that the start and end points of a time measure refer to the same element. In those cases, we allow overlap between the correspondences. Otherwise, we generate an alignment that contains distinct correspondences for the start and end points.

Finally, derived measures allow for the widest variety in alignments, because these measures can describe any function over other measures. To capture this, we do not impose specific restrictions on the size of their alignments. Rather, we align each extracted phrase $p \in P_F$ to its most similar process model element. This allows the approach to generate a broad variety of alignments, in line with the semantics of derived measures. For *fraction* measures, a specific sub-class of derived measures, we do impose restrictions on the size of their alignments. A fraction measure requires distinct process model elements to reflect its *numerator* and *denominator*. Therefore, the cardinality of these measures always equals 2.

To obtain the optimal alignment $\hat{\sigma}$ for a PPI, we construct the alignment that has the maximum sum of similarity scores for its correspondences, while it still abides to the alignment constraints imposed by Γ. This alignment then represents the final outcome of our approach.

4   Evaluation

To demonstrate the strength of our alignment approach, we conduct a quantitative evaluation that compares the generated alignments to a manually created *gold standard*. The goal of the evaluation is to learn how well the automated approach approximates manual alignments. Section 4.1 introduces the data set used for the evaluation. Section 4.2 describes the details of the evaluation approach. Finally, we present and discuss the results in Sect. 4.3.

4.1   Test Collection

To evaluate our approach, we use a collection of process models and accompanying natural language PPI descriptions from practice. To allow for a high external validity of the evaluation results, the data in the test collection has been obtained from various sources. Part of the test collection consists of an industrial data set stemming from prior research on the formalization of PPI definitions and service level agreements [23,24]. The request for change example, used throughout this paper, provides a fragment of one of the models included in this collection. The test collection furthermore includes a number of process models and PPIs from the SCOR (Supply Chain Operations Reference) and ITIL (Information Infrastructure Technology Library) reference frameworks. From these frameworks we selected processes from various application contexts and with a high number of associated performance indicators. The resulting test collection consists of 15 different process models and a total of 173 PPIs. The PPIs in the collection comprise 65 count, 28 data, 47 time, and 33 derived measures. Table 3 presents an overview of the characteristics of the collection per source, including the average number of elements per process model, and the total number of correspondences between the PPIs and model elements.

Table 3. Overview of the test collection

ID	Source	Process models	Elements/model	PPIs	Correspondences
1	Industry	9	11.2	47	65
2	SCOR	3	8.3	86	138
3	ITIL	3	13.7	40	48
Total		15	11.1	173	251

Aside from the broad variety of domains it covers, the heterogeneity of the test collection mainly manifests itself in terms of granularity. The SCOR and ITIL process models represent reference models that are intended as templates for implementations in organizations. The models from the reference collection are more abstract and, thus, provide less fine-granular process descriptions.

4.2 Setup

To conduct the evaluation, we implemented the alignment approach in the form of a prototype. The Java prototype uses the Stanford Parser [8] to assist in the PPI parsing, the semantic similarity implementation DISCO [10], and the WEKA toolkit for classification [6]. Specifically, we apply the C4.5 algorithm [21] to generate a decision tree, one of the most commonly used implementations for decision tree learning. We train the decision tree on a collection of 300 PPIs from the SCOR and ITIL frameworks, for which we manually defined the measure types. To avoid any bias, the PPIs in this training collection are distinct from those used in the test collection. Furthermore, because the training collection is obtained from different processes and does not include PPIs from the industrial sources, the PPIs in the training and test sets differ considerably in terms of their domain, terminology, and structure.

We use our prototype to automatically generate alignments for the PPIs in the test collection. To assess the quality of the generated alignments, we compare them to a manually created *gold standard*. We involved three researchers in the creation of the gold standard for the industrial and ITIL collections. Two of them independently created the alignments. The differences were discussed in detail, involving a third researcher to settle ties. For the SCOR framework, we directly obtained the gold standard from the relations that the framework itself specifies between performance indicators and activities. To perform the comparison between the correspondences contained in the generated alignments $\mathcal{A}$ and those contained in the gold standard $\mathcal{R}$, we computed *precision* and *recall* metrics as given by Eqs. (1) and (2).

$$pre(\mathcal{A}, \mathcal{M}) = \frac{|\mathcal{A} \cap \mathcal{R}|}{|\mathcal{A}|} \quad (1) \qquad rec(\mathcal{A}, \mathcal{M}) = \frac{|\mathcal{A} \cap \mathcal{R}|}{|\mathcal{R}|} \quad (2)$$

Precision here reflects the number of correct generated correspondences, i.e. the correspondences from $\mathcal{A}$ that are also included in the gold standard $\mathcal{R}$, divided by the total number of generated correspondences. *Recall* is the fraction of correspondences in the gold standard that are correctly identified by our approach, i.e. included in the generated alignments. We furthermore report the f_1-score as the harmonic mean of precision and recall.

As we are the first to present an automated approach for the alignment of PPIs to process models, there is no commonly accepted benchmark available. To demonstrate the performance of our approach, we therefore compare its results to a *baseline configuration*. For this baseline, we align each PPI to the process model element with the highest semantic similarity to the entire PPI description. Through this comparison, we are able to illustrate the added value of classifying and parsing the PPI descriptions instead of this straightforward, rough approach.

4.3   Results

Table 4 summarizes the evaluation results. It shows that the baseline configuration achieves a considerable precision for the total collection (0.75), but lacks in recall (0.51). This high precision can be attributed to the use of semantic similarity measures specifically suited to deal with specific terminology used in business settings. The lack of recall follows from the low number of correspondences the baseline configuration generates (173). The full approach avoids this problem by classifying the measure types of the PPIs. Through this classification, the approach much better approximates the number of correspondences to be included in the alignments. It generates 255 correspondences versus 251 included in the gold standard. The slightly higher precision achieved by the full approach (0.76) is remarkable, because it generates a significantly higher number of correspondences than the baseline. This achievement can be attributed to the extraction and filtering of phrases in the PPI parsing step. Because the parsing step removes extraneous information from consideration, the generated similarity scores are more accurate. The full approach therefore manages to maintain a high predictive precision. The increased number of correspondences, together with the stable precision, results in considerable improvements in recall (0.75 versus 0.51) and F_1 (0.76 versus 0.60).

Table 4. Evaluation results

Configuration	Source	$|\mathcal{A}|$	Precision	Recall	F_1-score
Baseline	Industrial	47	0.79	0.52	0.63
	SCOR	86	0.74	0.46	0.57
	ITIL	40	0.73	0.60	0.66
	Total	173	0.75	0.51	0.60
Full approach	Industrial	70	0.73	0.72	0.72
	SCOR	139	0.77	0.78	0.77
	ITIL	40	0.78	0.75	0.77
	Total	255	0.76	0.75	0.76

The evaluation results suggest that the classification of measure types and the tailored technique for parsing PPI descriptions greatly improve the quality of the generated alignments. A post-hoc analysis of the results reveals that alignments which depend on context-specific information present the most important challenge to the automated approach. This challenge manifests itself in the form of PPI descriptions that refer to process concepts that are only related in a specific context. For instance, the ITIL process on Service Design contains the *"Average duration of service interruptions"* PPI. This PPI relates to an *"availability monitoring and reporting"* activity in the accompanying process model. To identify the correct correspondence, it must be recognized that service *interruptions* affect the *availability* of services. Still, due to the usage of semantic similarity measures, our approach successfully identifies the vast majority of such cases, in which PPIs and process models do not refer to the same concepts.

5 Related Work

The work presented in this paper mainly relates to two research streams. One is focused on the problem domain and includes different models to define the relationships between PPIs and process models. The other is focused on the solution domain and includes techniques that have been developed to automatically align process information between different artifacts.

Concerning the former, there are a number of frameworks for modeling PPIs and their relationship with business processes. For instance, Popova et al. [20] present a framework for modeling PPIs within a general organization modeling framework. The framework provides an explicit mechanism to link PPIs with process models. Momm et al. [19] introduce an approach, based on the principles of Model-Driven Architecture, for the development of infrastructure necessary to instrument the monitoring of a set of PPIs in a Service-Oriented Architecture. Wetzstein et al. [26] introduce a Key Performance Indicators (KPIs) ontology to specify KPIs over semantic business processes as part of a framework for Business Activity Monitoring. Finally, PPINOT [24] presents a metamodel to define PPIs with a high degree of expressiveness and an explicit link with process model elements. Although these frameworks provide mechanisms to link PPIs with process models, it was found that in practice, managers often start out to describe relevant PPIs in an unstructured and ad-hoc manner [24, 26]. Our approach is, therefore, complementary to these frameworks. Based on these existing, unstructured PPI definitions, the approach can generate the links that are necessary to define PPIs in accordance with the structured notations of the frameworks.

To the best of our knowledge, there are no earlier methods that generate alignments in this context. By contrast, numerous approaches, referred to as *process model matchers*, exist that create alignments between different process models, e.g. [4, 9, 13]. To create alignments these matchers exploit different process model features, including natural language [9], model structure [4], and behavior [13]. Process model matchers face challenges similar to our approach in the form of different levels of detail and the usage of different terminology [1]. Contrary to the unstructured natural language descriptions used as input in this work, these matchers work with explicitly structured input. An exception to this is an earlier proposed approach, which aligns textual process descriptions to process models for the purpose of inconsistency detection [2]. However, the nature of the input considerably differs from the PPI descriptions used in the presented work. This results in distinct parsing and alignment challenges.

6 Conclusions

In this paper, we presented an approach to automatically align natural language descriptions of PPIs to process models. To achieve this, our approach combines machine learning and tailored natural language processing techniques to deal with the variability of natural language and the different measures types of PPIs. A quantitative evaluation, conducted using a test collection obtained from various industrial sources, demonstrated that the approach generates alignments of a high quality. These generated alignments show a high level of similarity to manually created ones. The approach thus accurately identifies relations between textually described PPIs and process models in practical settings. As such, it successfully supports the operationalization of process performance monitoring. Despite the promising results, we need to reflect on some limitations. First, the dataset we employed is not representative in a statistical sense. However, the obtained result quality is stable among the processes from different sources, which illustrates the approach's ability to deal with heterogeneous data. Second, the approach does not generate perfect alignments in all cases, especially not when the link between PPI and process model depends on a considerable amount of contextual knowledge. The approach, therefore, remains a means to support users. It does have the potential to greatly reduce the effort required to identify correct correspondences for a process collection.

In future work, we set out to further develop the alignment approach. A promising direction is to develop extraction techniques tailored to the different PPI measure types in order to further improve the results. Second, the approach can be extended by also parsing the information in a description that relates to the calculation of a PPI's value. As such, the generated alignments can be extended into fully formalized PPI definitions.

References

1. van der Aa, H., Leopold, H., Mannhardt, F., Reijers, H.A.: On the fragmentation of process information: challenges, solutions, and outlook. In: Gaaloul, K., Schmidt, R., Nurcan, S., Guerreiro, S., Ma, Q. (eds.) BPMDS 2015 and EMMSAD 2015. LNBIP, vol. 214, pp. 3–18. Springer, Heidelberg (2015)
2. van der Aa, H., Leopold, H., Reijers, H.A.: Detecting inconsistencies between process models and textual descriptions. In: Motahari-Nezhad, H.R., Recker, J., Weidlich, M. (eds.) BPM 2015, vol. 9253, pp. 90–105. Springer, Switzerland (2015)
3. Achour, C.B.: Guiding scenario authoring1. Information Modelling and Knowledge Bases X 51, 152 (1999)
4. Dijkman, R.M., Dumas, M., Van Dongen, B., Käärik, R., Mendling, J.: Similarity of business process models: metrics and evaluation. Inf. Syst. **36**(2), 498–516 (2011)
5. Gal, A.: Uncertain schema matching. Synth. Lect. Data Manag. **3**(1), 1–97 (2011)
6. Hall, M., Frank, E., Holmes, G., Pfahringer, B., Reutemann, P., Witten, I.H.: The weka data mining software: an update. ACM SIGKDD **11**(1), 10–18 (2009)
7. Islam, A., Inkpen, D.: Second order co-occurrence pmi for determining the semantic similarity of words. In: Proceedings of the International Conference on Language Resources and Evaluation, Genoa, Italy, pp. 1033–1038 (2006)

8. Klein, D., Manning, C.D.: Accurate unlexicalized parsing. In: Proceedings of the 41st Annual Meeting of the ACL, vol. 1, pp. 423–430. ACL (2003)

9. Klinkmüller, C., Weber, I., Mendling, J., Leopold, H., Ludwig, A.: Increasing recall of process model matching by improved activity label matching. In: Daniel, F., Wang, J., Weber, B. (eds.) BPM 2013. LNCS, vol. 8094, pp. 211–218. Springer, Heidelberg (2013)

10. Kolb, P.: Disco: a multilingual database of distributionally similar words. In: Proceedings of KONVENS-2008, Berlin (2008)

11. Kovacic, A.: Business renovation: business rules (still) the missing link. Bus. Process Manag. J. 10(2), 158–170 (2004)

12. Kronz, A.: Managing of process key performance indicators as part of the aris methodology. In: Scheer, A.W., Jost, W., Heß, H., Kronz, A. (eds.) Corporate Performance Management, pp. 31–44. Springer, Heidelberg (2006)

13. Kunze, M., Weidlich, M., Weske, M.: Behavioral similarity – a proper metric. In: Rinderle-Ma, S., Toumani, F., Wolf, K. (eds.) BPM 2011. LNCS, vol. 6896, pp. 166–181. Springer, Heidelberg (2011)

14. Luftman, J., Papp, R., Brier, T.: Enablers and inhibitors of business-it alignment. Commun. AIS 1(3es), 1–32 (1999)

15. Marshall, B., Chen, H., Madhusudan, T.: Matching knowledge elements in concept maps using a similarity flooding algorithm. Decis. Support Syst. 42(3), 1290–1306 (2006)

16. Mendling, J., Reijers, H.A., Recker, J.: Activity labeling in process modeling: empirical insights and recommendations. Inf. Syst. 35(4), 467–482 (2010)

17. Mihalcea, R., Corley, C., Strapparava, C.: Corpus-based and knowledge-based measures of text semantic similarity. In: AAAI, vol. 6, p. 775–780 (2006)

18. Miller, G.A.: WordNet: a lexical database for english. Commun. ACM 38(11), 39–41 (1995)

19. Momm, C., Malec, R., Abeck, S.: Towards a model-driven development of monitored processes. Wirtschaftsinformatik 2, 319–336 (2007)

20. Popova, V., Sharpanskykh, A.: Modeling organizational performance indicators. Inf. Syst. 35(4), 505–527 (2010)

21. Quinlan, J.R.: C4. 5: Programs for Machine Learning. Elsevier, Amsterdam (2014)

22. del-Río-Ortega, A., Cabanillas, C., Resinas, M., Ruiz-Cortés, A.: PPINOT tool suite: a performance management solution for process-oriented organisations. In: Basu, S., Pautasso, C., Zhang, L., Fu, X. (eds.) ICSOC 2013. LNCS, vol. 8274, pp. 675–678. Springer, Heidelberg (2013)

23. del-Río-Ortega, A., Gutiérrez, A.M., Durán, A., Resinas, M., Ruiz-Cortés, A.: Modelling service level agreements for business process outsourcing services. In: Zdravkovic, J., Kirikova, M., Johannesson, P. (eds.) CAiSE 2015. LNCS, vol. 9097, pp. 485–500. Springer, Heidelberg (2015)

24. del-Río-Ortega, A., Resinas, M., Cabanillas, C., Ruiz-Cortes, A.: On the definition and design-time analysis of process performance indicators. Inf. Syst. 38(4), 470–490 (2013)

25. Rosemann, M.: Potential pitfalls of process modeling: part A. bus. process manag. j. 12(2), 249–254 (2006)

26. Wetzstein, B., Ma, Z., Leymann, F.: Towards measuring key performance indicators of semantic business processes. In: Abramowicz, W., Fensel, D. (eds.) BIS, pp. 227–238. Springer, Heidelberg (2008)

A Configurable Resource Allocation for Multi-tenant Process Development in the Cloud

Emna Hachicha[1(✉)], Nour Assy[2], Walid Gaaloul[1], and Jan Mendling[3]

[1] Telecom SudParis, UMR 5157 Samovar, Université Paris-Saclay, Evry, France
{emna.hachicha,walid.gaaloul}@telecom-sudparis.eu
[2] Eindhoven University of Technology, Eindhoven, The Netherlands
n.assy@tue.nl
[3] Vienna University of Economics and Business Administration, Vienna, Austria
jan.mendling@wu.ac.at

Abstract. Cloud computing has become an important infrastructure for outsourcing service-based business processes in a *multi-tenancy* way. Configurable process models enable the sharing of a reference process among different tenants that can be customized according to specific needs. While concepts for specifying the control flow of such processes are well understood, there is a lack of support for cloud-specific resource configuration where *different allocation alternatives need to be explicitly defined*. In this paper, we address this research gap by extending configurable process models with the required *configurable cloud resource allocation*. Our proposal allows different tenants to customize the selection of the needed resources taking into account two important properties *elasticity* and *shareability*. Our prototypical implementation demonstrates the feasibility and the results of our experiments highlight the effectiveness of our approach.

1 Introduction

Motivated by the need of adopting agile, flexible and cost-effective business solutions, enterprises are looking for available business processes outside of their organizations to quickly adapt to new business requirements and also reduce process development and maintenance costs. Cloud Computing is recently gaining momentum due to its capability of outsourcing service-based business processes based on a scalable pay-per-use model. According to the National Institute of Standards and Technology (NIST), Cloud Computing is a model that enables providers sharing their computing resources (e.g., networks, servers, storage, applications, and services) and users accessing them in an ubiquitous, convenient and on-demand way with a minimal management effort [1]. In such a multi-tenant environment, using *configurable process models* [2] allows a cloud business process provider to deliver a customizable process that can be configured by different tenants according to their specific needs [3].

Different approaches for configurable process modeling have been proposed so far, mainly with a focus on configuring the control flow [4]. Even though the

S. Nurcan et al. (Eds.): CAiSE 2016, LNCS 9694, pp. 558–574, 2016.
DOI: 10.1007/978-3-319-39696-5_34

concept of configurable process models is highly complementary to cloud computing, there has been hardly any uptake in that area. The problem is apparently that specifics of cloud computing, specifically in how resources can be configured and integrated, are hardly considered in configurable process modeling. The few proposals on extending configuration to resources [5–7] do not cover required cloud concepts such as elasticity or multi-tenancy and focus on human resources and their dependencies [8–10].

In this paper, we address this research gap by proposing process configuration concepts for cloud computing. More specifically, we define a novel approach for modeling configurable processes with *configurable cloud resource allocation operators* that allow to explicitly model resource allocation alternatives in multi-tenant process models including elasticity and shareability. Our concepts have been prototypically implemented in the Signavio editor. We evaluate our approach using experiments, which demonstrate its effectiveness.

The paper is structured as follows. Section 2 motivates the problem with a real-world case of a Telco operator and identifies requirements. Section 3 defines our approach for configurable resource allocation. Section 4 describes our implementation and the evaluation results. Finally, Sect. 6 concludes the paper and presents an outlook on future work.

2 Preliminaries and Motivation

In this section, we describe the example from one of our industry partners. Then, we revisit essential concepts from configurable process modeling and cloud computing to identify requirements that are not yet addressed by prior research.

2.1 Motivation

Our research is motivated by a real business of the Telco operator Orange, one of our industry partners. In order to consolidate its expertise in service supervision processes, Orange affiliates share the configurable process in Fig. 1 in a common infrastructure[1]. According to its specific needs, each affiliate configures the process by taking into account the countries legislation and internal regulations. For instance, suppose that an affiliate A does not have access to the resource test management functionalities (the subprocess starting with the activity a_4) and does not have the right to neither perform manual tasks (activity a_6) nor trouble ticket escalation (activity a_{14}). Therefore, it configures the process in Fig. 1 to exclude these functionalities, resulting in a variant as illustrated in Fig. 2.

Since configurable process modeling approaches do not support the resource allocation in multi-tenant cloud environments, the affiliate defines the required resources for its derived variant in an *ad-hoc manner*. For example, for the derived variant in Fig. 2, the activity a_1 needs a *network resource* to communicate with a virtual machine via virtual networking. The network type is manual

---

[1] For understandability and confidentiality issues, an abstract and simplified version of the configurable process is shown in Fig. 1.

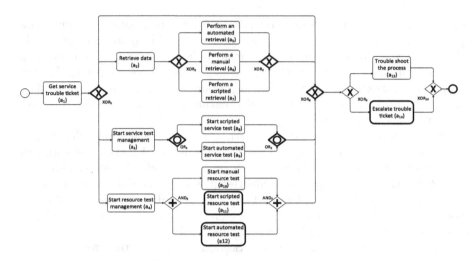

Fig. 1. A configurable service supervision process

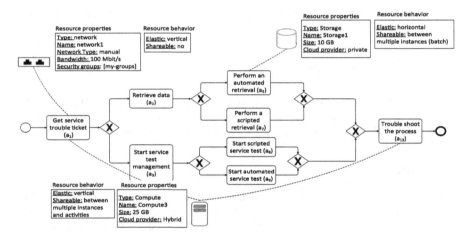

Fig. 2. Variant 1: A process variant derived from the configurable process in Fig. 1 and its allocated cloud resources

with a bandwidth of 100 Mbit/s and which is accessible for a specific security group. These parameters are identified in the "Resource properties" label in Fig. 2. Furthermore, the activity needs an elastic network resource (vertical elasticity), that for security issues is not shared with other activities or instances. These parameters are specified in the "Resource behavior" label.

Suppose that another affiliates B configures the process as shown in Fig. 3 including its required resources. Activity a_1 needs an elastic network resource (horizontally, vertically or both according to the run-time requirements). The network is dynamic with a bandwidth of 100 Gbit/s in order to support the workload from different variants' instances. We notice that the allocated resources for

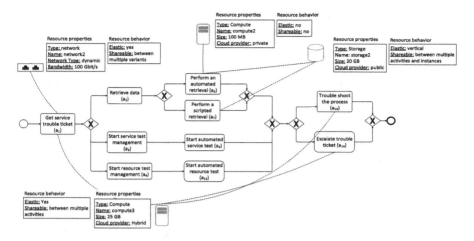

Fig. 3. Variant 2: A process variant derived from the configurable process in Fig. 1 and its allocated cloud resources

the remaining activities are similar to those allocated in the *variant 1* in Fig. 2 but with some variations.

This example shows that multi-tenant business processes do not only share commonalities between their executed tasks, but also between their allocated resources. In fact, different tenants allocate similar resources that slightly differ according to the resource properties and behavior. Up until now, these allocation parameters are hard-coded in an ad-hoc manner which is certainly undesirable in such a multi-tenant environment. Therefore, there is a need for a process configuration support at the cloud resource allocation level and which shifts the cloud resource allocation parameters from the tenant side (at the process variant level) to the cloud process provider side (at the configurable process level).

2.2 Configurable Process Models

The process in Fig. 1 has been modeled with the configurable Business Process Model and Notation (c-BPMN). A configurable process models such as in c-BPMN contain configurable elements whose configuration decision is made at design-time [2]. The configurable elements are graphically modeled with a thick line. In case of c-BPMN, *activities* and *gateways* can be configurable. A configurable activity can be included (i.e. *ON*) or excluded (i.e. *OFF*) from the process model. For example, in Fig. 1, the activity a_{11} is configurable. It can be configured either to *ON* in order to keep it in the process or to *OFF* in order to exclude it from the process. A configurable gateway has a generic behavior which is restricted by configuration. It can be configured by (1) changing its type while preserving its behavior and/or (2) restricting its incoming (respectively outgoing) branches in case of a join (respectively split) [2]. For example, the configurable OR (OR^c) can be configured to any gateway type while a configurable AND (AND^c) can be only configured to an AND. We denote by $c \sqsubseteq c^c$ iff the behavior of c is subsumed by that of c^c. For instance, $AND \sqsubseteq OR^c$, $Seq \sqsubseteq XOR^c$ etc.

Once the configuration choices are selected for all configurable elements, algorithms such as the one presented in [2] can be used to derive the specific variant by removing the nodes and edges that have been excluded. For example, the process variant in Fig. 2 is derived as a result of the following configurations:

– XOR_1 is configured to an XOR with the two outgoing branches starting with a_2 and a_3;
– XOR_2 is configured to an XOR with the two outgoing branches starting with a_5 and a_7;
– OR_4 is configured to an XOR with the same outgoing branches;
– XOR_8 is configured to an XOR and is the join of the split XOR_1.

Various configurable modeling languages with comparable capabilities as c-BPMN have been proposed [2,4,11–13]. These works have been focused on the control flow perspective. The general benefits of integrating cloud and BPM have been stressed by different authors [14,15]. If configurable process models have the potential to be an efficient solution for modeling multi-tenant business processes [3], they need to integrate the resource perspective.

2.3   Resource Perspective in Cloud-Based Business Processes

Not only for cloud-based business processes, but also for BPM in general, the research on resources has been scarce. Specific topics of investigation in this area are human resource allocation [9,10] and scheduling [16–18]. The workflow resource patterns [19,20] are often used as a benchmark for corresponding modeling concepts such as [8]. Some works consider cloud characteristics explicitly: S. Schulte et al. in [21,22] develop a platform that allow Business Process Management Systems (BPMS) to manage resource elasticity. L. Pufahl et al. in [23] handle batch activities and allow its flexible adjustments at run-time.

Relevant for configurable processes in the cloud are the following characteristics. The cloud offers three main types of resources at the Infrastructure-as-a-Service (IaaS) model which can be spread into virtual machines (VMs). They consist of *compute*, *network*, and *storage* resources. *Compute* resources are a collection of Physical Machines (PMs) where each contains one or more processors, memory, network interface and local I/O [24]. These PMs require interconnection with a high bandwidth network using *network* resources. Last, the *storage* resources provide persistent storage services where each service have varying levels of data consistency and reliability. Two main properties are specified to the Cloud resources: *elasticity*, and *shareability*. First, the Cloud infrastructure provides two types of elasticity, vertical and horizontal, in order to account for the run-time workload. The *vertical elasticity* is the possibility to scale up and down by adding or removing resources to an existing activity in order to increase its capacity. The *horizontal elasticity* is the possibility of adding or removing instances of activities with their consumed resources. Second, the resource share-ability represents one of the important features in cloud environments. According to security, availability and scalability issues in the process, an allocated resource may or may not be shareable between multiple activities, between multiple instances of the same activity or both. A resource shared between multiple activities is referred to as *shareable* and can be consumed by more than one activity instance at the same time within the same process instance. A resource shared between multiple instances of the same activity is referred to as *batch* and can be utilized by multiple instances of the same activity within multiple process instances. An *hybrid* resource is shareable and batch. These cloud resources can be specified using the RDF-based Cloud business Process Ontology (CloudPrO) [25], which extends in turn the Business Process Modeling Ontology (BPMO) [26]. Its properties are grounded in the cloud computing API Open Cloud Computing Interface (OCCI) [27], allowing statements such as resources of type *compute* contain *speed* which corresponds to the frequency of CPU Clock in gigahertz.

Recently, works in the area of configurable process modeling have been proposed towards such a configuration of the resource perspective [5–7]. In [5], La Rosa et al. propose the configurable integrated EPC (C-iEPC) with features for capturing resource, data and physical objects. Configuration of these elements is achieved using configurable connectors borrowed from the control flow perspective to model the variable allocation of resources. Their focus is, however, on human resources and there is no direct support for cloud resources including *resource sharing* and *resource elasticity*. Moreover, A. Kumar and W. Yao in [6] propose an approach for configurable business processes that integrates resource and data needs using process templates and business rules. Resources in cloud environment are not covered in their approach and flexible resources selection is not addressed. In [7], A. Hallerbach et al. extend the *Pro*cess *v*ariants by *op*tions (Provop) framework to adequately model and manage large collections of process variants. Concepts such as resource allocation and resource selection are not considered. Table 1 summarizes these approaches and relates them to properties that are important in a cloud setting. We observe that resource variability, cloud features, and allocation are only partially covered or not at all. In the following, we aim to fill these gaps by the definition of our novel approach.

3   A Configurable Cloud Resource Allocation

In this section, we present our *configurable cloud resource allocation approach* for multi-tenant business processes development. As mentioned before, cloud resources' allocation takes into account two main parameters: (1) the desired resources and their properties and (2) the desired resource behaviour (i.e. shareability and elasticity). Therefore, we identify three main operators related to the configuration of the resource properties and behavior: (i) configurable resource assignment operator denoted as A^c (Sect. 3.1), (ii) configurable resource elasticity operator denoted as E^c (Sect. 3.2) and (ii) configurable resource

Table 1. Evaluation of previous approaches

| Approaches | Criteria | | | |
	Control-flow variability	Resource variability	Cloud resources & features	Resource allocation
[2]	+	−	−	+
[7]	+	−	−	−
[5]	+	+	−	+
[6]	+	−	−	+
Our approach	+	+	+	+

sharing/batching operator denoted as $(S/B)^c$ (Sect. 3.3). Then, an excerpt of a configurable process model with the configurable resource operators is depicted in Fig. 4 and explained in the following.

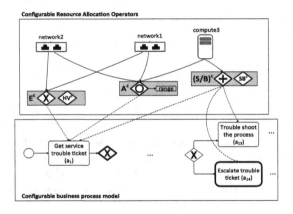

Fig. 4. Configurable resource allocation operators

3.1 Configurable Resource Assignment Operator

The configurable resource assignment operator A^c allows the modeling of *a variable number of resources allocated to a specific activity*. For instance, in our running examples in Figs. 2 and 3, the activity a_1 needs either (i) a network resource "network1" and a compute resource "compute3" or (ii) a network resource "network2" and a compute resource "compute3". Therefore, through A^c, we model a design-time choice in the configurable process that allows the tenants to select one of the available options. To do so, we define two main parameters for A^c: (i) a configurable type and (ii) a range (see A^c in Fig. 4).

The configurable type can be either a configurable OR (OR^c), a configurable AND (AND^c) or a configurable XOR (XOR^c). These connectors have the same behavior as the configurable control flow connectors. They are configured in the same way as the configurable connectors of the control-flow perspective (see Sect. 2.2). In our example in Fig. 4, the activity a_1 is connected to the cloud resources "network2", "network1" and "compute3" through an OR^c. A tenant may configure the OR^c to an XOR associated to "network2" and "network1" in order to specify that either "network2" or "network1" can be allocated to a_1 while "compute3" is not needed. The allocation decision between "network1" and "network2" is therefore left to the run-time depending on the environment requirements, availability of the resources, etc.

The second operator parameter (i.e. range) imposes an additional constraint on the configuration choice. It is specified by the cloud process provider as a *configuration guideline* for the tenants. A range specifies the minimal and maximal number of the resources that are recommended to be allocated from each resource type ($range_C$ for compute, $range_N$ for network and $range_S$ for storage). For instance, a cloud process provider recommends that at least one compute and one network resources are allocated to the activity a_1. This corresponds to set the minimum of $range_C$ and $range_N$ to 1. By default, the range minimum is set to 0 and the range maximum is set to the total number of the resources from a specific type that are available for the activity. The configuration of the connectors in the configurable type should respect this constraints. For example, having the minimum $min_{range_C} = 1$ and $min_{range_N} = 1$, the aforementioned configuration of the OR^c to an XOR associated to the resources "network1" and "network2" is not valid.

Table 2 summarizes the configurable resource assignment parameters and their configuration constraints. The configurable type follows the configurable connectors from the control flow perspective. Its configuration constraints are the same as described in Sect. 2.2. Each of the range parameters has a minimum min (set by default to 0) and a maximum max. We denote by $|R_C|$, $|R_N|$ and $|R_S|$ the number of compute, network and storage resources respectively provided for a specific activity.

Table 2. Configurable assignment parameters and configuration constraints

Parameters		Configuration constraints
Configurable type	OR^c	Follow the description in Sect. 2.2
	AND^c	
	XOR^c	
Range	$range_C$	$min = 0$, $max = |R_C|$
	$range_N$	$min = 0$, $max = |R_N|$
	$range_S$	$min = 0$, $max = |R_S|$

For instance, in order to derive the resources allocated to the activity a_1 in the process variant in Fig. 2, the configurable resource assignment operator in the process in Fig. 4 is configured as following:

– the configurable type OR^c is configured to an AND associated to the resources $network_1$ and $compute_3$;
– This configuration does not violate the range that is assumed defined by the cloud process provider as follows: $range_C$ ($min = 1, max = 2$); $range_N$ ($min = 1, max = 1$); $range_S$ ($min = 0, max = 0$).

The resource assignment operator is the main operator in the configurable resource allocation modeling. It allows to define the pool of resources that may be allocated to the process activities. Once it is specified, the configurable sharing/batching (see Sect. 3.3) and the configurable elasticity (see Sect. 3.2) operators can be used to model the behavior of the identified resources.

3.2   Configurable Resource Elasticity Operator

During resource allocation, an organization may have different requirements regarding the anticipation of its activities workload, and thus may request different elasticity configurations. For instance, in a specific organization, an activity may require a network resource of at least 100 Mbit/s but may go to 600 Mbit/s during pick hours. At allocation time, a network resource of size 100 Mbit/s which can scale up to a 600 Mbit/s by vertical elasticity is selected. In a second organization, the same activity requires a network resource of at least 100 Mbit/s but may go to a maximum of 150 Mbit/s. The organization requests an horizontal elasticity that adds multiple activities' instances to acquire a 150 Mbit/s.

In order to model such variability at the elasticity level, our proposed *configurable resource elasticity* operator E^c takes into account two parameters' configurations: (i) the set of resources to be elastic and (ii) the way they scale up and down (i.e. elasticity type). Table 3 summarizes the configurable resource elasticity parameters and configuration constraints. Similarly to the *configurable resource assignment* operator, the first parameter (configurable type) can be either an OR^c, XOR^c or AND^c and is used to model the number of resources to be elastic. For instance in our example in Fig. 4, either "network1" or "network2" can be elastic (they are connected through an XOR^c). An organization may configure the XOR^c to a "sequence" associated to "network2" in order to specify that only "network2" can be elastic. The second parameter (configurable elasticity type) specifies the elasticity behavior. Four elasticity types: (i) H (i.e. horizontal), (ii) V (i.e. vertical), (iii) HV (i.e. hybrid) and (iv) HV^c (i.e. configurable hybrid) are defined from which only HV^c is configurable and can be configured to H, V or HV.

Besides the configuration constraints in Table 3, additional *configuration guidelines* can be specified by the cloud process provider regarding the configuration of the elasticity type. These guidelines assist the tenants for selecting the right configuration of the configurable HV^c. They are derived according to the maximal capacity that is provided by the cloud provider during the scale up (vertical or horizontal elasticity) which is specified in the Service Level Agreement (SLA) [28]. In case a resource has a configurable resource elasticity type HV^c, two parameters C_H and C_V are specified in the SLA which correspond to

Table 3. Configurable elasticity parameters and configuration constraints

Parameters		Configuration constraints
Configurable type	OR^c	Follow the description in Sect. 2.2
	AND^c	
	XOR^c	
Configurable elasticity type	HV^c	H, V, HV
	V	-
	H	-
	HV	-

the maximal capacities provided by the cloud provider if the configurations H and V are selected respectively. We denote by C_a the maximal capacity required by an activity "a" for a tenant specific process variant. The configuration guidelines of the configurable HV^c type are defined in Eq. (1).

$$HV^c = \begin{cases} H & if \ C_a \leq C_H \ \wedge \ C_H = min(C_H, C_V) \\ V & if \ C_a \leq C_V \ \wedge \ C_V = min(C_H, C_V) \\ HV & if \ (C_a > C_H \ \wedge \ C_a > C_V) \ \wedge \ (C_a \leq C_V + C_H) \end{cases} \quad (1)$$

where $min(C_H, C_V)$ returns the minimal capacity. The configuration H is recommended to the tenant in case (1) the maximal capacity required by its activity is less than or equal to the maximal capacity provided by the cloud provider in the horizontal elasticity and (2) the capacity of the horizontal elasticity is less than that of the vertical elasticity. The configuration V is recommended in case the same aforementioned conditions are valid for C_V. The configuration HV is recommended in case C_a is greater than C_V and C_H but is less than or equal to their sum. For example, suppose that a tenant specifies that the activity a_1 in the process in Fig. 4 requires a maximal capacity of $100 \, uc$ (i.e. $C_a = 100$ unit-of-capacity where unit-of-capacity can be a storage, compute or network related units). The cloud provider specifies that a maximal capacity of $200 \, uc$ can be provided for the vertical elasticity (i.e. $C_V = 200 \, uc$) and a maximal capacity of $150 \, uc$ can be provided for the horizontal elasticity (i.e. $C_H = 150 \, uc$). Since, $C_a \leq C_H$ and $C_a \leq C_V$ then H and V are potential configurations. However, as C_H is the minimal ensured capacity, the configuration H is recommended.

3.3 Configurable Resource Sharing/Batching Operator

As different tenants sharing the configurable process may have different requirements, the shareability of a resource should account for variability. For instance, in our running examples in Figs. 2 and 3, the resource "compute3" is shareable between multiple instances of two activities in the first process (a_1 and a_{13}) (i.e. it is shared and batch) while it is shared between three activities in the second process (a_1, a_{13} and a_{14}). Therefore, we define the *configurable resource sharing* operator denoted as $(S/B)^c$ which allows to model the variability according to (i) the number of instances/activities that can share the corresponding resource and (ii) the way the activities share this resource (i.e. in a shareable, batch or hybrid manner) (see $(S/B)^c$ operator in Fig. 4).

Table 4. Configurable sharing/batching parameters and configuration constraints

Parameters		Configuration constraints
Configurable type	OR^c	Follow the description in Sect. 2.2
	AND^c	
	XOR^c	
Configurable shareability type	SB^c	S, B, SB
	S	-
	B	-
	SB	-

Table 4 summarizes the configurable resource sharing/batching parameters and their configuration constraints. The first parameter (configurable type) is similar to the configurable type in the configurable resource assignment and configurable elasticity operators. It can be either an OR^c, AND^c or XOR^c and allows to model the behaviour of the resource shareability. Referring to our example in Fig. 4, an AND^c is used to connect the resource "compute3" to the activities a_1, a_{13} and a_{14}. Since an AND^c can be only configured to an AND with possible restricted branches, one can configure the type by selecting only a subset of the activities to share the corresponding resource. For example, the AND^c can be configured to an AND associated to a_1 and a_{13} in order to specify that only a_1 and a_{13} may share "compute3". The second parameter (configurable shareability type) allows to define the way the activities share the resource. Four shareability types: (i) SB (i.e. hybrid), (ii) S (i.e. shareable), (iii) B (i.e. batch) and (iv) SB^c (configurable hybrid) are defined from which only SB^c is configurable and can be configured to S, B or SB.

For instance, in order to derive the shareability configuration of the resource "compute3" in the process variant in Fig. 2, the configurable shareability operator in Fig. 4 is configured as follows:

- AND^c is configured to an AND associated to a_1 and a_{13};
- The configurable shareability type SB^c is configured to a SB (as "compute3" in Fig. 2 is hybrid, i.e. it is shared between multiple instances and activities)

4 Proof of Concept

In this section, we first outline our extension of *Signavio Process Editor*[2] as a proof of concept to validate our approach. Signavio is an open source web application for

---

[2] Source Code at: https://code.google.com/p/signavio-core-components/.

developing process models in BPMN. Thus, it can support our context of cloud-based processes. More details on our application can be found at http://www-inf. it-sudparis.eu/SIMBAD/tools/Configurable-RA-BPM. We have added two main functionalities to *Signavio* as follows:

1. *Cloud resources' modeling:* We have extended BPMN 2.0 in order to allow for cloud resources' description and integrated it within Signavio (Area 1 in Fig. 5). The user can drag and drop the cloud resources needed for different activities in the process. He can also specify the different attributes and properties as defined in the OCCI standard.

2. *Configurable resource allocation operators:* This functionality allows to allocate the cloud resources to activities using the configurable operators presented in Sect. 3. The three configurable operators (i) assignment for A^c, (ii) elasticity for E^c and (iii) sharing/Batching for $(S/B)^c$ (Area 2 in Fig. 5) can be used to link the process activities to their allocated cloud resources. Their different configurable parameters (e.g. configurable type, configurable elasticity type, etc.) and configuration choices can be also specified (Area 3).

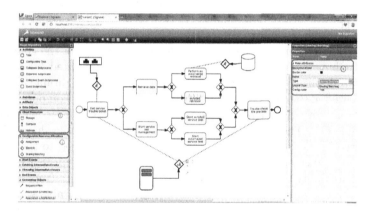

Fig. 5. Application screenshot

5 Experimentation

In order to evaluate the usefulness and effectiveness of our approach, we performed experiments using a real dataset of business processes from Orange, a french telecom industrial partner. Different variants of business processes for VoIP assurance in France are defined and used by Orange. These variants and their allocated resources are manually and separately described. In total, there are 28 variants of the same process using about 30 different resources. Some activities have the same allocated resources in multiple variants, while others have different allocated resources and different needs for shareability and elasticity. In order to consolidate their expertise in telecommunication domain,

Orange experts were interested in constructing one consolidate configurable model that also depicts the different resource allocation strategies.

To construct the configurable model, we proceeded in three different ways. First, using our approach, we designed a configurable process model that depicts the variability both at the control flow and resource flow levels. Second, we modelled a configurable process model with a basic approach that does not consider the variability at the resource level. Thus, whenever an activity has different resource allocation possibilities, it is duplicated in the model in a choice block to express that there exist different resource allocation possibilities and so one should be selected. Third, we designed the same configurable process model using the approach introduced by La Rosa et al. in [5] which is close to ours but does not consider the variability at the shareability and elasticity levels. Therefore, when such a variability occurs (e.g., an activity has the same allocated resources in different variants but with different needs for elasticity and shareability) the same strategy as in the second approach (i.e. duplication of activities) is used. Figure 6 shows three process fragments from Model 1, Model 2 and Model 3. An activity a_1 is assigned to a variable number of resources (network and compute). The compute resource can be shared between a variable number of the activities (instances) a_1 and a_2. According to our approach (represented by Model 1), a_1 is linked to the compute and network resources with a configurable OR via the configurable assignment operator. The compute resource is shared and therefore is linked to a_1 and a_2 with a configurable AND via the configurable Sharing/Batching operator. In the basic approach (represented by Model 2), there are two duplications. The first one is to model the configurable allocation. It is represented in the model by an activity a_1 assigned to the compute resource, and another activity a_1 assigned to the network resource which are connected by a configurable OR. The second one is to model the configurable shareability. It is represented in the model by the activities a_1 and a_2 assigned to the compute resource and connected through a configurable AND that represents the configurable shareability choice. In the approach of La Rosa et al. (represented by Model 3), there is only one duplication to model the configurable shraeability. The configurable allocation is supported and can be modelled as in our approach.

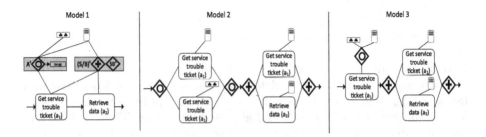

Fig. 6. Fragments of configurable processes of the three models

Thereafter, we assessed the quality of the three models in terms of their structural complexity. We computed the well known complexity metrics proposed in the literature: CFC (Control Flow Complexity), ACD (Average Connector Degree), CNC (Coefficient of Network Connectivity) and density. The CFC [29] metric evaluates the complexity of the process with respect to the presence of gateways OR, AND and XOR. The ACD [30] metric generates the number of nodes that a connector has as an average. The CNC [31] gives the ratio of edges to nodes. Whereas the density [32] metric relates the number of edges to the number of maximum edges that can exist among nodes.

The above metrics have been proposed to assess the complexity of the control flow perspective in business processes. We also use these metrics to compute the complexity of the resource flow perspective since we are using control-flow like operators (i.e. XOR, OR and AND). The obtained values for the three configurable process models are summarized in Table 5. Model 1 refers to the configurable process model constructed with our approach; Model 2 is the configurable process model constructed with a basic approach that does not take the variability at the resource level; and Model 3 is the configurable process model constructed using the approach in [5]. For Model 1 and Model 3, we separately compute the complexity metrics at the control flow (referred to as $[metric]_c$) and resource flow (referred to as $[metric]_r$) perspectives. This is a logical choice since the resource and control-flow perspectives are separately modeled.

The results show that the metrics of Model 1 have noticeably low values compared to values of Model 2. For instance, even by summing the CFC_c (28) and CFC_r (25) of Model 1, the result remains smaller than the CFC_c (128) of Model 2. Hence, separately modelling the control-flow and resource-flow variability decreases the complexity of the model. We also notice that the density $density_c$ (0.02), and $density_r$ (0.04) of Model 1 are greater than the density $density_c$ (0.01) of Model 2. However, as stated in [33], the density metric is negatively correlated with the complexity of the model.

By comparing the metrics' values of Model 1 and 3, we notice that Model 1 has better complexity values for the control-flow while Model 3 has better

Table 5. Structural Complexity metrics for different approaches

Complexity metric		Model 1	Model 2	Model 3
CFC	CFC_c	28	128	39
	CFC_r	25	-	14
ACD	ACD_c	3.30	7.37	5.61
	ACD_r	2.11	-	1.64
CNC	CNC_c	0.56	1.18	0.61
	CNC_r	0.51	-	0.78
Density	$Density_c$	0.02	0.01	0.01
	$Density_r$	0.04	-	0.03

complexity values for the resource-flow. This can be explained by the fact that Model 1 fully supports the resource variability modelling (i.e. allocation, shareability and elasticity). Therefore, we do not need to do duplications in the control flow and hence we obtained better complexity values for the control flow. Whereas, Model 3 is less expressive and only supports the resource variability modelling (i.e. allocation). So, it has better complexity values for the resource flow. Since we did duplications in the control flow to model the variability in the shareability and elasticity, we obtained worst complexity values for the control flow.

6   Conclusion

In this paper, we proposed an approach for configurable cloud resource allocation in multi-tenant business processes. Our aim is to shift the cloud resource allocation from the tenant side to the cloud process provider side for a centralized resource allocation management. Through configuration, different tenants can easily derive their allocated resources. The approach has been described through a real example from an industrial partner and implemented in Signavio process editor. Further, we conduct experiments that validate our proposal.

Some potential threats to validity exist in our study. First, we have been interested in IaaS resources since they are the raw resources on which all others (i.e. PaaS and SaaS resources) are built. Our approach can be easily extended to consider the PaaS and SaaS resources. Second, we have shown the feasibility of our approach through real examples from an industrial partner. The work requests a larger dataset to further evaluate the effectiveness of our approach. Third, the proposed configurable resource operators as well as dependencies among cloud resources should formally be described, which are of a high importance in a multi-tenant environment. We aim, in future work, at extending our previous work [25] so that we define these dependencies in a flexible way so that tenants can customize them depending on their needs. In fact, research on cloud resources' management in BPM still at its beginning stage.

References

1. Mell, P.M., et al.: The nist definition of cloud computing (Technical report) (2011)
2. Rosemann, M., van der Aalst, W.M.P.: A configurable reference modelling language. Inf. Syst. **32**(1), 1–23 (2007)
3. Aalst, W.: Business process configuration in the cloud: how to support and analyze multi-tenant processes? In: ECOWS, pp. 3–10. IEEE (2011)
4. Rosa, M.L., van der Aalst, W.M., Dumas, M., Milani, F.P.: Business process variability modeling: a survey (2013)
5. Rosa, M.L., et al.: Configurable multi-perspective business process models. Inf. Syst. **36**, 313–340 (2011)
6. Kumar, A., Yao, W.: Design and management of flexible process variants using templates and rules. Comput. Ind. **63**, 112–130 (2012)

7. Hallerbach, A., et al.: Capturing variability in business process models: the provop approach. J. Softw. Maintenance Evolution Res. Pract. **22**, 519–546 (2010)
8. Cabanillas, C., Knuplesch, D., Resinas, M., Reichert, M., Mendling, J., Ruiz-Cortés, A.: Ralph: a graphical notation for resource assignments in business processes. In: Zdravkovic, J., Kirikova, M., Johannesson, P. (eds.) CAiSE 2015. LNCS, vol. 9097, pp. 53–68. Springer, Heidelberg (2015)
9. Cabanillas, C., Norta, A., Resinas, M., Mendling, J., Ruiz-Cortés, A.: Towards process-aware cross-organizational human resource management. In: Bider, I., Gaaloul, K., Krogstie, J., Nurcan, S., Proper, H.A., Schmidt, R., Soffer, P. (eds.) BPMDS 2014 and EMMSAD 2014. LNBIP, vol. 175, pp. 79–93. Springer, Heidelberg (2014)
10. Kajan, E., et al.: The network-based business process. IEEE IC **18**, 63–69 (2014)
11. Mietzner, R., Leymann, F.: Generation of BPEL customization processes for SaaS applications from variability descriptors. IEEE Conf. SC **2**, 359–366 (2008)
12. Gottschalk, F., et al.: Configurable workflow models. IJCIS **17**(2), 177 (2008)
13. Ciuksys, D., et al.: Reusing ontological knowledge about business processes in is engineering: process configuration problem. Informatica **18**, 585–602 (2007)
14. Duipmans, E.: Business process management in the cloud: Bpaas (2012)
15. Wang, M., Bandara, K.Y., Pahl, C.: Process as a service. In: SCC, pp. 578–585 (2010)
16. Candra, M.Z.C., Truong, H.-L., Dustdar, S.: Provisioning quality-aware social compute units in the cloud. In: Basu, S., Pautasso, C., Zhang, L., Fu, X. (eds.) ICSOC 2013. LNCS, vol. 8274, pp. 313–327. Springer, Heidelberg (2013)
17. Sengupta, B., Jain, A., Bhattacharya, K., Truong, H.-L., Dustdar, S.: Who do you call? problem resolution through social compute units. In: Liu, C., Ludwig, H., Toumani, F., Yu, Q. (eds.) Service Oriented Computing. LNCS, vol. 7636, pp. 48–62. Springer, Heidelberg (2012)
18. Hoenisch, P., et al.: Workflow scheduling and resource allocation for cloud-based execution of elastic processes. In: IEEE 6th International Conference on SOCA, USA (2013)
19. Van Der Aalst, W.M.P., Ter Hofstede, A.H.M., Kiepuszewski, B., Barros, A.P.: Workflow patterns. Distrib. Parallel Databases **14**, 5–51 (2003)
20. Russell, N., van der Aalst, W.M.P., ter Hofstede, A.H.M., Edmond, D.: Workflow resource patterns: identification, representation and tool support. In: Pastor, Ó., Falcão e Cunha, J. (eds.) CAiSE 2005. LNCS, vol. 3520, pp. 216–232. Springer, Heidelberg (2005)
21. Schulte, S., et al.: Costdriven optimization of cloud resource allocation for elastic processes. Int. J. Cloud Comput. **1**(2), 1–14 (2013)
22. Schulte, S., Hoenisch, P., Venugopal, S., Dustdar, S.: Realizing elastic processes with ViePEP. In: Ghose, A., Zhu, H., Yu, Q., Delis, A., Sheng, Q.Z., Perrin, O., Wang, J., Wang, Y. (eds.) ICSOC 2012. LNCS, vol. 7759, pp. 439–442. Springer, Heidelberg (2013)
23. Pufahl, L., Herzberg, N., Meyer, A., Weske, M.: Flexible batch configuration in business processes based on events. In: Franch, X., Ghose, A.K., Lewis, G.A., Bhiri, S. (eds.) ICSOC 2014. LNCS, vol. 8831, pp. 63–78. Springer, Heidelberg (2014)
24. Jennings, B., Stadler, R.: Resource management in clouds: survey and research challenges. J. Netw. Syst. Manag. **23**, 567–619 (2015)
25. Hachicha, E., Gaaloul, W.: Towards resource-aware business process development in the cloud. In: 29th IEEE International Conference AINA, South Korea, pp. 761–768 (2015)

26. Cabral, L., et al.: The business process modeling ontology. In: SBPM, pp. 9–16 (2009)
27. Edmonds, A., et al.: Toward an open cloud standard. IEEE IC **16**, 15–25 (2012)
28. Rady, M.: Parameters for service level agreements generation in cloud computing. In: Castano, S., Vassiliadis, P., Lakshmanan, L.V.S., Lee, M.L. (eds.) ER 2012 Workshops 2012. LNCS, vol. 7518, pp. 13–22. Springer, Heidelberg (2012)
29. Cardoso, J.: Evaluating the process control-flow complexity. In: ICWS (2005)
30. Cardoso, J., Mendling, J., Neumann, G., Reijers, H.A.: A discourse on complexity of process models. In: Eder, J., Dustdar, S. (eds.) BPM Workshops 2006. LNCS, vol. 4103, pp. 117–128. Springer, Heidelberg (2006)
31. List, B., et al.: Evaluation of conceptual bp modelling languages. In: SAC (2006)
32. Reijers, H.A., Vanderfeesten, I.T.P.: Cohesion and coupling metrics for workflow process design. In: Desel, J., Pernici, B., Weske, M. (eds.) BPM 2004. LNCS, vol. 3080, pp. 290–305. Springer, Heidelberg (2004)
33. Vogelaar, J., et al.: Comparing business processes to determine the feasibility of configurable models: a case study. In: BPM Workshops, France, pp. 50–61 (2011)

Context-Aware Analysis of Past Process Executions to Aid Resource Allocation Decisions

Renuka Sindhgatta[1(✉)], Aditya Ghose[2], and Hoa Khanh Dam[2]

[1] IBM Research-India, Bangalore, India
renuka.sr@in.ibm.com
[2] Decision Systems Lab, School of Computing and Information Technology,
University of Wollongong, Wollongong, NSW 2522, Australia
{aditya,hoa}@uow.edu.au

Abstract. The allocation of resources to process tasks can have a significant impact on the performance (such as cost, time) of those tasks, and hence of the overall process. Past resource allocation decisions, when correlated with process execution histories annotated with quality of service (or performance) measures, can be a rich source of knowledge about the best resource allocation decisions. The optimality of resource allocation decisions is not determined by the process instance alone, but also by the context in which these instances are executed. This phenomenon turns out to be even more compelling when the resources in question are human resources. Human workers with same the organizational role and capabilities can have heterogeneous behaviors based on their operational context. In this work, we propose an approach to supporting resource allocation decisions by extracting information about the process context and process performance from past process executions. The information extracted is analyzed using exploratory data mining techniques to discover resource allocation decisions. The knowledge thus acquired can be used to guide resource allocations in new process instances. Experiments performed on synthetic and real-world execution logs demonstrate the effectiveness of the proposed approach.

Keywords: Resource allocation · Context-aware · Data-driven analysis · Process execution logs

1 Introduction

One of the critical determinants of process performance is the effectiveness (or even optimality) of resource allocation decisions (i.e., decisions on what resources to allocate to each process task). Process execution histories annotated with quality of service (or performance or outcome) measures together with the process context, can be a rich source of knowledge about the best resource allocation decisions. The optimality of resource allocation decisions is not determined by the process instance alone, but also by the context in which these instances are executed. This phenomenon turns out to be even more compelling when

© Springer International Publishing Switzerland 2016
S. Nurcan et al. (Eds.): CAiSE 2016, LNCS 9694, pp. 575–589, 2016.
DOI: 10.1007/978-3-319-39696-5_35

the resources in question are human resources. Human workers with same the organizational role and capabilities can have heterogeneous behaviors based on their operational context. In this work, we propose an approach to supporting resource allocation decisions by extracting information about the process context and process performance from past process executions.

The notion of *process context* plays a key role in this account. We define the process context to be that body of *exogenous knowledge potentially relevant to the execution of the process that is available at the start of the execution of the process, and that is not impacted/modified via the execution of the process* (in general, exogenous knowledge impacting the execution of a process can be dynamic, changing during the execution of the process, but our focus on only the knowledge that holds at the start of the execution of a process is a simplifying assumption). The process context can impact resource allocation decisions in a variety of ways. Consider a document printing process that takes as input a document and goes through a series of steps resulting in the document being printed. During office hours, the process might allocate a high-throughput (and high carbon-footprint) printer to the print task, but allocate a slower (but lower carbon-footprint) printer outside of office hours. The differential resourcing of the print task is driven by the context (specifically the time of day) which does not form part of the process data (generated or consumed by the process) but is exogenous. The context can also contain important information about resource characteristics (which, again, do not form part of the process data). Thus, for handling an insurance claim from a high priority customer, we might allocate an experienced employee as a resource (the experience or other attributes of employees do not form part of the process data - they are neither generated, impacted or consumed by the process - but have a bearing on the execution of the process). We note that processes can always be re-designed to incorporate context attributes as process inputs, but such an approach is not particularly useful given the complexity of the process designs that would result (consider, for example, the complexity of a process design that incorporates XOR branches for each distinct resourcing modality for a task).

Our proposed approach involves the use of two data mining techniques: (1) Decision tree learning and (2) the k-Nearest Neighbor (k-NN) algorithm. With the former, we take a process context and a history of past process instances (each instance consisting of set of tasks executed, the relevant process data and a set of outcomes or performance indicators) and compute a decision tree which enables us to predict the performance of a (potentially partially executed) process instance. The decision tree thus obtained can also be used to extract rules correlating contextual knowledge with process data when the intent is to guarantee a certain set of outcomes (in other words, a certain performance profile). Given that resource characteristics typically form part of the process context, these rules can be valuable in determining the attributes of the resources necessary for achieving desired performance. With the k-NN approach, we use k-NN regression to determine from the nearest neighbors of a process instance, those values of the process context attributes (and particularly those that characterize resources) that would likely lead to the desired outcomes. We present an evaluation of our approach using both a real-world dataset and a synthetic dataset.

The approach that we propose is of considerable practical value. Conventionally, the decision taken by a project or team lead (in many practical process resourcing settings) is based on human judgment, experience and on her implicit understanding of the context. Consequently, resource allocation activity is subjective and relies on the experience of a project or team lead. Automated, data-driven support can potentially serve as a game-changer in these settings.

The paper is organized as follows. Section 2 presents related work, while Sect. 3 provides a simple running example. Section 4 presents a discussion of the general setting. Our proposed approach is outlined in Sect. 5, and a detailed empirical evaluation is presented in Sect. 6, followed by conclusions and future work in Sect. 7.

2   Related Work

Context Modeling in Business Processes: Modeling of context in business process has been proposed by Saidani et al. [17] who define context as "... any information reflecting changing circumstances during the execution of a BP can be considered as contextual information". They introduce a taxonomy of contextual information for business processes consisting of four categories: (i) context related to location (ii) context related to time (iii) context related to resources and (iv) context related to organization. In more recent work [18], a meta-model for context has been defined. The meta-model comprises of context entity and context attributes. Context entities are connected to each other using context relationships. We have leveraged this meta-model in our work, we have used context entities such as process and resource, and their related contextual attributes. The contextual attributes of each process instance are used in conjunction with process outcomes to extract resource allocation rules. Ghattas et al. [4,5] use process context and process outcomes from execution histories to discover decisions taken in the past. In their work, the authors model the process context and outcomes. The definition of context is based on a Generic Process Model defined by the authors where, external events, that are out of the control of process execution are referred to as context (something we leverage in our conception of process context). Process instances, containing contextual information and process outcomes are clustered and a decision tree is built to discover decisions taken in the past. The approach has been validated for a clinical process [3]. Our work is similar, as it uses past execution histories and context information to further link with process outcomes. However, in our work we have focused in greater detail on specific contextual characteristics of resources, which has an impact on both the process outcomes and allocation decisions. Process context has also been defined by a different set of authors as "Minimum set of variables containing all relevant information that impact the design and execution of a business process." [16] (our conception of process context is somewhat more specific relative to this definition). A large body of additional work exists in context-aware approaches to information systems, as well formal approaches to the modeling of context, but space constraints preclude a detailed discussion of these.

Resource Allocation Recommendation: Some of the early work by Kumar et al. [12], proposed dynamic allocation of task to resources, considering factors such as suitability, availability, urgency and conformance. Further, their recent work [11] highlighted the use of cooperation among the team members involved in the process, and developed an allocation algorithm to maximized team cooperation. The authors, have highlighted the need for examining impact of cooperation on throughput and other process outcomes. In this work, we consider multiple such resource specific context, in addition to process outcome and discover resource allocation rules. Work experience is an important contextual characteristic of a (human) resource, that influences allocation of tasks. Sonja et al. [10], define various measures of experience. The authors, further describe an experience breeding model [9], for maintaining experience levels of the resources. Detailed modeling of experience enables better evaluation of resource allocation decisions. In our work, we have used experience as one of the contextual characteristics of a resource. In their work [13], Nakatumba et al. have analyzed the influence of workload on service times. The authors use event logs to extract service times and workload on a resource and build a regression model using workload as a single predictor of service time. While this model is useful to compare specific resources and their efficiencies, it is limited as there are several factors of resource influencing service times. In this work, we use predictors that are guided by the context model. Resource behavior indicators [14], has been defined by Pika et al. In their work, the authors provide a framework for extracting resource behavior indicators from event logs and highlight the change in these indicators over time. Huang et al. [7] present resource behavior measures for competence, preference, availability and collaboration. Enriching resource model, to include additional resource characteristics, has also been described in [22]. In our work, we use resource behavior indicators as resource context, and discover the influence of these behaviors on process outcomes. Recommending the next action to take, based on a user's current execution history and specific goal, has been described in [19]. The approach evaluates past history of executions to mine recommendations. The work focuses on the control flow and the context is not considered. Predicting process outcome in terms of duration of task has been evaluated by authors in [20]. However, the resources involved and the context of the executing process, has not been taken into account. In one of the recent works [1], the authors present a general framework to derive and correlate process characteristics. The framework does not consider contextual characteristics of process, resources, and its influence on the process characteristics.

3   Example

For the purpose of illustration, we describe an example process that is adopted throughout the paper. Consider a process for handling vehicle repair and maintenance in a garage. Figure 1 illustrates the business process. The process starts with a 'Receptionist' receiving the vehicle (task 'Receive Vehicle'). A 'Supervisor' inspects the vehicle (task 'Inspect Vehicle'). After inspection, a decision is made to either repair the vehicle or send it for regular maintenance. The vehicle is either repaired (task 'Repair Vehicle') or goes through maintenance (task 'Vehicle Maintenance'). These tasks are performed by a mechanic. The supervisor finally checks the vehicle (task 'Check Quality'). The process ends by the receptionist handing over the vehicle to the owner (task 'Hand over Vehicle').

In this process, there are certain attributes, defined as a part of the process design: the process type indicating whether a vehicle requires repair or maintenance, the models of the car that the process supports, the organization model of the process with resources, their roles and capabilities. There are certain aspects that are dependent on the environment or situation during process execution: the problem list associated to each car, the utilization of mechanics at a specific instance of time (the number of tasks the mechanic is currently working on, when multi-tasking or number of tasks waiting in the queue of a mechanic), the preference of a mechanic to work on a given model of car or collaboration of a mechanic with a co-worker. These aspects do impact the process execution but are not modeled as a part of the design and become contextual characteristics of a process instance or resource. In this process, if a problem of the vehicle has been handled by only one particular mechanic, in the past, then it is preferable to allocate task to that mechanic. Contextual characteristics of the resource and process instance are considered during task allocation and forms a part of the experience gained by person allocating tasks.

Process outcomes are another important aspect that are defined and need to be assessed during execution. In this process, there is a goal set for the completion time of the process: The repair of a car should take no more than 3 days while the car maintenance should take no more than 5 h. A process instance may be successful or may fail in meeting the goal. Our approach uses the process outcome, process instance attributes, contextual characteristics of the process instance and resources involved to discern allocation rules.

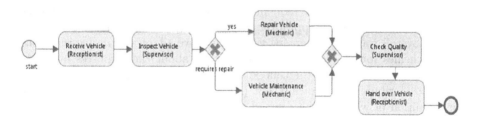

Fig. 1. Process model vehicle maintenance and repair

4   The General Setting

In this section, we explain the notion of process context and describe the key data items that are used by the data mining machinery we outline in the following section. We define the *process context* to consist of *exogenously determined knowledge potentially relevant to the execution of the process that is available at the start of the execution of the process, and that is not impacted/modified via the execution of the process.* The intent is to capture the knowledge/data that does not fall under the ambit of the traditional notion of *process data* (or *process attributes*) but can be an important determinant of the performance of a process instance. It is critical that only exogenously determined data (i.e., determined not by the process but by the "rest of the world") constitute the process context. In contrast, process attributes (or process data) include endogenously determined elements (i.e., attributes whose values are determined via the execution of the process) as well data provided as input to the process. In general, the process context can be dynamic, i.e., exogenously determined knowledge relevant to the process might change while the process executes. For the purposes of this paper, we make the simplifying assumption that only the context that holds at the start of the execution of the process is of interest. A particularly interesting type of contextual knowledge is knowledge about resources (resource characteristics are typically not determined, impacted, or provided as input to the execution of a process, and thus correctly belong to the process context). Thus the experience of a vehicle repairer (i.e., a mechanic) is part of the process context in the example in the previous section. Contextual knowledge unrelated to resources can also be of interest. For instance, a history of process executions of a insurance claim handling process might suggest that these tend to perform poorly (in terms of completion time, cost or number of problem escalations) during periods of financial market volatility. Thus financial market volatility might be an important contextual attribute that determines the performance of the claim handling process. The context can be of two types (i) generic and relevant to all processes and (ii) domain specific [17]. Some of the generic contextual characteristics defined in [17] are reusable across processes, while the domain specific contextual characteristics need to be identified by a domain experts.

We assume that the *process context* is modeled by a set of attribute-value pairs C. Other approaches to modeling the context are possible, such as truth-functional assertions in an appropriate logic, but our approach is quite general, and the overall framework remains valid even if we adopt alternative representation schemes for the context. Our knowledge about the resources available to a process is also part of the contextual knowledge that can brought to bear (resource attributes are typically not part of process data, and hence satisfy our definition of what can be deemed to be contextual knowledge). We sometimes find it convenient to denote knowledge about resources as $C_r \subseteq C$ and to denote those parts of contextual knowledge that do not pertain to resources by C_p where $C_p = C - C_r$. We use a set of attribute-value pairs X to denote *process data* in the usual sense, i.e., data provided as input to a process, data modified or impacted by a process and data generated as output by a process. We note that the *signature* of X (i.e., the schema for process data) is associated with a process design while an actual set of attribute-value pairs are associated with a process instance. We use A to denote the set of all activities that form part of a process design. Finally, we are interested in the (non-functional) *outcomes* (or *performance*) of a process (we aim to predict these for a process instance, and to provision processes to achieve desired outcomes). We use a set of non-functional attribute (or QoS factor)-value pairs O to denote the outcome of a given process instance. The *signature* of O is associated with a process design, and represents the set of non-functional attributes that can be used to assess the performance of an instance of that design.

Our approach relies on being able to mine an *execution history* represented by a set of *process instances* and their associated *process contexts*. On occasion, we will also leverage a record of a partially-executed process instance for determining the best resource to allocate to process task (based on knowledge mines from the execution history).

Definition 1 (Process Instance). *A* process instance *is a tuple* $PI = \langle v_x, v_a, C, v_o \rangle$, *where:*

- $v_x = (v_x^1, \ldots v_x^i) \subseteq X$, *is a set of attribute-value pairs representing available process data for that instance.*
- $v_o = (v_o^1, \ldots v_o^j) \subseteq O$, *is a set of* $\langle$*non-functional-attribute, value*$\rangle$ *pairs or outcomes.*
- $v_a = (a_i | a_i \in A \land f_{executed}(a_i) = true)$, *set of activities that were executed in that process instance,* $(f_{executed}(a_i) = true) => $ *activity* a_i *was executed in the process).*
- C, *is a set of attribute-value pairs of the process context.*

5   Proposed Approach

Our intent is to provide data-enabled decision support for allocating resources to process tasks. We achieve this in two ways: (1) By applying *decision tree learning* and (2) By deploying the *k-nearest neighbor algorithm*.

Decision Tree Learning: The key problem we solve is as follows. *Given:*

- An execution history of process instances and their associated process contexts as defined above and
- A description of the process context as defined above,

Compute:

- A decision tree which enables us to predict the performance of a (potentially partially executed) process instance.

Given the decision tree that is mined, we are able to answer the following questions:

- Given a specification of context and process data, we are able to predict the performance of the process. We can make predictions about performance even in the presence of partial specifications of context and process data.

– We can extract rules from the decision tree that identify what states of the context and what process data are likely to lead to a given process outcome. These rules provide important guidance in process provisioning decisions.

In both the above modes of leveraging the decision tree that is learnt, we rely on the important observation that *the context often contains detailed knowledge about the resources that might potentially be used in a process instance.* We also represent knowledge about resource-task pairs in the context (for example the experience of the resource used for the repair task in Fig. 3 is represented by the context attribute *Experience.RepairV* - this tells us what the experience of the *repairer* was, independent of the identity of the specific individual) and not about resources in isolation (e.g., a specific person, or a specific machine). We first cluster process instances using the process attributes (v_x) and process activities (v_a, indicating the path of the process). *Clustering*, groups the process instances in a way that similar clusters have similar process attributes and execution paths. Two-step clustering method [8] is used, as it is capable of handling both categorical and numerical data, and identifies the optimal number of clusters from the data. However, any Gaussian mixture model based clustering with a suitable distance metric to identify (dis)similar process instances can be used [2]. The intent behind clustering is to mine decision trees only from clusters of similar process instances, and not from across the board. The next step is to generate a decision tree model using the outcome(s) (v_o) as the target variable(s) and context attributes as predictor/independent variables (C). Our approach is best illustrated in the example in Fig. 3. The root node of decision tree in Fig. 3 is the process outcome. At each branch, a branching criterion is used for determining which predictor variable is best suited to split process instances. At the first branch, customerType is used to split the process instances. 35 % of the process instances have the value *customerType = premium*. The remaining 65 % of the instances have *customerType = normal* (the branches further on, has not been detailed due to lack of space). The next split of the tree, for premium customer, is based on the experience of the repairer. The percentage of process instances having a specific value of the process outcome, is available at each node. The next predictor used for splitting the tree is the preference of the repairer and the final split is based on the utilization of the repairer. Given the attributes of a resource-task pair, the tree helps predict the process outcome. In Fig. 3, if *customerType = premium* and if the experience of the repairer is low ($Experience.RepairV = LOW$), then the probability of meeting the service level is very low 0.3 %, ($0.19 * 0.02 = 0.003$).

k-Nearest Neighbor (k-NN): This approach is one of the options available when the intent is to provide decision support for allocating resources to process tasks in partially executed process instances. We provide as input the process data, the sequence of tasks executed thus far in the process instance and the desired outcomes (assignments of values to non-functional attributes). The k-nearest neighbor algorithm [6] identifies past process instances that are similar to the current instance. We use k-NN regression to identify the contextual conditions (specifically, those parts of the context that represent knowledge about the resource-task pairs) which would lead to the desired outcome/performance of the instance. k-NN regression thus provides the attributes of the resource to be deployed for a given task. Using the same setting as the example in Fig. 3, k-NN regression might tell, based on neighbors most similar in terms of process data and the partial sequence of tasks executed, that using a repairer with high experience is most likely to lead to a good outcome (in this case, service level being met). k-NN regression relies on averaging attribute values of the nearest neighbors. For discrete-valued attributes, we use majority voting of the nearest neighbors.

Figure 2 illustrates our approach to provide data-enabled decision support.

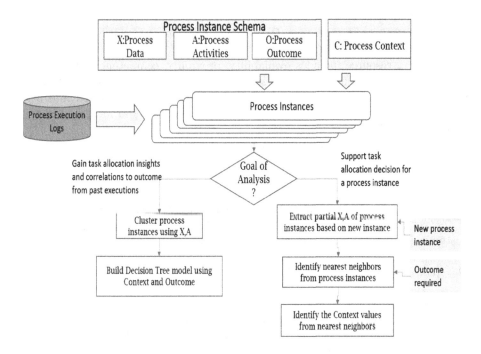

Fig. 2. Approach for Context-Aware analysis of Resource allocations

6   Evaluation

This section presents two evaluations: first using synthetic execution logs and second using a sub set of a real-world event log. Evaluation of the synthetic data aims to verify the ability of using the approach to discover context dependent task allocation rules. The real-world data, is used to validate the possibility of extracting context, and gain insights using event logs.

6.1   Evaluation Using Simulated Process Instances

The synthetic data is created by simulating process instances of the car repair and maintenance process, described in Sect. 2. The context comprises of the process context C_p and resource context C_r.

Attributes of $C_p = \{problemType, TimeOfDay, caseHandling\}$

$problemType$ is a problem reported by the customer that needs to be addressed. $caseHandling$ is a domain specific context attribute and is set to true, if the supervisor who has inspected the car is the same as the supervisor doing a quality check.

Attributes of $C_r = \{Experience, Preference, Collaboration, Utilization\}$

Context of a resource includes availability, proximity, competency, experience, collaboration sensitivity, age, gender and so on [17]. Further, some of these resource contextual characteristics include behavior of the resource such as utilization, preference and collaboration have been identified and measured in the previous work [7,14].
The schema for process data is given by

$X = \{isRepair, vehicleModel, customerType\}$

$isRepair$ indicates if the request is for repair. The $vehicleModel$ is the model of the vehicle to be repaired or maintained and $customerType$ depicts if the customer is a premium customer or normal customer.

$O = \{completionTime, metServiceLevel\}$

completionTime is the time taken for the process to complete. $metServiceLevel$ refers to the meeting service levels defined for customer type. In the example scenario, if a customer is a premium customer, metServiceLevel is defined as true if $completionTime \leq 18h$ for repair and $\leq 2h$ for maintenance. For a normal customer, metServiceLevel is true if $completionTime \leq 24h$ for repair and $\leq 3h$ for maintenance.

Process Instances Generated for the Model. A simulation model is used to generate process instances based on the process context model. Gaussian distribution functions are used to generate values for the context of process, resources and process attributes. The completion time is generated by considering the context and attributes of the process. There is additional randomness added to the generation of completion time to imitate real-world settings. 10000 process instances are simulated. The process instance data is used as follows:

Decision Tree Learning: This step starts with clustering the process instances based on process attributes. The process instances are clustered based on a

Table 1. Importance of Predictor with metServiceLevel as the target

Predictor	Predictor importance
customerType	0.57
Experience.Repair	0.23
Preference.Repair	0.19
Utilization.Repair	0.14
caseHandling	0.2
Team collaboration	0.1

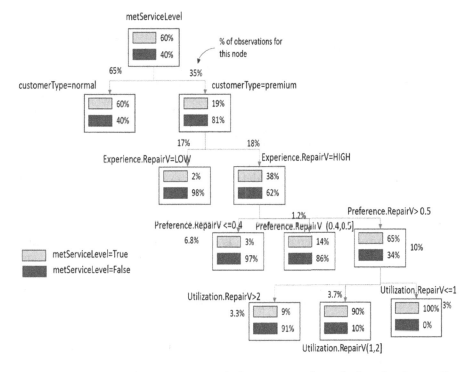

Fig. 3. Decision tree depicting one path from root node to leaf nodes for metServiceLevel prediction

process attribute *isRepair* indicating if a vehicle is for repair. A decision tree is built with the metServiceLevel as the target variable and context as predictor. Chi-square Automatic Interaction Detection (CHAID) algorithm is used to construct the decision tree [15]. Table 1 shows the predictor importance. The most important predictor is the customerType as the serviceLevel is stringent for a premium customer and relaxed for a normal customer. The other resource context variables such as experience of the resource performing the repair task, the preference of the resource, enable predicting the process outcome. The decision tree (Fig. 3) predicts the outcome with 95.3 % accuracy. The task allocation rules for a premium customer can be derived from the tree. One such rule for task allocation would be:

$if(customerType = premium) \land (Experience.RepairV = HIGH) \land$
$(Preference.RepairV > 0.5) \land (Utilization.RepairV <= 1)$
$then\ (metServciceLevel = true)$

The variable Experience.RepairV implies the value 'Experience', of the resource performing Repair vehicle activity. The rule indicates that for the repair task of a premium customer, a resource with high experience and higher preference and utilization of $<=1$ should be chosen for higher probability of successful outcome.

K-Nearest Neighbor: Another useful scenario would be in supporting the decision of task allocation, during process execution. In this scenario, a process may have executed partially (or is in its initial state). The *new* executing process instance and the target outcome of the executing process are given as input. In the example, we provide the $\{isRepair = false, customerType = premium, vehicleModel = XY\}$ and completionTime of 4 h, as input. The input values are matched against past process instances. K-Nearest Neighbor algorithm (K-NN), is used to find process instances that are closest to the current process execution instance. There are similarity distance functions that consider continuous and categorical data. For our evaluation, we use Euclidean distance measure. Statistical packages such as SPSS [8] provide an estimate of K. For our experiment, K is set to 5.

The context values of the nearest neighbors (average for continuous values and majority voting for discrete values), is used as input, to find the matching resources. Table 2 shows the key context attributes required for the maintenance of a vehicle for premium customer (process attribute) and an outcome or completionTime $= 4$ h. The matching resource is identified by selecting resources with the same experience, utilization and preference.

Table 2. Nearest neighbors and resource recommendations for a premium customer with 4 h completionTime

Collaboration	Experience	Utilization	Preference
1	HIGH	1	0.17
1	HIGH	1	0.82
1	LOW	1	0.91
1	HIGH	2	0.55
1	HIGH	1	0.81

A similar K-NN model, when built for a process requiring maintenance of a vehicle for a regular customer, with an outcome or completionTime =6 h, indicates that resource with lower experience and higher preference is capable of meeting the outcome. Hence, resource context required for a process outcome varies with the process attribute values.

Table 3. Importance of Predictor with metServiceLevel as the target

Predictor	Predictor importance
Utilization	0.77
Preference	0.15
Incident impact	0.12
Experience	0.08

6.2   Evaluation Using Real-World Event Log

The approach was evaluated on a real-world event log. To this end, we used the logs from the BPI Challenge of 2013 [21]. The data set comprises of logs from an IT incident management system. An incident is created where there is an issue in the IT application. Each incident or issue, has an associated impact and relates to a product of the enterprise. A resource, is allocated the task of resolving the issue.

Lack of information about the domain, limits our ability to model process attributes or the context of the process. Hence, the process context model is limited to generic attributes such as $TimeOfDay$ of the incident. The process attributes are the *impact* of the incident and *product* associated with the incident. The resource context is derived from event logs. We use resource behavior measures that are computed from event logs, for capturing the resource context based on the work presented in [7,14]. The evaluation is done on a subset of the instances where a single resource resolves an incident. Event logs involving multiple resources, do not provide clarity the time spent by each resource on the incident and hence is not used.

The process outcome is based on the completion time. A process with a completion time of < 1 day is set to have metServciceLevel (process outcome). A decision tree is build using the process attributes and context. The model predicts the process outcome with 88.2 % accuracy. Table 3 presents the predictor importance for the process outcome. The utilization of the resource impacts the outcome, followed by the preference of the resource. The impact of the incident, is a process attribute, that influences the outcome. Experience of the resource has lower importance in the model. However, in this model, we had two categories of experience levels (level1, level2), based on the organization or team the resource belonged to.

There could be several other factors, that could influence the outcome, which have not been used for the evaluation of real-world event logs. This requires us access to additional information available in the PAIS. However, the current results indicate, that process context has an impact on the process outcome.

7   Conclusion and Future Work

This paper shows how a history of past process instances and their associated contexts can be mined to provide guidance in resource allocation decisions for a currently executing process instance. Research in the past has analyzed resource behavior or context, but in isolation. The work presented here, uses it in conjunction with the process context and outcomes. This work further uses real-world event logs to derive resource context and discover the influence of the context on process outcome. The effectiveness of such approaches are limited by the insufficient information captured in real-world process systems. As an extension of this work, we would define a taxonomy for process execution logs that would support the ability to derive rich context information of a process. This would further enable us to evaluate the approach by applying it to real-world data and help better understand its applicability in wide variety of business processes.

References

1. de Leoni, M., van der Aalst, W.M.P., Dees, M.: A general framework for correlating business process characteristics. In: Sadiq, S., Soffer, P., Völzer, H. (eds.) BPM 2014. LNCS, vol. 8659, pp. 250–266. Springer, Heidelberg (2014)
2. Fraley, C., Raftery, A.E.: How many clusters? which clustering method? answers via model-based cluster analysis. Comput. J. **41**, 578–588 (1998)
3. Ghattas, J., Peleg, M., Soffer, P., Denekamp, Y.: Learning the context of a clinical process. In: Rinderle-Ma, S., Sadiq, S., Leymann, F. (eds.) BPM 2009. LNBIP, vol. 43, pp. 545–556. Springer, Heidelberg (2010)
4. Ghattas, J., Soffer, P., Peleg, M.: A formal model for process context learning. In: Rinderle-Ma, S., Sadiq, S., Leymann, F. (eds.) BPM 2009. LNBIP, vol. 43, pp. 140–157. Springer, Heidelberg (2010)
5. Ghattas, J., Soffer, P., Peleg, M.: Improving business process decision making based on past experience. Decis. Support Syst. **59**, 93–107 (2014)
6. Hall, P., Park, B.U., Samworth, R.J.: Choice of neighbor order in nearest-neighbor classification. Ann. Statist. **36**(5), 2135–2152 (2008)
7. Huang, Z., Xudong, L., Duan, H.: Resource behavior measure and application in business process management. Expert Syst. Appl. **39**(7), 6458–6468 (2012)
8. IBM. In (2008). http://www-01.ibm.com/software/analytics/spss
9. Kabicher-Fuchs, S., Mangler, J., Rinderle-Ma, S.: Experience breeding in process-aware information systems. In: Salinesi, C., Norrie, M.C., Pastor, Ó. (eds.) CAiSE 2013. LNCS, vol. 7908, pp. 594–609. Springer, Heidelberg (2013)
10. Kabicher-Fuchs, S., Rinderle-Ma, S.: Work experience in PAIS – concepts, measurements and potentials. In: Ralyté, J., Franch, X., Brinkkemper, S., Wrycza, S. (eds.) CAiSE 2012. LNCS, vol. 7328, pp. 678–694. Springer, Heidelberg (2012)
11. Kumar, A., Dijkman, R., Song, M.: Optimal resource assignment in workflows for maximizing cooperation. In: Daniel, F., Wang, J., Weber, B. (eds.) BPM 2013. LNCS, vol. 8094, pp. 235–250. Springer, Heidelberg (2013)
12. Kumar, A., van der Aalst, W.M.P., Verbeek, E.M.W.: Dynamic work distribution in workflow management systems: how to balance quality and performance. J. Manage. Inf. Syst. **18**(3), 157–194 (2002)

13. Nakatumba, J., van der Aalst, W.M.P.: Analyzing resource behavior using process mining. In: Rinderle-Ma, S., Sadiq, S., Leymann, F. (eds.) BPM 2009. LNBIP, vol. 43, pp. 69–80. Springer, Heidelberg (2010)

14. Pika, A., Wynn, M.T., Fidge, C.J., ter Hofstede, A.H.M., Leyer, M., van der Aalst, W.M.P.: An extensible framework for analysing resource behaviour using event logs. In: Jarke, M., Mylopoulos, J., Quix, C., Rolland, C., Manolopoulos, Y., Mouratidis, H., Horkoff, J. (eds.) CAiSE 2014. LNCS, vol. 8484, pp. 564–579. Springer, Heidelberg (2014)

15. Press, L.I., Rogers, M.S., Gerald, H.: An interactive technique for the analysis of multivariate data. Behav. Sci. **14**(5), 364–370 (1969)

16. Rosemann, M., Recker, J.: Context-aware process design exploring the extrinsic drivers for process flexibility. In: Proceedings of the CAISE*06 Workshop on Business Process Modelling, Development, and Support BPMDS 2006, Luxemburg, 5–9 June 2006

17. Saidani, O., Nurcan, S.: Context-awareness for adequate business process modelling. In: Proceedings of the Third IEEE International Conference on Research Challenges in Information Science, RCIS 2009, Fès, Morocco, pp. 177–186, 22–24 April 2009

18. Saidani, O., Rolland, C., Nurcan, S.: Towards a generic context model for BPM. In: 48th Hawaii International Conference on System Sciences, HICSS 2015, Kauai, Hawaii, USA, 5–8 January 2015, pp. 4120–4129 (2015)

19. Schonenberg, H., Weber, B., van Dongen, B.F., van der Aalst, W.M.P.: Supporting flexible processes through recommendations based on history. In: Dumas, M., Reichert, M., Shan, M.-C. (eds.) BPM 2008. LNCS, vol. 5240, pp. 51–66. Springer, Heidelberg (2008)

20. van der Aalst, W.M.P., Schonenberg, M.H., Song, M.: Time prediction based on process mining. Inf. Syst. **36**(2), 450–475 (2011)

21. van Dongen, B.F., Weber, B., Ferreira, D.R., De Weerdt, J.: Report: business process intelligence challenge 2013. In: Business Process Management Workshops - BPM 2013 International Workshops, Beijing, China, 26 August, 2013, Revised Papers, pp. 79–87 (2013)

22. Vanderfeesten, I., Grefen, P.: Advanced dynamic role resolution in business processes. In: Persson, A., Stirna, J. (eds.) CAiSE 2015 Workshops. LNBIP, vol. 215, pp. 87–93. Springer, Heidelberg (2015)

Author Index

Printed in the United States
By Bookmasters